ALTERNATIVE VIEWS

OF

LEARNING DISABILITIES:

ISSUES FOR THE 21ST CENTURY

EDITED BY

Mary S. Poplin
and
Patricia Tefft Cousin

8700 Shoal Creek Boulevard
Austin, Texas 78757-6897

Portions of this material previously appeared in
the *Journal of Learning Disabilities*

pro·ed

© 1996 by PRO-ED, Inc.
8700 Shoal Creek Boulevard
Austin, Texas 78757-6897

Library of Congress Cataloging-in-Publication Data

Alternative views of learning disabilities : issues for the 21st
  century / edited by Mary S. Poplin and Patricia Tefft Cousin.
        p.   cm.
  Includes bibliographical references and indexes.
  ISBN 0-89079-697-1 (pbk : alk. paper)
  1. Learning disabilities—United States.   2. Learning disabled
children—Education—United States.   I. Poplin, Mary S., 1951–
II. Cousin, Patricia Tefft.
  LC4704.A48   1996
  371.91—dc20   96-5374
                                                          CIP

Printed in the United States of America

1 2 3 4 5 6 7 8 9 10   00 99 98 97 96

Contents

Foreword

It has been an interesting, challenging, and at times frustrating and confusing experience for me as I read the 26 chapters that comprise this book. As I studied these pieces, particularly the first batch, I wondered, "Why did I agree to write the foreword for this book? This material isn't exactly the fare of a professed, if not devout, behaviorist." I pondered also why Mary Poplin asked me to author this foreword, knowing full well that I have been tagged as a behavioral chap. Perhaps she thought that I had gone through an epiphany and had abandoned my behavioral ways. Then, it occurred to me that her reason for engaging me to write this piece must have been that she wanted a person with old-fashioned lenses (bifocals) and a creaky voice to look at the pieces in this book that advance the notion of studying learning disabilities through modern lenses and other voices. Although this seems a bit optical and sonorous, it must have been why she called on me. Whatever her motivations, my beliefs have been seriously challenged. My paradigms have been pummeled.

I have never considered myself to be a radical behaviorist. In fact, in recent years I have seen myself as a soft behavioral person. (Survival in academe does strange things to people.) To illustrate, I have become more qualitative in my thinking and research. Moreover, I have argued for some time that our instruction and assessment should be authentic. Furthermore, I have long supported the idea of asking pupils what they thought about education, schools, and instruction. In addition, I have promoted the notion of self-advocacy, that children and youth should take charge of their lives to the extent possible. (There is a huge literature showing that children are highly motivated when given the opportunity to record and chart their behaviors, schedule the times they work on activities, select their own form of instruction, and arrange their own rewards.) Further evidence of my softening, along with the above modifications, is that I have tempered a few of my behavioral beliefs and practices. For one, I am not as task analytic as I once was, believing we should teach as we lay bricks—one at a time. I am not as keen on arranging complex token economies as I used to be, although I haven't scrapped the notion entirely.

But there are elements of the so-called reductionist, behavioral approach that would be extremely hard for me to discard. One has to do with the basic idea of reinforcement theory: the belief that individuals are greatly influenced by positive and negative contingencies. Another is that certain techniques advanced by behavioral folks are still ones to consider: time out, response cost, extinction, overcorrection. Yet another, related, belief I will keep is that many of the techniques promoted by the behavioral clan are suitable for not only mundane and simple behaviors (as many of the new wave concede) but are equally appropriate for higher-level cognitive activities, social skills, and beneficence as well. But the attribute from my behavioral colleagues I would be most reluctant to jettison, the one about which the new group is rather soft, is that some sort of data should be kept on whatever belief is advanced and put into practice.

While reading these chapters, all of which promote change, I asked myself, "Why should we change? Why should we abandon the old ways?" According to some individuals it seems that the traditional methods haven't panned out. Reid and Button (chapter 21 of this book) claimed that information they and others had acquired from children with learning disabilities "suggested that they [the children] felt isolated, victimized, devalued, and oppressed." If those data hold up across other situations and children, it would certainly be one reason to shift gears. Another motive for altering our methodological course was offered by Albinger (chapter 22 of the book), who claimed that "qualitative research may provide color to the gray areas about what is known regarding children's world—a world in which schools are often floundering in multi-biased, pedagogical ineptness."

These new lenses are indeed eye openers. In fact, some proponents of the new methodologies are saying that we should actually reverse our lenses; instead of seeking deficits and disabilities, we should look for strengths and successes. To exemplify that notion, I am reminded of Leon Fleisher, the pianist. His epic struggle to regain the use of a lost hand suggests that as we look for individuals' strengths we may find them to be very close to their weaknesses. In Fleisher's case, the weakness was his right hand, the strength his left hand. About 30 years ago, when Fleisher was touted as one of the rising young pianists, his right hand became nearly paralyzed. The more he practiced and exercised, the worse it got. It became so bad he could not use it at all. Instead of giving up, however, he mastered the considerable piano literature for the left hand. For several years he has concertized with that repertory. Only recently—

following surgery, therapies of all sorts, dedication and persistence—has his right hand come back. Now, at the age of 67, he is able to play not only the repertory for the left hand, but the literature for two hands as well. (*Note.* Although he temporarily put a weakness on hold and concentrated on a strength, he did not give up on the weakness. He later returned to it and resurrected it.)

In presenting their views, a few authors in this book could not resist the current trend toward conspiracy theories. According to this group, obviously influenced by Oliver Stone, educators have consciously (or at least unconsciously) set out to perpetuate the diagnostic–remedial "bring-them-up-to-standard" model. They give batteries of tests to detect deficits, prescribe treatments intended to deal with those deficits, and continue the treatments until the identified behaviors are dealt with and the person is "normal," or at least comes closer to being normal than before the process began. There have been times, when I was a bit more paranoid than usual, that I bought into this theory. Take a look at our business: There are the special education teachers, the psychologists, the other specialists who deal with children with disabilities, the publishers of textbooks and tests catering to special education, the guilds and societies that were spawned by the many disabilities, the university professors and the courses they teach. The bull market of special education would go into an October 1929 decline if current practices ceased.

It is at times a daunting experience reading about the new methods. We are told of the liberation pedagogy, discourse analysis, transformative philosophy, feminist pedagogy, critical pedagogy, and constructivism. We are encouraged to move from a mechanistic, linear world into a global, interconnected, systemic, and holistic one. Several of the constructs and commandments of the new group are formidable. A number of their terms are not readily grasped. But when we operationalize their ideas and bring them down to a folk level, the majority of them are sensible and practical.

I will note a few of the ideas discussed in this book and offer a comment or two on why I support them. In so doing, I could be accused of flying my behavioral colors by breaking up a paradigm into pieces, rather than looking at it holistically, but as Ian Fleming said, "paradigms are forever," and I've been with mine for so long I'm sure readers will forgive me.

Selecting Meaningful Tasks. Who could argue with this? It appears to me that if we teachers chose tasks for students to learn, or better yet, if they selected them, that of itself would do a great deal toward motivating them to learn more and stay in school longer. This is particularly true at the secondary level.

Seeking Strengths Rather Than Weaknesses. We are being asked to consider multiple intelligences, to expand the category of normal. I agree.

We have spent far too much time trying to locate things that folks can't do, and far too little has been devoted to finding and tapping into individuals' strengths. I can't think of anything more deadly than to be a remedial person who has spent years being informed tacitly and otherwise how inferior and off the mark he or she is.

Interacting and Collaborating with Teachers. By all means, let us do more of this. We should confer with children; ask them how we can help them; show them what they did wrong or how they could do it differently; ask them to explain how or why they did certain things; ask them for advice on what to teach them, when to do it, and under what conditions.

Reflecting and Keeping Journals. This goes with the above, and it, too, is a good idea. We should set aside times for groups of students to chat about their experiences, to tell others what they got out of their assignments, what went wrong, what was difficult for them. And we should ask teachers and students to keep a few notes, if not full-fledged journals, about what they have been doing. These narrations can provide the substance for reflective sessions.

Conducting Authentic and Contextualized Assessment. I certainly buy into this notion. For too long we have monitored the performances of children indirectly. We have asked them to draw circles when we should have asked them to write their name. We have asked them to check one letter or another on a multiple choice test instead of asking them to tell us about the story they read. As for context, we are all aware that an assessment of what we can do in one situation is not a fair appraisal of what we can do in another. Yet, we have abandoned this folk wisdom when dealing with children; we seem to think that one intelligence test score explains all their abilities, skills, and attributes, regardless of the circumstances.

Incorporating Students' Experiences and Background Knowledge. Again, this just makes sense. We should encourage and help children draw on their past experiences as they read new stories, compute problems, carry out science experiments, and study geography. Some children have rich experiences and are able to draw on them, whereas others have more modest backgrounds and are unable to tap into them. The latter must be given extra assistance.

I can bring all the above notions into my way of thinking without dumping my old paradigm. Although my methodological foundation was bruised and bent and clobbered and careened as I read these stories, it is still standing, just a bit worse for wear.

Dear readers, as you pore over these articles, you could, quite obviously, do as you please. You could take my course—retain your base and simply twist it around a bit. Or, you might dump your old foundation and latch onto the new one. Another option would be to dust off the new one you may already have and sprinkle in certain particles from these stories.

Indeed, that will "reinforce" your current beliefs. Or, you could chuck all the paradigms, the old as well as the new, and seek a newer one. Your quest could be referred to as the "advanced post-modernist paradigm."

In reading these reports and others of similar ilk, I speculated as to how the methods and means being promoted would play out in Providence and other state houses and in Peoria and other schoolhouses. Would our beloved governmental mavens be better able, using the new ideas, to understand and support education? Would classroom teachers, who have one score and two quartets of children in their classes, do a better job by operating with the new paradigm?

This is a refreshing collection of pieces, written by classroom teachers, by university professors concerned with teacher training, and by educational researchers and philosophers. There is a commendable balance of practice and theory. The authors have identified and discussed a number of different approaches, all of which are reasonably compatible, that differ from traditional methods. Their suggestions for practitioners, clinicians, researchers, and theorists are rich and deserving of attention. This book should be helpful to all those concerned with the education of children and youth, especially those with learning disabilities.

Lastly, I am overjoyed that these new visions and voices are bringing back John Dewey. Let us hope that we take in the full measure of his teachings this time around, including his deep thinking on multiculturalism and elitism. We might even hope that through him there will be a modest rise of liberalism.

Dr. Thomas C. Lovitt

1. Looking Through Other Lenses and Listening to Other Voices: Issues for the 21st Century

MARY S. POPLIN

The writings collected in this book range from the philosophic to the practical. Some bring new theory to bear on our assumptions. Some are teachers' stories, whereby teachers, both general and special education, come to understand students with learning disabilities in new ways by directly questioning their own assumptions and practices or by learning what is on their students' minds. This process has helped them create new spaces where they can work differently with children and youth. Other chapters describe individual or statewide programs that educate students with learning disabilities, some of whom are also bilingual. Also included in this book are three chapters that address teacher education in both preservice and inservice programs. Patricia Tefft Cousin and I have been greatly encouraged by the work going on around the country that is creating new ways of looking at learning disabilities that helps bring the individuals experiencing them into the fullness of their lives, rather than concentrating solely on their deficits. Cousin et al.'s chapter will appear at the end of the book and will tie the various works together

Reprinted, with changes, from "Looking through other lenses and listening to other voices: Stretching the boundaries of learning disabilities," by Mary S. Poplin, *Journal of Learning Disabilities,* Vol. 28, 1995, pp. 392–398. Copyright © 1995 by PRO-ED, Inc.

in terms of a sociocultural view of learning disabilities. In this chapter, I will simply introduce some common themes that emerge from these chapters.

A common ingredient in this book is an attempt to find new ways to educate students—ways that focus on students' lives such that the larger issues in their lives can become the focal point of our work. At the same time, the authors encourage us to be ever conscious of the role the field plays in the larger society. Children and adolescents with learning disabilities are people, like you and me. They have lives that go far beyond reading; they have abilities far beyond the range of what schools care about. They have needs that stretch beyond the boundaries of our reductionistic psychology. They have gifts that often lie dormant. They have reasons for being that we do not know, and they have questions that we cannot imagine. And they are impacted, as are we, by the society, the structure of schooling, and rules and practices we create and apply.

THE IDEOLOGY OF SCHOOLING AND THE LD FIELD

Our current diagnostic, placement, and instructional procedures for individuals with LD largely ignore the more important issues in people's lives and are driven more by ideology than by reason, and by deficits more than by talents. Mehan, Hertweck, and Meihls (1986) noted that we label children based on expectations, availability, funding, and finding the "right" test, rather than making instructional decisions based on who children are and what they can do. The instruments we use carry with them enormous cultural "baggage" (as does the education system itself), which makes it more likely that some people's children will be "disabled" (Valdes & Figueroa, 1994).

We also place children in instructional settings more on the basis of current vogue, most recent law, or latest method than on the basis of individual needs. This is ironic, because special educators have always clung (at least intellectually) to the spirit of individualization. But the letter of the law that mandates individualized programs is the same one that limits us and encourages us to make decisions based on what the current fad is. Is full inclusion a good thing? Yes and no, depending on whom you ask and when and where you ask it, and depending on the beliefs and desires of the students, their parents, and their teachers. In our field, in this house called school, there should be many mansions, many possibilities. In Chapter 2, Wiest and Kreil bring this reality home to us using excerpts from diaries of special educators who are writing about the very real legal, systemic, and personal impediments to making decisions for children based on what the most healthy alternatives would be. They state,

There is a dramatic gap between the thinking and conceptualization of special education in higher education and the actual practices of local school districts. . . . Again, a gap exists between levels of systems, with the law and its medical/dysfunctional model being pitted against the practitioners who interact daily with children.

This caution reflects the sentiments of Howard (1994), expressed in his controversial book *The Death of Common Sense,* revealing the ways in which laws often kill the spirit of good intentions. Bruce Matsui (Chapter 3) has provided for us another kind of analysis of the law and the spirit. As a former administrator in public school systems, he shows us the escalating costs of special education programs and warns us that the financial demands on school districts inhibit schools from being able to keep up with the current legal requirements. Giving examples from his experience, Matsui demonstrates the rising resentments inside the schools to the legal and economic demands of special education as it is currently structured and warns us that change is of the essence.

Healthy alternatives give way to systemic demands often because of imperatives shaped by a larger schooling structure that makes implicit assumptions about the nature of human learning and society. Curt Dudley-Marling and Don Dippo (Chapter 4) do an excellent job of making some of those implicit assumptions explicit, as do Lou Denti and Michael Katz (Chapter 5). Both chapters raise the problems we face as accomplices in creating and maintaining bureaucracies and other structures that contribute to the current injustices of "ableism," racism, and classism; the authors also suggest ways we might begin to move our field, over the long term, to a more tenable position, one that would not limit healthy alternatives for children. Dudley-Marling and Dippo suggest we can "work daily to remove the stigma of difference, to create classrooms where relationship and dialogue, as opposed to treatment and training, are central, and to create a conception of community based . . . on diversity, mutuality, and social justice." Denti and Katz, in a similar vein, call for us to develop "an alternative, normative conception of education that emphasizes the importance of caring, social relatedness, and community participation . . . the development of citizens."

GIFTS THAT DIFFER

The reconceptualization of learning disabilities will call on us to simultaneously subscribe to the seeming paradoxical notions of *unity* and *diversity.* To do this we must understand human diversity in its fullest sense and require our pedagogies to be responsive to all human gifts, so that education can help individuals with learning disabilities achieve full-ness of life. Raskind and Higgins (Chapter 6) begin to outline an ethics of technology in relation to learning disabilities that does just that: They call for our use of technology to be responsive to complex human needs and abilities by "fully contemplating the consequences of the ways technology is used with persons with learning disabilities."

Expanding the notion of human abilities will be crucial to our efforts to significantly broaden our narrow perspective of learning disability and the ultimate life needs and potentials of our students. Hearne and Stone (Chapter 7) encourage us to expand our notion of human abilities, and they provide empirical evidence that the students we label learning disabled are often gifted in areas the school cares little about. Using, in part, the notion of multiple intelligences, they suggest that "we need to consider the proposition that those with LD may well be in large part simply a group of students whose talents mismatch the primary values and expectations of the schools." This thesis is similar to the one expressed by Thomas West (Chapter 8), who suggests that in an increasingly visually centered and technological world, those we currently call learning disabled may be just the ones who will be most successful. West states, "When we understand . . . that for some the 'easy things' are difficult, but the 'hard things' are easy, then we may find that we are surrounded by much more talent than we could have imagined."

LIBERATION OR CRITICAL PEDAGOGY

Essentially, the authors whose chapters are included in this book call on us to see ourselves as liberatory educators, as teachers seeking to provide students ways to free themselves from worldly limitations and to awaken their full potential. Liberatory or critical education asks us to carefully examine how our assumptions and practices in learning disabilities might be oppressing the very students we seek to serve. To use a liberatory pedagogy is also to teach students to critically analyze their own situations and lives in the larger context of society. This kind of education calls for going beyond the cognitive and affective skills our current pedagogies address, to look at larger sociopolitical issues of liberation. The action demanded of teachers and students in liberatory or critical pedagogy is a larger action than is required in constructivism, and the tie to the larger world is stronger and more explicit (see also Poplin, Wiest, & Thorson, 1995; Rivera & Poplin, 1995). Indeed, liberatory pedagogy would have us engage the issues of having learning disabilities and "ableism" in society in the course of the classroom.

Taking the theory of liberatory pedagogy and relating it to special education and postmodernist thought, William Rhodes (Chapter 9) suggests we look differently at persons with disabilities—and simultaneously look more deeply into ourselves. He suggests that some of our biggest debates in special education are indicative of our "nibbling at the edges of postmodern thought." He is urging us to be more reflective of what we do and how it impacts the lives of the students we serve, and to use that reflection to think and act differently.

Paulo Freire and Myles Horton, the fathers of liberatory or critical pedagogy, each developed education projects that held forth larger implications. In teaching illiterate peasants to read and write in Brazil, Freire sought to use the peasants' lives and their thoughts about their lives in the context of the larger society, to both promote literacy (phonics and other written language composition and comprehension) and awaken sociopolitical action. This action was indeed born of the literacy program, which sought to liberate the peasants from the oppressive conditions of their dire poverty and to draw them into being active participants in state politics (Freire, 1970; Freire & Macedo, 1987; Horton & Freire, 1990). Myles Horton developed and ran the Highlander School in Appalachia for adults who came to study and work on specific political projects. For example, the early trade union and civil rights movements were born there. Rosa Parks, contrary to popular fiction, was not simply too tired to go to the back of the bus one day. Her action had been planned; it was a part of the larger education and social-action project developed with Martin Luther King and many others working together at Highlander. Many critical pedagogy projects in the public schools today center on ecology. As students and teachers study these issues, they find that they must not only study but act. Thus, many a school recycling program or other environmental project is born. The process of liberatory or critical education emphasizes the continuous cycle of reflection and action, reflection and action, that is involved in real learning.

Barbara Goldstein (Chapter 10) has captured the practice of critical or liberatory pedagogy in her first- and second-grade bilingual special class for Latino students who have been identified as having learning disabilities. In her chapter, she articulates the major principles of critical pedagogy (e.g., the development of student voice, linking critical issues to language development, going beyond constructivism) in a rich context of story and example by showing us her classroom and her students. In her classroom, children learn to read and write by sharing stories from their lives, such as immigration stories, and by being immersed in literature. She concludes,

If we are to truly provide an environment in which students benefit from formal education, it is imperative that we structure our classrooms and curriculum with the opportunities for students to engage in critical dialogue, so that true literacy . . . can develop.

In a year-and-a-half-long participatory project inside four schools in California, we found students echoing the pleas of critical educators, begging for their education to include serious conversations about real life (Poplin & Weeres, 1992). Alongside this was the biggest complaint of teaching: that it is boring, that it has little to do with what students call "real life." In 24,000 pages of data, students never complain that school is too difficult; but there are hundreds of complaints of boredom. Special education and remedial students echo these pleas even louder. For example, in a study of discipline and special and general education students, Thorson (1995) quoted two special education students on the same topic: "What's the big deal about dropping out? . . . If it's just special ed, cuz I used to see, like some of my friends they would carry books, they would carry, you know, like a folder and two books. And me, it was like, I never carried nothing. Like you know, I don't know, I felt like I'm [not] going to learn nothing." A second student with learning disabilities simply states, "I'm not learning nothing." Critical or liberatory education calls for our classrooms to be relevant and rigorous.

SOCIOCULTURAL CONSTRUCTIVISM

In earlier work, I described constructivism from a largely Piagetian framework, where the major concern is the child's individual construction of meaning around a particular topic or content. The view is heavily cognitive in its orientation and largely excludes issues of how the larger sociocultural environment influences learning and teaching. Recent work drawing more on Vygotsky's theories has emphasized the roles that sociocultural contexts play in the construction of meaning and the development of effective instruction (Moll, 1990). Constructivism as I previously described it calls on educators to make content more relevant and responsive to individual interests and existing knowledge, but sociocultural constructivism embeds this in larger contexts, as does liberatory or critical pedagogy. Several of the chapters in this book, including Pat Tefft Cousin et al.'s, broaden our vision of constructivism by including the essential sociocultural view.

To me, the project that best exemplifies the new pedagogies (constructivist, critical, multicultural, and feminist), new research on literacy instruction, concepts of sociocultural and linguistic difference, knowledge of learning disabilities, and teacher change in the learning disability classroom is the Optimal Learning Environment (OLE). The OLE program is being developed and tested in several schools in California with bilingual special students. Pat and I are pleased that Nadeen Ruiz and her colleagues are able to share some of the wealth of knowledge and understanding emerging from this project. In the first two of three chapters emanating from the OLE project (Chapters 11 and 12), Ruiz documents with extensive ethnographic research the premise that ability and disability are contextual, and that particular instructional procedures allow for children to perform optimally, while other procedures create obstacles to literacy development. Ruiz notes, "The context of the [instructional] situation profoundly affects behavior, and that behavior cannot be interpreted without taking into account those situational features [of the classroom]." She summarizes by detailing the conditions under which bilingual children of varying abilities perform optimally. Through her careful analysis of actual conversations in the classroom and instructional practices, she shares with us standardized and diagnostic data about the children she followed, in much the same way Taylor (1990) did in her book *Learning Denied* (Taylor documented the almost daily struggle of a child being diagnosed as reading disabled while he simultaneously wrote detailed science fiction stories at home).

Another study of instruction guided by sociocultural constructivism is presented by Palincsar, Parecki, and McPhail (Chapter 13), who provide us with an intensive look at a literacy unit that involves the issue of friendship. The authors show us how the unit came to be developed and its effects on both literacy and friendships in a special class for youngsters with learning disabilities. They conclude that

> the instruction began with the children both in terms of their concerns about friendship and in terms of their current literacy levels. These would appear to be useful guidelines in planning meaningful instruction for students identified as learning disabled—instruction that is adapted to their special needs without compromising the important social and communicative goals of literacy.

WHOLE LANGUAGE AND STUDENTS WITH LD

Prominent movements within constructivism that have been the most incorporated in the school environment are whole language, process writing, literature-based instruction, and project-based instruction. Most of the research on these approaches exists within the context of general education. Most of the arguments against constructivism in special education focus on specific uses of these methods (see the fall 1994 issue of *The Journal of Special Education*). In addition to the chapters previously mentioned, which are also related, several other authors in this book emphasize these processes in instructing students with learning disabilities. Hemming and MacInnis (Chapter 14) thoughtfully address whole language in the context of characteristics of learners with disabilities and suggest ways to link the specific needs of those learners to the whole language curriculum. Addressing the special literacy needs of students with LD, they note,

> Students considered to be learning disabled need assistance in the learning process. In a whole language curriculum this assistance is provided in a way that does not substantially take the ownership away from the student. However, it does provide the necessary assistance to facilitate growth in the learning process. It is this interactional support provided by the teacher that gently moves the child forward in his or her development.

In this chapter and the classroom research and stories that are also included in this work, a true picture of whole language for individuals with LD emerges—a picture that does not deny or exclude the teaching of explicit skill knowledge but, rather, integrates skill work into larger, literacy-rich environments. Indeed, regardless of mythologies to the contrary, the theory of constructivism adequately integrates "parts and wholes" into its whole–part–whole sequence. The classroom tales of real-life educators introduced below give life and meaning to our theories of language development and reveal the ways that expectations, language, family, and real lives interact with teachers' daily tasks of serving students.

The Foxfire method emphasizes not only the use of written language in literacy instruction, but also the integration of community and student concerns. This method, which produced the popular Foxfire books of folk culture from Appalachia, is now being extended across the country through a national network of public schools. Judy Kugelmass (Chapter 15) brings us an early progress report of some Foxfire projects that are integrating students with disabilities into general education programs. She describes some of the characteristics of these projects, as well as providing us with the theoretical background of the combination of literacy projects and community issues in the schools. The project approach to instruction advocated by Foxfire encourages, in Kugelmass's words, "enriched learning environments that resemble the cultures of the communities in which students will function and that have the flexibility to adapt the curriculum and the learning environment to the needs, interests, and abilities of all students."

CLASSROOM TALES

One of the most exciting aspects of this book is that it features several pieces of teacher research conducted by classroom teachers deeply enmeshed in the daily tasks of instructing children with learning disabilities in both special and general education settings. These chapters begin with the teachers' concerns about students with learning disabilities who are in their classes. Each teacher has posed questions for herself, developed alternative strategies, watched them, recorded students' responses, modified strategies, and reassessed progress. In the minute interactions of everyday life in the classroom, we are privileged to see the microscopic realities of how teachers think through, design, change, and monitor their own instruction. Their stories are reminiscent of Five's (1991) classroom studies recorded in her beautiful book *Special Voices*. It is often in listening to other people's stories that we are led to create our own. So, for those in the classroom, these articles will be especially encouraging.

Laura Lovelace (Chapter 16), a third-grade bilingual teacher, shares with us a "nonreader's" gradual involvement with writing. Laura, a second-year teacher with the wisdom and commitment of teachers much her senior, shares her doubts and struggles over implementing a writing workshop in her class. She demonstrates the importance of illustrations in text development and the importance of persistence and high expectations. She states,

> When R. entered third grade, he could barely read. He knew his name, but other than that, he would sometimes sound out the first letter of a word and then would give up. He was frustrated by reading and most of the time would not try. As R. became interested in reading his own writing aloud, his interest in learning to read was renewed. . . . I believe that the writing workshop method accelerated R.'s ability to read and write because he saw the connection between his written products and his life. . . . [The writing workshop] has taught me to have more faith in my students.

Ina Kau (Chapter 17), a second-year teacher of first- and second-grade children with severe language disorders, also uses a writing process. She provides us with stories of struggle; and it becomes clear that she overlooked the warning she received early in the year ("You have to understand these children aren't going to get better"). Kau concludes, after sharing the richness of children's progress, "The children have seen the use of language and want to use it in writing. They are pleased and proud of what they have done. And in the end we have moved past faith and the need for assurances. We now hold in our hands the things hoped for—beautiful little books."

Through her diligent efforts to serve a junior high student named Jimmy, Jessica Jackman (Chapter 18), also a special educator, demonstrates the dangers of accepting other people's perceptions of students and their families, and the relatively insignificant contribution formal tests and Individualized Education Programs (IEPs) make to the task of teaching. As Jackman comes to know and respect Jimmy and his family, the relationships between her and Jimmy, Jimmy and reading, and ultimately Jimmy and himself begin to shift. Her search to answer a simple question becomes her solution as Jimmy answers her question, "Why do you think you haven't learned to read very well?" with, "'Cause I didn't pay much attention, I'm sorry to say this but no one was there to encourage me and I couldn't encourage myself." Jackman, Kau, and Lovelace developed these pieces while working in a teacher research support group led by a teacher research specialist (Pine, 1992).

Like the authors above, Thorson (Chapter 19) directly challenged the lowered expectations of students who were labeled learning disabled in her high school resource room. As she taught *Macbeth*, she detailed the students' search for understanding, their interests and responses; and her chapter brings home the importance of special education students' having access to the themes and literatures of general education. Thorson concludes that in this work with classic texts, "academic growth becomes more than a list of memorized gains in grade-level skills. It refers to curiosity and research, literature and passion, composition and expression. Teacher and student become interchangeable in the exhausting, exhilarating experiences of intellectual growth."

In her chapter, Catherine DuCharme recalls for us two students she taught in her general primary classroom. Even years later, the details surface and the anguish over what was the best thing to do persists. She captures the issues of general and special education in the lives of Nate and Tanya and their families. DuCharme summarizes by calling on us as teachers to be advocates responding to children's differences. She states,

> Our job as teachers is to observe and assess what the child CAN do and build upon her or his own unique strengths in the educative process. Our focus must remain on responding to our students' differences, rather than looking for their causes or attempting to define them.

She raises the critical issue that teachers who seek to listen to students must also listen to themselves as professionals who can protect children from the damaging aspects of certain systems.

IMPACTS OF BEING LABELED LEARNING DISABLED

Following the theme of larger social contexts, Reid and Button (Chapter 21), using various narrative and linguistic analyses of a student's oral and written language, reveal the disturbing effects of labels, placements, and casual language about disability. The subject of the chapter, Anna, and other students reveal whom they think themselves to be as they talk about their lives in school and the beliefs they hold about their own abilities and disabilities. Reid and Button remind us through the words of students that "handicapping conditions are socially constructed." They warn us that the same words that answer questions such as "Who am I?" shape what students believe about "Who I can become."

Using interview and inductive analysis, Albinger (Chapter 22) adds another insightful picture of students' perceptions and coping behaviors regarding being labeled LD. She concludes, after both humorous and tragic stories, that "the children were not certain what was 'wrong' with them and felt they were to blame for not learning."

Both of these chapters raise the critical question of how much our students' low self-esteem, depressed performance, and lack of a sense of future are direct results of the system we have developed to "help" them.

TEACHERS AND TEACHER EDUCATION

To teach in tandem with seeing through different lenses, there must be different teacher education programs—programs in which the principles of different pedagogies are not only taught but also demonstrated. As Mallory and New (1994) stated,

> Social constructivist theory entails a new interpretation of the role of the teacher as one who is capable of and responsible for learning about the children within his or her care, and utilizing this knowledge to construct practices that are developmentally appropriate for particular children in particular contexts. (p. 334)

A number of institutions around the country have attempted to design teacher education programs that address these issues. Three such programs are described in this book. Nadeen Ruiz, Robert Rueda, Richard Figueroa, and Margaret Boothroyd (Chapter 23) share their experience in inservice teacher change with bilingual special education. They have developed a long-term model for teacher change and provide us with details of the process. They also reveal the disturbing insight that "the more special education training in the teacher's background, the stronger his or her reductionist orientation." The process they have developed looks at optimal processes for teacher change, with an eye toward better instruction for bilingual special education students based on the work and findings of the OLE project (discussed earlier). These authors' insights are critical to those who wish to engage with current teachers in changing instruction beliefs and practices.

In Chapter 24, Ellen Bacon and Lisa Bloom of the graduate teacher education program for special educators at Western Carolina University share their use of portfolios, collaborative work, student evaluation, and professional presentations to engender the professional growth of preservice teachers. Students in their program share the transformation of their thoughts that occurs as they involve themselves in these processes. These methods have been suggested by many for assessing students in K–12 classes. Bacon and Bloom have demonstrated their application to teacher education. They remark on the ways in which interactions inside the university change:

> By expecting all students to use their creative ability and power to solve their individual problems, all of us see ourselves and each other differently. Students see each other as professionals with important ideas to share, we see our students as serious contributors to solving problems in our region, and they see us as collaborators and assistants in solving these problems. Consequently, we are living all of these roles.

Taking another vantage point toward teacher education change, James Paul, Betty Epanchin, Hilda Rosselli, Brenda Townsend, Ann Cranston-Gingras, and Daphne Thomas (Chapter 25) describe the structural changes in their teacher preparation program that have been centered around constructivist philosophy. Integrating constructivist pedagogy, moral and social embeddedness, and a change in student–teacher relationships, these faculty at the University of South Florida lay out the principles around which they began the transformation of their program. Also using teacher portfolios, they suggest that the new aspects of the program look like a "collage rather than a snapshot approach to evaluation, to capture growth and change in the learner while incorporating reflection as a means of involving teachers in their own professional development and bridging the gap between research and practice."

CONCLUSION

Like the authors in this book, we all want to make our work more meaningful and more life giving. We are not alone: All disciplines are seeking to do the same, to reclaim the larger moral purposes of their work. We both know and fear that the energy we expend is not equivalent to the results obtained. None of us has the answer, but we can encourage one another in our search. Such are the hopes found in books such as this.

Special education is a field whose premise is to do great works for others—for the disabled, the poor, and the oppressed. It is a worthy quest. In one of the collections of her speeches, Mother Teresa remarks that we think too much about doing great things, that instead we should strive to do small things with great love. It is in these small moments of great love that we can transform what we do into the larger moral purposes for which we entered the profession. For us, as for Mother Teresa, love is not simply some sweet sentimental or humanistic emotion; it must be grounded in the day-to-day realities of schools and lives. Our work must be strong enough to confront oppressive forces, create new programs that focus on the entirety of a life, be responsive to the larger education environment, and inspire all of us to work toward constant growth for ourselves and our students.

2. Transformational Obstacles in Special Education

DUDLEY J. WIEST AND

DENNIS A. KREIL

For the past several years, it has been apparent in our professional circle (school psychologists, teachers in special education, program administrators, and even state officials) that special education is not meeting the needs of the students we have been mandated to serve. Not only have we questioned the efficacy of our practices, but also our feedback from parents and community members suggests an unimpressive level of satisfaction.

This discontent with our practice has also been supported by such authors as Poplin (1988a, 1988b), Reid (1988), and Heshusius (1989), who have provided arguments in favor of a complete paradigm shift away from current mechanistic, reductionistic views of the learner and learning process to what Poplin (1988a) described as a holistic–constructivist position. Others, including parent and professional organizations, are simply calling for reform in assessment and placement practices to better serve children with learning problems, without regard for the guiding principles of a particular paradigm.

Reprinted, with changes, from "Transformational obstacles in special education," by Dudley J. Wiest and Dennis A. Kreil, *Journal of Learning Disabilities*, Vol. 28, 1995, pp. 399–407. Copyright © 1995 by PRO-ED, Inc.

Those of us who are practitioners generally concede that considerable reform is needed, particularly in light of the staggering statistics demonstrating unprecedented growth in the identification of children with learning disabilities and the associated costs of providing special education services to these students. Our concerns are intensified by the philosophical change toward full inclusion of all disabled students into general education classrooms and the sudden, ever-increasing demand for special education services for students with attention-deficit disorders. Such dramatic transitions are making traditional approaches to learning difficulties problematic and impractical, and, coupled with the lack of identified achievement in many of the students placed in special education programs, this leaves us feeling perplexed, somewhat disheartened, and occasionally cynical. Simultaneously, our dissatisfaction with the current model of learning disabilities and special education inspires us to search for a better paradigm to use for our professional practices.

As we consider a new paradigm and begin to establish fundamental beliefs about learning and education practices within the new paradigm, it becomes essential that we understand the institutional realities that will inhibit or accommodate the transition in thinking and practice. As Heshusius (1989) stated, "fundamental change only comes about by naming, by continually resisting what stands in the way and by reinterpreting it" (p. 600). Heshusius also expressed optimism for the eventual transformation to holistic constructs. Such optimism is viewed with some skepticism by the practitioner who consistently must be accountable to the dominant philosophical, methodological, and sociopolitical structure. We must be careful to avoid the "sense of inertia and apathy" in paradigmatic change that was predicted by Poplin (1988b; p. 401) by providing systematic attention to these realities. The present article will discuss those systemic constraints that will influence the reframing of the field of learning disabilities into a more holistic approach to the education of students experiencing learning problems.

METHOD

Procedure

Although we have grappled with the paradigmatic transformation from mechanism to holism over the past several years, and, indeed, have specific thoughts about how this transformation affects the fields of learning disabilities and special education, simply exhorting a set of postulates and beliefs seemed inadequate for establishing a strong argument about what implications such a transformation has for schools. Because our perceptions were grounded in the daily work of addressing children's special needs, we kept diaries for 4 weeks that summarized both the specific vignettes of our work for that period of time and our internal and external responses to these experiences. It was our hope that by recording such daily information we would create a more cogent and systematic organization of our ideas, as well as establishing some sense of validity to our conclusions.

The specific accounts occurred at both the school-site and the district-office level. By integrating the experiences of a site psychologist with those of a central office administrator (director of pupil services), the framing of transformation becomes more systemic in nature and loses the perspective of being fragmented in roles and beliefs. We recorded the data on dictation devices daily for the 4-week period. The data were then transcribed in written form. Next, we read through the data in their entirety six times. Specific themes began to emerge from the whole of the document. We sorted the various vignettes and responses into logical sets of recurring subjects. This process was repeated three times so that the sorting responded accurately to the central theme of the vignette. Four preeminent themes emerged as primary in the obstruction of providing a holistic system of special education.

Setting and Participants

The district is suburban in nature and reflects the cultural diversity in Orange County, California. The district comprises more than 23,000 students; over 30 languages are spoken by the various households, and more than 30% of the population represents cultures other than Anglo. The variation in culture also reflects the stratification of the community, ranging from modest dwellings and hovels to million-dollar homes with views of the ocean. There are also three barrios, which have long and rich histories in the community. Family concern and participation in school activities is considered above average for the county.

The school experiences noted by the site psychologist occurred at two separate facilities. One school is middle class in nature and reflects stable families. It also houses a resource classroom, three special day classes for children who have severe language/communication disabilities, and another special class for children diagnosed as severely emotionally disturbed. Cultural diversity is approximately 20%. The other school, although in a middle- to upper-middle-class neighborhood, has many students bused in from outlying areas. Its population is over 70% minority students, and the school has many English as Second Language classes. Children are much less affluent in this school than in other areas of the district. Six special day classes for children with multiple disabilities (orthopedic handicaps, mental retardation, autism, seizure disorders, cerebral palsy, etc.) and 1½ resource programs make up the special education program at this site.

The director of pupil services works out of a central office along with other management employees, such as the superintendent, assistant superintendents, program specialists, personnel director, and various support staff.

School Site Themes

Four issues emerge as daily factors that have an impact on the efficacy of service delivery in a holistic manner to students in the school setting. The first area of concern is the focus on legal parameters that ensures justice within the school system. The second area is the systemic nature of schools and subsequent service issues that evolve with respect to children who struggle and may be considered disabled according to the law. The third issue involves the belief systems of parents and their advocates, as well as of the educational community. These beliefs, which are often rigid and narrow in scope, create an impasse for hope of collaborative resolution to the daily struggles many children experience in schools. They also impede the transformation to a more holistic and constructivist orientation within the educational setting. Fourth, lack of time is considered a pivotal barrier to working with children in an effective manner. Because there is the attempt to implement two contrasting paradigms simultaneously, professional educators struggle to implement either one adequately within the limits of the school day.

These factors dictate who is helped when problems arise in the education setting, when they are helped, how they are helped, and to what degree the assistance is beneficial. Paradoxically, these central issues create the impetus for legitimizing help for children who have difficulty succeeding in the general classroom program. At the same time, these areas are problematic for assisting *all* children due to the rigidity of their nature and inflexible interpretations by certain people in the various subsystems of the environment. Often these four areas weave together and are difficult to separate as individual entities. In fact, we should not attempt to understand them as individual phenomena, for they are constantly influential in a reciprocal fashion.

In our discussion, we will briefly review issues associated with the four dimensions that function as impediments. In addition, specific vignettes reflecting this viewpoint are presented. We also respond to these vignettes in a personal manner and, finally, conclude our position with a set of recommendations.

Special Education Law and the Dominant Paradigm

Educators not only teach children (a challenging task in and of itself), but also are anchored to a system of legal prescriptions that in many ways directs their programs and decisions. In no subsystem of education is this more evident than in the area of special education.

Laws governing learning disabilities and special education have as their main goal the assurance of justice for children who struggle in their educational setting. However, the legal parameters of special education have become irrepressible and now constitute the most fundamental impediment to the reframing of learning disabilities. Clearly, the perception by the majority of education professionals (e.g., general education teachers, specialists, administrators) at our sites and at the district level is that the law mandates a series of decisions (i.e., assessment, eligibility, and placement) that often fail to respect the interactional nature of family and school, and the professional judgment of educators wishing to transition to a different view of learning disorders. The legal framework, reflecting a specific view of learning disabilities, dictates reductionistic approaches that emphasize labels and placement outside of the general education classroom.

> This afternoon I met with a set of parents who were unhappy with the results of an assessment I conducted on their child. The boy is just five years old, comes from a traumatic birth, and the parents are worried that he doesn't have average intelligence, or worse, that I have underestimated his ability and that I will irresponsibly *label* him. He has motor and auditory impairments. The parents see him as much more advanced than I do, and they don't want to take my word that he has some delays in spite of the fact that I see many more children each year than they do. I am ambivalent and understand their point. I feel restricted by a legal path, mandated in my job, which dictates that I must decide the presence (previously determined) or extent of a disability. They do see their child for what he *can do* in many different contexts. Even though I tried to see this boy in as many different arenas as possible, noted his various strengths and possible contextual ways to learn, and interviewed as many other professionals in his environment to get as accurate an assessment as possible, I still see him through the lenses of an evaluator who has to make a legal distinction about the prevalence of a handicap. The father says, "I want as many services as possible, but I don't really think he is handicapped." That legal distinction, *impairment*, and subsequent decision is what funds their child's special program, which the parents advocate and renounce simultaneously.

When we reread this narrative, we were struck by how constant this dynamic occurs in the daily scope of our jobs. What we *want to do* and *know to be right* is often thwarted by the requirements of the law. Decisions are often driven by test scores and interpretations that fit within the legal framework. That is, test data that approach legal definitions of a learning disability are often sufficient to establish that disability in the child and preclude explanations that emphasize change within the caretaking and learning environments. These alternative views and holistic explanations of learning lack the support of the law and may not be defensible when challenged by reductionistic thinking and data. The practitioner experiences pressure to comply with many legal elements that reflect the dominant reductionistic model. These demands are often not congruent with what we experience to be true with regard to children's learning. Resistance, however, results in the risk of punishment by the legal system, or, minimally, pressure to conform in order to avoid disputes.

> Mr. and Mrs. _____ attended a meeting for their son who has learning disabilities as well as cerebral palsy. The parents are supportive and cooperative, but the staff is anxious because the father is a lawyer and has previously successfully sued the obstetrician. The staff is too obsequious and overly solicitous most of the meeting because of their anxiety of displeasing the parents. The threat of making a mistake and subsequent legal consequences keeps the IEP team guarded, and in that sense we cannot truly join their system and work together. We are too worried about being swallowed up if we authentically joined with them, rather than placating them. The parents don't overtly acknowledge this dynamic, but I sense that they receive an artificial sense of superiority over the staff because of our reaction. It's like the staff feels a relief that we are not going on trial for their son's disability and slow progress.

Has the legal quest to advocate fair and appropriate education for all children evolved into a dynamic in which parents seek refuge in judicial shelter when their children struggle, and practitioners cling to legal definitions in a convenient manner and abdicate responsibility for teaching children? Unfortunately, on a daily basis this concern appears to be validated in some schools. Many parents assume that the only way they can receive help is to demand an often recalcitrant system to respond to the timelines of assessment and placement. The assessment tools and practices themselves, however, are often dictated by the legal definitions of disabilities and inherently result in conclusions that are medical and reductionistic in nature.

It is evident that the predominant paradigm of learning disabilities evolved from a medical or child deficit model. This paradigm has been "institutionalized" through legislative definitions, case law, and agency interpretation of federal and state regulations, and it essentially confines practitioners to a path of reductionistic decision making. Deviation from this path puts the practitioner at risk for litigation and adversarial relationships.

In this medical paradigm, when a child is identified as handicapped, one infers that something is wrong or deficient in the child. Parents may feel a sense of relief by finally being able to label their child's difficulties, to put a name to the struggle he or she has endured. Nevertheless, a label is still a label; it suggests a form of permanence and intimates failure and worthlessness. In their search for help in teaching their child, parents may join a framework and interpretation that implies that the child is not capable. The child is blamed, and very little respect emerges for alternative modes of learning and environmental, contextual methods of instruction.

Education staff members may feel abused by many of the laws (e.g., P.L. 94-142, Section 504, California's Hughes' bill, etc.) that are systematically imposed by higher powered governing bodies; the paperwork, difficulty with scheduling special education programs, arduous meeting schedules, and feelings of being controlled and restricted through rigid IEP goals and objectives are all valid criticisms. But many of these same educators also are often proselytizers for the same legal framework that they criticize; they forget or ignore the many alternatives available for teaching children, hastily filling out referral papers for a child who "is obviously handicapped and incapable of succeeding in the regular classroom." These referrals often go unchallenged; even worse, if the description of learning difficulties holds that the child is incapable due to a "neurological deficit," the instructor may abdicate expertise in teaching such an "impaired" youngster. Rigidity in process and in the conceptualization of learning disabilities stifles creativity and represses changes in the art or science of teaching. The focus on adhering to the law creates a sense of frustration and even fear in professionals as they attempt to respond to what is mandated, avoid litigation, and repress instincts to change.

Everyone suffers as the legal framework comes to restrict professional judgment and inhibit education decisions and change. When laws intended to protect children become controlling and threaten punitiveness, they have lost their power to effect positive change and intervention. Educators, including teachers, administrators, and psychologists, who are imperative in the formation of a more organismic approach to education, will be thwarted in their attempts to provide a reframing of learning disabilities to more holistic principles when the law becomes preeminent. Holistic education, by definition, precludes a rigid, legalistic formula for ensuring an appropriate education within a school setting.

School Structure and Resistance to Change

Schools are complex structures, made up of myriad systems and subsystems. Among the various levels of organization, the process of decision making can become rife with conflict. This is particularly true when a student displays inadequate social or academic skills and the various participants in the child's life are called in to assist in problem solving. Unfortunately, this system often witnesses conflict and a lack of consensus regarding even the basics of clearly identifying the problems and coming up with reasonable solutions.

In our experience, most practitioners recognize that education works optimally when the various systems a child experiences collaborate. This cooperation is defined by reciprocal relationships that emphasize flexibility, dynamic behavior, interconnectivity, and problem solving as normal patterns of response. Ironically, we see many well-intentioned individuals from various systems advocating their personal beliefs exclusively, with little regard for students' individual needs. When various systems are rigid in their methods of interaction, the student becomes susceptible to failure.

Paradigmatic change compounds the problem of inadequate cooperation among systems. As the transformation to a different paradigm of learning disabilities is initiated, rigidity between the subsystems of education is likely to intensify, due to the lack of common values and ideals held by staff members. Practitioners in special education who advocate a shift in thinking regarding student learning problems must face the inevitable pressure that erupts in the face of nonconformity and disagreement among staff to maintain the current dominant model of student learning and intervention.

Our school intervention team meets on a second-grade boy who is being raised by his mother. This boy is large and appears to be a fourth or fifth grader, and this is his third school this year. The mother is on welfare, and while I like her in some respects, I also suspect that she is a drug addict struggling to survive every day and take care of this boy. The school staff's appraisal is that she has limited parenting skills, and there is a blaming mentality to our assessment.

The boy is disruptive in class despite many positive steps to intervene by the teacher. He is assaultive nearly every recess, has little sense of boundaries, masturbates publicly at times, and then regresses to the point of using baby talk with his mother. He doesn't know how to make friends, and even though he has been here only two months, kids loathe to be social with him. The teacher wants the boy out of the class. She remarks, "I have taught many years, and he is the most uncontrollable child I have ever had. He is too dangerous for all the children, and I have done all that I can to help him."

The principal thinks he needs a transfer to a more restrictive program. The parent wants the school to stop calling with negative reports or suspensions. The boy said to me, "I just wish I had some friends and could see my dad." After much wrangling and deliberation, most of it dedicated to providing an "appropriate education someplace else," the parent and staff agree to move the boy to another school and class for emotionally disturbed children.

This child's education experience is very familiar to us, in both the process of intervention and the subsequent solution. As the above vignette illustrates, the existence of diverse interests among parents, general education classroom teacher, principal, and special education staff results in a very narrow solution originating from the dominant decision-making power involved in the process. The most frequent resolution to such a disagreement in interests is the provision of an identified program and label that serve the interest of those groups having the positional power (i.e., the principal) and/or any decisional power the parents and their advocates might possess. This fragmentation of paradigms within education often results in rigidity of the local school and even the district systems. This child's behavior is certainly extreme and troubling, but perhaps even more discouraging is attempting to transition from "blame" to "reframe" by conceptualizing his behavior in a more global, systemic manner. Staff members who felt they had attempted their fair share of interventions moved into an accusatory stance, with the child and family as scapegoats. Once this dynamic was instituted, it deeply infiltrated the process of finding a logical solution.

We are mindful of several lessons illustrated by this case. First, families need a tremendous amount of support, particularly when one parent is assuming the primary parenting role. Transportation, day care, jobs that pay a decent wage, affordable housing, and emotional support from community and school were areas this mother identified as struggling with. She felt ungrounded in her community, and while she confessed her many weaknesses and shortfalls, she was also urging us to support her system—and even help her change it. It is difficult to conclude that all avenues for linking home, school, and community into an effective plan were exhausted before this boy was summarily transferred to his fourth school of the year.

Second, this inability to merge systems in a strong, intervening fashion at the boy's home school points also to a shortfall within our culture, or, as Bronfenbrenner (1979) referred to it, the macrosystem. This woman has a responsibility, as do all parents and individuals in society, to provide for herself and her family. From a cultural standpoint however, it appears that we have difficulty accepting the possibility that we are all members of the same structure. That is, we all are humans who function within this country on this planet. Our focus on *independence* instead of *interdependence* undermines many families, leaving schools to somehow provide what we are culturally unwilling to. Schools feed children, sometimes assist with clothing, provide values and moral training, and also carry out the primary mission of training children in the thinking process our culture deems imperative for survival. Our cultural focus on an independent mentality discourages unity and care for all people. In essence, the result is *intervention* for a disability or behavior as opposed to *prevention* through a care orientation that acknowledges our interconnectedness. Drug babies, homeless children, hungry children, high infant mortality rates, high rates of depression and suicide, proliferation of divorce, rising murder rates, and existential ennui point to a disdain of holistic conceptualization in culture that ultimately affects schools, as they are in fact interconnected.

When the umbrella of all systems, culture, does not respect its members and commit to empowering them, systems such as the school experience diverse problems, but many members ultimately respond with the implicit rule of the culture; that is, if a person has a problem, let him or her deal with it. In addition, there is the belief that one group's problems do not affect the other members of society. Once the inevitable problems arise, solutions (following the inflexible thinking of culture) are narrow in focus.

Rigid Belief Systems

The inability of separate systems to cooperatively solve problems and unitedly create an effective culture emanates from faulty and rigid belief systems. These mechanistic beliefs undercut the type of creative thought that is requisite for healthy systems. In education, an impasse between families and schools is created when one (and sometimes both) of the parties attempts to impose its uncompromising structures on the other party, a process typically sanctioned in some manner by the legal system. There are times when many people are gathered with the goal of assisting a child, only to have a single adult with an unyielding and constricted view of the problem and its ultimate solution obstruct a more palatable and healthy resolution *for the child*. The strength of such opposition is immense, for it shifts the creative group energy—which is necessary for changing the child's environment—from the child's needs to the need to repair the system fissure. If the opposition is forceful enough, energy shifts from group collaboration to placation of a member.

We have just concluded a meeting on one of my favorite students, R. Now a fifth grader, he has come such a long way from the emotionally explosive boy I first met three years ago, when his school diagnosed him as emotionally disturbed and transferred him to my program. He has since matured, calmed down, and been mainstreamed into regular education with support from a resource program. He reads like a second grader, and while he doesn't complain, being expected to perform at grade level is often humiliating for him. In addition, he continues to be plagued by a difficult family complicated by divorce, a father who is a gambling addict who can't hold a job, remarriage of mother to a man who both physically and emotionally abuses the youngster, and an ambivalent mother who can't commit to the safety of her son.

The teacher, who started the year with positive hopes of helping the boy, has written him off. She voices her fear of him in the IEP, although he has done nothing physical to any members in school or community. She interprets his quiet opposition and indifference to disrespect. His occasional outbursts simply justify her beliefs. She has done everything a teacher could be asked to do, she contends. Of course she has been patient, modified his work, tried to assist and understand him. What she doesn't say is how let down and disappointed she is in him. Her own needs for being a helper become the focus, and she has little sympathy for the boy's plight of now being forced to change schools. "He has to know consequences," she convinces the other committee members.

My reframing of this issue into another explanation for his behavior, such as that he is frustrated by his inability to feel successful with peers, falls on deaf ears. I know why. Most of the upper-grade teachers already have formed negative opinions of this boy, and they will oppose any effort to establish a positive and flexible classroom relationship if he is placed in their classroom next year. My peers at the table know this, and their looks suggest that we cut his losses and make the transfer to a teacher at another school who has a reputation for being talented and patient, and for healing such youngsters. Perhaps we can only help him by placing him with a healing teacher who loves such kids. The mother weeps softly and signs the papers to move him.

Few cases have troubled us more than this youngster. Certainly there have been more violent, assaultive, self-abusive, sociopathic, and dysfunctional students within our district. This youngster is a bright and often warm person. His chronicity and severity of problems improved dramatically before the aforementioned episode, but we could not seem to replicate whatever triggered the success. As of this writing, the boy is no longer mainstreamed at his new school, seldom appears interested in schoolwork, appears indifferent to adults, and has developed an attachment to gangs.

Children who have difficulty with the day-to-day complexities of school provide teachers with a tremendous challenge to educate them. However, academic and behavior problems are part of the task of being an educator. How adept one is at assisting a struggling child depends on the fundamental belief system of the adult. Naturally, this suggests the notion of paradigm and underlying meta-belief systems that daily influence decisions.

Unfortunately, our daily experience with teachers, administrators, and support staff suggests that several fallacious beliefs are prevalent among many educators. The first erroneous position is that if a child exhibits problems in school, he or she innately *is* the problem. Problems are framed as inherent and unchangeable, and teaching style, curriculum, classroom organization, family dynamics, culture, school climate, and learning techniques are easily overlooked as alternatives.

The second false belief is that once the educator has attempted the usual interventions for instruction and intervention, he or she is excused from further attempts. This mind-set presupposes a finite set of possibilities for explaining and understanding behavior. Site members skilled and open to consultation often discover other alternatives. However, an unalterable belief system limits the reframing of such issues (i.e., the provision of other explanations and subsequent solutions for problems).

The third fallacy involves the deification of the special education process. Problems are often conceptualized as needing special education to solve them. It is as if the process of testing and labeling a child and removing him or her from the general education program has a mystical, salutary benefit. In fact, it probably benefits the general education instructor the most, because he or she is released from much of the expectation of intervention. Attempts to change this process are slow at best, because many adults subscribe to this belief to some degree.

Parents want "extra help," teachers want "experts" to intervene, special education teachers feel it is their duty to assist "special" children, and administrators want a peaceful solution. It is not that special education cannot be beneficial in certain cases. However, too many adults embrace it as *the most* beneficial option, thus overfilling resource programs and special classes, instead of perceiving general education classrooms as optimal environments for learning. The reality is that rigid classrooms with little regard for individual, contextual learning are difficult places for many students to be successful. The emphasis on special education as the vehicle for intervention suggests that the general education teacher has less responsibility for modifying the general classroom program. In spite of the legal requirement that individual differences be accounted for in the classroom, many children are still expected to simply adjust.

> Mr. and Mrs. M_____ are seated around a large table with a team composed of their son's six junior high teachers, two psychologists, a resource specialist, a principal, the assistant principal, and the district special education administrator. The parents are angry and defensive, feeling that the school has been unresponsive to their concerns about their son's attention-deficit/hyperactivity disorder. The boy is characterized as bright in many areas, but he constantly misses assignments and is poorly organized. He has been disrespectful to certain staff members, who have allowed him extra time to finish work. The parents interpret his behavior as a logical reaction to the teachers.

The school has met with the parents over the previous year, but the result is that both parties feel maligned. The educators feel they have provided adequate modifications and help, without the provision of special education. The parents feel that only lip service has been provided. The team finally agrees to place the boy in special education—after they are threatened with a court battle—and the parents demand to write a Section 504 plan to further accommodate their child. The team agrees. As the parents pass out their proposal with over 25 components, many of which I can see are overwhelming and probably untenable for the staff, I can see the members of the school site contort with resentment and discouragement.

I try to temper the parents in such a way that they are not embarrassed, but they continue to beat the staff down. Their goal appears to be winning, not connecting or collaborating. They defy my efforts to have them create a joint process. The principal is defensive and falls into the trap of debating the parents, who righteously attack the school for failing their child.

The staff quietly seethes, for they perceive the parents as poorly organized, having a dysfunctional marriage, projecting blame upon them, expecting more out of the school than of themselves as parents, and bullying public servants who are doing the best they can. The parents decry the irresponsible and insensitive nature of school culture, and after the meeting, staff members mutter to themselves and shake their heads in disgust.

Although we are concerned about the often uncompromising and narrow belief structures of school staffs, we are equally distressed by parents' inflexible mind-set. Parents often embrace a set of reductionistic beliefs about education, which complicates the task of reforming special education. These beliefs may develop from a simple naïveté about education, predictable responses to insensitive school systems, or, in the extreme, blatant egocentrism and selfishness.

The previous example is reflective of many of these beliefs. The parents did not trust the school, and they doubted that their son's interests could be addressed. Thus, they became his "advocate" after a thorough orientation from a national advocacy group. In addition, they believed it to be their mission to create formal services for their child. Unfortunately, the parents' perception of advocacy included harassment until they got their way and did not consider the consequence of their son having to interact with staff they had just humiliated.

Formal service in special education is often not the treatment of choice, for it decontextualizes the learning experience from the general classroom and creates the context of the m¡edical, neurological model. In essence, this family wanted enough remediation and treatment to eradicate the "disease" of school failure. Their belief that *more is better* was the cornerstone of their strategy.

While we find it disconcerting to have school personnel blame parents and students for academic, social, and behavior problems, we find it equally unsettling to have parents condemn school personnel for these problems. In essence, blame is counterproductive when used by any party and simply complicates the situation. Some members *are* more culpable than others at times, but condemnation and accusation preclude a focus on solutions and involvement from *all* systems.

In this specific case, we are distressed by several dynamics occurring within the home microsystem. The parents could not get the youngster or his younger sibling to school on time, in spite of many suggestions from consultants. The interventions were seldom implemented. The parents had difficulty monitoring their son's homework and expressed distaste at assisting in writing and organizational aspects. Specifically, they noted that they expected someone (such as the teacher) to help with their adolescent son's secretarial skills, yet they felt it was beneath *them* to assist in this task. Finally, as one of the parents confided, they experienced marital problems and were enduring catastrophic financial loss in their business.

In many ways, we experience ambivalence involving this case. We empathize with these parents who no longer trust the school—their son has experienced failure for a long period, and in spite of various efforts to modify assignments, homework, time schedules, discipline, and organization, he continues to struggle. But the parents fend off any attempt by school personnel to explore and understand the issues at home and their subsequent impact on the son.

Fueled by their son's continued problems and the school's frequent blaming mentality and often insensitive attempts to intervene, the parents resort to using the law in the worst possible context, that is, as a club. Believing that the law is their only avenue for success, they insist upon the formal IEP process, which safeguards their child's rights. They then batter the school with implied or explicit threats of lawsuit, creating fear among the staff.

Parents often believe that it is their inherent right as taxpayers to receive service and assistance, without any consideration for cost to the total system. Although the law does state that education must be free and appropriate, at some point participants must acknowledge the finite fiscal situation in their state and the country. We do not deny that families need help; however, simply demanding more money and services does not address the child's strengths, identify possible learning styles and meaningful experiences, or create an optimal learning environment.

Lack of Time

When a school organization attempts to implement a more holistic paradigm, the issue of time becomes a battleground. Interacting with various systems and utilizing an ecological approach inevitably results in a collision, primarily because there are two diametrically opposed paradigms vying for the same finite set of time periods. Because the holistic paradigm is not supported by the legislative and judicial communities, the education community is forced into the onerous dilemma of providing service in both paradigms (an impractical and seemingly impossible approach), or simply ignoring the holistic world assumptions and committing to basic, legalistic requirements.

It is June, and I count 75 meetings that I have attended in the past four weeks. Tonight I will stay up late after the kids are in bed to write several reports that must be finished for meetings. I have just finished meeting with two separate families from 3:30 to 6:30. Both families have friction and tumultuous relationships. Previously, they have suggested that the problems are related to special education concerns.

The notion of "learning problems" dissipates quickly when the families come together and various systemic blocks become apparent. I work with them in the hope of referring them to an agency and avoiding the maze of special education, which only circumvents their need to function more efficiently as a family. Both sessions are fruitful, and I feel a sense of gratification. The families want to grow and relate in a loving and compassionate way.

I see the stack of phone messages on my desk, many related to scheduling the next round of IEPs, and the box of over 60 reports to dictate, and I shake my head. The satisfaction of the day is short-lived.

Whether we work at a school site or at a district office, we continually face the challenge of responding in a more global, holistic manner to students and their needed services. It becomes wearisome to address issues in a systems manner, only to be restricted by an exclusive focus on a legal structure or impeded by rigid beliefs and structure.

To address children's need for systems to adjust and change necessitates a consultative format. It is crucial for representatives from the child's various subsystems to collectively address the concerns and collaboratively develop some interventions. Changing curricula, teaching approaches, home/school organization, family dynamics, and classroom culture are just a few of the possible ways to reframe the difficulty, from seeing it as residing within the child to perceiving it as representing mismatches between the child and the ecology. Parents and educators may hail the benefits of consultation and a more holistic approach; however, the most typical result is the desire to have *both* models employed.

The change from the medical model to a systems–ecological perspective takes a great deal of time and perseverance. A tremendous amount of energy has been devoted to the implementation of the medical model. The desire to assist children has created a belief in faulty children, and it is often easier to conceptualize the problem as originating within the child than to expose problems within or between systems. Convincing educators and parents alike to risk changing is difficult, as the special education model has been promulgated, taught, and accepted by culture for a generation or more. To change entails balancing both paradigms until our culture sees the benefit of transforming the education system into a more beneficial model. In the meantime, the same legal requirements of the predominant mechanistic paradigm, such as timelines and IEPs, are expected.

CONCLUSIONS

Responding to the concerns of site- and district-level practitioners requires thinking at what Bronfenbrenner (1979) described as the "macro" level, that is, culturally. We must examine our current practices in education and special education and discern if they are congruent with what our culture believes to be true about learning. It must be a collective agreement, one that incorporates all elements of society. To attain such consensus, there must be leadership at various levels of systemic functioning so that agreements on law and education can be formulated. For change to occur, it is crucial to have professional agreement and subsequent leadership at various levels of service. This "consensus of ideals" will then be reflected in the laws and professionals' daily roles.

The dissonance, confusion, and consternation about roles and responsibilities for teaching and caring for children must be conceptualized as a normal feature of the change process. Thus, rather than condemning the experience of frustration, understanding it as being a normal aspect of change is crucial for the next step in development. It is more salutary to ask the question, "Are we going to restructure, or are we going to shift paradigms?" Paradigmatic shifting surpasses restructuring in scope. When changing paradigms, resources and responsibilities are not simply changed within the existing paradigm of professional thinking. Paradigm transformation includes examining how we think globally and systematically. Paradigms are metatheories and thus require us to reexamine our belief systems about reality. Clarifying the change of either paradigm or structure becomes an important component of the transformation. Until we decide to what extent we must transform, changes are simply temporary behaviors and lack the strength of reformation.

Transformation must also move beyond theory and postulation into the realm of the practitioner. Currently, there appears to be a great deal of discussion about transformation and paradigm shift in higher education. However, the day-to-day practice of professionals who actually interact with children does not typically reflect this reform. Our observations of ourselves, our systems, and other systems in the area suggest that there is a dramatic gap between the thinking and conceptualization of special education in higher education and the actual practices of local school districts. Administrators, teachers, psychologists, and special education personnel do not identify with a transformation. They do acknowledge the realities of law and the institution, with its various fluctuations in demands. To compound the problem, legal mandates often do not reflect the conceptualization of education and learning within the professional field. Again, a gap exists between levels of systems, with the law and its medical/dysfunctional model being pitted against the practitioners who interact daily with children. Practitioners must conform to this narrow definition of behavior and its implications for treatment, or risk being criticized for their beliefs and even punished by the law.

Thus, consensus involves the joining of higher education institutions and local school districts, as well as individual schools that represent the district. Consensus suggests that parents, advocates, lawyers, and politicians all merge with practitioners and administrators to define a model of special education. But developing a consensus will be impossible without examining the assumptions of our current paradigm. If we believe in a transition of paradigms from a mechanistic, linear world into a global, interconnected, systemic, and holistic world (similar to what Kuhn, 1970, and Capra, 1982, suggested), then we need to own that thesis and use it in our laws and policies. Our supposition is that most people agree with this postulate when it is explained. However, they have yet to examine the issue of whether their behaviors, policies, and laws are congruent with such a metabelief system.

Finally, we suspect that members of our society, after developing a consensus, will advocate a "care of culture" orientation. A care belief system includes recognizing the strength of independence within individuals, an attribute that served the pioneers and the cultivation of our young country well. However, just as this country has matured, so has our thinking, and we are now confronted with the assumption that there exists within humanity an interconnectedness and interdependence. A care orientation does not deny the responsibility of the individual, but it values the needs of the whole over the individual parts.

3. The Economic Lens: Serving the Needs of Students With Disabilities—Warnings From the Edge

BRUCE I. MATSUI

In California school districts, required levels of funding for programs that serve students with learning disabilities (LD) are woefully inadequate. The current level of funding in many districts fails to meet the requirements of laws such as the Education for All Handicapped Children Act of 1975 (P.L. 94-142) and the Americans with Disabilities Act of 1990 (ADA, P.L. 101-336) Office for Civil Rights (OCR) compliance regulations, and the costs of legal procedures that arise from continuous litigation. In order to remain compliant with such laws, the majority of California districts supplement the required level of funding with dollars from their unrestricted budgets. This comes at a time when, for most California districts, these types of budgets are stretched to the point of bankruptcy because they provide for employee salaries and fringe benefits, maintenance and operations of school plants, general equipment and materials, adequate student-to-teacher ratios, general transportation needs, and textbooks and instructional materials. Having to supplement the restricted budgets for mandated costs of programs for students with disabilities by using unrestricted funds forces districts to reduce services and programs and to deter possible salary increases.

⋈ The restricted categorical funds associated with mandated programs for students with LD can only be used to comply with established policies that call for the following:

- smaller class sizes supplemented by paraprofessional aides;
- special transportation requirements;
- additional support personnel such as nurses, speech and language specialists, school psychologists, central office administrators, and legal counsel; and
- unbudgeted tuition costs for required placement in private institutions that provide the least restrictive environment.

All of these required components comprise the enormous costs of maintaining programs that comply with current legislative mandates. Restricted funds that can be used only for service to students with LD are simply insufficient in California school districts.

TYPICAL DISTRICTS

The Montebello Unified School District (average daily attendance of 30,000) and the Pasadena Unified School District (average daily attendance of 24,000) are typical of districts feeling the effects of inadequate funding and growing costs. The Montebello Unified School District's unrestricted funds for the 1995–1996 school year total approximately $99 million. Total revenues that the district has budgeted for the costs associated with special education programs is $11,626,910. The Montebello school district expects to receive revenues in support of special education programs that will total $7,376,483, and the anticipated number of dollars that will be transferred from unrestricted funds to support and maintain special education programs is projected at $4,249,427. This funds transfer represents approximately 4% of the district's entire unrestricted budget.

In the case of the Pasadena Unified School District, the total unrestricted budget is approximately $78 million. Pasadena has budgeted $17,843,887 for the maintenance of their special education programs and expects revenues that support and maintain their programs for learning disabled students to total $14,872,631. This will result in a shortfall of $2,971,256. As in the case of the Montebello district, the funds for the projected shortfall will be transferred from the Pasadena district's unrestricted funds. This transfer represents a 3.8% encroachment upon the district's entire unrestricted budget (see Table 3.1).

TABLE 3.1
Level of Encroachment Upon District Funds
for Two California School Districts

Funding categories	Montebello U.S.D.	Pasadena U.S.D.
Total special education costs	$11,625,910.00	$17,843,887.00
Total special education revenues	$7,376,483.00	$14,872,631.00
Encroachment amount	$4,249,427.00	$2,971,256.00

STARK REALITIES FACING SCHOOL PERSONNEL

The reality of complying with program mandates is sadly different from the intent of the laws that govern placement and structural components of programs for students with LD. The following examples may better illustrate what those responsible for implementing programs face.

The Teacher

A sixth-grade teacher with a class of 36 students receives an additional student for part of her (teacher) day—a mainstreamed student designated as Learning Handicapped (LH). This teacher, who has not had the benefit of special training, is also aware that the teacher (a trained specialist) who is transferring this student now has fewer students with whom to cope. The teacher is also aware that the school's resource specialist (RSP) is provided with an instructional aide. The mainstreaming program at this school is considered by many to be an exemplary program; however, the realities of mainstreaming students with special needs into general education programs are quite the opposite.

By the end of the day, the sixth-grade teacher may well be angry, contemptuous of the program, and resentful of the additional burden of teaching a student with special needs. This teacher is considered to be one of the best teachers at the site, a caring individual who has been chosen as a mentor teacher on five different occasions.

The District Coordinator

The district's special education coordinator is preparing for a hearing that may result in a parent's right to have the district be responsible for providing and paying for the schooling of a student in a private institution that will cost upwards of $17,000 per year. Although the coordinator believes that the district has a program that will serve the student well, she is fearful that the hearing officer may agree with the parents and their legal advocate. The coordinator has spent 2 entire days with her staff preparing for the hearing.

District support services personnel are often called upon to prove that their programs are adequate, and their time is often usurped by cases that may cost the district large sums of money. Current rules and mandates hold districts responsible for tuitions at private institutions that can "better" serve students with learning disabilities.

The coordinator is frustrated because time used in preparation of such cases takes support personnel away from the classrooms that house students with LD. She is fully aware of the need to support and develop classroom environments that work.

The Business Manager

After a careful audit, the business manager in the same district has discovered that sustaining the district's current level of support for students with LD will require additional funding from the unrestricted budget because state and federal allocations for such programs have not kept pace with inflation. The business manager also is preparing to negotiate with the teachers' union over a fringe benefit package that will affect all employees. When the union negotiators ask about encroachment on the general funds by categorical programs, he will share the results of the audit. This in turn will cause a great deal of resentment by union members who see their fringe benefit costs increasing. They are not placated by the rationale for such programs. They see the program as an added burden to the overwhelming majority of their membership.

The Instructional Aide

A paraprofessional aide has been assigned as an interpreter to a sixth-grade classroom where a student who is hard of hearing is assigned. The principal and personnel from the Special Education Division have warned the teacher not to ask the aide to do anything else but interpret for the student. At times when the student does not need this assistance, the interpreter does crossword puzzles, much to the chagrin of the classroom teacher. The aide, however, is simply following the dictates of her job description.

None of these vignettes are unusual. In fact, each is commonplace and, taken together, the vignettes demonstrate the downside of a well-intentioned program.

WARNINGS FROM THE EDGE

If we are not careful, special education services for students who have disabilities may collapse under their own mandates—and school districts themselves may become "disabled." Barker (1988), a futurist, warned that organizations must constantly look to the edges of change for omens about new paradigms and realities.

Mandates Require Funds for Monitoring

For those concerned about the changing economic and pedagogical requirements for students with LD, recognition of the angry voices at the edge is a much needed first step for the development of effective programs. Far too many of those who are vested in the current programs fail to see the future because they have become blinded by the untenable tenets of the law. They have chosen not to look at or heed the warnings from those who are responsible for the delivery of solutions—the teachers, administrators, and parents of the students. The moral spirit embodied by well-intended laws such as P.L. 101-336 are endangered by those who live and die by the text, rather than by the spirit, of such laws.

The voices of mainstream classroom teachers who take special education students into their already large classes should be acknowledged instead of shamed. The charge by the same group of teachers that they lack quality time for professional development is legitimate and requires a professional response. Rosenholtz (1991) stated, "with teacher uncertainty comes the need to avoid situations that threaten to disclose it" (p. 43). Rosenholtz continued, "For teachers, technical knowledge encompasses the skills, procedures, and methods that help pupils progress academically. A technical culture is labeled *uncertain* if the outcomes of work are highly unpredictable; where, because of variability in their students, for example, teachers do not reach automatically for solutions to the myriad of learning problems they confront" (p. 4).

That the growing costs of special education programs have led to fiscal encroachment on every district's unrestricted budget is a legitimate concern that must be addressed. The rigid specialization of job descriptions, although understandably well meant, must be adjusted to the context of every situation. Specific class size requirements, detailed job descriptions that create narrow specializations, and prescriptive structural components of a program that cannot be uniformly applied to every situation all lead to a climate of rules and regulations instead of one of support and compassion.

The actions of monitoring legal and compliance issues are counterproductive to the expressed goals of such programs and often lead to the inappropriate allocation of limited funds. Learning disability specialists who are needed to guide both students and teachers find themselves swamped with testing requirements and compliance requirements for annual, biennial, even triennial reports. Teachers rarely receive much needed help from specialists; instead, they feel the increased burden of having to provide additional evidence and data to support the results of a specialist's recommendations. Because the results of special education personnel's tests trigger placement into specially designed programs, general education teachers have come to view these personnel as major obstacles that prevent the transfer of problem students into other settings. The fiscal game of remaining compliant to receive augmented restricted funds increases the need for monitoring and reduces the available funds for direct professional service to the deliverers of solutions. The net result of current programs is a highly bureaucratic rules-based program that requires additional enforcement resources.

The growing anger of general education teachers adds to the frustration of parents who want equitable access to a quality educational program as promised by the law. Parents' unhappiness in turn has led to lawsuits by legal advocates that further deplete school district funds. This vicious cycle is rooted in the ill-advised action of mandating a uniform set of policies without understanding the unique organizational environments that house each student.

Supporters of specially designed programs for students with LD must come to understand that many districts are perched on a precarious ledge that separates solvency from bankruptcy. Districts are or soon will be in the unenviable position of becoming noncompliant in order to remain fiscally solvent. Ironically, noncompliance may produce greater gains for students with LD—because funds can be applied directly to the classroom without the burdens of monitoring.

Avoidance of Organizational Defensiveness

Remaining blind, hard of hearing, and mute in the face of realities is a formula that will lead to an implosion similar to the ones happening in the areas of welfare and health reforms. Those who are responsible for the well-being of students with LD must rethink programs instead of standing steadfastly behind organizational defenses that take up so much of their time.

Argyris, in his powerful book *Overcoming Organizational Defenses* (1990), chronicled the saga of the futile attempts by David Stockman, director of the federal Bureau of Management and Budget, to air concerns during Ronald Reagan's ill-fated supply-side theory of economics. Argyris described both "the norm" of Ed Meese's White House role of protecting the president from bad news during executive cabinet meetings and the tragic existence of internal norms during the space-shuttle Challenger disaster that institutionalized mechanisms of silencing those who knew of problems with the "O" rings. In both of these cases, those who were entrusted with the mission's success were so busily engaged in defense mechanisms that the warnings of impending disaster were never heeded. In fact, Argyris pointed out the presence of a norm that "makes the undiscussability of the undiscussable also undiscussable" (p. 27).

In education we have had our share of similar disasters. New math, whole language, and open classrooms are but a few of the examples of programs with great potential that now are synonymous with failure. They failed in large measure because people with knowledge about problems remained silent or were not heard. The recent California Learning Assessment System (CLAS) also failed, in large part because the public and the majority of practitioners were kept out of the process. When the examination came under attack, proponents of the test simply hunkered down and defended it without acknowledging their errors. Instead of postponing the test for a year to allow for greater inclusion of various individuals and organizations, they marched blindly ahead. The CLAS exam today is interred alongside the "grave" of new math. The same can be said of the whole language and open classrooms reforms. The energy expected by defenders of these programs would have been better spent by listening to what was being said rather than wearing the shield of organizational defensiveness, righteousness, and secrecy.

Those who are charged with implementing inclusion for every student with a learning disability must be neither blinded to nor silenced about the fiscal realities of maintaining programs of equity. This applies equally to the cries of frustration from those who are directly involved with students with LD.

Special education as a whole stands at the brink of self-immolation because the warnings about its mandates, program requirements, and concomitant funding shortages are being defended against, rather than heeded. As Fullan (1993) warned, "problems are our friends, only if we are willing to do something about it" (p. 28).

HARD SOLUTIONS REQUIRE NEW WAYS OF THINKING

What can we do? We can begin by "graying" the black-and-white issues that are accompanied by mandates leading to bureaucratic, rules-based practices. We have to practice what mathematicians are calling "fuzzy thinking"—thinking that has the capacity to adjust to an environment. The environmental context of each student must be matched with the resources of his or her community. Arguing over what "ought to be" according to mandates will not necessarily meet the needs of students with LD.

The shrinking dollar base must be wisely allocated so as to meet students' needs rather than comply to the rigid texts of the law. Reinventing programs around the needs of students with LD will require a healthy reexamination of our sources of authority. We can no longer afford to rely solely on bureaucratic rules and regulations to justify our actions.

As Sergiovanni (1992) pointed out, bureaucratic and technical sources of authority do not lend themselves to lasting changes that benefit an organization's clients. As a group, those who would create equity must look to the moral and spiritual sources of authority rather than to the technical or positional sources that dominate our current decision-making processes. The whole education community must assess the *systemic* consequences of actions or inactions when applied to decision making. The leaders who are responsible for the well-being of students with LD may be better served by promoting what Sergiovanni called the "virtues of moral leadership." These virtues include (a) a commitment to practice in exemplary ways, (b) a commitment to practice toward valued social ends, (c) a commitment not only to one's way of teaching but to the professional craft itself, and (d) a commitment to the ethic of caring.

Developing practices that exemplify virtues and an efficacious sense of professionalism will cause an institution to better meet the needs of all its students. Not paying attention to these virtues and relying on compliance measures will result in efforts to meet the letter of the law but not its substance.

The history of students with LD is not filled with stories of success. The fact that most students in special education programs seldom exit from these programs prompted Slavin, Karweit, and Wasik (1994) to design programs in which students are "never streamed. . . . One major goal of Success for All is to keep students with learning problems out of special education if at all possible, and to serve any students who do qualify for special education in a way that does not disrupt their regular classroom experience" (p. 182).

Slavin et al. (1994), who designed the early primary program Success for All, explicitly stated that an element of success for early primary students is avoiding placing them in programs that have been specially designed for students with LD.

> A major goal of the Success for All program is to keep students with learning problems out of special education if at all possible. When a child is having serious learning problems in a Success for All school, the staff exhausts all other possibilities before beginning the formal referral process that may lead to special education. Only after tutoring, family interventions, adjustments in curricular approaches, and other interventions have been tried is a child considered for special education, and even at the referral stage every effort is made to find solutions other than special education for students who have IQ's above 70. (p. 195)

Slavin et al. have concluded that entering such programs inevitably leads to failure. This conclusion, echoed by others, cannot continue to be ignored. That it has been ignored is symptomatic of attempts to legislate what is "right" and therefore necessary. The exercise of power by proponents of programs for students with LD has manifested itself in laws and their concomitant policies and mandates. This in turn has led to the creation of a bureaucratic structure with the primary responsibility of determining whether or not policies and mandates are being implemented in an appropriate and timely manner. Categorical programs such as Title I or California's former specialized bilingual mandates have also suffered from an attempt to legislate complex policies.

Fullan (1993) stated, "You cannot mandate what matters (the more complex the change, the less you can force it)." Fullan went on, "you can effectively mandate things that (i) do not require thinking or skill in order to implement them; and (ii) can be monitored through close and constant surveillance" (p. 22).

Across the nation, most programs for students with LD violate these points. Such programs are highly complex and should engender a great deal of careful thought. Based on Fullan's requirements, they are impossible to monitor closely where it counts most—in the classrooms. Success or failure in these programs should be determined in the context of classroom effectiveness, not in the bartering halls of legislative bodies.

A prime artifact of the ills of mandating and monitoring "things that are important" is exemplified by an examination of the role of school psychologists. For years these professionals fought to remove the term psychometrist from their job title in order to send a message that the importance of their role went well beyond the task of testing. Ironically, when one examines the role of the school psychologist today, one finds that they are buried under a sea of testing deadlines and compliance paperwork, and many of them are working beyond the school day to complete testing requests because the bulk of their time is devoted to filling out yearly compliance instruments. A large proportion of California school districts must hire additional psychologist time to complete their triennial compliance reports to remain eligible for funding. Sadly, it now appears that psychologists have evolved into specialized psychometrists who also serve as compliance officers—hardly ever using their skills in psychological support with the frontline deliverers of program instruction and functioning in a reactive manner rather than a proactive one. They are trapped by the mandates of the program.

Backward Planning

This maladaptation of the spirit of the laws would be better served by new ways of planning and implementation. Elmore (1980, 1983) and Odden and Odden (1984) have advocated the use of "backward mapping" strategies that could result in an efficient and more appropriate use of funds. Backward mapping, which begins with the desired outcome and then requires that planners examine obstacles, solutions, and resources that enable the deliverers of the solution (teachers) to bring about success, is governed by knowledge and the early inclusion of the teachers.

At the heart of this new way of planning lies the allocation of time and money. The community that seeks equity for its students must recognize the need for professional development among the district's teacher corps. Mandating a structure does nothing to guarantee that significant learning will occur. Instead, teachers, parents, and experts must come to an agreement about what students will know, do, and believe. The allocation of funds should follow the outcomes of such agreements. As Fullan (1993) pointed out, "Connections with the wider environment is critical (The best organizations learn externally as well as internally)" (p. 38). Too many of our structures and policies in the area of students with LD have been shaped and formed by the few who fought the courageous battle in the courtroom to win equity in the classroom. In many instances, the law has spawned counterproductive practices that do not serve the students for whom it was intended.

The alternative of establishing learning communities that are committed to the spirit of equity, excellence, and choice will require a systemic view by institutions such as public education. Resolution of the current fiscal crisis in school systems across the nation will require the inclusion of all stakeholders in the community. The consequences of remaining segmented in our approach to students with LD may spell fiscal disaster for entire systems. The danger signals are clear:

1. Current mandates, policies, and specific guidelines are not supported by the level of program funding in school districts' restricted funds, and they are transferring dollars from their unrestricted general funds

to their categorical restricted funds to support and comply with legal mandates.

2. These mandates and their specific administrative policies require districts to expend a large portion of funds and precious time to monitor compliance.

3. Although programs may be in compliance, support services for classroom teachers are lacking, and the quality of instruction does not incorporate the virtues and "spirit" that initially created the laws.

4. District personnel are angry and frustrated at meeting the letter of the law in spite of their unique fiscal and programmatic situations.

5. Dissatisfied with the quality of programs, parents are seeking legal help to provide access to "quality" programs, thus adding to the fiscal burdens of school districts.

The signs of an impending fiscal and programmatic crisis are clear if we honestly examine programs for students with LD from the perspective of the classroom. When taken as a whole, it appears that the growing anger and dissatisfaction may stem more from bureaucratic rules and compliance sources of authority than from the unavailability of systemic solutions.

Programs in education that work do so because the classroom interactions that touch students are nurturing and effective. The current methods of allocating funds for serving students with LD not only exacerbate the fiscal problems, but they drain the sense of efficacy from those who are asked to implement the program.

Left unchanged, the current set of specific mandates and compliance provisions will result in another well-intentioned program caught in the snafus of faulty implementation practices. Many California districts soon will be faced with the choice of disobeying legal statutes for students with LD or making larger cuts in programs that service the general school population. This can be avoided only if we heed the warnings and reexamine the entire approach to serving students with LD.

4. What Learning Disability Does: Sustaining the Ideology of Schooling

CURT DUDLEY-MARLING

AND DON DIPPO

Individuals must be equipped to reflect upon the knowledge structures we provide, to identify themselves with respect to them, to penetrate their mystiques. They must be equipped as well to reflect upon the erosion of community. (Greene, 1978, p. 122)

Critical lenses have often been brought to bear on the field of learning disabilities. Heshusius (1982), Poplin (1984, 1988), Iano (1986), and Skrtic (1991), for example, have challenged the behavioral theory that underlies much of the work in learning disabilities. Coles (1987) and Kavale and Forness (1985) questioned the research base of learning disability theory and practice. The work of Franklin (1986) and Sleeter (1987) offered alternative understandings of the historical roots of learning disabilities. The analyses of Carrier (1986) and Sleeter illustrate the role learning disabilities may play in the practice of sorting students on the basis of race, culture, and ethnicity.

It is difficult to gauge the effect of these critiques, but published responses have ranged from indifference to defensiveness to ridicule (Ulman & Rosenberg, 1986) to near hysteria (Rourke, 1989). There is

Reprinted, with changes, from "What learning disability does: Sustaining the ideology of schooling," by Curt Dudley-Marling and Don Dippo, *Journal of Learning Disabilities*, Vol. 28, 1995, pp. 408–414. Copyright © 1995 by PRO-ED, Inc.

little evidence that these critiques stimulated the kind of self-reflection that would affect the way learning disability professionals view themselves, their field, or the children and adults they serve. The field of learning disabilities, although enriching itself by drawing on various traditions in medicine and cognitive psychology, remains isolated from developments in sociolinguistics, critical theory, anthropology, feminist studies, literacy education, philosophy, and literary studies that challenge basic understandings in learning disabilities.

Critical analysis is often unwelcome, but it may be crucial to ensuring a diversity of ideas as a means of protecting a field of study from intellectual and moral isolation and decay, and to maintaining the vitality of communities that come together to explore questions and ideas. The ability of a field such as learning disabilities to shield itself from criticism may seem reaffirming, but the skill with which a field of study deflects criticism in the short term may seal its fate in the long term. The health of any field of human study depends on persistent and penetrating criticism.

Although a critique of the field of learning disabilities is worthwhile in its own right, learning disabilities may be a particularly good place from which to engage in a broader critique, of schooling and society. Foucault (cited in Skrtic, 1991, p. 24) has argued "that the most insightful way to understand society is to consider it from the perspective of the professions that have emerged to contain its failures." Clearly, the field of learning disabilities emerged to contain the perceived failure of society's principal institution for educating and socializing its youth.

In this chapter, we critique learning disabilities theory and practice through the lens of discourse theory (Fulcher, 1989; Gee, 1990; Macdonell, 1986). We use discourse analysis not to test learning disability "truths," but to see what the social practice of learning disabilities can tell us about taken-for-granted assumptions about schooling and the social and political context in which schools are situated. We begin with a brief overview of discourse analysis.

DISCOURSE ANALYSIS OVERVIEW

Discourse theory arose, in part, because of the inadequacy of language alone in accounting for meaning. To illustrate, consider an example adapted from Gee (1990): An urban professional in a three-piece suit steps into his neighborhood "biker bar." He orders a beer and then asks his leather-jacketed companion, "May I have a match for my cigarette, please?" (p. xv). The man's words alone indicate a simple request. But what the man says, how he says it, where he says it, and how he is dressed combine to signal an additional meaning: "I do not belong here. I am not one of you." Similarly, the formal tests used by school psychologists communicate meanings about children's ability *and* the status of people who administer them.

Discourses are "saying (writing)–doing–being–valuing–believing combinations" (Gee, 1990, p. 142); or, more formally, "discourses are ways of being in the world, or forms of life which integrate words, acts, values, beliefs, social identities, as well as gestures, glances, body position, and clothes" (Gee, 1990, p. 142). They are social "identity kits" (Gee, 1990, p. 142), the means by which individuals define who they are (and who they are not).

Individual identities are complicated by the fact that each of us belongs to many different primary and secondary discourses. Primary discourses are those into which we were apprenticed as part of our socialization within our homes and families; secondary discourses are public discourses, beyond home and family (Gee, 1990). You might, for example, simultaneously be an American, a Democrat, a learning disabilities teacher, a runner, a pianist, and a member of the National Organization of Women. Associated with each of these roles is a discourse that constructs individuals in different and sometimes contradictory ways.

The meanings we make as humans (including the meanings, "Who am I?" and "Who are you?") can be understood only within the context of discourses. Discourses determine who counts as the right sort of person (Gee, 1990) and who does not. Determining who the right sort of people are also helps regulate who is entitled to the benefits that accrue to participants in a discourse. In that sense, discourses are inherently ideological (Gee, 1990; Macdonell, 1986), involving "a set of values and viewpoints about the relationships between people and the distribution of social goods" (Gee, 1990, p. 144). (Gee defines "social goods" as "anything that the people in the society generally believe are beneficial to have or harmful not to have . . . including life, space, time, 'good' schools, 'good' jobs, wealth, status, power or control" [1990, p. 23].) Control over certain discourses, such as the discourse of schooling, can affect the acquisition of social goods like money, power, and status.

The work of discourse analysis is to uncover "the tacit theories [that] underlie the common-sense generalizations people make" (Gee, 1990, p. 73) and determine "what aspects of the present social order are sustained by, and which social actors are able to realize their objectives via, dominant discursive practices" (Fulcher, 1989, p. 12). In other words, discourse analysis attempts to explicate the ideology, the "tacit or overt theories of the distribution of social goods" (Gee, 1990, p. 73), underlying discourse practices. In this chapter we use discourse analysis to see what learning disabilities can tell us about the ideological meaning of schooling and the role the field of learning disabilities plays in sustaining that ideology.

Sustaining Schooling Assumptions: The Need That Creates the Category

We begin with the observation that the category of learning disabilities exists within the institution of schooling and must, therefore, fulfill some need within the schools. It is commonly believed that the classification of learning disabilities arose in response to the unique needs of a group of students for whom school was especially challenging. That is no doubt true, but it is not the whole story. To assume that the LD field *just* supports students assumes that schools *just* educate children. Schools do educate children, but underlying schooling are ideological assumptions that affect both the way children are educated and the role education plays in the distribution of social goods. The field of learning disabilities may serve the needs of individual children, but it also serves ideological needs. The meaning of learning disabilities, that is, how the field of learning disabilities operates to sustain the ideology of schooling (Gee, 1990), can be ascertained only by uncovering some of the taken-for-granted assumptions underlying contemporary schooling and considering how the category of learning disabilities operates to sustain those (ideological) assumptions. As Carrier (1986) stated:

> Learning disability theory's truths are not self-evident. If we are to make sense of it we must go beyond an agenda of scientific questions of truth, evidence, and interference, extend our inquiry to include an analysis of the content and context of learning disability theory. (p. 124)

Three Assumptions

There are three powerful, taken-for-granted assumptions of schooling that are particularly relevant to uncovering the ideological meaning of learning disabilities:

1. *Compulsory schooling is justifiable, reasonable, and beneficial.* It is a basic belief among Americans that the key to maintaining a democracy is an informed and responsible citizenry. Compulsory attendance laws charged schools with ensuring that all Americans received instruction that fostered the attitudes (e.g., respect for authority) and skills deemed necessary for responsible citizenship. Compulsory education attests to the importance placed on the role of education in creating opportunities for every American to be what they want to be: With hard work and a good education, "anyone can grow up to be president" (see Note 1). The Education for All Handicapped Children Act reaffirms the value Americans place on schooling.

2. *Each learner comes to school with a unique intellectual endowment.* Most people assume that each child comes to school with an intellectual endowment, or "capacity," that is strongly predictive of school success. This endowment—operationalized as IQ—is understood to distribute normally; that is, a few gifted individuals have a lot of it, a similar number of individuals have less, with most people in between. Effort is also seen to play an important role in school success, enabling an "average" student to do quite well. Similarly, without effort, an intellectually gifted student may do poorly in school.

Other factors—understood as individual differences—can also affect achievement. An assumption underlying tracking, remedial education, and special education, for example, is that not everyone learns in the same way or at the same rate. There is, however, an assumption implicit in the age-graded, factory model of education common in most of our schools that all children learn pretty much the same way, at the same time. It seems that common assumptions about differences among learners contradict other assumptions implicit in traditional models of school organization. These sorts of contradictions (in this case, that schools assume that children are simultaneously the same *and* different) are not unusual in discourses, but can be troubling nonetheless.

3. *Competition is good and natural.* The almost exclusive use of normative evaluation to determine grades, school placement, admission to college, and so on attests to the importance placed on competition in schools. Competition is valued as the "natural" way to motivate students to do their best and the *only* way to prepare students for life in a competitive world. In a meritocracy, competition is also assumed to be the only fair way to determine who is entitled to the rewards of schooling (e.g., occupational choice, college, graduate school).

Historically, there has also been a sense that it is unfair, even unkind, to expect some people to compete. This humanitarian rationale has often been used to assign some students to special schools or classes, basic tracks, or work study programs. For the privilege of being relieved from the brutality of competition, students enter into an implicit bargain with the schools. They no longer have to compete, but this accommodation comes with a cost—the expectation that students forfeit the opportunity to be adequately prepared to compete for the jobs that carry the highest pay, security, and prestige.

Learning Disabilities: Satisfying a Need

One of the principal needs fulfilled by the category of learning disabilities is that it *explains an anomaly in the discourse of schooling.* One of the most powerful tenets of schooling that is taken for granted is that effort and capacity are what count. There is, however, a group of children who appear to have the potential (IQ) but do not succeed in school even with effort. The theory of learning disabilities—generally understood as a discrepancy between ability (IQ) and achievement presumed to be due to neurological factors—explains this anomaly by adding another factor, (dis)ability, to the achievement equation. Normally, capacity plus effort results in school success, *unless a disability intervenes*—in this case, a learning disability.

Learning disability theory also functions to *preserve conventional assumptions about the role of potential and effort in school achievement* by placing responsibility for school failure within individual students. This enables schools to explain the anomaly of learning disabilities without having to consider more troubling explanations for school failure—for example, that factors such as race, class, culture, gender, and ethnicity are as important in school success as either effort or capacity. Stories that are part of learning disabilities folk wisdom about eminent men like Rodin, Einstein, and Edison who overcame their learning disabilities (Coles, 1987; Lerner, 1981) further reinforce the role of effort in school discourse by providing tangible evidence of the value of schooling and hard work.

Learning disability theory also functions to *sustain beliefs about the role of individual differences in schools.* The very presence of school programs for students with learning disabilities—understood in terms of both *inter*- and *intra*individual differences—supports the belief that schools recognize, accept, and accommodate individual differences. However, contradictions in the discourse of learning disabilities—which mirror contradictions about individual differences in the discourse of schooling—reveal another meaning of "difference" in schools. Learning disabilities rhetoric may be about difference, but learning disabilities practice, which stresses (a) adaptive behavior; (b) coping strategies; and (c) right (i.e., normal) ways of thinking (abstract, not concrete; Carrier, 1986), talking, and interacting, has the effect of "normalizing" students while leaving unchallenged conventional notions of what is normal or natural. The assumption that learning disabilities persist throughout life (American Association for Children and Adults with LD, 1985) means that individuals labeled as learning disabled need to learn strategies to overcome their disabilities. But there is the sense that "overcoming" means minimizing or eliminating differences (i.e., "passing for normal"). So at the same time that the field of learning disabilities accommodates diversity by providing for the needs of individual children and adults, it *limits* diversity in the schools by reinforcing a rigid, narrow definition of what counts as normal behavior. Learning disability theory, at least the way it is constructed in schools, reveals the true meaning of difference and diversity in our schools: Differences, in the name of education, are to be leveled.

A key assumption in the discourse of schooling, that "competition is good," depends on the corollary, "competition is fair." Presumably, competition is acceptable only if everyone has an equal opportunity to succeed. The behavioral, skills-based instruction that is the foundation of learning disability practice *sustains the belief that school curricula are culturally neutral* (i.e., fair) by limiting the discussion of teaching practice to "method." However, "disputes about . . . correct procedures, whether in medicine or in teaching, are never merely technical" (Fulcher, 1989, p. 263). They are located within a moral system of values and a political system that has established a hierarchy of values (Fulcher, 1989). But, if instruction equals method, then there is no reason to consider the cultural or moral content of what is being taught. From this perspective, the strong relationship between family income and school achievement (Edelsky, 1991) is seen not as a challenge to the cultural fairness of school curricula, but as an affirmation of the values of middle- and upper-middle-class homes.

Another contradiction in learning disability discourse further reinforces the myth that school curricula are unbiased. The behavioral technology that dominates learning disabilities practice acknowledges individual differences through its promise to "begin where the child is." However, the claim that behavioral laws are universal—applying to everyone, all the time—effaces individual differences based on factors such as race, class, culture, ethnicity, and gender. Behaviorism sustains assumptions of fairness by implying that, because we are all the same anyway, questions about cultural fairness do not really matter.

Finally, learning disabilities *provide a practical solution to a dilemma created within school discourse* when provisions are made to offer humane alternatives to the rigorous competition of schooling. Historically, many middle- to upper-middle-class parents, who had certain aspirations for their children, were willing, even anxious, to accept extra support for their children when they struggled in school. However, these same parents were unwilling to accept the price of existing special education programs, which included giving up any realistic chance of high-paying, prestigious, secure careers for their children (Carrier, 1986; Sleeter, 1987). The field of learning disabilities, by constructing its clients as "normally intelligent," provides support for individual students without necessarily blocking either their own or their politically influential parents' aspirations (see Note 2).

Assumptions about schooling do not exist, and cannot be understood, apart from the social context within which schools reside. In the next section we examine the ideological context that creates the need for such a category as learning disabilities by explicating the relationship between school-based discourse and dominant discourse outside of schools.

IDEOLOGY OF SCHOOLING: THE CONTEXT THAT CREATES THE NEED

The field of learning disabilities has arisen in a context in which discussions of schooling are increasingly limited to the role of schools in serving the needs of the economy. In this section we take up both the economic conception of schooling and the issue of who benefits from such a view.

✴ The Needs of the Economy

Critics of public education who view schooling through the lens of economic competition conclude that schools are not adequately preparing students for the rigors of the workplace. Education reforms emerging from governments and the business communities stress bringing schooling even more closely in line with society's economic needs. Historians of education in Canada and the United States have observed that the motivating forces behind compulsory schooling have always been some combination of social control and economic development (what the British liked to call "gentling the masses"; see Cremin, 1988; Houston & Prentice, 1988; Osborne, 1991). The production of responsible citizens and productive workers has long been touted as the only legitimate goal of compulsory public schooling.

In current social, political, and economic contexts, there are certain versions of "the responsible citizen" and "the productive worker" that are more highly valued than others. Media pundits, politicians, and business leaders make daily pronouncements about the knowledges, skills, and attitudes needed to be responsible and productive in a postindustrial society. These authorities seem clear on the kinds of adults the future will require, and schools are very much implicated in the process of producing them. According to this vision, the responsible school citizen (and future productive worker) is one who has learned, among other things, to do homework on time, to not question the authority or expertise of the teacher, to compete for grades, and generally not to make trouble. It matters little in the long run (though one would never surmise this from the current debates) whether classrooms are organized around texts and workbooks or activity centers, as long as the expectations for students focus on obedience and conformity.

To better serve the needs of the economy, promote productivity, and enhance international competitiveness, education institutions, from departments of education to classrooms, are increasingly expected to become more accountable, to ensure effectiveness of instruction, and to enforce uniform standards of excellence. Such "reform" measures, we are assured, will create a "win/win" situation both for society (through the economy) and the individual. The economy benefits by being continuously provided with a high-quality human resource, and the individual benefits by being provided with a learning environment that supports individual growth and achievement—"where everyone can be the best they can be and develop to their true potential."

These images of good citizenship and productive workers, and the kinds of learning environments based on efficiency of instruction and individual achievement they require, both assume and promote an understanding of the person that Apple (1982), following MacPherson (1962), called "possessive individualism." From within this frame of reference, Apple (1982) noted that

> the mark of a good pupil is the possession and accumulation of vast quantities of skills in the service of technical interests. As an ideological mechanism in the maintenance of hegemony this is rather interesting. In the larger society, people consume as isolated individuals. Their worth is determined by the possession of material goods. . . . The accumulation of such goods or of the "cultural capital" of technical competence—here atomistic bits of knowledge and skills measured on pre-tests and post-tests—is a technical procedure, one which requires only the mastery of the prior necessary technical skills and enough time to follow the rules, at one's own pace, to their conclusion. (p. 262)

Within this dominant discourse of schooling (based on the twin pillars of "normal distribution" and "meritocracy"), every student can achieve to her or his full potential (not equal, but normally distributed) when placed in a competitive environment that supports and encourages each student to put forth her or his own best effort, while making allowances for individual differences in rate of accumulation (i.e., working at one's own pace). It is important to note how difference is acknowledged in this account. Difference in capacity (as determined by IQ) is recognized; hence equality of achievement or outcome is never expected. Rather, the claim is that schools can provide equality of *opportunity* for each student to achieve to her or his full potential. Difference in ability is also recognized but is defined as a matter of pace—some are fast and some are slow, but all can get there (to a uniform standard or to their true potential?), given sufficient time. Given differences in capacity and differences in ability, the determining factor in achieving to one's full potential is effort. And here is where individualizing is most insidious: Best effort is required and best effort is expected, and a competitive environment is what really brings out best effort. Those who do not achieve to their full potential, given sufficient time and the right learning environment, have only themselves to blame—they are lazy, unmotivated, not willing to put forth the effort, and, therefore, deserving of their fate (low academic achievement and the consequent lack of social and economic rewards).

Who Benefits?

So who benefits from this dominant discourse around schooling? A significant body of research indicates that the prime beneficiaries are those who enter schools with a certain kind of "cultural capital" (Bourdieu & Passeron, 1977) and who accumulate conventionally valued skills and knowledge in highly competitive environments—that is, White, able-bodied, middle- and upper-class men (Bowles & Gintis, 1975; Curtis, Livingstone, & Smaller, 1992; Jencks, 1972). In other words, those who have the most to gain from school-based discourse are those who benefit most from preserving a status quo in which a relatively small number of individuals control the lion's share of the social goods.

Of course, while the status quo benefits some, it also disadvantages others. Critics of dominant discourse detail how schools, by sustaining the status quo, participate in the perpetuation of social and economic injustice. Feminist scholars, for example, describe how schools, in favoring certain ways of knowing, doing, thinking, believing, and interacting, distort, marginalize, and denigrate young girls and women. Similarly, African-American, Caribbean-Canadian, and First Nations educators, gay and lesbian activists, and people with disabilities have decried the unwillingness of those who speak within the dominant discourse to hear other voices.

What is the problem with opening things up? First and foremost, it would challenge theories and practices that legitimate White male privilege. The claim, however, is that to acknowledge a broader range of differences would slow down efficiency of instruction and obstruct individual achievement. Within the dominant discourse, sameness is what is desirable. Differences in capacity and ability can be accommodated, but only insofar as they do not disrupt the fundamental assumptions of normal distribution, meritocratic principles, and the achievement of full potential. The dominant discourse imagines communities of difference based on essential sameness within a normal distribution.

The dominant, humanistic discourse of schooling sustains these assumptions. In school-based discourses, everyone is a unique individual within the limits imposed by assumptions of normality. We can recognize and celebrate our uniqueness together because essentially we are all the same—normal human beings with a range of capacities and abilities who, through our own efforts, achieve a measure of academic success and reap concomitant social and economic rewards.

CONCLUSIONS

We do not doubt that the field of learning disabilities provides needed and welcome support for many children and adults. However, it also satisfies another need: to preserve fundamental assumptions in the discourse of schooling about what schools are for and who should succeed in them. As Sleeter (1987) pointed out:

> In accepting commonly used categories for children, we also tacitly accept an ideology about what schools are for, what society should be like, and what the "normal" person should be like. Far from being objective fact, ideology rests on values and assumptions that cannot be proven, and that serve some people better than others. (p. 211)

Our analysis indicates that learning disabilities theory, despite its progressive rhetoric, is fundamentally conservative in that it functions to preserve ideological practices in schools by reinforcing taken-for-granted assumptions of schooling and explaining anomalies in school-based discourse. Learning disabilities practice, by "normalizing" clients to conventional standards of behavior, reinforces narrow conceptions of normality that will never be congenial to individual differences. By protecting school discourse against claims that school practices are unfair, that gender, race, culture, and ethnicity are at least as powerful as effort or capacity, the field of learning disabilities participates in school practices that tend to preserve the inequities that exist in the larger society (Bowles & Gintis, 1975). In the final analysis, the field of learning disabilities, by reinforcing the discourse of schooling, serves to preserve ideological practices that

> privilege us who have mastered them and do significant harm to others. They involve us in foolish views about other human beings and their Discourse. They foreshorten our view of human nature, human diversity, and the capacities for human changes and development. They render us complicit in the denial of "goods", including full human worth, to other humans, including many children. They imply that some children—

including many black, Chicano, native American and other children who disproportionately fail in school—*mean* less than other children. (Gee, 1990, p. 191)

If we find this state of affairs unacceptable and take seriously Gee's (1990) charge to closely examine any discourse—in or out of school—that we suspect advantages oneself or one's group over other people or other groups, what in the field of learning disabilities is to be done? What is the most reasonable course of action for those who are otherwise different (and for those who work with and care for and about them): to challenge the dominant discourse at the risk of being further marginalized, or to pass oneself off as the same, as normal, as willing to participate and partake in the bargain (provided some reasonable accommodation is made)?

Our analysis suggests a course of action that is both strategic and principled. In the short term, LD practitioners ought to continue to work in ways that directly benefit the students to whom they are accountable and for whom they care. In the longer term, however, LD practitioners ought to consider spending less time and energy in efforts to expand the category of normal (or to create a category of "qualified normal") and instead seek to assert the value of difference in ways that apply not just to marginalized "others," but also to those whose difference is effaced within the category of normal. Difference is, after all, what makes us who we are, and the "normalizing" tendencies of schooling (and their marginalizing effects) must be challenged by those seeking to create the kinds of classrooms Greene (1993) imagined possible, where

> individual identity takes form in the contexts of relationships and dialogue; our concern must be to create the kinds of contexts that nurture—for all children—the sense of worthiness and agency. The stigma of "disabled" or "low IQ" or "lower socioeconomic class" too frequently forces young persons into being the recipients of "treatment" or "training," sometimes from the most benevolent motives on the part of those hoping to "help." (p. 229)

To really help, then, is to work daily to remove the stigma of difference, to create classrooms in which relationship and dialogue, as opposed to treatment and training, are central, and to create a conception of community based not on normalcy, competitiveness, and "just deserts," but rather on diversity, mutuality, and social justice. As Greene (1993) framed the question:

> How are we to comprehend the kind of community that offers the opportunity "to be otherwise"? Democracy, we realize, means a community that is always in the making. Marked by an emerging solidarity, a sharing of

certain beliefs, a dialogue about others, it must remain open to newcomers, those too long thrust aside. (p. 227)

Inclusive, democratic communities are marked by a willingness to acknowledge difference and an openness to the possibility that inclusive communities will affect not only how we construct the "other," but also how we construct ourselves.

NOTES

1. The reality, of course, is that <u>anyone</u> means any <u>White</u> man.
2. The speedy success parents of children with LD had in obtaining official recognition for the category of learning disabilities from state, provincial, and federal governments attests to their power and influence (Carrier, 1986; Sleeter, 1987).

5. Escaping the Cave to Dream New Dreams: A Normative Vision for Learning Disabilities

LOUIS G. DENTI AND

MICHAEL S. KATZ

During a recent period of sleepless nights, I remember falling into a deep dream state. The images were so vivid that I can recount the reverie with some accuracy. I was sitting on top of a mountain on a secluded island observing a terrible injustice being done to a group of workers. The workers were garbed in tattered purple overalls with large "O" insignias sown on their right sleeves. On the back of the uniforms the following was scripted in bold gold letters: "Your greatest adversary is your own creation." As the laborers toiled, the work bosses scurried about in carts with sketch pads, dropping little notes reminding the workers they were inferior. There were no chains, whips, or slave-like forms of doctrinal obedience, just constant reminders that the workers were less capable and less significant. Periodically a loud speaker would boom out, "Your greatest adversary is your own creation" and the famous Pogo variation— "You have met the enemy and he is you." Everyone seemed oblivious to these obnoxious, repetitive loudspeaker messages except me.

As I watched from my perch, I was stirred to action. I wanted to help the workers by making them aware that they had indeed helped create an

Reprinted, with changes, from "Escaping the cave to dream new dreams: A normative vision for learning disabilities," by Louis G. Denti and Michael S. Katz, *Journal of Learning Disabilities*, Vol. 28, 1995, pp. 415–424. Copyright © 1995 by PRO-ED, Inc.

inferiority complex and were accentuating the self-fulfilling prophecy. It was apparent that the bosses might be persuaded to act differently. However, a dream-master, who reminded me of the Magister Ludi in a Herman Hesse novel, would not allow me to help unless I could master the glass bead game. The game, with its thousand glass beads on strings in a perfect line, required that I take the first glass bead and, with a perfect motion, recoil and let go. If the bead struck the subsequent bead perfectly, a chain reaction would be set into motion whereby all 1,000 beads would be hit, and I would be allowed to interact with the workers and bosses. As I recoiled, I was jolted out of the dream (see Note 1).

The dream haunted me for weeks before I began to realize that each bead represented an isolated piece of propositional knowledge in the field of learning disabilities, the field I have plowed and contoured for 25 years. To reshape the field and recast its grounding assumptions would require nothing less than "living the truth." But what would this involve? Was it possible that in spite of all that I had learned, I might know everything and understand nothing? Perplexed, I wondered aloud, "Have we missed the point in the field of learning disabilities? Have we built a house of cards? Could our greatest enemy be our own creation? Was Pogo right?"

Images of reality, both dreamlike and nondreamlike, inform our everyday understandings, influence our sense of what is possible, and determine, in part, our vision of what is desirable. If we adopt a critical stance, these images invite us to examine the hidden dangers embedded in the status quo and question whether we are being deceived by the legitimizing mechanisms of our field's dominant view of reality and its underlying core assumptions. If we are like Plato's prisoners in the cave, watching the shadows of the fire against the wall and not seeing them as shadows, how shall we break out of our chains, see the illusions and false images for what they are, and then gain a clearer grasp of an empowering new reality (see Note 2)?

This chapter proposes that we must liberate ourselves, as prisoners, from the cave-like condition that characterizes the field of learning disabilities. Our article is predicated on two beliefs: (a) that teachers of students with learning disabilities must critically examine the dominant view of reality undergirding the field of learning disabilities to see the false images built into it, and (b) we must seek a new, empowering, alternative vision of the purposes of education as we move into the twenty-first century. Thus, our purpose here is twofold: first, to examine critically how the dominant image of reality in the field of learning disabilities is derived from what we call the "diagnostic model," and second, to propose an alternative, normative conception of education that emphasizes the importance of caring, social relatedness, and community participation—what we will call the "development of citizens."

RE-HUMANIZING THE LEARNING DISABILITIES FIELD

Skrtic's insightful book, *Behind Special Education,* offers the field an opportunity to examine critically its grounding assumptions. Skrtic (1991) synthesized key components of research and formulated the following four assumptions that have guided, and continue to guide, the field of special education:

1. Disabilities are pathological conditions.

2. Differential diagnosis is objective and useful.

3. Special education is a rationally conceived and coordinated system of services that benefits diagnosed students.

4. Progress results from incremental technological improvements in diagnosis and instructional interventions.

Specialized fields are undergirded by patterns of conduct based on implicit and explicit models that have acquired significance. If one were to ask a working professional, "Why are you doing that?" or "Why do you say that?," justificatory responses would invoke these models. Special education, and the field of learning disabilities in particular, has borrowed on the credibility of scientific terminology, diagnosis, and medical research to establish a complex set of labels and a body of esoteric discourse accessible only to the initiated. Regardless of whether these labels are used appropriately, or whether their application benefits the persons so named, the clients—parents and students with disabilities—are not privy to the esoteric body of knowledge that generated the labels. Moreover, if one views special education in general and learning disabilities in particular as reasonably new fields trying to establish their academic and professional credibility, one can clearly see why a diagnostic model that borrows on the established reputation of medicine as a field of applied science has much to recommend it. Without question, at a certain end of the continuum, wherein students have specific genetic and metabolic disorders dictating medical treatment and education prescriptions, it should be acknowledged that a diagnostic model is quite appropriate. Furthermore, we would also acknowledge that for many families, a diagnosis seems to alleviate the state of anxiety that stems from not knowing what the child's problem is or how to solve it. However, the labeling process is seldom cut-and-dried, and students often have a host of concomitant medical disorders, such as epilepsy, heart problems, and physical anomalies, associated with the initial medical diagnosis. Clearly, parents and students with disabilities are in no position to judge the adequacy of the label or its preceding diagnosis.

On the other end of the continuum, students with learning *problems* are likely to be subject to the same diagnostic procedures. For these students, the diagnostic model can be terribly inappropriate; through a harsh tagging process, these labels can destroy the students' self-esteem. From one critical perspective, labeling students' problems runs the risk of promoting the naming fallacy—claiming one has solved the problem because one has named it. From another perspective, one might go further and suggest that the labels invoke a pseudoscientific reality that bears little resemblance to what the students' actual problems are based upon (Reynolds & Lakin, 1987). In this regard, some researchers have dismissed the entire field of learning disabilities, with its elaborate taxonomy of diagnostic labels, as "instructionally irrelevant" (Coles, 1987; Heshusius, 1982; Iano, 1987; Sleeter, 1986; Stainback & Stainback, 1984).

If what we have just argued is correct, a noteworthy paradox of special education seems to be the following: Some of the diagnostic model's potential strengths (clear diagnosis for specific syndromes and psychological support for families based on a specific diagnosis) are also bound up with two potential weaknesses, namely, (a) the danger that misleading labeling will lead to inappropriate treatment, obscuring the complexity of a student's problem by oversimplifying the problem with a label, and (b) the danger that the diagnostic model and its application justify the isolation, or at least the stigmatized separation, of special education students from their mainstream peers.

One peculiar feature of the diagnostic model that we believe has not received adequate attention is its individualistic theoretical underpinnings. Unfortunately, in our view, the diagnostic model makes all problems appear to be individualistic: Problems are always *the individual's problems*. Thus, the student with a disability is viewed as an atomistic unit, to be studied and treated apart from his or her social relations. In our view, the diagnostic model allows little room to examine a student's interpersonal or group relationships, for these relationships are not seen as essential to what the individual needs to become a socially productive group member or "citizen" (see Note 3). The diagnostic model places a diminished emphasis on students as social beings (Tomlinson, 1982). As a result, a concern for group and interpersonal relations is seldom viewed as central to the special education process. Because the grounding assumptions of special education and learning disabilities seem to reduce the individual to a person with particular cognitive deficits, it is difficult for the field of learning disabilities to address the central normative issues of what it is that a healthy social person does, what competencies she has acquired, and what character traits she has developed (see Note 4). The paradigmatic views of special education and learning disabilities diminish the possibilities for thoughtful dialogue on what we regard as central to the development of a healthy social person. In the second half of this chapter we shall raise more explicitly what we regard to be the central normative questions for both special education and regular education: What kind of person should school be trying to develop? In particular, what does a healthy social person look like? What kinds of experiences does a child with or without learning difficulties need to become a functioning citizen at a minimum, and a flourishing citizen as an idealized goal? We shall say more about how special education, and learning disabilities in particular, should focus more attention on students as social beings who need to acquire the capacity to care for others, relate effectively with others as individuals and within groups, and learn to function productively as citizens within diverse communities. Our main point here is that the discourse of special education makes such a focus on the social dimensions of learning conceptually difficult.

Ironically, a central problem created by applying the diagnostic model with students with learning disabilities is an unintended one, namely, reducing students to "second-class citizens." The intention of labeling, appropriate diagnosis, and "special" education was to target resources, as well as to individualize instruction for students with learning disabilities. However, the unintended result has been the transformation of students with learning disabilities into second-class citizens who are entitled to something less than other students, or who are thought of by others as "less." An abiding sense of inferiority is thus reinforced, albeit unintentionally. That is, if we think persons with disabilities are inferior because they belong to a particular group, we have engaged in psychological discrimination. We have acquired a negative view of a person because of her group affiliation. It is a short step from such psychological discrimination to discriminatory treatment and its justification. Hence, segregated educational arrangements of students with learning disabilities are legitimated (Dunn, 1968; Madden & Slavin, 1983).

It should also be clear at this point how hard it often is for the prisoners of these practices to separate the shadows of the fire on the wall of the cave from the fire itself. Images, however distorted, may provide a person with her only sense of reality. According to Berger and Luckman (1966), "institutional meanings are impressed powerfully and unforgettably on the unconscious of the individual in the system" (p. 70). Institutional meanings in the field of special education are derived from diagnostic, prescriptive formulas. Thus, the dominating image is the following: Ministering to children who might need special help requires trained specialists to execute a series of tests and exams to find out what is wrong and prescribe an individualized education treatment plan (Ysseldyke & Thurlow, 1984). Are there difficulties with this image? We think there are.

As Ysseldyke et al. (1983) pointed out, significant problems underlie current assumptions and practices in the assessment of, and decision-making for, students with learning disabilities. Ysseldyke and his colleagues argued that the challenge lies in how to address the problems, question the assumptions, and suggest alternative approaches for providing services to students in school. After 5 years of extensive research, Ysseldyke's team concluded the following: (a) The description of students with learning difficulties lacks precision; (b) students with learning disabilities are best defined as "whatever society wants them to be, needs them to be, or lets them be at any point in time"; (c) researchers have compiled an interesting set of findings on a group of students who are experiencing academic difficulties and who bother general classroom teachers; and (d) sanctioned labelers classify students as having learning disabilities in order to remove them from the general classroom mainstream.

Ten years after the Ysseldyke research and analysis, the diagnostic model remains intact, even though the disability-rights movement has been instrumental in criticizing the deficit model, in shifting attitudes so that they are more inclusive of special needs students in mainstream school environments, and in emphasizing alternative modes of assessment (Shinn & Hubbard, 1993). In fact, since Mercer's (1973) seminal book 20 years ago that challenged the phenomenon of labeling, the diagnostic model has changed in very minimal ways. Seemingly with every decade, a major new treatise attempts to shed light on the inadequacy of the diagnostic model (Skrtic, 1991). These critical efforts bring about a renewed defense of the model or an intensive interrogation of its critics' intentions (Fuchs & Fuchs, 1994; Kauffman, 1991; Scruggs, 1993). It is interesting to note that because the model is resistant to change, the noninitiated today come to understand it through as vigorous and agreed-upon a transmission process as was the case years ago. Persons entering the field of special education are introduced uncritically to the diagnostic model and other special education formulas via institutes of higher education, school staff-development programs, and the propaganda of special interest groups (Glass, 1983). Furthermore, the curricula and instructional programming via which students come to apprehend the social reality of special education obscure the way in which the taken-for-granted reality of special education, and, more specifically, learning disabilities, is intellectually reproduced. Using our Plato cave analogy, we can say that the special educators are led to their positions in the cave with blindfolds on. Once they are chained with their backs to the fire, they do not know how they got there or that there is any other place they could have been taken to. Thus, the model maintains its intellectual and institutional dominance in uncritical form. However, as the decades pass, many more prisoners can be found in the cave.

For a moment, let us revisit my dream and the notion of living the truth. The interpretations and application of the diagnostic model's mechanisms—assessment, labeling, placement, treatment, and cure—have often led to a state of disenfranchisement for students with learning disabilities and their families. A close, honest look reveals that de facto segregation and primitive shunning responses toward students with learning disabilities are the norm in most schools (Slavin, 1990). This may be the unwitting result of having institutionalized the diagnostic model and having created a false image of reality. It may also be that the special education legitimization process is a sophisticated initiation rite into a false view of the world. As a process based on a falsehood, this legitimation process is unwittingly dangerous for students with significant challenges, because it denies them the life-affirming aspects of participation, engagement, and involvement in the mainstream of public schools (Ensminger, 1991). If it is likely, or even possible, that much of special education is based on an invented set of pseudoscientific categories (e.g., learning disabilities), analogous to labels on the shadows on the cave, then it behooves special educators to liberate themselves from their intellectual and institutional chains. It behooves them to critique basic assumptions and to systematically challenge any reductionistic view of human capacity and capability (Poplin, 1988a, 1988b). This is not an easy task, and they risk oversimplifying a complex set of conditions and problems associated with diverse learning needs.

However, it is important to enter the dialogue or critique if we seek to discover particular truths and realign our angle of vision. If we seek to see more than illusory shadows and step into the sunlight, we will need a new angle of vision, or better yet, a new vision of reality. In this regard, we seek to make a cautious first step in that direction by advancing a conception of education that does not pigeonhole students, for it applies to nondisabled students and those labeled "special education students" alike. Furthermore, it does so in a way that seeks to remove the label itself for most of these students. If we are successful in our cautious first step, we will have moved a short distance on an important journey—a journey aimed at replacing the diagnostic model with something more adequate.

In our view, living the truth requires the courage to challenge the status quo and to act upon an alternative vision of what is desirable. It requires the capacity to dream more fulfilling dreams. It is to that alternative vision and the possibility of having those more fulfilling dreams that we now turn.

TOWARD A NEW, NORMATIVE VISION IN SPECIAL EDUCATION

In the first part of this chapter, we suggested that the field of special education in general, and learning disabilities in particular, has acquired an intellectual and institutional life of its own, both in universities, which prepare special educators, and in schools, where special educators assume their traditional roles. One might say that there is a "culture of special education," wherein the culture's dominant beliefs, values, rituals, and practices are reproduced and transmitted to new generations of special educators. We have argued that special educators, for the most part, do not have a critical perspective on the dominant, taken-for-granted view of reality that undergirds this culture, and as a result, are not able to criticize their culture effectively or change it in fundamental ways. We have compared special educators to the chained prisoners in Plato's cave because they are unaware of how their dominant view of reality is based on the false images of education that emanate from the diagnostic model.

In the second half of this chapter, we shall conceptualize an alternative, empowering vision of special education and argue for the importance of serious dialogue dealing with the normative foundations of special education. Before we do so, we need to clarify our own views of the concept of a "normative vision" and discuss what would be required for such a vision to guide special educators in acting differently. A normative vision, in our view, is a reasonably clear view of how the world, or some portion of it, should be. It is an idealized conception of what things would be like if our fundamental goals, value commitments, and deepest longings could be brought to fruition. How much specificity of detail such an idealized picture requires is open to question. Moreover, we reject the notion that only one enlightened normative vision is possible. Quite the contrary. It is possible to conceive many humane, empowering visions of how special education students might be educated, and we encourage our colleagues to join in this normative dialogue; our vision represents simply one plausible example.

The position we shall take here is based on the following presuppositions: (a) A normative vision should be informed by central normative values or general normative principles, such as caring for others, caring about one's work, and supporting the communities to which one belongs (see Note 5); (b) people who share a commitment to these normative values or principles may have somewhat different visions of how these values should be implemented; (c) the normative values embedded in a single vision, or in different but related visions, must not merely be *understood* but be *thoroughly internalized* so that a fundamental integrity exists between the commitments of the individuals and the social practices they engage in; put another way, the values of the vision must be manifest in the lives of those committed to it. Or, as we stated earlier, people must live their truth.

Without doubt, changing an institutional culture that has developed over many years will be a formidable task. However, we believe that any culture can change if the following conditions are present: (a) A compelling normative vision of the culture is articulated, (b) the members of the culture *embrace* this vision and agree to be guided by it, and (c) an ongoing dialogue among members of the culture occurs. This dialogue must be sustained by the sincere efforts of special educators to translate their normative commitments into their social practice, their professional roles, and their personal lives.

To begin a dialogue among special educators working with students with learning disabilities on possible normative visions of special education, let us imagine the following idealized condition. We have a culturally diverse community with people of different ages and ethnic backgrounds working together both indoors and out, in a richly variegated schooling environment. Students, teachers, parents, administrators, and interested members of the community are enthusiastically working on many different learning projects, all of which seem to require effective thinking and interpersonal cooperation (Collins, Brown, & Newman, 1990). Many of the projects require exploring issues outside of school that are very significant to the students (e.g., how toxic waste is effectively disposed of; how effective drug rehabilitation programs work). The community participants and the students view themselves as responsible learners, expected to demonstrate a mastery of effective reading, writing, computing, reasoning, and communication skills. But no one seems fearful, anxious, or alienated. Everyone is treated with dignity and respect, thoughtfully listened to, morally appreciated, and emotionally supported. All seem intently focused on the work at hand. Moreover, there seems to be virtually no random, nonpurposeful conduct. Ongoing discussions are occurring among interested participants, who are informally evaluating the progress of the projects with interpersonal cooperation. Some decisions to make midcourse adjustments are being made. A few formal conferences are being held among teachers, parents, administrators, and community members to determine how cooperatively the students are working with others toward common ends, and to determine whether any skills need further development.

Some individuals seem to be working in several heterogeneous groups on different projects. In addition, a few individuals are tutoring their peers and younger students in particular skill areas such as algebra, creative writing, and graphic design. Some students are engaged in school "work apprenticeships" at the end of the regular school day. Most students, teachers, and community members have decided to work with the same group of people for several years to develop lasting, caring relationships and an abiding sense of community.

This brief sketch of an education reality is open to diverse interpretations. Moreover, we hope it inspires our readers to dream of what might be possible if we were to conceive of education as something radically different from traditional schooling in bureaucratically structured, age-graded institutions filled with alienated students and an increasing number of burned-out teachers. Our vision is not a vision of schooling that emphasizes grading and ranking students, ability groupings, passive listening, disconnected subjects in discrete time periods, or paper-and-pencil versions of mastery. The purpose of painting a different picture of learning is to suggest it as *one possible example of an alternative view of reality.*

Underlying our alternative vision are some central normative values that we believe are critical to any effective, empowering vision of education. Thus, we shall now explain what we regard as the central values that provide the normative framework for our idealized education condition. One critical structural component in our vision is that every member of our education community must *care deeply* about other people and the work to be done. It is not enough to simply care about others, or to simply care about the projects to be accomplished. One must care deeply about both. Let us consider each form of caring separately and explain its importance.

What does caring for others consist of, and why is it so important to education for all children, even those who would otherwise be labeled as special education students? Caring, in our view, is the emotional and moral glue that enables individuals to grow, to feel supported in themselves as persons and in the projects they work on. To be cared for, in any meaningful sense of this term, is to be accepted as a unique individual with strengths and weaknesses, with fears and aspirations, with goals, desires, and hopes. According to Mayeroff (1971), "to care for another, in the most significant sense, is to help him grow and actualize himself. . . . Caring is the antithesis of using the other person to satisfy one's own needs" (see Note 6). In Mayeroff's view, caring requires the commitment to help another person grow to be her own person, not to be one emotionally dependent on the caregiver. It means not taking away decisions that the other can make on her own. It means struggling to understand the other—how she thinks and feels, what she fears and values—without losing one's own identity in the process. Finally, it requires the kind of commitment to the other's well being that would lead one to be there for the other, to be on call, so to speak, if the other is in need. The one cared for understands that a crisis will cause the caring person to rearrange her priorities to meet the other's need.

Noddings (1984) suggested that caring is not merely a positive attitude toward another individual, but a form of reciprocal relatedness that requires the cared for to give something back in return. The caring person, in her view, is committed not merely to the growth of the other, but to the sustenance of the caring relationship, for it is the quality of our relationships with others that determines the quality of our lives. The challenge of caring, especially involving those to whom we are not naturally attracted, is to call upon our best self, our "ethical self," which may be brought forth by recollecting how we had acted toward others in the past when we cared for them naturally. According to Noddings, ethical caring often requires extra effort, simply because it does not flow from naturally liking the other person (see Note 7).

What would schooling organized around the value of caring look like? Noddings (1992) provided a different, more richly detailed vision than ours in her recent book entitled *The Challenge to Care in Schools: An Alternative Approach to Education.* In it she expresses her commitment to the value of multiyear caring relationships between teachers and students:

> These days, tragedies strike school campuses fairly often. Children are murdered, killed in accidents, commit suicide. When these tragic events occur, "grief counselors" are dispatched to the affected schools. I am not arguing that there is no need for specially trained people to advise administrators and teachers, and, perhaps to listen to severely disturbed students. But the best grief counseling should come from teachers who know and care deeply for their students. They are the people who should comfort, counsel, and express their common grief. In contemporary schools, teachers and students do not know each other well enough to develop relations of care and trust.... Students and teachers need each other. Students need competent adults to care; teachers need students to respond to their caring. (Noddings, 1992, p. 69)

Although caring for one's students often contributes to their taking their learning more seriously, we do not believe that caring for students should be viewed as an *instrumental* pedagogical value. Why do we believe that caring should not be justified merely as an instrumental good designed to heighten the student's level of intellectual seriousness? Simply because we view the disposition and capacity to care for others as integral to becoming a healthy social person and productive group member, or citizen. In our view, the central normative question that must be addressed by an adequate alternative vision of schooling is, "What is a socially healthy person?" Having asked that question, we must ask two other related questions: (a) What kinds of relationships does she maintain with others? (b) What kinds of understandings, skills, and character traits does she possess?

In asking these questions, we think it is appropriate to reinvoke the older, pre–nineteenth-century notion of education as training or bringing up children. Prior to the middle of the nineteenth century, when mass schooling became widespread in the United States, to "educate" someone meant to bring up that person properly. Accompanying the older, broader meaning of education was the view that the moral responsibility for bringing children up properly fell primarily to the parents and only secondarily to the schools, the church, and the community. Many still share that view.

If our goal as a professional field is to insure that every young person is brought up properly, we should not adopt a reductionist, cognitive-deficit model of the person, a model that ignores, or places a diminished value upon, a person's fundamental attitudes and dispositions. Although we do not seek to diminish the importance of skills in a person's journey toward becoming a socially productive citizen, our own normative vision emphasizes the importance of attitudes. In this regard, we now turn to our second critical normative value: caring deeply about one's work.

People who care deeply about their work are much more likely to take pride in doing it well and, as a result, are more likely to acquire the skills, insights, and understandings to do that work well. We want our students to succeed in the critical learning tasks of schooling, but we want them to succeed for the right reasons, so their successes will be part of the continuous development of their character. In his compelling classic, *Zen and the Art of Motorcycle Maintenance*, Pirsig (1974) dramatized the cultural problem of a society in which so many people had become alienated from their work. The picture Pirsig painted of motorcycle maintenance workers working carelessly on motorcycle repairs with music blasting in the background was symptomatic of his view that something about American culture was fundamentally wrong, that Americans were suffering from a crisis of the spirit growing from a deep rift between the mind and the heart. In the symbolism of Pirsig's motorcycle repair shop, we have a glimpse into the malaise of many schools, where large numbers of students remain alienated from their work, take little pride in it, and, as a result, do not do it very well. In this regard, we see so many of today's students passing through the critical years of youth and adolescence viewing schoolwork as meaningless, as unimportant, as nothing to care for in its own right. One of the most destructive features of contemporary schooling, in our view, is that many teachers, parents, and administrators have accepted the students' uncaring attitude toward their school work. How often have we heard teachers complain, "We don't assign homework because the students simply won't do it"? How often do we see teachers resigned to the fact that students simply do not care about learning (Levin, 1988; Slavin, Karweit, & Madden, 1989)?

In contrast, in our normative vision of education, students, teachers, parents, and community members all take pride in the work of learning. They care deeply about the projects they are working on. They are focused and disciplined in their efforts to get the job done well. One has merely to think about those situations in which a person really wanted to learn something that was important to her, or in which one really wanted to complete a project that was significant. The power of those positive attitudes brings much in its wake, not the least of which is acquiring the skills necessary to do one's best.

The significance of caring for others and caring for one's work is enhanced if one final normative value is present—the value of community. Community is the social correlate of caring for others and caring for one's work, and it is central to the development of citizens. We conceive of community as the inclination and ability to work cooperatively in many different kinds of groups. Upon what foundation does our emphasis on citizenship and community depend? First, we believe that underlying all normative views of education is some conception of "personhood." In our view, we see persons not as atomistic individuals seeking to expand their personal liberty and materialistic well-being, but as citizens, that is, socially related persons, who will flourish if they can sustain caring interpersonal relationships and participate in communities they can identify with (Sandel, 1982; see Note 8).

What notion of community are we advancing? The notion of community that we have in mind here is one well developed in Dewey's (1916) classic, *Democracy and Education*. A community, for Dewey, was not merely a collection of individuals who lived in close physical proximity to each other, but, rather, a socially cohesive group united by common purposes and values. Moreover, democratic communities required that people respected each other's individuality and granted each person both a voice and a vote on matters of common interest.

Democracy, Dewey (1916) reminded us many years ago, was more than a political form of government; rather, it was primarily "a mode of associated living" (p. 101). As a social way of living, democracy requires a set of well-established dispositions and understandings that enable persons not merely to solve their problems effectively, but to work cooperatively to solve the group's problems, to achieve the community's purposes, and to promote the common good. Our normative vision of schooling emphasizes the abilities, dispositions, and virtues central to a person's being effective in several different kinds of groups. These virtues include respect for others, tolerance, caring, and loyalty, among others. In emphasizing group problem solving and teamwork, Dewey expressed the hope that we develop socially intelligent persons, persons who can help others in the group to clarify problems, seek mutually agreed upon ends, and discover the best means to achieve those ends.

The value of community is being rediscovered in both positive and negative ways. The growing social despair over violent crime in America has made politicians, pundits, and ordinary folk speak out about reviving a sense of moral community, especially in our inner cities. In the area of the global workforce, both big and small companies have begun experimenting more seriously with project teams, often based on democratic principles. It would not surprise us if in future years more and more areas of modern social and economic life emphasize the value of positive group membership—that is, citizenship, defined as the disposition and ability to work well with diverse others in multiple communities or groups.

A compelling argument for the importance of developing the skills and attitudes necessary for cooperative work can be found in the research on developing self-regulated learners. Researchers have quite convincingly argued for teaching students with learning disabilities self-regulation procedures, such as goal setting, self-monitoring, self-instruction, and contingent self-reinforcement (Graham, Harris, & Reid, 1993). Instruction in self-regulatory behavior coincides with many of the skills needed to be successful in the work world as well as in the community. It also reinforces the notion that students with learning disabilities can learn the social skills necessary to participate meaningfully with their age-appropriate peers in school. These skills, we believe, can be transferred to the workplace through such activities as planning, problem solving, and participation on work teams. Although these skills appear individualistic in their conceptualization, once learned, they seem to allow for more positive group membership for students with learning disabilities. Clearly, more research would need to be done to validate this belief in the transfer of skills from school to work. However, the rapid changes in the nature of contemporary work warrants both the research and our guarded optimism underlying it.

In many areas of contemporary work, hierarchical, multilayered structures of bureaucratic organization are being replaced by smaller, more flexible organizations, by cooperative work teams assigned to special projects, and by cyberspace communities whose members interact regularly through long-distance telecommunications. We believe that any adequate normative vision for special education must emphasize educating young people to become good citizens, to become the kinds of social persons who understand how to communicate well with diverse others, know how to support colleagues and co-workers in productive ways, and know how to be flexible enough to adapt effectively to several kinds of groups in different kinds of settings.

Most important, the field of learning disabilities has adopted a narrow trajectory focused on improving students' deficits. The broader sociological context of participation in school life and membership in schooling cultures appears to have been sacrificed for a rational–technical approach to remediating individual problems. In our view, the rational–technical approach has failed significantly, for it has sanctioned a separate, segregated educational system with limited benefits to the identified students (Will, 1986). Certainly, efforts to enhance instruction and improve our understanding of the social liability of being labeled learning disabled warrant considerable praise. However, what we have learned from these progressive efforts need no longer remain the exclusive preserve of a labeled group or a separate field (Gardner, 1991;

Marzanno, 1992). Our insights as professionals working in the field of learning disabilities can benefit all learners, and it is ethically incumbent upon us to try to effect such an outcome.

Let us summarize what we have said about our alternative vision. In our interpretation of the structural normative dimensions of an alternative vision for special education, and, particularly, for the field of learning disabilities, we have emphasized three critical ideas: (a) the noninstrumental value of caring for others as valuable persons, (b) the importance of caring about one's work, and (c) the abilities and dispositions to work cooperatively in diverse groups and communities. While all three features can be talked about separately, they reinforce each other quite powerfully when they are united into a vision that allows for a creative tension between individual growth and social cohesiveness. In our normative vision, individuality and personal liberty are not suppressed. Individuals will not have their identities submerged by group projects. Many opportunities will exist for individuals to develop their own skills, independent of group projects and community endeavors. Nevertheless, implicit in our view is the rejection of an individualistic, competitive model of schooling focused predominantly on the achievement of grades through alienated work (Oakes, 1985). Our vision has people working and learning together for the right reasons in ways that promote their individual growth and the well-being of the community. In a model schooling culture, caring is not merely a condition of the relationships between teachers and students, but infuses itself throughout the schooling culture, characterizing relationships between and among students, between administrators and students, and among administrators, teachers, staff, and parents. Everyone is valued as contributing members of the culture and entitled to the full dignity of such membership.

In our normative model, individuals are not stigmatized by labels that deny their humanity or give them any sense of second-class citizenship. There is only one kind of citizenship, namely, first-class citizenship, and it is shared equally by all, regardless of ability. Intellectual skill development is viewed as something that should be demonstrated through tasks, projects, and problem-solving activities that are challenging in their own rights. Thus, our vision requires that teacher-educators become effective facilitators of caring interpersonal relations, of community, of intelligent social reasoning, of interpersonal cooperation, and of focused teamwork. Our vision, then, is clearly a part of the progressive tradition of American educational history.

In the first part of this chapter, we argued that the discourse of special education and its reliance on the diagnostic model placed a diminished emphasis on an individual's social relatedness. It is our view that any normative vision that does so remains fundamentally inadequate, for a life not supported by meaningful, caring relationships is a life that cannot be fulfilling for most people. Children with learning disabilities must participate in a caring universe that respects their fundamental humanity and does not diminish their personal value through stigmatizing labels and separated treatment. Our normative vision is not a form of inclusion that is simply rhetorical. Rather, it is a form of inclusion that necessarily embodies the growth-producing integration of persons into social communities. It is a form of inclusion that emphasizes the life-enhancing possibilities of ongoing, continuous, viable, caring relationships with others. Our goal is to develop educated citizens who have learned how to care for others, how to care for their work and take pride in it, and how to participate meaningfully in various communities that treat them respectfully.

Education has both its minimalist and maximalist versions. On its minimalist side, it aims to produce persons who can survive, who can adapt to society's demands without causing too much harm to themselves or others. On its maximalist side, it seeks to develop persons who can flourish and contribute to others' human flourishing. Our normative vision emphasizes an environment where nonalienated learning contributes to the individual's and the community's flourishing.

CONCLUSION

In this chapter, we have argued that special educators need to reexamine the taken-for-granted worldview underlying their professional culture and consider new normative visions for educating persons, especially ones that emphasize the values of caring for others, caring for one's work, and participating in diverse communities. In making this argument, we invite our colleagues in special education and general education to join us in the dialogue over reforming American education in its oldest and broadest sense—as the effort to bring up children well. Education remains, as always, a normative enterprise, not a technical one. It aims at producing better people, better lives, and a better society. As an enterprise, it always stands in need of dialogue over its fundamental normative vision. What is at stake in producing or bringing about better people, better lives, and a better society? Certainly far more than higher scores on standardized tests! Such reductionism does little toward improving our own education culture.

One of the features of special education, both as an academic field and as a professional culture, is that it presumes to be morally concerned about the students' well-being. It is that concern that requires, we think,

critical self-examination, fresh approaches, new thinking, and a fundamental reexamination of the normative underpinnings of present practice. But that is merely the first step. As we argued earlier, ultimately we
need a new normative vision of the possibilities of good education, a
willingness to embrace such a vision and internalize its core values, and,
finally, a commitment to translate those values into personal and institutional practices in the context of ongoing dialogue.

If we are correct in our views here, the culture of special education
needs some shock therapy. This chapter was inspired by the shock therapy
of a disturbing dream, a dream about workers in tattered purple overalls
with large "O" insignias sown on their right sleeves and the following
gold letter inscription on their backs: "Your greatest adversary is your
own creation." It concludes with both a brief sketch of a different reality
and an interpretation of some central values of that reality. In actuality,
the alternative picture is somewhat like a new dream, a different dream,
one that clarifies an important ideal. The ideal is a society in which all
students can flourish through caring, learning, stimulating work, and
social community.

Education, as James (1962) reminded us, "enlarging as it does our
horizon and perspective, is a means of multiplying our ideals, of bringing
new ones into view" (p. 142). In James's view, ideals by themselves are not
worth much. However, when combined with courage, pluck, and "the
sterner stuff" of virtue, ideals are what make a life significant. Moreover,
they are what give educators their sense of direction and purpose. They
can, if embraced by others, lead to significant cultural change.

The ideal of education as the development of caring citizens, socially
grounded and connected to others they care about and to communities
with which they identify, is not a new ideal. However, it *is* one that deserves
renewed consideration if we seek to revitalize our education practices
and renew our education culture. To those who would dismiss this invitation to reconsider our normative ideals, it is useful to remember the
lines from Thoreau (1971): "If you have built castles in the air, your work
need not be lost; that is where they should be. Now put the foundations
under them." Special education requires a critical examination of its
culture and its dominant images; moreover, it cries out for new normative
foundations and multiple normative visions based on those foundations.

However, in our view, all of that will not be sufficient to change the
professional culture. We need to embrace the normative commitments of
our new visions, translate these commitments into personal and institutional practice, and begin an ongoing dialogue over how to enhance
these values in our culture. Only then will special educators be able to
live their truths. Perhaps then we will all be able to dream happier
dreams.

NOTES

1. *The reason the dream and its aftermath are written of in the first person, even though the chapter is co-authored, is simply that it is the dream of the first author. The reactions to the dream are those of the first author as well.*

2. *In Book VII of Plato's Republic, Plato describes the human condition as analogous to that of prisoners in a cave: "Imagine an underground chamber, like a cave with an entrance open to the daylight and running a long way underground. In this chamber are men who have been prisoners there since they were children, their legs and necks being so fastened that they can only look straight ahead of them and cannot turn their heads. Behind them and above them a fire is burning, and between the fire and the prisoners runs a road, in front of which a curtain-wall has been built, like the screen at puppet shows between the operators and their audience, above which show their puppets" (pp. 278 280). Although we draw upon Plato's metaphor for the condition of special educators, we are not committed to Plato's metaphysics of idealism or his education utopia.*

3. *In this chapter we shall use the term citizen to stand for "socially productive group members." We understand that the term generally carries with it a lot of additional connotations regarding participation in the political life of the society, but that is not our primary focus here.*

4. *In this chapter we shall avoid the awkward "he/she" form by using the feminine singular in those instances in which we can clearly be referring to both males and females.*

5. *In our view, the normative values constitute the structural framework of the normative vision. Believing that we can have a core structural framework in any adequate normative vision allows us to accept a form of relativism regarding other normative visions without falling into an extreme form of relativism, wherein all normative visions are as good as any others. The normative values mentioned here are the ones we use in this essay.*

6. *Mayeroff used the first person masculine throughout his book, a stylistic convention at the time but increasingly offensive to female students in recent years.*

7. *Noddings suggests that the ethical self is guided not by principles functioning as moral obligations, but by an ideal derived from one's sense of oneself acting in caring ways. See Noddings, 1984, chapters 5 and 6, for a fuller discussion of this ethical self.*

8. *In his book Liberalism and the Limits of Justice, Sandel describes what he calls "a constitutive conception of community" (p. 150). In this conception, individuals do not simply belong to communities and share communitarian sentiments, but conceive of their personal identity as defined to some extent by their membership in the community. This strong sense of community makes much sense, in our view.*

6. Reflections on Ethics, Technology, and Learning Disabilities: Avoiding the Consequences of Ill-Considered Action

MARSHALL H. RASKIND AND

ELEANOR L. HIGGINS

The welfare of humankind requires a creative technology that is economically productive, ecologically sound, socially just, and personally fulfilling. (Ian Barbour, "On human values and technology," *Ethics in an Age of Technology*)

In the ancient Indian fable "The Lion-Makers," four Brahmans (scholars) were traveling through a forest, where they found the bones of a dead lion. They decided to test the powers of their scholarship by bringing the lion back to life.

The first Brahman said: "I know how to assemble the skeleton." The second said: "I can supply skin, flesh and blood." The third said: "I can give it life."

So the first assembled the skeleton, the second provided skin, flesh and blood. But while the third was intent on giving the breath of life the

Reprinted, with changes, from "Reflections on ethics, technology, and learning disabilities: Avoiding the consequences of ill-considered action," by Marshall H. Raskind and Eleanor L. Higgins, *Journal of Learning Disabilities*, Vol. 28, 1995, pp. 425–438. Copyright © 1995 by PRO-ED, Inc.

[fourth] advised against it, remarking: "This is a lion. If you bring him to life, he will kill every one of us."

"You simpleton!" said the other, "it is not I who will reduce scholarship to a nullity." "In that case," came the reply, "wait a moment while I climb this convenient tree."

When this had been done, the lion was brought to life, rose up, and killed all three. But the man of sense, after the lion had gone elsewhere, climbed down and went home. (The *Panchatranta, "Ill-Considered Action,"* Book 5, pp. 380–381)

Like the fable, this chapter is concerned with the importance of adequately reflecting upon the consequences of one's actions. Specifically, we will address the importance of critically analyzing and fully considering the ethical implications arising from the use of technology among persons with learning disabilities (LD). Over the last several years, ever-increasing attention has been directed toward the use of technology with individuals with LD. According to Hresko and Parmar (1991a), "during the last decade, no area [in the field of LD] has grown as significantly as high technology" (p. 45). Computers and other electronic devices have been integrated into resource rooms and mainstreamed classrooms, in the hope of improving methods of instruction and remediation; postsecondary LD programs are promoting the use of assistive (or compensatory) technologies to help ensure the academic success of their students; the Americans with Disabilities Act (ADA; 1990) has prompted employers to provide "reasonable technological accommodations" for employees with LD; technologically based psychoeducational assessment systems have been devised to diagnose learning problems (Fifield, 1989); and researchers are addressing the efficacy of technology in remediating (e.g., Torgesen & Barker, 1995) and circumventing (e.g., Raskind & Higgins, 1995) the difficulties faced by individuals with LD. Although technology has moved rapidly into the field of LD, little discussion has appeared regarding the ethical issues that surround technological utilization among persons with LD. Consequences that may have a profound effect on the lives of those with LD have not been given due consideration, perhaps because they have been shrouded by our infatuation and fascination with technology. Although literature exists that addresses ethics and LD (e.g., Adelman & Taylor, 1983; Council for Exceptional Children, 1978, 1983; Larsen, 1978; Lenz & Deshler, 1994; Vaughn & Lyon, 1994), little focuses specifically on the ethical issues related to technology and LD. This is in sharp contrast to other fields, such as medicine and environmental studies, which have given considerable attention to questions of ethics and technology.

A word is in order regarding the intentions of this chapter. It is *not* the intention of the authors to paint a pessimistic or negative view of technology, or to imply that technology is the "lion" of the Indian fable. Alternatively, this chapter does not aim to portray technology in a strictly positive or optimistic light. Rather, the present discussion is intended to stimulate thought in such a way that we begin to adequately reflect upon the larger ethical issues that accompany technological utilization, issues that may often be unintentionally submerged by our desire to remain technologically "in vogue." Although technology is not the lion created by the Indian scholars, failure to adequately reflect upon the ethical issues surrounding its use may have negative consequences.

Ethical issues related to the use of technology with individuals with LD will be addressed within a framework of the major ethical principles of beneficence, justice, and autonomy. These principles will be applied to a number of topics, including instructional/remedial, assistive, and diagnostic technology; technology and special abilities; health-related concerns; social/psychological impact of technology; technological access; and medical technologies. A short discussion of particular views of technology also will be included.

MAJOR ETHICAL PRINCIPLES

A discussion of the history of ethics or contemporary ethical theory is well beyond the scope of this chapter. However, a brief discussion of several basic ethical principles is fundamental to establishing a framework within which to view issues pertaining to technology and LD. The ethical principles of beneficence, justice, and autonomy are derived from the field of general normative ethics and play a major role in normative ethical theory. According to Beauchamp and Walters (1989), "general normative ethics attempts to formulate and defend basic principles and virtues governing the moral [ethical] life" (p. 2). The ethical principles derived from this field are frequently employed in discussions regarding such issues as abortion, widespread hunger, and racial discrimination. The application of these principles, or moral-action guides, to specific moral problems, including moral problems that arise in various professions, is referred to as "applied ethics" (Beauchamp, 1991).

The present discussion is not intended as a philosophical analysis or elaboration of these principles, or as an endorsement of a specific theory of beneficence, justice, or autonomy. Rather, these ethical principles are introduced in an attempt to provide a framework within which to reflect upon and evaluate a number of issues emerging from the ever-increasing use of technology with persons with LD; we hope to offer a new approach for analyzing issues pertinent to LD and technology. A brief discussion of each of the three major ethical principles to be used in this chapter is presented below.

Beneficence refers to acting in a manner that benefits others. It involves doing good and the active promotion of goodness, kindness, and charity. In the field of medicine, nursing, and public health, this concept is often expressed in terms of an obligation to come to the assistance of those in need of treatment. Beneficence also involves helping others to further their legitimate and important interests, largely by preventing or removing possible harm. Inherent in the principle of beneficence is *nonmaleficence,* which refers to not inflicting evil or harm. This notion is one of the most frequently quoted maxims in medical ethics: *Primum non nocere*—"Above all do no harm" (Beauchamp & Walters, 1989).

Justice pertains to treating a person according to what is fair, due, or owed. The denial of goods, services, or information to a person who has a right, or is entitled to them, is considered an injustice. According to Beauchamp (1991), "justice is explicated in terms of 'fairness,' 'desert' (what is deserved), and entitlement" (p. 342). The more restrictive concept of "distributive justice" often accompanies discussions on the general topic of justice. Beauchamp further contended that distributive justice refers to the proper or "just distribution of social benefits and burdens in accordance with the implicit and explicit terms of cooperation in society" (p. 342). The underlying concept in distributive justice is that persons should be treated equally because they are fundamentally equal. However, unequal treatment can be considered just if it serves to alleviate other forms of inequality or is necessary to ensure the good of all (Barbour, 1993). Although discussions on distributive justice have historically been directed toward such areas as economics and political rights, they are also considered fundamental to the analysis of a broader range of contemporary issues (Beauchamp & Walters, 1989), including technology (Barbour, 1993).

Autonomy (from the Greek terms *autos* ["self"] and *nomos* ["governance"]) and "respect for autonomy" are loosely associated with such ideas as individual freedom and choice, privacy, voluntariness, consent, and self-mastery (Beauchamp & Walters, 1989). For a person to act autonomously, he or she must be free and independent of the controlling influences of others (external control). These controlling influences range from weak forms of influence, such as rational persuasion, to coercion, which attempts to completely control or dominate another person (e.g., rape). Manipulation through lying, withholding of information, and exaggerating to mislead would fall somewhere in the middle of this range. In addition, freedom (as well as encouragement) to choose activities that an individual deems important or of particular interest has also been equated with the principle of autonomy. Respecting the autonomy of an individual requires refraining from intervening with his or her beliefs or actions, even if they are thought to be wrong, foolish, deviant, or harmful to the individual.

It is important to emphasize that these three principles do not always operate in harmony. Although in some instances specific actions serve to simultaneously uphold all three principles, in other situations they come into direct conflict with one another. It should also be noted that not all ethical principles are applicable to all of the topics presented in this chapter. Conversely, although several of the topics could be discussed under more than one ethical principle, as they overlap (in fact some are, e.g., instructional technologies), an attempt was made to limit discussions to the intersections of principles and topics that appeared to be most pertinent and have the greatest implications for the field of LD. A case could certainly be made regarding the analysis of specific issues with regard to other ethical principles. Such considerations might well be considered in subsequent writings.

ETHICS AND VIEWS OF TECHNOLOGY

Historically, discussions on technology and ethics have tended to center around a number of major areas, including the military, politics, industry, agriculture, and energy. More recently, a heated ethical debate has surfaced in the areas of medicine, genetic engineering, ecology, work, and communication/information. We find the media replete with such stories as the morality of using technology to sustain life in the terminally ill, and the ethics of gene therapy; we are also hearing how technology is destroying the environment, yet how it also may provide the means to eradicate pollution; how technology can increase efficiency in the workplace while simultaneously carrying the potential to dehumanize workers; and how the "electronic superhighway" will provide access to virtually unlimited information while it also threatens to invade our privacy.

The manner in which one approaches, analyzes, and potentially resolves such complex issues is a result of many factors, including religious beliefs, cultural background, gender, societal position, and economic status. Collectively, these factors determine our view of technology. In his book *Ethics in an Age of Technology*, Barbour (1993), a leading scholar in the area of science and religion, suggests that there are three fundamental views of technology: (a) technology as a liberator, (b) technology as a threat, and (c) technology as an instrument of power. These three categories can be roughly interpreted as optimistic, pessimistic, and contextual (an instrument of power dependent on its context), respectively.

According to Barbour (1993), the optimists stress that technology (a) has raised standards of living; (b) has enhanced opportunities for individual choice; (c) promises to eradicate disease and ensure adequate food for the world population; (d) may serve to promote psychological well-being, social relationships, and even spiritual development; (e) has increased time for leisure activities; and (f) has improved communication and transportation. In contrast, those with a pessimistic view see technology as a threat to humankind and warn that it (a) breeds uniformity, loss of identity, impersonality, and alienation, and restricts individual freedom; (b) contributes to a narrower criterion of efficiency within society, emphasizing quantity over quality; and (c) has created pollution and the potential for nuclear holocaust. Finally, Barbour identified a third technological view, which sees technology as "neither inherently good nor evil," but as "an ambiguous instrument of power whose consequences depend on its social context" (p. 15). For example, nuclear technologies have the capacity to heal or destroy; television can be used to educate or manipulate. It is imperative for anyone examining the ethical issues surrounding the use of technology with individuals with LD to be aware of his or her own view of technology. Viewing technology from an optimistic, pessimistic, or contextual perspective will undoubtedly influence one's response to the ethical issues and questions surrounding technology and LD.

The reader is urged to become cognizant of his or her inherent technological biases while wading through the complex issues and questions in the following sections. What is construed as upholding the ethical principles of beneficence, justice, and autonomy is likely to vary depending on one's basic attitude toward technology. It must also be stressed that this chapter is not intended to foster a particular view of technology, but rather to provide an ethical framework from within which to reflect upon specific issues in the use of technology with persons with LD. Although perhaps not always successfully, the authors have attempted to present issues and questions, rather than to provide resolutions or answers.

BENEFICENCE

Instructional/Remedial Technology

As previously discussed, beneficence refers to acting in a way that benefits others. In health-related fields, this concept is often expressed as a professional duty to come to the assistance of those in need of treatment. This emphasis on acting in a manner that will benefit others also appears in special education (e.g., Principles 1 and 2 of the Council for Exceptional Children's [1983] "Code of Ethics and Standards for Professional Practice," and the Council for Exceptional Children's [1978] "Code of Ethics and Competencies for Teachers of Learning Disabled Children and Youth"). Historically, the primary acts aimed at benefiting persons with LD have taken the form of educational programs/interventions based on models designed to provide instruction/ remediation in academic areas of deficit, such as reading, writing, and math, as well as remedial efforts aimed at improving or alleviating difficulties in specific areas of cognitive functioning, such as memory and attention. Although many of these programs/approaches have been instituted with the intention of benefiting individuals with LD, their efficacy in reaching this goal has recently been questioned by several authors (e.g., Heshusius, 1989; Poplin, 1988a; Reid & Hresko, 1981). Poplin emphasized that historical models for remediating/alleviating LD have essentially failed. According to Poplin, even when specific skills appear to have been learned through traditional approaches, those skills do not generalize across situations or over time.

Critics of traditional approaches in treating LD attribute the failure of these approaches to the underlying assumption of a deficit-driven, mechanistic, and reductionistic paradigm that breaks up learning into smaller and smaller pieces and skills and proposes instructional/ remedial procedures (aimed at improving deficient skills) that are sequential and tightly controlled (also see Heshusius, 1991, for a discussion of mechanistic–reductionistic thinking and LD). These authors propose an alternative, holistic/constructivist paradigm for approaching LD, which emphasizes that (a) learning is larger than the sum of its parts; (b) learning involves a process of moving from whole to part to whole; (c) learning is transformative rather than additive, with the learner constructing meaning; and (d) learners learn best from experiences in which they are actively involved, passionately interested, and able to self-regulate (Poplin, 1988b; Reid & Hresko, 1981).

The above controversy has a bearing on the discussion of technology and LD, because the use of technology with individuals with LD has predominantly followed the traditional mechanistic–reductionistic instructional/remedial approach (Lewis, 1993; Okolo, Barh, & Rieth, 1993). Such approaches generally take the form of computer software and include both tutorial and drill-and-practice programs (e.g., Sentence Master, New Math Blaster Plus; Lewis, 1993; Margalit, 1990). Lewis, while acknowledging that there are a number of different kinds of educational software (e.g., educational games, discovery, simulation, problemsolving, databases, desktop publishing, utilities), cited research by the U.S. Congress, Office of Technology Assessment (1988), indicating that 66% of available educational software is of the drill-and-practice type, and 33% is tutorial in nature. Similarly, Hresko and Parmar (1991a) stressed that although computers and other technologies have several applications in the education of students with LD, "computer use in the schools has traditionally been limited to drill and practice" (p. 46). Given that the majority of educational technology currently being utilized with children with LD is operating from a mechanistic–reductionistic paradigm, and the objections that have been raised to such a paradigm by those supporting a holistic model, questions arise regarding the extent to which such a technological approach is benefiting individuals with LD. In regard to the benefits of computers in special education, Hresko and Parmar (1991b) stated the following:

> Although much has been expected of computers in the education of the exceptional child, those expectations have not been realized. Research to date has failed to substantiate significant or even moderate gains in the academic areas. Furthermore, although some researchers have focused on the potential effects of computers on thinking and reasoning ability, research has failed to show significant gains. Thus the widespread hopes for educational uses of the computer remain to be realized. (p. 47)

It is not the aim of this discussion to suggest that the use of mechanistic–reductionistic technology (e.g., drill-and-practice programs) is in some manner maleficent. Such a contention would be unfair because the intent of such technology has always been to promote the welfare of persons with LD. However, such intentions must be accompanied by results. If mechanistic–reductionistic technologies are not living up to their promise of helping persons with LD, can they be considered in accord with the principle of beneficence? This is an important question, given that these forms of technology are the predominant mode of technological intervention with persons with LD. And, at least for now, there is no definitive answer to the question. Considerable debate occurs as to the efficacy and overall benefits/value of these programs (see Lewis, 1993; Okolo et al., 1993), and it may be some years before a verdict is reached.

Then what about holistic/constructivist instructional technologies (e.g., simulations, problem-solving software), which are learner centered and allow students to generate their own problems and solutions—are they more beneficent than those considered to be mechanistic–reductionistic? Several authors have in fact suggested that learning through the more holistically oriented exploration and discovery technologies has its limitations and may lead to the acquisition of isolated facts and erroneous conclusions (Charney, Reder, & Kusbit, 1990; Woodward & Carnine, 1988). However, it should be stressed that although the majority of exploration and discovery programs seem to be more holistic and offer greater opportunities for the student to construct knowledge, they are often rooted in mechanistic thought, which engages students in "a sequence of increasingly difficult problems or activities with specific performance feedback" (Okolo et al., 1993, p. 13). Once again, the aim of this discussion is not to suggest that one instructional technology paradigm is more beneficent than the other, but rather to offer the principle of beneficence as a means to examine current approaches in the use of instructional technology with persons with LD, in an effort to ensure the well-being of this population.

Unfortunately, an awareness of the limits of various instructional technologies may not, in and of itself, be enough to preclude their use. Fundamental flaws in an approach are often clouded by a "technological veil." Technology carries with it a certain intrigue and mystique; technology-coated approaches may appear more credible or scientific than their past nontech forerunners, despite the fact that they are based on the same educational principles. A technology, with its electronic bells and whistles, may serve to sugarcoat approaches that are, in fact, ineffectual. To ensure that specific technologies and technological approaches are in accord with the principle of beneficence, it is imperative that their implementation be based on sound educational models and valid research, rather than on the fact that they are intriguing or fashionable.

Although the use of technology for persons with LD has been traditionally focused on instruction/remediation, the greatest benefits might not be found within this area. Rather, the benefits of technology may be more fully realized through its capacity to enable persons with LD to accomplish something that could not have been done before, or reach a specific goal that otherwise would not have been possible. It is to some of these possibilities that we now turn.

Assistive Technology

Raskind (1993) emphasized that technology can be used to compensate for LD as well as for the purpose of instruction or remediation. This compensatory, or assistive, technology has tremendous potential for enhancing the quality of life for persons with LD and thus may be viewed as acting in accord with the principle of beneficence. Assistive technology offers a means by which to circumvent weaknesses while capitalizing on strengths. For example, an individual with a reading disability yet strong receptive oral language abilities might be able to "read" through the use of an optical character recognition (OCR) system with speech synthesis. Similarly, an individual with difficulty in the area of writing may be able to bypass the problem through the use of a speech recognition system that converts spoken language to computer text. The use of such technologies has the potential to increase independence, enhance self-concept, and even promote social interaction (see Raskind, 1994).

Although at first glance assistive technology appears to have all the makings of a beneficent intervention, J. K. Torgesen (personal communication, July 1993) pointed out the difficulties and ensuing ethical conflicts that arise when one is determining at what point an assistive technology (rather than an instructional/remedial approach) should be introduced to an individual with LD. If an assistive technology (e.g., an OCR system with speech synthesis for a child with a reading disability) is introduced too early, either before an adequate number of instructional/remedial methods have been attempted or before a particular approach has had time to take effect, then perhaps we are robbing the individual of the opportunity to improve his or her skill deficits. This in turn may serve to make the person technology dependent, rather than self-reliant. Furthermore, if the use of the assistive technology were to delay the implementation of instructional/remedial strategies to young children, then critical learning periods during the early years might also be lost.

The intention of this discussion is not to determine the beneficence of assistive technology. Such a determination is dependent upon the individual, the technology, the specific disability, and the context. However, it is imperative that we reflect upon such considerations in our attempts to use assistive technology to benefit those with LD. This is particularly important at a time when ever-increasing attention (e.g., Raskind, 1994; Raskind & Higgins, 1995; Raskind & Scott, 1993) is being directed toward assistive technology as a means for enhancing the quality of life for persons with LD.

Special Abilities/Talents

Helping someone to foster his or her special talents could certainly be considered promoting the welfare of the individual and thereby fitting into the parameters of beneficence. However, as previously discussed, the use of technology with persons with LD has been primarily deficit driven. Such an approach presupposes a dysfunction that needs to be corrected, remediated, or alleviated and does little to foster special abilities or talents. Although the primary use of technology among persons with LD has been to correct deficiencies, it should be noted that a number of persons (including those with LD) have suggested that a learning disability may in fact be a gift that needs to be nurtured, rather than a defect that needs to be fixed. West (1991) suggested that LD might be thought of as a "pathology of superiority" (p. 19), and that many persons with LD "have achieved success or even greatness not in spite of but because of their apparent disability" (p. 19). He continued,

The complex of traits referred to as "learning difficulties" or "dyslexia" may be in part the outward manifestation of the relative strength of a different mode of thought, one that is available to everyone to one degree or another, but one that a few children (and adults) find it difficult to suppress. Too often, the gift is not recognized and is regarded only as a problem. (p. 19)

For example, Smith (1987), a leading economist with The Conference Board in New York, referred to his dyslexia as "plus-lexia." Smith stressed that despite a history of school failure, his dyslexia is really a special ability that has enabled him to view the world in a different light, a light that has provided him with insights and perceptions that are often not available to persons without LD. He believes that it is this different way of looking at the world that has been instrumental in propelling him into the position of being one of the world's leading economists. The idea that persons with LD may possess special abilities and talents has also been used to account for the creativity and genius of such notable persons as the English physicist Michael Faraday and French mathematician Henri Poincaré (West, 1991).

Poplin (1995) also raised the issue that persons with LD may have special abilities in such areas as visual arts, music, and divergent thinking, and suggested that technology can be utilized to foster these talents. Similarly, West (1991) suggested that the real benefits of technology for persons with LD lie in its potential to accentuate their distinctive abilities:

Indeed, in some cases, these machines may come to be used as extensions and amplifiers of the imagination, permitting gifted visual-thinkers [dyslexics] to work in a visual–spatial language on fast and powerful graphics-oriented computers, developing and communicating their ideas in novel ways. (p. 43)

If we are to use technology in accord with the principle of beneficence, then perhaps greater emphasis should be placed on technology's potential for fostering and nurturing special talents. Possibilities for cultivating special abilities are virtually limitless, considering emerging technologies, which possess enlarged memory capacities, increased speed, and enhanced graphic and sound capabilities. At present, however, there is a paucity of research and practice in this area.

Social and Psychological Issues

Questions of beneficence can also be viewed relative to the social and psychological welfare of individuals with LD. Reflection in this area is particularly important considering the social and psychological difficulties experienced by many persons with LD (Bryan, 1974, 1982; Dudley-Marling & Edmiaston, 1985; Gresham & Reschly, 1986; Heavey, Adelman, Nelson, & Smith, 1989; Margalit & Zak, 1984; Stone & La Greca, 1990). In this regard, it is imperative that we ask whether technology promotes the social and psychological welfare of persons with LD, or is in some ways detrimental to them.

Several authors have emphasized that technology can increase self-confidence, promote independence, decrease learned helplessness, and empower persons with LD (e.g., Collins, 1990; Ellis & Sabornie, 1988; Margalit, 1990; Raskind, 1994). Lewis, Dell, Lynch, Harrison, and Saba (1987) reported that the use of technology by students with disabilities (including LD) can also increase motivation and enhance self-concept. Raskind (1994) asserted that assistive technology may serve to "facilitate the move toward independence by reducing reliance on others" (p. 160) as well as "reduce the psychological stress and possible social ramifications of having to continually rely on others" (p. 160).

With regard to the social benefits of technology utilization among persons with LD, Raskind (1994) also suggested that technology has the potential to enhance social relations by providing support for organizing time (e.g., personal data managers), providing access to information necessary for interpersonal communication, and providing assistance for participation in recreational activities (e.g., calculators for games). Similarly, Margalit (1990) emphasized the social benefits of technology for individuals with LD: Computer games and simulations may "serve as a source of acceptable social interactions with peers, such as sharing and exchanging games or discussing successful strategies for solving adventure games" (p. 14). Telecommunication networks, which can link individuals with LD via computer, modem, and telephone lines also offer the potential for enhancing communication and social interaction. Persons who may not be readily willing to engage in face-to-face communication may feel quite comfortable carrying on electronic conversations with others, thereby reducing feelings of isolation and loneliness.

The use of technology with persons with LD appears to be in accord with the principle of beneficence in regard to social and psychological implications. However, there are a number of other possible social and psychological consequences of technology utilization that may not be as apparent—consequences that most assuredly would not be promoting the welfare of persons with LD. For example, Margalit (1990), in a discussion of home computing for children with LD, acknowledged the potential psychological benefits of computer use, but stressed that technology can also be a source of frustration, anxiety, anger, and helplessness, depending on the specific context. Similarly, S. Larsen (personal communication, July 1993) asserted that a technology (e.g., a computer) may become a best friend to a child with LD, to the extent that it may act as a substitute for relations with "real people." Some children with LD may be more comfortable relating to a machine than to another person. For example, a child might be more at ease playing a computer game than he or she is attempting to participate in sports or other recreational activities with peers. Similarly, although communicating via electronic networks does foster an interaction of sorts, an individual with a fear of social interaction might use this "safer" (but not necessarily psychologically healthier) alternative to face-to-face communication. The concern that technology will serve to alienate people from one another and impoverish human relationships has been voiced by sundry authors (Barbour, 1993).

Health-Related Issues

As previously noted, inherent in the principle of beneficence is the principle of nonmaleficence, or not inflicting harm. Although the idea that LD professionals might be using technology to intentionally harm individuals is obviously unfounded, it may not be out of place to question whether all professionals are aware of, or at least have given serious thought to, the potential health risks associated with the use of technology. In our fervor to explore technological approaches to helping individuals with LD, we may not always give due consideration to the possibility of concomitant dangers, and as Barbour (1993) suggested, the "human risks associated with technology are dismissed too rapidly" (p. 8) by technological optimists.

For example, there is considerable debate about the safety of the electromagnetic fields (EMFs) emitted by personal computers, with several studies suggesting that EMFs may adversely affect a person's biochemistry and circulatory processes, and even place an individual at greater risk for developing cancer (e.g., London et al., 1991; Omura & Losco, 1993). Other health-related risks associated with computer use include (a) carpal tunnel syndrome (compression in the median nerve in the wrist resulting in paresthesias in the hand and pain in the wrist, palm, forearm, and/or shoulder, as well as atrophy in the muscles controlling the thumb; Berkow, 1992) (e.g., Grant, 1992; Schmaus, 1990); (b) headaches, tension, and fatigue associated with poor ergonomic design (Kroemer, 1993); and (c) visual problems, including eye strain and pain from consistent use of video display terminals (Sheedy, 1992). Although research in several of these areas is not conclusive, there is indeed enough evidence to suggest that these risks must be considered, given the LD professional's responsibility to avoid inflicting harm. The intention of discussing these health-related concerns is not to foster a pessimistic view of technology utilization but, rather, to bring to light issues that may be clouded by our intrigue with, fascination with, or, at times, overly optimistic views of technology.

A number of topics have been considered relative to the principle of beneficence, and most assuredly other topics could be discussed. However, further discussion in this area is beyond the scope of this chapter. At this point, the discussion will be directed toward issues in LD and technology relative to the ethical principle of justice.

JUSTICE

Access

According to Beauchamp and Walters (1989), justice requires equal access to goods, services, or information to which a person has a right or is entitled. To deny access is not acting in accord with the principle of justice. Many of the goods, services, and information available in our society are technologically based and promise to be even more so in years to come. Unfortunately, persons with LD are at risk for being treated unjustly in regard to technological access and the benefits such access may bring.

There are two components of technology access for individuals with LD: (a) availability of technologies and (b) operational access. In the first instance, technology access requires that the technology needed to reap the full range of benefits afforded others in the society is available to persons with LD. Operational access requires that once a technology is physically present, it is effectively and easily operated by the individual. These two components of access work hand in hand, as total access requires availability of operationally accessible technology. Operational access will be considered first.

Specific learning disabilities may in and of themselves preclude or restrict access to certain technologies. For example, problems with visual–motor operations may make the use of a computer keyboard or mouse difficult for a student with LD in the classroom or an employee with LD in the workplace. Memory difficulties may affect an individual's ability to carry out a series of operational commands on the keypad of a pocket-sized electronic personal data manager. Organizational difficulties may cause problems in utilizing the menu system of an on-line electronic database. Reading difficulties may inhibit access to the "help" and "tutorial" portions of education and business software programs.

These specific problems in operationally accessing particular technologies have the potential to significantly diminish the quality of life for individuals with LD. Such difficulties as those described above might jeopardize a person's employment, livelihood, or ability to live independently. Equal access to education could be restricted by difficulties in the ability to utilize education technology. Participation in recreational activities (e.g., electronic games) could also be restricted by limited access to technologies. Even access to basic needs, such as food and shelter, has the possibility of being hampered if specific learning disabilities were to interfere with using technologically based banking services (e.g., automatic tellers, on-line banking) and shopping services (e.g., online, interactive television). The promotion of justice through operationally accessible technologies becomes increasingly important in a society that is building an electronic superhighway of networked telecommunications, databases, financial services, and interactive entertainment. Although a society with increasingly technology-based goods, services, and information has the potential to promote justice for persons with LD, without due reflection and thought, even more barriers may be created.

To ensure the accessibility of specific technologies, products will have to be developed with the individual with LD in mind. This will require that manufacturers/developers directly involve individuals with LD and LD professionals in the development process. Although several manufacturers have made an effort to solicit input from end-users with LD (e.g., Xerox-Kurzweil, Humanware, Franklin Learning Resources), they are relatively few in number. Furthermore, although an increasing number of technology manufacturers are involving persons with disabilities, they tend to be from disability groups other than LD (Raskind, 1993).

In many instances, only minor modifications (e.g., a more intuitive command sequence) are necessary to make a technology accessible to an individual with LD. In other situations, however, substantial changes may be required (e.g., addition of a speech synthesis or speech recognition system)—changes that may be costly. A basic question thus arises: Who is ultimately responsible for ensuring that technologies are operationally accessible to persons with LD? Moreover, who is ultimately responsible for bearing the costs of making specific technologies accessible? Is it the individual, the manufacturer, the government, the education system, or society as a whole? If the individual is choosing to use the technology, should it not be his or her responsibility to pay for it? Yet, if the manufacturers will ultimately reap a profit, should they not absorb the cost? Is it perhaps the government's responsibility, as it must ensure justice for all citizens?

There has been an attempt to answer some of these questions in both the private and public sectors. For example, several companies have taken steps to solicit information from users with LD, with the intention of incorporating some of these suggestions in the design of their mass-market computer technologies (e.g., IBM, Apple, NeXT). Such steps may serve to curtail the cost of "retro-designing" technologies. Additionally, legislation (i.e., ADA, Individuals with Disabilities Education Act of 1990 [IDEA], Rehabilitation Act of 1973, Technology-Related Assistance for Individuals with Disabilities Act of 1988) has attempted to provide some initial mechanisms for distributing the financial burden across the educational system, the government, manufacturers, and employers (depending on the situation).

In a just system, accessible technologies will need to be available. Distributive justice demands that there be proper or just distribution of social benefits. If technology is the primary means of access to particular social benefits (e.g., school, employment), then failure to provide individuals with these technologies would be unjust. For example, if a student with LD can gain the full benefit of instruction afforded nondisabled children only through the use of a computer with a speech synthesizer (text-to-speech conversion), then failure to make this technology available within a classroom could be considered an injustice. Similarly, individuals with LD might have difficulty reaping the same rewards in an employment setting if they lacked the technology (e.g., an OCR—a "reading machine") necessary to be judged on the basis of their ability rather than disability. Fortunately, such concerns over the provision of technology to persons with disabilities are being addressed in recent legislation. The IDEA deals with this issue by requiring school districts to provide assistive technology to "eligible children with disabilities." The ADA (1990) requires employers to provide "reasonable accommodations" to employees with disabilities, including the acquisition and modification of equipment and devices such as adaptive hardware and software for computers. Although such concerns are being addressed in legislation, it is not yet clear how they will be operationalized in regard to specific cases.

As with the concern for making technologies operationally accessible, the question of financial responsibility emerges regarding the availability of operationally accessible technology. In the purest sense, a just system of access to goods, services, and information available through technology would require that technology be available to individuals with LD, regardless of cost. Unfortunately, despite price decreases in commercially available technologies, many are still not affordable. Although it is possible to buy a personal computer system for $1,000 (or less), this is a formidable amount for some individuals. Ensuring just distribution becomes even more difficult when considering devices with higher price tags, such as OCR/speech synthesis systems, which cost as much as $4,000 (excluding the computer). These costs may be especially prohibitive for individuals with LD, who have been identified as the lowest paid among all the disability groups (Tindall, Gugerty, Heffron, & Godar, 1988).

Who, then, bears the costs? The individual, public/private insurance companies, employers, or the government? As previously discussed, although legislation exists that to some extent addresses the question of financial responsibility, it is too early to tell how this legislation will be enacted. However, at some point, these questions will have to be answered. Otherwise, we may be at risk for creating a society in which technology is available only to the privileged few—a society of technological haves and have nots.

Even if the tab for a technology is picked up, the maze through the bureaucratic funding process (or just saving up for a technology) may take considerable time and effort. As the National Council on Disability (1993) reported to the President and Congress regarding the funding of assistive technology, "There are long delays as the result of cumbersome procurement practices before [potential users] actually gain access to appropriate assistive technology devices" (p. 42). By the time a product is placed in the hands of an individual with LD, it may already be obsolete. The potential for receiving outdated technology is further complicated by rapid advancements in technology, which often are not modified/adapted until after they have been introduced to the general public (if at all), once again leaving persons with disabilities behind. Would a *just* system of technology access provide the LD population with yesterday's technology?

Awareness, Literacy, and Support

Availability of operationally accessible technology will not in and of itself create a just system. To ensure accessibility, several other components have to be in place. Persons with LD also need to be aware of the technologies and technology-based goods, services, and information that will enable them to reap the same benefits as others in society. They also need the technological literacy necessary to utilize technologies. This means that they should have access to educational programs designed to promote technological literacy, and to knowledgeable and trained professional service providers. Finally, they will need a system of technical support that is readily available (e.g., toll-free numbers), as well as support materials that take into consideration their special needs (e.g., manuals written at their reading levels).

Justice, or Unfair Advantage?

Thus far, issues have been addressed that point to the necessity of having technologies accessible to persons with LD in order to ensure equality in attaining goods, services, and information. However, the opposite case could be made: Does the provision of certain technologies create an unjust system by giving individuals with LD an unfair advantage? How can we ensure that a technology is only an equalizer, giving an individual with LD the same level of opportunities and benefits that others enjoy (and therefore also operating in accordance with the principle of beneficence), rather than an inequitable means to outdo others? For example, some faculty and staff at postsecondary institutions have raised the question of the fairness of allowing postsecondary students with LD the use of a word processor during essay examinations, or calculators during math tests, as it has been asserted that other students (although not disabled) could also benefit from the use of such technologies (S.A. Vogel, personal communication, February 1994). How do we ensure that the technology is matched to the disability in such a way that it is only an equalizer for the student with LD? How do we know it has not provided a means of enhancing academic performance that has gone beyond what he or she needs to compete on an equal basis? How can we be sure that we have only provided a method by which students with LD can be judged on the basis of their abilities rather than disabilities, and that we haven't tipped the scales in favor of the LD population?

Similar questions could be posed with regard to the workplace: Would the provision of a speech recognition system to a secretary with LD merely provide the same opportunity for success as provided to nondisabled coworkers, or would it shift the balance to the point of inequity? Once again, the intention here is not to answer such questions, but, rather, to reflect upon them, in an effort to ensure that we are acting in accordance with the principle of justice.

AUTONOMY

Educational Technology

As previously discussed, the principle of autonomy is associated with such concepts as freedom from external control, opportunities for choice, voluntariness, pursuit of interests, and self-mastery. Similar concepts are also appearing in the growing body of LD literature on holism/constructivism (e.g., Heshusius, 1991; Poplin, 1988b). Proponents of the holistic/constructivist teaching/learning process assert that children with LD need the opportunity to self-regulate their learning, be active in their own learning, and pursue learning experiences in which they are passionately interested and that have relevance to their own lives. Such notions appear to be in contrast to the mechanistic–reductionist beliefs of traditional approaches to LD. In discussing this difference, Heshusius stated the following:

> Once the meanings of self-organization, self-regulation, and dynamic inter-action are grasped, it becomes clear that externally controlled, programmed ordering of progress contradicts these crucial holistic principles (indeed contradicts natural learning) and can, in fact, thwart authentic progress. . . . Meaningful progress can be fostered, but not forced or programmatically controlled. (p. 452)

However, as noted earlier, the majority of instructional technology used with children (and adults) with LD tends to be highly program-matic, sequential, and tightly controlled. These technologies often leave little room for the individual to pursue learning experiences that are self-directed, self-regulated, or of passionate interest to their lives. Further-more, these technologies promote passive interaction and offer the learner little control over what takes place in the program (Maddux, Johnson, & Willis, 1992; Russell, Corwin, Mokros, & Kapisovsky, 1989). The ethics of using such technologies in the teaching/learning process comes into question, as they may tend to restrict choice, impose external control, and limit pursuit of interests.

To ensure that we do not limit the autonomy of individuals with LD, perhaps we would be wise to see that other types of educational technolo-gies are available. Specifically, more open-ended and learner-centered technologies would allow for greater freedom, self-direction, and pursuit of personal interests. These technologies might include software/ hardware designed to foster exploration, discovery, and construction of knowledge. Technologies of this kind have become increasingly possible with the advent of interactive-CD, multimedia, hypermedia, electronic information/communication, and virtual reality systems. Greater avail-ability of such technologies will also increase these individuals' opportu-nities for choice (in the selection of technology), also acting in accordance with the principle of autonomy.

When considering education technology relative to the principle of autonomy, it is important to consider the origin of technologies and the notion of external control. Educational technologies come from develop-ers and manufacturers who, for the most part, are driven by the potential economic success of a product. Most teachers and students are not in a position to develop their own technologies, and, in fact, in many cases they lack general knowledge in the area of special education technology (Penso, 1991). As a result, they are often highly dependent upon the makers and sellers of technology for recommendations on the best tech-nology to purchase. This places LD professionals and individuals with LD in a vulnerable position, a position that may make them subject to exter-nal control in the form of persuasion and even manipulation.

Attractive packaging, fancy graphics, engaging sounds, and testimonials promising improved learning performance may entice professionals, parents, and persons with LD to purchase technologies that are not necessarily in harmony with particular learning needs. Teachers and administrators may be further drawn to the programmatic formats of many instructional software programs, which offer discrete, sequential, easy-to-use steps. Such programs, while fitting quite readily into conventional special education models of curriculum planning (e.g., IEPs) and management, may in actuality have limited educational value.

Many companies make generous equipment and software donations to educational institutions. However, in some cases it may be valuable to reflect upon the incentives for such philanthropy. While not dismissing the generosity of the companies that have donated their technologies to institutions and persons with disabilities, we think it is important to recognize that such actions may simultaneously serve as excellent marketing strategies that help to ensure the purchase and institutionalization of a company's products—products whose value in promoting the welfare of individuals with LD may be questionable. Although it is wonderful to receive "free" technology, such actions may ultimately limit choices in the products selected for use with persons with LD.

This discussion is not meant to paint technology developers, manufacturers, or sellers in a negative light. Apple Computers and IBM (as well as others) have given millions (if not billions) of dollars in donations to enhance the quality of life for individuals with disabilities, and such generosity should not be discounted. Nevertheless, we need to be sure that the selection of specific technologies is being made on the basis of sound educational principles and research, and not merely on enticements offered by manufacturers.

To help ensure that technologies are consistent with the needs of persons with LD, manufacturers will need to solicit input from the LD population. The thoughts and ideas offered by persons with LD should be taken seriously, even if manufacturers consider their ideas foolish or wrong, because respect for autonomy demands, at a minimum, due consideration of an individual's beliefs and judgments (Beauchamp, 1991). Although companies manufacturing special education technologies generally test their products with potential users toward the end of the development process, there is frequently little input from the end-user in the beginning stages. Neglecting to involve persons with LD in the planning and development process may be a result of the manufacturer's, as well as the special educator's, fundamental lack of respect for the ideas, beliefs, and thoughts of those with LD. Persons with LD may be viewed as less competent and not capable of making decisions or recommendations regarding technology that may assist in enhancing the quality of their lives. This failure to listen to persons with LD regarding their own treatment was highlighted by Adelman and Taylor (1983). They stated, "Children and individuals with problems are often treated in ways which diminish their autonomy, which occurs because of assumptions about their relative lack of competence and wisdom. Even when they are treated autonomously, their decisions may not be respected" (p. 291).

Perhaps it is time that technology developers (and LD professionals), in an effort to respect the autonomy of persons with LD, start listening more attentively to what persons with LD believe they need, rather than merely what manufacturers and educators deem appropriate technologies and technological interventions for them.

Medical Technologies

The advent of medical technologies was a major factor in the rise of the field of bioethics, raising new questions in the "bio-realm" (Clouser, 1989) regarding abortion, euthanasia, reproduction, and genetic engineering (Beauchamp & Walters, 1989). In turn, considerations in these areas prompted a number of ethical questions related to autonomy and concerns for freedom, choice, voluntariness, consent, and self-mastery.

Recent advances in medical technology have found their way into the LD arena, offering great promise for persons with LD, yet simultaneously provoking ethical query. These technologies have been directed primarily toward the study of brain anatomy and functioning (see Bigler, 1992; Flowers, 1993; Hynd, Marshall, & Gonzalez, 1991; Swanson & Bray, 1991) and include computed tomography (CT) scanning, magnetic resonance imaging (MRI), positron emission tomography (PET), brain electrical activity mapping (BEAM), electroencephalography (EEG), and cerebral blood flow (CBF) studies. Technologies have also been employed to study the genetic factors associated with LD (e.g., Pennington et al., 1991), as well as in postmortem studies of people with LD (e.g., Galaburda, 1989; Humphreys, Kaufman, & Galaburda, 1990). Although no technology currently exists that can definitively diagnose LD (Hynd et al., 1991), several hold considerable promise, and some have already documented differences between "normally achieving and learning disabled individuals" (Hresko & Parmar, 1991b, p. 19). Prospects for the future are promising.

Until this time, the diagnosis of LD has been approached primarily from an educational, psychoeducational, or neuropsychological perspective. Such diagnoses have been based upon soft evidence and inferences made from (a) standardized and informal "paper-and-pencil" tests of cognitive and academic performance, (b) reviews of academic work, (c) observations, and (d) interviews. The inability of these procedures to conclusively diagnose the presence of LD is perhaps one of the most frustrating factors related to LD practice—for professionals and nonprofessionals alike. In contrast, medically based diagnostic technologies have the potential to provide hard evidence (e.g., misplaced neurons). The generation of such scientific evidence has the potential to prompt a wide-scale push for technology-based diagnoses from professionals, parents, and persons with LD. Such a push also triggers a number of ethical questions related to autonomy.

First of all, who should decide, and on what grounds, who is to be assessed through these technologies? Although the final answer will probably lie with a physician, other questions still arise in this regard. For instance, should a school district be permitted to require that a child be assessed by such means in the course of determining eligibility of services? Should private schools be permitted to require such testing as part of their admittance requirements? Then there is the issue of employers: Should they be allowed to mandate such testing to ensure that they are not hiring an individual who may be a potential liability? Does an insurance company have the right to require such testing as part of procedures for issuance of a medical policy? Might the armed forces make it a part of their medical screening of recruits? Or in the extreme, should the federal government mandate technology-based genetic screening (and counseling) with prospective parents in an effort to forestall the birth of children with LD and the costs to society associated with serving/treating them? These are all questions related to external control, choice, and voluntariness that lie at the very heart of the principle of autonomy. In each of these instances, the individual's freedom to choose whether or not to be tested has the potential of being compromised by external mandates or requirements.

If a diagnosis of LD is made through one of these technologies, or testing reveals that prospective parents are likely to have a child with LD, another fundamental question emerges: Who should have access to this information? This question involves key components of autonomy—privacy, consent, and, ultimately, questions of beneficence and justice relative to what is eventually done with the information. For example, should insurance companies have open access to this information, or must the individual give consent to release the information? If insurance companies have such access, could they not use it as a basis to raise rates or deny coverage? Yet, is it not an insurer's right to be aware of information that may have a significant financial impact on their business? Similarly, would providing a private school with such information result in its refusal to admit students with LD or requiring parents to pay supplemental funding? Yet, should the school not have a right to know about a student that may place substantial demands on its program? Do employers have the right to know if they are hiring an employee with LD, and would such information inhibit that employee's advancement or prevent initial opportunities for employment? Yet, do employers not have the right to know about potential difficulties that may affect the operation of their business?

Then there is the individual who undergoes technology-based diagnostic procedures. Should they have access to the results? At what age? Should we wait until there are manifestations of symptomology? How might knowledge of these results affect them? Is it different than presenting the results of pencil-and-paper diagnostic measures? It is important to emphasize that in each of these cases, concern for fostering the autonomy of the individual with LD may also have ramifications regarding beneficence and justice, not just for the individual, but for institutions as well. Such questions form a complex web in which multiple ethical principles interplay and often come into conflict with one another.

The information derived from medically based diagnostic technologies may also be suggestive of specific medically based interventions for treating LD. Among the future possibilities for such procedures are brain tissue/cell transplantations (as in the case of Parkinson's disease; Brundin, Odin, & Widner, 1990); biotechnology implantation (as has been used in the treatment of ALS; Sutter, 1988); and gene therapy. Considering the research that has documented structural/anatomical abnormalities in the brains of individuals with dyslexia (e.g., Galaburda, 1989), and the ongoing advances in medical technology, the possibility of such future interventions most assuredly exists and will inevitably raise a multitude of ethical questions, including those of autonomy. Genetic intervention is a case in point.

Genetic Intervention

Although initial efforts in gene therapy have focused on such severe disorders as sickle-cell anemia, muscular dystrophy, and cystic fibrosis (Beauchamp & Walters, 1989), future efforts may also include conditions such as LD. In fact, efforts to identify the genetic factors associated with LD are already under way (see Olson, Wise, Conners, Rack, & Fulker, 1989; Pennington et al., 1991; Smith & Pennington, 1987). It may not be long before the prospect of genetic therapy for the alleviation/ prevention of LD becomes a reality. These genetic interventions may involve somatic-cell therapies, in which only the individual is treated, as well as germ-line therapies, which involve egg and sperm cells and affect future generations.

The ability to control individuals' specific traits, and ultimately those of future generations, provokes a number of considerations regarding autonomy. For example, would germ-line therapy aimed at preventing LD in an unborn child be a basic infringement of that child's freedom of choice? If parents are to make such decisions on behalf of the child, how do we know that they possess the knowledge and understanding to make such decisions? How do we ensure that parents will not be subtly persuaded or even manipulated by professionals in making such decisions? Similarly, would somatic-cell therapy with a newborn compromise a self-directed life course? And, again, who is to make such decisions, and on what bases?

Then there is the child who has begun to experience the problems associated with having LD. At what age does a child have the knowledge, understanding, and wisdom to consent to genetic intervention? Should a child have the right to overturn the decision for genetic intervention made by a parent or guardian? These questions are further complicated by the fact that they may come into conflict with the principle of beneficence, since it could be argued that interventions designed to prevent or alleviate the constellation of problems associated with LD are acts of beneficence. At what point does or should the principle of beneficence override the principle of autonomy, and who is to make that decision? Answers to such questions are made even more complex by the realization that although a child may inherit the genetic characteristics of a specific LD, he or she does not necessarily develop the disability. And, even if the disability develops to some degree, other factors may be at work that diminish its manifestation. As Olson et al. (1989) stressed in discussing genetic factors in dyslexia, "genetic influences may constrain the speed or ease of reading development, but environmental factors such as improved reading instruction and greater reading experience may compensate for genetic constraints" (p. 347).

Further complications arise, in reflecting upon the ethics of gene therapy, when one considers that many persons with LD (as previously noted) think of their disability not as a defect, but, rather, as a gift or attribute that enabled them to gain insights and achieve success that would have not been possible without the "disability." How do we justify genetic intervention with a gifted individual who believes the full rewards of life are reaped not in spite of an LD, but because of it? Then there is society as a whole. If learning disabilities are eliminated, might not the special talents and abilities that often go hand in hand with the disability (Geschwind, 1982) also disappear? Will society not be deprived of the benefits that might have resulted from the gifts of those individuals who see the world in a different light? Might society not have already been robbed of the contributions of some of the world's most distinguished scientists, athletes, artisans, business leaders, and political figures if efforts had been made to eradicate LD?

CONCLUSION

By design or by accident, the field of LD has been thrust into the technological revolution. Technology is being used at an ever-increasing rate, in the hope of improving academic abilities, ensuring employment success, and promoting social and psychological well-being. Although the primary objective of using technology with persons with LD has been to enhance the quality of their lives, we have perhaps failed to adequately reflect upon the full range and depth of the consequences of such use. This failure could result in consequences that are not only less desirable than anticipated, but actually harmful to individuals with LD. The field of applied ethics, with its basic principles of beneficence, justice, and autonomy, has been offered as a framework within which to reflect upon the larger issues inherent in the use of technology with persons with LD. These principles have been employed to open a dialogue regarding technology utilization in an effort to ensure that we are moving in a direction that offers the greatest possible rewards while minimizing potential negative consequences. Although the use of this ethical framework does not provide definitive answers, it has the potential to ensure that we have adequately contemplated the repercussions associated with technology utilization with persons with LD. Adequate reflection will also require awareness of preconceived views of technology, both positive and negative.

Like the surviving scholar in the opening fable, who took a moment to reflect upon the consequences of bringing the lion back to life, we also need to pause for a moment and fully contemplate the consequences of the ways in which technology is used with persons with LD. Failure to do so may not only diminish the opportunity for persons with LD to live satisfying and rewarding lives, but also be detrimental to society as a whole.

AUTHORS' NOTE

The authors would like to thank Dr. Michael Kerze of Occidental College for his insights on ethics and technology.

7. Multiple Intelligences and Underachievement: Lessons From Individuals with Learning Disabilities

DIXON HEARNE AND

SUKI STONE

The schools allow millions of imaginative kids to go unrecognized and let their gifts remain untapped simply because educators focus too much attention on numbers, words, and concepts, and not enough on images, pictures and metaphors. Many of these children may be ending up in learning disability classes and many more may be wasting away in regular classrooms, at least in part because nobody has been able to figure out how to make use of their talents in a school setting. (Armstrong, 1987, p. 85)

In their provocative book, *Cradles of Eminence*, Victor and Mildred Goertzel (1962) explored common bonds and recurring themes in the lives of 400 eminent twentieth-century men and women. Their research revealed that clearly 60% of the 400 held a strong dislike for school and had serious problems while there. Primary in the list of dissatisfactions with school were the curricula, followed closely by their problems with "dull, irrational, or cruel teachers" (p. 241). Many of the 400 were them-

Reprinted, with changes, from "Multiple intelligences and underachievement: Lessons from individuals with learning disabilities," by Dixon Hearne and Suki Stone, *Journal of Learning Disabilities*, Vol. 28, 1995, pp. 439–448. Copyright © 1995 by PRO-ED, Inc.

selves thought dull because of their general lack of interest in school-work. Goertzel and Goertzel noted that many of these intellectually capable children who failed in school did so because they limited their interests to particular subjects and neglected others altogether. Others managed only to irritate their teachers with their originality and imagination.

Today, many of those individuals would no doubt be referred and perhaps assigned to learning disabilities (LD) programs or remedial instruction. This is due in great part to the widespread use of, and frequent overreliance on, IQ measures in determining school placements. Even the performance components of respected tests such as the Wechsler Intelligence Scale for Children-Revised are laden with the need for metalinguistic thought and reasoning. Examinees engaged in the block design, object assembly, or picture completion subtests, for example, can be observed "thinking in language" as they approach the tasks (e.g., whispering, talking to themselves, using body language that suggests inner conversation). This preoccupation with verbal and logico-mathematical ability has generally diverted our attention from other aspects or kinds of intelligence that reside within every child.

Following Alfred Binet's groundbreaking work, concern about the effects of intelligence testing on our views about creativity has been a perennial topic of debate in education and psychology. Binet's testing met with a backlash of skepticism and a wave of alternative intelligence measures—measures of talents, creativity, and even imagination. Simpson (1922), for example, argued the need for "tests designed to give us more direct and dependable information upon this essential element of progress—creative imagination" (p. 5). He developed several creativity tests himself. Subsequent research by Andrews (1930) resulted in the creation of three "tests of imagination," which were used with preschoolers. In 1931, McCloy and Meier constructed a "re-creative imagination" test.

In a set of related studies among college students, Welch (1946) found no statistical basis for equating intelligence with imagination. Despite the high intelligence of students in his studies, they displayed a lack of imaginative thinking. These results were consistent with findings by Dearborn (1898) in his pioneering research among college students.

In more recent research, Torrance (1967, 1991), Guilford (1968), Welsh (1975), and Barron (1968, 1991) have studied aspects of original-ity, fluency, flexibility, and problem-solving ability as indicators of creativity. Such traits provide both a broad, enhanced picture of an individual's abilities and valuable feedback about the act of learning itself. In 1962, Getzels and Jackson wrote, "Once we accept the notion, however provisionally, that creativity and intelligence as measured by the I.Q. are not synonymous—an almost limitless number of exciting problems present themselves for systematic study" (p. viii).

There have always been questions as to the efficacy of true intelligence measures and subsequent concerns about basing our instructional approaches solely on them—as if problems in short-term memory or auditory discrimination, for example, predict lack of success in all areas of one's life (Coles, 1987). At least some current research in the field of learning disabilities has begun to focus on creativity and nontraditional strengths and talents that have not been well understood or highly valued by the schools. In this chapter, we briefly summarize the findings in our search for the talents of students labeled learning disabled, evidence of their *abilities*, implications of these for the schools, and a beginning set of practical recommendations.

PAST IS PRESENT

Ironically, much of the existing research on the talents and strengths of individuals with learning disabilities has appeared not in learning disabilities journals, but, rather, in journals devoted to study of the gifted. In 1989, a group of researchers (Boodoo, Bradley, Frontera, Pitts, & Wright) at Texas A & M University sent survey forms to all 353 special education centers in Texas, to find out "whether any LD students were enrolled in gifted programs, the characteristics of such children, who nominated these children, and the reasons why they were/were not admitted to the gifted program" (p. 112). A second survey was sent to 444 directors of gifted and talented (GT) programs across the state, requesting information about districts' definitions of giftedness, the types of gifted programs that were available, and the eligibility criteria used for placement of students in GT programs. Of the 180 responses received, 91% of the districts reported no gifted–learning disabled (GLD) students, 91% did not respond to questions about special aptitude characteristics, 3% did not specify the special aptitude characteristics, and 3% felt the GLD have no special aptitude. Twenty-three percent of the districts nominated students with above-average aptitude for the gifted program. However, the authors noted that "the separation of SPED [special education] and GT programs and the fact that LD children have reading problems were other reasons given for not admitting LD students to GT programs" (p. 119). Surveys from directors of GT programs also contained comments to the effect that "LD children cannot be in a gifted program and that students with high aptitude are not LD" (p. 119). Such misconceptions seem to permeate our education system at all levels, due in great part to a general lack of knowledge and direct experience with those individuals who have been labeled by the schools as learning disabled. We suspect that many administrators, district personnel, and even some teachers know students only by numerical representations or categorical labels—rather than by their unique human qualities and gifts.

At the conclusion of her editorship of the *Learning Disability Quarterly*, Poplin (1984) noted that "the horrifying truth is that in the four years I have been editor of the LDQ only one article has been submitted that sought to elaborate on the talents of the learning disabled (Tarver, Ellsworth, & Rounds, 1980)" (p. 133). Even though our learning disability journals have carried almost no information on the capabilities of students with learning disabilities, special educators have always begun with the assumption that these students were average or above in "intelligence" and/or that there were tremendous discrepancies between their school achievement and their intelligence.

According to Poplin (1993), learning disabilities literature can be divided into roughly three broad philosophical and pedagogical domains: (a) remedial education, characterized by schools' efforts to "fill in" missing knowledge and skills (e.g., remedial reading, remedial math); (b) intervention, characterized by efforts of research and "specialists" within the schools to identify methods that presumably help the learner circumvent or better deal with a "learning problem" (e.g., computer-assisted instruction, cognitive strategies approach, resource specialist programs); and (c) compensatory education, which is characterized by efforts to "equalize" educational opportunity among all learners in the schools (e.g., Head Start, Title 1, Sheltered English, and bilingual programs).

Somehow, the field of learning disabilities has evolved into a deficit-driven enterprise, much as have the fields of compensatory, remedial, and even, in some cases, bilingual and English-as-a-Second-Language (ESL) education. (The fact that we have often assigned "remedial" strategies to nonremedial second-language learners is a political, as well as pedagogical, problem [see Benesch, 1988; Sleeter, 1986].) In "special" programs, educators look for students' deficits in their research, in their diagnoses, in their assessments, and throughout the school day. Once these are found, they define their roles as remediators of deficits. The students' days are then structured to be filled with activities based on their weaknesses rather than their strengths. Poor readers, for example, are frequently assigned multiple sessions of reading instruction (e.g., regular class, special class, and even afterschool and summer tutoring clinics). In addition, remediation is defined reductionistically, with the large and inherently interesting tasks, such as reading, broken down into small, often disconnected and uninteresting tasks. The small reductionistic skills are selected for instruction, as is true in most special programs

(Sooho, 1991). The data on this form of remedial instruction are well known and do not support the notion that such approaches are widely or even mildly successful in affecting the lives of students with learning disabilities.

Many of us know individuals with learning disabilities from our classrooms, and, regardless of what they look like in the research journals, we know they have incredible talents generally undervalued or not well represented in our curricula. The curricula, even most art and music curricula, require linguistic intelligence (largely reading and some writing) for access to all knowledge and/or proof of knowledge. So the student who knows more about ants than anyone in the class, perhaps even more than the teacher, may fail the second grade science test on ants. The adolescent who knows much about the politics of power may fail political science. Knowing this, special educators are left with a number of dilemmas, including the issue that we do not understand the talents of students with learning disabilities or how we might use these talents in their education. Quinn (1984), Moss (1989), Weinstein (1994), and Stolowitz (1995) have all documented the painful results of our not understanding or nurturing the strengths of students with learning disabilities. In recent years, however, some research has begun to examine—even emphasize— what learners can *do*, rather than what they cannot.

MULTIPLE INTELLIGENCES: AVENUES TO SUCCESS

There is a growing body of research and discussion, most notably in Gardner's (1983) work, that strongly suggests the need to revise our views about intelligence and our roles as educators. Gardner's groundbreaking work has advanced our knowledge beyond simplistic and naive definitions of intelligence. His theory of multiple intelligences offers a more holistic accounting of individual potential and talents.

According to Gardner (1983, 1993), each person possesses at least seven kinds of intelligence (linguistic, logico-mathematical, musical-rhythmic, visual–spatial, bodily-kinesthetic, interpersonal, and intrapersonal), and the degree to which each develops is dependent upon many variables. The most important, however, is freedom to pursue the intelligences. Because schools are deficit driven, they generally devalue or ignore intelligences other than the logico-mathematical and linguistic. This perspective is based on the seemingly fallacious assumption that one's general success in all areas is somehow predicated on one's development in these *two* areas (Gardner, 1983, 1993). Although the notion of a general intelligence measure has been widely replaced by verbal and performance composite measures in recent years, there is still a fascination with numerical representations of individuals' abilities in our schools. We continue to use them to segregate populations and to dictate special curricula. Grouping for instruction exists primarily as a function of time, economics, and student ability (verbal and mathematical), rather than of individual talents, strengths, or interests.

The kinds of schools Gardner (1993) advocated exist only as pilot programs, such as "Project Spectrum," which is a preschool collaboration between Harvard and Tufts universities; these programs allow students to demonstrate their particular strengths and interests through their play activities, number games, creative movement exercises, and storytelling activities. Another collaborative project, between the Educational Testing Service and the Pittsburg Public School System (ARTS PROPEL), involves junior and senior high school students whose latent abilities are assessed from project and process-based portfolios in music, creative writing, and visual arts. Students are taken into the community every day, and every day the community is brought into the school. The same is true at the Key School, an Indianapolis public school where video documentation of every student's projects, teacher observations, and personal preferences form the basis for the apprenticeships he or she selects at the end of third grade.

There is, however, no wide-scale plan at the national, state, or local level for nurturing the various intelligences. We know a lot about what students do not know because we look for it directly throughout the day. We perseverate on the things *we* want them to know and generally ignore things *they* want to know, forgetting that only when they are immersed in their own personal interests and passions are they honing their strengths and talents. As Gardner (1983, 1993) submitted, schools should be a place where learners go to nurture their personal intelligences, a place rich with choice, opportunity, and an accessible and varied curriculum. Eisner (1988), too, lamented that "as long as schools operate on an essentially linguistic modality that gives place of privilege to a kind of literal, logical, or mathematical form of intelligence, schools limit what youngsters can learn" (p. 37).

We have no statistics on student possibilities that are *not* nurtured in our schools; we cannot reconstruct what might have evolved. Nor do we have much information on the students' talents or interests, what is truly important to them, or what they truly know. Conversely, we know a tremendous amount about what *educators* think is important to know and do. Despite the dialectic on "restructuring," state- and district-level discussion seems to focus more on the politics of reason and economics than on institutional change, more on *teaching* than on *learning*.

Teachers who look for points of overlap or connections between their students' interests and the dictates of district-imposed curricula, however, may find surprisingly rich and interesting projects in which to immerse all their students, projects that nurture several or all of the multiple intelligences. Conversely, teachers who presume that all their students' learning begins with what they (teachers) do and how they think learning takes place, express a general belief that students are incapable of identifying their own right ways of learning and knowing. In reading and written language, for example, Leland and Harste (1994) submitted that "a good language arts program is one that expands the communication potential of all learners through the orchestration and use of multiple ways of knowing for purposes of ongoing interpretation and inquiry into the world" (p. 339). If we do not believe that students have multiple ways of knowing, it is because we have not looked for evidence of it, and it is a fallacious assumption to believe that creative problem solving is necessarily a by-product of good teaching.

In his study of six child prodigies, Feldman (1986) concluded that the creative powers of individuals stretch beyond the traditional classroom's ability to accommodate them. He asserted that creativity such as that of Mozart and Mill and the pure genius of an Einstein arise in their own time as a matter of the combined forces of their own talents and the zeitgeist of the age in which they live and operate. In light of the lessons learned from our past and the prodigies and geniuses it has produced, we should create every opportunity in the lives of individuals in our charge to allow *all* their unique gifts and talents to come forth. Because we cannot calculate or predict the advent of geniuses in our midst, schools should abound with opportunities for talents or genius to materialize, as if the time is always right for such things to happen.

Such reasoning presents several dilemmas for the schools. First, they must reexamine their primary role in the personal lives of their inhabitants, versus their role as impersonal agents of change. Schools must reexamine the reasons and procedures by which students are segregated into categories. Moreover, they must acknowledge the fallacies and limitations of testing and the fallacious assumption that remediating academic deficits is preparation for life. We must also set aside purely reductionist assumptions, at least temporarily, if we are to let an array of alternative views emerge. Inviting peers from other disciplines to tinker with the problem says much about the value we place on objectivity in our quest to understand learning disabilities, and much about our integrity in general.

EVIDENCE OF ABILITIES: A SUMMARY OF RESEARCH

To begin to address some of the dilemmas and issues raised by educators with respect to the abilities of students with LD, several studies have been conducted over the past decade. Although our current diagnosis, assessment, and instructional practices remain oriented toward locating and curing deficits rather than capitalizing on talents, our cure rate has been abysmally low (Coles, 1987; Poplin, 1988a, 1988b), suggesting that it might be time to rethink our direction. Propitiously, Gardner's pivotal work on multiple intelligences emerged to lend more structure and impetus to research in the field of learning disabilities. Below, we summarize some findings from relevant research and the issues they raise for both general and special educators.

In 1988, Baum and Owen conducted a study of 112 elementary school students (Grades 4 through 6) to "investigate what characteristics distinguish High Ability/LD students from learning disabled students with average cognitive ability and from high ability students" (p. 321). The researchers examined six types of motivational and cognitive predictor variables (Self-Efficacy for Academic Tasks, Creative Potential, Interests, Disruptive Behavior, Self-Concept, Attributions for Academic Success or Failure) using a variety of tests, for example, the Self-Efficacy for Academic Tasks (Owen & Baum, 1985); the Group Inventory for Finding Talent (Rimm, 1976); the Williams Scale (Williams, 1980a, 1980b); and the Torrance Tests of Creative Thinking (Torrance, 1972). Among other findings, the high ability/LD group performed higher than other groups at tasks involving problem solving and abstract thinking. Owen and Baum reported that "in nonacademic settings, they have been observed to be creative and productive. They can show extraordinary abilities and are highly motivated when completing challenging tasks based on their own interests" (p. 321). Clearly 36% of the students labeled LD "simultaneously demonstrated traits of gifted behavior" (p. 324). Rather than further dichotomizing instruction for the gifted and for the high ability/ LD students, Owen and Baum argued the need for the *same* kinds of challenging learning experiences—experiences based on their common creative and intellectual characteristics.

In a subsequent study, Minner (1990) asked 197 teachers of gifted students in four midwestern states to read vignettes describing hypothetical gifted students with and without learning disabilities from varying socioeconomic backgrounds. Although most of the teachers had little knowledge or training in the area of learning disabilities, results from this research revealed that teachers of gifted students were "less inclined to refer learning disabled and poor children than identically described children without those particular traits" (p. 37). The author noted that this research supported similar findings from a former study (Boodoo et al., 1989) indicating that general classroom teachers are also less inclined to refer such students for possible placement in gifted programs. Such attitudes leave entire segments of school populations unserved by appropriately challenging programs.

In our search of the past literature on learning disabilities for indications of talents and strengths, four areas emerged: conceptual writing, divergent thinking, computer aptitude, and musical ability. Researchers interested in exploring strengths and talents among students with LD typically have begun their study with the assumption that such students have many talents that remained unrecognized by the schools and/or the students themselves. Many researchers (e.g., Hearne, Poplin, Schoneman, & O'Shaughnessy, 1988; Kerchner & Kistinger, 1984; Tarver, Elsworth, & Rounds, 1980) also held that special educators' jobs had historically been defined as a deficit-driven enterprise, and that this course had caused us to miss many important aspects of students' lives.

In 1980, Poplin, Gray, Larsen, Banikowski, and Mehring published an article suggesting that the writing difficulties of students with learning disabilities lay more in the mechanical aspects of writing than in the conceptual ones. Using a test that separated these areas, Poplin et al. found that students who had learning disabilities, particularly in the early grades, did not differ from their nondisabled peers in thematic maturity or vocabulary, but had problems in spelling, grammar, and punctuation. However, as these students progressed through school, they lost their edge in the conceptual areas. Researchers hypothesized that this, in part, might be related to the emphasis on mechanical skills dominant in typical remediation programs. Atwell (1988) lent more support for that hypothesis with her documentation of the progress of a student with learning disabilities in a whole language program.

Kerchner and Kistinger (1984) looked at several groups of students with learning disabilities, some in traditional remediation programs and one group in a process-writing program that used word processing as well. Those students who received process writing instruction versus traditional remediation made significantly more academic progress during the year, further suggesting that skills remediation may not be the answer. Additionally, Kerchner and Kistinger noted that by drawing illustrations *prior* to writing, some of the students showed improvement in both organization and elaboration of their themes (see also DuCharme, 1990, on young children's use of drawing in writing).

By 1984, some researchers, interested in frequent reports by teachers that their students with LD were often mechanically talented (e.g., Poplin, Drew, & Gable, 1984), had begun to explore how these talents might relate to computer aptitude. A test was subsequently developed that could assess computer aptitude without requiring complex linguistic skills: the Computer Aptitude, Literacy, and Interest Profile (CALIP; Poplin, Drew, & Gable, 1984). Using the CALIP, Hearne et al. (1988), in their study of a matched group of junior high students with and without learning disabilities, found that the students with LD had computer aptitudes equivalent to those of their nondisabled counterparts. Results also indicated that no significant difference existed in computer aptitude scores between male and female participants in the sample. What is most significant here is the idea that learning disabilities may not automatically preclude a learner's success at programming or other complex computer tasks. Moreover, areas in which students with LD can excel might prove to be excellent avenues to academic success.

In 1980, Tarver et al. conducted a comparative study of divergent thinking skills among students with learning disabilities and their non–learning disabled (NLD) peers at the first-, third-, fifth-, and seventh-grade levels. Using the Torrance Test of Creativity and the Alternative Uses Test, they sought to examine both figural and verbal creativity. The Torrance test asks the child to complete an incomplete figure and make it tell an interesting story, all within 10 minutes. Results of the Figural Creativity subtest indicated that the students with LD were higher than their NLD counterparts in originality, and that the NLD students were significantly higher in elaboration. The results of the verbal creativity comparisons indicated that the NLD students scored higher on five of the six measures. Tarver et al. concluded that the students with LD showed ability in the area of "originality/uniqueness" (p. 13). They also suggested that lack of motivation or persistence may have contributed to the lower elaboration scores for students with LD.

In a more recent study, applying a different measure of divergent thinking, Stone, Poplin, Johnson, and Simpson (1992) looked for differences in divergent thinking and feeling in 60 matched elementary school students with LD and NLD peers from 10 schools in the southern California area. Using the Test of Divergent Thinking and the Test of Divergent Feeling, the researchers found no differences between scores for the students with LD and their NLD counterparts. In fact, results suggested that the students with LD actually scored higher on both the Titles and the Elaboration subtest, as well as showing better total test performance. Stone et al. pointed out that while divergent thinking is characteristic of creativity, it is not necessarily characteristic of success in school.

In a concurrent two-facet study among the same sample, Stone et al. (1993) examined the musical and visual-artistic talents of students with LD as compared with their NLD peers. Utilizing the Barron-Welsh Art Scale–Revised and the Welsh-Barron Figure Perception Test, Stone et al. asked students to state whether they liked or disliked a series of pictures. Responses were recorded and compared to scaled scores obtained from responses by artists and nonartists in the standardization sample. Results revealed no significant differences between scores earned by the students with LD and their NLD counterparts.

The second facet of the study compared students with LD and their NLD peers on the Seashore Measures of Musical Talent. Six areas of musical ability were explored: pitch, loudness, rhythm, time, timbre, and tonal memory. Students were presented with pairs of sounds, tones, and rhythm patterns, and with tone lengths and sequences of notes. They were asked to make judgments about them, and responses were converted to scaled scores. Again, results indicated no significant differences between students with LD and their NLD peers in this sample.

In related studies utilizing the Test for Creative Thinking–Drawing Production, Stone (1992) found that the average of combined scores on the Humor subtest for elementary students with LD were significantly higher than the average for their general education peers ($p < .05$). Ziv (1988) distinguished humor from other forms of creativity, although the forms are positively correlated. He submitted that even though humor is a cognitive process, it is more adequately described as "cognitive playfulness" (p. 109), which is an indicator of creativity. Bleedom (1988) described the intricacy of humor as the process of bringing together different ideas from two distinct planes, which then interplay in the mind to form a relationship. That process, identified by Koestler (1964) as *bisociation,* is creativity. Again, those of us who know these students from our own classrooms can attest to their leaps of insight, use of double entendres and parody, and creative solutions to both textbook and teacher-posed problems, despite confidential records that reflect intellectual and academic inadequacies. The research findings of Jellen and Urban (1988), Ziv, and Bleedom might then suggest humor as one productive line of inquiry into the strengths (cognitive and otherwise) of students with LD, and humor's role in subsequent pedagogical considerations.

Authors of studies reported here are quick to point out limitations of their research, but it should be noted that until relatively recently there has been a lack of both interest and instruments for productive research in these areas. The creation in recent years of such instruments as the CALIP, the Krantz Talent Identification Instrument (Krantz, 1982), and the Multi-Dimensional Screening Device, along with multimodal approaches to assessment (e.g., Gardner, 1993; Lazear, 1992), suggests a growing interest in nontraditional strengths and talents. The concurrent dialectic on constructivism (see, e.g., the entire Fall 1994 issue of *The Journal of Special Education*) and critical pedagogy offers perhaps even greater evidence of interest in "ways of knowing" other than the linguistic and logico-mathematical, which have dominated our research to date.

IMPLICATIONS

Taking these studies together, one sees many implications for developing new instructional strategies for individuals with LD and, potentially, implications for a whole host of students who fail to achieve in today's schools. It seems we must admit that being learning disabled in the schools today says much about our obsession with teaching and assessing solely through written language. If music, art, and divergent thinking were valued, would we not have a different group of students labeled learning disabled (see Sleeter, 1986, and Coles, 1987)? Are other remedial students also plagued by our overemphasis on written language and intelligence testing? Are second-language learners also placed at a significant disadvantage because of our holding all content ransom for skills in written English? Research clearly documents an overrepresentation of non–English-speaking students in learning disabilities programs and remedial programs (Barken & Bernal, 1991). Barken and Bernal suggested that IQ measures (widely used in student placement) serve to eliminate many able learners from gifted programs, "a disproportionate number of whom are students from nonmainstream cultures. These children, if they are 'identified' at all, are typically admitted only after they have mastered English and can receive instruction in an all English classroom" (p. 144). Many cultures, such as the Hmong, have stronger oral traditions than written ones, and some have no written language at all. In our new restructuring efforts, is there a way we can honor oral traditions as well as written ones?

Certainly, in our traditional teaching and assessment practices we validate the skills of convergent thinkers. Getzels and Jackson noted this in 1962, Torrance in 1967. Even our new definitions of critical thinking rarely take into account the creative divergent thinker, who is more likely to come up with a number of interesting solutions to a problem than to logically and narrowly focus his or her analyses. Is divergent thinking characteristic of a host of remedial students? Is divergent thinking a gift of some of our second-language learners as well? The work of Ramirez and Castaneda (1974) suggested that Latino learners might be gifted in some of these areas. It seems we must work hard to make sure our curricula and instruction are responsive to multiple ways of thinking and to multiple talents.

Key findings from intelligence research (e.g., Feldman, 1986; Gardner, 1983, 1993; Sternberg, 1988) suggest the need for several changes in traditional assessment and instructional practices in our schools, particularly as they are used to identify and segregate special populations. There seems to be a need to expand our study of learning disabilities, for example, to include other voices. Heshusius (1988) has urged that

> social scientists (and special educators) open up their self-imposed boundaries of scientific inquiry, and invite the arts and humanities in to provide a broader vision within which to ask questions and formulate answers.

Including such insights in special education would restore the importance of recognizing and justifying appropriate values as *a way of knowing*. (pp. 62–63)

THEORY INTO PRACTICE

A whole host of new instructional approaches should help the divergent and multiply talented learner, especially the learner for whom traditional language instruction and school requirements are problematic. Both whole language and interdisciplinary curricula, for example, emphasize the "whole" of what is to be learned and encourage multiple ways of conceptualizing, organizing, and demonstrating knowledge; divergent thinkers should be far more successful with interdisciplinary instruction that brings diverse information to bear on single topics, particularly topics of special interest to the learner.

In their discussion of multiple ways of knowing, Leland and Harste (1994) appealed to semiotic theory for support of multiple modes of individual inquiry: "According to semiotic theory, they [ways of knowing] are sign systems which we have created to express meaning and to mediate our world. These sign systems include art, music, mathematics, drama and language; they offer different perspectives" (p. 339). Different perspectives offer different ways of framing questions and conducting inquiry. If learners are allowed to frame problems in their own way, perhaps they might better identify their own unique means of making sense of the world around them. Consider, for example, the student who experiences a sudden flash of understanding about multiplication right in the middle of a poetry lesson. For all the teacher's efforts to teach the concept of "times" during math class, it took the interplay of language, meter, rhyme, and repetition to create within the child an epiphany, in which all past knowledge was suddenly transformed and a revised worldview was created. Although poetry provided the unique framework this student needed to construct the concept of multiplication, no doubt countless other students routinely make such connections between seemingly dissimilar pieces of information and among disciplines to construct meanings in areas other than the one presently being studied.

Cooperative learning also offers students a way to think through curriculum issues in their own way and to understand one another's thought processes and insights, rather than just the teacher's. The emphasis on active learning should aid students who seem to thrive on activity and suffer in passive classrooms. In addition to these current activities, other specific suggestions fall into two general areas: teacher preparation and instructional practices. However, paramount to the success of any set of plans for improvement is the assurance of strong commitment along all lines of the educational hierarchy.

Teacher Preparation

1. Teachers are potentially powerful catalysts for transformation in our schools. They bring to the classroom their own unique talents and intelligences. Teacher education and staff development should encourage the existing multiple talents and strengths of teachers to be integrated into the curriculum. Teacher preparation programs should develop artistic, musical, and kinesthetic talents of teachers *at all levels,* to encourage the cultivation of these in their own students.

2. All teachers should be encouraged to use, in the general classroom, the same kinds of divergent thinking strategies that are often learned and practiced only in gifted programs. A project approach, for example, engages both teachers and learners in stimulating work (experiential) for authentic purposes (functional, relevant, meaningful). Students are immersed in the exploration of language, the arts and humanities, the study of mathematical principles, and scientific inquiry. They must read, write, revise, edit, translate, calculate, predict, construct, and perform to degrees far superior to those fostered by textbook curricula. Because student-selected projects *begin* with high levels of interest and commitment, they frequently reflect students' personal strengths rather than deficits. Teachers, too, are honing their own learning, planning, and instructional skills.

3. We must question more seriously the reductionistic practice of breaking down tasks and knowledge for every student having problems. Perhaps it is the narrow definitions we give to the phenomena of learning and knowing that cause many of our students to look "deficient." The array of skills required to demonstrate learning and success outside the schools often differs fundamentally from those required for school success. This is certainly evident to such highly successful individuals as Bruce Jenner, Cher, Tom Cruise, and any number of other prominent persons from all walks of life who had difficulties in the traditional classroom and were identified as having learning problems.

4. Teachers of art, music, drama, dance, and physical education must take a leading role in helping other teachers integrate these disciplines into traditional academic subject areas. If we accept that the act of learning is the construction of new meanings from both familiar and unfamiliar information, then it is incumbent upon us to help students explore problems, issues, and questions from the unique perspectives offered by the various disciplines. Through team-teaching, mentor-teacher, and other incentive programs, districts and schools can foster an

atmosphere of professional sharing that offers opportunities to grow in areas other than the purely academic. Art, music, or athletic ability may well be the most marketable skills for future employment that some students with LD take with them when they leave us.

5. We must constantly critique our overdependence on assessments of all our students' deficits and our underemphasis on their talents and varied intelligences. Such thinking is at the very heart of constructivists' appeals for holistic assessments. In contemplating what constructivism has added to traditional educational assessment, Meltzer and Reid (1994) noted several new characteristics, including that assessment is becoming more holistic, dynamic, and multidimensional. This stands in sharp contrast to Meltzer and Reid's criticisms of traditional psychometric testing, which they say has failed to (a) consider the influence of motivation, personality, and social factors on learning; (b) consider the processes and strategies learners use to approach problems; and (c) distinguish between learners' performance measures and their potential to change and grow.

Instructional Practices

1. As an approach, interdisciplinary education seeks to explore broad concepts or ideas across many disciplines, for the purpose of better understanding both the concepts and their applications and meanings across the various disciplines. Teachers sometimes give priority to the disciplines themselves, however, and their eagerness to "stretch" learning across all subject areas is sometimes counterproductive, particularly when the concept or idea is of little interest to the students (Leland & Harste, 1994). Alternatively, Leland and Harste suggested that curricula organized around guiding inquiry questions framed by students themselves encourages them to explore their personal relationships to the topic, to use the various disciplines as heuristic devices for discovering more about the topic, and to come to recognize the unique perspective each discipline presents to them. "In the final analysis," wrote Gerber (1994),

> curricula are social constructs, consensual theories of learning and learner, that impinge upon and constrain all students' opportunities to construct their own knowledge. For that reason alone, *the* curriculum must be critically examined and distinguished from the simple sum of knowledge domains (e.g., reading, writing, mathematics) it purports to portray. (p. 372)

For students whose school problems are created by their problems with reading and writing, inquiry presents opportunity for both broad and deep-level learning, as well as ways of demonstrating it.

2. Programs for the individuals with learning disabilities and remedial students should seriously question the use of traditional techniques that simply maintain student status and matching delivery models. We must begin to offer activities that draw on students' talents in other intellects. Individualized Education Programs should include somewhere in their goals and objectives opportunities for learners to nurture their strengths and talents. Language objectives, for example, might be embedded in an art project or studied within the context of an inquiry-based social studies project. Written properly, such objectives are certainly observable, measurable, and perhaps immensely more appealing to the student (and the teacher) than when presented in reduced, segmented, and decontextualized instruction. Student interests and talents might well serve as the content for teaching the skills required by the curriculum.

3. Although whole language has been instrumental in helping learners (including students with LD) see themselves as readers and writers, Leland and Harste (1994) urged that we extend this principle across other disciplines. "Specifically, we need to ask, 'How can we set up classroom environments that support children in thinking like artists?. . . like mathematicians?. . . like musicians? . . . like dramatists?" (p. 341). Such "thinking in sign systems" is particularly encouraging for students with LD, who often remain ignorant of spheres of knowledge outside the curriculum in which they are forced to operate. Creating such environments can help students with learning disabilities to more accurately appraise their own talents and interests—one of the most promising starting points for teachers.

4. We must provide students who have difficulty with test taking with alternative ways of "proving" knowledge, such as demonstrations, performances, oral reports, and projects (in many forms). Just as knowledge is multidimensional, so too should be our ways of demonstrating it. Additionally, such alternative forms of evaluation/assessment can provide insights into why and how specific skills and knowledge have not been acquired. Piaget (1926) was more interested in errors children made than in their correct responses. The errors revealed more about the ability of the mind to grasp, organize, and integrate information into existing structures. Rarely do we find classroom teachers creating situations to study student failure, and yet the information to be gained from such study is valuable, if not essential, in planning individualized instruction. How we assess a learner's understanding should be a negotiated process.

5. Bilingual and English-as-a-Second-Language programs should seriously question reductionistic, remedial-like approaches, which emphasize deficits and serve to further stigmatize these students in our schools. The curricula for these learners can be infused with other intellectual and artistic pursuits that nurture multiple intelligences.

CONCLUSION

In conclusion, we need to consider the proposition that individuals with LD may well be, in large part, simply a group of students whose talents mismatch the primary values and expectations of the schools. Given the research findings presented in this chapter and other current studies, we suggest that learning disabilities may be socially and culturally determined, based on the values structured into the requirements of a deficit-driven educational system.

> Old paradigms do not retire gracefully, and the avatars of new ones are often scorned and savaged. . . . Many educators are still confident that the old paradigm will solve the problems that beset us, sort out the puzzles that perplex us, and place stubborn "anomalies" into context. There is, to be sure, some self-interest evident both in educators' devotion to an input-based conception of the enterprise that employs them and in their resistance to paying the consequences for poor results. In this sense, the old paradigm is manifestly more comfortable and less demanding than the new. (Finn, 1990, pp. 589–590)

The field of learning disabilities, like education in the main, is undergoing upheaval, a shifting in the landscape of educational thought brought on by the forces of opposing paradigms—the mounting tension between traditions of reductionism and eclecticism and the equally compelling force of constructivism. Evidence of this tension can be found in the ongoing, and sometimes heated, dialectic among representatives from many fields of thought and reported in topical issues of professional journals, such as the Fall 1994 issue of *The Journal of Special Education*. The editors of that special issue, Harris and Graham (1994), noted that

> many of the concepts underlying the constructivist reform of educational practice today have a long and distinguished history. . . . Current instructional approaches with constructivist roots include whole language, cognitive strategies instruction, cognitively guided instruction, scaffolded instruction, literacy-based instruction, directed discovery, and many more. (p. 233)

We would certainly add to that list evolving assessment and instructional approaches from both semiotic and multiple intelligences theory. These roots of constructivism are taking hold, and they challenge traditional pedagogy that has in many ways failed students with LD in both general and special education classrooms. What truly propels and advances us, according to Gerber (1994), is the infusion of challenging new views, such as constructivism. The new paradigm brings with it other ways of critiquing our past research and progress, framing questions and problems, and identifying new lines of inquiry. We are left to contemplate the field of learning disabilities (and perhaps the existence of learning disabilities as a verifiable phenomenon) in the greater context of its history in special education—a field both guided and constricted by social and political forces over which the schools that serve these individuals exercise limited control.

Nonetheless, the paradigm of power influences educational decision making and the belief system adopted by the schools. Although the schools still operate in a paradigm structure that is deficit driven, students caught up in the physical and pedagogical manifestations of our rhetoric probably care little about definitions and the elusive constructs we build to study their disabilities. Moreover, they continue to learn things—many things—that are important and useful to them. We see evidence of this both inside and outside the schools. Some of us still shake our heads in awe at the wonderful things our students with LD can do, things that defy the results from their psychological and academic testing. While certainly the research must continue, especially to test the hypothesis that other special learners show similar profiles, there are a number of things we can do now to make sure our newly restructured schools will be restructured for everyone. Most important, the schools must meet the unique needs of students whose strengths and talents lie outside the narrow view of knowledge as being purely linguistic.

8. A Future of Reversals: Dyslexic Talents in a World of Computer Visualization

THOMAS G. WEST

New technologies and techniques currently being developed in computer graphics, medical imaging, and what is now called "scientific visualization" are already having important effects on our society and will in time have profound consequences for education and work at all levels.

A side effect of these advances may be that certain visual–spatial abilities often found among dyslexics may come to confer special advantages in those fields which are coming to rely more heavily on visual approaches and techniques. Ironically, these special advantages may result from the same pattern of traits that has long caused so much difficulty for visually oriented dyslexics in traditional verbally oriented educational systems. Thus, it is proposed that many dyslexics will find themselves on the right side of a major set of trend reversals—ones that could dramatically affect their lives and the lives of their children.

Historically, some of the most original thinkers in the physical sciences, engineering, mathematics, and other areas have relied heavily on visual modes of thought, employing images instead of words or numbers. Some of these thinkers have shown evidence of a striking range of

Reprinted from "A future of reversals: Dyslexic talents in a world of computer visualization," by Thomas G. West, *Annals of Dyslexia*, Vol. 42, 1992, pp. 124–139. Reprinted with permission of The Orton Dyslexia Society, Inc., November 14, 1995.

learning difficulties, including problems with reading, spelling, writing, calculation, attention, speaking, and memory. In recent years, neurological research has suggested that some forms of early brain growth and development tend to produce verbal and other difficulties at the same time that they produce a variety of exceptional visual and spatial talents (Geschwind & Behan, 1982; Geschwind & Galaburda, 1985).

Visual approaches have long been a rich source of insight for certain creative thinkers (Bogen & Bogen, 1969; Gardner, 1983, 1987). These approaches have been major factors in the work of some of the most creative and innovative physicists, chemists, mathematicians, inventors and engineers, including Michael Faraday, James Clerk Maxwell, Albert Einstein, Thomas Edison, Henri Poincaré and others (Hadamard, 1954; Miller, 1986; West, 1991). Visual approaches, however, have been largely ignored or denigrated in many fields for about a hundred years. Recently, there has been a revival of visual approaches at the forefront of several scientific, mathematical, and technological developments creating in certain areas dramatic reversals in the way research is being conducted. The problems have changed. The tools have changed. The methods have changed.

Thus, with these new tools and methodologies, a revival of long-neglected visual approaches is already underway in several fields. The continued spread of increasingly powerful and inexpensive graphic computer hardware and software—together with interactive media, "personal learning workstations," computer simulation, and "virtual reality" systems —can be expected to further accelerate these trends (Brown, 1991; Jaffe & Lynch, 1989; Jolls, 1989; Rheingold, 1991). Before long, these developments should make it possible for many people to use visually oriented methods and approaches that previously only a small number of extremely gifted people could apply through their own mental models alone.

As these changes affect society and the workplace, some professions are beginning to recognize that those with high visual and spatial talents may have moderate or severe difficulties with verbal or lower level mathematical material—and that professional training programs that do not (formally or informally) acknowledge this pattern may eliminate some of the most talented (and ultimately most productive) individuals.

For some time, studies have suggested linkages between certain dyslexic traits and strong visual–spatial abilities, especially among those in fields such as engineering, mathematics, or architecture. But, only recently have practicing professionals begun to recognize the implications of this pattern for the educational requirements of their profession as a whole.

A professional journal for electrical and electronic engineers recently published an opinion article (Frey, 1990) arguing that engineering schools are screening out some of the best future engineers because they are mild or "compensated" dyslexics. If this assertion is true (or one might say to the extent that it is true), current professional schools, through a laudable but misplaced zeal for high academic standards, may be unintentionally eliminating some of the most talented students, possibly helping to degrade over time the overall quality and innovative capabilities of some professions. That is, the newer programs may be selecting students based upon their course management and test taking skills rather than on their ability to devise elegant design solutions in a real working environment.

People working in the dyslexia field are, of course, concerned with children who cannot read; some, however, now see that we need to be equally concerned with a reservoir of talent that is not being allowed to assert itself in a society that needs those talents to do jobs that are undergoing fundamental transformation. Perhaps the problem is not so much how to help certain children measure up, but, rather, how to identify and develop widely varied but often substantial talents, talents that appear to be well-suited to provide novel and integrated solutions to extremely complex modern problems.

The task is made more difficult because many of the visual skills previously considered unimportant will become more essential in the future, while many of the verbal skills will become inconsequential or merely utilitarian. Children at the bottom of the class may have much more potential than anyone now realizes. Furthermore, if these talents are not applied to the needs of the society, they often can be applied in ways that are injurious to the society.

Accordingly, professionals in the field of dyslexia—in addition to dealing with remediation of their clients' difficulties—should follow the examples of Samuel T. Orton and Norman Geschwind by beginning to focus more on a variety of substantial skills, skills that are likely to become increasingly important as our technological world culture changes in dramatic ways (Geschwind & Galaburda, 1985; Orton, 1966).

It is time to be attentive to gifts as well as problems. It is becoming more apparent that a substantial number of extraordinarily gifted people in different fields have some varied set of learning difficulties which have never been properly identified and which would seem to have been only minor impediments in an otherwise highly successful career. Yet, when we listen to the observations of these remarkable people, we see that often a novel form of thinking has played a major role in both the special insights and the surprising difficulties these people have experienced— and that this novel form of thinking often reflects a distinctive style relating directly or indirectly to visual and spatial (or right hemisphere) modes of thought.

GIFTED HISTORICAL VISUAL THINKERS

This paradoxical mix of visual strengths and verbal difficulties is best understood through reference to the life experience of several well-known persons. It is argued that in these persons mixed talents can be seen as major factors in both the accomplishments and the difficulties. A few highlights will be provided below for illustrative purposes. Accounts of greater depth can be found in Thompson (1969), in Aaron, Phillips, and Larsen (1988), and, most recently, in West (1991).

Albert Einstein

Albert Einstein did not have an evident reading problem, but he did exhibit a set of verbal difficulties and visual talents that seems to fit within the general pattern of traits we are considering. Gerald Holton, a noted historian of science, wrote an article in the early 1970s about the sources of Albert Einstein's genius. Holton sees Einstein's abilities as something of a trade-off between competing capacities:

> An apparent defect in a particular person may merely indicate an imbalance of our normal expectations. A noted deficiency should alert us to look for a proficiency of a different kind in the exceptional person. The late use of language in childhood, the difficulty in learning foreign languages . . . may indicate a polarization or displacement in some of the skill from the verbal to another area. That other, enhanced area is without a doubt, in Einstein's case, an extraordinary kind of visual imagery that penetrates his very thought processes. (Holton, 1972, p. 102)

In his own writing, Einstein makes references to what he saw as two very different modes of thought, especially with regard to his own most creative and productive work. He pointed out that when he did really productive thinking, he always used "more or less clear images" and what he called "combinatory play," as the "essential feature" in his "productive thought," as well as of some "visual and some muscular type" (Hadamard, 1954, pp. 142–143). But he explained that if he wanted to communicate these thoughts to others, he had to go through a difficult and laborious translation process, proceeding from images to words that could be understood by others. Einstein's description fits neatly into a bimodal, two-hemispheric approach.

Concerning Einstein's early life there is a debate among biographers as to whether he was a brilliant student or a dullard. To some extent he was both—a pattern that is typical of highly gifted dyslexics and those who are more or less like them. One needs to understand this pattern because one scholar will produce evidence to show that he was really brilliant, while another scholar will point out evidence to the contrary. But the evidence proves neither position, only that he exhibited traits that were apparently contradictory.

In school, Einstein encountered great difficulty because of his poor memory, especially for words and texts. In the traditional school systems of Europe at that time, a great deal of recitation and memorization was expected. Einstein was not good at recitation, but he did very well with conceptual or philosophic thinking. In school he was beyond the curriculum in mathematics, physics, and philosophy. (When you read his essays, you realize that they are very philosophical. He does not write the way most physicists write.)

In a recently published account, his sister Maja comments about Einstein's late speech; his slow answers but deep understanding in mathematics; his frequent calculation errors even though he had a clear understanding of the main ideas involved (Einstein, 1987, pp. xviii–xxi). In secondary school, he dropped out of school in Germany to follow his parents when they moved to Italy. His reason was that because of his poor memory, he preferred to endure all kinds of punishments rather than to have to learn to "gabble by rote" (Hoffman & Dukas, 1972, p. 25). After he failed his first set of university entrance examinations, Einstein went to a new and unconventional school based on the highly visually oriented ideas of a Swiss educational reformer (Pestalozzi, 1801, 1973). Here his abilities began to blossom and the great theories of a few years later began to take their initial shape (Holton, 1972; West, 1991).

As a university student, Einstein respected highly the work of two British scientists who were unusually visual in their orientation, Michael Faraday and James Clerk Maxwell. These two scientists are now acknowledged to be giants of 19th-century physical science.

Michael Faraday

Michael Faraday did his most important work at the Royal Institution in London during the early part of the 19th century. A blacksmith's son, he was entirely self-educated. He was known for his extremely visual scientific conceptions. He started with chemistry but moved on to physics and the study of electricity, light, and magnetism. He thought of himself as a "philosopher" and disliked being called a "chemist" or a "physicist" because he hated the limited perspective of the specialist approach. Among many original discoveries, he developed the first electric motor. But most important, he developed original ideas about the fundamental nature of energy and matter, the electromagnetic "field" and "lines of force." These ideas were later translated into proper mathematical form by Maxwell and later still became a powerful influence on the young Einstein. These ideas have proved to be valid and useful since they were first developed in the middle of the last century. With each new scientific revolution, many old theories and concepts become dated, but on the whole, those of Faraday and Maxwell just keep looking better and better (Agassi, 1971; Jones, 1870; West, 1991).

Like Einstein, Faraday had no apparent reading problem. However, he did observe that he "could not imagine much progress by reading only." Rather, he said he was "never able to make a face [his] own without seeing it." Also, he did have a slight speech problem in his youth, was notably erratic in his spelling and punctuation, and had an extremely unreliable memory, which forced him to keep detailed journals and diaries of nearly everything he did.

As a youth, he explained that he was not precocious or a deep thinker. But he said that he was a "lively imaginative person" and could believe in the "Arabian Nights" as easily as the "Encyclopedia." However, he found a refuge from this too lively imagination in experimentation. Known as a physicist who was a great experimenter, he found he could trust an experiment to check the truth of his ideas as well as to educate and inform his intuition. In the experiment, he said, he "had got hold of an anchor" and he "clung fast to it" (Tyndall, 1870, pp. 7–8).

Another trait that is intriguing in this context is Faraday's skill as a performer. Dyslexics often show heightened abilities in performing, acting, or in using lively speech, full of voice modulation, hand gestures, and animated facial expression, all abilities thought to be largely controlled by the right hemisphere. In the early 19th century, to be a successful scientist, you had to be a good lecturer and performer. Part of Faraday's fame resulted from his ability as a lecturer and performer. Observers of the time commented on his "wonderful mobility of countenance" and his "moving hands." Another observer said that "his audience took fire with him, and every face was flushed" (Forgan, 1985, pp. 62–63).

Finally, Faraday is seen by later scientists as being like Einstein in that he "smells the truth." They thought he had an "unfailing intuition." They wondered at "his inconceivable instinct" (West, 1991).

James Clerk Maxwell

James Clerk Maxwell, a Scot, was trained in science and mathematics at Cambridge University in England. He was brilliant in the conventional way and got top grades, but he also could deal with two different worlds in an extraordinary way. He converted Faraday's ideas into mathematics for what are now known as "Maxwell's equations." But Maxwell's work was based on the same "fields" referred to earlier, Faraday's electromagnetic fields that involve radio and light (West, 1991).

Maxwell had severe, life-long speech problems. Although he is thought to be the most brilliant physicist of the 19th century, he was a stutterer and had continuous career difficulties as a result. In fact, the Nobel prize-winning American physicist, Feynman, said that

> from the long view of the history of mankind—seen from, say, ten thousand years from now—there can be little doubt that the most significant event of the 19th century will be judged as Maxwell's discovery of the laws of electrodynamics. The American Civil War will pale into provincial insignificance in comparison with this important scientific event of the same decade. (Feynman, Leighton, & Sands, 1963)

But, of course, as Maxwell says over and over again in his books, these laws are based upon Faraday's ideas.

While Maxwell was an especially clear writer, he had remarkable difficulty answering unexpected questions quickly on demand, what some who work with dyslexics call "demand language," the term generally referring to similar difficulties among dyslexic children. If Maxwell were asked such a question, he would not only stutter, but would also stumble excessively, making what some of his friends would call "chaotic statements." However, when he had had time to make whatever translations he had to make to respond to the question, he would then provide answers that were clear, thoughtful, and unusually perceptive (Schuster, 1910). He just could not do this on demand, which suggests something about the way his mind worked.

It is easy to show that Maxwell was a strong visual thinker—there are many references in the biographies and letters as well as the commentaries of historians of science (Campbell & Garnett, 1882; Everitt, 1983; Tolstoy, 1981; West, 1991). He could understand Faraday's highly visual ideas much better than others, presumably because his visualization abilities were as exceptional as Faraday's were. He was familiar with the mathematics required, as Faraday could not be, and was able to translate the conceptual clarity of Faraday's theories into the language of mathematics. He much preferred Farday's conceptions to those of the professional mathematicians of his day. Indeed, he felt that following Faraday's lead produced a conceptual clarity and simplicity impossible through the other more acceptable approaches of the time.

Maxwell's visual orientation was evident in many aspects of his work. In mathematics and physical science, his starting point was often geometry. He used mechanical analogies and resorted to diagrams and pictures wherever possible. Much of his work involved the interplay of force and substance in a largely visual–spatial arena. One historian of science, writing of Maxwell, puzzled at the appearance of artists in his family, generation after generation, although the family seemed to be otherwise a uniformly practical group (Everitt, 1983).

Leonardo da Vinci

Recent studies have argued that the journals and manuscripts of Leonardo da Vinci show distinctive signs of what is called "surface disgraphia" (Aaron, Phillips, & Larsen, 1988; Santillana, 1966; Sartori, 1987). There is evidence that he used the phonological rather than lexical route in his spelling. Although Italian (whether Renaissance or modern) is phonetic and highly regular in its spelling, da Vinci still made many errors. Several scholars observed that his spellings were "by ear" or they were "bizarre" or "inconsistent." His writing was characterized by consonant doubling, letter substitutions, additions, blending, and word splitting. He made unusual kinds of errors when he was copying material from another text. He made homophonic errors in his letters which were not corrected.

Da Vinci was evidently aware of the nature of his difficulties. In one place he observed: "They will say that, being without letters, I cannot say properly what I want to treat of . . ." In another passage he cautioned that "You should prefer a good scientist without literary abilities than a literate without scientific skills" (Sartori, 1987).

Of course, he was very strong in the visual–spatial area. He was not only a painter and sculptor, but used sketching and drawing as the main vehicle for his scientific investigations and innovative engineering designs. There is much evidence of his use of mental rotation of three dimensional objects. For example, in one elegant and long-standing design, he rotated a triangular architectural arch down flat into a canal to form the common canal lock gate that is still standard today, some 500 years after his original conception (Ritchie-Calder, 1970).

He was ambidextrous as a young man, but eventually shifted to and remained with left-handed writing and drawing. Of course, he is well known for his use of mirror image writing, but it is not so well known that much of his drawing and painting consisted of mirror images as well. Cook (1979) points out that a familiar village skyline that Leonardo sketched would not be recognized by a modern observer familiar with the village until the observer realized that the image is reversed left to right.

Einstein, Faraday, Maxwell, and da Vinci all show a varied mix of traits consistent with a larger pattern of verbal difficulties and unusually powerful visual–spatial abilities.

NEW TECHNOLOGIES, REVIVED OLD APPROACHES

The curious mix of traits exhibited in these remarkable individuals takes on new importance in today's changing technological and intellectual context. With new technologies, sophisticated analytic techniques based on visual and graphical approaches are now possible. At the same time, there is a renewed appreciation of the value of visual approaches. In the physical sciences, mathematics, and other fields, nonvisual approaches have held the dominant position for some time. Scholars and scientists preferred words, numbers, and formulas to images, diagrams, and moving pictures. However, with current computer graphic technologies, there is more and more evidence of major change in these deeply rooted attitudes.

For some years now, articles have appeared describing the new possibilities when computers were used to visualize statistical data. Scientists at research centers at Stanford and Harvard, for example, noted that they were "seeing patterns in data that never would have been picked up with standard statistical techniques." The intent of statistical data analysis techniques is to uncover "patterns," to discover "non-random clusters of data points." This was previously done "by using mathematical formulas." However, with the coming of "computer motion graphics," it is now possible "to look at three-dimensional projections of the data and to make use of the uniquely human ability to recognize meaningful patterns in the data" (Kolata, 1982, pp. 919–920).

There is growing evidence that visual approaches are moving back into center stage in mathematics and in certain related new fields such as "system dynamics" or "chaos" (Abraham & Shaw, 1984, 1988; Gleick, 1987; Steen, 1987, 1988; Zimmermann & Cunningham, 1990).

The late 19th-century British biostatistician Karl Pearson and his son E. S. Pearson both relied heavily on visual images in their statistical work (Pearson, 1966). They were puzzled to discover that their professional associates and students used visualization rarely, if at all. These latter believed that visualization was useful only for presentations to lay persons or a popular audience. It did not occur to them that visualization could be a powerful tool for professionals—indeed the essential wellspring of deep and original scientific perceptions. Yet the Pearsons saw visualization as the essential source and grounding for their most creative work.

E. S. Pearson (1966) quotes from Karl Pearson's lecture notes: "Contest of geometry and arithmetic as scientific tools in dealing with physical and social phenomena. Erroneous opinion that geometry is only a means of popular representation; it is a fundamental method of investigating and analyzing statistical material" (p. 252). E. S. Pearson lamented that "the prestige of mathematical procedures based on algebraic formulae is deeply entrenched in our lecture courses and our textbooks, so that few mathematical statisticians will use to the full their visual faculties unless they are trained to do so" (p. 253).

Even with the rapid spread of visualization techniques in many fields in the past few years, similar difficulties are evident in some areas. For example, visual–spatial approaches to investigating and teaching thermodynamics have been revived in recent years by some chemists. These researchers are using powerful graphic computer workstations to construct three-dimensional surface plot graphs of the interaction of changes in temperature, pressure, and other variables for various substances. While employing the most advanced technology, these researchers are well aware that they are employing methods and approaches that were used extensively about a hundred years ago.

Previously, these approaches required an unusually powerful visual imagination as well as the use of modeling clay and plaster of Paris, each model developed over weeks or months by hand instead of microseconds by computer. Although this older approach has been neglected for nearly a century, it has recently shown itself to be ideally suited to powerful new graphic workstations. Researchers in this area are finding their new (and old) approach is producing substantial results in both novel teaching methods as well as original research findings, for example, allowing investigation into mixtures of substances never possible before. But these researchers have also encountered varied levels of resistance to their innovative approach among more traditionally-oriented professional colleagues (Jolls, 1989; Jolls & Coy, 1990).

Thus, in the early 1990s several trends appear to be converging to promote a gradual but dramatic change in education and work, along with corresponding changes in the roles and methods for using information in the larger economy. Several interrelated trends appear to be especially significant.

Some of the problems, such as those of large atmospheric or ecological systems, are vast and extremely complex. Voluminous data from satellites and other automated sources overwhelm traditional methods of analysis (Richards, 1989; Wolkomir, 1989). Graphics-oriented computers, as they become more powerful and less expensive, promise to be effective tools for original work in many fields. Such systems, by focusing on a visual representation of the whole rather than the parts, are inherently better suited to dealing with such complex phenomena (DeFanti, Brown, & McCormick, 1989; Schultz, 1988).

This trend is supported by the recent emergence of new methods and techniques for the analysis of complex systems, such as chaos theory and dynamical systems studies. The rise of interest in fractals and related visual approaches serves to heighten awareness of the importance of these developments (Abraham & Shaw, 1984).

In addition, many mathematicians have come to see their discipline less as a matter of symbol manipulation and logical rigor and more as a science of patterns, shifting their emphasis toward more visual and experimental approaches (Steen, 1988). Many fields of mathematics have long accorded high status to spare and rigorous symbol manipulation; diagrams and pictures have had low status. However, some highly creative visual thinkers have always had a passion for geometry and other visual–spatial approaches to mathematics.

In recent years, advanced mathematics research has again focused on geometry. One layperson's breakthrough in the mathematics of tiles ("combinatorics") used direct visual–spatial methods that had previously been considered unacceptable by professional mathematicians, but have since been shown to be powerful and effective and are now used widely by professionals who would not have stooped to such questionable methods earlier (Rival, 1987).

Another significant trend is the growing awareness within certain professions that some of those who are very talented visually may perform rather poorly in conventional professional educational systems. As briefly noted above, a recent article in a magazine for professional engineers claimed that "the engineering profession in the United States is being denied potentially innovative engineers" because the educational system "screens out and discourages" talented students who are "right-brain-dominant and/or compensated dyslexics" (Frey, 1990). The author argues that some of the finest engineers are intensely visual in their way of working, but often have difficulties with words or even numbers. These difficulties are seen as resulting inevitably in unimpressive academic performance. As a consequence, the author states that some who could become talented engineers either drop out of demanding academic programs or fail to move into the most important job positions because of mediocre grades.

After the article appeared, a number of letters (Frey, 1991) to the editor and to me have indicated that this pattern may be more prevalent than previously expected. One PhD electronic engineer at a prominent national laboratory thanked the author for "letting the bogeyman out of the closet," observing that it had been "a shameful secret until now." Another engineer responded: "I can emphatically agree . . . 100 percent valid . . . Regrettably, I didn't come to this realization until after . . . graduate school." In another letter, a student currently in engineering school said that he had been ready to give up. Once he read the article, however, he saw that his special abilities were more important than his difficulties and he resolved to finish his professional training. Similar patterns of strengths and difficulties have begun to be observed among those in other professions such as medicine, architecture, and music (Götestam, 1990; Guyer, 1988).

IMPLICATIONS

The consequences of the coming changes may be far greater than we can easily imagine. We need to realize that for some 400 or 500 years our schools essentially have been teaching the skills of a medieval clerk—reading, writing, counting, and memorizing texts. With the more pervasive influence of increasingly powerful computers of all kinds, we could be on the verge of a new era when we will be required to develop a very different set of talents and skills, those of a Renaissance man such as Leonardo da Vinci rather than those of the clerk or lay scholar of the Middle Ages.

As part of this change, past ideas of desirable talents and skills are likely to be transformed, gradually but dramatically. Of course, the conventional skills will always be needed and valued, but they will not be considered as important or as useful in themselves as they were previously. Before long, we may find that semi-intelligent machines will be more "learned" and better read, with more complete and accurate memories, than even the most experienced and most conscientious of the traditional scholars in any field.

In the future, instead of the qualities desired in a well-trained clerk, we may find far more desirable talents and traits similar to those associated with Leonardo da Vinci: a facility with visual–spatial approaches and modes of analysis instead of mainly verbal (or numerical or symbolic) fluency; a propensity to learn directly through experience (or simulated experience) rather than primarily from lectures and books; a habit of continuous investigation in many different areas of study through ceaseless curiosity (perhaps with occasional but transient specialization); the more integrated perspective of the global generalist rather than the increasingly narrow specialist; a predisposition to innovation by making connections among many diverse fields; an ability to rapidly progress through many phases of research, development and design using imagination and "intuitive" mental models, now incorporating modern three-dimensional computer-aided design systems (Aaron, Phillips, & Larsen, 1988; Ritchie-Calder, 1970; Sartori, 1987).

Leonardo da Vinci's predisposition to investigation and analysis through visualization may come to serve us as well as it served him, providing innovative results well in advance of those competing groups which follow other more conventional approaches.

Thus, in the foreseeable future, we might come full circle, using the most advanced technologies and techniques to draw on some of the most old-fashioned approaches and capacities to simulate reality rather than describe it in words or numbers. To learn, once again, by doing, rather than by reading. To learn, once again, by seeing and experimenting, rather than by following memorized algorithms and routines. In so doing, all of us will learn greater respect for abilities and intelligences that were always vitally important but were generally eclipsed by a disproportionate emphasis on the traits and skills most valued by traditional schoolmen and scholars. Sometimes, the oldest pathways and most primitive patterns can be the best guides into uncharted waters.

As we contemplate these possible changes, we may reflect that there could be little choice about the coming transformations in education and work. If we continue to educate people who have primarily the skills, perspectives, and attitudes of the medieval clerk (no matter how advanced or specialized their fields of training), we may be turning out people who, like the unskilled laborer of the last century, will be unable to compete with intelligent machines, will have less and less to contribute to the real needs of our culture, and will have less and less to sell in the marketplace. Many of the most routine functions of the copy editor, bank clerk, and bookkeeper are already being handled more rapidly and cheaply by machines. In similar fashion, it may not be long before "expert" computer systems reliably replicate the more routine professional judgments of engineers, physicians, attorneys, and investment bankers (Moravec, 1989; Knaus, Wagner, & Lynn, 1991).

One of the pioneers of information and control theory, Norbert Weiner, saw the almost inevitable consequences from the very beginning. He pointed out in 1948 that the first industrial revolution, in producing goods with mechanical power, resulted in the "devaluation of the human arm by the competition of machinery." Similarly, he predicted that the second industrial revolution, involving computers in their many forms, is "bound to devalue the human brain, at least in its simpler and more routine decisions." Although some specialist workers will always be needed in specific areas, he explained that on the whole, "taking the second revolution as accomplished, the average human being of mediocre attainments or less has nothing to sell that is worth anyone's money to buy" (Weiner, 1961, pp. 27–28).

Some four decades later, it is clear that soon machines will be the best clerks. Consequently, we must learn, as teachers, parents, and workers, to appreciate and cultivate in ourselves and in our children those human capabilities that are most important and valuable and which machines cannot replicate. In the face of much uncertainty, it seems clear that many of these valued talents and skills will involve the original, insightful, intuitive, and broadly integrative capabilities associated with visual and spatial modes of thought, ironically, traits that are frequently associated with dyslexia or learning disabilities in their many variations.

Accordingly, we should pay more attention to gifted dyslexic individuals, not only for what they can tell us about dealing with the difficulties, but also, and more importantly, for what they can teach us about how to educate and apply a wide range of special talents to achieve innovative solutions to a variety of urgent and complex human problems.

When we understand the implications of the paradoxical pattern, that for some the "easy things" are difficult, but the "hard things" are easy, then we may find that we are surrounded by much more talent than we could have imagined.

This new approach will, of course, be difficult since it involves reeducating ourselves about the demands of a changing world as much as educating others. But if we can do this, we may find that some of the children clearly ill-suited for the educational system and workplace of the 19th century are superlatively well-suited for the educational system and workplace of the 21st century.

9. Liberatory Pedagogy and Special Education

WILLIAM C. RHODES

Liberatory pedagogy is embedded in the emerging worldview of post-modernism. Like all of the postmodern models, it can be used to con-struct, deconstruct, and/or reconstruct, simultaneously, knowledge and its reality context. What makes liberatory pedagogy postmodern as a way of thinking, rather than modern, is that it takes an activist stance vis-à-vis influencing history, rather than a passive stance of accepting the power of history; that is, it is oriented toward change and transformation rather than accepting things as they are. What makes it liberatory is that it frees us from encrustations of the past. We use our minds to free our minds from past, or traditional, learnings. For example, we can use liberatory thought to free ourselves from a strictly deficit-oriented model.

Liberatory pedagogy is a way of using pedagogy to free ourselves from the undue authority of texts and cultural contexts so that we can gain new, or deeper, insights and more complex meanings from them. It aims at transforming, rather than simply accepting, knowledge and its reality context. This makes it a constructivist pedagogy and not a pedagogy of transmission. It is consciously self-transforming at the same

Reprinted, with changes, from "Liberatory pedagogy and special education," by William C. Rhodes, *Journal of Learning Disabilities*, Vol. 28, 1995, pp. 458–462. Copyright © 1995 by PRO-ED, Inc.

time that it is culture-transforming. It is not oriented toward passing on knowledge, which seems to be the major orientation of modernist pedagogy, but to building onto the self and its world through knowledge-making.

Liberatory education is also concerned with freeing oneself and others from excessive internal/external control or determination. Liberatory educators are aware that although knowledge itself is frequently used as an instrument of control or personal determination, it is also used to free us from such influences. The radical shift from modernism to postmodernism involves an awakening into such awareness. The postmodernists believe that we have been taught to be spectators, rather than constructors, of knowledge. We have reified knowledge and thus have subjected ourselves to its oppression. Without having been aware of it during the long era of modernism, we have used knowledge both to define who we are and to separate ourselves from others by using knowledge to determine who others are.

Postmodernism attempts to use knowledge as a connector rather than a divider and oppressor. Postmodern pedagogy reflects that shift.

SPECIAL EDUCATION

Special education can be advanced as an exemplar of the use of knowledge to define and separate. In that exemplar, knowledge separates "them" from "us" to create "others" that are not "ourselves." We use reductionistic psychological knowledge to spoil "their" identity and distance them from "ourselves."

"Special" education, "Title I," and similar federally mandated programs provide an ideal context for delivering and developing liberatory pedagogy. Because of their ongoing social justice intent, these programs provide the fertile ground in human experience that is needed to nurture liberatory consciousness, knowledge, and school culture as an integrated whole.

From the point of view of liberatory pedagogy, special education is a subsystem of the school community set aside for differences, for separateness, for children treated as other than ourselves. They are outsiders. At the same time, special education is an example of the relationship of social power to social powerlessness, of oppressor to oppressed, and of how special meanings and understandings develop within this relationship.

Throughout the ages, we have feared the "other," even as we have created the "other." To a significant degree, we have built whole societies, whole cultures, on walling out the "other." In the extreme, as in Bosnia and Nazi Germany, we have attempted ethnic cleansing, trying to wipe out the "other," whose spoiled image we have made in our own minds. From the perception of liberatory pedagogy, special education could be viewed as a modernist version of walling off the "other," the different ones. Although special education is more complex than that, it offers a good exemplar of what we are talking about in pedagogical liberation.

The "other" we construct represents the dark side of ourselves—our unacknowledged sins and fears. According to depth psychology, we construct the image of others that uses the part of ourselves we cannot bear to face. Depth psychology (that group of psychologies that tries to go beneath the surface mask of self or person that we adopt socially) does not play so easily into the notion of an objective "other" who can be diagnosed and remediated. Instead, it raises the issue of how what is inside us colors what we see inside others. The sins of commission and omission that loom inside us threaten an inside peace, and we try to expel them by casting them into an outside presence—the "other"—a spoiled identity. Our rational and irrational fears of imperfection and social rejection are thus personified. "They" exist "out there," not "in here." And yet, at a very deep level, there is a nagging suspicion that "they" may be connected to us and we to them. We cannot seem to get rid of *them* anymore than we can get rid of *ourselves*. They symbolize reparation for our sins.

It is this confusing, ambivalent human condition that makes dogmatic certainty and absolute objectivity so appealing to us in our relationship to others. We can become spectators rather then participators in the perceived evil of imperfection. The philosophical doctrine of positivism, which contends that sensory perceptions are the only admissible basis for human knowledge and precise thought, shields us from any possible knowledge of how we are connected to "them." We use our eyes to see only outward, not inward; thus, we are shielded from "knowing" if anything inside of us reflects or reciprocates with things we can see in "them." Consequently we can disconnect and declare "them" something other than ourselves—the "other," the different ones. We can put "them" outside—outside ourselves and our living contexts. We do not have to worry about "their" meaning to us. We do not have to reflect philosophically or psychologically about how we may be connected to "them" and "them" to us. This strange disconnecting/connecting process is institutionalized into separate spaces, places, programs, diagnoses, treatments, and so forth.

In postmodernism, we cannot do this. We cannot pretend that only the eyes "know." We are forced to look inside ourselves and examine how we are connected, how we are alike. In liberatory pedagogy, this is the necessary condition for our own growth and transformation.

Within the school system, both inside and outside special education, there are all sorts of disconnecting/connecting processes at work—the same contradictory forces come into play in all federally mandated programs for special kinds of students. These same forces also operate, though less visibly, in general education. However, let me use special education as an exemplar for how schools construct, treat, understand, and act toward differences in their midst, and how knowledge is used to oppress. The meaning and structures given to exceptional children in the schools did not originate in the schools. As a social institution, schools borrowed these meanings and structures from the larger society. In 1975, the metaphor of illness (e.g., diagnosis, treatment, clinical organization features) was codified and imported directly into the school system by the authority of P.L. 94-142, the Education for All Handicapped Children Act of 1975. The imported medical metaphor of illness constructed differences in learning style as "pathology," "handicaps," and "deficiencies." All sorts of new categories of learning pathology have crept into federal and state legislation every year since then.

At one level, the intent of this act was to insist that public schools include all children, without exception. However, the law itself assumed that the ideology of pathology was the only way to read the reality of the lives of children with disabilities. Because these lawmakers saw reality as "given" rather than socially and historically constructed, they assumed this was the only way to think with regard to these children. In this chapter on liberatory pedagogy, the reader is being presented with an alternative way of viewing "them" that, within the postmodern worldview, is equally valid—or *more* valid, because it unmasks the psychosocial dynamics that separate "them" from us. From the perspective of this worldview, history becomes open to change and transformation. "They" are no longer separate from us. "They" are "like" us. "They" *are* us. "They" are accorded equality.

By seeing the "other" in an altered, declassified, light, we might be able to reduce both the intended and the unintended cruelty to "them." We can see these lives as more normal, "their" needs in larger pictures, like our own. At the same time, we can reclaim our connection to "them" by reassuring ourselves that if *they* cannot be "othered," *we* cannot be "othered" (as we feared.) With a changed view, our actions toward "them" can change and, in a complementary way, "their" own self-concept will be changed.

As things now stand in special education, there has been a constant proliferation of categories of pathology. In the controversial ones, like "behavioral disorders" and "learning disabilities," we have isolated all sorts of subtle differences, to the point where we could include most of the school population. It is not surprising that a major portion of the individuals and groups we consider to have pathologies in learning also come from populations and cultures we have "othered" on the basis of color and socioeconomic status.

Having internalized this psychomedical and social conceptual system in the operation of our perceptions on the world, we use the privileged status of science to justify its reality. We do not take into consideration that the science we use, and its methods, is very questionable in view of the scientific revolution. Postmodern, or postrevolutionary, science says that most of what we "see" in the world is colored by what we expect to see. Our "outward" gaze, our observations, are filtered through our mind-sets. When our mind-sets are changed, our views are changed. To a significant extent, we find in the world what we expect to find. There is no actual objective observation, free of our framework of thought. We become participators, not "observers," in actualizing what is "there." It is like refluent mirrors—the mind mirroring the world mirroring the mind, which can be changed only by a new system of thought.

Imminent Collapse

Such a change in thinking seems to be occurring in special education, and in all school programs isolating differences in children. Hierarchical thinking seems to be under attack vis-à-vis education. This antithetical thinking not only is a private spectacle, within education, but also is a public spectacle outside of special education. For instance, in the December 13, 1993, issue of *U.S. News and World Report*, the outside cover reads: "SEPARATE AND UNEQUAL—A U.S. News Investigative Report—How Special Education Programs Are Cheating Our Children and Costing Taxpayers Billions Each Year." The lead story inside the magazine is headed, "Separate and Unequal. America's Special Education System Was Intended to Give Disabled Kids the Edge. But It Is Cheating Many and Costing the Rest of Us Billions." The "exposé" contained in this attack on special education makes public what private professional publications have been revealing over the years. However, even though such public exposure is bound to accelerate the collapse of special education as we know it, that story in *U.S. News* can still be pegged as a product of the modernist, outdated worldview that created the field of special education in the first place.

The text of the article, as critical as it is, does not lay bare the critical basic assumption of special education: that there is only one way to look at these children—through the modernist spectacles of pathology, deficiency, disability—a one-dimensional view of who they are and what education is all about. These are flat, either/or spectacles. Their perspective of children is that they are either disabled or not disabled, leaving out all other dimensions of their lives. This modernist view backs up its myopia with "science"—modernist science. Postpositivist, or postmodern, science is multidimensional, or holographic, and no longer uses the either/or logic of classic or modernist investigation. Since Einstein, "science" has realized that even physical scales, measuring time and space, are colored by (or change their measurement depending on) the context of measurement.

The postmodernists would say that even more questionable than physical scales measuring time and space are socially constructed scales used to measure socially powerless children according to educational criteria that just happen to characterize the designers of the scales as superior. They would say that the personal values and status of the designer are bound to influence the dimensions chosen as the measure of these children. Furthermore, the postmodernist liberatory pedagogy would say even the chosen ideal characteristics of the educational final product are colored by such egocentric narcissism. For instance, Jean Piaget (1986), a constructivist if there ever was one, believed that the acme of growth and development attained by the child's mind approaches that of a scientist. He did not mean a scientist, in fact, but rather a person who can think like, and look upon the world like, a modernist scientist. This is arrogance, says the postmodernist, and it ignores the contributions to the commonwealth of great politicians, musicians, poets, writers, singers, and dancers. It ignores the contributions of all other citizens who collaborate to make our world go around. They are all participants in the moment-to-moment creation of reality according to the new 20th-century science.

The postmodern liberatory educator accuses education of having operated at a one-dimensional level and producing what Marcuse (1968) called a one-dimensional person in a one-dimensional society. Marcuse claimed that society as a whole is irrational. Its productivity is destructive of the free development of human needs and faculties; its peace is maintained by the constant threat of war. Its growth depends on the repression of the real possibilities for easing the struggle for existence—individual, national, and international. Marcuse was a member of the Frankfurt School, the early developers of critical theory, out of which liberatory theory evolved.

Internal Conflict

From the beginning, special education has been filled with contradictions and conflict—within itself and within the school system. Taken either separately or together, the conflicts could suggest a dawning awareness of the power that mutually constructed mental schemata or theories have in shaping the reality we experience. For schools, this is particularly important: Schools play a major role in molding the minds that shape the everyday theories that construct our conceptions of reality.

Special educators, very early on, derided the medical model under which they were constrained to work. This is probably what drove them to accept the positivist philosophy of science, even after natural science had already discarded it during the first quarter of the 20th century. Special education embraced behavioral learning theories with great enthusiasm; behavioral analysis, behavioral research, and behavioral control became its centerpiece. Although general education has been influenced somewhat by this modernist psychological perspective, most special educators, particularly in the areas of behavior disorders and mental retardation, saw it as a panacea for all disabilities. There were, however, many special educators who rejected behaviorism as "animal training" rather than education.

The point being made here, however, is not that there was disagreement within special education over behavioral learning theory. Rather, my emphasis is on the implication of the rejection of the medical model very early in the development of special education. The facility with which the medical model was rejected in favor of behavioral learning theories indicates the power of mental models in shaping reality as we live it. Even though these educators had not been exposed to the postmodern mode of thought or liberated from deterministic, absolutistic, positivistic, subject-object, modernist thought processes, or from the single reality of dogma—they were still aware of the power of the mind in nature. What they were not aware of was the inherent facility of the mind in metamorphosing into a new, holographic paradigm, a new worldview. Although these educators did not take the postmodern leap, they seemed to be dissatisfied with the certainty and absoluteness of modernist thinking. They were trying to free themselves from the overriding schemata of "pathology."

Special education, very early on, also was split over the issue of labeling theory. Part of the profession saw labeling as demeaning and as undermining not only the child's self-concept, but also the perceptions and actions of others with regard to him or her. The label itself was meaning-making. One could say that this was a forerunner of postmodern constructivism in special education. However, this point of view was not unanimous. Some special educators thought of the label as a "thing"—an independent reality existing *in* the child. However, those who believed the label to be detrimental did so both on the basis of research on self-fulfilling prophecy, whereby the child internalizes the label and thus makes it real or true, and because the label itself determined how others related to the child bearing it. The rejecters of labeling theory, although they were able to undergo an altering of perception regarding the belief in the "thing-ness," absoluteness, or "given-ness" of the label, did not take the next step, which was absorbing the fact that by invalidating the label, they had opened the way for invalidating the whole system of thought governing deficiency or disability thinking. If they had realized this, they might have leaped into postmodern thought and liberatory pedagogy. Nevertheless, they were nibbling at the edges of postmodern thinking.

Another related issue that divided special education in the beginning was categorical versus noncategorical special education. Coming from a slightly different angle, followers on either side also questioned the labels, but argued simply that all children in special education could be taught together. They did not advocate total inclusion of these children in the general education classroom, but indicated two different mindsets—one that took the child's category seriously, and one that did not. One treated the category as an absolute "thing" within the child; the other showed a liberation from such thinking, treating the category only as a mental construct. Here again, special education verged on postmodern and liberatory thinking.

To an extent, special education also was somewhat divided over the concept and procedures of mainstreaming. Some special educators, out of sympathy for their charges, suggested that children who were "different" would benefit more in a school totally separated from general education. There they would be free of the expectations of the general education school and of the hazing and teasing of the nondisabled students. This seems more a protectionist attitude than the divergent thinking of a postmodern, liberatory perspective.

A more sweeping divisive concept, similar to the *U.S. News and World Report* "Separate and Unequal" exposé, went beyond the idea of mainstreaming and took on the egalitarian argument. Arguing that all children should be included in the general class, it opened the way to postmodern thought and liberatory pedagogy. The issue of inclusion also divides special educators. Some do not agree that special children can get an equal break in the general class. From the point of view of modernist thought and liberatory pedagogy, much of this internal controversy signals the more serious inadequacies, and perhaps breakdown, of modernist thought as related to schools, education, and children. It shows in particular that there is a need for a radical paradigm shift in special education, a new way of thinking about these children and their educational needs. It suggests there is something wrong with our general mindset with regard to what education is all about. The so-called special children concept forces this to our attention.

MODERNIST SCHOOL IMPERIALISM

Postmodern liberatory pedagogy would say that modernist thought imposes imperialism upon social institutions, like the schools. In fact, the organization and educational processes of the schools both model and teach imperialism. The practice of tracking and differentially mandating for special children not only is undemocratic, but also institutionalizes the self-fulfilling prophecy. It trains the developing minds of all children to accept social and psychological layering as inevitable. Children are indoctrinated into "other-ness," "differences," "alienation," "disconnection," and "belonging" and "not belonging." The inherent anxiety around not belonging, of being cut out, not only in special children, but in all children, is thus reinforced.

Children are being taught, by the school's example, to not only see privileged and underprivileged people and culture in the world, but also to classify knowledge itself as either privileged or unprivileged. In special education, for instance, the information that is taught is considered less privileged than that taught in the general education class. The voices of nondisabled children are considered privileged voices. What they say, how they think, has been given privileged status. The actions and way of being of these children in general education are likewise being given privilege. Even the teachers in the general education class are being given privilege in the school. Special educators frequently feel like second-class citizens. General educators, particularly those with administrative power in the system, are privileged in that they make all decisions about special children, even to the point of countermanding decisions made by the special educator with regard to particular children. The grounding in direct, empathic experience that special teachers share in the lives and needs of special children is frequently ignored by such administrators and by education in general.

THE POSTMODERN CONDITION

Within the emerging postmodern condition, this mind-set of privilege is a serious impediment to any reform of the educational situation. Yesterday's needs, yesterday's values, and yesterday's organization of so-called regular education no longer seem germane to the changing social situation in the United States as the 21st century approaches. A massive shift in population characteristics, growing cultural diversity, and changing (albeit controversial) attitudes and laws vis-à-vis such diversity is instituting a new reality. Within this context, many of our previous certainties in education, as in science, become uncertainties. For instance, what is considered the "regular" student is no longer clear-cut. The "exceptional" can no longer be clearly distinguished as such. Our way of thinking about "special" and "regular" students is collapsing. In the postmodern condition, education, out of necessity, becomes much more multidimensional. The teachers in "nonregular" programs may be much more grounded in the reality of the multidimensional needs and diverse perspectives of the child of the dawning century. They know that schools can no longer afford to throw away or put away children who do not fit the narrow confines of modernist, or classic, education. They know that the curriculum, so prized in classic education, is much too unidimensional—that a multipurpose, multidimensional curriculum is more appropriate for the postmodern condition.

Transforming, rather than simply *informing*, the child has been the task of special education. If, because of changing population and social characteristics, "exceptional" and "regular" are becoming more difficult even for our categorically conditioned modernist to distinguish between, a mind-change is imminent. Our framework of thought has to be freed of encrustations of the past in order to inform, and be informed by, this changed reality. *Inclusion* cannot mean simply folding all children into the status quo of the general classroom, to be fed predigested information. In postmodernism, the educator has to be liberated from that classic, or modernist, idea of what knowledge is. Acquiring knowledge is active, not passive. It has to transform—and this requires the child's participation. It is a constructivist project in which the child has to be engaged. As in the special education project of transforming the child, "knowing" and "being" have to be amalgamated. The educator's mind must be liberated, to enable him or her to see the logic of this way of thinking. It is a different logic than that of the modernist era. It is the "both/and" logic of quantum thinking, not the "either/or" logic of modernist thinking: Education has to both change and inform the child. We cannot place child development in one category and information transmission in another. Both must be accomplished simultaneously. Such is the experience-informed wisdom of special education. This is what special education has to offer to "regular" education in its latest project of inclusion.

10. Critical Pedagogy in a Bilingual Special Education Classroom

BARBARA S. C. GOLDSTEIN

The education of Latino children with special needs, specifically those who have been identified as having learning disabilities (LD), has traditionally focused on addressing the students' disabilities rather than their language needs. Students with limited English proficiency (LEP) are routinely placed in monolingual (English-only) special education programs, and little or no attention is paid to primary language development. Often what passes for English language development is a form of English submersion, also known as the "sink-or-swim" method of English language learning. In larger urban school districts with large bilingual populations and a somewhat active advocacy constituency, students with LEP placed in learning disabilities programs are assisted by a bilingual resource teacher, a bilingual aide, a community volunteer, or a bilingual classroom peer. Rare is the limited English proficient student with LD who is in a bilingual special education program with a certified bilingual special education teacher.

Service delivery models for students with LEP and special education needs have been limited in scope and design with respect to meeting the specific cultural and linguistic needs of this growing population (Baca &

Reprinted, with changes, from "Critical pedagogy in a bilingual special education classroom," by Barbara S. C. Goldstein, *Journal of Learning Disabilities*, Vol. 28, 1995, pp. 463–475. Copyright © 1995 by PRO-ED, Inc.

Cervantes, 1989). However, because a greater willingness to discuss multi-cultural issues has gradually been shown in the mainstream of special education circles, and because of the rapid change in demographics, innovative programs based on alternative pedagogies are reaching a wider and more diverse special education faculty and student population.

CONSTRUCTIVIST AND HOLISTIC EDUCATION

Research by Lerner, Cousin, and Richeck (1992), Poplin (1988a), and Rueda (1989) suggests that those characteristics that mark a highly effective general education and bilingual program are also manifest in classrooms that are effective for children with learning disabilities. Those characteristics include the incorporation of students' experiences, background knowledge, authentic tasks that are meaningful to the students, and student interests into the teaching/learning process; an emphasis on meaning rather than form; an emphasis on creativity and divergent thinking rather than correctness; interactive/dialogical teacher/student interactions rather than teacher-centered instruction; and assessment that compares the students' unassisted performance with their assisted performance in authentic tasks. Poplin (1988a, 1988b) described these characteristics as elements of a constructivist and holistic educational approach to the teaching process (for a more thorough discussion of constructivist and holistic education, see Poplin, 1988a, 1988b).

Research by Rueda (1989) and Ruiz (1989) indicates that whole language methods not only are effective for bilingual and/or LEP students with learning disabilities, but also are critical to promoting language, reading, and writing abilities in *all* students. Further, there is evidence to suggest that skill-based instruction does not work in most instances, and may even contribute to the creation of a "learned learning disability" in LEP children (Figueroa, 1989; Poplin, 1988a, 1988b; Rueda, 1989). Delpit (1990), however, cautioned us to continually assess our interactions with bicultural students as these students struggle to learn the rules implicit in academic settings. She stated that successful teachers identify the skills and information required for students to benefit from meaning-centered tasks, and then the teacher explicitly teaches those skills and that information.

CRITICAL PEDAGOGY AND BICULTURAL DEVELOPMENT

What becomes increasingly clear as critical bilingual and special education teachers explore innovative practices for their bilingual/LEP students with learning disabilities is that there is a gap, a missing piece in the theory and practice of bilingual special education that is not being acknowledged. Bicultural students continue to make little or no progress in or out of our special education classrooms despite the efforts of those general and special education teachers, who provide opportunities for language and literacy development in both the first and the second language. The 53% dropout rate for Latino students (U.S. Bureau of the Census, 1992) is tragic evidence of the failure of our institutions to educate poor, limited-English-speaking Latino students with and without LD. I believe the missing piece that educators desperately need to address with respect to the education of our so-called multicultural population is the influence of race, class, and power, and the relationship of these to the education of poor bicultural students.

Nurturing the Development of Students' Voices

Students often respond to literature stories by connecting or contrasting their own experiences with those in the story. Issues that emerge in class discussions may reflect the relations of power between the subordinate and dominant communities, specifically as the issues reflect the social, cultural, and economic positions and realities of the school and the community. These power relations are often drawn along class, ethnic, and racial lines. When young children identify these issues at circle time, they are effectively silenced. The young child who brings issues of power to the classroom is often ignored, receives a pat answer, or is labeled a troublemaker. Teachers are not prepared to deal with issues of power and subordination, especially when stated in terms of race and class—terms not used comfortably in educational circles, yet uncritically discussed under the guise of "cultural" or "multicultural." A few examples follow of how children strive to bring their stories to their classrooms and how they are silenced:

Colleagues and student teachers in southern California have told me of how some of their elementary-school students wanted to discuss the original Rodney King verdict and the turmoil that ensued. However, teachers had been instructed not to discuss what was happening right outside their classroom doors for fear of a classroom melee.

Several students in a resource specialist program for students with mild learning disabilities voiced concerns regarding the impact of a proposed state initiative on their immigrant community. This initiative would require that school administrators, based on teacher information, submit the names of suspected undocumented students or undocumented parents of U.S. citizens to immigration authorities. The students were told not to worry because the school knew that this particular set of students had green cards. End of discussion.

After returning from a field trip that necessitated driving through a wealthy neighborhood, a group of first graders said that their parents were working hard to buy them a big house like the ones they had seen. One child said that no matter how hard the parents worked, they would never be able to live in that type of house because the parents could never make that much money, spoke no English, and were Mexican. The teacher promptly scolded him and said that in this country, if "you" work hard enough "you" will achieve your goals, *even if you are Mexican*. Whose "truth" is closer to the reality of the lived experiences of the children of that community?

How can teachers begin to actively engage in dialogue on the issues with which their students struggle daily but which they themselves are prevented from discussing in their socially and politically neutral class-rooms? It is much easier and less taxing to deal with the technical aspects of language and literacy development, instead of trying to probe those links between race, class, culture, and power and their effect on language and literacy development.

Linking Discussions of Race, Class, Culture, and Power to Language Development

According to Bartolome (1994), the preoccupation with methods, and even methodological theory, without a critical analysis of the socio-cultural and historical context of the teaching/learning environment serves only to perpetuate the miseducation of poor students of color. She stated that

> although it is important to identify useful and promising instructional programs and strategies, it is erroneous to assume that blind replication of instructional programs or teacher mastery of particular teaching methods, in and of themselves, will guarantee successful student learning, especially when we are discussing populations that historically have been mistreated and miseducated by the schools. (p. 174)

Bartolome explained that student teachers (and, I believe, seasoned teachers as well) see the academic failure of bicultural students as a technical issue, devoid of political content; therefore, technical answers, such as a new method, should solve the problem. That perspective brings with it an underlying assumption that all is well with the existing educational system and its programs, and that what needs to be changed is the student. Once the student is sufficiently transformed to fit the academic structure, he or she will succeed. Bartolome contended that a myopic focus on methodology often serves to obfuscate the real question—which is why in our society, subordinated students do not generally succeed academically in schools. In fact, schools often reproduce the existing asymmetrical power relations among cultural groups . . . . By taking a sociohistorical view of present-day conditions and concerns that inform the lived experiences of socially perceived minority students, prospective teachers are better able to comprehend the quasi-colonial nature of minority education. By engaging in this critical sociohistorical analysis of subordinated students' academic performance, [teachers] are better situated to reinterpret and reframe current educational concerns so as to develop pedagogical structures that speak to the day-to-day reality, struggles, concerns, and dreams of these students. . . . Command of a content area or specialization is necessary, but it is not sufficient for effectively working with students. Just as critical is that teachers comprehend that their role as educators is a political act that is never neutral. (p. 179)

Darder (1991) provided a framework and theoretical construct for bicultural development that describes how bicultural development is enmeshed in the cultural relations of power between the subordinate and dominant cultures, and how bicultural students might react to the pressures of having to contend with two different cultural realities. Darder's bicultural development theory explains why students are reluctant to engage with the dominant language and culture. But it can also explain why they are eager to adopt the dominant language and culture, at the expense of their primary language and culture.

Freire's (1970) and Freire and Macedo's (1987) work on critical literacy provides teachers and students with an analytical mode of inquiry that attempts to describe the lens through which we see the world. According to Freire and Macedo, literacy is not just a set of decoding skills or the ability to read a newspaper. It is the ability to examine and critique the printed word in order to identify the origins of and assumptions behind the ideas presented. Critical literacy attempts to strip away the layers of obfuscation in order to examine ideas within the social, political, economic, and cultural contexts. Freire stated that

> reading does not consist merely of decoding the written word or language, rather, it is preceded by and intertwined with knowledge of the world . . . . The understanding attained by critical reading of a text implies perceiving the relationship between text and context. (p. 29)

Furthermore, critical literacy casts light on the relationship between the learner and the world, how knowledge is produced, and how subjectivities are constructed, so that students can begin to see themselves as historical beings and as prime movers in their expanding world. I believe that a thorough understanding of critical literacy and bicultural development can provide educators with a vehicle for beginning to address the issues of race and class that our students bring to the classroom.

Darder's (1991) work on critical bicultural education and bicultural development, Freire's (1970) work on critical pedagogy, and Freire and Macedo's (1987) work on critical literacy can help us build a framework for integrating those race, class, ethnic, and language issues into the constructivist/holistic bilingual special education classroom. Critical bilingual special educators need to actively discuss these taboos, which have been virtually censored from the research literature with respect to the education of poor LEP students with learning disabilities.

INTEGRATING PRACTICE

As a general education and special education teacher working with adults and children, I have grappled with the issues of power and subordination by creating an atmosphere for genuine dialogue, particularly with those who historically have been marginalized by the dominant community because of disability, culture, language, or socioeconomic status. Those students must have an opportunity to participate in the discourse that is determining the shape of their lives.

Following is a description of what occurred when I attempted to integrate practice rooted in language-acquisition theory, holistic/constructivist notions of learning, bicultural development, and critical pedagogy. What emerged is not meant to become a model or step-by-step manual to be replicated in other classrooms. It *is* meant to illustrate the dialogical process between and among students and teacher and the students' subsequent recognition of their own abilities to name their world, engage with and critique existing knowledge, and create new forms of knowledge that will enable them to actively change their world.

Participants

The class was composed of 11 Latino, Spanish-speaking first- and second-grade students who had been designated as having learning disabilities according to the California Educational Code. In California, students meet eligibility criteria according to the following definition:

> A severe discrepancy exists between intellectual ability and achievement in one or more of the following academic areas: oral expression, listening comprehension, written expression, basic reading skills, reading comprehension, mathematics calculation, mathematics reasoning. The discrepancy

is due to a disorder in one or more of the basic psychological processes and is not the result of environmental, cultural, or economic disadvantages. The discrepancy cannot be corrected through other regular or categorical services offered within the regular instructional program. (California Education Code—Part 30, 1980)

The decision as to whether or not a severe discrepancy exists shall be made by the individualized education program team, including assessment personnel in accordance with Section 56341(d), which takes into account all relevant material which is available on the pupil. No single score or product of scores, test or procedure shall be used as the sole criterion for the decisions of the individualized education program team as to the pupil's eligibility for special education . . . . When standardized tests are considered to be invalid for a specific pupil, the discrepancy shall be measured by alternative means as specified on the assessment plan. (California Code of Regulations—Title 5, 1981)

Students were identified by a district assessment team that specializes in the psychoeducational assessment of students with limited English proficiency. The Individualized Education Program (IEP) team, in conjunction with the district LEP assessment team, determined that the language of instruction for the students should be in the primary language—in this case, Spanish. Both the full-time special education aide and I are bicultural, bilingual, and biliterate, so we had firsthand experience with what it was like to live all our lives on a cultural and linguistic border. The class was composed of three girls and eight boys and had an age range of 6 through 8 years. The class was situated in a school that has a strong bilingual educational philosophy and an academic program that supports this philosophy. The school's strong support for bilingual education enabled my aide and me to more easily mainstream the students in bilingual classes with fully certified bilingual teachers.

The school is 85% Latino, 12% African American, 2% Anglo, and 1% Asian, which reflects the ethnic composition of the surrounding community. The school qualifies for Chapter 1 federal funding, and the majority of the students qualify for the federally funded free lunch program.

Program

Students were instructed in Spanish the majority of the day except for a 30- to 45-minute daily English-language–development lesson. The language arts program consisted of shared literature, daily writing through interactive journals, individual reading time, and writing and publishing of original work. Content areas in math, science, music, social studies, art, dance, and physical education were integrated with the language arts program. Students were given opportunities to pursue individual interests within the unit of study that was being presented. I designed units that were expanded and modified through the interactive dialogue between the students and myself. As the students and I moved through the units of study, themes that emerged from the classroom discussion and activities were identified. These often recurred throughout the year as students made connections with ideas that surfaced in previously studied units. A description of the themes, activities, discussions, and student responses follows.

Units were built around literature that depicted cultural and social themes that the children could immediately relate to and respond to personally. (See the Appendix for a bibliography of children's literature that can initiate classroom discussion on critical themes and issues.) Some of the books studied, along with the emergent themes, are listed in Table 10.1. All of the books are written in Spanish or are bilingual except for "Fly Away Home" and "At the Crossroads," which are written in English. All of the books were read in Spanish.

Students were read a book at story-time every 2 to 3 days. During the reading, students were encouraged to respond to a particular point of interest. At the beginning of the school year, the children were reluctant to orally share their thoughts with the whole class. They were more willing to take a chance on speaking publicly when I framed the discussion by asking specific questions, such as "What did you like best/least about the story?" "How are you like the character in the book?" "What might you have done differently?" I recorded their responses, using their exact words, on a large chart of tagboard or butcher paper. Students could also choose to write or depict their responses on the chart themselves.

The charts served several purposes: They reinforced reading vocabulary and were read daily; they served as a point of reference for discussions and story comparisons. Finally, they served as a reading log for the whole class. Charts were kept, bound, and placed in the classroom library to be used as references as well as independent reading choices. In addition, students rewrote their statements from the charts in individual folders so that they could practice writing and reading their own sentences. Key vocabulary generated by the students' discussion and writing, and vocabulary provided by the teacher based on the discussions, was incorporated into a vocabulary word bank, which students kept on rings. After each book was read, students discussed their feelings about it, identified key events in the story, and then shared personal experiences that they thought were similar to those of characters in the book. Students could later use the word bank to write original sentences. Students also illustrated their experiences, and the aide or I recorded their original dictated statements on those papers. Students could choose to read their statements and share their illustrations with each other. These dictated statements

TABLE 10.1
Literature Titles and Emergent Themes

Titles	Themes					
	Prejudice	Poverty	Illness/medicine/death	Authority	Family/community	Immigration
"Cuadros de Familia"			X		X	
"Diego"			X	X		X
"Wilfredo"	X				X	X
"Cesar Chavez y La Causa"	X	X			X	
"Yagua Days"	X				X	
"Fly Away Home"	X	X		X	X	
"At the Crossroads"	X	X		X	X	
"La Calle Es Libre"				X	X	

and illustrations were kept in their journals, and students could periodically "re-read" the literature book to the class.

A narrative description of this program highlighting the use of specific texts follows. The students' inquiry into issues of race, class, ethnicity, and language is presented and discussed.

"Cuadros de Familia."   This story depicts a woman's childhood experiences while growing up in a Texas town near the Mexican border. The detailed illustrations depict the heroine going to the marketplace, picking oranges, being cured by a local medicine woman, and cutting and preparing cactus leaves for cooking.

All of the students in the class had experienced picking and cooking cactus with their families. They knew how to cut, skin, and cook the leaves to make a cactus leaf soup. The students described their family outings and identified places in the surrounding community where we could find wild cactus growing. They generated suggestions on how to cook cactus and what side dishes might go with it. What resulted was a book of recipes.

> *Primero té pones los guantes y cortas el nopal con el cuchillo y entonces le quitas los picos, y entonces lo lavas, y entonces lo cortas, y entonces lo pones en agua y le hechas sal, ajo, y cebolla, y chile, y entonces lo pones en la lumbre, y entonces té lo comes con tortilla y huevos.*

> (First you put on the gloves and cut the cactus with the knife and then you take out the spines, and then you wash it, and then you cut it, and then you put it in water and put in salt, garlic, and onion, and chili, and then you put it on the stove, and then you eat it with tortilla and eggs.)

One of the illustrations in "Cuadros de Familia" is of a healer woman, or *curandera*, tending a sick woman in bed. She is burning incense, saying prayers, and using herbs to cure the woman's ailment. The students had little experience with U.S. medically trained doctors. Because of limited financial resources or lack of insurance, students have little access to mainstream medical care and often rely on alternative health practitioners in their families or communities to treat their illnesses. They shared ways in which parents, grandmothers, and other family members treated fevers, stomachaches, earaches, and warts. (See Table 10.2 for dictated responses students recorded in their journals.)

Some students began questioning why so many of their peers had never seen an "American" doctor. The lack of access to mainstream medical care and why they see a medical doctor only when it is an emergency became part of the discussion. Students shared experiences of rushing to the local county general hospital when a neighbor or relative was gravely ill. They concluded that lack of money was one of the reasons

TABLE 10.2
Examples of Children's Oral Responses to "Cuadros de Familia"

Cuando yo tengo dolor de oido mi abuelita me pone un rollo de papel del periòdico y me lo pone en el oido y parece trompeta y le pone el fuego y ¡pum! se me quita el aire y ya no me duele.
(When I have an earache my grandmother rolls up a newspaper and places it in my ear and it looks like a trumpet and lights the paper and pum! the air goes away and it doesn't hurt anymore.)

Mi mamà me lleva con el señor que cura y èl me pone medicina en las cortadas y ya se me quitò.
(My mother takes me to the man who cures people and he puts medicine on my cuts and it goes away.)

Aquì estoy enfermo y mi tìa me da un tè de yerba buena para sentirme mejor.
(This is where I'm sick and my aunt gives me herb mint tea so that I can feel better.)

Note. Themes: Illness and medicine.

why they did not go to a U.S. doctor. They also affirmed their trust in the alternative health care practitioners they visited. As students began to question and discuss these issues, they became increasingly aware of the distribution of resources and the lack of affordable medical care in their communities. At this point in the discussion it became critical for the students to be provided reassurance about their parents' ability to provide medical care—that if they were ill, their needs would be adequately met. Activities with older students might have included researching the local medical care facilities and the percentages of families in the surrounding school communities who had some form of medical insurance. These research projects have the potential to change students' perceptions, and perhaps their lives.

"Wilfredo." This is the story of a Salvadoran boy who tells about what his life was like before the most recent civil war, what happens to him when the fighting starts, and his journey to the United States. He talks about school, his friends, his village, and his family. When his father disappears and his mother has to leave for *el norte,* he stays with his grandmother, who eventually decides he must also leave because it is becoming too dangerous for him to remain. In the United States, Wilfredo slowly becomes accustomed to the new language, school, and friends.

Students studied maps and pictures of the United States, Mexico, and El Salvador. Although most of the students were born in the United States, they often visited Mexico and El Salvador to see relatives and friends. Students recounted, illustrated, and shared stories of their own and relatives' border crossings (see Table 10.3 for examples of their stories).

TABLE 10.3
Examples of Children's Oral Responses to "Wilfredo"

Mi primo vive conmigo y despues cruza la mamà sola. Él tiene igual que yo.
(My cousin lives with me and his mother crosses [the border] alone. He is the same age I am [8 years old].)

El aviòn lo sigua. La mamà y el papà estan en el carro. Los niños estan dormidos. Yo le pege a mi hermana cuando cruzamos.
(The airplane is following him. The mother and the father are in the car. The children are asleep. I hit my sister when we crossed [the border].)

El helicòptero ve al señor. Tiran balazos y lo matan y los otros los demas ya cruzaron.
(The helicopter sees the man. They fire bullets and kill him and the other, the rest, already crossed.)

Es la bandera de los niños. Es de Mèxico.
(It is the children's flag. It belongs to Mexico.)

Se lo trajo el coyote y la migra no lo agarrò. Trabaja con mi papà en el restaurant.
(The coyote [smuggler] brought him and immigration didn't catch him. He works with my father in the restaurant.)

Mi mamà llora porque la migra no la deja ver a mi abuelita.
(My mother cries because immigration won't let her see my grandmother.)

Note. Themes: Prejudice, poverty, immigration, and family and community.

Many of the students were aware of the antagonism of those they called *los Americanos* toward undocumented people. When I asked them what they thought about the need for green cards in order to live and work in the United States, many of them expressed opinions that reflected negative impressions of undocumented immigrants, whom they called *mojados* (literally, "wetbacks"). Undocumented people were seen as lazy or stupid, or as *cholos* (i.e., gang members). They told me that Mexicans got jobs nobody else wanted, like cart vending or selling flowers on street corners. I became increasingly aware that for them, the term *mojados* was synonymous with *Mexican nationals,* and, in fact, when students became angry with a classmate and wanted to insult him or her, they would call him or her a "Mesican," using an American accent. Although I did not ask questions regarding the residency status of family members, students readily shared that there were *mojados* in the family, but in fact they only meant that these family members had come from Mexico or El Salvador and were not necessarily without legal documentation. In effect, someone who was Mexican or El Salvadoran, for them, automatically meant someone who was undocumented, that is, someone who had no right to be in the United States. Upon further questioning, I discovered that the students felt they themselves did not have rights like "the Americans," nor did they feel entitled to those rights.

During the discussion I pointed out the various ways the word *American* could be used, for example, to describe a U.S. citizen, or a citizen from the American continent. The students insisted that *los Americanos* were different from them, referring to and describing a White, middle class, Euro-American population. In their hierarchy, African Americans, Asian Americans, Native Americans, and other darker skinned people were not Americans. Students called themselves Mexican or El Salvadoran even if they were U.S. citizens. When I asked them why they could not also be called Americans, as well as Mexican and El Salvadoran, their answers included the following:

Porque no nos parecemos. (Because we don't look like them.)

Porque vivimos en este barrio. (Because we live in this neighborhood.)

Vamos a diferentes escuelas. (We go to different schools.)

Mis padres hacen diferente trabajo. (My parents do different kinds of work.)

Los Americanos en la televisión se parecen diferentes. (The Americans on TV look different [from us].)

Mis padres son de México/El Salvador. (My parents are from Mexico/El Salvador.)

The children were a mass of contradictions. Their statements, if we were interpreting them correctly, meant that they viewed who they were with such shame that to be called Mexican was an insult. Yet, their pride in their families, and especially in their parents, was evident in how they spoke of family accomplishments. My students' internalization of how the dominant media and culture perceived them became clear when I placed their answers in the context of Darder's (1991) work on bicultural development. The themes of immigration, identity, and prejudice kept appearing throughout the semester, particularly after we studied the life of labor leader Cesar Chavez and, later, the history of the early Chinese immigrants in California.

"Cesar Chavez y la Causa." This book recounts the life of American labor leader Cesar Chavez, founder of the United Farmworkers Union. We studied his life and the labor movement a few months before his death. Although my students were not from migrant-worker families, they had relatives who had worked in the fields, or they themselves had had experience picking fruit in nearby fields. During discussions, the

students marvelled that someone with Chavez's background had gained international fame and had built a union that crossed racial and ethnic lines. One child, a second-grade boy of 8, told the class, *"Todavia tratan mal a los Mexicanos"* ("Mexicans are still badly treated"). Students drew parallels between their lives and Chavez's early life and recorded these on a chart. One first-grade girl stated that when she grew up she also wanted to help poor people.

The class decided that they would make a mural about the farm-workers and invite other classes to see it. When two other general education primary classes toured our room to see the mural, the students gave short presentations about what the mural depicted. It took about a week and a half for students to do the research, prepare presentations, and practice their talks. To assist the students in their project, my aide and I outlined topics or provided questions based on the students' initial discussions. These included Chavez's early life, the farmworkers' strikes, and the conditions in the fields. Students worked in groups of three or four and discussed, dictated, and wrote paragraphs that depicted pieces of the mural (see Table 10.4).

About 2 months later, we studied the history of the early Chinese immigrants in California. The students learned about their work in the mines and railroads. Two students pointed out that the experiences of the early Chinese were similar to the farmworkers' experiences in the fields. Taking their cue, my aide and I assisted them in comparing and contrasting the Chinese and farmworker experiences. The students again shared a mural and presentations with the school at the annual multicultural fair. At one point, I overheard one of my second graders

---

TABLE 10.4
Examples of Children's Oral Responses to "Cesar Chavez y La Causa"

Cesar Chavez naciò en 1927 en Arizona. Ellos tenìan una familia grande. A su familia le quitaron sus tierras y no tenìan dinero. Eran pobres y se pusieron a trabajar como campesinos.
(Cesar Chavez was born in 1927 in Arizona. They had a large family. They took away the family's land and they didn't have money. They were poor and they worked as farmworkers.)

Los campesinos trabajan en la cosecha. No tenìan baños. No tenìan escuelas. No les pagaban bien. Cesar Chavez les ayudò para que los patrones les pagaran bien.
(The farmworkers worked with the harvest. They had no bathrooms. They had no schools. They were not well paid. Cesar Chavez helped them gain a good salary from the owners.)

Note. Themes: Prejudice, poverty, and family and community.

chastising a student in another class for making fun of the way Chinese people talk. *"A los chinos tambien los trataron mal. Así como los campesinos. You shouldn't be prejudiced about Chinese. ¿Té gusta si se reían de tí porque hablás español?"* ("The Chinese were also treated badly. Just like the farmworkers. You shouldn't be prejudiced about Chinese. Would you like it if they laughed at you because you speak Spanish?")

"Yagua Days." In this book, a Puerto Rican child living in New York visits his family in Puerto Rico for the first time. He is amazed to find that members of his family vary in their skin color and hair texture. He explores the family ranch and learns something special about his family's village.

The students began to talk about the farms and ranches where their own families lived in Mexico and El Salvador. The discussion generated activities on geography as students mapped out where the ranches and farms were located. Science activities revolved around farm animals, and growing vegetables and other crops. Students made several class big books that they planned and illustrated using key words they identified from their written dictations and responses to the story and discussions. They began a classroom garden and talked about starting a school garden, so that they could share the food with people who had none.

> *La casa de México. Omar es el nombre del caballo. Tengo dos mas en la casa de mi abuelito Enrique. Aquí está la puerta. Aquí le sale humo. Aquí deben meter los carros. Aquí está mi caballo Rosa. Aquí estan los puercos. A los puercos los matan para hacer chicharones.*

(This is the house in Mexico. The horse's name is Omar. I have two more in my Grandfather Enrique's house. Here is the door. Here smoke comes out. Here is where we park the cars. This is my horse Rosa. Here are the pigs. We kill the pigs to make crispy pork rind.)

Students also discussed how some family members were treated by relatives and friends according to the color of their skin or eyes, or their hair texture. For all of the students but one, being light skinned was better than being dark skinned. Being dark skinned with straight hair meant an Indian background, which was seen as undesirable. Students generally agreed with one another that lighter skin and hair meant more attention and being perceived as more attractive.

I proceeded to place skin color in the context of our discussion about being Mexican, El Salvadoran, and American. The students concluded that Mexicans and El Salvadorans could be light-skinned, but that undocumented people were more likely to be dark-skinned. When we asked them why they thought this, one student said that it was probably because poor people were Indian. Most of the students felt that if Mexicans or El Salvadorans were light-skinned or fair-haired they could become "American" because "the Americans" would like them because they were attractive. One child, a first-grade boy who was indignant at the thought that someone might judge him because of his dark skin and hair, said that everyone in his family had dark skin and hair and he thought they were very attractive people. He put his arm up and compared it to mine and said, *"Teacher, usted es café con leche y yo soy café con chocolate"* (Teacher, your skin is like coffee and milk and mine is like coffee and chocolate"). (See Table 10.5 for other responses.)

"At the Crossroads" and "Fly Away Home." These two books were written in English, but we told them to the class in Spanish. Both stories brought out themes pertaining to family integrity and solidarity. Interestingly enough, the students' focus during the discussions and writing centered on how children can contribute to the family's welfare by working alongside parents to help make ends meet. "At The Crossroads" is a story about a group of South African children waiting for their fathers to return home from working in the mines for 10 months. The story is about their vigil at the crossroads while they wait for the truck that will bring their fathers to them. "Fly Away Home" is a story about a boy and his father who are homeless and live at the airport. The story is told from the boy's point of view; he tells how he and his father live their day—how they wash and eat, when and how they sleep.

Many of the students had experienced a father's absence when he went to work away from the family for extended periods of time. Also, most of the students in the class work with their parents after school and

---

TABLE 10.5
Examples of Children's Oral Responses to "Yagua Days"

Yo no soy India. Mi mamà dice que soy blanca.
(I'm not an Indian. My mother says I'm white.)

Yo tengo la piel morena como mi mamà y mi papà y a mì me decen "el indio."
(My skin is dark like my mother and father and they call me "the Indian.")

Yo tengo una prima con ojos azules y pelo huero y se llama Carolina. Dicen que parece muñeca.
(I have a cousin with blue eyes and blond hair and her name is Caroline. They say she looks like a doll.)

Miguel [another student in the class] es mas prieto que yo. Él es feo.
(Miguel is darker than I am. He's ugly.)

Note. Themes: Prejudice, and family and community.

on weekends. They help their parents cut grass, care for younger siblings, wash dishes and fold napkins in restaurants, clean houses, collect aluminum cans, and paint houses. After students wrote, revised, and published their stories, they talked about possible kinds of jobs they might have when they became adults. They read and researched which skills were needed for preparation and began to identify some obstacles they might face in the future (see Table 10.6).

"Diego." Different stories elicit different types of responses and activities, and they sometimes are not the responses and activities the teacher might have thought of on his or her own. After reading "Diego," a story

---

TABLE 10.6
Examples of Children's Oral Responses to "Fly Away Home" and "At the Crossroads"

Estoy vendiendo mis juguetitos. Tambien estoy vendiendo chicle. Voy a comprar una casa para mi familia con el dinero que voy agarrar.
(I'm selling my little toys. I'm also selling gum. I am going to buy a house for my family with the money I get.)

Estaba cortando el zacate. Estaba cortando el àrbol. Estaba cortando los palos pa' ir a Mèxico con la familia.
(I was cutting the grass. I was cutting the tree. I was cutting the branches to get money to go to Mexico with the family.)

Yo le ayudo a mi mamà limpiar casas. Estan bien grandes las casas. Ella me da un "quarter" para mì pero yo le digo que no.
(I help my mother clean houses. They are really big houses. She gives me a quarter but I tell her no.)

Yo y mi papà fuimos a Taco Bell y alli trabajamos de hacer $1.29. Yo y mi papà le decimos si quieren comprar tacos y dicen que sìs y luego se hizo noche y nos fuimos.
(My father and I went to Taco Bell and we worked there for $1.29. My father and I ask people if they want to buy tacos and they say yes and then it gets late and we leave.)

Le estoy ayudando a mi papà. Estoy lavando la olla. Me dijo mi papà "No lo agarres. Te quemas." Le puso la lumbre y hicimos tacos, burros, hamburguesas, y muchas cosas. Ya se hizo noche. Ya nos fuimos.
(I am helping my father. I am washing the pot. My father tells me "Don't touch it. You'll burn yourself." He put it on the stove and we made tacos, burros, hamburgers, and lots of things. It gets late. We leave.)

Ando trabajando con mi papà. Es mi papà y yo. Anda trabajando con las màquinas. Un cerrucho para cortar el àrbol.
(I am working with my father. This is my father and me. He is working with the machines. A saw to cut the tree.)

Note. Themes: Poverty, family and community, and authority.

about Mexican muralist Diego Rivera, the students decided that they could make the school look beautiful if they could paint murals on the walls. They did not realize the amount of bureaucratic research and paperwork this would involve. I suggested they practice painting some murals on butcher paper on some of the themes they had already studied. This would give them an opportunity to practice and develop some skills with paints and planning the mural, and would also give me time to track down what the district would require in order for a mural to be painted on school grounds.

Students painted murals about farms, their neighborhoods, and the cultural holiday *Día de los Muertos* (Day of the Dead), also known as *Día de los Difuntos* (All Souls' Day). They wrote words to go with their murals. While they waited for official word on their project, the students began to discuss other ways they might improve their immediate community and how they might get adults to listen to their ideas for making positive changes in the neighborhood.

"La Calle Es Libre." In this book, a group of children who struggle to get a children's park constructed face obstacles from public officials and some of their neighbors. My students and I discussed some similarities and differences in the problems they were facing with their proposed mural and those that the characters in the book faced. Students suggested ways that some of the problems might be solved, and possible action plans were listed. My aide and I helped them develop and frame their strategies by (a) asking them key questions with regard to their planning, (b) critiquing their ideas, and (c) showing them how to critique their own and each other's ideas.

My efforts at *problematizing* the situation, through interactive dialogue journals and discussion that focused on modeling analyses of their problem and strategies, generated what Freire (1970) referred to as *generative words* and *codifications*. (To problematize is to create a forum for discussion that allows participants to inquire into the nature, background, and assumptions of an idea, person, or object. To problematize is to "understand existing knowledge as an historical product deeply invested with the values of those who developed such knowledge" [Shor, 1987, p. 24].) Codifications are pictorial representations of a real-life experience. Generative words are the words that can be constructed from the syllables of the codification label. In class, one codification consisted of the possible murals that might be painted on the school buildings; another codification was an illustration of a group of children on one side of a heavy dark line and a group of adults on the other side of the line. A third codification pictured the adults, children, and murals all in one setting. The label for the mural illustration was *escuela,* or "school," and the other two codifications were labeled *comunidad,* or "community." The words *escuela* and *comunidad* were defined and analyzed for meaning as well as for syllables. New words were generated from the component syllables. (See Table 10.7 for definitions and generative words.)

In addition, students wrote autobiographies that described their families, friends, particular interests or talents, and hopes for the future. They drew pictures of themselves, their homes, and their communities. As we began to share the autobiographies, one student suggested that we write stories about family members. The discussion that resulted identified what kinds of interview questions might be asked and who might be possible subjects of the biographies. Another student suggested we make a mural of our neighborhood and interview people in the neighborhood who were not family members.

DISCUSSION

As the student responses illustrate, even young children with the added challenges of learning disabilities and language differences are aware of those economic and social barriers that education often cannot bridge. Although the students may not be totally aware of or able to label the obstacles they face, their personal experiences and observations about their world lead them to the conclusion that school and formal education will not always provide the answers to the problems they face in their communities. If we truly are to provide an environment in which students benefit from formal education, it is imperative that we imbue our classrooms and curricula with opportunities for students to engage in critical dialogue, so that true literacy such as that described by Freire and Macedo (1987) can develop. Fostering student voices in educational institutions can provide bicultural students with the opportunity to bring their lived experiences into the classroom. Using information grounded in daily life can serve to enhance and support the students' emerging language, communication, and academic abilities. Using storytelling within the cultural context, such as folktales, myths, religious stories, and life stories, acknowledges and validates the knowledge that students bring with them into the classroom.

To provide a critical pedagogical classroom environment, elementary school teachers in particular need to be well informed regarding community history, the history of the bicultural group with whom they are working, and the community resources, including people and community centers, that can provide additional information and support to the teacher and students. Teachers should have at least a basic philo-

---

TABLE 10.7
Examples of Children's Oral Responses to "La Calle Es Libre"

Definitions of escuela [school]
> *Un lugar donde se aprenda a leer y escribir.*
> (A place where one learns how to read and write.)

> *Donde trabajan los niños y los maestros.*
> (Where children and teachers work.)

> *Donde hay amigos.*
> (Where there are friends.)

> *Es para hacer la matemàticas.*
> (It's to do math.)

> *Es para aprender y tener un buen trabajo.*
> (It's to learn and have a good job.)

> *Donde juegan los niños.*
> (Where the children play.)

Generative words/phrases included
> *estar juntos* / be together
> *escribir* / write
> *la maestra* / the teacher
> *escoger* / to choose
> *el niño* / the boy
> *la niña* / the girl
> *el libro* / the book

Definitions of *comunidad*/community
> *Donde vive la familia.*
> (Where the family lives.)

> *Donde juegan los niños.*
> (Where the children play.)

> *La escuela està en la comunidad.*
> (The school is in the community.)

> *Aquì vivo yo.*
> (I live here.)

> *Donde se compra la comida.*
> (Where we buy food.)

> *Aquì està la lavanderia.*
> (The laundromat is here.)

Generative words/phrases include
> *comer* / to eat
> *mural* / mural
> *niño* / the boy

Note. Themes: Family and community, authority.

sophical understanding of the major theories that inform this type of practice. Works by Freire (1970), Freire and Macedo (1987), Giroux (1992), and Shor (1980) are excellent places to begin to explore critical pedagogy. Research by Darder (1991) and Ramirez and Castaneda (1974) examines bicultural development issues that involve key components for creating a critical educational program.

Teachers working with bicultural, non–English-proficient, or LEP students must thoroughly understand first- and second-language acquisition theory and know how to translate the theory into appropriate classroom activities. Students who also have language/learning disabilities will need teachers who are familiar with special education programs, models, and research and holistic/constructivist notions of language learning that bilingual/bicultural special education researchers see as a viable alternative to traditional special education approaches to remediation.

Knowing when and how to problematize an event in the classroom and use it for teaching, or how to modify an activity for a student in the language-emergence stage of English acquisition who also exhibits language/learning difficulties in his or her native language, and who is striving to develop an understanding of the bicultural issues at work in his or her own life, requires more than a "multicultural night" in a teacher education course. It requires intensive study of theory and practice and, most important, a partnership/mentorship with a teacher who is already engaged in this type of practice. Although apprenticeships and university student teacher programs have been diminished somewhat in their ability to provide this education, team teaching, informal teacher support groups at local levels, and staff development offer opportunities to begin the dialogical process at the professional level. Like the young students in our classrooms, we need to engage in discourse in a collaborative environment to develop our own capabilities and voice in the educational institutions.

Teachers interested in creating a critical environment in their classrooms should not replicate the lessons described here. Instead, teachers must create a classroom environment in which students can develop their confidence in their legitimate right to voice their honest reactions to their world. Teachers must listen and respond to their students in ways that will encourage dialogue that validates, challenges, analyzes, and critiques assumptions, ideas, and conclusions without silencing voices. As students and teachers begin to recognize students as decision makers in their own learning, lessons and activities will emerge from the dialogue. These lessons will be meaningful, powerful, and transformative for both the students and their teachers, because they will come from the willingness and commitment of both parties to struggle through the difficult issues our students face every day.

AUTHOR'S NOTE

Many thanks to Joni Enriquez, friend, colleague, and classroom aide in the bilingual special day class, and to the Pasadena Unified School District LEP Assessment Team, for their support in the creation of this project.

APPENDIX
Bibliography of Children's Literature

Acuna, R. (1971). *The story of the Mexican Americans.* Sacramento: California State Department of Education.

Adoff, A. (1973). *Black is brown is tan.* New York: Harper & Row.

Anaya, R. (1987). *The farolitos of Christmas.* Santa Fe: New Mexico Magazine.

Bunting, E. (1988). *How many days to America?* New York: Clarion Books.

Bunting, E. (1991). *Fly away home.* New York: Clarion Books.

Cohen, B. (1983). *Molly's pilgrim.* New York: Lothrop, Lee & Shepard Books.

Cowcher, H. (1988). *Rainforest.* New York: Farrar, Strauss & Giroux.

De Paola, T. (1981). *The hunter and the animals.* New York: Holiday House.

Doppert, M. (1981). *La calle es libre* [The street is free]. Caracas, Venezuela: Textos Kurusa.

Dorros, A. (1991). *Abuela* [Grandmother]. New York: Dutton's Children's Books.

Dragonwagon, C. (1990). *Home place.* New York: Scholastic.

Franchere, R. (1970). *Cesar Chavez.* New York: Thomas Y. Crowell.

Garcia, M. (1987). *Las aventuras de Connie y Diego* [The adventures of Connie and Diego]. San Francisco: Children's Book Press.

Garcia, R. (1987). *Los espiritus de mi tìa Otilia* [My Aunt Otilia's spirits]. San Francisco: Children's Book Press.

Garza, C. L. (1990). *Cuadros de familia* [Family pictures]. San Francisco: Children's Book Press.

Gaspar, T. R. (1974). *La aventura de Yolanda* [Yolanda's hike]. Berkeley, CA: New Seed Press.

Golenbock, P. (1990). *Teammates.* New York: Harcourt Brace Jovanovich.

Hopkinson, D. (1993). *Sweet Clara and the freedom quilt.* New York: Alfred A. Knopf.

Isadora, R. (1991). *At the crossroads.* New York: Scholastic.

Johnson, A. (1990). *When I am old with you.* New York: Orchard Books.

Jordan, M. K. (1989). *Losing Uncle Tim.* Morton Grove, IL: Albert Whitman.

Levine, E. (1989). *I hate English.* New York: Scholastic.

Levine, E. (1993). *If your name was changed at Ellis Island.* New York: Scholastic.

Lionni, L. (1963). *Swimmy.* New York: Scholastic.

Martel, C. (1976). *Yagua days.* New York: Dial Books for Young Readers.

Maury, I. (1978). *My mother and I are growing strong.* Stanford, CA: New Seed Press.

Mendez, P. (1989). *The black snowman.* New York: Scholastic.

Miles, M. (1971). *Annie and the old one.* Boston, MA: Atlantic Monthly Press.

Moss, M. (1991). *After-school monster.* New York: Lothrop, Lee & Shepard Books.

Nava, J., & Hall, M. (1974). *Mexican American profiles.* Walnut Creek, CA: Aardvark Media.

Nodar, C. S. (1992). *El paraìso de abuelita* [Grandmother's paradise]. Morton Grove, IL: Albert Whitman.

Ortiz, S. (1988). *The people shall continue.* San Francisco: Children's Book Press.

Perez, T. (1991). *Portraits of Mexican Americans: Pathfinders in the Mexican American communities.* Carthage, IL: Good Apple.

Ringgold, F. (1991). *Tar beach*. New York: Scholastic.

Roberts, N. (1986). *Cesar Chavez y la causa* [Cesar Chavez and the cause]. Chicago, IL: Children's Press.

Rylant, C. (1982). *When I was young in the mountains*. New York: E. P. Dutton.

Say, A. (1993). *Grandfather's journey*. New York: Scholastic.

Sendak, M. (1993). *We are all in the dumps with Jack and Guy*. New York: HarperCollins.

Shigekawa, M. (1993). *Blue jay in the desert*. Chicago, IL: Polychrome.

Spier, P. (1980). *People*. New York: Doubleday.

Stanek, M. (1989). *I speak English for my mom*. Niles, IL: Albert Whitman.

Steig, W. (1986). *Brave Irene*. Canada: HarperCollins Canada Ltd./Farrar, Strauss & Giroux.

Stolz, M. (1988). *Storm in the night*. New York: Harper Trophy.

Teachers' Committee on Central America. (1986). *Wilfredo: The story of a boy from El Salvador.* Los Angeles, CA: United Teachers of Los Angeles.

Tsutsui, Y. (1983). *Anna's special present*. New York: Puffin Books.

Turner, A. (1990). *Through moon and stars and night skies*. New York: Harper Trophy.

Vasquez, E. P. M. (1985). *La historia de Ana* [The story of Ana]. Pasadena, CA: Hope.

Walker, A. (1967). *To hell with dying*. New York: Harcourt Brace Jovanovich.

Williams, S. A. (1992). *Working cotton*. New York: Harcourt Brace Jovanovich.

Williams, V. B. (1982). *A chair for my mother*. New York: Scholastic.

Williams, V. B. (1990). *More, more, more said the baby*. New York: Greenwillow Books.

Winter, J. J. (1991). *Diego*. New York: Knopf.

Yarbrough, C. (1979). *Cornrows*. New York: Coward-McCann.

Zak, M. (1992). *Save my rainforest*. Volcano, CA: Volcano Press.

11. The Social Construction of Ability and Disability: I. Profile Types of Latino Children Identified As Language Learning Disabled

NADEEN T. RUIZ

Recently, when researchers in special education turned an ethnographic eye toward special education classrooms and the larger context of the special education system, many of their studies produced a fundamentally similar theme: The abilities and disabilities of children in special education vary according to the context of interaction (Gleason, 1989; Mehan, Hertweck, & Meihls, 1986; Rueda & Mehan, 1986; Ruiz, Figueroa, Rueda, & Beaumont, 1992; Taylor, 1991, 1993). On the surface, this theme may seem to be only another tributary of special education research, one that will be followed by a few, who will basically talk among themselves about its importance and continue to pursue its course. And, at present, this ethnographic research is just that, except for sporadic splashes in the mainstream special education journals (e.g., Poplin, 1988a, 1988b). But the theme needs to be recognized for what it is: a powerful working theory with a strong explanatory function. It is a theory that extends across macro and micro contexts of special education to explain the anomalies found therein—from the arbitrary nature of national incidence

Reprinted, with changes, from "The social construction of ability and disability: I. Profile types of Latino children identified as language learning disabled," by Nadeen T. Ruiz, *Journal of Learning Disabilities,* Vol. 28, 1995, pp. 476–490. Copyright © 1995 by PRO-ED, Inc.

figures of handicapping conditions (Ortiz & Yates, 1983; Ruiz et al., 1992), to the very personal stories of misdiagnosed and misplaced children (Figueroa, 1986; Ruiz, 1988; Taylor, 1991). It is also a theory that undergirds a longitudinal research project, the Optimal Learning Environment (OLE) Project (Figueroa, Ruiz, & Rueda, 1990), which seeks to create effective learning contexts for bilingual children in pull-out special education programs. Finally, it is a theory that explains the success stories emanating from the OLE Project and others, which have radically altered the nature of instruction for special education students (Cousin, Weekley, & Gerard, 1993; Figueroa & Ruiz, 1993; Figueroa, Ruiz, & García, 1994; Scala, 1993).

A broad goal of this chapter is to examine this working theory using the case of 10 Latino children who were labeled language learning disabled and placed in a self-contained, bilingual special day class. The data discussed here are part of a larger ethnographic study that looked at the social-organization patterns across recurring events in this bilingual special education classroom (Ruiz, 1988). One of the major findings of the larger study was that as the organization of the classroom events varied, so did the picture of the children's language and academic abilities. The primary purpose of this chapter, along with its companion piece (see Chapter 12 of this book), is to pull out the contextual features of the classroom events and discuss those that revealed the upper range of children's language and academic skills, as well as those that showed the lower range of their skills. This discussion is organized around case studies of three students in the bilingual special education classroom; each student represents one of three profile types that emerged from the study: Profile Type 1—severe to moderate disability; Profile Type 2—mild disability to normal ability; and Profile Type 3—normal ability.

On the theoretical level, my intent is to build on a theoretical framework recurring in the special education field. On the applied level, I hope to add to the small group of studies identifying effective learning environments for Latino children identified as mildly handicapped (Echevarría & McDonough, 1993; Flores, Rueda, & Porter, 1986; Ortiz, Wilkinson, Robertson-Courtney, & Kushner, 1991; Ruiz, 1988; Viera, 1986; Willig & Swedo, 1987). For educators concerned with assessment, it is within those optimal learning contexts that the most complete and useful picture of children's language and learning abilities emerges; for educators concerned with instruction, it is within optimal learning contexts that individualized instruction needs make themselves apparent.

THEORETICAL FRAMEWORK

The classroom is identified as one place where social transmission and construction of knowledge occurs (Cook-Gumperz & Gumperz, 1982;

Green, 1983). Yet, the classroom is a unique context that requires special language and interactive skills, some patterns of which may be shared in the home and community settings, and some of which may not (Heath, 1983; Wilkinson, 1982). Essentially, students are expected to show *communicative competence*. Communicative competence, as defined by ethnographers of communication (the originators of the term), is what a speaker needs to know to communicate appropriately—what may be said and what should not be said; when, where, and by whom; and for what purposes—in addition to the linguistic knowledge necessary to produce grammatical utterances (Hymes, 1964; Saville-Troike, 1982).

During classroom interaction, problems with communicative competence can impede the social transmission and construction of knowledge just as effectively as if the class were taught in a foreign language. Because an important function of classroom talk is to enable teachers to evaluate student learning and performance (Cazden, 1988), what is viewed as communicative incompetence in students can have serious consequences: assignment of them to the "slow group," retention, or special education referral.

In the past, responsibility for the breakdown was assigned to the children. Specifically, the problem, be it a language learning difference or a disorder, was viewed as internal to the child. Poplin (1988a), Rueda (1989), and other special education researchers pointed to this as a critical component of the reductionist, or medical model, paradigm that has dominated the special education field to the present. But naturalistic studies of special education classrooms and children over the last 12 years have clearly refuted that view. This research has consistently found that, depending on the way the classroom events are organized, a child displays both competence and incompetence (Gleason, 1989; Hood, McDermott, & Cole, 1981; Rueda & Mehan, 1986; Taylor, 1991). Within the medical model paradigm, this finding would have been interpreted as simply the characteristic peaks and valleys of the profile of a child with a language learning disability (Kirk, 1972). But the people doing the naturalistic research see this phenomenon connected to what the fields of anthropology and sociolinguistics have documented for years: the fact that the context of a situation profoundly affects behavior and that behavior cannot be interpreted without taking into account those situational features.

The impact of context on children's language and academic performance is the thread running through the present study, as well as what connects it to previously published studies. As readers are introduced to three students in Mrs. Dixon's special day class for children with language learning disabilities, and as they are presented with seemingly contradictory evidence on the children's abilities and disabilities, this theoretical construct will explain the variability of their language and literacy behaviors.

METHOD

Studying a group about which we have few intensive investigations is a challenging task. Latino children identified as language learning disabled (LLD; Wallach & Liebergott, 1984) constitute such a group. Experimental researchers trying to "control" the various linguistic, cultural, educational, and socioeconomic variables that must be accounted for when working with U.S. Latino children have an especially hard time of it: When confronted with this variation, many have ignored it or chosen a certain variable, to the exclusion of others, to control. (See Figueroa, 1990, for a review of studies of Latino children's intellectual abilities that have followed both of these paths.)

A search for research methodology that is associated with exploration rather than control of linguistic, cultural, and social diversity led me quickly to ethnography. Ethnography is the extensive study of sociocultural aspects of a group from the point of view of its members (Green & Wallat, 1981; Spradley, 1980), produced through participant observation in regularly occurring cycles of events (Lutz, 1981). Ethnography of special education was relatively new at the time of the data-collection period of this study; however, a book published during its course, *Handicapping the Handicapped* (Mehan, Hertweck, & Meihls, 1986), served to illustrate the important insights that ethnography can produce about education for children with LLD. Using a research design that looked at both micro and macro structures of schooling—that is, the immediate contexts of classroom participation and the wider social system of which they are a part—Mehan et al. found that special education labels were not simply a function of student behavior, but, rather, were based on program availability and funding, expectations that evaluators brought to verify the original referral reason (the "test until find" approach), and the enactment of interactional routines associated with the referral and placement processes. Mehan et al. wrote,

> Learning disabilities are more like touchdowns and property rights than like chicken pox and asthma. They are defined as real by a complex set of legal and educational practices and governed by school rules and policies. They are objects that are culturally constructed by the rules of the school, its laws and daily educational practices. Just as the rules of football constitute touchdowns, so too the tools of special education constitute learning disabilities and educational handicaps. (p. 85)

The Mehan et al. (1986) ethnographic study focused on the referral and placement processes in special education. The present study looks at another aspect of special education: classroom language and literacy patterns of students identified as LLD. (For additional discussion of this study's research methodology, including the topics of reliability and validity, see Ruiz, 1988.)

Setting and Participants

This study took place in a bilingual special education classroom in the central agricultural valley of California during a 20-month period. Bilingual special education has been defined as "the use of the home language and home culture along with English in an individually designed program of special instruction for the students" (Baca & Cervantes, 1984, p. 18). This particular classroom is a self-contained class, or special day class, for children identified as LLD.

The teacher and instructional assistant use Spanish and English with the students in a very structured and routinized way. They employ an "alternate-day" method of bilingual instruction known to the classroom participants as the "Language of the Day" (Legarreta, 1979). Specifically, the teacher alternates daily between Spanish and English during class openings and for other classroom routines and procedures occurring after it, such as directions to the class as a whole. Whole group lessons in science and health, although not occurring daily, also follow the language-of-the-day rule. For example, Monday, Wednesday, and Friday of a particular week might be "English days" and follow the pattern described above; Tuesday and Thursday of that week would be "Spanish days."

The only formal context of language use in the classroom that follows another pattern is small group lessons. There, what has been designated as the students' primary, or dominant, language is always used for math, reading, and language arts, regardless of the particular language of the day. Again, as an example, a Spanish-dominant student would be expected to adhere to English, if that were the language of the day, for all whole group, teacher-directed activities. Small group lessons, however, would be conducted that day and every day in the student's dominant language, Spanish.

The teacher, Mrs. Dixon, is a licensed language, speech, and hearing (LSH) specialist. She is of Euro-American descent and began learning Spanish about 3 years before this study. The primary instructional assistant, Ms. Chaparro, is a native speaker of Spanish who speaks English proficiently.

The students in this bilingual special education classroom range in age from 6 to 11 years. Their Spanish and English proficiency and preferences vary considerably, from some who speak Spanish almost exclusively to those reluctant to speak Spanish at all. Almost all of the children are of Mexican or Chicano background; one is of Honduran and Puerto Rican heritage.

A typical day in Mrs. Dixon's class shares the social organization of many classrooms. Once the class officially begins, the students primarily participate in two teacher-directed events, whole group and small group lessons (Mehan, 1979). But Mrs. Dixon widens the range of ways that her students can use language. She encourages, and gives her students time to engage in, sociodramatic play (essentially, symbolic play around a peer-negotiated theme; Smilansky, 1968). Mrs. Dixon also encourages her students to dictate or write storybooks when they finish the tasks in their individual work folders. These storybooks are simply scratch paper stapled together, illustrated, and placed in a decorated shoe box on the classroom book shelves. These two contexts for interaction—sociodramatic play and making storybooks—along with the more typical whole group and small group lessons, showcase the children's oral and written abilities and disabilities.

Data Collection

Data collection for this study was divided into two stages. During Stage 1 (the first 16 months), I acted as a participant-observer. I observed and audiotaped all the students during the course of their normal classroom activities on either a weekly or a biweekly basis. These activities included the class openings, whole class science and social studies lessons, small group language and mathematics lessons, lunchroom conversations, sociodramatic play, and storybook writing.

Field notes were equally important as a source of information. I noted contextual information for the classroom interaction and, in general, anything of interest that might help describe the participants, their personal histories, and the social structure shaping their interactions.

Stage 2 data were collected in the final 4 months of the study. I reviewed the students' school files and their Individualized Education Programs (IEPs), interviewed their parents, and continued to participate in the classroom on a monthly basis. In contrast to the data generated by fieldwork, the information contained in the files constructed the "official" school view of the students and their abilities.

RESULTS AND DISCUSSION

From this ethnographic study of Mrs. Dixon's bilingual special education classroom, three distinct language and learning profiles among the Latino children in this classroom emerged. These profiles were constructed by observing the students' communicative and academic competence across a range of classroom events, some which were teacher directed, some student directed. Further, the teachers signaled the different profile types by varying their behavior according to the children's levels of language learning abilities.

Emerging Profiles

There is substantial diversity among the students in Mrs. Dixon's class. Victor is 6 years old; Rosemary is 10. Nelly shows a 4- to 5-year language and academic delay across a battery of tests, Victor, a 1- to 2-year delay. Esteban is thought to be mildly mentally retarded; Gina has average intelligence. Virginia, age 7, is struggling with kindergarten work; Cristina, age 9, is working at third- and fourth-grade levels.

This diversity, although surprising to those who solely do experimental studies of LLD children, is nothing new to school personnel. Mehan et al.'s (1986) naturalistic study of special education documented the variety of handicapping conditions within special education classrooms. Those authors noted that special education personnel would shift the children's labels to be able to serve them: For example, a child who originally qualified for a learning handicap program was requalified, when that classroom was full, as communication handicapped. The child could then immediately receive services.

Mrs. Dixon also commented to me early in the fieldwork that she knew the students brought a mix of language and learning problems, but as the only special education classroom in the county that was able to instruct Spanish-speaking children in their primary language, she needed to accept this range. A recent classroom study of a bilingual special education classroom also documented a range of handicapping conditions and abilities (Echevarría & McDonough, 1993).

Table 11.1 illustrates the diversity among Mrs. Dixon's students. It lists how the school views the children in terms of a number of dimensions, such as ascribed cognitive and linguistic ability and level of academic work. However, even with this range of age and skills, patterns among the children emerge. Specifically, the present study shows that the students represent three groups in terms of language learning abilities and disabilities: (a) children with a severe to moderate language learning disability, (b) children suspected of having a mild disability who possibly have normal abilities, and (c) children with normal ability who are misdiagnosed as disabled. Figure 11.1 represents the groups' profile types along a scale of language learning ability and disability.

TABLE 11.1
The Students: The School's View

Student	Age (yrs)	IQ	Language delay (yrs)	Academic delay (yrs)	Language dominance
Victor	6	Low average	1–2	0	English
Anita	7	Average	3–4	2–3	Spanish
Francisco	7	Low average to borderline	3	2–3	Spanish
Virginia	7	Slow	2–3	2–3	English
Esteban	8	Mildly retarded	4	4	Spanish
Nelly	9	Borderline– mildly retarded	4–5	3–4	English
Cristina	9	Average	2	0–1	Spanish
Pilar	9	Average	2	1–2	Spanish
Gina	9	Average	2–3	1–2	English
Rosemary	10	Low average	4	2–3	English

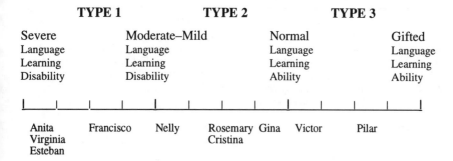

Figure 11.1. Emerging profile types of Latino children identified as language learning disabled.

Profile Type 1: Moderate to Severe Disability.   Four children in Mrs. Dixon's class represent Profile Type 1: Anita, Francisco, Virginia, and Esteban. On a scale of language learning disability (see Figure 11.1), they all show a severe to moderate degree of disability. Although the degree is similar, the actual nature of their disability varies considerably (Ruiz, 1988). Anita illustrates this profile type:

Anita is a vivacious 7-year-old of Honduran and Puerto Rican heritage. She lives with her parents and younger sister in a small town about 15 miles from the school. Her mother is a young housewife and her father is disabled from a work injury. They speak Spanish at home.

Anita's speech is largely unintelligible. When she was first referred for special education, her parents reported that she began talking late and that they were concerned about her language problem. They also reported that Anita is asthmatic. She has been hospitalized for this problem and must take medication to control it. She also has various allergies and a history of ear infections.

Various assessment personnel found Anita to have average intellectual ability and a severe communication disorder. They recommended placement in Mrs. Dixon's bilingual special day class.

Anita is trying to learn the letters and sounds of the Spanish alphabet, without much success. She can recognize about a third of the alphabet but can neither associate sounds with the letters nor write them. In math she is at the kindergarten level, learning the names of shapes and such concepts as "more" or "less." She is working on counting objects of a set up to 10, and writing the numerals up to 20.

Anita's work folder contains a variety of dittoed worksheets: cut-and-paste and coloring activities focusing on visual discrimination, and visual-motor tasks, such as drawing lines through paths. Occasionally she is given worksheets on the numbers 1 through 5.

TABLE 11.2
Anita's Communicative Competence in Class Openings

Participant	Verbal text	English translation
Mrs. Dixon	Today is Friday, good, and what is the date. Anita?	
Anita	Mm.	
Mrs. Dixon	*Anita, mira acá.* What is the date?	Anita, look here. What is the date?
Anita	*¿Domingo?*	Sunday?
Mrs. Dixon	The date. (9½) *Okay, quiero que escuches.* Okay, Pilar, what is the date today?	The date. (9½) Okay, I want you to listen. Okay, Pilar, what is the date today?

Note. The numbers in the transcript refer to seconds of silence between conversational turns.

In predictable whole class events, such as class opening (lunch count, calendar, weather discussion), Anita's contributions are usually brief, filled with pauses, and often off-target, as seen in Table 11.2. Her incorrect responses are usually followed by a reprimand from the teacher to listen. On the rare occasion that Anita supplies the response Mrs. Dixon needs, she is praised enthusiastically.

Because student responses in class openings are so predictable, one of Anita's typical communication problems—unintelligibility—diminishes in those situations. The narrow range of teacher questions and acceptable student answers facilitates comprehension of her speech. In small group lessons, however, the instructional aide seeks to elicit as much language as possible from Anita. She does not have the luxury of routinized language to aid in understanding Anita. In the example in Table 11.3, Anita wears a nurse puppet that she has made and responds to questions about what a nurse does. Note Anita's topic shifts, from doctors to shoes to parties.

Even during sociodramatic play, an informal event in which the students socially organize most of the interaction, Anita's language disability manifests itself. In the example in Table 11.4, she tries to imitate Nelly's successful purchase of a book from bookstore proprietor Pilar. Pilar has to supply Anita with the appropriate question: *"¿Cuánto vale?"* ("How much is it?"); a quantity concept: *"No es mucho dinero"* ("That's not a lot of money"); and the appropriate action: *"Llévate tu libro"* ("Take your book with you").

Though Anita struggles through this particular interaction sequence, she learns the appropriate form of a price request over the course of this sociodramatic play. Anita begins by simply using the deictic form *"Este"*

TABLE 11.3
Anita's Communicative Competence in Lessons

Participant	Verbal text	English translation
Mrs. Chap	¿Qué tienen? ¿Por qué están enfermos?	What's wrong with them? Why are they sick?
Anita	Tiene ama.	They have asthma.
Mrs. Chap	Tienen asthma, ooh, ¿qué mas tienen?	They have asthma, ooh, what else is wrong with them?
Anita	[XX] yo no sé.	[XX] I don't know.
Mrs. Chap	Pues usted es la enfermera, usted tiene que saber.	Well, you're the nurse, you have to know.
Anita	[XX] allí al doctor.	[XX] there to the doctor.
Mrs. Chap	Usted trabaja con el doctor.	You work with the doctor.
Anita	Sí.	Yes.
Mrs. Chap	¿Y qué pasa con el doctor?	And what's going on with the doctor?
Anita	El - mm - e - allá. [XX]. El pone mis zapatos.	He - mm - uh - there. [XX]. He puts on my shoes.
Mrs. Chap	¿Cómo?	What?
Anita	Pone zapatos.	He puts on shoes.
Mrs. Chap	Usted le pone los zapatos.	You put on his shoes.
Anita	Sí.	Yes.
Mrs. Chap	No, usted es una enfermera.	No, you are a nurse.
Anita	(2½) No sé.	I don't know.
Mrs. Chap	¿Qué hace una enfermera, Anita?	What does a nurse do, Anita?
Anita	La enfermera, [XX]? Doctor Ramos, mañana mañana voy a irme.	The nurse, [XX]? Doctor Ramos, tomorrow tomorrow I'm going to leave.
Mrs. Chap	¿A dónde?	Where?
Anita	A una party, [XX] un niño.	To a party, [XX] a boy.
Mrs. Chap	Okay, quiero que me hable de la enfermera, Anita.	Okay, I want you to tell me about the nurse, Anita.

Note. [XX] refers to unintelligible utterances in the transcript.

TABLE 11.4
Anita's Communicative Competence in Sociodramatic Play

Participant	Verbal text	English translation
Anita	*Esta, señora, ésta.* (no response) *Este. ¿Qué nombre este libro. Este. ¿Qué nombre este?* (no response) *¿Qué número?*	This one, ma'am, this one (no response). This one. What name this book. This one. What name this one? (no response) What number?
Pilar	*Uh, ¿cuánto vale? Vale dos dolares.*	Uh, how much is it? It's two dollars.
Anita	*Ay, no.* ((Imitating Nelly, who protested the high price of $100 just a minute ago.)	Ay, no.
Pilar	*No es mucho dinero.*	That's not a lot of money.
Nelly	*¿Qué? ¿Siete dolares?*	What? Seven dollars?
Pilar	*A ver. Déjeme ver si trae las libretitas.* (Pilar pretends to take some imaginary money or a check from Anita.)	Let's see. Let me see if you have the checkbook.
Anita	*Yo no lo tengo.*	I don't have it.
Nelly	*Te digo.*	I told you.
Pilar	*Anita, illévate tu libro!* (As Anita leaves without taking her purchase)	Anita, take your book!

("This one") and progresses to *"¿Qué nombre este?"* ("What name this one?") to *"¿Qué número?"* ("What number?") to *"¿Cuánto vale?"* ("How much is it?").

With persistent and intense scaffolding (Applebee & Langer, 1983), or mediation, Anita is able to show some verbal strengths, as revealed in the story she dictated to me (see Table 11.5). Notice the multiple action episodes, dialogue, insertion of personal information (Lillian is her sister's name), and resolution. The first two characteristics make it a relatively advanced story, whereas the naturalistic ending ("They got married and had babies") suggests an early stage of story development (Applebee, 1978).

Anita, like the four other children in this profile type, clearly gives evidence of her language learning disability. For anyone with a background in child development and a proficiency in the children's native language, it is easy to spot the disability soon after one begins to interact with children with this profile. Their language and learning patterns are clearly different from normal-ability Latino children with similar sociocultural backgrounds. The difference cuts across formal and informal contexts.

However, even among Profile Type 1 children, the effects of context on the picture of their abilities and disabilities apply. If one looks solely at Anita's test results and work folder, a picture of a child with very limited abilities emerges. However, certain contexts just as clearly reveal Anita's strengths. When Anita can use her native language, when she can interact in a peer-oriented and peer-structured event, such as sociodramatic play, when she can choose the topics for her dictated storybooks, when she can insert her personal experiences into the preceding activities, and when the activities have an authentic end product (such as a book or social interaction with her peers), Anita shows another side. She is a child with a strong story sense (or narrative schema) in spite of the severity of her language learning disability and the infrequency of being read to at home. She can adapt her language to be more pragmatically and grammatically appropriate as she interacts with peers. In short, Anita and peers who share her degree of disability show that in certain contexts, with certain situational features, their strengths related to language and literacy make themselves apparent.

Profile Type 2: Mild Disability to Normal Ability. Three children represent Profile Type 2: Cristina, Rosemary, and Gina (see Ruiz, 1989, for a discussion of Rosemary). Some of their language and literacy characteristics overlap with reported characteristics of children with LLD (Donahue, 1983, 1985; Donahue, Pearl, & Bryan, 1980; Donahue & Prescott, 1984). However, these same characteristics have been associated with children of normal ability with culturally and linguistically diverse back-

TABLE 11.5
Anita's Book: "Wonderwoman"

Page	Story text	Translation
1.	Wonderwoman fue en el avión.	Wonderwoman went on the airplane.
2.	El avión chocó.	The plane crashed.
3.	Ella estaba yendo a casa de su abuelita.	She was going to her grandmother's house.
4.	No sabía la casa de ella.	She didn't know which house was hers.
5.	Superman vino.	Superman came.
6.	Dijo, "El avión tuyo se chocó."	He said, "Your airplane crashed."
7.	Wonderwoman dijo, "Oye, Superman. Yo tengo otro avión."	Wonderwoman said, "Hey, Superman. I've got another plane."
8.	Superman dijo, "Mira, Wonderwoman. Allí abajo hay una niña chiquita llorando. Su nombre es Lillian."	Superman said, "Look, Wonderwoman. Down below there's a little girl crying. Her name is Lillian."
9.	Superman fue abajo y levantó a Lillian, y tiró al hombre malo.	Superman went below and picked up Lillian, and threw the bad man.
10.	Wonderwoman dijo, "Mira. Superman ayudó a Lillian."	Wonderwoman said, "Look. Superman helped Lillian."
11.	Otra vez el avión de Superman chocó en el agua.	Again, Superman's airplane crashed in the water.
12.	Superman y Lillian se casaron.	Superman and Lillian married.
13.	Tenían bebitos.	They had babies.
14.	Se divorciaron Lillian y Superman.	Lillian and Superman divorced.
15.	Lillian tenía otro novio. Su nombre era Jose Luis.	Lillian had another boyfriend. His name was Jose Luis.
16.	Wonderwoman y Superman tuvieron 8 bebes.	Wonderwoman and Superman had 8 babies.

grounds (Heath, 1983, 1986). The children in this profile type show more situational variability in their skills and problems with language: In certain contexts they seem to have marked problems with language use; in others, they give evidence of normal language ability. In this article, I focus on Cristina.

Cristina is a heavyset 9-year-old girl who gets along very well with her classmates. She was born in a very small town near the school, the fourth of four daughters. Cristina, her parents, and an unmarried sister live in an isolated and impoverished but neat and brightly decorated house. Her father does fieldwork, her mother seasonal work in the canneries. They speak only Spanish at home. In contrast to Anita's parents, Cristina's parents never noted anything amiss in the way she developed.

The school, however, suspected language and learning problems from the onset. Cristina was retained in kindergarten and deemed at risk by an LSH specialist. She fit the pattern of children in this profile type, as well as that found in other studies of Latino children in special education (Maldonado-Colón, 1984). The school reported a concern that Cristina was not learning English fast enough; teachers also cited problems with gross motor coordination and confusion in spelling, writing, and following directions.

Mrs. Dixon confided to me that an early psychological assessment had determined Cristina to be in the "trainable retarded" range of intelligence. Luckily, by the time Cristina was placed in Mrs. Dixon's classroom, she had been reassessed by a psychologist and two LSH specialists and determined to have normal intelligence with an auditory processing problem. (In certain tests of language, especially those that purportedly tap visual abilities, Cristina scored *above* 1 standard deviation; this was interpreted as further evidence of Cristina's weak auditory skills and her need for visual cues.)

In Cristina's first year in Mrs. Dixon's class, where for the first time she is being consistently instructed in the language arts and math in Spanish, she has jumped up a year as measured by a Spanish achievement test. Cristina's IEP shows that her instruction includes a focus on communication skills, such as using sentences of at least six words in written assignments, and on auditory memory skills through a commercial program in Spanish. The IEP also pinpoints final sounds in words as an area for improvement, along with auditory discrimination of sounds. In summary, Cristina's days in Mrs. Dixon's class are spent working on reading, math, spelling, written assignments, a special self-paced auditory memory program, and occasional articulation exercises, and participating in regular classroom routines.

Cristina functions relatively well on verbal tasks across both the formal and informal events. When she is the focal child in classroom openings, she supplies correct responses most of the time. When she is not the focal child, and the child who is cannot answer Mrs. Dixon's question, Cristina is quick to raise a hand and supply the correct response.

When formal classroom contexts call for extended turns of talk, Cristina is more hesitant, and the teacher must actively encourage and shape her discourse. The example in Table 11.6 takes place during Cristina's reading lesson. Mrs. Dixon has directed Cristina to write an essay on her sister; here she asks Cristina to talk about what she will write. The pauses before Cristina speaks, as long as 27 seconds, are especially marked.

In direct contrast to the almost painful dialogue in Table 11.6 is a storybook that Cristina dictated to me (see Table 11.7). The topic was of her choosing. Her oral rendition of the story flowed smoothly, with none of the long pauses so marked in the previous transcript. Cristina's story includes a minor setting (page 1), a central problem presented to a main character and its resolution (pages 3, 4, and 5); a clear sequence of temporally related events; and cohesive markers that clarify relationships (pages 2, 4, 5, and 7).

As much as our limited time would allow, Cristina proved herself to be a fairly prolific story writer. Her sense of story is good, whether it be an original narrative, a retelling of "The Three Billy Goats Gruff," or a recounting of the events of Halloween night; her word fluency is entirely adequate. Again, these examples were in marked contrast with her struggles in describing her sister in the earlier transcript.

So, with Cristina, the pattern of language learning disabilities is less clear. We found evidence of adequate language skills in certain contexts, yet in certain other, formal contexts for extended talk, Cristina appeared to be struggling with language—the same sort of contexts that are typically troublesome for students with LLD (Silliman, 1984). This fact, coupled with her academic delay of about 2½ years, explained her presence in the bilingual LLD classroom.

This second group of children, children with either a mild disability or normal ability, present the greatest challenge to bilingual special educators. They show characteristics of students with mild language learning disabilities, but these particular characteristics are also shared by normal-ability Spanish-speaking students who are from rural, socioeconomically depressed backgrounds with extremely limited opportunities to use language in ways that the school expects. The Profile Type 2 children in this study all had difficulty with oral and written language performance in some classroom contexts. However, in other contexts they showed very normal ability, such as when they independently wrote or dictated a story whose topic they chose. Experts in the field of learning disabilities talk about the characteristic word-finding problems of children with LLD, for example, "great difficulty in turning his bright ideas into verbal form" (Chasty, 1985, p. 20). In writing the storybooks "El Osito Pandita," "El Libro de la Maestra Enojona" ("The Grouchy Teacher Book"), and

TABLE 11.6
Cristina's Communicative Competence in Lessons

Participant	Verbal text	English translation
Mrs. Dixon	Di, dime algo acerca de su uh:, su uh hermana.	Tell, tell me something about uh:, your sister.
Cristina	¿Cual? Any one?	Which one? Any one?
Mrs. Dixon	Hm-hm. Adelante. Usted [XX].	Hm-hm. Go ahead. You [XX].
Cristina	Rita?	
Mrs. Dixon	Okay.	
Cristina	(3) Ella? Va a:, River School?	(3) She? She goes to:, River School?
Mrs. Dixon	Mm-mm.	
Cristina	(14) Y:. Tiene? Catorce años?	(14) An:d. She is? 14?
Mrs. Dixon	Mm-mm.	
Cristina	Se llama Ana Roberta Jurado?	Her name is Ana Roberta Jurado?
Mrs. Dixon	Mm-mm.	
Cristina	Y:.	An:d.
Mrs. Dixon	(5) ¿Es alta? O: :. ¿Baja? O::. ¿Qué.	(5) Is she tall? Or::. Short? Or::. What?
Cristina	Mediana?	Medium?
(This exchange continues for nine more conversational turns, until Cristina moves to end it)		
Cristina	Tiene el pelo negro? (5) Morena?	She has black hair? (5) A brunette?
Mrs. Dixon	Mm-mm.	
Cristina	Y:. (27) That's all.	

Note. Rising intonation at the end of an utterance is marked with a ? [XX] refers to unintelligible utterances in the transcript. : indicates lengthened syllable (each : = one "beat").

TABLE 11.7
Cristina's Book: "Un Osito Panda" ("A Panda Bear")

Page	Story text	Translation
1.	El osito pandita estaba jugando con una pelota.	The panda bear was playing with a ball.
2.	Luego se subió a la pelota.	Then he climbed up on the ball.
3.	Y luego se cayó.	And then he fell.
4.	Estaba llorando porque se cayó de la pelota.	He was crying because he fell off the ball.
5.	Luego vino su mamá, y los dos estaban jugando con la pelota.	Then his mom came, and the two of them were playing with the ball.
6.	Luego, un niño estaba cargando al Pandita chiquito.	Then, a boy was carrying the little panda bear.
7.	Y luego todos los niños estaba con los Panditas.	And then all the children were with the Pandas.
8.	Fin	The End

"Cinderella," Cristina and peers sharing her profile type certainly found the words to express their bright ideas.

Children like Cristina expose the futility of deciding on the presence of a handicapping condition on the basis of a few testing sessions with a psychologist and speech therapist (Neal, 1993). They need to be observed in a variety of contexts, to ascertain if contextual features of instruction are behind their occasional poor language and literacy performance (Taylor, 1993). These children require the very best instructional techniques and materials available to bilingual students. Only with such an optimal instructional program will educators be able to distinguish between those children who progress rapidly and thus illustrate normal ability (which seemed delayed in certain instructional contexts), from those children whose continued struggle across multiple contexts suggests a language learning disability. These findings indicate that answers to eligibility questions lie not in finding a better, "nonbiased" test but, rather, in powerful instructional contexts (Ruiz & Figueroa, in press).

Profile Type 3: Normal Ability.   Victor and Pilar represent the third profile type. Although they score low on standardized language tests and occasionally have problems with academic discourse forms, records of their language skill across a variety of classroom contexts make the case that they are children who have normal ability and have been misdiagnosed.

Victor is 6 years old. Like his sister, Gina, who is also in Mrs. Dixon's class, Victor was born in the area and speaks English much more proficiently than Spanish. His family speaks both languages at home. Victor's parents occasionally have to leave their children in their trailer as they do fieldwork.

Victor is a very pleasant boy. He is kind, fair, and sociable. He often plays with English-speaking boys from the general education classrooms, but will sometimes play with his Spanish-dominant classmates. On occasion, Victor withdraws from peer play and sits quietly, perhaps manipulating a little toy, seemingly lost in thought.

In the middle of Victor's kindergarten year, his teacher referred him for special education testing. She reported that Victor seemed oblivious to what went on around him. He had problems attending, got lost in group situations, and blankly stared when asked to speak during a class activity. The teacher was not sure which language, English or Spanish, Victor understood best; she wrote that he confused both while speaking. Furthermore, Victor cried easily when interacting with peers.

The school psychologist who evaluated Victor reported that on an intelligence test, Victor attained a composite score that "fell within the borderline range of mental retardation." Victor had no difficulty with subtests in the areas of visual–motor coordination, nonverbal reasoning, or gross and fine motor coordination. However, he scored at the severe-deficit level in verbal and quantitative skills. The psychologist also reported that Victor did not seem to understand the concepts of "more," "each," or "same." In contrast to these intelligence test scores, Victor scored at the 9-0 age level on tests of visual–motor integration and perceptual tests when he was not quite 6 years old.

The psychologist noted that the intelligence test she used to evaluate Victor was normed on an English-speaking population, but did not discuss how this affected the validity of the scores she used to infer a language learning disability or borderline mental retardation. She did list some contributing factors to the delays she found during testing: "bilingual confusion, cultural background, auditory/memory difficulty, and possible hearing loss." (Victor's hearing was later found to be normal.) She also recommended special education placement for him.

A speech and language therapist evaluated Victor around this time. On receptive language tests tapping grammatical and memory abilities, Victor scored at or slightly above his age level. However, on a receptive vocabulary test he scored at the 4-0 age level. Victor also performed at the 4-year level on expressive language tests, including grammatical and memory tests. The therapist scored his language sample at the 5th percentile for his age group, or, put another way, at the mean for children aged 2½.

At 6 years old, Victor is doing first-grade-level work in Mrs. Dixon's class. He also uses a self-paced, taped auditory–perceptual program. He often has difficulty following the instructions on the tapes and has to redo them. At times, Victor receives special small-group instruction in problem areas, such as formulating *who* and *what* questions, and using descriptive words. Victor's work folder resembles those of the older girls in the class. He writes book reports and sentences with his reading words; in one report card, Mrs. Dixon wrote that he has difficulty creating these sentences.

In formal instructional contexts in the curriculum, Victor's oral language performance is variable. He correctly answers most of Mrs. Dixon's questions during class openings—answers that are very predictable, given the repetitive nature of this event. However, Victor often gives these responses without raising his hand, or when the elicitation is directed toward another child. Mrs. Dixon seldom overtly chastises these turn-taking breeches, preferring to ignore Victor's responses or pointedly thank other children for raising their hands. In small group lessons, where turn-taking is less strictly constrained by the teacher, these problems diminish while another surfaces: dealing with decontextualized and form-oriented language tasks. In the example shown in Table 11.8, Victor must look at an illustrated card and formulate a *what* question, appropriately incorporating the lexical items indicated by the picture into the interrogative form. (The girl in the picture is cutting paper with scissors.) Throughout this lesson, Victor has a difficult time not only coming up

TABLE 11.8
Victor's Communicative Competence in Lessons

Participant	Verbal text
Aide	Okay, Victor, your turn.
Victor	What i-, what is she doing.
Aide	Okay, almost. I want you to ask me the question, something about, this part, right here=
Victor	=Oh, I know, um: What, is, she's cutting.
Aide	Okay, almost.
Victor	Oh. What is she. Holding.
Aide	No: Wha-, say what you said before, okay?
Victor	What. Wh:at.
Aide	What?=
Victor	=What.
Aide	Is she?=
Victor	=Cutting.
Aide	What is she cutting. Okay:, very good.

Note. The symbol = denotes that one conversational turn is simultaneous with the following one. : indicates lengthened syllable (each : = one "beat").

with the response desired by the instructional aide, but also figuring out what was wrong with his attempts—whether it was using the wrong word or using the wrong grammatical form. Victor always assumed it was the former, perhaps because during this lesson the instructional aide did not directly address the children's tendency to use inappropriately the contracted form "she's."

Victor also struggles with grammatical forms in written work. The next example consists of sentences he wrote using his reading words. Victor has already turned these sentences in twice for grading and teacher correction.

1. He got a knife
2. I got live fish.
3. He's alive.
4. I have a wife.
5. I have lot of wives.

6. My cat has life.

7. The fireman saved the people lives.

8. I have 1 leaf.

9. The meat is even.

10. Is he Steven.

11. Is he seven.

12. I has a lot of leaves in my tree.

The view from certain instructional contexts is a young boy struggling with the forms, fluency, and word meanings of the English language in school tasks. In other contexts, however, two of these problems—difficulty with fluency and word meanings—disappear. Figure 11.2 is a story Victor dictated to me and illustrated while in the first grade, in Mrs. Dixon's room. His original story contains the narrative elements of a setting, an initiating event followed by other temporally and causally related events, and a resolution. There is a clear logic to the story. The difficulty Victor had in "creating his own sentences with spelling words" is not in evidence here; he created, instead, a well-developed story with many story grammar elements.

Victor wrote a number of charming adventure stories about whales, lost airplanes, football games, and, of course, Superman. I include the story found in Table 11.9 because of the unusual circumstances under which it was written. Near the end of the active fieldwork stage for this study, Victor "drew" a story: He made illustrations on the cover, title page, and each page of the blank booklet I had left for him in his work folder. Then he patiently waited for the day that I could sit with him to fill in the text. At least 3 weeks elapsed before we had that opportunity.

One effect of having the story illustrated before it was dictated was that Victor's language is not as colorful or specific as in the other stories; he depends on the pictures to provide the interest and detail. For example, on page 9 of his story, Victor dictated only that the police almost shot the robber, but the picture shows a moon, a starry night, ladders going up the side of a prison, and the robber jumping off the building toward his getaway car. Page 11 talks about shooting the airplane down, but the picture shows the robber parachuting out of a burning airplane.

Obviously, then, this story is not representative of the upper limit of Victor's language ability. Its function here is to contrast it with what a speech therapist wrote about Victor 2½ years after he dictated the story: "The greatest area of concern continues to be his expressive language skills. He has difficulty retelling a story in order and organizing consequences logically." "Superman and the Lost Girl," "Cops and Robbers,"

Figure 11.2.   Victor's book: "Superman and the Lost Girl."

and every other story dictated by Victor when he was 6 and 7 years old provide stark counter-evidence to this therapist's report.

Victor's case is just as complex as those representing the second profile type. However, his relative success in formal instructional events, his near-grade-level academic performance, and his strong narrative ability suggest to me that Victor is not language learning disabled.

The children representing the last profile type (Victor and Pilar) show normal language ability if one looks at their performance across a range of instructional events. Pilar's communicative skill cuts across all formal and informal situations; Victor's does not. He often struggles

TABLE 11.9
Victor's Book: "Cops and Robbers"

Page	Story text
1.	One day some police were trying to catch some of the robbers.
2.	Then the police was chasing the robber inside the car.
3.	Then he shot the man and the car jumped.
4.	And he crashed!
5.	And the car started to have fire.
6.	Then the robbers and the cops were trying to kill each other.
7.	Then the robbers were climbing up the ladder. One cop was running up on the building.
8.	Then one police shot a robber.
9.	Then the police *almost* shot the robber.
10.	Then the robber went in the car and he had a key, and he drived the car.
11.	And they shot the airplane down, and someone was trying to kill the robber.
12.	But the man didn't die. So then they took him out of the airplane, and the airplane exploded.
13.	Then they took the man to the car.
14.	Then the police put the robber in jail.

according to the degree of context-embeddedness of the classroom event, but at other times he excels in decontextualized tasks, such as conceiving creative, well-developed narratives. There is no doubt that both Victor and Pilar have serious educational needs. But their strengths in certain areas of language learning ability, despite social conditions antipathetic to the development of classroom language skills, make the case that these needs should be pursued in the general education classroom, not special education.

How did Pilar and Victor end up in a segregated class for students with disabilities? And if some Profile Type 2 children, such as Cristina, also have normal abilities, how did *they* get there? Beyond the reports in the cumulative folder, this study does not have data from the key decision-making events in the past that led to the children's classification for special education—the events that formed the focus of Mehan et al.'s (1986) study. But the school files examined here support their contention that some distorted syllogistic reasoning (e.g., "Men die. Grass dies. Men are grass"; p. 108) is partially responsible for these special education placements. The reasoning that emerges from the school files is as follows: "Victor and Cristina (children with Profile Types 2 and 3) score low on tests of verbal ability and academic achievement and have problems with classroom discourse. Children with language learning disabilities score low on tests of verbal ability and academic achievement and have problems with classroom discourse. Victor and Cristina have a language learning disability." If this reasoning is typically behind the special education placement for Euro-American students, then for students from linguistically and culturally diverse backgrounds, who have an established poor track record in test performance and problems with some aspects of academic discourse, we can expect this reasoning to be enacted with even more frequency.

CONCLUSIONS AND ISSUES FOR FUTURE RESEARCH

For the children of this study, the paths that led to the bilingual special education classroom are diverse. Their experiences probably represent the continuum of educational services, from the very worst (using an intelligence test to assess English language ability) to the suspect (trying to take into account cultural and educational factors that impinge on standardized test scores) to the best (creating optimal instructional contexts in which children can show the upper range of their language and literacy competence). Yet, all the children share placement in a relatively restricted special education setting, a special day class.

The discussion of these three children, based on a larger compilation of 10 case studies, suggests that there may be three profile types of Latino pupils in bilingual special education: (a) those with disabilities in the moderate to severe range; (b) those with mild disabilities or of normal ability in conjunction with certain socioeducational factors, and, finally, (c) those with normal ability.

These case studies seem to temper Mehan et al.'s (1986) findings, which state that all educational handicaps are in the cultural eye of the beholder. Consider Anita and her peers with Profile Type 1: A large percentage of their language is so unintelligible, telegraphic, or delayed that effective communication is negatively affected in many situations. Even people from cultural and educational backgrounds very different from those of the school personnel making special education placement decisions (e.g., Anita's parents) agree with the school that their child has problems talking and learning.

The medical model in special education (e.g., viewing educational handicaps as a disease), which Mehan et al. (1986) and Mercer (1973) criticized, unfortunately does serve as a metaphor for children with very severe problems in language and learning. However, a more critical issue is whether children with severe learning handicaps need an educational setting apart from the mainstream. In effect, the medical metaphor may have little or no utility from an instructional perspective. There may be a problem *within* the student under these circumstances, but the educational treatment need not be different than that given to children who are gifted, nondisabled, or bilingual, when the treatment is enriched instruction rather than remedial (Figueroa & Ruiz, 1993). For all learners, optimal educational contexts may be sufficient to promote optimal achievement.

At the same time, this study lends credence to a critical point of Mercer's (1973) research: that the medical model as applied to special education overidentifies children from diverse backgrounds as handicapped (e.g., Profile Type 3, children with normal ability). These children offer convincing evidence of normal language and learning skills in almost all contexts, with one crucial exception: formal testing situations, even when the tests are in the child's dominant language (see Valdés & Figueroa, 1994, for a detailed explanation of why this occurs).

The present investigation raises issues for future research with similarly defined populations. Case studies in this chapter provide a picture that is in considerable contrast with the school's view of the children (see Table 11.1). The contrast derives from the different sources and types of information tapped. On the one hand, the school relies on the psychologist's and speech therapist's reports for special education classification decisions, reports that are "anchored" by commercial test scores (Mehan et al., 1986; Neal, 1993). These scores in turn are anchored on normative frameworks that assume homogeneity of experience (Figueroa, 1990). All the children, even Victor and Pilar from the third profile type, show problems with performance in formal testing situations. On the other hand, the case studies in this investigation rely on observing the children's language and literacy performance across a variety of contexts. The results further make the case for situational variability in special education students' competence (Hood et al., 1981; Rueda & Mehan, 1986), and the need for observing them in multiple contexts to construct a more accurate picture of their communicative and academic competence.

This overview of the different profile types of children in a bilingual special education classroom has begun to point out some school contexts that might serve to showcase the upper range of children's language and literacy abilities, particularly storybook writing. Such features would include students being able to choose the code (English or Spanish), the topic, and the genre of the book; having opportunities to insert their personal experiences; and concentrating on constructing a meaningful text without a prior emphasis on correctness of mechanics. Ruiz (see

Chapter 12 of this book) looks at three other contexts besides storybook writing to further elaborate on the features of lessons that construct the case for either ability or disability. Taken together, these studies of Latino children identified as language learning disabled directly challenge the educational relevance of the medical, diagnostic metaphor in special education. They also redirect our focus, to the instructional setting and to the construction of optimal learning environments for all children.

AUTHOR'S NOTE

This chapter was supported in part by a grant from the California Department of Education, Specialized Program Branch. The opinions expressed herein are the author's and do not reflect those of the funding agency.

12. The Social Construction of Ability and Disability: II. Optimal and At-Risk Lessons in a Bilingual Special Education Classroom

NADEEN T. RUIZ

Naturalistic studies of bilingual children in special education classrooms are few and far between. Yet, children who come to school speaking a language other than English constitute the fastest-growing group of children in our most populous states (U.S. Department of Education, 1993). Contact between children with diverse linguistic backgrounds and the special education system will only continue to increase.

In the mid to late 1980s, a handful of bilingual special education researchers answered the call to describe and explain what really happens to bilingual students in special classrooms. These researchers moved away from large-scale psychometric investigations and self-report studies of special education, from which it was difficult to understand what students' educational experiences and needs looked like, to investigations that focused on the day-to-day interaction between teachers and students. Most of these latter studies were either case studies or ethnographic studies.

Reprinted, with changes, from "The social construction of ability and disability: II. Optimal and at-risk lessons in a bilingual special education classroom," by Nadeen T. Ruiz, *Journal of Learning Disabilities*, Vol. 28, 1995, pp. 491–502. Copyright © 1995 by PRO-ED, Inc.

Table 12.1 lists these studies and provides a brief description of each. The majority were naturalistic in that they attempted to explain the classrooms in the most authentic way possible, without significantly altering the students' and teachers' patterns of interaction. A few had an intervention component. However, all of the studies can be viewed as supporting a theory that is gaining prominence among special education researchers doing ethnographic work (Gleason, 1989; Mehan, Hertweck, & Meihls, 1986; Rueda & Mehan, 1986; Ruiz, 1988; Ruiz, Figueroa, Rueda, & Beaumont, 1992; Taylor, 1991, 1993), namely, that the context of interaction dramatically affects children's abilities and disabilities. Essentially, the children in these ethnographic studies could look like they had serious communication or literacy problems when lessons were constructed in a certain way, but with lessons of a very different kind, a new picture of the same children's abilities emerged.

The present chapter reports the findings of a study that shares that emerging theoretical framework. The study (Ruiz, 1988) was an ethnographic investigation of a bilingual (Spanish–English) self-contained classroom for students identified as language learning disabled. I spent 20 months in this classroom acting as a participant-observer, as well as audiotaping class-room interaction and keeping field-notes. Based on an extensive review of those tapes and fieldnotes, I identified a number of themes, one of which is highlighted in this chapter: Language and literacy in this bilingual special education classroom are socially organized into various communicative or classroom events (see Note), which can be identified through situational and discourse features of classroom language (e.g., turn-taking). Depending on this organization, one can see either the upper range of students' language and literacy skills, or the lower range.

METHOD

The unit of analysis for this study was the classroom event, a socially organized unit of classroom discourse. I identified classroom events through a two-step process. First, I categorized the database to initially account for every interaction sequence recorded in the classroom. The database comprised 28 day-long observations of the classroom, 32 hours of audiotaped classroom interaction, and extensive fieldnotes. Second, I selected contextual features used by other ethnographers (Gumperz, 1982; Hymes, 1964) to identify classroom events. I then adapted their methods of analysis to describe and explain the particulars of interaction in this bilingual special education classroom (see Table 12.2). For example, "Degree of language learning disability" is not usually a subcomponent of "participants" in ethnographies of communication. In the present study, however, it was an important feature that was highly associated with discourse patterns and interrelated with other situational features, such as spatial organization, turn-taking, code choice, pause time, fixed lexical sets, and so on.

From the audiotapes, I transcribed over half of the instances of each classroom event. The remaining untranscribed episodes were reviewed aurally. I took detailed notes as to whether they were additional evidence or exceptions to the patterns noted in the transcribed events.

Though all the contextual features listed in Table 12.2 were used for the identification and analysis of classroom events, I chose to emphasize certain features in my descriptions. Those features are associated with *formality*—a construct discussed by Irvine (1979) and applied to the classroom by Dickinson (1985). Briefly, formal events have increased structuring of the rules governing communicative behavior. These include (a) increased structuring of linguistic and nonlinguistic codes, such as spatial organization; (b) emergence of a central situational focus; and (c) more consistent *co-occurrence relationships* between language choice and social connotations. The situational features most directly associated with these dimensions of formality are noted in Table 12.2.

The first characteristic of formal events, increased code structuring, refers to the "tightening up" of what is acceptable communication on many levels. For example, during very formal events, students need to raise their hand to get a turn, not just speak. They may be constrained to a certain space in the room, such as at their desk, rather than being free to move about as classroom talk goes on. The second feature of formality listed above, a central focus, keeps classroom talk bound to certain topics. In a very formal event, a teacher may censure a student who talks off topic and thereby strays from the desired lesson focus. The third feature, more consistent co-occurrence relationships (a term borrowed from sociolinguistics; Ervin-Tripp, 1972), refers to the tendency in very formal events to use socially acceptable language forms and tone, or register. Breaking away from this socially approved language is rare. Irvine (1979) related this dimension of formality to the seriousness of formal events.

Using this analytic approach, I found that three classroom events in the bilingual special education classroom align themselves along a continuum of formality, from the most formal—class opening—to the moderately formal—lessons—to the least formal—sociodramatic play. Taken together, they provide a range of occasions for students to display their language and literacy skills.

My specific interest was to look among these classroom events for instances of when the children showed their communicative competence,

TABLE 12.1

Qualitative Studies of Bilingual Special Education Classrooms

Reference	Summary
Beaumont (1990)	Beaumont took a random sample of IEPs from three bilingual resource specialist programs (OLE classrooms before intervention). She found that, in general, the children's difficulties were interpreted without real attention to their previous contexts of instruction, and that a reductionist orientation prevailed in the instructional goals.
Echevarria & McDonough (1993)	A teacher-researcher team implemented a different approach to reading instruction, called *instructional conversations* (ICs), in a self-contained, bilingual special education classroom. Essentially, ICs link text themes to the students' schemata, allow children to self-select conversational turns, emphasize real- rather than known-answer questions, and encourage conversational style exchanges rather than recitation scripts. In comparison with traditional reading lessons, children participating in ICs showed both lengthened and increased engagement, as well as greater numbers of student conversational initiations and negotiations.
Flores, Rueda, & Porter (1986)	Using the example of interactive journal writing by an 11-year-old trilingual (Spanish, English, and Yaqui) boy labeled learning disabled, the authors make the case that there is more promise in instructional activities that are holistic in nature than in skills-oriented approaches.
Goldman & Rueda (1988)	This article cites theoretical grounds for establishing effective writing contexts for bilingual students with learning disabilities. Those contexts include (a) student-chosen topics, (b) student personalization, (c) an emphasis on meaning over evaluation, (d) assistance at a level just beyond students' current levels, and (e) assistance in developing self-regulatory aspects of writing. Data from two studies in two computer-based settings—interactive journals and narrative writing—support those effective writing contexts.
Rueda & Mehan (1986)	The authors studied a Latino boy labeled LD in school and out-of-school contexts. They found that his competence (or incompetence) varied according to the situation he was in.
Rueda, Figueroa, & Ruiz (1990)	Among the OLE teachers (before intervention), the authors found a medical model orientation toward their students' problems (i.e., teachers believed that all their students, Latino and non-Latino, had learning disabilities). Instructional assistants, however, viewed the source of the problems as either ineffective instructional contexts or family difficulties.

(table continues)

TABLE 12.1 (cont.)

Reference	Summary
Rueda, Betts, & Hami (1990)	As part of the OLE baseline study, the authors analyzed a sample of student work products from three resource specialist programs. They identified a reductionist orientation in the writing tasks given to the children.
Ruiz (1990)	As part of a baseline study of OLE classrooms, the author analyzed a random sample of videotaped instructional events along a continuum of holistic constructivism and reductionism. The lessons generally had a reductionist orientation.
Trueba (1987)	The author observed limited English proficient students in special education. He found that much of the classroom social organization and many of the academic tasks actually contributed to the students' poor performance.
Viera (1986)	The author followed the case of a Latino 7-year-old boy, identified as LD and reading below grade level. The boy participated in a one-on-one reading program that asked him to read whole texts and focus on self-monitoring. Post assessments showed that he could read at a proficient level for his grade and made miscues that preserved the meaning of the text. Intervention component included in design.
Willig & Swedo (1987)	The authors videotaped a variety of self-contained and pull-out special education classrooms, examining lessons for student engagement. They found that when students could choose the language of the task, insert their personal experience, and cooperate with others, students were highly engaged.

TABLE 12.2
Selected Contextural Features for the Identification and Analysis of Classroom Events

Participants	Code Choice
Teacher/aide[a]	English–Spanish
Student	Imposed[a]
Language dominance	Elected
Degree of disability	Surface linguistic signs/forms
Space	Fixed lexical sets[a]
Constraints/organization[a]	Syntactic restrictions[a]
Positional identity[a]	Intonation[a]
Relation to event boundaries	Pause time between turns
	Phonological accuracy[a]
Time	Code switching
Time of day	
Length allotted	**Topic**
Relation to event boundaries	Imposed topical framework[a]
	Negotiable framework
Channel	Central situational focus[a]
Oral	Relation to turn-taking[a]
Written	Personal topic
Mixed	
	Message Genre
Interactional Norms	Conversation
Student turn-taking	Instructional sequences[a]
Teacher nomination[a]	
Invitation to bid[a]	Elicited narrative
Student reply	Story
Student initiation	Recount
Conversational structure	Description
Initiation–response	Forecast
Initiation–response–evaluation[a]	
Turn length	**Goal/Intended Outcome**
Openings and closings	Evaluation[a]
Sequencing	Action-oriented
	Invoking of social identity[a]

[a]Identifies features that are linked to formality.

that is, their understanding of and ability to use socially appropriate language (Volk, 1992). Evidence for communicative competence or weakness was based on a variety of aspects of discourse, such as appropriate use of language forms (vocabulary and grammar), functions (speech acts), turn-taking, conversational initiations, fluency, topic-centered language, code switching (use of two languages within or between utterances), and extended turns of talk. Other classroom ethnographies of communication have studied these aspects of student discourse but not within a bilingual special education classroom (e.g., Cazden, 1988; Saravia-Shore & Arvizu, 1992). I was also interested in the occasions when students showed their academic competence. Within the three literacy-oriented events highlighted in this study, students gave evidence of their academic competence when they used written language that was comparatively advanced for them. Advanced features of written language included appropriate use of language forms and functions, fluency, extended texts, coherent texts, and well-developed story grammar.

RESULTS

Over the course of the ethnographic study I identified three profile types of students in Mrs. Dixon's special day class (Ruiz, 1988, Chapter 11 of this book). I based the profiles on the students' degree of disability as they interacted in a range of classroom contexts. Profile Type 1 students have moderate to severe disabilities; Profile Type 2 students include students with mild disabilities to normal abilities; and Profile Type 3 students have normal abilities. As the students sharing these profile types participated in a range of classroom events, certain features of those events covaried with the upper range of their language and literacy abilities, and others with the lower range (see Table 12.3). Following is a discussion of how the classroom participants display these abilities in three events.

Class Openings

Class openings are the most formal event in Mrs. Dixon's classroom; they are also the most ritualized. In the following narrative description of a class opening for March 28, the profile type of each child is given in parenthesis.

When Mrs. Dixon arrives at school, her students follow her in. The children engage in various conversations with their peers and teachers. A few minutes before 9:00 a.m., Mrs. Dixon checks the sign in front of the classroom to remind herself of the language of the day and directs the children to put away their things. The children quickly move to their desks, where they wait quietly as Mrs. Dixon moves to the front of the room, lunch count in hand, and inquires what will be served for lunch. Mrs. Dixon selects Victor (3) "since he raised his hand," to read the school menu from the back of the room. Mrs. Dixon begins to determine which children will eat in the cafeteria by calling the children by their last names, in alphabetical order (e.g., Miss Anguiano, Miss Gonzalez). All answer, "Yes, please."

Mrs. Dixon asks Anita (1) to lead the children in the flag salute. After the salute, Mrs. Dixon moves to the calendar corner, where she

TABLE 12.3
Contextual Features of Classroom Events Associated with the Upper and
Lower Ranges of Children's Language and Literacy Abilities

Upper range	Lower range
Emphasis on communication, not language forms	Syntactic and lexical constraints
Topic choice	Topic constraints
Increased student initiations	Few student initiations
Student-directed discourse	Teacher-directed discourse
Functional use of language	Language use for teacher evaluation
Whole texts	Fragments of texts
Centered on students' experiences and background knowledge	Centered on prepackaged curricular materials

begins to query the children with a set of questions that is asked daily, in the same order. Mrs. Dixon first asks Esteban (1) in English to name the day. Two seconds later she repeats the question in Spanish. After 19 seconds with no response, Mrs. Dixon allows Nelly (2) and Victor (3) to try and help him. Their answers are incorrect. Pilar (3) is able to supply the sought-after response, "Today is Wednesday." Mrs. Dixon continues her questioning about the date, this time selecting Virginia (1) to respond. Only after a series of attempts to elicit the correct response, characterized by pauses of around 20 seconds between each teacher elicitation and student response, is Virginia able to say the date with a rising intonation pattern: "Twenty-eighth?"

Gina (2) is selected next, to answer the question about the number of remaining days in the month. She does so correctly, after being prompted to phrase her answer in a complete sentence. Mrs. Dixon then calls on Pilar (3) to write the day's date on a strip of paper that will be placed next to the calendar, and to tell the class about the weather.

Pilar (3) makes quick work of reporting the weather, while Mrs. Dixon records her observations on the board. Her responses very nearly echo those that have been given in the past on an English day: "It's sunny. It's a little breezy. [Mrs. Dixon writes only "It's breezy"] It's warm. There are a few clouds. There was dew on the grass." Mrs. Dixon thanks Pilar, who goes back to her seat.

Class openings have a marked degree of code structuring of language use, a primary characteristic of a formal event. Students must adhere to the language of the day and either translate responses they give in the "wrong" language, or pass their turn on to someone else. (Only Profile Type 1 children, such as Esteban, are allowed to waive this rule, as in the narrative above.) In general, only specific behaviors, such as hand-raising, will get the students a turn at the floor without censure. Conversational structure is largely the typical tripartite sequences—teacher initiation, student response, teacher evaluation—noted by other classroom researchers (Mehan, 1979). In fact, Mrs. Dixon initiates up to 93% of the conversation in certain phases of this event, and 81% overall.

Class openings also have very fixed topic sequences and lexical sets. If children begin to bring up topics other than the date and the weather, Mrs. Dixon brings them back to the central situational focus. If they use vocabulary outside of the preapproved sets, Mrs. Dixon prompts them to return to those sets, as in the transcript of Pilar's (Profile Type 3) reporting of the weather found in Table 12.4. In that exchange, Pilar was shown that *"Hace poquito viento"* (It's a little windy") is not an acceptable variation of *"Hace brisa"* (It's breezy").

Classroom openings also call for specific syntactic forms. Mrs. Dixon expects certain students, generally those with Profile Types 2 and 3, to answer in complete sentences. Essentially, students in Mrs. Dixon's class learn that in class openings their responses to elicitations and their talk in general is up for evaluation. Class openings, then, are a very formal event that emphasizes the students' verbal performance.

Most of Mrs. Dixon's students tend not to show the upper range of their communicative competence in this event. They produce long pauses and responses that have high terminal rises (ending with a rising intonation)—both features of discourse that make the students seem hesitant. In short, the lexical, syntactic, topic, conversational, and code constraints

TABLE 12.4
Class Opening: Fixed Topic and Lexical Sets

Participant	Verbal text	English translation
Pilar	*¿Hace poquito viento?*	It's a little windy?
Mrs. Dixon	*Mm-hm. ¿Qué es, qué es la palabra=*	Mm-hm. What is, what is the word=
Child	*=Brisa=*	=Breezy=
Mrs. Dixon	*=¿Qué es la palabra?* (ignoring other child's utterance) *¿Qué es la palabra?*	=What is the word? What is the word?
Pilar	*¿Brisa?*	Breezy?
Mrs. Dixon	*Uh-huh. Hace Brisa. Excelente.*	Uh-huh. It's breezy. Excellent.

Note. The symbol = denotes that one conversational turn is simultaneous with the following one.

on language use in class openings paint a picture of limited communicative competence. Class openings possess many features that are associated with the lower range of children's communicative competence (see Table 12.3).

Lessons

Each lesson has features that establish it as a distinct classroom event with its own goals, participation structures, and discourse patterns. But a unique characteristic of a lesson is that there are two subtypes: lessons for Profile Type 1 children, and lessons for Profile Types 2 and 3 children. I will refer to the former as Lessons A and the latter as Lessons B. First, however, I describe what all lessons have in common.

All lessons involve small groups of children sitting around a small teacher's table in the classroom's perimeter to work on either language arts or mathematics. Children not participating in lessons at a particular time stay at their desks to work on tasks in their individual work folders.

Lessons in general present a mixed bag in terms of formality. Teachers organize the space used for lessons, select a code (English or Spanish, according to the school's determination of the children's language dominance), and determine a central situational focus—all characteristic elements of a formal event. However, only 65% of teacher-initiated conversational turns take the form of initiation–response–evaluation sequences in lessons, as compared to 93% in certain phases of class openings. Also, students initiate more conversational turns: 29% in lessons as compared to 19% in class openings. Both of these features indicate that talk in lessons begins to look more like conversational or everyday discourse, that is, a series of initiations and responses, without evaluations and with children, rather than solely adults, initiating conversation.

Also in lessons, the number of student responses ending with rising, hesitant-seeming intonation drops to less that 17%, as compared to 60% in class openings. Teachers relax the turn-allocation system, allowing children to respond to elicitations without formal bidding for a turn (i.e., hand-raising). In general, lessons emphasize students' verbal performance much less than do class openings. On the formality continuum, then, lessons are less formal than class openings.

Lessons A. Although all lessons share the features described above, lessons for Profile Type 1 children—Lessons A—have a distinct character. Following is an example of a Lesson A.

Francisco and Anita are at Miss Chaparro's teaching table for their language arts lesson in Spanish. Miss Chaparro takes out four puppets that the children have made earlier: a letter carrier, a nurse, a policeman, and a teacher. She asks Francisco to put on the letter carrier puppet and talk about his work in that role. Francisco relates how he goes to Miss Chaparro's house to deliver letters. She in turn asks him if a dog is going to bite him today, and Francisco launches into a narrative about being bitten by a Chihuahua. When asked what is sold in his office, Francisco first replies "food" but readily accepts Miss Chaparro's suggestion of stamps, and again begins a long turn of talk, rather hard to follow, regarding envelopes, money inside them, and books that he will give the children and teacher.

Miss Chaparro ends Francisco's turn by thanking the letter carrier politely. She turns to ask Anita, the nurse, about the situation in the hospital. Anita replies that things are going badly, that many patients have asthma. The conversation then takes many unexpected turns as Anita suggests that, as the nurse, she puts on the doctor's shoes, walks a lot, is going to a party, and other actions that are difficult to understand because of her articulation difficulties. Anita's extended sequence of turns finishes with another difficult-to-follow narrative about her real stay in the hospital for asthma. Miss Chaparro ends the sequence by thanking the nurse and calling for the police officer, Francisco.

With a siren-like sound and a lowered voice, Francisco begins his stint as the police officer explaining his job. He asks to see the nurse, Anita, and he and she talk in their roles, with Miss Chaparro occasionally clarifying. When the nurse states that she is looking for a husband and leans over to kiss the policeman puppet, Francisco and Miss Chaparro move on to safer subjects, like robbers and the dog pound.

The last sequence of turns involves Anita as a teacher. With frequent questions from Miss Chaparro, Anita talks of writing names on the board and, again, of a boyfriend.

Francisco, still in the police officer role, threatens to put the boyfriend in jail if he does not have a license for his guns. Anita tries to end her turn by saying "Adios" repeatedly. Miss Chaparro finally lets her off the hook when Anita says that her students have gone outside. Again, Miss Chaparro politely thanks the teacher, and the lesson is over. (Later in the day, Miss Chaparro has Francisco and Anita put on their puppets and talk in role in front of the whole class, to everyone's enjoyment.)

Lessons for Profile Type 1 children avoid fixed topic sequences or lexical sets. There is little restriction of syntactic form. Teachers do not place an emphasis on students' responding with phonological and grammatical accuracy; instead, they simply model correct usage. The conversational structure is punctuated by longer turns from students, facilitating narratives. While the teachers' and students' code consistency in terms of English or Spanish is quite stable, sometimes they shift their register or tone, which lends a playful tone to Lessons A, as illustrated in the narrative above.

Lessons A also stand out as a time when students' personal identities are highlighted. The learning tasks call upon them to verbally encode their background knowledge and personal experiences. When students participate in Lessons A, we begin to see the upper range of their communicative competence, even when that competence is impaired with a severe language learning disability. Students more frequently initiate conversational turns, produce longer turns of speech, and produce a greater range of language forms (statements, questions, imperatives) and functions (describing, explaining, negotiating, etc.).

In Lessons A, the children's enhanced communicative competence co-occurs with certain contextual features of the event, including (a) activities centered on students' background knowledge and experiences; (b) opportunities for verbal activity versus passivity (student initiations, longer conversational turns, greater range of functions and forms); and (c) an emphasis on communicating meaningful messages, not on language forms. Thus, Lessons A suggest optimal features of classroom events—"optimal" because they are associated with Latino students' showing the upper range of their communicative skills (see Table 12.3, left-hand column).

Lessons B.   Quite another type of lesson occurs with children sharing Profile Types 2 and 3. Here, Victor (Profile Type 3) and Nelly (Profile Type 2) participate in a reading lesson. An example of a Lesson B follows.

After the first recess, Nelly and Victor are called to Mrs. Dixon's teaching table. Mrs. Dixon has written the following words on the board: Column 1—*I'll, We'll, the seal, I, the meat, me;* Column 2—*fry, fly, sees.* Mrs. Dixon first provides an example, *I'll fly,* and then asks the children to write sentences using these words from the two columns. Victor writes, *The seal sees. We'll fly. I fly.* Nelly writes, *The seal sees. I fly. sees the seal. fly I'll we'll.*

Mrs. Dixon notices Nelly's last few sentences and requests repeatedly, "Tell me what you're doing." When Nelly does not reply, Mrs. Dixon shows her how to begin with the first column. Nelly erases her last sentences and begins to write another, *We'll the seal.* Mrs. Dixon asks her to read the first word in her new sentence (*we'll*) and Nelly guesses first *wagon,* then *lamp.* Mrs. Dixon instructs her to stop guessing. When Nelly starts to slowly say *wagon* again, Mrs. Dixon snaps her fingers and says, "Get *wagon* out of your mind, okay?" Nelly reads, "We'll."

Mrs. Dixon asks Victor and Nelly to read their first and second sentences, which she approves. Then Nelly reads her third sentence, *sees the seal.* Mrs. Dixon acknowledges Nelly's good idea for a sentence, "See the seal," but explains that the word in the column is *sees* and she must use *sees* not *see*.

Mrs. Dixon notices that the children have not used *the meat* or *fry*. She asks for a sentence with these words and Nelly excitedly suggests, "Fry the egg" and "I fry eggs." Mrs. Dixon rejects these sentences because *egg* is not currently a reading word for Nelly and Victor. After an 8-second pause, Nelly offers again, "Fry the egg," to which Mrs. Dixon replies, "Nelly, get eggs out of your mind." Nelly suggests "eggs" one final time during the following sequence, but finally comes up with "the meat."

Victor informs Mrs. Dixon that he has finished another sentence: *Sees me*. Mrs. Dixon writes *see* next to *sees* and asks Victor if they are the same. He says no and is told, "That's why we can't use this word (*see*) in the sentence." Nelly, too, has trouble with her next sentence, *I fry I meat*, but Mrs. Dixon helps her insert *the* and praises her good idea for a sentence. Mrs. Dixon then gives a few more examples of combinations the children could have used. Mrs. Dixon moves to end the lesson with an extended turn.

> This is how we can use, in sentences, the words that we've already had in reading. In our reading book, okay? So, we usually don't need to look for more words that we don't know how to spell. We can just use all the words, the ones we've already had in our reading lessons. And use them to make the sentences because you already know how to spell those words.

The narrative above portrays an obviously different subtype of lesson than the one described earlier. The most distinguishing characteristic is the lexical and syntactic constraints. For example, when Victor and Nelly use a word or inflected form not on their reading list (*see* instead of *sees*), Mrs. Dixon does not accept their contributions. In essence, the children in this context are asked to construct meaning given a limited set of grammatical and lexical tools. The process entails the teacher first giving the form in which the students' response is to be fashioned, and then asking them to construct meaning using that form. Many of the children's struggles with language emerge with this distinctive feature of Lessons B. In the transcript shown in Table 12.5, Victor tries to formulate a sentence with the word "mine." At the end of this lesson, Mrs. Dixon tries to protect Victor from problems similar to the above with the seatwork task she will assign—writing sentences with their reading words: "The words in 3 and 4 you need to write sentences for. Victor, you be very careful with words like *sneeze* and *please* that you don't use *he* with these words. Or *she*. Okay?"

Using *sneeze* with *he* results in the ungrammatical *He sneeze*. In this lesson and others revolving around reading words, it is not an option to add an "s" to make *sneezes;* the reading word is *sneeze* and that is the word

TABLE 12.5
Lexical Constraints in Lessons B

Participant	Verbal text
Victor	Um: I'll say. That's is my recorder.
Mrs. Dixon	No, the word is mi:ne, Victor.
Nelly	Look at mine.
Mrs. Dixon	(Ignores Nelly's suggestion.) (8½ second pause) Can't say that is my. (2-second pause) Nelly, hold your feet still.
Victor	That book is mine?
Mrs. Dixon	That book is mine, sure. That book is mine. Uh-huh.

Note. : indicates lengthened syllable (each : = one "beat").

that must be used in the sentence. As it happens, I collected Victor's sentences the following week and found that he had written the following: *He's sneeze.*

The lessons taught here certainly go beyond how to decode, spell, and use "sneeze" in a sentence. These excerpts from Lessons B suggest a particular view of learning to read, write, and speak, one that stresses the importance of linguistic form over meaning. Linguistic forms become the focus in these lessons. They are broken down and separated from contexts with real communicative intent. They are practiced until the children's "bad" language habits become "good" ones.

The behaviorist, or reductionist (Poplin, 1988a), model of instruction is easy to detect here. This is not surprising: That model, with its emphasis on behavioral objectives and behavior modification, pervades much of special education instruction. But the behaviorist model ignores important developmental aspects of language and literacy learning. It does not recognize certain "bad" behaviors, or "errors," as simply developmental indicators of language and literacy learning. Furthermore, the behaviorist model of teaching is in direct opposition to current thought on learning to read, write, and speak a second language (Cambourne & Turbill, 1987; Freeman & Freeman, 1992).

There is no doubt that in Lessons B the students are learning an important message tied to academic success: The written form of language must be specific and precise. Essayistic forms of discourse possess these characteristics; children struggling with oral and written aspects of academic discourse seldom do. But again, most of the recent work on helping children become more proficient in using academic discourse emphasizes how the students must build a bridge to the school's communication and literacy events with their own ways of speaking, their own experiences, and their own cultural organization (Au, 1993; Heath, 1983). Lessons A seem to actively build that bridge to children's background knowledge and personal experiences. Lessons B assume that the bridge is in place when children are ready to read and write, and that it no longer needs to be addressed.

Participation in either lesson type has direct and important consequences for the children's language and literacy lessons. In Lessons A, children learn that their personal experiences and knowledge have an important place in the learning task. The talk in this lesson type revolves around it, as do art and dramatic activities. The children practice longer turns of talk, with less emphasis on appropriate phonological or grammatical form, or on a fixed topic sequence. But there is no direct link to reading and writing in Lessons A; children do not write down their ideas or see words being written down by the teachers, nor do they hear the conventions and purposes of written forms discussed or instructed.

Lessons B, on the other hand, offer powerful literacy lessons on the importance and specificity of texts. They emphasize fixed lexical and topical sets and accuracy of phonological and grammatical form. But Lessons B have little relation to the children's ways of using language for making meaning or to encoding their background experiences into writing and reading texts. The forms, constraints, and meaning of the curricular materials take precedence. Lessons B contain many features associated with the lower range of students' communicative and academic competence (see Table 12.3, right-hand column).

In stark contrast to Lessons B, another event in Mrs. Dixon's class—storybook making—shows us the upper range of the students' literacy skills (see Ruiz, Chapter 11 of this book, for a description of this event and student work samples emerging from it). Briefly, Mrs. Dixon encourages her students to make storybooks when they finish independent work in their work folder. They actively choose their own topics, code, syntax, and vocabulary. They create whole texts, inserting their personal experience and background knowledge. The product, the book, is not solely for teacher evaluation of their language and literacy skills. It has a real-life function: It goes on the class bookshelf as a book to be enjoyed by peers and parents. Essentially, this event contains all the features located in the left-hand column of Table 12.3. It is also an event that showcases the sometimes surprising abilities of the students even when they have a severe language learning disability (Ruiz, Chapter 11 of this book).

It is important to note that when I began this study, the bilingual special education classroom was only in its second year of operation. In the time since then, Mrs. Dixon has reported to me that she has radically changed her reading and writing curricula lessons to look much more like storybook making. So, although this section is critical of Lessons B in terms of this study, Mrs. Dixon and her colleagues have shifted their instructional practices in the direction of optimal instruction for Latino children in special education (Ruiz, García, & Figueroa, 1995).

Mrs. Dixon made substantive changes in her approach to literacy instruction, but many other teachers have not. Recent research points out that special education classrooms with high concentrations of Latino children continue to provide instructional services that are highly reductionist in nature (Rueda, Betts, & Hami, 1990; Ruiz, 1990). Further, even general education teachers assign such writing tasks as creating sentences or stories with spelling words, and, for a number of students, this demand to construct meaning with fixed lexical and syntactic constraints creates a risk context: Students are at risk of showing a lesser level of language and literacy competence.

Sociodramatic Play

Mrs. Dixon proved to be a highly innovative teacher in another classroom event. She encouraged her students, both before school and at certain times during the school day, to engage in sociodramatic play. Sociodramatic play occurs when two or more children engage in thematic pretend play based on their experiences, that is, act as if they are another person, animal, or object (Sachs, Goldman, & Chaille, 1985; Stern, 1984).

Sociodramatic play is an informal context for language and literacy learning in Mrs. Dixon's class. It is also a time when the upper range of her students' communicative competence emerges. In the following narrative I describe a sociodramatic play occurring after a celebratory lunch for having filled a jar with marbles, each marble representing a good behavior.

Narrative of a Sociodramatic Play, "La Tiendita" ("The Store"). Mrs. Dixon's class is having a party today because the marble jar is filled. The children and adults have brought food for a luncheon buffet. Mrs. Dixon says that after lunch they may play store.

Mrs. Dixon and Miss Chaparro busy themselves at their desks while the children begin their play. The older girls, Rosemary, Cristina, Pilar, and Gina, begin moving tables and books to set up the store. Anita asks me to help her make money out of little pieces of paper she has cut, which she promptly gives to Nelly. Pilar directs Anita to give some money to Francisco. Pilar also begins a conversation with me, labeling and explaining her props for the play: pads of paper for the receipts she will write out, a box for the cash register. Amid the bustling and conversation, Mrs. Dixon jokes with me about her unnecessary presence from across the room, saying that she will be back around 3:00, at the end of the school day.

Preparations continue, with Pilar asking Rosemary about the sign they had made a few days earlier which says *Abierto* (Open) on one side and *Cerrado* (closed) on the other. Pilar remembers that she took it home in her purse and Rosemary directs her to enlist my help in making a new one.

During these preparations, Rosemary responds to Cristina's and Pilar's questions about roles, boundaries, and procedures. For example, she says that Cristina will be the person in the back of the store who gives the prices over the intercom system when there is no tag on the item.

Nelly, in the meantime, flits back and forth between the store and the money-making table. When she suggests that there be more than one store, Rosemary informs her that no, there will be only one store with different cash registers. However, Gina begins to make her own *Abierto/Cerrado* sign. This sparks questions about the owner of the store and whether there is one owner or two. An argument ensues between Pilar and Gina, with Pilar asserting that there is only one central store and Gina that she has her own separate store. Gina wins.

Mrs. Dixon lets the children know that they may line up for some soda. A while later, Miss Chaparro informs them that she has a 7-Up store and that she charges for sips. Most of the children collect their drinks and move back to the stores.

Anita is solicited by Pilar, Nelly, and Virginia as a purchaser of books. Later, she and Victor try to enter Gina's store, only to find out that it is closed. Victor respects Gina's directive but Anita does not (Gina occasionally complains about Anita throughout the episode).

When the stores officially open, Rosemary makes the whirring and beeping sound of computerized cash registers. Nelly tries to buy a Bambi book from Pilar, but when she is told that it costs $100, Nelly replies "*Híjole, no!*" ("Heavens, no!"), and Pilar quickly lowers the price to $1, even giving change. Mrs. Dixon and I overhear, and laugh and comment about the exchange. Soon after, Anita tries to buy a book from Pilar. Pilar tells her that the price is $2, and Anita tries to imitate the previous interaction by replying, "*Ay, no.*" It is not successful in getting the reaction that Nelly and Pilar's exchange did. Pilar says that $2 is not very much money. Anita walks away without her book.

Later, Anita once again wants to buy a book. Pilar states the price, $100, and Anita says to give her two. Now Pilar tells her that $100 is a lot of money and that she does not have enough. Anita again walks away without a purchase.

Early on, Francisco states that he is going to rob the stores, but he is repelled by the store owners. Esteban enters as a drunk and accidentally knocks over one of the girls' sodas. Amid giggles and shushing sounds, the girls and I clean up the mess.

Victor enters Pilar's store through "the back." Pilar, who is very Spanish dominant, chases Victor out with, "Get out of here, you runt!" The rest of "La Tiendita" alternates between play in role and negotiation about the play.

The informality of sociodramatic play manifests itself in many ways. The children can decide on the use of space. Adults do not control turn-taking or the topic framework; in fact, their participation is usually invited by the students. No teacher initiation–student response–teacher evaluations occur. There are no fixed lexical sets or syntactic constraints. Teachers do not impose code choice, nor do they group children by language dominance. In this heterogeneous, bilingual setting, the result is a fluid and dynamic use of both languages, called "code switching." Even when students are not yet very proficient in their second language, sociodramatic play encourages them to use the language as they move along with the others through the play. For example, In "La Tiendita," the very-English-dominant Gina writes her store sign in Spanish and chases Anita out of her store in Spanish, too.

Another aspect of code structuring concerns intonation patterns of student responses to teacher elicitations. Numerous terminal-rise responses are an important indicator of the relative degree of formality of events; they are tied to the children's responsibility to perform verbally for teacher evaluation. In sociodramatic play, this high-pitch pattern never occurs. Teachers and aides seldom make elicitations in this event, and on the minute number of occasions that they do, students always respond with a natural, falling-pitch pattern typical of everyday conversation. Obviously, this event does not emphasize the evaluation of student verbal performance. Intonation patterns are one of many ways that this is made clear.

During sociodramatic play, the students also show their control over different speech registers associated with the different roles they play. In another occurrence of this event, playing house, Anita and Virginia give their version of baby talk (high-pitched whining and telegraphic utterances), while Nelly is alternately a directing mother with crisp orders for her pack of children going off to school or a sympathetic caretaker using very high-pitched talk as she soothes their crying. In "La Tiendita," Nelly and Pilar very politely use the *usted* form of address (connoting distance or formality in Spanish), until Nelly learns the stiff price of the Bambi book and responds with an interjection and suprasegmental pattern typical of informal contexts of talk in the local community. Francisco and Esteban take on the pitch patterns occasionally heard among men in their community: They lower their voice and use an emphatic pitch pattern noted among Spanish speakers from Mexico (Cruttendon, 1986).

In general, the children make use of speech registers typical of their (home) communities in sociodramatic play. Some, like Nelly and Pilar, exhibit a wide range of registers; others, like Virginia and Esteban, both Profile Type 1 children, show less variety across their roles in sociodramatic play. The latter group may lack skill with the structure and lexicon of the language, as when Anita says, "*¿Qué número esto?*" (What number this?") instead of "*¿Cuanto cuesta?*" ("How much is it?"). This group might also lack the social knowledge behind speech registers that comes from observing their parents interact frequently with secondary institutions, such as banks (Heath, 1986). Scripts such as these are important elements for successful sociodramatic play (Sachs et al., 1985).

The "La Tiendita" narrative also illustrates how cooperation is crucial to this play and how that, in turn, affects language interaction (Heath, 1985; Pellegrini, 1985). Even children who are not normally sought after as playmates, such as Anita and Francisco (Profile Type 1 children), become important. The older girls need book buyers, so Anita is called over to enter their store, and Francisco is given money without his asking. In sociodramatic play, Profile Type 1 children are engaged in language practice with more proficient language users.

In summary, this study supports others' contentions that older children (over age 4) engage in fantasy play that is highly symbolic, and that the symbolic nature creates potentially ambiguous situations (Pellegrini, 1985). During sociodramatic play, children in this classroom use elaborated language to explain object and person transformations that occur during pretend play. In a sense, they tell a story (Heath, 1982); they construct a fantasy narrative line that is related temporally and causally, with language that reflects these connections (Sachs et al., 1985). Thus, sociodramatic play is a good display of explicit language, an important component of academic discourse. It is also an excellent display of what children know about the range of language forms and use in their homes and community. Finally, sociodramatic play is a good source of peer language and experiential teaching under meaningful and motivating conditions. For play to continue smoothly, breakdowns in these areas have to be repaired. The payoff is not only immediate, that is, making a successful conversational interchange during the event, it is also long term: Children with LLD are given lessons from their more language-proficient and socially skilled peers on the forms and uses of language, along with the associated background knowledge needed to communicate with nonintimates in contexts outside of school. Classroom instructional contexts that share characteristics of sociodramatic play and, by extension, the features listed in the left-hand column in Table 12.3, will likely constitute a similar optimal context. Cooperative learning is a natural example.

Sociodramatic play in this bilingual special education classroom provided a look at the language use of Latino children identified as language learning disabled that is unique in two ways—ways that are associated with some fundamental problems in bilingual special education. First, sociodramatic play is an excellent context for viewing the upper range of the students' language skills. This context dramatically differs from the context usually used to ascertain Latino children's language abilities— standardized tests. Scores are almost invariably low due to myriad social factors affecting the validity of these tests with the U.S. Hispanic population (Figueroa, 1990; Ruiz, 1987). The tests provide little information as to the range of language forms and functions these children are capable of using in social situations other than testing or formal academic ones, all of which have very different participation structures and ways of using language than those at home. With regard to this study's theme of abilities covarying with context, sociodramatic play is a peer-structured event that allows for verbal participation patterns different from those in any other event-patterns that add to the picture of the student's language abilities. The event features of sociodramatic play overlap with those listed in the left-hand column of Table 12.3—features associated with the upper range of students' abilities.

Second, this study supports Figueroa's (1993) contention that in optimal contexts, individual differences are even more clearly displayed. Even in this informal, peer-directed event, children with severe LLD give evidence of their language learning disability by less frequent verbal participation and more instances of communication breakdowns needing repairs. Observations of sociodramatic play can confirm diagnostic and other educational decisions; however, they can also call them into question. Records of Pillar's verbal participation during this event make the label originally applied to her, "a nonverbal child," seem ludicrous. Rosemary's and Nelly's records call into question the decision to teach them language arts and math solely in English: Their Spanish is more grammatically correct and more varied in its style and function. (Readers should remember that Rosemary and Nelly are exposed to Spanish every other day through Mrs. Dixon's alternate-day approach.)

CONCLUSION

In Mrs. Dixon's bilingual special education class there is a range of ways in which the children use their language and literacy skills, from the teacher-structured, formal class openings to the student-structured, informal sociodramatic play. Examining this range led to the identification of classroom contexts that revealed both the upper range and lower range of the children's language and literacy skills. For teachers and assessment personnel alike, features associated with the upper range of student language and academic competence are critical to creating optimal learning environments—optimal in that they paint a more valid picture of student ability and lead to accelerated student progress.

This study of Mrs. Dixon's class was the catalyst for selecting the instructional strategies for the OLE Project. Charged with developing an effective curriculum for Spanish-speaking students in learning handicapped programs, I sought out instructional techniques that aligned themselves with the optimal features identified in this study, as well as those emerging from the studies listed in Table 12.1. Some of those strategies are Interactive Journals, Writer's Workshop, Shared Reading with Predictable Books, Literature Study, and Drop Everything and Read (D.E.A.R.) Time (Ruiz, García, & Figueroa, 1995). Far from selecting these instructional techniques at random or from passing bandwagons, the OLE Project used research from bilingual special education classrooms to collaboratively construct, with teachers, optimal learning environments for students.

Besides the possible help this study may lend to the applied realm of special education, it has something to say about theory and paradigms. It suggests that those who view learning abilities and disabilities as internal to students, without acknowledging their powerful interaction with the situational context (essentially, the medical model view), would have trouble explaining the varying pictures of children's language and learning abilities. Those subscribing to a contextual performance view (e.g., Ruiz, Rueda, Figueroa, & Boothroyd, Chapter 23) would have no trouble.

This study also suggests that those who favor reducing the curriculum to smaller fragments (essentially, the reductionist paradigm; see Poplin 1988a) would have trouble explaining why the Latino children in this study in fact did poorly in instructional contexts with reductionist features. Those observing the success of special education students, second-language learners, and bilingual learners in holistic–constructivist contexts (Poplin, 1988b) would have no trouble.

Depending on their organization, classroom lessons can either put bilingual children at risk or optimize their language and literacy performance. We need continued classroom research on the social organization of language and learning among bilingual children receiving special education services. These studies will add to and refine our knowledge of the contextual features of language and learning that showcase bilingual children's abilities. They will also help us select instructional strategies with a record of success with bilingual children.

AUTHOR'S NOTE

I would like to thank Mrs. Dixon and Miss Chaparro, the teacher and instructional assistant in this study (though Miss Chaparro is now herself a bilingual special education teacher). My admiration for them only increased during the course of the study. I especially appreciated the humor with which they carried out their formidable task, that of pioneering what has thankfully now become slightly more common: a special day class that respects and promotes bilingualism. Fieldwork was never "work" in their company. I would also like to thank Carolina Oropeza, graduate research assistant with The OLE Research and Dissemination Project, for her critical help in the preparation of this article.

NOTE

The term __classroom event__ in the study overlaps in a general way with others' conceptions and definitions of the units of analysis in classroom research, for example, __lessons__ (Mehan, 1979) and __activity settings__ (Gallimore & Tharp, 1988). But it draws most heavily from __communicative event__, a term used in ethnographies of communication for describing communication patterns of communities (Hymes, 1964). A communicative event is a sociocultural construct for studying speech that is derived from the community's own social organization. It consists of recurring communication, bounded in time and space, for the same general purpose, and involving the same general topics, participants, language variety, tone or key, and norms for interaction (Saville-Troike, 1982). These basic event components combine to portray the situational or contextual features of communication. I decided to change the term from __communicative event__ to __classroom event__ to more clearly encompass the written or literacy aspects of the events and not lead the reader into thinking that only oral communication was up for analysis.

13. Friendship and Literacy Through Literature

ANNEMARIE SULLIVAN PALINCSAR,

ANDREA DeBRUIN PARECKI, AND

JEAN C. McPHAIL

This chapter describes exploratory research involving the use of thematic instruction in an upper-elementary, self-contained special education classroom for students identified as learning disabled. The literature and instructional activities were organized around the theme of friendship, a theme that emerged as a response to the students' concerns about their own abilities to make and keep friends. This research had several purposes, one of which was to examine the development of children's understandings related to friendship in the course of reading and responding to fantasy, realistic fiction, and nonfiction texts about friendship. A second purpose was to determine what an array of activities, broadly conceptualized as *responding to literature,* would reveal about the students' literacy learning. Supporting these purposes are claims that thematic instruction enables children to form more integrated knowledge bases, leading to richer conceptual understandings (Lipson, Valencia, Wixson, & Peters, 1993; Perkins, 1989).

Reprinted, with changes, from "Friendship and literacy through literature," by Annemarie Sullivan Palincsar, Andrea DeBruin Parecki, and Jean C. McPhail, *Journal of Learning Disabilities,* Vol. 28, 1995, pp. 503–510. Copyright © 1995 by PRO-ED, Inc.

THEORETICAL FRAMEWORK

There are numerous challenges in providing literacy instruction to students identified as learning disabled. Etiology aside, these students may demonstrate a host of difficulties variously characterized as problems of selective attention, metacognitive awareness, strategic engagement, and perspective taking (Englert, Raphael, & Anderson, 1988; Graham & Harris, 1992; Williams, Brown, Silverstein, & de Cani, in press). Perhaps in response to the nature and seriousness of these difficulties, it is not uncommon for instruction in these classrooms to focus on the mechanics of reading and writing, typically in a decontextualized, reductionist manner, which, in turn, constrains the opportunities these learners have to experience reading and writing in holistic and meaningful ways (Allington & McGill-Franzen, 1989; Needels & Knapp, 1994; Poplin, 1988; Rueda, 1990).

Our search for an alterative conception of literacy instruction with special education students has been informed by the tenets of the sociohistorical school represented principally in the work of Soviet psychologists. One of the most important achievements of Soviet psychology in the late 1930s was its introduction of the concept of *activity* into research on the genesis and development of the mind and consciousness. Leont'ev (cited in El'konin, 1972) wrote, "Thus, in studying the mental development of the child we must proceed from the development of his activity as that activity arises from the given, concrete conditions of the child's life"(p. 226). In other words, mental processes are dependent upon the motives and tasks of the activity in which they are involved; they are determined by the place they occupy in the structure of the activity (the action or operation). Two sets of activities are proposed within activity theory: those that are related to learning the objectives, motives, and norms of human relations, and those that shape the intellectual powers of the individual.

Activity theorists argued for the need to overcome the dichotomy between the development of the need–motivational aspects and the intellectual and cognitive aspects of the personality. Activity theorists further proposed that certain activities are leading, or dominant, in the development of the individual. For the young child of preschool age, the lead activity is play. For the child entering school, instruction becomes the dominant activity; and the lead activity of adolescence is the activity of social contact: the building of relationships with friends on the basis of moral and ethical norms (Vygotsky, 1978).

One aim of our work was to create settings in which these two leading activities, instruction and social contact, would assume prominence. Hence, while we were conscientious about exploring story structure with students as a tool for aiding text comprehension, we were equally attentive to the possibilities each story provided for connecting with students' experiences and emerging notions of friendship. Just as the students were encouraged to generate predictions about the story based on what they knew about the characters, or based on what they knew about that particular text genre, so were they encouraged to make predictions based upon the feelings of the characters, or their projected feelings. In addition to writing about the theme of each story, students were asked to indicate how each story enhanced their own understanding of, and experiences with, friendship. In this manner we hoped to achieve an interplay between the two leading activities that mark this time of development and learning.

Additional tenets of the sociohistorical perspective (as represented in the works of Leont'ev, 1932; Luria, 1976; and Vygotsky, 1978) suggest that literacy learning is best understood and approached as cultural practice; the cognitive processes related to literacy are best acquired in holistic, contextualized activity; and literacy processes are constituted in social interactions with others (Englert & Palincsar, 1991). Hence, the literacy activities in the research we report on here were conceptualized as social and collaborative enterprises. For example, to situate literacy learning in a holistic and contextualized manner, retellings were conducted for the purpose of planning how one would tell the story to others who were unfamiliar with it. Preparing a script that would capture the story (where the story was retold using puppetry or a play) required considerable collaboration and negotiation among the members of the class.

TRANSLATING THEORY INTO PRACTICE

In this next section, we will describe the implementation and outcomes of an instructional intervention that was informed by the theoretical principles described above. We begin by describing the special education classroom serving students identified as learning disabled in which this research was conducted; then proceed to describe the instructional activities, the questions that guided our study of how the children responded to the intervention, and a selection of outcomes.

Context

The school in which this class was located serves a population of working poor families, a number of whom had been employed in an automotive manufacturing plant that had recently closed. The 10 children in this class were between the ages of 8 and 12 and were considered to be third and fourth graders. Seven of the children were from racial-minority families; five of the children were girls. All but one child spoke English as his or her first language. Each child had been in a self-contained classroom for children identified as learning disabled for at least 2 years at the time of this project. Their reading and writing achievement was considerably below grade level, with reading achievement assessed to range from mid-first to mid-second grade, based on the results of the Qualitative Reading Inventory (Leslie & Caldwell, 1990). Their writing achievement was also significantly below grade level; 70% of the children used preconventional forms of writing, whereas the remaining children wrote in conventional forms. The literacy program in place in this classroom included daily guided, oral reading from a children's anthology and journal writing. During journal writing, the students were encouraged to make entries of their own choosing.

We had the good fortune to have spent the previous year and a half in this classroom, observing the students' responses to literacy instruction, before launching the friendship unit. Therefore, we were quite familiar with the students and the curriculum. As we studied the journal writing in this classroom the previous year, we were struck by the fact that the range of purposes, and the kinds, of writing in which the children engaged was somewhat constrained, despite the fact that the teacher was careful to include journal feedback sessions and to encourage more diverse uses of writing through the questions she raised in each student's journal. Furthermore, although the teacher used a children's anthology, only 2 of the 10 children were able to identify a favorite story during interviews that were administered prior to beginning the unit of instruction. Our decision to investigate the use of thematic instruction was prompted, in part, by the considerable evidence we had gathered that although there were opportunities that we associate with a rich literacy environment, these children had not embraced those opportunities, nor did they demonstrate anticipated gains in literacy learning.

Hence, the instruction was designed with multiple goals in mind, including increasing interest, engagement, and achievement in reading and writing. We will first describe the broad strokes of the curriculum and then detail the enactment of it, referring to the principles that informed the instruction.

Instructional Intervention

The instructional activities included (a) interactive readings from literature on friendship, (b) personal written responses to the literature, (c) supported retellings of the literature for the purpose of preparing a performance to share the literature with others, (d) performance related to the literature, and (e) journal writing on the topic of friendship.

The selected literature included fantasy, realistic fiction, and nonfiction—all of which addressed different facets of friendship (see Note). Our goal was for the students to acquire increased understanding of, and shared experiences with, the theme of friendship. The texts were also selected because they represented an array of text structures; for example, while each story contained typical story elements (characters and setting), they also were organized using cause and effect, problem/solution, and sequences of events.

The specific instructional activities included the following: In preparation for reading each story, the students generated predictions based upon the title, the cover illustrations, and their developing understandings of friendship. This preparation was followed by an interactive reading of the story (the teacher read the text aloud as children followed along), during which the students were encouraged to comment on the developments in the text and to relate the story not only to their personal experiences as friends, but also with the other stories they had read in the friendship series. The teacher scaffolded these discussions by initially modeling interactions with the story, for example, commenting on how the story reminded her of a friendship she enjoyed, how the story suggested a different aspect of friendship, or how the friendship depicted in one story compared with that in another. In each case, the teacher was careful to justify her statement by drawing upon the literature or personal experiences. Over time, the teacher made fewer of these comments and instead would pause opportunistically in the reading, to give the students the chance to comment or raise issues.

The interactive reading of the text was followed by each student generating a personal response to the piece of literature; the children were encouraged to write about the ways in which the story added to or changed their ideas about friendship. These responses were for personal use and were written using whatever forms of writing the students had in their repertoires, with the teacher providing such support as holding ideas in memory for the child, reminding the child where the spellings could be found in environmental print, and helping the child sound out words that were phonetically regular.

The day after the interactive reading and personal response to the story, the group engaged in a teacher-led retelling of the story. The retelling activity was for the purpose of teaching the students to make use of the story structure to support their recall and retelling of the story. For example, the students always began their retellings by identifying the characters, setting (where appropriate), and problem in the story. They then completed, as a group, a graphic that best depicted the events in the story. Through discussion, the students determined the key ideas or events in the story to be captured in the retelling. Although these retellings were initially heavily directed and led by the teacher, over the course of the 6-week unit of study the students required less and less teacher assistance in generating their retellings.

Following the retelling, the children prepared a script for a performance of the story; the performances varied from a puppet show to a dramatic reenactment of the story. In some cases, the class drew a mural depicting the events and narrated the story, with their narrations assisted by the mural. The purpose of this activity was to provide the students an array of opportunities for making the story their own. Converting the retellings to scripts provided the students with multiple opportunities to determine what was most salient about the stories and how to best communicate those ideas in their own words. In addition to writing in response to the literature, the students also maintained a "friendship journal," for the purpose of reflecting on themselves as friends and on what they valued in friendships. These writings were more extensive than the brief responses made following the stories, and were read aloud to the class for the purpose of soliciting feedback from the other members about their writing and their ideas. To draw the 6-week, six-story unit to a close, the class formed a critics' circle. In preparation for critics' circle, the children wrote their opinions of each of the six stories read, presented their critiques, and then voted for their favorite story, to which they awarded the Class Newbery Award.

RESULTS

In keeping with the exploratory nature of this research, we will address the outcomes by describing a number of observations that emerged in the course of studying the pre- and postinterviews, the writing that the children engaged in following the reading, and transcripts of all the group interactions (e.g., the reading, the retellings in preparation for the performances, the performances themselves). Guiding our observations was the following set of questions:

1. What are the opportunities for students with learning disabilities to learn about reading, writing, and themselves in the course of reading and responding to a series of stories related to the theme of friendship?

2. How do the students make cumulative reference across stories?

3. Given different kinds of opportunities to generate responses to literature, what do these children reveal about themselves, their responses to literature, and their literacy skills?

Guided by these questions, we made a number of observations. Given the nature of our work, we will first report observations using the group as the unit of analysis; this will be followed by the cases of 3 children.

Class Responses to the Unit

Use of Intertextuality.   Hartman (1991), among others, has observed that good readers generate interconnections, or links, between texts, which result in webs of meaning, providing the reader with a multidimensional network of textual resources. Indeed, as we examined the transcripts of student conversation in the course of the interactive readings, we noticed a number of occasions when the children drew upon one text to help them bring meaning to a second. For example, having read (the previous week) the story of a unicorn that gives up her horn to a friend (a sheep who longs to have a horn), Carolyn begins to anticipate a similar scenario for a story entitled "A Place for Everyone"—a story about two elephants, one of whom has pink ears. "I think the big elephant with pink ears isn't happy because her ears aren't gray, but they might be gray at the end of the story. I think the little one is gonna give him his ears, and the little one will disappear." In this instance, Carolyn has transposed two features from the previous story onto this story—the sharing of a coveted possession, and the price of this sacrifice (the unicorn in the previous story does indeed disappear upon sharing her horn).

We are aware of very little work attempting to determine how students with comprehension difficulties respond across multiple texts; yet, the instances that we observed of children making resourceful use of intertextuality suggests that intertextuality may provide both a tool for enhancing the achievement of these children and a richer picture of how children with comprehension difficulties approach text.

The Emergence of Theme as a Salient Feature of Literature.   The question of how children with learning difficulties draw generalizations from literature for the purposes of moving beyond the plot to identify themes, or "underlying ideas that tie the plot, characters, and setting together into a meaningful whole" (Norton, 1991, p. 98), was of considerable interest to us. In part, this interest arose from the difficulties that researchers have reported in attempts to teach theme to children identified as learning disabled (e.g., Dimino, Gersten, Carnine, & Blake, 1990; Guerney, Gersten, Dimino, & Carnine, 1990). In addition, we were mindful of the admonitions of Williams et al. (in press), who have speculated that students with learning disabilities have a lot to lose, rather than gain, from curriculum reforms that move us toward holistic, integrated curricula and instruction and away from highly structured, direct instruction. We decided in advance of beginning the unit that we would not provide direct instruction relative to the theme of friendship but, rather, would use the literature in an opportunistic manner, providing multiple occasions for the teacher and children to comment on and compare what they learned about friendship across stories.

The clearest evidence regarding the development of individual children's notions of the theme across the stories arises from the writing in which the children engaged immediately following the reading of the story. It is important to remember that they were encouraged to write about the ways in which the story added to or changed their ideas about friendship. As we examined the writings across time, we were interested to note that, with few exceptions, the initial writings of the children depicted events in the story. For example, when responding to the first story, 7 of the 8 children for whom we have data (data are missing for 2 children due to absences) recorded events in the story (e.g., "They play and run together." "He wanted to give the horn back to have his friend back."). One child made an entry that might be viewed as thematic: "Friendship is love." With the second story, we see several other children responding in a thematic fashion (e.g., "Friends help each other." "Friends are sad when they are not together."). Toward the end of the unit, 7 of the 10 children were consistently writing about the story in reference to a theme of friendship (e.g., "Friends stand up for each other." "Race doesn't matter in friends."). Furthermore, we were interested to note that in the group-generated retellings of the stories (which followed the independent writing), the children consistently punctuated the retelling with a thematic statement. This interested us because, although friendship was central to these stories, the ideas presented about friendship were implicit, and, certainly, thematic statements were not a device used to conclude any of the stories themselves.

Clearly, any conclusions about these children's ability to identify and build upon themes in the context of holistic instruction must be tempered by the acknowledgment that there are themes in narrative literature that vary in complexity, and that the theme of friendship as presented across these stories may be, in comparison, quite simple. Nevertheless, given the difficulties that researchers have reported in attempts to teach theme, we are intrigued by the emergence of theme in these children's writing, and in their efforts to capture what they regarded as important in the stories to share with others who are unfamiliar with them.

Evidence of Change in Children's Conceptions of Friendship. Data to address this outcome are derived from the pre- and postinterviews, as well as from the journal writings and discussions that were held in the context of the friendship unit. In the pre- and postinterviews the children were asked to identify some of their friends, discuss why they called them their friends, describe how they showed them that they were friends, and discuss what made a friend really special.

There is a fairly comprehensive developmental literature describing the transformation of children's conceptual understandings regarding friendship from childhood to adolescence. Whereas young children (10 years old and younger) principally describe friends in external and behavioral terms (Bigelow & LaGaipa, 1980; Smollar & Youniss, 1982), older children's descriptions reflect more psychological depth (Furman & Bierman, 1984; Youniss & Volpe, 1978). We were interested to note that in the context of this 7-week unit, two outcomes were suggested by the responses to the interview questions, both of which speak to the development of a richer sense of friendship over time. First, across all of the children, the number of descriptors they used in responding to the friendship questions during the preassessment numbered 23. This is in contrast to the 88 descriptors provided during the postassessment interview. The number of descriptors in the preinterview ranged from 1 to 6 and averaged 3 per child; the number of descriptors in the postinterview ranged from 4 to 15 and averaged 7.5 per child. In addition, whereas the majority of responses on both the pre- and postassessments referred to the external, or sharing, activities that young children typically use to characterize friendship (e.g., "They're nice." "I play with them." "We go to each other's house and ride bikes."), postassessments showed a 16% increase in responses reflecting conceptions of friendship that were psychological in nature and reflected the intimacy, support, and reciprocity that is true of friends (e.g., "They help you and you help them." "Trust each other." "Standing up for each other.").

Additional group outcomes included the following: At the conclusion of this unit of study, each child successfully identified and retold a favorite story, using all of the story elements. Although they were not prompted to do so, they each retold one of the friendship stories. Recall that only 2 of the 10 children identified a favorite story in the preinterview setting. The sheer amount of writing in which the children engaged increased significantly; this is illustrated in the cases that follow. Finally, interest in the stories themselves prompted the children to independently engage in repeated independent readings.

Case Studies: Three Children

To further illustrate the children's development of understandings about friendship and their uses of writing across the unit, we present the cases of 3 students. Two girls and a boy, all 10 years of age and all African American, were chosen to represent the class. These children were selected on the basis of having varying literacy levels, as well as differing responses to the activities within this unit. After introducing each of the children separately, we will examine their oral responses to pre- and postinterview questions, a sample of their written responses to a question about friendship, and their selection of themes for several of the stories read.

Tamika was the highest achieving student in this class. Her teacher reported that her reading and writing performances were actually quite close to her grade level, although on formal reading measures her reading was assessed to be equivalent to that of a child at the end of second grade. She participated regularly in class discussions and activities.

Jay was a quiet child, somewhat withdrawn in comparison to the other students. His reading and writing were assessed as comparable to those of a child beginning second grade. Although he struggled with both his reading and his writing, he readily participated when the activity was of interest to him.

Tamara was a child whose attitude and attentiveness to the unit fluctuated daily; moody and uncooperative one day, she could be attentive and engaged the next. Tamara's reading level was assessed to be comparable to that of a child at the end of first grade, and her difficulty with writing resulted in very sparse written responses.

As described earlier, after each initial interactive reading of a story, the children were asked to generate a personal response in writing that addressed the ways in which the story added to or changed their ideas about friendship. This writing was done on index cards and was intended to be focused and brief. We have suggested that over time, the children's decisions regarding what to write became more focused on the themes of friendship, and also become more elaborate and complex. Using our case-study children, we shall provide examples of this development.

The first story, "Morgan and Yew," concerned the unicorn who shared its horn with the sheep. Tamika's responses to the friendship issue in this story was "you can be yourself," whereas Jay wrote, "They are friends and they play games." Tamara wrote, "They was running." Tamika addressed the overarching theme of the story, Jay related his ideas to the overall theme of friendship, and Tamara did neither. Instead, she concentrated on one of the primary activities that took place in the story (the animals did a lot of running).

The fourth and fifth stories in the unit featured human characters, as opposed to animals. One, "Jamaica Tag-Along," depicted the story of a young girl who pesters her brother by tagging along. One day, as she is playing, she is pestered by a younger child who wants to join her. Finding herself sounding much like her brother as she rebukes the younger child, she relents and invites the younger child to join her. The next story, "Teammates," is a piece of historical nonfiction that relates the friendship of Jackie Robinson and Pee Wee Reese, whose friendship persisted in a climate of racism.

In response to "Teammates," Tamika wrote, "Friendship is when you stand up for someone especially someone in that time." When asked what "that time" meant, Tamika said she was referring to a time when White and Black people did not get along and often were not friends. She said it took a special kind of person to do what Pee Wee had done—someone who was not afraid to stand up for a friend when times were like that. She added that being a friend was not always easy. Jay was hopeful in his response; he wrote, "In those days, people did not like White and Black. Now people like White and Black." As he read his response to the class, he added that there were children of all colors in the school and in his neighborhood, and they were friends, so things had changed. With the story of "Jamaica Tag-Along," Tamara, after focusing exclusively on events and actions in the first three stories, now wrote about her feelings as she read the story: "I like when she be sad cause I be sad too." She added to her response a note regarding friendship: "Age doesn't matter."

The last story of the unit was "Elizabeth and Larry." This is a funny and poignant story about a woman and alligator who befriend one another and experience considerable difficulty adjusting to one another's worlds—culminating in Elizabeth joining Larry in his world when the ridicule he experienced in her world simply becomes too much for him. There was animated discussion during the initial reading, and when asked to fill out their cards, the children did so eagerly. Tamika wrote, "I thought it was sad that they threw food at Larry because he was different. Larry helps out around the house." In this response, she speaks to the problem posed by Larry's differentness and comments on one attribute of friends, their helpfulness. Jay wrote, "They were friends. They cared about each other. They could not be apart." With this response, he summarized the special qualities he associated with friendship. Finally, Tamara, continuing to move beyond simply the action of the story, wrote, "They was happy because they was friends."

The children's immediate responses to individual stories provided but one way to trace their understandings of the theme of friendship. After reading and discussing the first three stories, the class began entries to their "friendship journals," describing, for example, their special friends. (See Figure 13.1 for Tamika's engaging response in her first journal entry.)

Jay's first entry in the friendship journal resulted in more writing than he had ever generated on a single occasion in class. As he read his

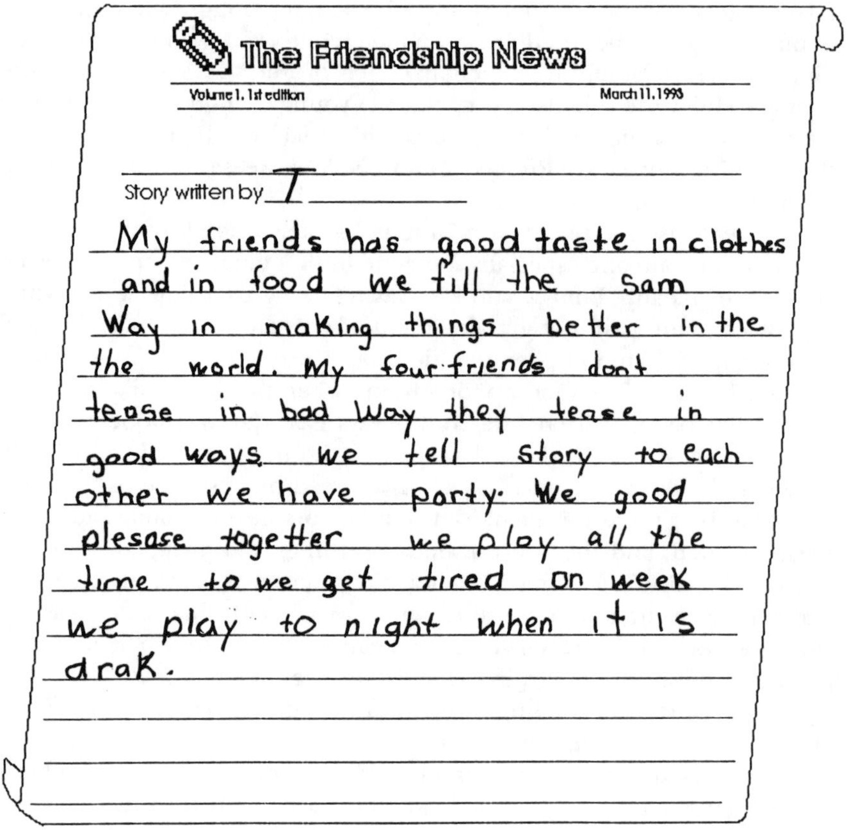

The Friendship News

Volume 1. 1st edition   March 11, 1993

Story written by _I_____

My friends has good taste in clothes
and in food we fill the Sam
Way in making things better in the
the world. My four friends don't
tease in bad Way they tease in
good ways we tell story to each
other we have party. We good
plesase togetter we play all the
time to we get tired on week
we play to night when it is
drak.

Figure 13.1. Tamika's journal entry.

entry, the source of his inspiration became clear (see Figure 13.2). In the journal-sharing session that followed, the class listened nervously as Jay read his entry. The teacher commented that this was the first time that Jay had mentioned in class the accidental drowning of his father, an event that had occurred over a year ago.

In the second of Tamara's friendship journal entries, we read shades of the message she derived from "Teammates." Her entry is given in Figure 13.3. This entry, which is more than Tamara had written since the unit began, indicates the connection she drew from the story to events in her own life: Friends stick up for each other, as she had done for her cousin.

At the close of the friendship unit, before doing our postinterviews, we asked the children to critique the books we had read and vote for the

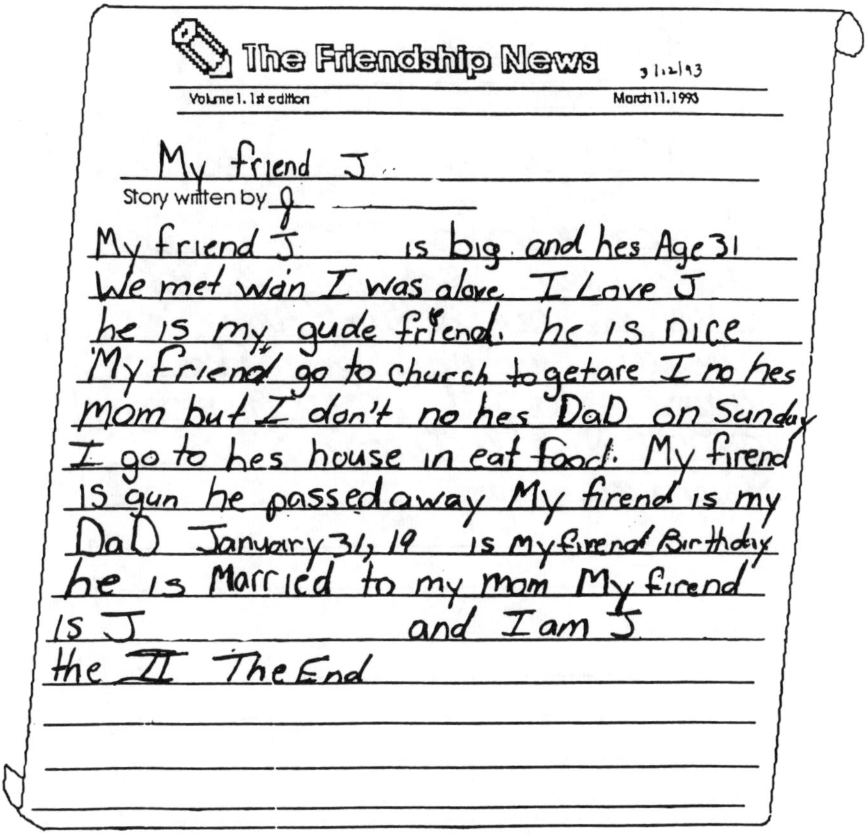
The Friendship News 3|11|93
Volume 1. 1st edition March 11.1993
My friend J..
Story written by J
My friend J is big. and hes Age 31
We met wan I was alone I Love J
he is my gude friend. he is nice
My Friend go to church togetare I no hes
mom but I don't no hes DaD on Sunday
I go to hes house in eat food. My firend
is gun he passed away My firend is my
DaD January 31, 19 is My firend Birthday
he is Married to my mom My firend
is J and I am J.
the II The End

Figure 13.2. Jay's journal entry.

one they liked best and wished to award the class Newbery. This activity was called "Critics' Circle" and was compared to the process critics went through before deciding which children's books would win an award, such as the Caldecott. Although "Elizabeth and Larry" won the award hands down because it was funny, Tamika insisted on explaining why "Teammates" was her choice. She wrote, and then read to the class, "I like it because someone like Jackie Robinson, had got a friend. Jackie was different. He was a different color than his other teammates." Pointing to the bulletin board with pictures of Martin Luther King, Jr., and Rosa Parks, she added that Jackie and Pee Wee belonged with the historical figures depicted there.

As a final assessment of what the children had learned about both the theme of friendship and their emerging notions of story, we con-

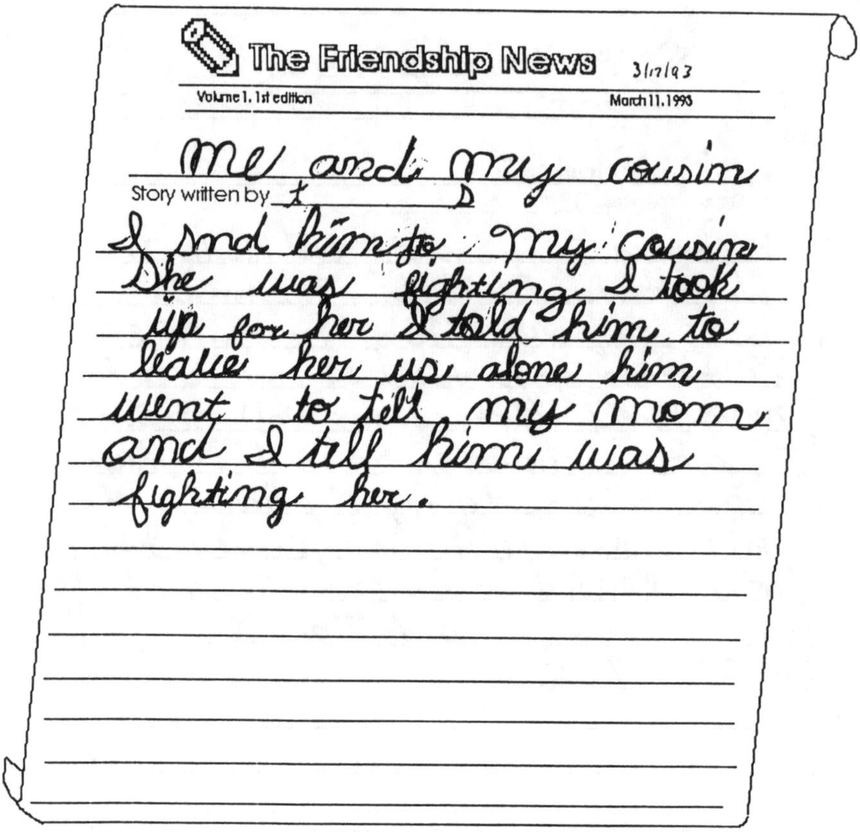

The Friendship News 3/11/93

Volume 1, 1st edition   March 11, 1993

Story written by _t_

Me and my cousin

I and him to my cousin
She was fighting I took
up for her I told him to
leave her us alone him
went to tell my mom,
and I tell him was
fighting her.

Figure 13.3.   Tamara's journal entry.

ducted the postinterviews described earlier. Tamika, who in the pre-interview indicated that "friends were kind and friendly, but some were mean," and they "lik[ed] to sleep at each other's houses," now provided us with an elaborate list of what a friend is and does. She said, "Friends stand up for each other. They have good times together. Friends should be able to be themselves. Friends shouldn't fight. Friends spend time together, play and go places." In response to the probe concerning what makes a story a story, Tamika, in the preinterview, responded, "Good scenes" and a "good ending." During the postinterview, she elaborated that a story has "a name, something that happens, has why the book was written, someone who wrote it, characters."

Like Tamara, Jay also indicated deeper understandings of friendship as well as stories. During the preinterview, Jay described friends as "people who play games together, and help each other when they are in trouble." In the postinterview he suggested, "Friends care about each other. Friends stand up for each other. Friends can be different from each other. Friends are funny. Friends share. Friends spend time with each other. Friends help each other." His description of a story changed from "when you like it and it tells about something" to "a story is a story when it has a title, setting, characters, and tells you something."

Finally, Tamara, who at the start of this unit had said friends were friends because "they play together," in the postinterview responded, "Friends are nice. Friends help each other. Friends like each other. Friends do things for each other. Friends do stuff together."

CONCLUSION

This research was conducted for the purpose of exploring the design and implementation of instruction, guided by the tenets derived from a sociocultural perspective. In the various activity settings that we have described, the children read and wrote for a broad range of purposes, including indicating their understanding of the stories, expressing their own opinions, creatively representing the stories to others, and reflecting on their own beliefs about friendship. They experienced reading and writing in holistic and integrated ways. They assisted each other during activities, sharing their expertise and knowledge. Finally, from a developmental standpoint, the instruction began with the children, both in terms of their concerns about friendship and in terms of their current literacy levels. These would appear to be useful guidelines in planning meaningful instruction for students identified as learning disabled—instruction that is adapted to their special needs without compromising the important social and communicative goals of literacy.

AUTHORS' NOTES

1. This research was supported in part by a grant from the U.S. Department of Education, Office of Special Education Programs (No. H023C90076). The opinions and statements in this chapter are those of the authors and in no way represent positions of the U.S. Department of Education.
2. The authors express their gratitude to Ms. Carol Brozo, who gave us the opportunity to conduct this research with her students.

NOTE

The literature used in this unit includes the following: "Morgan and Yew," by Stephen Cosgrove; "A Place for Everyone," by Barbara Resch; "Amos and Boris," by William Steig; "Jamaica Tag-Along," by Juanita Havill; "Teammates," by Peter Golenbock; and Elizabeth and Larry," by Marilyn Sadler.

14. Whole Language: A Promising Framework for Students with Learning Disabilities

HEATHER HEMMING AND

CAROLE MacINNIS

During the last decade, a whole language approach to curricula has become a focus of research and practice. The purpose of this article is to examine why a whole language approach to curricula in language arts can be effective in meeting the needs of students considered to be learning disabled. First, we develop a rationale by examining the characteristics of students with learning disabilities (LD) as documented in the published literature. Second, the characteristics of a whole language curriculum are outlined, and explicit links to the needs of students considered to be learning disabled are explored. The implications of the analysis suggest that when a curriculum is approached from a whole language perspective, many of the needs of students characterized as learning disabled can be effectively met.

In reflecting on the appropriateness of a whole language curriculum for students with learning disabilities, it is important to first identify what

Reprinted, with changes, from "Linking the needs of students with learning disabilities to a whole language curriculum," by Carole MacInnis and Heather Hemming, *Journal of Learning Disabilities*, Vol. 28, 1995, pp. 535–544. Copyright © 1995 by PRO-ED, Inc.

the typical needs of this population of students might be. Outlining these characteristics is a complex process because an examination of the literature suggests that the characteristics used to describe these learners has varied considerably (Hallahan, Kauffman, & Lloyd, 1985). Because the cognitive strategies approach is the most prevalent model of instruction in the field of learning disabilities at the present time, it is those characteristics most commonly identified within this framework that will be examined in relation to the whole language curriculum.

LEARNER CHARACTERISTICS

Dependency

Researchers have increasingly noted that students with learning disabilities tend to be dependent on others for direction in their learning (Hallahan et al., 1985). On examination of the conditions under which their learning has typically taken place, it becomes apparent that many of the approaches used with these students have been highly teacher directed. This predominance of teacher-controlled curricula may have unintentionally reinforced these learners' dependency. In attempts to help students considered to be learning disabled, the learning process has been divided into sequential instructional objectives. This simplification of the instructional material may have taken away the opportunity for the students to take control of their learning, as a broader understanding of the material is required to initiate learning (Palincsar, David, Winn, & Stevens, 1991; Poplin, 1988b).

Because independence is necessary in lifelong learning, the student with learning disabilities should be exposed to an environment that encourages independence by allowing him or her to share ownership of the curriculum. This would require a more open-ended curriculum, whereby the students, regardless of their background, could experience success and participate in learning activities that were meaningful to them.

Difficulty Monitoring Performance

Another identified characteristic frequently mentioned in the literature is these students' difficulty with evaluation and monitoring of their own performance (Reid, 1988; Reid & Stone, 1991; Swanson, 1990). Self-monitoring is an awareness of whether one has understood a task, be it reading, writing, or a similar academic task. It involves assessing when learning is breaking down and determining what strategies should be employed. Not only is self-monitoring critical to independence (Brown, 1980), it is also crucial to becoming a proficient learner. Students with learning difficulties often fail to adopt a flexible, strategic approach to learning (Reid & Stone, 1991). Self-monitoring typically occurs in situations wherein the student has developed some ownership of the curriculum. As previously mentioned, the curriculum typically used with the students with LD is often highly structured and teacher controlled; therefore, the student is not given many opportunities to develop self-monitoring strategies.

Because students with learning disabilities are often not aware of the strategies that should be employed (Brown, 1980; Derry, 1990; Palincsar et al., 1991), not only should they be given the opportunity to develop these strategies, but they also may need to be given instruction on the use of self-monitoring strategies within the context of their academic work.

Strategy instruction has relied primarily on direct instructional methods for teaching the strategies. However, Reid and Stone (1991) maintained that the type of guidance that is required is not provided through direct instruction but should be"functionally contingent" on the student's need to know (p. 9). This type of guidance often occurs in parent–child relationships when the parent assists the child in the parts of a task that have not been mastered. The parent provides guidance by modeling the correct procedure and encouraging the child to extend her or his competencies. The entire process is one wherein assistance is offered at a time when it appears that the child might be ready to master a new level of skill or understanding. If the child does not take advantage of the parents' input at the time, the assistance is offered again at a later date. This type of facilitation is not as efficient as the direct instruction approach, because it does not lend itself to a predetermined type of intervention. However, in the long run, it may be more effective, because it is linked closely with what the child needs to know. This link to the child's existing strategic ability and desire to learn provides a framework from which he or she can evaluate and monitor the use of strategies.

In the strategy instruction models little attention has been paid to students' existing strategic abilities once it is determined that they are not proficient readers or writers (Anderson & Roit, 1993). In defining strategy instruction as "a thoughtful and effortful mental act designed to maintain existing mental competencies when those competencies are taxed" (p. 126), Anderson and Roit provided a definition that respects the student's existing strategic knowledge. This type of strategy instruction, which puts less emphasis on prescribed strategies and more emphasis on the modification of students' existing strategies, would appear to facilitate students' self-monitoring, as they are actively involved in the process of developing more effective strategies by consciously modifying or abandoning their existing strategies.

Failure to Modify Strategies in Response to Critical Task Changes

The failure to modify cognitive strategies in response to changes in the critical task is another characteristic that interferes with learning (Derry, 1990; Torgesen, 1979). Because there does not appear to be any one strategy for use within or across academic domains (Swanson, 1989), the need to vary strategies is unavoidable. For example, when students are reading a science text as opposed to a novel, different strategies are necessary. If students do not realize they need to alter their approach to a task depending on the material and the reason for engaging in the activity (e.g., reading for enjoyment vs. for an exam), their performance will be inadequate. Although research studies have documented the effectiveness of strategy instruction in improving academic performance, the ability to select the appropriate strategy for a task still remains problematic (Borkowski, Johnston, & Reid, 1987). The students need to develop a repertoire of strategies and learn when to apply each one. The need to contextualize strategies seems apparent. Students identified as learning disabled need numerous opportunities to apply strategies to various academic activities.

Difficulty with Memory

Another characteristic associated with students identified as learning disabled is difficulty with memory. This characteristic has been well documented throughout the history of the field (Ceci, 1987; Mastropieri & Scruggs, 1987; Smith, 1983; Swanson, 1987). This difficulty results in the learner's depending on others to provide the necessary links for remembering material. In an attempt to facilitate memory, there has been a move to simplify material into discrete, sequential steps, but in so doing, the necessary semantic information that allows the learner to make links between concepts has been stripped from the activity (Gavelek & Palincsar, 1988; Poplin, 1988a). When the conceptual links in the information are unclear, the student will have more difficulty remembering the material. This dilemma has generated research on the lack of strategies for remembering (Reid, 1988). Research on the use of strategies of verbal rehearsal and classification with students with learning disabilities has demonstrated the positive effect of these strategies on the performance of memory tasks (Swanson, 1991; Torgesen, 1979). It appears that verbal mediation can play a significant role in facilitating the learning process. This suggests that students who experience difficulty with accessing information would benefit from an environment in which oral language is encouraged and meaningful strategies are modeled.

Difficulty in Acquiring Elementary Units

A characteristic of these learners that is tied to memory involves a difficulty in acquiring elementary units. Elementary units involve such skills as recognizing the alphabet, reading words in isolation, and symbolic representation in mathematics (Reid, 1988). It has been documented that poor readers frequently enter the intermediate grades with a basic sight vocabulary but an undeveloped understanding of sound–symbol relationships (Gaskins, Gaskins, & Gaskins, 1991; Zivian & Samuels, 1986). Even when the skills are acquired, students with learning disabilities often fail to use them in context. This relates to their problems with storing and retrieving information. As was mentioned in the prior description of memory, the students need a meaningful base to link new information to their previous knowledge and experiences. The more disconnected and abstract the material, the more difficult it is to store and retrieve. Brown (1978) cautioned against the teaching of isolated skills without a contextual basis:

> The learning of isolated material for a purpose neither understood nor appreciated is not an easy task for the skilled and far less so for the novice. . . . The aim should be to "recontextualize" . . . early school experiences, to breathe meaning into school activities in order to alleviate the transition difficulties of the disadvantaged child. (p. 95)

Difficulty with Generalization

The next characteristic is integrally entwined with all the previously mentioned characteristics. Difficulties with generalization have been a concern that has surfaced in all the models of instruction used with students who exhibit learning disabilities. These students' ability to demonstrate their understanding of a concept or skill in one context but failure to transfer what they have learned to a different context has puzzled many researchers and practitioners. This difficulty in spontaneously transferring newly acquired skills across settings and tasks has been well documented (Borkowski, Carr, & Pressley, 1987; Keogh & Hall, 1983). Generalization rests on an understanding of the function served by a given skill (Stone & Wertsch, 1984), which highlights the importance of teaching strategies in a meaningful context for these students. Even though students may be able to verbally explain the steps of a strategy, it does not necessarily mean that they will *use* that same strategy. Palincsar et al. (1991) suggested that there is a relationship between "inert knowledge" and difficulties with generalization. "Inert knowledge" refers to the knowledge that students can recall on request but fail to use spontaneously within or across tasks. The work of Palincsar et al. suggests that difficulties of transference are due to a lack of instructional environments that encourage the real use of knowledge. Those authors suggested that a major goal of instruction needs to be the "creation of shared environments in which students and teachers explore meaningful problems that provide occasions for real use of knowledge" (p. 44). These shared environments create opportunities for dialogue that can provide feedback on and enrichment of strategy use for the student.

Difficulty in Approaching a Task Positively

A final characteristic that has been repeatedly used to describe students with learning disabilities involves difficulties in approaching a task with a positive mind-set (Brown, 1978; Hallahan et al., 1985; Weins, 1983). Often, these students approach a task expecting to fail. Their resistance to attempting tasks may be the result of repeated incidents of being asked to perform tasks for which they are not developmentally ready. Inappropriate curricula, based on content objectives rather than the students' needs, have created frustration, failure, and dependency. After repeated failures, they need to have their confidence restored. By recontextualizing the learning experience, the student can begin to feel in control, which in turn restores his or her self-confidence and motivation to learn (Weins, 1983). An environment that focuses on the student's interest and knowledge, while still being sensitive to his or her developmental level, seems essential to creating a positive learning experience for these students.

All the above characteristics are interrelated; each feeds into the other in a highly complex network of interactions. To address these needs individually would be impossible; therefore, instructional approaches for students with learning disabilities should be carefully integrated with the ongoing curriculum, while always taking into consideration the whole child.

WHOLE LANGUAGE CURRICULUM

Currently, in the field of learning disabilities, there is a growing interest in understanding the needs of the learner and the necessary ingredients of the curriculum from a holistic perspective (Cousin et al., 1991). Heshusius (1989), Poplin (1988b), Rhodes and Dudley-Marling (1988), and others have raised questions about approaches to the field of learning disabilities that have arisen from reductionist frameworks, and have suggested that an alternate approach, whose basic tenets can be labeled holistic/constructivist, is more suited to the needs of students with LD. Perhaps the most prevalent form of this approach to education is represented by the practice in the language arts area known as *whole language*. The whole language movement has risen to a position of prominence during the last decade. Pearson (1993) suggested that as whole language has become widespread, there has been a movement away from some of the mechanistically driven approaches. Some have questioned whether whole language is appropriate for all children, often citing the need for more structure and a greater emphasis on phonics (Chaney, 1990; Stahl & Miller, 1989). However, by examining the principles of education that are represented in the whole language approach and how they relate to the previously mentioned characteristics of students with learning disabilities, the suitability of the whole language curriculum for these students can be understood, and a clearer understanding of their relationship emerges.

Child Centered

Researchers who have attempted to define whole language (e.g., Altwerger, Edelsky, & Flores, 1987; Edelsky, Altwerger, & Flores, 1991; Goodman, 1989; Harste, 1989; Newman & Church, 1990; Pearson, 1990; Watson, 1989) have without exception stated, either explicitly or implicitly, that the curriculum needs to be child centered. As Shannon (1990) suggested,

> Whole language advocates still uphold many of the basic assumptions of the child-centered position that G. Stanley Hall proposed during the 1880's. They maintain that children's language develops naturally according to the child's interests in communicating and that self-expression is the goal of language learning. (p. 164)

A child-centered orientation typically means that the child's interests and needs are central to the curriculum. The focus is on the child, as an individual who is a member of the social community within the classroom. The learner's background of experiences, both in terms of what she or he brings to the learning process and what the learner's needs are for future learning, is the key determinant of the curriculum. The teacher's responsibility in this process is to help students to participate in experiences that are within a critical range, such that they can move forward in their learning. When there are minimal links between existing knowledge and the new experiences, growth will be difficult. This is particularly the case for students with learning disabilities, as they have difficulty making connections to their previous knowledge when material is presented in isolation.

Basic to the rationale for keeping the child central to the curriculum is the belief that students do not acquire and integrate knowledge from outside information being given to them but, rather, learn by integrating their existing knowledge with the new information. In other words, for the curriculum to be of maximum benefit, it needs to intersect with the child's world—his or her knowledge base, strategies, interests, needs, and difficulties. When the teacher or materials control the curriculum, the likelihood of this intersection is significantly reduced. Reid and Stone (1991) described the limitations of a highly structured instructional environment for the development of self-monitoring strategies with students with learning disabilities:

> To impose external structure, however, is to avoid the issue altogether . . . .
> When internal structure is lacking, children who are not helped to achieve
> better organizational strategies are at the mercy of others, because they
> must rely on others to organize their thinking and activities for them.
> (p. 16)

Embedded within the view that the child should be the center of the curriculum is the image of the child taking control and ownership over her or his learning. One of the purposes of education is to develop lifelong learners. It is believed that when students assume a position of control over their learning, they will have repeated experiences of making decisions about their learning in a way that is empowering. Through these experiences of being in control of learning in a whole language curriculum, a mind-set is established that results in the learner seeking motivation and direction internally, rather than looking for others to assign the next activity card or worksheet. It is important to keep in mind that even though students are given control in the curriculum, the teacher still plays a valuable and significant role.

For the child who is considered to be learning disabled, numerous possibilities are created. First, as suggested in the section on characteristics, developing a positive mind-set has been problematic for these children. When the curriculum is based on the student's interests, there is the likelihood that it will connect with the child in a meaningful manner, thereby reducing his or her dependence on the teacher. Further, this reduces the passivity and frustration that is characteristic of dependent learners when decisions about what, when, and why learning events are to take place are made by someone else. In addition, when the learner has control over decision making, opportunities are created that encourage self-monitoring. Given that difficulty with self-monitoring is seen in students with learning disabilities, it seems essential that these students be in an environment in which they can make decisions about their own learning.

When instruction is developed based on the students' needs and interests, there is greater likelihood that the student with a learning disability, like all learners, will be able to relate the new experience to his or her existing knowledge. To use Dewey's (1938) terminology, the new experience becomes integrated into a continuum of learning. As a result, the learner takes what is learned in one context and uses this to make sense of a new situation, thus facilitating the process of generalization. This would, of course, be advantageous for the learner who has difficulty transferring what is learned in one context to another.

Language Based

An assumption basic to whole language curricula is that literacy learning involves learning language. As children become effective readers and writers, they learn an endless number of things about how written language works. These understandings are as diverse as how to predict patterns of rhyme in stories, how authors use quotation marks to signal conversations in texts, how the writer's voice affects meaning, and the power of the written word. Because learning to read and write involves learning language, the position is taken within a whole language framework that students need to be allowed to develop the processes of reading and writing in a manner similar to that observed in the development of oral language (Edelsky, 1990; Holdaway, 1979; Weaver, 1988).

When educators adopt the view that children become competent readers and writers in the same way that they learn to talk, several implications for the curriculum are born. Embracing this assumption requires that the curriculum be developed in a manner that is sensitive to the developmental nature of language and literacy learning. When children learn to talk, they are not expected to produce accurate vocalizations that demonstrate command over the language on a predetermined time schedule that is exactly the same for each child. Instead, children are given plenty of opportunities to try out sounds and vocalizations as they attempt to communicate. There are variations in when children talk, but, with few exceptions, the drive to communicate with others propels their development forward. Within a literacy curriculum there is no predetermined clock that establishes when and how children learn to read and write. As Toomes (1990) suggested, age is not an accurate determinant of a child's development. For that reason, the whole language curriculum is often perceived as open-ended (Harste, Woodward, & Burke, 1991). Basically, this means that there would be different entry and exit points within activities, enabling students at various developmental levels to have the opportunity to engage in similar learning events. For the student who approaches new learning situations with an expectation to fail (which is often the case with students with LD), a curriculum that is sensitive to the student's developmental level will help him or her feel in control and, as a result, will assist in the building of self-confidence and risk taking. As Lindquist (1990) pointed out, risk taking is critical to the learning process. To demonstrate that the teacher values and supports children in their risk taking, she or he would need to view what might be thought of as errors in a different light. Instead of mistakes, these errors should be thought of as developmental achievements on the path to gaining control over the process. Plenty of time would need to be allocated for children to experiment with the processes involved in meaningful communication.

The benefits of embracing this assumption as foundational to the curriculum are numerous. First, by achieving an open-ended curriculum that is appropriate for the developmental levels of all children, an experience for learning would be created that was inclusive. For example, during writing process time or literature reading time, all students would be participating in the same kind of activity, although the levels at which they would be working (in terms of skills and strategies) would vary. One student, for example, might be working on a story involving an elaborate discussion of a hilarious family outing using rich vocabulary and invented spelling to communicate the family's predicament. At the same time, another student who had had difficulty generating a connected piece of discourse might be constructing a meaningful message with a sequence of pictures. A belief in the developmental nature of language learning allows the teacher to view both of these students as writing and participating in the same curriculum. For students with learning disabilities, an experience is created that includes their peers, and it is likely that it will be successful, given that it is based on individual developmental levels. This ultimately will affect the student's attitude toward learning.

The feelings associated with being a member of the learning community and the opportunity to successfully participate in a curriculum would be beneficial in helping to establish positive rather than aversive attitudes toward learning. In addition to facilitating a positive mind-set via success with appropriate-level activities, an open-ended curriculum allows for the child to experience independence. As suggested earlier, a curriculum with different entry and exit points gives the student an opportunity to engage in activities when he or she is developmentally ready. This would set up a situation in which the learner could operate on her or his own most of the time, reducing the likelihood that the student would need to ask for assistance or direction; consequently, the dependence on others often cited as a characteristic of learning disabilities is less likely to occur.

Social Interaction

Whole language curricula are based on the assumption that social interactions are critical to learning language. The root of the belief is that all language use is triggered by genuine attempts at communication (Deford & Harste, 1982; Edelsky, 1990; Halliday, 1975; Vygotsky, 1978; Wells, 1981). Reflections on the process of learning to talk suggest that utterances develop out of meaningful attempts to communicate with others. The implication of this assumption for the language arts curriculum is that the learning events in which children participate need to be personally significant and linked to communication. As previously mentioned, the creation of shared environments creates opportunities for the real use of knowledge (Palincsar et al., 1991). In other words, learning to read and write optimally occurs when the purpose is genuinely motivated by communication, between author and reader, writer and audience, or reader and listener, as opposed to a need to fulfill a teacher's objective of practicing reading and writing (Edelsky, Flores, & Altwerger, 1991).

For the learner, the concentration on socially triggered communication provides a conceptual framework within which learning is linked to function. Although this is essential to all literacy learning, it is important to note that it is particularly relevant to the teaching of the parts of language. As mentioned earlier, whole language has been criticized because of its perceived lack of attention to the parts or skills of language. However, the focus on function sets an important stage for examining parts (Calkins, 1980). Take, for example, the use of an elementary unit of language, such as quotation marks or exclamation marks in writing. Removed from the context of trying to communicate to someone that an individual is speaking or that there is enthusiasm and excitement that needs to be relayed, the task becomes abstract. When the use of quotation marks is placed within this act of communication, it is likely that a meaningful context is provided for the learner.

As previously mentioned, children considered to be learning disabled have frequently had difficulty with their ability to generalize use of strategies and skills from one context to another. What typically becomes problematic for these learners is that they learn the how-to of the part or skill in a mechanistic manner, separate from the dynamic process in which the use of the strategy actually occurs. If the how-to is explored within the context of why it is important to the communication process, it is possible that links can be established that encourage the learner to see similarities and differences in situations. The overall result would be a greater chance for generalizations to other, similar contexts. Further, there is a likelihood that the child will understand that different strategies are needed to perform different tasks, depending on the situation. The feedback process, which is integral to any communication, helps the learner to know when strategies need to be modified. The benefit for the student characterized as learning disabled is that within this context, the stance the learner must adopt is one that makes meaning.

Whole-to-Part Relationship

Within a whole language curriculum there is a delicate relationship between wholes and parts of language (Newman, 1985; Poplin, 1988b). For many, understanding this relationship has been problematic and all too frequently has resulted in one of two behaviors. Many have rejected the notion of a whole language curriculum for students with learning disabilities because they felt that working within the framework would not allow them to attend to skills or parts of language. Still others, working within a whole language perspective, have had a phobia about anything that resembled teaching phonics. However, because some theorists have integrated the whole-to-part relationship, the door has been left open for dealing with skills and parts of language (Freppon & Dahl, 1991; Poplin, 1988b). Understanding this component of the whole language curriculum is important for meeting the needs of individuals with LD. Researchers continue to suggest that not all students become readers merely by immersing themselves in reading and writing. This applies particularly to poor readers (Gaskins et al., 1991). These students need learning experiences that help them discover the patterns of our language and use them effectively in their literacy learning. It is important to note that in a whole language curriculum, the focus on the parts of language is attended to differently than in a curriculum established from reductionist principles, the most significant difference being that in a whole language curriculum a child is taught a skill or about a part of language when she or he needs it, not when the teacher wants it learned (Edelsky, 1990). Further, the process of learning to read and write is not approached as a hierarchy of skills to be mastered.

Drawing on the work of Whitehead (1929), Poplin (1988b) suggested that learning optimally moves from the whole to the parts to the whole. She maintained that first there needs to be an initial phase of "romance," in which curiosity and a craving for new information is developed. This is followed by a second stage of precision, which is driven by the need to gain control over the form or details. It is within this context, after the student has become emotionally attached to reading and writing, that elementary units such as letter recognition, grapho-phonemic relationships, and control over grammatical structures might be addressed. Real reasons are created for the student to want to gain control over the elementary unit. This is typified in the case of the young reader who has become convinced that she or he can read, yet wants to be more exact in reading by attending carefully to the print. After the love for constructing the meaning is satisfied, readers start to slow down and allocate extra time and energy into gaining control over the processes of word identification. No longer is the reader content to read by constructing a message based on the recalled meaning of the story. He or she becomes more concerned with precision. In this case, there is a need established to move from the meaningful whole of the story to gaining control over the parts of word recognition. It would be on occasions such as these that the focus on parts would be meaningful for the learner. The recent work of Winsor and Pearson (1992) suggests that when teachers encourage students to use invented spelling (approximations) in writing, a medium is created in which phonemic awareness and phonetic knowledge develop. When students engage in the process of using invented spelling, they have to segment the speech stream of spoken words in order to focus on the phoneme. This information then becomes a base of knowledge about the relationships between sounds and letters that can have substantial transfer value in reading. Further, if the child is not given the opportunity to become attached to the process of reading and writing, there will be little drive or purpose to gaining control over the parts. Poplin (1988b) outlined that the next stage in the process is the movement back to the whole through generalization.

Given the characteristics associated with individuals with learning disabilities, and their difficulty with acquiring elementary units and problems in generalization, the importance of creating the flow among romance, precision, and generalization becomes obvious. In the whole/part/whole framework, the learner gains control over the parts of language, and, as those parts are clearly linked to the whole, this facilitates the likelihood of generalization.

Teacher As Mediator

Another important feature of a whole language curriculum is that the teacher plays an active role, to ensure that the learners' understanding and use of language strategies should not be left to chance. This is particularly important in meeting the needs of students with learning disabilities. This point was demonstrated by Lindsay (1990), who conducted an observational study that focused on students with learning disabilities and those being considered for referral and/or grade retention. She noted that when given the option of either generating a story or copying the one generated by the teacher and the class, the at-risk students invariably copied. Thus, she concluded, they spent a good deal of time each day performing a task with little meaning and little potential for cognitive development. In addition, Lindsay noted the behaviors of children during silent reading time in which they self-selected books: Two of the three targeted low-achieving students consistently picked books that were too difficult for them and had little success reading them. These behaviors indicate that the children had difficulty evaluating and monitoring their performance. Lindsay's research suggests that the teacher needs to play a vital, yet delicate, role in evaluating, monitoring, and facilitating the growth of learners. While students who are considered learning disabled need to experience independence and control, they also need a teacher who is not on the periphery of their learning. This teacher would need to work in a collaborative manner to provide the students with strategies for evaluating and monitoring their performance (Staab, 1990).

There is considerable debate about the nature of the teacher's role in this process. Due to the belief by some that complete teacher dominance has a crippling effect on learners, there is resistance to examining how the teacher can facilitate the learner's ability to gain control over strategies and yet not strip away the necessary ownership (O'Brien, 1987). Critical to the effectiveness of mediation is the nature of how it evolves, because learning how to lead (teach) without taking control and ownership away from students is difficult (Newman, 1991). It appears that one of the critical features of mediation is sensitivity to timing. To be most effective, it requires that the teacher volunteer information in response to what students are actually doing; questions are asked or suggestions are made to those particular individuals when they are likely to prove immediately helpful (Newman, 1991). The instruction should not be systematic but rather flexible, based on the learner's characteristics and the demands of the task. For example, reading many of the books in the early elementary curriculum is greatly facilitated if the child has a rhyming strategy within her or his repertoire of knowledge. Consider the case of the second-grade child with a learning disability who has difficulty manipulating sound patterns in such a way that allows her or him to identify rhyming patterns or produce rhyming words. In this case, it would be essential for the teacher to provide explicit explanations and create learning events that focus on rhyme and the manipulation of language. This mediation would likely be conversational in nature, whereby the teacher might ask questions that would encourage the learner to focus on the relevant details. It is important for the teacher to view students' use of new knowledge from a developmental perspective, so that there would be a gradual movement toward competency.

In her analysis of implications for instruction for students with learning disabilities in a whole language curriculum, O'Brien (1987) suggested that teacher intervention needs to occur along a continuum, from less to more teacher control, depending on the student's characteristics. She explains that the need for the direct or more explicit instruction is particularly important for students with LD. Delpit (1988) suggested that certain attempts at creating a whole language curriculum have disadvantaged some students by not making the curriculum explicit. As she has pointed out, this is a problem, particularly for students who do not internalize the patterns and conventions of the language represented in the classroom, which she refers to as the standard English. O'Brien suggested that to make certain aspects of the curriculum more explicit, teachers must develop "enabling strategies" that encourage the students to extend and clarify their understandings. These enabling strategies can vary from something as direct as a minilesson focusing on a particular aspect of language for students who require more explicit explanation, to something as indirect as changing the material to encourage the use of various strategies. For the teacher interested in meeting the needs of students considered to be learning disabled, enabling strategies are an important construct. When the role of the teacher is conceptualized in this way, it enables the teacher to give specific attention to helping learners become more strategic and flexible in their language use.

CONCLUSIONS

For the last decade there has been concern by educators over how to meet the needs of students with learning disabilities within a whole language classroom. A number of documented characteristics that have an impact on the instructional needs of students with learning disabilities must be considered. With regard to academics, these students have been described as dependent learners. They have been characterized as having difficulty with self-monitoring strategies, which results in problems in identifying when, how, and why strategies are used. Furthermore, these students have been shown to have difficulty with memory and with acquiring elementary units, both of which contribute to their lack of success in specific areas of the curriculum. All of the previously mentioned characteristics are thought to contribute to these students' problems with generalizing concepts, skills, and strategies. Further, repeated difficulties in academic learning have resulted in these students' expecting to fail. Because the needs of these students are varied and complex, special educators have questioned whether students with these characteristics could be accommodated in a whole language–oriented classroom.

However, an analysis of the nature of a whole language curriculum suggests that it does hold promise for creating an effective learning environment for students considered to have learning disabilities. Within this child-centered context are ongoing opportunities for students to have control over their learning, thus allowing them some ownership of decision making within the curriculum. Likewise, in a curriculum that focuses on how children learn oral language, students are encouraged to experiment and to take risks in their learning. This fosters independence and supports the child in the refinement of knowledge. In addition, within the whole language classroom, there are ample opportunities for development of self-monitoring strategies that are critical to the learning process. Also, memory is enhanced in a whole language curriculum, because learning occurs in a context that is meaningful for the child. When the needs and interests of children are central to the curriculum, there is a greater likelihood that the child with learning disabilities will relate new information to existing knowledge. For example, new information regarding the parts and elementary units of language are explored in the context of existing knowledge about communication. Further, children do not learn strategies, skills, and information in isolated segments; instead, the learning is linked to function and meaning, thus enhancing memory and facilitating transference.

When teachers develop curricula based on the principles of whole language, an environment is created that facilitates learning. Essential to this environment is a consideration of the role of the teacher as mediator. Without the teacher playing an active role as mediator, the children will not benefit from his or her expertise. All students, but particularly students considered to be learning disabled, need assistance in the learning process. In a whole language curriculum, this assistance is provided in a way that does not substantially take the ownership away from the student. However, it does provide the assistance necessary to facilitate growth in the learning process. It is this interactional support the teacher provides that gently moves the child forward in her or his development.

Overall, a curriculum guided by whole language principles broadens the learning opportunities for all students. It provides the type of atmosphere that enhances students' growth, one in which they are treated with respect and carefully nurtured throughout the learning process.

15. Educating Children with Learning Disabilities in Foxfire Classrooms

JUDY W. KUGELMASS

In "The Child and the Curriculum," Dewey (1964) argued against the either/or debate that was raging between the traditionalists and the progressives in education at the turn of the century, with the former insisting on discipline-specific subject matter as the center of education and the latter focusing on the child as "furnishing the standard" (p. 343). These issues are central to the present debate surrounding inclusion and are particularly relevant to the education of children identified as having learning disabilities.

The belief that the content of the curriculum should be fixed and uniform—that there is a best way for children to learn and that all children need to be learning the same things at the same time in the same way—has been central to the assumptions that historically have guided public education, thereby requiring the segregation of children who could not follow the set curriculum because of differences in the ways in which they processed and understood information. Dewey (1964) described these ideas as those of "traditionalists" who believed that the curriculum should focus on "stable and well ordered realities":

> Subdivide each topic into studies; each study into lessons; each lesson into specific facts and formulae. Let the child proceed step by step to master

Reprinted, with changes, from "Educating children with learning disabilities in Foxfire classrooms," by Judy W. Kugelmass, *Journal of Learning Disabilities*, Vol. 28, 1995, pp. 545–553. Copyright © 1995 by PRO-ED, Inc.

each one of these separate parts, and at last he will have covered the entire ground. . . . Thus emphasis is put upon the logical subdivisions and consecutions of subject matter. Problems of instruction are problems of procuring texts, giving logical parts and sequences, and of presenting these portions in class in a similar definite and graded way. Subject matter furnishes the end, and it determines method. The child is simply the immature being who is to be matured; he is the superficial being who is to be deepened; his is narrow experience which is to be widened. It is his to receive, to accept. His part is fulfilled when he is ductile and docile. (p. 342)

These beliefs not only have guided general education, but also have directed special education practice (Carini, 1991; Ensminger & Dangel, 1992). Because in most traditional school settings subject matter had taken ascendency over developing children's learning abilities, special education, in its early years, moved away from teaching subjects and toward the teaching of skills. In spite of the fact that the "topics" to be taught were not the same, the instructional processes used in both special and general education continued to be guided by similar assumptions. In both cases, lessons were selected, designed, and developed by teachers and presented to students in a prescribed, step-by-step fashion. Certainly, systematic instruction and behavioristic strategies are appropriate tools for teaching some discrete skills and for shaping some behaviors; these strategies should not be abandoned completely. Rather, it is their *exclusive* or predominant use in both general and special education settings that is at the heart of the debate surrounding school reform today.

To function as mature adults, students need much more than an ability to understand subject matter that has been presented in a logical and sequential manner in a classroom with few distractions. Our children do not live in a world that is logical, sequential, or free from distraction. Functioning in today's world requires flexibility, critical thinking skills, and the ability to problem solve in new or ambiguous situations (Sizer, 1984). The current school restructuring movement, which includes the creation of inclusive educational settings, is based on that premise and recognizes that strict adherence to linear methods of instruction will not meet the needs of any child. Addressing the needs and interests of the child without attention to the content and context of learning can be as problematic as attending only to subject matter and discrete skills (Carini, 1991; Ensminger & Dangel, 1992; Stainback, Stainback, & Moravec, 1992).

Many students in general education programs and those identified as having mild disabilities, including learning disabilities, share similar perceptions regarding the traditional structure of school. Particularly at the secondary level, students lack enthusiasm about both the process and the content of their educational experiences (Ensminger, 1991; Sizer,

1984). In a study of 10 high schools in five school districts in the Atlanta, Georgia, area, Ensminger found that students in special education resource room programs saw little connection between what they were being taught and their lives. They were not provided with any opportunity to have control over what was going on in their classrooms. As was the case in many of the general classrooms he observed, special education programs were not providing environments that enhanced motivation. Students were not permitted to work with one another. Rather, silence prevailed, and instruction was delivered to students through individual assignments in textbooks or worksheets designed to correspond with assignments from their mainstreamed general education classes.

Today, special educators concerned with the development of inclusionary practices are recognizing that instructional approaches that focus solely on remediation and/or isolated skill development, whether in a general classroom or in a special education setting, stand in the way of attaining authentic education (Poplin, 1988). Besides failing to provide learning environments that motivate and empower children, this kind of teaching deprives students who rely on it of needed opportunities to acquire both the skills and the knowledge base essential for becoming successful, independently functioning individuals. It also interferes with their development of age-appropriate social skills (Ferguson & Ginevra, 1993; Stainback et al., 1992). To achieve an appropriate, inclusive education, a balance must therefore be developed among the child, the content, and the process of instruction.

Dewey (1964) proposed that this could be achieved if education would move away from the either/or debate and find a balance between the needs of the child and those of the curriculum.

> Abandon the notion of subject matter as something fixed and ready-made in itself, outside the child's experience; cease thinking of the child's experience as something hard and fast; see it as something fluid, embryonic, vital; and we realize that the child and the curriculum are simply two limits which define a single process. Just as two points define a straight line, so the present standpoint of the child and the facts and truths of studies define instruction. It is continuous reconstruction, moving from the child's present experience out into that represented by the organized body of truth we call studies. (p. 344)

There is now, almost a century later, an opportunity to continue Dewey's (1964) discussion and move beyond the debate between content and skills. Recognizing the necessity of providing a balance between both has moved the conversation on curriculum to a focus on the development of instructional processes. This chapter will describe the ongoing development of an active, learner-centered process that incorporates Dewey's notion of balancing the child and the curriculum in the context

of schools that are reframing the way education is being conceived and delivered. Examples from several elementary classrooms will provide illustrations of instructional processes that have facilitated the creation of classrooms that are integrating content with skill development and are including children identified as having learning disabilities. The work reported here represents the beginning of a collaborative research program with teachers who are developing restructured programs, and should therefore be viewed as a preliminary report on a work in progress.

THE FOXFIRE APPROACH

In 1990, I began an affiliation with the Foxfire Teacher Outreach program as the coordinator of its Network of Empire State Teachers (NEST). Foxfire Teacher Outreach grew out of work that started in rural Appalachian Georgia 27 years ago. Beginning as an attempt to engage rural youth in relevant, community-based experiences that would both develop their literacy skills and preserve local cultural traditions, Foxfire became a nationally recognized leader in the use of cultural journalism as an approach to the teaching of English. The Foxfire Outreach program began in 1986, to promote and support the overall approach to teaching that had emerged from Foxfire's earlier focus. By 1993, over 4,000 practicing and preservice teachers had received Foxfire training through courses designed to prepare teachers to develop a learner-centered approach to curricula. These courses were offered through colleges, universities, and staff development programs. The initial training was linked to teacher networks that provided follow-up support and resources to teachers for refinement of the approach in specific settings (Foxfire Fund, 1994).

Teachers who became involved in Foxfire were drawn together by their mutual interest in developing approaches to education that are learner centered, experiential, and linked to the communities and real-life experiences of their students. They included educators working at all grade levels and in all subject areas; general classroom teachers and special educators; and teachers and administrators from rural, urban, and suburban communities. They recognized and appreciated the impact of current school reform and restructuring on the development of instructional strategies for children who experience special learning challenges. Many have been involved with other national initiatives for school reform, such as the Coalition for Essential Schools; Project Zero; The Institute for Democracy in Education; and the National Center for Restructuring Education, Schools and Teaching (NCREST); as well as state and local reform initiatives.

The Foxfire approach to teaching provides an instructional framework for the integration of other instructional practices that share its Deweyan philosophy. The special education and general classroom teachers with whom I have worked teach both in restructured settings and in traditionally organized and administered schools. All share a vision of education and a way of thinking about teaching and learning that can be described as learner centered and constructivist. It is an approach to teaching that involves students in the development of the curriculum and allows for their strengths and talents to be included in academic instruction, while providing experiences that will develop new and emerging skills. It incorporates many practices that have been identified as meeting the needs of students with learning disabilities (Ensminger & Dangel, 1992).

Diversity among students is a given in the mind of the Foxfire-trained teachers. Their work is guided by the following set of core practices, which are neither a recipe nor a formula for teaching but, rather, provide a guide for the development of instructional practices that balance the child and the curriculum:

1. All the work teachers and students do together flows from student desire, student concerns.
2. Therefore, the role of the teacher is that of collaborator and team leader and guide rather than boss.
3. The academic integrity of the work should be absolutely clear.
4. The work is characterized by student action, rather than passive receipt of processed information.
5. A constant feature of the process is its emphasis on peer teaching, small group work and team work.
6. Connections between the classroom work and the surrounding communities and the real world outside the classroom are clear.
7. There is an audience beyond the teacher for student work.
8. As the year progresses, new activities should spiral gracefully out of the old.
9. As teachers, we acknowledge the worth of aesthetic experience.
10. Reflection—some conscious, thoughtful time to stand apart from the work itself—is an essential activity that takes place at key points throughout the work.
11. The work includes unstintingly honest, ongoing evaluation for skills and content, and changes in student attitude. . . . Students should be trained to monitor their own progress and devise their own remediation plans. (Foxfire Fund, 1991, pp. 3–4)

When applied in classrooms that include students with learning disabilities, the core practices assist teachers in providing educational experiences that address subject area givens, while at the same time teaching academic, social, and functional skills in the contexts in which they need to be applied. Teachers engage their students in educationally and age-appropriate ways in the active construction of the curriculum and in the creation of a classroom community that appreciates diversity and provides opportunities for all children to develop their talents and to make connections between the content of academic learning and their life experiences (Kugelmass, 1991). Children are provided with opportunities to approach the curriculum through their strengths while being supported by the classroom community for stretching their skills and developing new ways of approaching tasks.

It is always difficult to describe a typical Foxfire classroom. Given the basic premise that each classroom represents a unique ecology, it follows that no two will ever look precisely alike. The structure of the school and community in which they are situated provides a unique dimension to each classroom. What does characterize all Foxfire classrooms, however, is that children are actively engaged with one another, their teacher, and the instructional materials in shaping the culture of their classrooms. They talk openly and knowingly about what they are learning and about why and how it is being learned. The curriculum becomes learner centered, with students making decisions about how they will structure their learning, thereby enabling the inclusion of all learning styles, abilities, interests, intelligences, and cultures. Through ongoing negotiations, the children and their teacher shape what goes on. Much of the work is done in groups, with a good deal of peer interaction. Children's lives and experiences in the world outside the classroom, including their communities and families, are actively and consciously integrated into academic work, as are the arts and aesthetic considerations. Assessment is ongoing and integral to instruction. Children are asked to reflect upon and evaluate their own learning.

I am currently collaborating with several Foxfire-trained elementary teachers in different schools in order to discover how this approach assists in developing strategies that meet the needs of children identified for special education services who are included in their general education classrooms. In each case, the special education students in their classrooms have been identified as having learning disabilities. My observations took place during the first 6 weeks of the school year. Observing early in the year and discussing the program with parents, students, teachers, and other school personnel has demonstrated the significance of developing a classroom and school-wide culture that supports collaboration and diversity for the successful implementation of inclusion.

The schools in which the classrooms described in this chapter are located provide the kind of climate that is supportive of inclusive classrooms. Diversity is viewed as offering richness rather than providing an obstacle to learning. The teachers see the presence of a child with learning disabilities as an opportunity to create a new perspective for the class.

Because the teacher's role includes assisting all the children in understanding their own, and everyone else's, learning styles, intelligences, goals, and needs, small- and large-group projects (which are often the culminating event in a Foxfire classroom) will need to accommodate the strengths and needs of the child with a learning disability in the same way they do every other child's abilities. These classrooms have explicit norms that foster and reward collaboration and cooperation throughout the day, and not just during lessons that are identified as "cooperative learning" activities. Other shared practices include a strong focus on parental involvement and collaborative decision making among the entire staff.

THE FULLER SCHOOL: A MULTIPLE INTELLIGENCES PROGRAM

Two of the teachers in the "school-within-a-school" program at the Fuller School in Gloucester, Massachusetts, are trained in the Foxfire approach. The curriculum of the program (kindergarten through Grade 5) is built around the theory of multiple intelligences (MI) as articulated by Gardner (1993). Gardner identified seven discrete "intelligences." Depending on cultural context, one or more are more valued in a given society and are rewarded accordingly. In the United States and most Western cultures, linguistic and logical mathematical intelligences have been selected as those most indicative of an "intelligent" person. School curricula are therefore organized to develop the attributes and skills associated with these intelligences. The Wechsler and Stanford-Binet tests of intelligence that are used throughout the United States in the identification of children as learning disabled reflect this premise.

Children who do not exhibit strengths in these intelligences will not perform well in traditionally structured schools or on standardized tests, nor will they be provided with adequate opportunities to develop their other talents. When significant discrepancies exist between their primary intelligence and those valued in American schools (linguistic, logical mathematical), children may become identified as learning disabled. The deficit-based remedial approach that has typified special education further compounds the problems facing students whose strengths are in areas other than language as they try to learn the content of a curriculum that is taught primarily through the written and spoken word. Rather than using the child's intelligence as the entry point for the curriculum or acknowledging other intelligences as valid ways of knowing, traditional models of teaching have stigmatized these children and missed the opportunity to provide an environment whereby all children can develop their musical, visual, kinesthetic, interpersonal, and intrapersonal intelligences.

Julie Carter's combination first- and second-grade MI classroom at the Fuller School began the year in a Foxfire fashion: having the children involved in establishing the norms for the classroom while building a learning community. Unlike previous years, when she was less consciously trying to build a learner-centered classroom in the Foxfire sense, she started this year with few materials or decorations visible to the children. Instead, she and her students designed the learning centers in the room together. These centers, which are to be built around the different intelligences, will continue to be developed throughout the year.

Julie began by informing the children that they would be creating seven learning centers that would be places where they could design work that focused on being "word smart," "math smart," "music smart," "art smart," "body smart," "people smart," and "self smart" (Armstrong, 1994). The class brainstormed the meaning of these concepts and then decided what items, in addition to the few items Julie had brought to class, should be included in each center.

Eventually these learning centers will become integrated into the thematic projects the children will design around the program's theme for the year, "Relationships and Connections." Julie and all the other teachers in the program have collaborated on selecting this theme. They will meet with one another in grade-level teams on a regular basis throughout the year, to determine units through which to develop this theme. Subject-specific material, academic skills, and all seven intelligences will be integrated into activities that will be developed in collaboration with students. Curriculum is understood as a process that unfolds as the children interact with one another, their teacher, the materials, and the content of their learning.

Julie's first and second graders began the year with a unit on self, home, and family. Their first assignment was to draw pictures of their families. This was followed by storytelling and story writing. They then were asked to bring a box from home that contained objects that represented themselves. The children shared these objects with one another in cooperative groups and then came together in a large group to tell about all the "symbols." The concept of "symbol" was discussed, and concrete examples were provided.

Although these activities seem similar to the way many primary classrooms begin the year, there are significant differences in the meaning and purpose of the process used. They are designed to introduce several concepts to the children and to build a classroom community. Following these introductory activities, the children were paired, a first grader with a second grader. The mixed-age grouping of first and second graders provides an opportunity for peer teaching and learning that will further build a classroom community in which a wide range of abilities and interests are the norm. Although these initial pairs were chosen by the teacher, the children will be given many other opportunities to choose their own partners.

The pairing, peer teaching, and self-examination that are built into these first lessons are designed to develop the children's intra- and interpersonal intelligences. As partners in learning, the pairs of children select and rotate through each center, working on writing, reading, mathematical, artistic, kinesthetic, and musical activities that they complete at their own level of competence. As the year proceeds, the learning centers will become more integrated with one another. The beginning of the year is consciously designed to teach these young children the specific vocabulary of MI and to develop the norms that will guide the development of this classroom community.

Cherylann Parker's fifth-grade classroom in the MI program also began the year with the goal of building community. However, because the majority of the children in this class have been in the program since it began 3 years ago, they more automatically integrate multiple intelligences in the work they develop. The development of the classroom culture includes involving students in self-assessment. In this classroom, as in all the other MI classes at Fuller, assessment is imbedded in instruction, not separated from it. Beginning with the question, "What does a good learning environment look like?," students generate the criteria for the structure of their classroom. Students are also asked to identify the criteria upon which their work should be assessed *before* they begin to work. In the fifth-grade classroom, the students also developed individual learning contracts for their roles in group projects. They began the process by generating criteria for the contracts, and then moved to the criteria for the work itself. These contracts were hung on the wall in the classroom. All were written on 8½-inch × 11-inch paper, glued onto a work of art created by each student. Each contract was unique in both its form and its content, but each met the criteria set by the class for a "good" contract and a "good" work of art. Although specific, the criteria were still broad enough to accommodate the diversity that existed among the students in the class, and resulted in very creative visual displays as well as stimulating learning projects.

Both of these teachers have been trained in special education and general education and have previously taught in segregated special education settings. Their special education backgrounds have prepared them to expect and accept differences in children's learning styles, behaviors, needs, and abilities. They both left work as special education teachers because they found that special education was not providing the kinds of learning environments they believed could provide optimal educational opportunities. Both welcome the challenge presented by students who do not learn in traditional ways and both are comfortable in dealing with children whose behavior is troublesome to other teachers. In addition, they incorporate a variety of behavioral approaches as management strategies and recognize the necessity for balance among skill development, content, and the child's intelligences and talents. Neither teacher wants to return to working in a segregated special education setting that focuses on the remediation of isolated skills.

Cherylann and Julie are working in a situation that is ideal for the inclusion of children with learning disabilities. Not only does the framework of multiple intelligences provide a variety of entry points to learning for children with poor linguistic, mathematical, and/or perceptual–motor skills, but it provides opportunities for the development of kinesthetic skills. Foxfire adds the dimension of choice to all the activities and promotes problem solving and peer interaction for modeling and reinforcement. These teachers are operating in a school community that is guided by a philosophy of learning that places diversity at the center of the curriculum. In the MI program, curriculum development is seen as an evolutionary process and not as a predetermined "scope and sequence" for teaching a specific subject area. There is a shared and articulated vision for both the process and the content of curriculum.

A COALITION OF ESSENTIAL SCHOOLS

Sharon Weaver's second-grade classroom offers another example of curriculum development in a classroom that operates in the context of a collaborative school culture. The Belle Sherman Elementary School in Ithaca, New York, is one of 22 elementary schools that have recently joined the Coalition of Essential Schools. Following the work of Sizer (1984), Coalition schools develop their educational programs and school cultures around a set of common principles. These principles are focused on the purpose and organization of schools and were originally designed for the restructuring of secondary schools. They include (a) helping students learn to use their minds well; (b) focusing on essential skills and questions; (c) tailoring the school's goals to apply to all its students; (d) personalizing instruction; (e) promoting "student as worker" and "teacher as deliverer of instructional services"; (f) graduating by exhibition; (g) focusing on the values of "unanxious expectations, trust, and decency"; (h) teachers and administrators functioning as generalists first; and (i) reducing student–teacher ratios and providing substantial time for planning (Coalition for Essential Schools, 1992).

At Belle Sherman there is a commitment to providing an approach to education that is inclusive. All teachers see themselves as responsible for all students. Neither teachers nor students are viewed as special. One structural aspect of the school that supports this principle, and which has assisted Sharon and other teachers in their work, is its adoption of a "blended-services" model. There are no special education classrooms in this K–5 school. Rather, the funds for all support services have been pooled, and "specialists" are included as team teachers in general classrooms. All classes have two full-time teaching professionals. Sharon's teammate is a teacher of English as a second language.

The blended-services model has addressed one of the greatest problems faced by Foxfire-trained teachers in general classrooms: Students identified for special education are included, but the schools have not redesigned the way they provide support. In more traditionally structured schools, teachers often find themselves in situations in which pull-out programs interfere with building the sense of community that is essential to the collaborative classroom environment that characterizes Foxfire classrooms. When the general classroom teacher receives the support of a special education resource teacher who works from a consultant model, but operates under a behavioristic framework, conflicting paradigms and priorities interfere with real collaboration. In such instances, it is often difficult to include "labeled" students in ongoing, interdisciplinary class projects because of the pressure put on the general classroom teacher and special educator to demonstrate the achievement of specific, predetermined behavioral goals, as listed in an Individualized Education Program (IEP). In these situations, general classroom and special education teachers are working in schools that are attempting to address parental and legislative pressures for inclusion, while still operating under a school culture that is guided by the deficit model that has traditionally characterized special education.

In Sharon's classroom I have observed a well-developed community of learners who are actively involved in shaping their own educational experiences. Although there are some differences, there are even more similarities between how this second-grade class and Julie Carter's first-and-second-grade classroom operate. Although Sharon does not talk about multiple intelligences with her students, and has not identified Gardner's (1993) work as guiding her practice, the integration of and appreciation for visual arts, music, kinesthetic, and intra- and interpersonal intelligences are evident in the work the children do every day. Student choice, active learning, an appreciation for diversity, and authentic assessment characterize this classroom, much as they did Julie's MI classroom.

Sharon's students are all second graders, and this is the second year that the majority of these children have been her students. She believes that multiple-year placement with the same teacher builds a stronger classroom community, as well as providing continuity of instruction and the time for her and her students to build a strong relationship with each other. Her second graders, like those in Julie's class, were able to jump into the school year familiar with the collaborative and learner-centered approach of the classroom. Visiting during the second week of school, I found the students working diligently on writing short stories individually, seated in the clusters of four that make up their five base groups. Occasionally, children would turn to one another for help or for brief conversation. The children in this class bring a wide range of interests, abilities, socioeconomic backgrounds, races, cultures, and languages to the group. Among them are two children identified as having learning disabilities.

A lesson that began with Sharon's reading a story grew into several activities that included reading, writing, math, and social studies, as well as an exploration of the diversity of the families and communities represented by the class. This provides an excellent example of Sharon's constructivist approach to the curriculum and her natural manner of including issues that are relevant to students with learning disabilities, as well as to all young children. The book *Don't Forget the Bacon* (Hutchins, 1989) tells about a boy being asked to go shopping for

SIX FARM EGGS,
A CAKE FOR TEA,
A POUND OF PEARS
AND DON'T FORGET
THE BACON

After reading this first page, Sharon asked the children, "What does this mean?" A child with strong linguistic skills explained that it was a list of the things the boy was being asked to buy. Sharon next asked the children to identify and count the number of items on the list. This question pushed the children to sort out the words and describe the items. The problem of whether "six farm eggs" was one item or six was debated, and the group counted the items several times. The story proceeds with the boy in the book repeating these words to himself as he walks to the store. However, he confuses words and substitutes others, a situation that all the children in the class can relate to, and one that provides an opening for those children identified as having learning disabilities to talk about their learning difficulties in and out of school. A short discussion about being confused about words and forgetting things ensues, with Sharon facilitating the children's sharing of personal stories.

The story moves to a discussion about the usefulness of lists as organizers and helpers for remembering things. Sharon then guides the class in sharing with one another the ways in which they have seen lists used outside of school. They talk about how writing the items beneath one

Figure 15.1. The "shopping list" of a child (identified as having a learning disability) whose work is at a less developed level than his classmates'.

another makes it easier to remember. The discussion becomes an entry into a writing lesson in which the children are asked to develop their own lists for things they would like. Sharon suggests, but does not require, that they write each item underneath the preceding one. Every child then works on producing a list that is unique in both form and content.

The figures included in this chapter illustrate the range of responses in this classroom. Figure 15.1 is the work of a child who has been identified as having a learning disability; Figure 15.2 was produced by a child whose work typically exceeds that expected from most of the other sec-

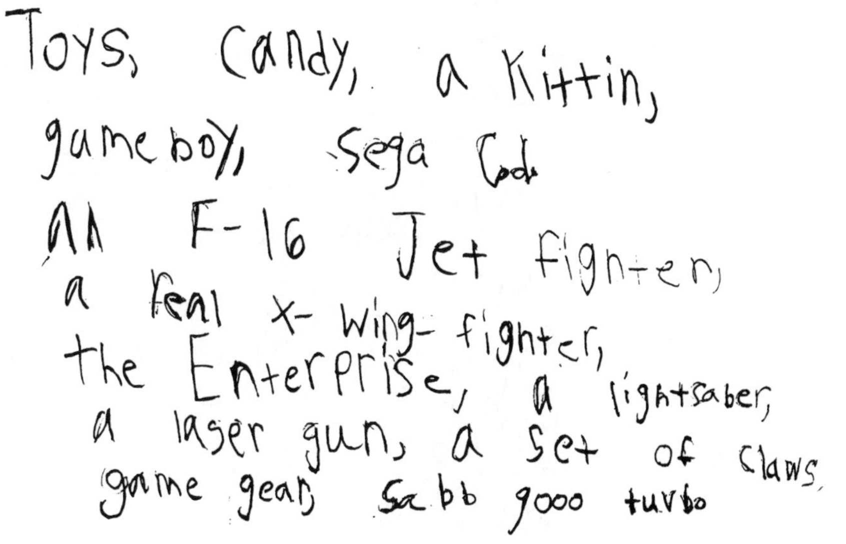

Toys, Candy, a Kittin, gameboy, Sega Cd, An F-16 Jet fighter, a real x-wing-fighter, the Enterprise, a lightsaber, a laser gun, a set of claws game gear Sabb 9000 turbo

Figure 15.2. The "shopping list" of a child whose work typically exceeds that of his classmates.

ond graders. Figure 15.3 represents a response that typified the work of most of the children in the class.

In this whole language classroom, the inability to spell a word correctly does not keep any child from participating. If a child wants assistance, he or she asks another child or calls on one of the adults to write the word in his or her personal dictionary. Sharon later explained that she did not ask the children to draw pictures of the items on their lists because she knew that they all were capable of writing something. She felt that offering the option of drawing would have kept the less able writers from pushing themselves: "I often use art as an entry point into writing. I'll use whatever brings all the children into an activity. However, I know that sometimes, kids need a push to do things that are hard for them."

Figure 15.3.   The "shopping list" of a child whose work represents the typical responses of her classmates.

When I asked Sharon what goals she had planned to address when she selected this story, she responded,

> I knew I was going to read the story, but I really didn't have a "plan." When I got there and I saw what was there and I thought about the kids, I stopped and moved right into what you saw happen. It's intuitive. I look for entry points for the curriculum and here I saw lots of opportunities. I will extend this to include more math activities.

For this teacher, the Foxfire approach is integrated into how she thinks about her teaching on a day-to-day basis. The core practices are woven into minilessons, group activities, and classroom design, assisting in the development of an inclusive classroom. In other inclusive class-rooms, Foxfire-trained teachers frequently use interdisciplinary class projects, designed by students and guided by the teacher, to meet general learning goals and specific academic objectives. Certainly, participation in class projects by special children is not unique to these classrooms. It has frequently been used in more teacher-directed classrooms as a strat-egy for mainstreaming. However, in many cases, projects may provide only token involvement for some children. For example, the student with special educational needs may get to draw a flower on the cover of the project brochure or pull the string on the curtain at the close of a play, but may not have been involved in the overall development of the project in the authentic way they will be in Sharon's classroom.

In Foxfire classrooms such as this one, the curriculum is woven into small-group and class projects throughout the year. A final project will be an activity that can be seen as an exhibition and celebration of children's learning. Although a project can be an impressive showcase of the children's work, it will be the *process* that the students engaged in throughout the year and used in designing and completing their project that will provide the most significant education. Social and academic development will have been integrated into the work, as students col-laborated with one another, provided peer support, and modeled appro-priate behavior and learning strategies. All students will have been acknowledged for their talents and provided with opportunities to dem-onstrate and develop new skills in an integrated, authentic, and func-tional manner.

CONCLUSIONS

In the coming year, several other teachers will join in the collabora-tive research that has been initiated with the teachers described in this chapter. We will continue to document the development of their classroom practice and the growth in these classrooms of students who have been identified as having learning disabilities. In each child's case, assessment will constitute a process of continual documentation and reflection on the child's learning. Data will be collected through portfolio assessments; running records; anecdotal reports; interviews with the children, their peers, their parents, and their teachers; and systematic observation. The compilation of these data will provide the information needed for the ongoing development and improvement of the instructional strategies that have been described.

The variability in school cultures across the nation, among school districts, among schools within districts, and within individual classrooms has frequently been ignored by educators when they are considering the development of instructional approaches for students identified as having learning disabilities. In fact, some special educators have argued that the emphasis on "place" articulated by advocates for inclusion is merely a distraction from what should be the major concern of special educators, that is, providing empirical evidence for the success of systematic instructional strategies (Kauffman, 1993). Few would disagree that any educational approach must demonstrate effectiveness. The purpose of the work in progress reported here is to do just that. Defining "empirical" evidence only as information gathered in a highly controlled environment fails to consider the real world of schooling and the lives of children beyond the context of the classroom.

Ecological investigations of children's growth and development have clearly demonstrated the significance of context to all aspects of learning (Bronfenbrenner, 1979; Garbarino, 1992; Vygotsky, 1962). Educators are now aware of the ways in which a mismatch between a child's culture of origin and the culture of the school affects his or her cognitive and language acquisition and social development (Anastasiow, 1986). Special educators have become sensitive to the difficulties many children face when they are required to move from one environment to another. Generalizability of learning across settings often does not happen automatically. Highly distractible children and those with language disorders and/or processing difficulties who have been "succeeding" in highly controlled classrooms, where stimulation was minimized, have difficulty functioning at the same levels when suddenly placed in more open, active learning environments.

Rather than being an argument against inclusion, the dialogue on context asks educators of children with learning disabilities to work toward the development of general education contexts in which all children can learn effectively. Enriched learning environments that consider the cultures of the communities in which students will function, and that have the flexibility to adapt the curriculum and the learning environment to the needs, interests, and abilities of all students, need to be developed. This development will not be manifest in a single event, but will be an ongoing process. The outcome will yield a flexible model of schooling that can provide the "place" where children with learning disabilities can receive the enriched educational experience that all children deserve.

16. Exploring Writing—From Rebellion to Participation

LAURA LOVELACE

We need to write, but we also need to be heard.—Lucy McCormick Calkins

I did not think writing workshop would work for my class. I did not think my students could handle the freedom of this program, which allows them to choose their own topic, write at an individual pace, and address writing concerns in teacher-directed minilessons, group conferences, and individual conferences. I had heard other teachers talk about how much their students enjoyed it, I had even been to a workshop on how to implement a writing workshop program in a classroom; but I was sure my students would kill each other if I even tried. So my first year of teaching, I did not try. By my second year, I was ready. I was tired of trying to force my students to write about subjects that were irrelevant to them. And, if it turned out to be a disaster, I could always revert to my old ways.

We started writing workshops the second week of school. I was teaching a third-grade bilingual class. The students were at a variety of skill levels and at varying degrees of English-speaking ability. My program was a combination of that of Lucy Calkins (1986) and of recommendations of a fellow teacher who had used a similar method previously.

Reprinted, with changes, from "Exploring writing—From rebellion to participation," by Laura Lovelace, *Journal of Learning Disabilities,* Vol. 28, 1995, pp. 554–559, 568. Copyright © 1995 by PRO-ED, Inc.

I started with basic rules. For a finished product, my students needed to produce nine lines or more of writing and to complete an illustration with at least four colors. When their story was ready, they placed it in a basket. I took it home, added corrections on a sticky note, and passed it back the next day. They were then supposed to correct their pieces.

The new program started well. At first, my students could not believe I was letting them work together and talk while working. We work approximately an hour per day. The hour was broken into three parts—a 10-minute teacher-focused minilesson, 45 minutes of writing, followed by 15 to 20 minutes of sharing time. It worked wonderfully. Students who refused to do anything else during much of the day sat down and wrote. There were some problems at first: high noise level, writing rude stories about each other. We worked on solutions to these problems as they came up.

What struck me the most about the difference between my conventional writing program of the previous year and my new program was the increased student interest in the new program after using it for approximately 1 month.

In March, our schedule shifted because of an added mandatory English Language Development program. We were limited to only 40 minutes, 3 days a week, for writing workshop. It still worked decently, but I could feel the effects of less time for writing and sharing of the stories by the student authors. Our schedule evolved into 40 minutes of writing and 40 minutes of teacher/student conferences on Tuesday, 40 minutes of writing on Wednesday with 20 minutes for me to check student progress (students received a plus, a check, or a minus), and on Thursday, they wrote for 20 minutes and shared with the class for 20 minutes. Each writing folder had a list of titles and the date each piece was completed. Once students conferenced with me and completed their pieces, I put their names on a wall chart for completed published works.

For this case study, I decided to focus on one student, Student R, because of the success he has had with the writing workshop program. His work is not the most advanced conceptually or grammatically, but he now loves to write and will not do anything else in my class. Before that, he did nothing in my class.

Student R is 9 years old. He does not know when his birthday is. He is in the third grade; he skipped second grade this year because his true age was discovered. His first language is Spanish. He knows some very basic English. R had a close relationship with his first-grade teacher. When she decided to skip him, she consulted with me. She said his math skills were solid but his reading and writing were very basic. When he started in my class, he could barely read. He knew the sounds of letters but had a hard time putting the sounds together, and he displayed almost no comprehension. His writing was restricted to his name and words he could copy from the classroom. He was very uneasy about putting words on paper if he did not know for certain they were spelled correctly. If he became frustrated (because I would not tell him what I wanted him to write about or how to spell something), he would throw his paper on the ground or rip it up and refuse to work. If he got frustrated when reading, he would throw his book down, walk out of class, and stand outside until he cooled down.

Within the first month of writing workshop, R discovered working with partners. Unlike other students with low writing skills, who often choose highly skilled partners to work with, R chose to work with students who, although a little more advanced than he, were also at a very basic writing level. His first writing pieces were usually dictated to another student, who would write while R illustrated. These early works were very basic labeling of his drawings (see Figures 16.1 and 16.2). Cars, trucks, and helicopters figured prominently in his early pieces (and still do). R did not treat his pieces well. He would shove them in his desk instead of his folder, or rip them up if he was unhappy with the results.

Toward the end of February, he signed up for a teacher conference with me. Because it was the first time he showed interest in sharing his

Figure 16.1.   "This is R and J's book."

R   *tenia   una camione da*

Figure 16.2.   "R has a truck."

writing, I saw him immediately rather than making him wait for his name
to come up on the conferencing list. This was irregular procedure, but
R tends to lose interest if he does not receive immediate feedback, and
I wanted to take advantage of his new interest. He read me his piece,
which explained that it was his favorite day because he got to play kickball
(see Figure 16.3). I was impressed. To my knowledge, this was the first
piece of this length that he had written almost independently. He was
very proud. During our conference, we discussed kickball and how much
I liked his story. When I asked for volunteers to share, he raised his hand
and I let him share. He read his story to the class, and they responded
with their typical responses: "It was good," "It was funny," "It was fresh,"
"I like your illustration." R looked as though he would explode with
pride.

   I believe that this was a big turning point for R. He made a transition from seeing writing as something the teacher made him do and that
he was not very good at, to seeing it as a way to communicate with his

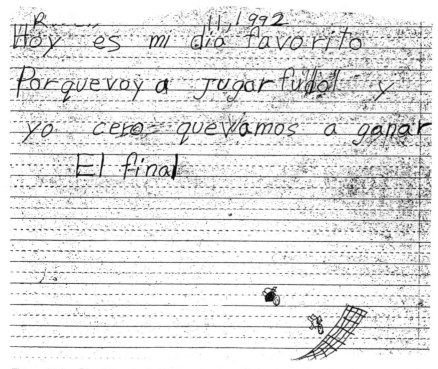

R
11, 1992
Hoy es mi día favorito
Porquevoy a jugar fuĺbol y
yo cero quevamos a ganar
El final

Figure 16.3. R's piece about his favorite day: "Today is my favorite day because I'm going to play soccer and we're going to win. The end."

peers. "A sense of authorship comes from the struggle to put something big and vital into print, and from seeing one's own printed words reach the hearts and minds of the readers" (Calkins, 1986, p. 9). R had discovered the power to communicate with written words. From that day on, it seemed as though his main purpose in writing was to share the stories he wrote. If he did not get to share his stories on the exact day that he finished them, he either lost interest in that story or got frustrated and crushed his story into a little ball or ripped it up. Unfortunately, our writing workshop time was shorter than any of us would have wanted. Sharing time had been greatly reduced because of other school demands. The effects of shortening this time was apparent: Without the instant interaction with the class, authors often lost interest in their pieces and the excitement level decreased. For Student R, who usually took about 10 minutes to get himself settled enough to write, the shortened time meant less actual writing time. The limited sharing time greatly affected him. If R did not get to share his writing with the whole class, that work seemed to become worthless to him.

Along with discovering that the power of words can be used to share ideas, R soon discovered that the power of words can be employed to bother other students. In an interview conducted in April, R said that one of his stories of this latter genre was his favorite (see Figure 16.4). When I asked him why it was his favorite story, he said that Student A wrote about *him* (R). R wrote several similar stories, some quite long. For a while, these stories were the rage in my classroom, and followed a predictable pattern. A student would write about two students kissing or getting married, and jump up and read the story aloud to the people whose names were involved. They, in turn, would express appropriate horror and proceed to write something more horrifying about the author. R loved to be on the author side but would get very angry when a story was written about him. Although a lot of writing was occurring, I had to intervene with a rule that an author needed a student's permission to use his or her name in a story.

After R discovered the power of print, I believe the second big change for him occurred when I decided to focus on him for the present project. At first, I was very frustrated by his haphazard way of treating his stories. When I started investigating, I found that many of his pieces were missing. A lot of his works had been done in collaboration with other students, but neither author knew what had happened to the actual piece of writing. R also had a habit of not putting his name on a piece that he dictated or was helped with. When I searched for pieces that I found very interesting, they were missing. For example, he had worked with a student who spoke only English. They stapled two pieces of paper together; on one paper, R had written his part in Spanish, while on the other side, Student A had written the same sentence in English. The sentences were very basic: *Aqui es un avion* ("Here is a plane"). I was struck by this collaboration, because both R and A had difficulty settling down and were easily distracted. Yet, when working together, they kept each other on task, and together created a piece that was specifically geared to our bilingual classroom audience, which does a lot of translating during sharing time. R had the idea and enlisted A, who has trouble initiating any writing and looks for people with ideas to work with. When I looked through R's writing folder for this piece, it was not there. I asked him where it was, but R did not know. I told him to look for it because it was very important. I told him that I had described how good it was to another teacher, who wanted to see it. He looked for about 10 minutes, in his desk and in his collaborators' writing folders, but he could not find it. He finally asked me if he could do another one. I said yes, and he went to work. Student A was working with someone else, but R grabbed him away and said they needed to do a new story because it was very important to me. They started but did not have time to finish it all. R seemed very upset that they had not had enough time to finish it. The next day, instead of writing, the students were putting together new writing folders. R put his together rapidly, then asked if he and A could finish their piece.

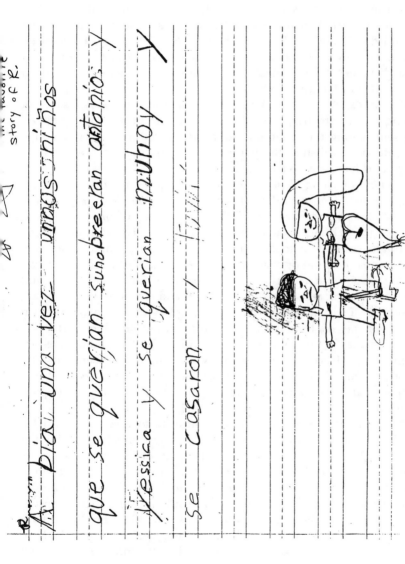

Figure 16.4. R's use of words to annoy other students: "Once upon a time there were some children who were in love. Their names were Antonio and Jessica and they loved each other a lot and were married."

While the rest of the class decorated their new folders, R and A made a replica of their original (see Figure 16.5).

The day after R and A finished their bilingual piece, during recess I interviewed R about his writing. He seemed nervous. The only times he was used to conferencing with adults during recess was when he was in serious trouble. He relaxed a little and was very impressed that I had made photocopies of his writings. I learned that he and Student A had had a third collaborator for their English/Spanish piece. I had been curious about how they managed to work together, because R knows very little English, and A knows next to no Spanish. R explained that a third student had translated for them.

Afterwards, R stayed and helped me in the classroom instead of returning to the cafeteria, where he was supposed to be cleaning tables. During our writing time that afternoon, he wanted me to play the tape of our interview and show the photocopies to the class. I chose to show the copies to his main collaborator.

The next morning, R presented me with a drawing of the classroom (see Figure 16.6). On it he had written, *Este el cuento de mi maestrar y de R ___. (the school) esta es mi clase* ("This is the story of my teacher and of R ___. [the school] is here. this is my class.") The drawing was in many bright colors and looked very happy. I do not think I can adequately express how out of character this was for R. His usual pattern was to act as though he hated school. He hardly ever did his homework and expressed disgust at students who tried hard and enjoyed spending extra time with me. I am still overjoyed with this gift. Not only had he drawn a picture for me, his teacher, on his own time, but he added a story, as well as the names of the students who sit at his table. This showed me that not only had he learned the power of words among his peers, but now he felt that I valued his writing. An adult who took extra time to let him know that what he wrote and felt was important made a very big impression on him.

At present it is May. R's writing continues to revolve around his illustrations. The pictures come first, and the text usually explains the illustrations. His first writings were the labeling of his drawings. In my April interview, I asked him what he liked to write about. He answered, "Planes, cars, and basketball." This answer interested me because he did write about planes and cars frequently, which he also practiced drawing during much of his free time and during the time when he should have been doing other classroom work. To my knowledge, however, he had not written anything about basketball. The day before the interview, we started basketball in P.E., so possibly he was planning on starting a story about basketball.

I have been very impressed by the connection between the improvement of R's writing and his reading. When R entered the third grade, he

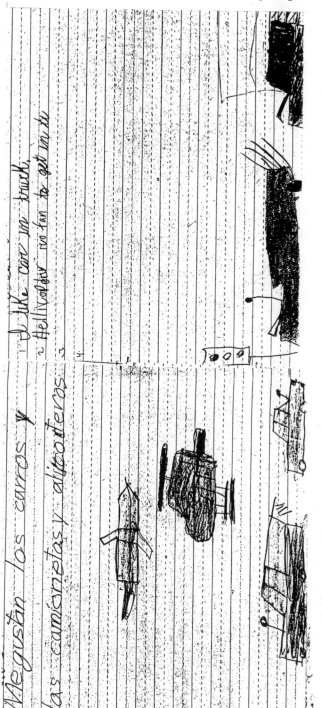

Figure 16.5.   Bilingual piece written by R, who spoke Spanish, and Student A, who spoke only English, with the help of a third student, who translated.

Figure 16.6.   R's present to me, done on his own time. The original was drawn using many bright crayons.

could barely read. He knew his name, but other than that he could only sometimes sound out the first letter of a word but then would give up. He was frustrated by reading and most of the time would not even try. As R became interested in reading his own writing aloud, his interest in learning to read was renewed. In the beginning, he read his writing very slowly and deliberately. He sometimes found his own work difficult to read because he did not leave any spaces between his words; there was just a flow of letters. Gradually, he learned the words he used the most: *dibujo* (drawing), *cuento* (story), and *avion* (plane). Around the same time, he chose an old first–grade Spanish language reader for his reading book. He kept the same book for about 3 weeks, reading it over and over again. Between this reading activity and learning the words he wanted to use the most in his writing, I believe R gained an understanding of words representing more concrete ideas. "Eventually young authors realize that the choice of letter depends on the sound it represents, and they develop a growing repertoire of sight vocabulary words" (Calkins, 1986, p. 39). I believe R now has a well-developed sense of this concept, which gives him a greater sense of self-assurance to try and do his own writing. He reads traditional literature in the same way he reads his writing—in a slow and conscientious manner. When he finishes reading successfully, the pride he takes in himself is obvious.

It does not seem to bother R that the majority of students in our class are at a more advanced writing level. For R, it is no longer a case of being a nonliterate student among literates. Now, he is literate also. Likewise, he sees himself as an author just like the authors whose books we read; his stories are just different kinds of stories.

Using the writing workshop program in my class has changed my perceptions. It has taught me to have more faith in my students. If I can give them an assignment that they enjoy, most will do it with pleasure. My exploration of R's writing has also shown me the difference it makes when someone thinks a student is important. R is now more conscientious about his writing because he knows that I am paying attention to it, that I know what he has written and will be very sad if he loses it. Just last week, another student accidentally tore a paper R was writing. He got so upset that he grabbed what that student was working on and ripped it to pieces. I am not proud of how R expressed his anger, but expressing such strong feelings about a piece of writing is a big change from when he used to rip up his own writing or just throw it away. As a reader and a writer, R is still below grade level, as measured by traditional methods. The big change is that he now perceives himself as both a reader and an author who has interesting and important ideas to share with the world.

AUTHOR'S NOTE

Thanks go to the students in my class for being active participants in my investigation of learning.

17. The Assurance of Things Hoped for: Coping Behavior of Children with Language Disorders in a Process-Writing Environment

INA J. KAU

The pencil leads are worn flat, right down to the wood. I'm trying to find six pencils so that I can do a collective writing project with my students—yet another plan to help this little group of first and second graders with severe language disorders make some sense of the jumble of sounds and letters in the English language. But these stubbed-down pencils trip me up for a moment. I stand looking through the box, pencil after pencil a mute witness to the struggle my students experience as they etch meaning onto a page.

I so often find myself this way—caught midflight through a teaching day, suddenly stopping short in wonderment as my students show me new dimensions of the terrain they journey. This is my first year as a teacher of children with severe language disorders and aphasia. My supervisor came to visit me early in the year to give me some advice and guidance. "You have to understand," she said, "these children aren't going to get better." It seemed a harsh judgment at the time. And in fact, the children in some ways did get better. I think what she meant, however, was that I

Reprinted, with changes, from "The assurance of things hoped for: Coping behavior of children with language disorders in a process-writing environment," by Ina J. Kau, *Journal of Learning Disabilities*, Vol. 28, 1995, pp. 560–568. Copyright © 1995 by PRO-ED, Inc.

shouldn't expect to cure them. I've remembered her advice from time to time, and it has helped. I feel so relieved and excited when I think my students have crossed some boundary, reached some understanding about the function and power of language. But I have learned now to expect the same child who "knew" yesterday to show me that this was just knowing for a while and not for all time.

I try to keep before me the metaphor of travel to faraway places to help me imagine what life must be like for my students. When traveling in a country where we know only a few phrases and scattered words, we try to listen, to hear our special words said by someone, just so that something in this unending stream of language will make sense. It is exhausting. After a while it becomes a relief to look at the landscape and the people and let the language flow on by, without processing any of it. Then there are the times when we know what is being said but can't remember how to *respond*—yes, we would like another cup of coffee, but we can't remember what to call the cup, even though we may have just heard the word, and where do verbs go in this language? On second thought, we've had quite enough coffee, thank you. Sign language, a shake of the head, will do for an answer.

And so it goes in my classroom. Gilberto stares blankly into a vacant space, midair; Eduardo, peering down his pencil shaft to watch the light glint off the end, crooks his fingers into strange patterns; Nolan rolls about eating nonfood items off the carpet; Martin, frustrated over the smallest error in his work, flings himself rigid on the floor, screams, and hits himself on the head; Marina curls into a ball under the table. I keep calling them back.

We work on what our bodies look like when we listen, read, write, or share at group time. "Show me you are ready to listen," I say, sitting flat on the carpet, crossing my legs, putting my hands in my lap, and looking intently at the child in question. Bit by bit they learn to do this. It wears us all out, this business of achieving the appearance of things. But without this constant insistence on "normal" behavior, most of my students slide rapidly off the spectrum of acceptable activity. Weary of speaking or unable to retrieve the words they want, they find whole body responses to life the easiest way of communicating. Stemming this tide, insisting on acceptable, productive behavior, being constantly willing to follow a child until I get the behavior I want, is an unending, enervating part of the job of teaching in this classroom. But I learned fairly quickly that without this, my students simply cannot control themselves well enough to work.

We are supposed to look like we are reading and writing because I am supposed to teach the children things. Some of these things are outlined laboriously in eight-page-long Individualized Education Programs (IEPs), but none of these plans promise much. "Joey will learn to read a book as measured by teacher records" is an extravagant assertion found nowhere in my students' IEPs. Instead, Joey's goal is to learn 15 letters of the alphabet. But students have to learn how to read and write. This is what teachers live for, and I am no exception. Our classroom is full of books; I read to my students every day, we memorize poems and songs, and I seize every opportunity to demonstrate reading and writing. Summaries of group discussions hang on the walls. Group poetry projects decorate the doors. Supplies for writing—paper, pencils, markers, crayons, laminated alphabet sheets, alphabet books, and word books—are all located in places readily reached by children. Because there are so few children in the class, we have plenty of space for cozy reading and writing corners. Sofas, bean bag chairs, little desks, and window seats are tucked around the classroom, inviting solitary or group exploration of literary endeavors. Every day, for 1 hour, we implement what we know about letters and words by participating in writing workshop.

Early on in the school year I read *Coping with Chaos* (Cambourne & Turbill, 1987). I liked the title, because chaos was what we seemed to have for writing time: Nolan would moan and shake his head and work himself up into an angry temper. When threatened with loss of recess, time out, and general misery, he would finally come up with a row of letter-like shapes to accompany his scribbling. Marina cheerfully filled up pages with colorful patches, and in any blank spaces she wrote a series of up and down wavy lines (see Figure 17.1). Omar made a few squiggles with markers using first his left and then his right hand, switching hands midpage when he felt bothered by crossing his own midline. He wrote some letters from his own name but didn't always remember all of them or the order of them when putting his name on his paper. Jason's writing was illegible due to his inability to make curved lines, and for the most part he wouldn't even try to write. Martin could print neatly and went around copying every word he could find. I started putting up labels— *Plant, Fish Tank, Blocks, File Cabinet*—and Martin copied. I didn't complain. At least it was writing I could read.

My image of what was supposed to happen during writing workshop—that the children would draw a picture and write about it, stick to a theme for 4 days or so and thereby produce a little book (see Note)— crumbled in the face of my students' realities. In an effort to improve our workshop time, I tried a variety of approaches to writing: having my students dictate sentences, having them copy over dictated sentences, writing their sentences out on sentence strips and trying to get them to read them, and using canned story-making dittos from a language development company. I learned several things in this process. None of my students understood the boundaries of words. Initially, many of them thought that each letter, in and of itself, was a word. When reading a known text, they would point to each letter and say the next word. That there would be

Figure 17.1.   An early example of Marina's "writing."

many letters left over when they used this method of reading was just one of the impenetrable mysteries of language and didn't concern them much. Spaces between words disappeared when they copied.

None of my students knew, in any reliable sort of way, the names of the letters of the alphabet, even though many of them could chant it. They could write their names but could not tell someone how their names were spelled. They could not write letters from dictation. "I don't know how to write *dog*, Teacher." "It's d-o-g," I say. "What letter is *d*? What else you say? How you make that?" And one day Martin, who is 7½, asked me where "elemeno" was in the alphabet. He was very annoyed at my explanation.

My students could not remember from day to day what their stories were about, and some of them could not remember from the beginning of a word to its end what word it was they were writing. They had trouble with the order of all the little words in a sentence, and would want instead to write only the last word. And none of them could actually read what they had written or even achieve the *appearance* of reading by pointing to each word and saying what they thought it was.

But in the midst of all this "chaos," small, unexpected events occurred. "Look, teacher, an *f*." Marina was awestruck. An *f*. Painted right there on the door of the school office. We could see it on our way back from the library. And then we passed the door that said "staff" and got to experience magic all over again. After a month or so of finding letters here and there in her environment, Marina took one of the class's laminated whole alphabet sheets home and taught herself the alphabet from start to finish. It took her only a few weeks to get fairly good at letter recognition and only 2 to 3 months to be efficient at both reading and writing the alphabet.

Marina was not the only one beginning to make some sense of her experiences with books and letters. Nolan brought his mass of scribbles and wispy, letter-like lines and circles to me one day and "read" the story he had written. Omar decided his left hand worked better than his right and quit trading off between the two. He began to make representational pictures with figures that could be recognized as people. He began to imitate Martin, copying from the pocket chart and calendar corner. And one day, Martin, having made an error of some sort on his paper, got an eraser, erased his mistake, and fixed it. Then he went on working; no screaming, no tantrums.

All of these small miracles happened without much direction from me. The children took more and more responsibility for the shape and progress of their writing. The exception was Jason, who would spend 45 to 50 minutes creating an extravagant work of art and then badger my instructional assistant into writing a sentence for him, which he would copy over. Jason had lots of ideas and seemed impatient and even embarrassed by his inability to find the words he needed to express himself. He would work privately on skills he was unsure of and avoided tackling projects he felt he couldn't do, including reading books. Sometimes he would behave very badly in hopes of being put in time out, thereby avoiding any activity at all. My instinct was to leave Jason alone for the most part.

By early December, I began thinking of ways to study my students and their writing behavior. These children had severe delays in language at every level. I didn't think I could afford to waste their time trying to get them to do things they weren't ready to do or could not do. I wanted evidence of progress, and I wasn't sure I would see that in their finished products alone. Omar's scribbling with his left hand doesn't look that much different from Omar's work when he scribbled with both hands. But that he finally settled on a hand was significant progress. Similarly, the result of goofing off by hiding behind the piano is the same as the result of going around the room looking intently at our alphabet cards. In either case Jason produced nothing, but in the latter case his behavior was at least relevant to the subject at hand. I felt I needed some way to view this behavior as steps in a process of learning to write. So I took *Coping with Chaos* as a starting point for beginning to study my students.

Cambourne and Turbill's (1987) thesis is that if given an environment structured to encourage language development through reading, writing, and speaking, children will in fact devise ways to do exactly that. The children develop a set of behaviors intended to teach themselves how to read and write, and these behaviors are fairly consistent in any group of children beginning to write. The authors call these behaviors "coping strategies" and extensively outline the types of behaviors and the use of them in a process-writing environment. From those strategies, I developed a check sheet; this included the category "Use of Related Activities," which comprises, among other things, drawing, making a title page, and getting ready to write by spending a lot of time finding supplies; "Using Environmental Print"; "Use of Repetition" in pictures, themes, and letter groupings; "Assistance From the Teacher"; and "Use of Temporary Spelling" (see Figure 17.2).

The plan was to look through the children's work and mark on my form for each the categories they were working on and things I had observed about their writing. This helped me to keep track of the children's activities. But it was even more helpful to me in other, unintended ways. It gave me the courage to leave my kids alone, to let them work at their own chosen tasks. Someone besides myself had studied children closely enough to know what behavior they indulged in to help themselves learn to write. That's what I wanted—some assurance that all this scribbling and copying was going to lead someplace. I didn't know whether these coping strategies would eventually lead to writing when exhibited in a child with language disorders. But, because I knew such strategies went somewhere with other children, as long as my students exhibited behavior that I could locate somewhere on my form, I decided to let it happen. Astonishingly enough, after a couple of months of observing coping behavior, I began to see something else that enabled me to drop the check sheet altogether.

It was Gilberto who showed me that, yes, indeed, we were going to move from just coping to actually reading and writing. I started working with Gilberto because he simply sat quietly and stared, his mouth partway open. When he needed to talk, his voice was so soft I could hardly hear it. He seemed to run out of breath before he got to the end of his short sentences. More of a somnambulist than a healthy 6-year-old, Gilberto moved slowly and dreamily, as though he had forgotten where he was headed before he even got out of the chair. For the first several months of school he would just sit and stare blankly as the rest of the children got busy on an assignment. "Gilberto, you need to get to work," I would say. "No crayons," he would murmur. "Do you know where the crayons are?" He would point to the supply table. "Well, you need to get some and get to work." He would drift away and then drift back, with or without crayons, in a sort of sleepy confusion. He would look at other

Coping Strategies of Language Disordered Children in a Process Writing Environment

Time Sampling Form

Use of Related Activities

1. picture drawing *&nonsymbol*
2. making title pages
3. other— *letter like shapes*

Using Environmental Print

1. random use of letters
   a. are the letters connected to writing not drawing?
   b. can the child "read a story" from the letters?

2. copying environmental print but giving it another meaning
   a. one to one correspondence with words
   b. textually appropriate pictures?

3. copying words the child knows but with no attempt at storyline.
   a. did the child draw a picture?
   b. can the child tell a story about the picture?

4. drawing pictures and copying appropriate lables

5. constructing a story from words that can be read

6. finding needed words and copying them to expand a storyline

Use of Repetition

1. repetition of picture items

2. repetition of letter groupings (differs from random use of environmental print in that letter groupings are "in their head," related to their name, or all of one type—straightlined or curved)

3. repetition of whole sentences or

sentence portions (use of basic patterns—"I like to...,my fish can...)

4. repetition of these

Assistance from/Interaction with the Teacher

Use of Temporary Spelling

Figure 17.2.   Chart developed after reading *Coping with Chaos* (Cambourne & Turbill, 1987), filled out for Nolan.

children's work to see if he could figure out what to do, and then he would take a stab at it. He had a complete lack of expressiveness about his face—simply blank most of the time. Of all my students, Gilberto seemed the most confused and hardest to reach. I wasn't sure how much talking or comprehending Gilberto could do. I started with a wordless picture book and asked him to tell me what he saw. I was surprised at how much English this bilingual child (who spoke Spanish to his mother) knew. Next I had him draw pictures and tell me about them. I would write down his sentences, ask "What comes next?" and give him a piece of paper for his next picture. He "wrote" a little story this way: A boy wanted a bat, caught the bat, took it home, played with it, and then took it to school. Afterward, Gilberto wrote a number of stories in this manner.

I don't remember how I discovered that Gilberto could write words himself, but he could, if I said a word slowly, produce appropriate consonants to match the sounds. He would leave spaces between his words because I told him to. When he was done, his writing could be read by anyone passingly familiar with invented spelling. The only problem was, Gilberto couldn't read it. When asked to read his writing, he would stare into midspace and recite what he remembered of what he had intended to write. When I told him he needed to look at, and point to, the words he was reading, he seemed very confused. He showed no recognition of any of the words he had written and would simply point randomly to letters and again recite his sentence. But by now I was beginning to get used to trafficking in the appearance of things. We continued to follow this routine daily.

"Faith," wrote the author of the Letter to the Hebrews, "is the assurance of things hoped for." I was developing a little faith as I watched Gilberto's facility with sound–symbol relationships outstrip the information I was presenting in class. "Did I teach you these?" I asked just to make sure. "No." "Did your mother?" "No." "So how did you learn the sounds all these letters make?" "I don't know. I just learn them." So, somehow, Gilberto, all by himself, was acquiring the knowledge he needed in order to write.

I tried various ways to help him see words and connect the letter sounds with the sentences he dictated. As often as possible, I referred him to environmental print. Out of a background of book titles, pocket chart poems, or the printed page, we would search for the word he needed. I would mask it off with adhesive notes, so he would see its beginning and end and not confuse it with other words. Then he would copy it on his page. I also recopied his sentences onto sentence strips. We practiced "reading" until he could match voice with printed word, pointing to each word as he said it. I cut up the sentence strips and put them on a pocket chart we labeled "Class Dictionary." Eventually Gilberto was able to recognize many of the words he needed to construct his patterned sentences. "The dinosaur is fighting" and "The fish is eating" were sentences he could write independently by the end of March. However, he still had not realized the importance of word order or of using all the words needed to convey the meaning he was after. One of the sentences from this time reads, "and the dinosaur rish." I asked him to read it to me. "The dinosaur is playing with the fish." He had pulled all the words he needed from the pocket chart and had them lying all over the table in front of him plus the word *and*. He had picked them up from the table at random and copied them. He was completely unconcerned about the fact that he didn't copy all of them, they were not in the order he said them, and he had written an extra word he didn't need. Even after we talked about what he had written and read it over exactly as he had written it, he still showed confusion over the whole process by writing *is* and *with* directly on top of the word *dinosaur*. "Start over," I told him. This time he produced "The dinosaur is playing fish" (see Figure 17.3). It was recess time, so I let him go.

Gilberto was showing me how much needed to be explained. We practiced making sentences from the words in the chart. Then we prac-

Figure 17.3.   Gilberto's writing using primarily pocket chart words.

ticed reading them, making sure the sentences had all the words we wanted, in the order we wanted them. He caught on quickly. A month later he had quit, for the most part, using the pocket chart words. He had learned to spell most of the words he needed. He began sounding out the rest of them, spelling them as best he could. Sometimes he wrote backwards; sometimes he just pulled letters out of the air. "KFPING" was "jumping" because *j* was one of the consonant sounds he didn't know. But for the most part he found a place to work, made a picture, and tucked his words in around tree trunks and sunbeams—an independent writer who knew what he wanted to say, wrote it, and read it. Not bad for a bilingual first grader with severe delays in all areas of language.

I began implementing the routines Gilberto and I worked out together with the other students. I would read to each student the work he or she had done the day before. I would ask what they were going to do today. Each child had to make a plan and tell it to me, then my instructional assistant and I would work individually with the students, slowly repeating their words back to them, helping them remember the symbols we use to represent sounds, telling them ones they didn't know. We encouraged the children to help each other by pointing out when one child used a word that another child needed. "Ask Nolan," we would say. "He just wrote that word." Or, "Remember that word? We saw it in the title of the book we just read. Jason can help you find it." I also kept writing out their sentences on sentence strips. After they read one several times, we would cut it up and store it on the pocket chart for future use. This turned out to be quite handy, as the children tended to write patterned sentences and needed the prompt "This is a" over and over. As some children acquired sight vocabulary, this also provided another way for them to help each other by searching for the words they needed among the growing number accumulating on the chart.

As Gilberto became increasingly independent, I began to focus more intently on other children in the room. Jason was one child who presented interesting challenges. His behavior fell under the category of "Related Activity" on my chart on his good days. He would just stand around in the company of books, letters, and words, or draw pictures, or copy the alphabet. Jason was a child with diagnosed attention-deficit disorder complicated by hyperactivity. He needed very loud auditory stimulation, which he usually provided for himself by yelling everything he said. He also suffered extreme articulation problems and delays in expressive language. Jason had a problem attending to any task that was not self-chosen.

But one day he came to writing time ready to work. We were in the midst of a pouring rainstorm that had pounded the city for hours. Jason rides to school each day on a miniature yellow school bus in the company of other children in need of language remediation. The little bus trundles through a number of surrounding school districts collecting these children. Jason, one of the first to be picked up, rides the bus for nearly an hour before arriving at school. Today the flooded streets and heavy rain of this dark, stormy winter morning had frightened him. He drew a bus full of children who were trapped in a rainstorm. "This bus is trapped," he wrote (see Figure 17.4). For the rest of the week in late February he did what he was expected to do in writing time—he drew pictures and wrote about them. "The tehlr TKA PKtr F The KlS" reads one entry (which translates to "The teacher took a picture of the class"). Clearly, immersed in "Related Activity" (his preferred coping strategy), Jason had been absorbing information about writing. Through all his drawing, he was mastering the curved line—the main problem in his illegible writing. He was also learning letter names and shapes and was mastering sound–symbol relationships. And he was able to find the word *the* on the pocket chart. But he hadn't felt obliged to make use of any of this information until the one day that he really wanted to record something about his fears on the bus. From that time on, he worked regularly and even enthusiastically on writing projects. He also frequently sat and read during reading time. His embarrassment over his disability lessened considerably, possibly because he realized he was actually overcoming it.

As I watched Jason, I concluded that he had followed Cambourne's and Turbill's (1987) research about young writers. Jason self-prescribed a line of study. Last fall he made himself a set of alphabet cards in his funny, broken writing. Most of his letters looked alike to me, but he seemed to be able to match them to the set of alphabet cards he helped me tack up on the chalk railings all around the room. He would dash about the room matching up his cards in a sort of frenzied physical education–writing activity well suited to his hyperactive state. He carried on during writing time in his loud, acting-out mode until he felt he had mastered enough skills not to embarrass himself in the job of writing. He waited until he had something to write about, and then he wrote.

Marina also took off on her own to master the skills of writing. Marina has severe delays in her receptive-language abilities. She has a difficult time hearing, processing, and following directions. But she also took home the alphabet chart and taught herself the alphabet. Her writing time was spent practicing the letters; she made endless rows of random letter sequences. However, she did not "read" her writing, even if it accompanied a picture. She viewed her writing as practice in letter-making, not story construction. For a time in February she tried representational drawing, and I had hopes this would lead to storytelling. It didn't. Marina has trouble remembering what she is drawing, and even if it vaguely resembles the object she intended to make, by the time she covers it over with patches of color, it is impossible to know what she had started to make. Even if I remind her ("OK, you've finished making the

Figure 17.4. Jason's bus story.

horse you said you were making"), she denies it. "It's not a horse. I made a hand." Her pictures have a fractured, broken look to them, with curly, wavy lines drifting about, perhaps a reflection of what she sees of the world through thick lenses designed to correct strabismus.

I didn't work very much with her as long as she seemed to have a plan of her own to occupy her writing time. I did notice that she could track words well, and could at least give the appearance of reading with good one-to-one correspondence when she had a memorized text in front of her. She could also match words easily.

None of my experience with Marina prepared me for the day when I asked, in a general sort of way, "Who can help Sandra find the word *the*?"—expecting someone to pop up and get it out of the pocket chart. Marina looked up from the letter strings with which she was filling a page of her journal. "You spell *the* t-h-e," she said, very matter of factly.

"How do you know that, Marina?"

"I just do," she said, as though there was nothing very remarkable about it at all.

"So can you write it?" I asked.

"Sure." T-h-e appeared in her letter string. "There." (Giggle, giggle.) "Now I'm going to write, 'The dog wrote this.'" At the bottom of her journal page, with some help from her teacher, she got her sentence written.

I decided to spend more time with this child, just to see what she could do. Marina didn't like this at all and spent some part of writing workshop sitting angrily in time-out. She was very annoyed by the structure of it—figure out a story, draw a picture for it, write one sentence about it, and do it every day for at least 4 days. This required her to stick with the theme regardless of what the drawing looked like. I was astonished at the results, however (see Figures 17.5 and 17.6). First, I learned that Marina could also spell *is*. And she knew many of the sound–symbol relationships we had learned in class—she wrote *trtL*, for instance, as well as *he* and *was*. Marina also demonstrated that, when pushed a bit, she could indeed produce organized, representational drawing and accompany it with clear writing that was related to the overall theme. She also found out that her teacher liked this immensely, showed it to Marina's mom, and Marina subsequently got taken to McDonald's for dinner. Dad took off work the next day just to come see this marvelous retelling of the story of the turtle who took off his shell.

I used this writing workshop model for about 5 months. I learned that despite learning differences, these children with language disorders can learn reading and writing using a process-writing approach. They self-prescribe courses of study. They use coping strategies identical to those of other emergent writers: These students copy endlessly from environmental print; they make letter strings, read from them, gradually

Figure 17.5. Day 1 of Marina working with me. This is the beginning of her turtle story. (I told her how to spell *crawling*.)

differentiate between letter strings and "book writing," and then either ask for, or are told by me that they need, assistance in crossing over from their private mode of writing to one more generally shared by a reading public. They invent sentence patterns and use them over and over until they know them by heart; then they slowly branch out. Their sentences become varied. They can write these sentences if the words are slowly dictated to them by the teacher, and they can imitate this strategy, eventually, on their own. From their use of repetition they have developed a small sight vocabulary, and from their copying they have developed an awareness of environmental print. This gives them three major strategies to use in their writing: phonics, sight vocabulary, and a kind of dictionary skill—looking up in their environment words they want to use. If I'm busy, and all else fails, they have learned to ask Gilberto and, more recently, Marina.

My assistant and I remain always ready to help children through the difficult parts. Children with language disorders have some extra miles to travel before language begins to make sense. Learning can take a long

neputhis chellON.

Figure 17.6. Marina's turtle story, Day 6. She wrote using information from the previous pages and drew the turtle without a model. It says, "He put his shell on."

time for them, and as a teacher I needed to watch and listen closely to see which information wasn't getting hooked up to a usable fund of general knowledge. "The dinosaur is . . . ," Gilberto writes over and over. He can find these words on the pocket chart. He can read them now after he has written them. But when he looks at a book, *the* and *is* are hard for him to recognize on a printed page. Jason can sound out a word on a printed page, and often, if an adult is saying the word very slowly, he gets the letters in his writing close enough to right that his words can be read easily. But he hasn't put these two skills together so that he can become independent in his writing. Marina knows how to spell certain words, but she never uses this knowledge. As a matter of fact, she kept this information completely hidden from me. And, initially, she did not appreciate being made to use this information.

Reversing a process is also very difficult. My students can guess letters from sounds but cannot say the sounds represented by the letters. They can write words but cannot read them afterwards.

Some of these breakdowns in the continuum of learning can be repaired by simply explaining and practicing. Gilberto did not know that word order made a difference. But just by having it pointed out and being given practice, he was able to remember this fact.

Other problems seem more built in to their language disorders, and they need much help. For instance, figuring out a sentence, holding each word of that sentence in suspension, in proper order, in one's mind, while at the same time figuring out which word is needed next on the page, saying that word, guessing at the letters needed, and then writing them down before going on to the next word, is a huge task for any child. For a beginning writer with word-recall and processing problems, this is just too hard to do. For me to take over some of the work by holding the sentence in my own memory for them, helps them focus completely on getting each word on the page.

When left on their own to write, only Gilberto and Nolan write independently. Nolan produces, "This is a" sentences and can usually find an appropriate noun in the room somewhere to complete it. Gilberto's sentences are a bit more complex, and sometimes there are even two sentences on his page. The other children still need an adult to help them sequence and complete their writing activities. Jason grows angry because he doesn't want to write any old thing—he wants the words he wants, and he wants them done right. But he isn't ready to employ the strategies we have been using on his own. Martin cries and moans and eventually produces letter strings that are broken into word-like groups. Marina cheerfully produces row after row of letters. Omar scribbles, claims to be done, and goes off to the listening center.

But if my assistant and I are there to help, to keep pulling them back to the task at hand and talking them through the steps of writing, they all write. The children choose their topics, choose the art supplies they will use for their pictures, sometimes decide to select a coauthor, choose their words, and once in a great while, even choose not to write, working instead on "Related Activities."

The children have seen language being used and want to use it themselves in writing. They are pleased and proud of what they have done. And, in the end, we have moved past faith and the need for assurances. We now hold in our hands the things hoped for—beautiful little books about whales and dinosaurs, caterpillars and butterflies, turtles, gardens, and Nolan's sister Whitney.

NOTE

This simple approach to process writing was given to me by a fellow teacher, Mary Mazmanian, who developed it in her own first- and second-grade classroom.

18. In Knowing Our Students Ourselves

JESSICA A. JACKMAN

This is the story of my relationship with one student, Jimmy Gonzales, and how I changed my perception of him. It was the beginning of my third year of teaching, my third school, and my third district. My school was located in a suburban southern California city with a predominantly Latino population. This was my first year with an actual teaching credential, and it was also my most difficult year. I was given a class of 16 sixth-, seventh-, and eighth-grade boys with learning disabilities (LD).

I began the year feeling hopeless after reading through their Individualized Education Programs (IEPs); all but three members of my class tested for reading at the first-grade level. How could they have made it this far and not have learned to read?

This was not my first year teaching special education at this grade level. In my last class of seventh and eighth graders, I had had only two students whose reading levels were that low, and they were twin refugees from El Salvador who barely knew English. I felt hopeless because this year's kids had been coming to school for so many years. What could I possibly offer that hadn't been done? Or how could I undo the damage that had been done? Either way, it seemed like an impossible responsibility.

I knew that I needed to investigate what had happened to these children—where had they been left out or hurt in the system of edu-

Reprinted, with changes, from "In knowing our students ourselves," by Jessica A. Jackman, *Journal of Learning Disabilities,* Vol. 28, 1995, pp. 569–574. Copyright © 1995 by PRO-ED, Inc.

cation? I began interviewing students and parents. What I learned heightened my sensitivity and prepared me to teach my students. This chapter focuses on Jimmy because my feelings changed more toward him than toward any other student throughout the year. He also became the most willing participant in my investigation, and from his interviews I developed insights into education, particularly related to students with LD.

THE BEGINNING

The first week of class was easy; I tried to find a feel for the school and the kids. Mainly, I wanted to learn what I could ask them to do without having them feel humiliation or anger. Jimmy stood out right away; he did not sit still and he continuously coughed, his face reddening. From his records I learned he was a twin, born full term but weighing only 3 pounds, whereas his fraternal twin weighed 7 pounds. His mother was a heroin user; Jimmy had lived with an aunt and uncle since he was 1½ years old. It was also noted in his records that at one point Jimmy believed his aunt to be his mother. He had had meningitis at 1 month, which the doctor felt might be the reason for his hyperactivity. Jimmy was in Headstart, where problems of hyperactivity were also noticed, and remained in kindergarten for 2 years because of poor social behavior.

Jimmy's story inspired pathos. He said he didn't know who his father was, his mother was in jail, his aunt and uncle didn't care about him, he hardly ever got to see his twin or his grandmother (with whom his brother lived). All this information burst forth in the middle of class activities. I contacted his uncle once concerning Jimmy's lack of Ritalin®. We met for the first time in front of the school. I said, "Hello, are you Jimmy's uncle?" I realized right away I had made a giant mistake. His expression completely changed for a minute as he calmly pointed out to me that he was just like Jimmy's father. This was my first indication that what Jimmy was telling me and others at school was not exactly the truth. It was obvious that his aunt and uncle truly loved and cared for Jimmy as their only son.

The meeting for developing Jimmy's IEP and for reviewing the annual goals was held in the first week of November. He had only partially met one of his goals—he could write his full name, address, and phone number correctly, except for his zip code. He did not meet the goals of improving time on task, writing the months of the year in order, reading consonant blends, subtracting four-digit numbers, or knowing multiplication facts. On the Piers-Harris Self-Concept Scale, Jimmy had a raw score of 12/80, which placed him in the 0 percentile and stanine in the nation. This surprised his aunt and uncle, who said they read with him every night.

In the beginning of the year I had nothing to guide me in controlling Jimmy's erratic actions; I had to learn about him on a daily basis. From Jimmy's turbulent behavior and the information in his IEP, I initially felt I would never bring him to literacy. He propelled himself around the room in quick, tense bursts of movement. When asked to read, he shut down, halting all of his energy. I was frightened that he would not even show progress, because he hadn't for so many years. Fortunately, I allowed the student to guide his own learning. Jimmy showed me that he could make lengthy efforts at writing when he was motivated by personal feelings (see Figure 18.1). He spent entire writing workshops (lasting more than an hour) on love letters. He wrote letters to his girlfriends, as well as the occasional favor for a friend having a girlfriend crisis.

First Interview

During the first few weeks of school I interviewed all of my students about reading and had them read to me individually. Jimmy's interview still stands out in my mind.

T: *How do you feel about reading?*
J: I don't read, I'm illiterate.

I asked Jimmy about his feelings toward school. He used this opportunity to complain about students in the class who bothered him. Jimmy said he hated one child because he was "a liar"; he disliked another because he was "crazy." This is a descriptor that Jimmy applied to himself. He said his own nickname was Loco. Jimmy professed to hate another boy because he was picky and constantly complained about school. I'm not sure how this related to Jimmy, but he did not try to spend time with this student.

T: *All right, Jimmy, I want you to tell me how you feel about school.*
J: I don't like it.
T: *Why not?*
J: I don't know.
T: *Well what don't you like about it?*
J: Kids.
T: *Okay.*
J: The kids in the class.
T: *In this class particularly?*

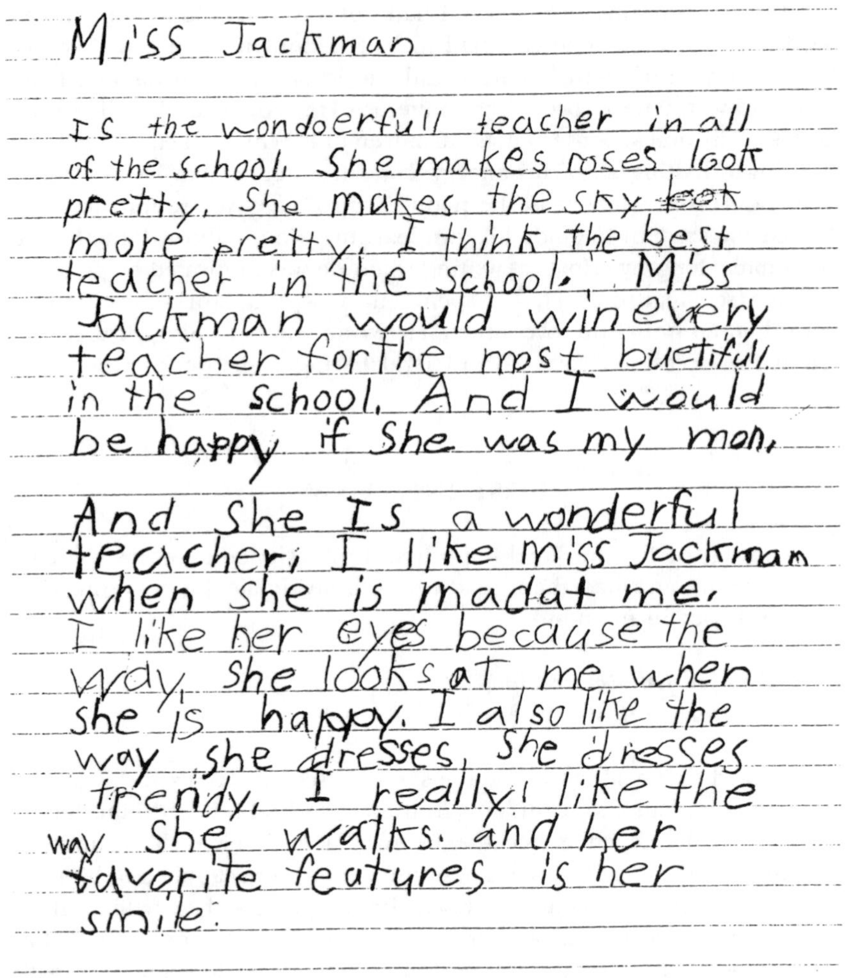

Miss Jackman

IS the wondoerfull teacher in all of the school. She makes roses look pretty. She makes the sky look more pretty. I think the best teacher in the school. Miss Jackman would win every teacher forThe most buetifull in the school. And I would be happy if She was my mom.

And She IS a wonderful teacher, I like miss Jackman when she is madat me. I like her eyes because the way she looks at me when she is happy. I also like the way she dresses, She dresses trendy, I really like the way she walks and her favorite features is her smile.

Figure 18.1.   Jimmy's letter to his teacher.

J: Yes.
T: *Okay, what bothers you about the kids?*
J: [pause] Steven, Steven bothers me a lot.
T: *What does he do?*
J: He's a liar.
T: *What do you mean?*
J: I don't know, lots of stuff.

T: *What does he lie about?*

J: Everything.

T: *You mean while you're having conversations? Or . . . .*

J: Yeah.

T: *What does he tell you?*

J: About sex.

T: *Do you know he's lying or is he playing around?*

J: Lying, everything he says.

T: *When he's bragging, or . . . .*

J: That's the word out there, bragging.

T: *Okay, so what else bothers you about this class?*

J: Jaime.

T: *Why does Jaime bother you?*

J: What? [laughter] He is just outta there.

T: *What do you mean?*

J: He's crazy!

T: *He's not crazy, he's just younger than the rest of you.*

J: Younger?!?

T: *More boyish.*

J: In a boyish kind of way. Oh God.

T: *It's sweet.*

J: It's sweet.

T: *Well, it's irritating, at least he's not bad.*

J: He's bad.

T: *No, he's not.*

J: He got his name on the board the other day.

T: *Well, probably because he was singing.*

J: Singing? He constantly talks too much.

T: *Yeah, well, other people do too.*

J: Not as much as him.

T: *All right, why does it bother you? Why can't you just ignore it?*

J: I don't know. I can't [mumbled]. It annoys everybody else.

T: *What does it make you feel like?*

J: Beating him up. At him. Get in trouble for that, huh?

T: *Um hmm.*

J: [laughter] Well [pause]

T: *Okay so who else bothers you? Jaime and Steven—because of those two people you hate school?*

J: Dave.

T: *What's wrong with Dave?*

J & T: [laughter]

T: *Well, you don't have to go around Dave, he doesn't get up and talk to you. You only go talk to him.*

J: He's picky.

T: *But you go and talk to him. Otherwise you could ignore him. He doesn't bother people who aren't around him.*

J: I don't know. I like to bug him.

T: *So you put that on yourself.*

J: True. Too many trues.

As this interview continued, Jimmy revealed that the other thing he hated about school was the teachers. He named the other SDC teacher to whom he went for math, because she "yells too much." I reminded him that I also yell, but he said it was not the same, because when she yelled, it hurt everybody's feelings. He said, "She doesn't stop until she makes a point, like my dad." Then he said more about his dad yelling at him in the morning and that's why he came to school in a bad mood. When I asked him why his dad yelled at him early in the morning, Jimmy said it was about waking up, and eating breakfast.

Second Interview

This second interview was about reading, and it is a good representation of how Jimmy has managed to avoid reading all of these years. In the first part, we were sounding out words together, and I was amazed that he could comprehend right away. It was going so slowly, however, that I thought it would be nearly impossible for him to get any meaning from the text. Toward the end of the interview, Jimmy admitted that he didn't feel he had improved in his reading during the year. This was hard for me to accept because sometimes he had been doing incredibly well. I reminded him that in March he had read from a book very well. Some of the words he read independently at that time were *baseball, powerful, form, even, dust, ice,* and *freeze.* In the previous October, on the other hand, he had been tested reading words such as *must, his, then, open, deep,* and *spell.* Despite this obvious improvement, he felt he was not really reading, that I was helping him. When I began to describe to him how I perceived his reading and to suggest some strategies for reading, he clearly led me off the subject.

T: *Tell me why you avoid reading?*

J: Uh.

T: *Why?*

J: Uh.

T: *You tell me, let's get at it, let's talk about it.*

J: Uh [not a comprehensible response], I don't know.

T: *You said to me that you hate reading.*

J: I don't like it.

T: *Can you tell me why you don't like it.*

J: Uh uh. I don't know.

T: *When did you first learn how to read?*

J: Today. Uh, fifth grade.

T: *Fifth grade.*

J: Um hm.

T: *When did you first go into special ed?*

J: When I got there.

T: *What grade?*

J: When they found out that, uh, third, when they find out that I couldn't spell and read good.

T: *Um hm. Did you ever? You didn't ever read and write in Spanish, did you?*

J: [negative response]

T: *Do you speak some Spanish? Not really.*

J: Little bit.

T: *When you first went into special ed, did they first do RSP and then, when's the first time you went into a small class like this?*

J: Oh, it was me and Jennifer and Maricela in there. Now they're still in it.

T: *Yeah.*

J: For a long time.

T: *All of you guys, huh. What grade was that?*

J: Third, I, I knew Maricela when she was in third grade and Jenny and Cathy and Shane. . . . Ah, forget those guys.

T: *Oh! That's how you know Shane!*

J: How do you know him?

T: *That's the one you wrote love letters for.*

J: Uh hm, so he can give all his. . . .

T: *I know him because he's famous around this school, because he's always getting detention.*

J: He's famous for being a jerk. Yeah. He has that little kid attitude.

T: *Oh really. So, do you feel like your reading's improved this year?*

J: No.

T: *No? What about the other day, when you read a whole page?*

J: You helped me.

T: *What?*

J: I didn't do it on my own.

T: *Oh, like three or four times I helped you, but you were just cutting up those words, you were tearing up the lines.*

J: I'm against reading, I don't know why.

T: *You're against it. Is it hard to see it, does it. . . .*

J: Well I, I need glasses anyway.

T: *I asked because, see when I was in third grade I had problems reading, too, and I still do sometimes, because sometimes to me the lines jiggle around. Does anything like that ever happen to you?*

J: Once in a great lifetime.

T: *Does it seem like kinds of letters change around?*

J: I just can't see them real good.

T: *You know what I think, 'cause, look at this word, when you were reading this, you read it as* <u>his</u> *and when you read* <u>bill</u> *you read* <u>beak</u>. *So you put words in that make sense and that's a good skill that you have, it's a strategy you have, of figuring out what words make sense. And sometimes you are so worried that you only use that strategy, you don't use other strategies. What are other strategies you could use?*

J: [uncomfortable grunt and "I don't know"]

T: *Well I could tell you some.*

J: Name.

T: *One would be trying to sound it out. Like with the* try *you did, you tried to sound that out, because you went* "tr" *(together* "ttrr tttrrrr") *"try." You want to, you're really not into this interview today are you? You don't want to talk; it's all me talking.*

J: [laughter]

T: *Oh, oh, this must be boring.*

J: Let's talk about, let's talk about baseball.

T: *Okay.*

J: You know anything about baseball?

T: *No, I don't, so you'll have to do all the talking.*

J: That's real cool. (And the interview continued with a discussion of baseball.)

Jimmy and his fraternal twin brother both played on the same Little League team, because his parents said, "Two people from the same family shouldn't play against each other." The boys' grandmother paid to enroll them both, to keep them occupied in a wholesome activity. The family is in full support. I attended two games, and both times at least five family members were there, including Jimmy's adoptive parents (his aunt and uncle). Jimmy definitely seemed to be the favored twin at these games—especially by his father and grandfather, although the women—Jimmy's sister and mother—defended the other twin. Jimmy's brother, Rudolfo, was living with his grandmother and attending another school in the district. He has never been in special education classes, and their difference from birth in weight has prevailed, as Rudolfo is quite overweight. Jimmy's parents seem completely dedicated to him; they try to help and understand him. I imagine they have struggled through many difficult times with him.

Still, Jimmy seemed uncomfortable when talking about his family. When specifically and seriously asked about his relations with his family, he replied, "It just doesn't click. It's not as good as my real family, 'cause my mom's in jail."

THIRD INTERVIEW

In the beginning of this interview, Jimmy talked about kindergarten, and getting into trouble, and going to the principal's office all the time. The same was true for first grade; he spent a lot of time in the principal's office, and got suspended. Jimmy's school records show that he hit and bit other students. He said that in first grade they did not learn how to read, they just drew pictures. When I asked him about reading in second grade, he said, "We learned *it, sit, at* and easy words like that." What he liked best at school at this time was beating up the girls and getting beaten up by them. I believe this interview really got to the heart of the experience of having an attention-deficit disorder, and of how children with this disorder manage in the school system.

T: *We talked about what you liked best. What did you like best?*

J: Nothing, nothing at all, don't like teachers 'cause you get into trouble. I don't like teachers 'cause if you get in trouble they get right away strict. It's like breathing down your neck.

T: *So how was reading in the third grade? Oh, did I already ask you that? How about math?*

J: Math!

T: *We haven't talked about math.*

J: It's easy, it can get easy.

T: *What were you doing in third grade? What type of math?*

J: Hm, reading storybooks.

T: *You were reading storybooks? Were you writing?*

J: Yeah, just a little bit.

T: *What kinds of things would you write?*

J: Uh, read about or write?

T: *Both.*

J: Reading *Indian in the Cupboard.*

T: *In third grade you were reading* Indian in the Cupboard?

J: No, the teacher read it to us. . . . We had this one table that you go around taking turns and, um, we would take turns, you know, with reading, we'd go in order. Somebody does one line and then the teacher does another. And some other kid does another line, you know, and. . . .

T: *Did you like that?*

J: It's okay, but when it got to me I got nervous.

T: *Yeah.*

J: Cause I'm not that much a good reader back then because we just started.

T: *Did you feel like other people were better than you were?*

J: Everybody had a hard time reading, but I was getting used to it.

T: *Do you feel better about it now?*

J: Yeah, it's okay.

T: *How about fourth grade? What was fourth grade like?*

J: [pause]

T: *Who was your teacher in fourth grade?*

J: He was funny, he used to give everybody wedgies. If you got in trouble he used to get them by their underwear and pick them up, and give them wedgies. . . . And they still have him there, too. After all these years they still have him. . . .

T: *So what else did you do that was interesting?*

J: [laughter and pause] Make you sit in front of the class.

T: *Why?*

J: If you got in trouble or get you by your underwear and take you to the front. . . .

T: *Front of what?*

J: The class.

T: *And what do you do?*

J: Just sit there in the front.

T: *Facing the class or facing the chalkboard?*

J: Facing the class. While he's doing something, while he's explaining something to the class.

T: *If he was teaching?*

J: I'd just be sitting there behind him making all these little funny things behind him, even bunny ears.

T: *He didn't know?*

J: Nah, nobody told. They just had to laugh.

T: *Didn't he think it was funny that the kids were laughing?*

J: Cause when something funny, I then do something behind his back, then they could really laugh. Making him think, making him think that they were having a good time with him.

T: *[laughter] You are so bad. What other little things did you figure out to do in fourth grade to amuse yourself?*

J: How to, um, how to get into a fight and blame it on somebody else. If I was having a fight, I hit that person on the ground, and then I'd lead them out. Then I'd make them start beating me up, until they got in trouble. [pause] Then make them get in trouble.

[Some interruption to the interview]

T: *What were we talking about? Oh, you did that funny thing to your teacher. So how was the reading going in fourth grade?*

J: Well, it was going a little better.

T: *How did [this teacher] do his reading? What did you do?*

J: Well . . . he'd have us read in pairs, you know, and later on after we got used to the words and all, he would choose us to read. Like if it was us, he'd make us stand up and read.

T: *Stand up and read, huh?*

J: At your desk.

T: *What did it feel like?*

J: Nervous.

T: *What did you do when you got nervous?*

J: Nothing, say I feel sick, see that's how, that's how I got into SC [meaning SDC, i.e., Special Day Class]. I start coughing, making it sound real and get on a table and lay down and they'd send me up to the office and then I'd be walking up to the office all comical. And they'd say you're fine and I'd say oh my stomach was hurting or something like that, you know. It started getting after she'd send me to the office, she'd tell me to go back to class. She'd shut the door. I'd sit, I'd sit right there for a, a little bit, wait to the bell rings. Then got to class five minutes later, it's time to go home.

T: *How many times would you say you did that?*

J: Fifteen, fifteen times after I got caught, I stopped.

T: *What else did you do to try to get out of reading? Or just when you felt nervous?*

J: Get in trouble.

T: *What would you do to get in trouble?*

J: I would, I'd be looking around the class to see if anybody's doing anything. If somebody's laughing at me, saying he'd not going to do it, I'd tell him to shut up. . . . Then I'd get sent out of class. That's why I'm always nervous, 'cause I'm always looking around, that's how I got the idea for always, for looking around and getting myself in trouble.

T: *Did you have many friends in that class? No?*

J: Everybody hated me 'cause I got them in trouble. They still don't trust me after all these years.

T: *Do you still know the kids from that class? Who was in that class that go here now?*

J: I forgot all of them after they don't like me. I just put them away, you know, I just put them behind my mind.

T: *So they didn't like you all year? Really?*

J: Not even for the next year, 'cause I had them in my class again.

T: *What was the next year like?*

J: Same thing. No, not the same thing, but just switching, but switching two classes—math and regular class.

T: *Oh, you had a regular class?*

J: Well, yeah, RSP. We still had RSP in there 'cause um. . . . [RSP is the Resource Specialist Program, which has a requirement that a student spend 49% of the day or less in special education]

T: *Was it RSP or SDC?* [SDC stipulates that 51% of the day is to be spent in special education]

J: I think it's SDC, 'cause she, my other teacher, used to go to my class. When it was time to, um, you know, the reading, she picked me up from that class. Everybody was in RSP because after they found some of the kids don't know how to read and all that, you know—they were just hiding themselves. Some of the kids back in third grade, they used to say I don't want to read, you know. I'm not used to reading the book, they'd be sitting there looking at the book, you know, pretend, pretending and moving their eyes around pretending they're reading it. Getting used to it. Then after they found out that they put them in the RSP an, um, they had a teacher come to the classroom and pick up a couple kids like Jennifer and Maricela and some other girls and we used to go into one classroom with these, all these other kids that didn't know how to read in that row, and, um, she'd help us all.

T: *What would she do in that class?*

J: Well, um, she would have, she would have us sound out the words first. Then make it go fast, you know.

T: *Did you like what she did?*

J: She was, she liked me, especially because I was a good kid to her, I respected her.

T: *But did you like her helping you learn to read? Did it help?*

J: I made her laugh a lot. Yeah, and she'd say, "It's time to stop laughing and get down to work," you know. She was a cool teacher. [We stopped the tape here, because he wanted to remember her name, so I looked it up on his IEP]

T: *Okay, so you had Carole Matthews in fifth grade as your RSP teacher and you like her. So, did you feel like you were making progress in learning how to read?*

J: Yeah.

During this interview I pushed Jimmy for information about his class the previous year, which I suspected had been traumatic. It had also been Jimmy's first placement into SDC. His comments in the interview showed that he handled the experience by forgetting everything.

END OF THE YEAR

It is now May, and at this point in the year it is impossible to think about Jimmy without a smile. He is the first child to greet me with a robust "Good morning, Miss Jackman." He always asks about my welfare and gives gifts of praise and abundant compliments. I call him the King of Kiss-up, a name of which he is very proud.

He is a person of great intensity—highly emotional, excited, extreme in all his undertakings. I had never noticed how distinct his stuttering was until I scripted our interviews. The motion of his words matches exactly the motion of his body and the flow of his reading. In walking, he moves with great velocity and halts abruptly, spins on his heels to change direction, and sets forth again with a speed and determination not suited for short distances. To come up behind Jimmy in the school halls is an unnerving experience—he nearly collides with seven or eight different people in a 30-foot distance through a crowded hallway. Yet, at the same time, his movements are absolutely, finely, and quietly controlled. I used to call him "The Ghost," because he could move all the way across the room, soundlessly, in a moment's turn of my head. In out-of-school situations, Jimmy's ability to move is esteemed; he looks like a star during his baseball games. If he relaxes enough from his nervousness, he will hit home runs, or at least doubles or triples.

I have seen how Jimmy's reading mimics his general approach to movement, and to life. He is either in love or his heart is broken, he is extremely good or horribly bad in class; in reading, he plunges ahead depending upon context clues and his knowledge of language. Then he freezes up at small words that he cannot recognize or establish meaning from well enough to guess. After writing most of this article, I asked Jimmy, "Why do you think you haven't learned to read very well?" Jimmy's reply was, " 'Cause I didn't pay much attention. I'm sorry to say this, but no one was there to encourage me and I couldn't encourage myself." I knew Jimmy to be hard on himself concerning his ability to pay attention; he does feel responsible for his behavior. He knows the limitations of his medication and feels he should not have to take it.

Conclusions

I gained much as a teacher from this study. Healthy skepticism, for example—if I had not seen Jimmy's parents in a variety of settings, I probably would have continued to believe that they did not care about him. I learned that Jimmy needs personal and emotional feelings to motivate his learning or his ability to pay attention. I am hoping that, with the relationship we developed throughout this year, I can be the teacher that encourages him to literacy. At the end of this school year Jimmy spontaneously read instructions to a paper out loud, but to himself, and then said, "Hey, Miss Jackman! I guess my reading really has improved."

19. Macbeth *in the Resource Room: Students with Learning Disabilities Study Shakespeare*

SUE THORSON

My students in a high school resource room had learned that when it came to English class, "difficult" was synonymous with "impossible." Although we coaxed them into reading and enjoying poetry at a college-prep level, they firmly clung to their simplified versions of other literary works, such as novels and plays.

I have always wondered how Shakespeare came to be such a scholastic ogre, when he wrote for the uneducated masses of rural England. Surely our students were more sophisticated than the illiterate citizens of the Tudor age. But one look at the difficulties of Shakespeare made my guys dig in their heels and screech. I supposed that with an average reading level at the fourth grade, a record-best attention span of three class sessions, and a cultural abyss of race, class, and time, they were probably right.

For some mysterious reason, my instructional assistant, Kathy Zepka, and I decided to give *Macbeth* a try, in spite of all logic, common sense,

Reprinted, with changes, from "*Macbeth* in the resource room: Students with learning disabilities study Shakespeare," by Sue Thorson, *Journal of Learning Disabilities*, Vol. 28, 1995, pp. 575–581. Copyright © 1995 by PRO-ED, Inc.

and experience. It was one of the most successful units I have ever taught and became a much-anticipated part of our triennial curricular cycle.

When teachers meet, we complain and we boast, in story after story, about our classrooms. Our success stories resound with our pride and love for our students. Each success is a discrete event, to be celebrated over and over again. Sharing stories is an important part of our search for ways of duplicating good lessons and engaging units.

Academics talk theory. Their pedagogical panaceas, clinical proofs, and esoteric research projects often fail dismally when applied to daily classroom realities. There are, however, a few theories that will enhance a wide variety of classroom practices. Behavioral strategies, although confining and reductionistic, can provide some students with a sense of security, a clarification of the academic arcana. The search for opportunities to reinforce reminds adults to seek out and build on strengths instead of bemoaning weaknesses. Critical pedagogy, with its insistence on respect for students and *their* realities, the sharing of power in the classroom, and the nurturing of student voices, encourages students to invest personal interest and increased effort in their own learning by addressing their needs instead of the requirements of an alien curriculum. Feminine pedagogy permits caring and passion to enter the classroom. As learning becomes less sterile, students respond with gusto. Constructivism posits an epistemology that recognizes individual needs and experiences, the social nature of learning, and the learner's control of personal growth. When these theories are consistently applied to classroom procedures, a new environment evolves. Extrinsic control and motivation move toward intrinsic rationales; silent, stubborn resistance to schoolwork becomes friendly social interaction that is a vehicle for academic growth; the challenge of the teaching–learning process becomes a pleasure for all of the participants.

The following story recounts a successful experience in our room. I hope that it will give teachers the pleasure of a shared memory and perhaps a practical idea or two; academics may enjoy picking out the theoretical underpinning that I am just beginning to discover.

THE GROUP

In our learning disabilities resource room, I was truly a teacher–learner. I had never heard of Freire, and I probably espoused the concept of the teacher as expert dispenser of information, but I didn't know a lot about traditional curricula. My background in Spanish literature left me no more prepared to teach high school subjects than any other high school graduate. Students were already used to helping me figure out algebra and science lessons. My only exposure to Shakespeare was *Hamlet* and *Julius Caesar* in high school; I had never read *Macbeth*. So, as usual, the students and I were on equal footing when it came to figuring this drama out.

Besides assisting in instruction, Kathy was our cheerleader, pushing me ahead when I got nervous and encouraging the students to try assignments. As we constructed class learning plans, her curiosity and enthusiasm served as a constant model for us to emulate.

The students were 10th, 11th, and 12th graders, ages 15 to 20. Most had been in special education for 3 to 7 years, although a few started in the resource room in high school. They often remained with us for English and/or math for 3 years. Test scores indicated reading levels from 2.0 to 13.0. Writing skills varied from words and phrases to fairly coherent paragraphs. Spelling, punctuation, and grammar were universally poor. Some students were apathetic, others aggressive; none were "academic." The few students who appeared to be motivated had poor skills.

Of course, our first priority involved rules of behavior, from no fighting to appropriate work habits. A behavior modification system based on grade points and positive reinforcement was a central part of the classroom management system. Students who weren't interested in school gradually became avid accumulators of points, then sporadically decreased their interest in scores, and even grades, as they learned to participate in their own education. Due to the variety of ages, interests, skills, and behaviors in any class period, students usually worked individually on a selection of tasks. We actively solicited their input in planning their work. As their work habits improved, their choice of activities and assignments expanded.

Although our focus was on academic achievement, Kathy and I worked hard to make the class a safe, pleasant place to be. We didn't have the talent to make the room look pretty, but the casual chaos of papers, books, and scattered desks did provide a comfortable, relaxed atmosphere. The interesting book and magazine covers that were strewn about tempted students to read. There was an air of friendly teasing, offhand challenges, unabashed affection, and an unswerving belief in their abilities. Group and individual conversations included, but were not led by, the teacher and instructional assistant. We constantly prodded each other to think, explain, guess, and grow.

PREPARATION

Over the years, we tried several methods to introduce the students to the differences in language and customs found within a Shakespearean play. One thing that always interested them was my comments about the disgusting violence, teen sex, blue jokes, and disagreeable adults prevalent in these works. Mysterious references to the crude dialogue in *The Taming of the Shrew*, what Hamlet was *really* saying to Ophelia, or the bawdy behavior of Juliet's nurse made the class curious and slightly interested in attempting to explore the mazes of Elizabethan English.

During October and November I told them the plots of famous plays whenever we had 10 or 15 minutes to spare. (Lamb's *Tales From Shakespeare* helped me prepare.) Most students enjoyed listening to these bizarre stories, but some continued their seat work without seeming to pay attention.

The first year, we read a few sonnets together and spent several days reading and discussing Shylock's "If you prick me, do I not bleed?" speech from *The Merchant of Venice* (III, i, 51–63). The quotation generated serious conversations about issues of racism and prejudice. Then we watched films on the staging of *Shakespeare in the Park* productions. Meryl Streep was a hit in *The Taming of the Shrew.*

The most successful approach, however, was a research project, designed by the students, on Shakespeare and his times, in which they posed about 30 questions pertaining to Shakespeare and his works, did library research, and shared answers. Poor readers found valuable information in illustrations, filmstrips, records, and videos. With their interest piqued, they were enticed into reading and writing snippets way above their tested grade level. Results could be presented for evaluation in the form of one-paragraph answers to questions; illustrations and models of sets, clothing, the Globe, housing, and so forth; maps of the times; the locations in *Macbeth*; or music recitals.

Besides developing students' research skills and increasing their interest in the study of the play, this project had several unexpected benefits. Of course, our librarian was an invaluable resource, but other teachers also became actively involved in the research as they entered the media center to pursue their own projects. Their spontaneous involvement impressed the students more than any "modeled" research would have. The students were also amused, then impressed, as they watched the librarian and me spend 3 days searching for the answer to what had seemed like a fairly straightforward question. We finally combined facts located by students in history books, an essay on the Globe, and an encyclopedia article on economics to compute an approximate answer to the ticket price of a play in Shakespeare's time in current dollars (1990 cost: $2.36 for a groundling, $7.08 for a seat with a cushion, or a minimum of $14.14 for a private theater ticket). In the course of their research and sharing, students picked up literary terms, historical data, and a picture of Elizabethan England that I could never have "taught" them.

THE PLAY

The first rule we made was that nobody was required to do the play. Students were free to work on standard journal entries, vocabulary research, book reports, and reading/writing projects instead of doing the play with the group. However, they were expected to be quiet during our group work. Most chose to do the alternative activities at first, but found it difficult to resist watching the video of the play. I made sure that part of each *Macbeth* homework assignment was extremely easy, so almost all of the students were drawn into the group by the end of the first act.

We quickly established a daily routine. First, we viewed a *Macbeth* video, borrowed from the English department, of the scenes read for homework. We discussed those scenes as a group, concentrating on plot, linguistic explanations, and production values at first. As the students became familiar with the language and involved in the plot, they raised increasingly sophisticated discussion topics about mood and theme. I followed their lead, at first to avoid discouraging them, but finally because I couldn't keep up with their references to street activities, current events, and school politics. After our discussion, we rewound the video, amid moans and groans, to watch what we had discussed and continued through to watch the next section assigned. Tension mounted as we neared the end of the homework assignment, where they knew I would stop the video in spite of their protests. Although they hated watching scenes a second and third time, I think the multiple viewings enabled the students to develop new insights into the play. I assigned three to five questions for homework. One or two were factual, the answers to which were obvious from the action in the video. The others probed higher level thinking. (The next time I do this unit, I will ask the students to pose and answer their own questions, a technique that was successful when we read *A Raisin in the Sun* [Hansberry, 1959]). The students usually had enough class time to begin, but not to complete their homework. A few never did any more than that, but as the play progressed, more and more began reading at home.

The play begins with an irresistible scene: creepy, rhythmic, suspenseful. What is going on here? The students seem excited as they use the text to figure out the content of the strange language, but they are still convinced that the play is too hard for them. Discussions crop up about witches, the old lady down the street, voodoo customs of recent immigrants, New Age and ancient beliefs and customs. Does Shakespeare really believe this stuff? Do we? We go on to scenes 2 and 3.

Gert was a quiet, awkward girl in my class, whose tests and behaviors, including her rare efforts at speech, indicated fairly serious retardation, but activist parents raised a fuss about EMR placement, so resource teachers had helped her struggle through school. She shyly proffered an insightful paper, in her childish handwriting. Each homework question had been answered clearly, in perfect English: complete sentences, paragraphs where appropriate, spelling, punctuation, the works. Help at home? I watched her begin, and sometimes complete, every assignment from the play in the ensuing classes. Once she started writing, Gert never reverted to her "retarded" behaviors, but slowly increased her class participation and made tentative social advances.

Sorting out the characters and battle results in *Macbeth* is easy work for kids accustomed to war movies and the complexities of street politics. Figuring out what the witches are talking about takes more group effort, but is almost worth the time. Is Macbeth really thinking what we think he's thinking? This video is gray and creepy.

As the plot develops, the students are carried along in spite of themselves. Lady Macbeth's sensuality shocks even these worldly young people. Splashes of red in the grayness are noticed and discussed.

Act II. Will he or won't he? The students enter the room eager to see the next installment. More and more are following the video with their texts. This Macbeth guy is a total jerk: a coward, a sneak, a liar, a cheat. An argument rages over Lady Macbeth's role in the murder. She is defined as cold and heartless. Students comment on the use of loud noises in the quiet of the night.

Most students are impatient with the porter's comic relief. They want to know what will be done to Macbeth and are outraged at Lady Macbeth's deceit. Are the murders of the grooms believable? Only Malcolm and Donalbain see the truth, and of course the adults won't believe them. What would it be like to have to run away at night? Some students identify only too well with the young princes' terror.

King Macbeth instigates Banquo's murder, but still suffers from guilt. His queen is despised by the class as an amoral woman who is the antithesis of their idea of what a woman should be. We chat briefly about the difficulty of removing a corpse from a curtainless stage and the use of rhyming couplets to end a scene.

The ghost is greeted with delight. The students predict the beginning of the end. Obviously, Macbeth is going to go completely mad and either confess or commit suicide. They hope he confesses, so that his heartless wife can also be punished. The lords' conversation is not terribly interesting, just typical adult slowness. . . .

The class analyzes the witches' prophecies while Kathy and I sit back and beam. We challenge them to use a history resource to figure out the procession of kings. (I'm thinking books, they wisely go to teachers. Several return with an explanation.) A friendly competition is instituted to figure out the other prophecies as the play continues.

Streetwise Ellen, who has been in class for a record 3 consecutive days, is outraged at the murders at Fife. She demands the address of this Shakespeare guy so that she can write him a letter. He has just gone too far. The class cheers Macduff on, straining to understand the complex dialogue, then mourns with him as Ross tells him the horrible news from Scotland.

Linda comes in, shocked by and proud of the time she spent on homework last night. She even read ahead, because she just had to find out what happens to Lady Macbeth. The other students revel in Lady Macbeth's disintegration and discuss Macbeth's concurrent strengthening. The Scottish lords are finally wising up.

Although mad, Macbeth is strong. He expresses an astonishing love for his wife. The class discusses his feelings at length. Presenting arguments from their own experiences and television, they decide that Shakespeare is believable, and better than any soap. Billy catches the reference to Birnam Wood. There is a frantic flipping back to the prophecies. But Macbeth is deemed safe, because no one can kill him. Tentative hypotheses of wild horses or vicious dogs are put forth, because it is obvious that Macbeth *must* die.

Mario enters the discussion with a triumphant explanation of cesarean birth. Can it be? Kathy and I give him a secret thumbs-up but refuse to tell the others whether or not he is right ("Macduff was from his mother's womb untimely ripped"). He glows. The students wonder how Lady Macbeth died. They go back to previous scenes to prove or disprove options. A general education English teacher is stymied by my frantic request for an answer—no general-track student has *ever* raised that question. The English department grapples with the issue long after we each choose our favorite interpretations and move ahead.

By now, almost everybody has read ahead to glory in Macbeth's bloody end. Young Siward's death is still greeted with shock; his father's reaction is hotly debated. They are disappointed by the obvious fakery of Macbeth's bloody head, and discuss ways to make it more realistic. The letdown of finishing the play and ending our involvement with ancient Scottish feuds is leavened by the discovery that we have, indeed, read and understood a play by William Shakespeare. Casual discussion leads to comparisons with the modern world. Besides the local gangs and drug lords, there is always a "Macbeth" in the news: Khamenei, Amin, Noriega. Young people wrestle with the demands of their lovers versus the standards of parents and church. Occasional examples of the supernatural come up for discussion.

AFTERWARD

The results of challenging ourselves did not end with the play. Some students chose to develop their answers from the informal I-Search into a standard research paper. It was their first experience with writing a lengthy paper without copying from an encyclopedia. After Christmas, the seniors in public and parochial schools began to wrestle with *Macbeth*. Imagine the glee of "retard room" kids as they became respected Shakespearean experts in the cafeteria and the neighborhood.

The first year, just for kicks, we gave the multiple choice Shakespeare portion of the regular English midterm to our students (What the hey . . . one less section for me to write . . .). When the 10th graders in our room outscored the seniors across the hall, we decided to make up our own test in the future. (One student had refused to do any of the play, making up his grade on the optional assignments. He had not, however, been able to ignore the video or the class discussions. He only got a B on the test.)

As the year continued, students proudly reported answering "Jeopardy" questions before the "smart" sibling, watching a Shakespeare play on PBS, and even understanding sitcom references that had previously gone over their heads. By June, requests for free-time videos included *Romeo and Juliet* and *Othello*.

The students' increased self-confidence and newly established work habits, and the thrill of success, led to improved grades, increased mainstreaming, and a slow blossoming of interest in postsecondary education programs. The following September, one of Aaron's goals was "to learn to find things in the library, like Ms. T. did last year."

THE THEORIES

The *Macbeth* unit was a wonderful experience for my students, but, because I had the students for 3 consecutive years, we could do it for only one quarter every 3 years. My attempts to create other units met with varying degrees of success. Good teachers constantly try to recreate magic moments in the classroom, but my efforts were sporadic and chaotic. We could never quite duplicate the *Macbeth* experience with other topics. Academic and personal growth occurred, but never as dramatically or completely. What made this unit work so well?

Looking back, it is clear that the success of the unit was due not to a five-point lesson plan, or clever organization, but, rather, to a classroom environment and procedures that had been developing for years. Increasing respect for student abilities, combined with student participation in planning, regularly led us to the library, where informal research procedures evolved. After an introductory week in the library in September, students were sent on "treasure hunts" for information ranging from questions about words and current events to why I named my cat Carrie. The Shakespearean research and studying *Macbeth* simply polished skills that had been developing in the resource room for years.

Behaviorism was an integral part of the entering student's experience. I am distracted by wandering, head-banging, and put-downs, so these behaviors were extinguished in favor of the development of on-task, in-seat, socially acceptable behaviors. Tokens and points were faded as soon as students approached a minimal standard of behavior. (This fading was not planned, but as the students learned that doing work carried its own rewards, they gradually lost interest in extrinsic reinforcement.) However, the habit of looking for positive traits, improvements, and successes led me to an appreciation of subtle talents and multiple intelligences. My ideal, clinical, engineered classroom never got off the ground, but it was the basis for a complex contract system, which, in the process of teacher survival, became a simple, student-driven system of choice.

The years of trial and error led to a management style that almost replicated Deci and Ryan's (1987) model of the use of intrinsic motivation to enhance both the quantity and the quality of learning. From the first day, students were offered choices of activities; they were never required to complete specific assignments, as long as they were working. Although extrinsic, positive reinforcement was important in helping students begin to engage in classwork, it was usually paired with informative feedback or a challenge for growth (Deci and Ryan discuss in more detail the use of choice, information, and challenge to encourage intrinsic motivation).

Feminist pedagogy includes the emotional and spiritual needs of the classroom community and posits that adults should treat students with the care and respect they would extend to their own children (Grumet, 1988). Kathy and I were uncomfortable with many of the demeaning materials and activities recommended for special education adolescents. Besides challenging them and believing in them, we showed them how much we cared. We closed the door furtively and dropped our professional masks whenever we could. Feminist pedagogy offers many valuable theories to teachers, but I believe its greatest gift is the permission to show feelings in the classroom. The students' passionate reactions to the play enriched their experience after the emotional atmosphere in the room had already enabled them to risk the academic stretches demanded from any student of Shakespeare.

Critical pedagogues espouse a student-centered program, in which the teacher is a resource person who facilitates the students' journeys of discovery, rather than directing them (Freire, 1990). I have realized that student involvement and learning almost always had an inverse relationship to the amount of structured teaching activities I presented. However, students enthusiastically welcomed and remembered my participation. The research project and *Macbeth* discussions exemplify students' ability to direct their own learning with great success. The theories of critical pedagogy also emphasize the importance of connecting content to students' social realities. As they discussed the play, the class consistently related plot, characters, and theme to their families and community and the national news. The direction of their discussions validates the importance of social connections to learners.

Understanding how adolescents with LD learn has long been a challenge to educators. Constructivism offers a useful explanation: Each learner builds a meaningful picture of the world based on individual experience, a variety of cognitive styles, interests, and social interactions (Poplin, 1988). Although this theory answers a lot of questions for me, it also raises a potential problem. Left to themselves, what kinds of knowledge will these students construct? They designed a research project based on their interests and knowledge of literary interpretation. As they wandered around the library, chatting and exploring, they developed a picture of Shakespeare and his times richer than that presented by most literature texts. Although still excessive, teacher guidance was minimal as we watched and read the play, but the students did better than general classroom students on a test of standard required knowledge (the type of test most of them generally failed). It seems as if, left to their own devices, they not only learned what they were supposed to—a rare enough occurrence—but also acquired a very unusual appreciation for a difficult author.

The application of these theories on a day-to-day basis enables students to develop not an abstract self-respect based on pop psychology and the mere fact of existence, but, instead, a strong self-concept, rooted in successful experiences of challenges met and failures overcome. Academic growth becomes more than a list of memorized gains in grade-level skills; it refers to curiosity and research, literature and passion, composition and expression. Teacher and student become interchangeable in the exhausting, exhilarating experiences of intellectual growth.

APPENDIX A: STUDYING A SHAKESPEARE PLAY

Preparations

Activities that lay a foundation for reading a Shakespearean play

Month 1: Build a classroom environment that encourages work and mutual respect. Prove the possibility of success to each student. Establish standard learning/assessment opportunities, such as journal writing, vocabulary development, reading and writing options, television and video critiques, etc.

Month 2: Use extra class time to tell students Shakespearean plots. Begin research in the middle of the month.

Month 3: Research and/or readings from sonnets and plays once or twice a week.

Month 4: *Macbeth*

Month 5: Optional assignments due. Final assessment.

Beginning to Study Shakespeare

An activity to introduce the language and customs of Tudor England

Read a selection written by William Shakespeare or a contemporary aloud with the students. Initiate a discussion based on vocabulary, context and imagery. As students demonstrate contextual understanding, move into small-group discussions of imagery. Stimulate conceptual development with a general question about the applicability of the reading to reality. Assess with an oral debriefing or a quick write.

Optional assignments may include a translation of the reading into modern English, a poster or illustration, or resetting the scene into your school and time.

Stimulating Intellectual Curiosity

Some considerations in constructing a research project to enrich students' understanding of Macbeth

1. Ask the students what they want to know about Shakespeare and his times, Macbeth and his times, etc.

2. Combine student lists to make a master list of questions, leaving room for additions. Distribute the master list to the students.

3. Allow a minimum of 3 days in the library. Once the students have started working, the teacher, too, should research a question. Publicly ask the librarian and other teachers for research advice.

4. Students write a minipaper; draw pictures, maps, and diagrams; and make models, tapes, or videos to answer each question they choose to work on. Sources *must* be listed, in the bibliographical format used by the school. Sharing information is permitted, but the student who located the information must also be cited as a source.

5. Students have the option of rewriting minipapers as one coherent academic research paper and/or writing detailed explanations of their pictures, maps, or models for additional credit.

Reading Macbeth in Three Short Weeks

A daily routine and reading schedule for reading the play in 45-minute class periods

Day	Acts, Scenes
1.	I, i–iii
2.	I, iv–vi
3.	I, vii
4.	II, i–ii
5.	II, iii–iv
6.	III, i–ii
7.	III, iii–iv
8.	III, v–vi
9.	IV, i
10.	IV, ii–iii
11.	V, i–iv
12.	V, v–vii
13.	V, viii

At the bell, begin the video with homework reading. View the tape, discuss homework questions and other issues raised by the students. (We often discussed staging and production values.)

Either distribute questions for the next reading or assign students to write and answer their own. Rewatch the scenes, adding those for the next assignment. I generally assigned three questions per scene: a really easy one (who? where?), one of medium difficulty (translate, list), and a really difficult one (explain, predict). Next time, I will ask the students to write their own questions more often.

APPENDIX B: RESOURCES

Behavior Modification

Bryan, T., & Bryan, J. (1975). Understanding learning disabilities. New York: Alfred.
Cartwright, P. G. et al. (1989). Educating special learners. Belmont, CA: Wadsworth.
O'Leary, K., & O'Leary, S. (1972). Classroom management. Elmsford, NY: Pergamon Press.

Intrinsic Motivation

Gilbert, T. (1978). Human competence. New York: McGraw-Hill.

Feminist Pedagogy

Gilligan, C. (1982). In a different voice. Cambridge, MA: Harvard University Press.

Critical Pedagogy

Horton, M., & Freire, P. (1990). We make the road by walking. Philadelphia: Temple University Press.

Constructivism

Bruner, J. (1990). Acts of meaning. Cambridge, MA: Harvard University Press.

The Research Process

Elbow, P. (1981). Writing with power. New York: Oxford University Press.
Graves, D. H. (1984). Writing: Teachers and children at work. Portsmouth, NH: Heinemann.
Macrorie, K. (1985). Telling writing. Upper Montclair, NJ: Hayden.

Macrorie, K. *(1976)*. *Writing to be read*. Rochelle Park, NJ: Hayden.
Moffet, J. *(1968)*. *A student-centered language arts curriculum, Grades K–13: A handbook for teachers*. Boston: Houghton Mifflin.
Moffet, J. *(1981)*. *Active voice*. Montclair, NJ: Boynton/Cook.

Macbeth

British Broadcasting Company. *(1978)*. *Shakespeare Series, Macbeth*. Paramus, NJ: Time-Life Film and Video.
Calandra, D. *(1979)*. *Cliffs notes on Shakespeare's Macbeth*. Lincoln, NE: Cliffs Notes.
Caldwell, S. *(1987)*. *Macbeth*. Princeton, NJ: Films for the Humanities.
Evans, M., Anderson, J., & Schaefer, G. *(1961)*. *Macbeth*. Chicago: Macmillan Films.
Lamb, C., & Lamb, M. *(n.d.)*. *Tales from Shakespeare*. New York: George Routledge and Sons.
Mowat, B., & Werstine, P. *(Eds.)*. *(1992)*. *Macbeth*. New York: Washington Square Press.
Polanski, R. *(1971)*. *Macbeth*. New York: Evergreen Video Society.
Royal Shakespeare Company. *(n.d.)* *Macbeth*. Princeton, NJ: Films for the Humanities, Inc.

20. Valuing Differences: The Children We Don't Understand

CATHERINE C. DuCHARME

Nate's tongue was curled up on the right side of his upper lip as he moved his pencil to write. He carefully wrote, "Me and my mom went to Disneyland and it was my birthday." Nate's story seems typical for a first-grade child; however, I remember being confused at first, because Nate had written the entire sentence backwards, with each letter appearing in mirror image! "How did he do that?" I wondered.

After school that afternoon I sat down and tried to write like Nate had earlier in the day, but I found it to be impossible. "How did he do that?" I thought.

The following day I observed Nate during our morning-workshop time. While Nate's peers drew pictures and wrote stories, Nate drew pictures, too. When he began to write his story, I noticed that he began writing from the right-hand side of his paper. I watched as he carefully wrote each letter. I was in awe of this unique child.

I went home that afternoon thinking about him. What should I do? How should I respond to his reversals? Should he be tested for a learning disability?

Reprinted, with changes, from "Valuing differences: The children we don't understand," by Catherine C. DuCharme, *Journal of Learning Disabilities*, Vol. 28, 1995, pp. 582–585. Copyright © 1995 by PRO-ED, Inc.

When Nate began to compose his story the following day, I asked to sit beside him. When he began to write backwards just as before, I stopped him and told him there are different ways to read and write depending on the language. I told him about Chinese characters that are read vertically. Then I told him that in English we read left to right. I'm not certain that Nate was necessarily impressed by my little speech, but afterwards he smiled. I pointed to the left-hand side of his story paper and showed him that he could start writing there.

I wasn't sure if I had done the best thing for Nate by intervening, but that day his writing contained only a few letter reversals. It was readable.

During the course of the next few months, Nate occasionally wrote his story completely backwards (whenever he began writing from the right-hand side of the paper). I continued to remind him when I noticed him doing this, and each time that Nate wrote from left to right, his writing showed only a few letter reversals.

I abandoned the idea of submitting referral papers for testing.

During several parent conferences with Nate's mother, I learned that she also had had a difficult time in school. Her parents and her teachers were very worried about her and believed that she might be suffering from a learning disability. We conferred regularly to discuss Nate's progress and review samples of his writing. Nate's mother cried during several of our conferences and expressed guilt for possibly having passed on a dreaded learning disability. I, too, remained concerned about Nate, although his writing behavior was rather predictable and his errors systematic. For example, he reversed *b*s, *d*s, and *p*s regularly, and everything was reversed when he began writing from the right to the left instead of from the left to right.

I recall asking Nate's mother during one of our afternoon conferences if she could tell me more about her own perceived learning disability. Through tears she told me that she had a terrible time in first and second grade. She wrote backwards, just like Nate, and learning to read was difficult. Then, in third grade, she told me, everything changed. The letter reversals just disappeared.

I wondered . . . would Nate's reversals simply disappear with age?

Nate had not been placed in any special program. He remained in my classroom for 2 years. Like all of my students, Nate grew and developed during those years. He developed fluency in reading and writing, and although he occasionally wrote backwards, from right to left, he began to monitor himself in this regard.

I felt fairly confident as Nate entered third grade. But I worried a little about how he would be perceived by the third-grade teacher.

The new school year began and I often saw Nate on the playground. What a wonderful child he was! Full of energy and enthusiasm, full of curiosity.

I ran into Nate's mother while doing my grocery shopping one weekend. After some small talk, I inquired about Nate's reversals. "Do you still see reversals in Nate's writing?" I asked. "You know," she said, "I hadn't really thought about that. He's doing so well. He loves his teacher and school. I don't think I have noticed it anymore."

I felt validated by Nate's mother's response. I felt as if we had done the best thing for Nate by allowing him to grow in a supportive environment. What might he have suffered had he been referred for special education? Would he have felt the same way about himself? I know that he had been spared the humiliating school experiences his mother had endured. He had not been relegated to the "bottom reading group," nor had he been admonished for writing letters backwards. Perhaps Nate's mother had suffered more from "dysteachia" (Armstrong, 1987) than from dyslexia!

I taught kindergarten and primary-grade children for 10 years in the California public schools. I can't say that I ever had another student quite like Nate. And I can't say I never had doubts about my professional decision not to refer him for special testing. It wasn't until Nate finished third grade successfully that I felt reassured.

I have taught other children that I didn't fully understand: Jeff was a very angry child; Juan communicated in a way that made sense only to Lucio; Tanya was an extremely articulate 8-year-old but became frustrated when she couldn't remember her friends' names or how to spell *my*. I didn't understand the cause of the children's differences, but I believed that my role was not to understand them, but to find an appropriate way to *respond* to those differences that would facilitate individual, unique growth.

When I met Tanya, she was 8 years old. She was placed as a second grader in my first-and-second-grade classroom. Tanya's mother had moved her from their neighborhood school to this model school site, where she hoped things would be better for her child. I learned that as early as preschool, Tanya had had trouble remembering such things as directions and her friends' names. In kindergarten, she struggled with letter names and sounds. She was referred by her kindergarten teacher for special education but did not qualify for special help at that time. She was referred again in first grade, but when she did not qualify, she was retained. Near the end of her second year in first grade, Tanya began receiving special education, although neither she nor her parents really could explain what was "wrong" with her.

I was quite surprised when the resource specialist informed me that Tanya would be visiting the resource room on a daily basis. Tanya and I had spent 2 weeks together in our classroom and I had observed her to be an extremely articulate, strong leader. I *had* noticed that her invented spellings were more like those of a first grader, but she was functioning quite well in our multiage grouping.

Tanya did not like leaving our classroom. She usually didn't say much, but this time she didn't have to because her feelings were written all over her face. Some days she refused to go at all; and tears flowed down her cheeks occasionally. I tried to find out why she didn't want to go to the resource room; once she told me, "I don't learn anything there. I just have to say baby words." Another day she said, "What's wrong with me?" These times were very difficult for the two of us. I wanted to shield her from the pain she was experiencing. I wanted to tell her she didn't have to ever leave our classroom.

Eventually the resource specialist, who was a very kind young woman, agreed to come to our classroom to work with Tanya. She worked with some of the other children, too. But the scheduled visits could not be continued due to the resource specialist's time demands.

Tanya's parents became concerned about Tanya's emotional well-being, and after a conference with me and the resource specialist, it was decided that Tanya would be allowed to choose to go to the resource room or to stay in the classroom. This solution proved to be acceptable to all concerned, and Tanya did frequent the resource room throughout the year. However, as the year progressed, Tanya became more and more aware of her differences. She noticed that all of her classmates seemed to be able to communicate well through writing with invented spellings. She noticed that her drawings looked crude in comparison to her peers'. Tanya cried and was often frustrated in reading and writing, though she was a natural leader and extremely articulate in class discussions.

Tanya knew she was different, and even though I tried to provide the most supportive, caring learning environment possible, I could not protect her from her pain and suffering. Most school days were busy and productive, but some days were filled with sadness, disappointment, and frustration.

As the school year ended, I wondered how different Tanya's life could have been if she had not been tested over and over again since kindergarten. Would Tanya have developed her own ways of compensating had she experienced an early schooling experience with teachers that held high expectations for her success, rather than questions regarding the type of her learning disability? Did Tanya sense early on that she was "different" from other children her age because she left the classroom to take tests?

Tanya had been told by her parents and her former teacher that her brain didn't work the same as other children's brains. Did she interpret this difference as positive? Did she blame herself for being different? Did she blame herself when her parents fought about her "problem"? Tanya had heard her parents fighting and she thought it was her fault. These questions haunt me. Tanya didn't know what was "wrong" with her—but, then, I'm not sure that anyone else did, either.

Is there really anything "wrong" with Tanya and Nate, or is it that we just don't fully understand the complexities of human behavior? Perhaps the human mind, in all its complexity, is a mystery of life that still eludes us.

My experiences with Nate and Tanya suggest some important things for teachers to consider each day that we live and learn with a group of young children. First and foremost, we can *expect* great variability in individuals and *value* these differences. As Gardner (1983, 1991) and his associates at Harvard's Project Zero have shown, each child is a genius in her or his own right, with a particular blend of multiple intelligences. Western culture has traditionally placed a higher value on linguistic and logical–mathematical intelligence, often to the detriment of other intelligences, such as spatial, musical, personal, and bodily/kinesthetic. As teachers, we must adopt a broader view of intelligence, one that goes beyond the archaic idea of IQ as a fixed biological trait (Gould, 1981). The theory of multiple intelligences assumes that all children have gifts and strengths in ways of thinking that can be cultivated. Linguistic genius is just one of many valuable gifts.

Our job as teachers is to observe and assess what the child CAN do, and build upon his or her unique strengths in the educative process. Our focus must remain on responding to our students' differences, rather than looking for their causes or attempting to define them. In the case of Nate, would his education have been enhanced or hindered had I searched for explanations for his differences? I believe his interests were better served by responding to his uniqueness, by exploring ways to help him accomplish his own learning in his own way.

Tanya was labeled as LD early on, and the destruction to her self-image was devastating. We know too well the danger of labeling children (Albinger, 1993; Hrncir & Eisenhart, 1991). And, again, the energy spent on searching for the causes of her differences did not affect her education positively. Tanya was perhaps a victim of her kindergarten and first-grade teachers' expecting less of her, failing to try to understand her, and rejecting her for her differences.

Tanya's story also sensitizes us to the value of involving the child in placement decisions. As a special education student, Tanya was expected to go to the resource room each day for remediation. Prior to her second-grade year, Tanya had not been involved in the decision-making process. No one had considered her an integral part of the child study process; rather, she was the *subject* of that process. She was an outsider in the process even though it was her life that was being affected the most.

As I listened to Tanya explain why she wanted to stay in the general classroom, her reasons made sense. She knew she wasn't learning as well in the small resource room cubicle, doing tracking exercises in which she circled the appropriate letter. She knew how she felt about being singled out as different and in need of special help: She felt sad and lonely. Furthermore, she believed what she had been told—that her brain worked differently from other children's brains and so she needed special education in order to learn. The ambiguity of her "disease" was extremely problematic for her, and she often suffered from negative feelings of self-blame. I learned much about how to respond to Tanya in the classroom by carefully listening to her; she taught me a great deal.

There are many children in our public schools that we don't fully understand. Nate and Tanya are not isolated cases; others have been documented in great detail (Albinger, 1993; Taylor, 1991). Will we continue to search for and label their differences, or will we begin to value their differences and search for ways of responding to them?

In my own quest to respond to the children I do not fully understand, I have learned that I must listen to the children and I must listen to myself. Only by doing so can we become professional educators; as professional educators, we become child advocates, protecting our students from a system that is founded upon reductionism and reductionistic learning theory. As a teacher, I became aware of the important knowledge I possessed about the children I taught; I had lived with them day after day and had observed them in our learning environment. I had constructed detailed knowledge of their strengths and the ways in which they approached learning in all its complexity. My observations yielded portraits of individuals engaged in problem solving, each with his or her own unique patterns of behavior. Similarly, I learned that the children were my teachers and informed my quest to be responsive to their needs. Taylor (1993) stated that "our task is to insure that the voices of children become embodied in the ways in which we teach" (p. 49). Listening to ourselves and to our students is an important way by which we can be sure that the children's voices will guide our teaching.

A student advocacy model of instructional assessment (Taylor, 1993) is a valuable alternative to the present-day methods of viewing differences among individual children. As child advocates, we adopt a broad view of human development and behavior, and we expect great variability in the ways in which children learn (Perrone, 1991; Taylor, 1993). We look for strengths and focus on what each child CAN do. Through careful observation, portraits of individual children emerge, and this information allows us to teach to the child's strengths (Ayers, 1993). Rather than trying to explain a child's differences by looking for causes or disease, child advocates search for ways to help the child develop (Martin, 1988; Poplin, 1988). We vary our teaching approaches and utilize the child's interests (Five, 1991). Child advocates utilize the child's parents as informants to gain understanding of him or her (Spodek & Saracho, 1994). When working with children who are receiving special education, child advocates are sensitive to the importance of involving the children themselves in decisions about their school life (Taylor, 1991, 1993). Many inspiring books have been written by creative professional teachers, relating their personal experiences about responding to unique children in the classroom (Ashton-Warner, 1986; Kohl, 1984; Paley, 1981, 1991).

The lives of many children are in jeopardy; negative school experiences are long-lasting. We can no longer afford to label and sort children on the basis of their differences—a practice that may be well-intentioned but may in fact simply be a legal way for our schools to structure inequality (Crux, 1989; Shepard, 1991). Not only are these practices harmful, but they also "might in fact aggravate prejudice and interethnic hostility" (Nieto, 1992, p. 253). We need to accept and value differences, listen to children and observe their ways of problem solving, and utilize their strengths and interests.

> If such a student advocacy model were adopted, students who learn in ways that do not meet traditional school expectations would not be labeled. Students who are poor would not be penalized. Students of color would have a chance to succeed. Students whose young lives have been damaged by life's circumstances would have the opportunity to recover. (Taylor, 1993, p. 176)

21. Anna's Story: Narratives of Personal Experience About Being Labeled Learning Disabled

D. KIM REID AND LINDA J. BUTTON

There are two irreducible modes of cognitive functioning—or more simply, two modes of thought [i.e., paradigmatic science and narrative knowing, respectively]—each meriting the status of a "natural kind." Each provides a way of ordering experience, of constructing reality, and the two (though amenable to complementary use) are irreducible to one another. Each also provides ways of organizing representation in memory and of filtering the perceptual world. Efforts to reduce one mode to the other or to ignore one at the expense of the other inevitably fail to capture the rich ways in which people "know" and describe events around them.

Each of the ways of knowing, moreover, has operating principles of its own and its own criteria of well-formedness. But they differ radically in their procedures for establishing truth. One verifies by appeal to formal verification procedures and empirical proof. The other establishes *not* truth but truth-likeness or verisimilitude. It has been claimed that the one is a refinement of or an abstraction from the other. But this must either be false or true only in the most trivial way, for in their full development, the one seeks explications that are context free and universal, and the other seeks explications that are context sensitive and particular. Moreover, there

Reprinted, with changes, from "Anna's story: Narratives of personal experience about being labeled learning disabled," by D. Kim Reid and Linda J. Button, *Journal of Learning Disabilities*, Vol. 28, 1995, pp. 602–614. Copyright © 1995 by PRO-ED, Inc.

is no direct way in which a statement derived from one mode can contradict or even corroborate a statement from the other. As Rorty has recently put it, one mode is centered around the narrow epistemological question of how to know the truth; the other around the broader and more inclusive question of the meaning of experience. (Bruner, 1985, pp. 97–98)

It is ironic that in special education, a field devoted to improving the quality of life for people with disabilities, we have almost no acquaintance with those *people* in our literature. We have an array of means and standard deviations that characterize students with disabilities as "subjects" in groups or subgroups, and a significantly smaller set of case studies that report investigators' observations about these "subjects," but it is difficult to find instances in which we hear from the people themselves (Mishler, 1993). We do not know how *they* understand their problems and needs. We have studied them, planned for them, educated them, and erased them. We have not listened to *their* voices. In this study, we examine the role that personal-experience narratives play in one adolescent woman's understanding of her learning disability. During our discussions with six adolescents, it was Anna who was the most open about describing her experiences as a student labeled learning disabled. It was for this reason that we selected Anna's interview for in-depth study. The other students, although more reticent, echoed her concerns.

To give voice to Anna and her peers, we chose to elicit the less well-known, less well-studied mode of thought described by Bruner (1985) in the epigraph. (The other mode of thought is, of course, paradigmatic science.) Humans throughout the ages and in every culture have understood their lives and created their identities by emplotting life events into stories (Bruner, 1990; Mishler, 1992). Consequently, narrative is the "root metaphor" for human meaning making (Sarbin, 1986), and narrative inquiry focuses on individuals' stories.

Narrative inquiry is important for at least two reasons: First, people experience time as it unfolds in events (Ricoeur, 1981); by endowing life events with temporal and causal relations, they both answer the question "Who am I?" and define the range of possibilities for their futures. Second, narrative gives voice to the persons we study. Although it has a long and honored tradition in history and literature, the value of narrative inquiry for psychology and education is just being discovered (Carter, 1993; Polkinghorne, 1988). Narrative inquiry is one means of addressing Flavell's (1992) musing that we might want to add personal profiles to our knowledge base, to discover "what it is like to be them [in this case, students with language/learning disabilities] and what the world seems like to them, given what they have and have not achieved" (p. 1003).

Students with language/learning disabilities have long been reported to demonstrate sustained difficulties with narrative structure. The research suggests that those problems might be related to (a) difficulty knowing when to use acquired cognitive strategies (Swanson, 1992); (b) lack of linguistic sophistication in using such devices as cohesive organization (Liles, 1985) and/or causal inferencing (Ackerman, 1986); (c) constructive memory errors (Prawat & Jones, 1977); or (d) developmental delays (Roth, 1987).

Yet, since Labov's (1972) landmark study of Black Vernacular English, we have become increasingly aware that all humans learn the discourse of their homes quite easily and that these discourses are each coherent, consistent, and equally viable systems of language. As Gee (1985) remarked,

> There are some things that all human beings, barring rather severe handicaps, are good at. One of these is mastering a native language.... It is simply perverse to say that one native speaker has mastered the grammar better than another. Similarly, though this is less well recognized, all human beings are masters of making sense of experience and the world through narrative.... We are all given this gift in virtue of our humanness, though in some of us it may be atrophying under an avalanche of rational nonsense. (p. 27)

The "rational nonsense" to which Gee refers embraces the myth, so pervasive in our schools and in our society, that we can measure all human activities and then rank order people along a continuum. In schools, to make assumptions about students' language competence, we compare it to clearly articulated, middle-class, Standard English discourse. Students like Anna, who become labeled as people with language/learning disabilities, are usually assessed via decontextualized, standardized tests, which do in fact reflect the expectations most teachers have about what kind of language is appropriate and acceptable in school (Edwards, 1989; Gee, 1990).

Michaels and her colleagues (Collins & Michaels, 1986; Michaels, 1981, 1985; Michaels & Collins, 1984), for example, have shown that teachers have rather narrow and rigid expectations for classroom discourse, including writing, and that they strive to "teach" their students to conform to those expectations—often unconsciously. Michaels (1991) argued that nonnarrative discourse—description, explanation, and justification—are accorded a privileged status in school, even during sharing time (Show and Tell) in early elementary classrooms. Teachers, she says, "are looking for a certain kind of narrative account, with literate-like characteristics, closer to simple descriptive prose" (p. 309).

Because Anna had been labeled as having language/learning disabilities but was not severely impaired—and is in fact quite articulate—we decided to analyze the nature of her responses to our interview questions to determine how well they conformed to linguistic expectations for the structure of narratives deemed acceptable for use in school. Furthermore, we conducted a content analysis of the interviews with Anna and her peers to identify themes associated with the presentation of self (McAdams, 1993; Mishler, 1986).

Of course, in any interview, the questions and listening attitude of, as well as the power relations between, the interviewer and the participant affect the story that is told. The participants knew that we were university professors who taught teachers of both general and special education. We elicited the interviews by telling the students that we wanted them to tell us what they would like the teachers in *our* classes to know about them.

ANNA

At the time of our interview, Anna was a tall, 13-year-old, White, middle class European American adolescent with dark red hair and a shy smile. Anna was labeled as having language disabilities at the age of 5. In Colorado a language disability is defined as a disorder that prevents the student from receiving reasonable educational benefit from general education. Language disability is related to functional communication or delayed language development (Colorado Code of Regulations 301-8, 1992). Anna's mother recounted to us that at the time Anna was diagnosed, she and her husband were told "not to bother" saving for a college education for Anna, because she would never have the requisite academic ability. They were instead advised to take their savings and "go on a vacation." We refer to Anna as having language/learning disabilities because she was later diagnosed as having both disabilities.

Anna began first grade in a self-contained classroom for speech/ language and communication disorders and was educated in resource rooms nearly exclusively through the fifth grade. In sixth grade, she was mainstreamed into a fifth/sixth-grade class for science and social studies. She and her family moved several times because of changes in her father's place of employment (he was the manager of a supermarket chain). At the time she attended our summer special needs program, Anna had completed the sixth grade. Her tested reading level was 3 years below her grade placement level, and her math was 2 years below. Anna's intelligence, however, was well within the normal range. In the paperwork the school personnel forwarded to the summer program, they indicated that Anna needed help with reading, math, and her low self-concept. Her school report also noted that Anna had difficulty with written language skills, particularly spelling.

During her interview and the subsequent discussions, Anna told a number of disturbing stories about her school-related experiences.

Through Anna's pain, however, there emerged a dignity and determination that impressed her peers as well as us. It was because of our respect for her that we asked for, and were granted, permission by Anna and her family to use her real name.

OTHER PARTICIPANTS

Five other student volunteers (three boys and two girls) in Grades 6 and 7 participated. All of the students had applied for the summer program, but because of high demand, only Anna and Lisa could be accommodated. All of the students were diagnosed as having severe difficulties related to listening, speaking, reading, writing, reasoning, and/or mathematical abilities (Morris et al., 1994; National Institute of Child Health and Human Development, Interagency Committee on Learning Disabilities, 1987).

The students had all received special education services in public school settings and were designated as having perceptual or communicative disabilities, the terminology used in the state of Colorado to describe language/learning disabilities. These disorders are described as being present in the psychological processes that affect language learning and are evidenced by (a) a significant discrepancy between estimated intellectual potential, usually based on the results of the Wechsler Intelligence Scale for Children–Revised (Wechsler, 1974) or the Woodcock-Johnson Psycho-Educational Battery (Woodcock, 1977) and actual levels of performance, or (b) language or cognitive processing that results in impaired achievement in reading, written language expression, and the comprehension, application, and retention of math concepts (Colorado Code of Regulations 301-8, 1992).

During the discussions, when the students were working on their collaborative essays, Lisa, a middle class Chicana, and Sally, a middle class European American, were very attentive to what the others in the group had to say, but contributed little. Lisa, age 14, who had long, beautiful, dark hair, would often lean down and literally hide behind her hair during the discussions. Sally, age 13, sat, resolute, her head filled with ideas she chose not to share, unless we asked her specifically to contribute.

Pedro, one of two 13-year-old, working-class, Hispanic American boys, was also very reticent, especially when talking about school. But he became animated when recounting adventures with his family and meeting his friends at the local shopping mall. Fernando, age 13, a seemingly jovial, articulate, and outgoing youngster, repeatedly described incidents at school when he was ridiculed for being in special education. He made it clear that as a "special ed kid" you had to learn to stand up for yourself.

His greatest disappointments involved teachers and students who had treated him unfairly. Wayne, a 14-year-old, middle class European American, appeared to be very thoughtful. He also spoke with some displeasure about school, but his most profound messages were found in the drawings he made of his classroom experiences, one of which is presented later. We are using his real name with his and his family's permission in order to give him credit for his expressive artistic talent.

INTERVIEWS AND THE ESSAY

In the summer of 1992, we invited these 6 young adolescents to tell us what being called learning disabled meant to them and to write a collaborative essay to help teachers better understand all students with learning disabilities. The second author, who had met 2 of these students previously, conducted the individual videotaped interviews, 1 student a day over a 6-day period. She asked questions similar to those that are interspersed in Anna's interview. Our intention was to make the students as comfortable as possible and to make the interviews as fluid as possible, so the questions were not always asked in the same way or in the same order. These narrative interviews constituted our first data source. For their analysis, we followed the successive steps of the narrative inquiry process described by Mishler (1990):

> interviews with a small, varied group . . ., repeated listenings to taped interviews and readings of transcripts, discovery of parallel trajectories in . . . histories, development and refinement of a model . . ., selection of a respondent as a representative case, and specification of [her] narrative for detailed analysis and interpretation. (p. 427)

The first author (although both of us were present) led the discussions (also videotaped) through which the essay was created. The students worked together 2 hours a day for 4 days. The first day they were asked to brainstorm ideas they would like to see included in the essay. These were recorded on a board and then transcribed into a typed list, a copy of which was made available to each student during the second meeting. The students organized the list of items into categories by selecting the most important ideas. Nominations were listed on the board. After the students were finished listing the "most important ideas," they were asked to determine under which of those ideas each of the remaining items on the list would be included. There were discussions about their earlier selections, and some of the most important ideas were combined, some eliminated, new ones added. In the end, 16 categories were outlined into main ideas and supporting details. On the third day, the students were asked to discuss their categories of ideas and to rank order them: Which were most important to include in an essay to be shared with teachers? The top categories were then fleshed out into paragraphs: Students suggested sentences; others made recommendations for their revision or elimination. The order of the sentences was discussed and sometimes reorganized. When the students were satisfied with one category/paragraph, they went on to another. On the fourth day, the students reviewed their work for clarity and mechanical accuracy. Ideas were once again discussed, important ideas that had been previously left out were added, and a few words and sentences were deleted. The essay was typed and distributed to students on the fifth day, when we met for a pizza party. The essay provided us with a second data source, the discussion through which the essay was constructed, a third, and Wayne's cartoon, a fourth.

Analysis of Anna's Transcript

We used a linguistic approach (Gee, 1985, 1986, 1989, 1991) for the analysis of Anna's interview—a series of short narratives that, taken together, show how she uses stories to make sense of her experience as a person labeled learning disabled. We chose this means of presentation because, as Gee, Michaels, and O'Connor (1992) noted, cultural and linguistic strengths are more easily recognized from the idealized, formatted version.

Anna's protocol is a sample of her discourse as she takes on the role of student in a rather formal interaction—a videotaped interview—with a woman she knows to be a teacher. Gee et al. (1992) noted that dialogue reflects "expectations about the roles participants will play and the characteristic ways in which people playing these roles are expected to act, interact, and appear to believe, value, and think" (p. 234). Because Anna is talking with a teacher in such a formal setting (a university classroom), the language she uses in this interview approximates the discourse patterns she uses in school (see Gee, 1989).

How It Feels to Be Called Learning Disabled

The opening couplet of the text presented in Table 21.1 summarizes the feelings that Anna illustrates in her subsequent story. She is angry and frustrated about being "in there." By responding with the deixic term *in there*, rather than the term we used to ask the question, *learning*

TABLE 21.1

Idealized Realization of Anna's First Story: What It Is Like to Be Learning Disabled

What's it like to be called learning disabled?

Stanza 1: Feeling Abstract
1. I usually feel mad.
2. Sometimes I feel frustrated, because I'm in there.

Stanza 2: Story Abstract and Orientation
3. There are regular kids that were in there last year that had almost the same problems.
4. But, we all did not get along.
5. Because other sixth graders are in the regular class.
6. And we go there only for science or social studies.

Stanza 3: Challenge: You're Retarded
7. And they're like, "Why aren't you in here?"
8. "Like why aren't you?
9. "We know why you're not in there.
10. "You're not in there because you're retarded."

Stanza 4: Defense and Rebuff
11. And it's like, "I'm not in there because I'm retarded.
12. "I'm special ed."
13. And they're like, "No, you don't know where I'm at.
14. "You can't do stuff like us."

Stanza 5: Evaluation
15. And I couldn't even sit at their desks with them.
16. I couldn't even share a table.
17. I always had to be by myself at a different table when I had science or something.
18. And I was pretty sad.

Stanza 6: Episode Orientation
19. And then Mickey [a general education teacher] said, "I need somebody to help Anna."

Stanza 7: Second Challenge: They Thought I Could Do It
20. They helped me, but they didn't really want to help me.
21. Because they thought, "Oh, come on, dummy!"
22. (They thought too that I could do this.)
23. They thought, "Yeah, you can do this.
24. "You're a regular sixth-grade kid."

Stanza 8: Second Defense
25. It's like, "No, I'm special ed.
26. "I can't do this."

Stanza 9: Coda
27. So I get along with it sometimes.
28. And it's pretty hard.

disabled, Anna distances herself from the label. *Learning disabilities* is a place, a distant place, the place she goes in school, and not a personal characteristic.

Anna frames her story by including an abstract (Labov, 1972) that both provides its essential point, "We are isolated from the regular sixth graders," and orients the listener to the context—the setting (sixth grade), time (last year), and characters (regular kids). The source of her anger and frustration is the "regular kids," including students who, last year, were "in there," who had problems much like her own but who now are regular sixth graders. Lest we think that these students are her friends, she is quick to note that they did not all get along. She attributes her isolation to the fact that whereas other sixth graders are in the regular class for a full day every day, "they" go there only for science or social studies (see Note).

Stanza 3 is a clear example of a structure that Anna repeats again and again throughout her interview—parallelism between lines and groups of lines (see also lines 1–2 and 3–4). She begins with a verb, saying, "And they're like" (an expression typical of the current adolescent vernacular), then follows with a quotation, in this case, the sixth graders' question that serves as the initiating event in her story, "Why aren't you in here?" In line 8, she repeats that question in paraphrase. In line 9, she again quotes the sixth graders, but this time with a declarative sentence that indicates that the previous questions have been rhetorical. The sixth graders know why she is not in there—again, a distancing, as she prepares to follow with an expansion (increasing in loudness and rapidity) in which the sixth graders accuse her of being retarded. The overall structure of the stanza, then, takes a semantic *aabb* form.

Anna's response in this minidrama occurs in Stanza 4, which has a structure very similar to that of the previous stanza. She begins the first and third lines with a syntactic parallelism: "And it's like" and "And they're like." In the first couplet, she loudly and in staccato asserts "I'm *not* in there because I'm *retarded*" and then explains, "I'm *special ed*." The second couplet takes exactly the same form—an assertion, "No, you don't know where I'm at," followed by the explanation, "You can't do stuff like us."

Stanza 5 serves an evaluation function (Labov, 1972); that is, Anna tells us why she is telling the story. What is so out of the ordinary? She has to sit by herself. She is isolated. She could not even sit among the sixth graders at their desks, or share a table. Lines 15 and 16 have the same parallel form as the couplets in the previous stanza. In line 17, Anna emphasizes the pain associated with this outcome by repeating again, "I always had to be by myself at a different table when I had science or something." In line 18, she expresses her internal response to this state of affairs: "And I was pretty sad." In this expression, she reiterates the negative feelings with which she opened her response but does not bring us back to the present tense, because she is not finished with her story. There is more to tell.

A new and contrasting episode begins in Stanza 6. The teacher, Mickey, asks the sixth-grade students to help Anna. As she notes in Stanza 7, line 20, they did help her, but they did not want to. Line 22 is an evaluation, which interrupts the flow of the narrative. Anna is making certain that the listener understands why she is quoting her classmates. This time the problem is not that they think she is retarded—on the contrary: These students make the mistake of thinking that Anna is like them, a regular sixth-grade kid. Again, we see the extension of the first line (20) of the couplet in the second (21): "They didn't want to help. *Because* they thought, 'Oh, come on, dummy'. . . . They thought (line 23), 'Yeah, you can do this'" *because* (line 24) "You're a regular sixth-grade kid." The lines in which the quotations occur are said both more loudly and more rapidly than the lines surrounding them or the evaluation (line 22) inserted between them.

The story ends in Stanza 8 with Anna's asserting once again that she is "special ed" and cannot do what they expect of her. Anna's solution to these dilemmas, presented in the Coda (lines 27 and 28), is to "get along with it sometimes," but at great personal cost, which explains the feelings of anger and frustration she addressed in her opening couplet.

Anna's interview (see also the sections reported in other tables) stands midway between the oral tradition and the type of decontextualized, essayist style of narrative expected in school. Michaels (cited in Gee et al., 1992) reported that her data from the early elementary sharing-time studies indicated that even in the primary grades, teachers were looking for

> a decontextualized account centering on a single topic, whereby (1) objects were named and described, even when in plain sight; (2) talk was to be explicitly grounded temporally and spatially; (3) minimal shared background or contextual knowledge was to be assumed between speaker and audience; and (4) thematic ties needed to be lexicalized if topic shifts were to be seen as motivated and relevant. (p. 255)

And, in her study of the teaching of composition writing in a sixth-grade classroom, Michaels (1991) reported that the teacher typically edited personal, concrete anecdotes out, particularly in the beginning of the school year, when she was trying to establish her expectations.

Anna's story in Table 21.1 is more like a play than a decontextualized prose description. She first sets the tone and sketches out the cast of characters. When she plays the roles of the sixth graders in her dialogues, she assumes a derisive tone of voice that is more high-pitched than her personal voice; her speech also becomes louder and more rapid. The questions she raises are rhetorical; they are there for their dramatic effect and they are grounded neither spatially nor temporally (she refers to some general group of sixth graders in some unspecified sixth-grade class). In her abstract, she mentions the students who had the same problems as she did *last year*, but one gets the sense from her story that she is presenting a dramatized description of life, rather than a specific event. The second episode is juxtaposed, rather than lexically connected, although she does *imply* a shift of scene in line 19, with her use of "*And then* Mickey said, 'I need somebody to help Anna.' " This second episode does not follow the first in time. It simply is another vignette that dramatizes a contrasting, although still troublesome, misunderstanding that her classmates (this time, the ones in Mickey's class) have about her problem. Again, she adopts a mocking, rhythmic, and emphatic prosodic pattern, except for her external evaluation and the final couplet. And, again, the dramatization is of business as usual.

On the other hand, in keeping with school-based expectations, Anna's narrative is topic centered. She relates two contrasting reactions to her disability and her response to them—an unmistakable insistence that she is neither retarded nor a regular kid who learns as easily as the others. Instead, she is "special ed." And although the situation saddens her and is "pretty hard," she manages to "get along with it." The semantic, and occasionally syntactic, parallelism in her *aabb* stanzas is reminiscent of, although not as sophisticated as, the narrative of Sandy, an 11-year-old, White, middle class girl whom Gee (1989) described as an example of someone using a "language style highly compatible with school-based values in regard to the use of language in speech and writing" (p. 287). Sandy's story, however, is a series of episodes consecutively ordered in time and does not rely on dramatization like Anna's oral tradition does. In Anna's narrative, the dialogue carries the story. In Sandy's narrative the prose description carries the story and the dialogue embellishes it.

In summary, in this narrative (as well as in the others presented in this article), Anna has communicated both effectively and forcefully. The vast majority of her stanzas are four lines in length, as is also typical of English speakers. The narrative has a clearly defined overall form—a description of the problem, followed by two vignettes that illustrate it, and a return to the feelings articulated in the opening. The text has structure and coherence.

When compared to school-based expectations for language use, however, Anna's narrative is seen as lacking. It does not conform to the narrow expectations that govern teachers' instructional interventions and assessments of competence. It is far too personal and dramatic. Michaels (1991) noted an inherent catch-22 for students like Anna:

Those children whose oral style and narrative schemata were at variance with the teacher's were not able to establish the kind of engagement and cooperation with the teacher that seemed to be a prerequisite for successful collaboration and practice. . . . These results suggest a kind of Catch-22 for these children. You have got to start out having elements of a topic-centered narrative schema if you are going to get practice in developing it. If not, the narrative schema you have will be devalued, and you are unlikely to receive help in producing narratives of any sort—topic-centered or other wise. It is for this reason that I see the process as one of *dismantling* narrative abilities. (p. 326)

Although Anna's narrative is topic centered, it is still sufficiently different from school expectations to be devalued. But, because it is in fact well structured and coherent, we must ask whether Anna's oral style has been cast (in light of the measurement myth) as deficient when in fact it is adequate language that is simply *different* from the narrow band of styles that are valued and accepted in schools.

CONTENT THEMES

Our second purpose in this study was to identify the themes associated with these students' presentation and understanding of the selves that they construct through the stories they tell. Interviews of students with learning disabilities have traditionally been driven by a deficit model in which the questions address the investigators' purposes, such as planning programs, conducting assessments, and so forth (Thiessen, 1987). Few investigators have interviewed students with disabilities in order to hear from them, to give them voice. These students are the forgotten element in the educational equation. Few sources have acknowledged the importance of a student's previous knowledge and experience in the active construction of knowledge (Gallagher & Reid, 1983; Poplin, 1984). Even fewer recognize the roles they play in the social construction of their selves (Polkinghorne, 1991).

Students are active participants in the interpretation of themselves and their world, not mere reactors (Ferguson, Ferguson, & Taylor, 1992). In the interviews and discussions we engaged in with Anna and the other students, several themes about being learning disabled emerged. The students unanimously reported feeling isolated, victimized, and betrayed. A second theme related to the misunderstanding and devaluing they experienced in school. Finally, it is not possible to interpret the negative comments we heard as unpleasantness or mild distress. These students repeatedly reported feeling what is more accurately labeled as oppression, in its political sense.

Isolation, Victimization, and Betrayal

Like her peers, Anna expressed anger and frustration at being isolated from her classmates by being put in a different physical space when she was staffed into a special education classroom (see Table 21.1). During the discussions and interviews, all of the students, but especially Anna, Lisa, and Fernando, indicated that it was hurtful when other students, whom they hardly knew, misunderstood their problems: "People call us retarded ... or tell lies about you [and] it makes you feel bad. We get mad" (see Table 21.3). For Anna, being in special education might have meant being "disabled a little" (see Table 21.2), but she wants people to recognize that in most ways she is just like everybody else. And this isolation is pervasive. Even on the playground she stands around talking to the aides, "because I have nobody to play with" (see Table 21.2). She laments, "I had almost no friends ... I mean nobody really cared about how I felt" (see Table 21.2), and, "I only have one friend 'cause I've got a disability" (see Table 21.1). The way Anna makes sense of her loneliness and isolation is to connect it with her disability. The other students, except for Sally, revealed similar sentiments.

Anna and her peers not only have been isolated, but have often been victimized. During our discussions while writing the essay, the boys especially mentioned that being taunted (and sometimes even attacked) was commonplace. The girls talked about being called names and being made fun of. They all talked about how they had to learn to stick up for themselves (see Table 21.2). But it was not just their classmates who victimized them: They reported incidents in which teachers blamed them for things they did not do and failed to give them credit for things they did. There were also numerous stories of being punished by teachers who refused to help them with work they missed while they were out of the room for special education services. For example, in their essay in Table 21.3, the students reported that teachers just say, "If you weren't here, that's too bad."

Even family members, unless they too had been labeled as disabled, seemed to be insensitive to these students' plight. Several students told stories about how siblings, and even parents, could be the instruments of betrayal. Anna's brother, for example, denied that Anna was in a special education program. At a Valentine's Day party (see Table 21.4), when a student in her brother's school asked Anna, "Why don't you go to this school?," her brother distanced himself from Anna and her disability by making fun of her ("Yeah, she doesn't even know her times. What's this plus this times this?"). The incident represented a childish but cruel test that Anna failed to pass and that galvanized for the students in her brother's class her image of being unacceptable.

TABLE 21.2
Idealized Realization of Anna's Responses to Questions About Personal Relationships

Friends

I've had almost no friends.

(I almost always have two, three, or one friend.)

I only had one friend that was in my class.

'Cause she had to go in there for reading and cause I was in there in the afternoon, she knew that I am disabled a little. (But, that does not mean that I can't do *other stuff* like everybody else.)

I mean nobody really cared about how I felt.

They always called me names.

Has it gotten any better since you've gotten older, or is it the same as it was?

[Shakes head] It kind of got badder.

'Cause nobody cares for me now.

And now, 'cause I came up . . .

(I mean I'm older now and I'm coming up here)

I only have one friend 'cause I've got a disability. [Near tears]

I see. What do you think could have made it better?

[Shrugs] I don't know.

I guess being in a regular class a lot.

Teachers and Instructional Assistants (Aides)

How have teachers treated you?

Well, some teachers know that I'm special ed.

They treat me, "You're just like a regular student still."

And it's like, "Yes."

And I get along with it.

And sometimes they forget that I'm special ed.

And they think I can do this.

But, I can't do this.

I just can't do it.

How would you like them to treat you?

That I need help.

You need help, but you just want to be . . .

Like everybody else.

What about the help that you got? Did that help? I mean was there enough that . . .

[Nods] We always had an aide.

And a teacher [special education], Mr. Jones, wanted to work with everybody.

'Cause he had kids first grade through sixth grade go in there.

And he needed a lot of help.

Two years ago we had a kid named Tommy.

He had seizures a lot.

(We cared about him.)

So we had an aide in there a lot to help us go through the stuff that we needed help with.

And we got along with her.

Other Students with Learning Disabilities

What about other kids with LD? How is that, being with other kids in the program?

Pretty good, 'cause I'm with other kids.

TABLE 21.2 (cont.)

I usually don't like being by myself.	And they're still like, "You have to stick up for yourself.
When I was littler, I was usually by myself in the class.	"We can't go out and tell the principal to tell these kids to
Nobody was really like me.	stop."
They weren't my age to play with out on recess, so I had no	And we had spelling homework to practice
friends.	(Because we're in special ed, we got 10 spelling words.
I still like stand around out on recess.	Because we can't do a lot.)
I stand around and talk to the aides, because I have nobody to	And my dad made me
play with.	(Because he's like, "You can't do it like everybody else."
	Because I can't usually keep it in my memory a lot.
Parents	I mean sometimes I can keep it in my memory, but sometimes
Well, tell me about your parents and how they feel about the	I forget it a lot.
program you've been in a lot since you have disabilities.	And I can't think of the letters.
I don't really know.	And I get a different letter in there.)
I don't know what they	Well, my dad makes me do my spelling words five times.
You never talked to them about it?	And he makes me write it and say the word.
Yeah, I've said, "Kids make fun of me."	And the letters with it sometimes.
(I stick up for myself, but they don't care.)	

TABLE 21.3
The Students' Collaborative Essay

Being Learning Disabled: Sally, Anna, Pedro, Fernando, Lisa, and Wayne

We don't like it when people call us retarded. When people call you names or tell lies about you it makes you feel bad. We get mad.

It's fun to meet new friends, except the first day you meet them you are pretty shy. It's fun to learn new things. Teachers care about us. Some teachers know how we feel.

When you are learning disabled, you feel different because you are not with the same teachers as the regular students. You can't goof off. Some kids are really nice to you. Some kids are mean. They make fun of us because we are in special education.

Some parents talk to you about school and that helps a lot. But sometimes it doesn't help. When some parents talk to you about school, it's usually, "Do better!" But we are trying already to do our best. It's good when your parents know how you feel. Sometimes parents love you too much and do your work for you instead of letting you do it yourself. Most brothers and sisters don't understand, but some do, because they went through the same thing.

School is boring. Teachers should go faster because when they go slow, we fall asleep or we can't get our work done. Sometimes they talk too fast and talk too much. They repeat too much and that's another thing that stops us from doing our work. When you come from another class and they say something, they won't repeat it. They say, "If you weren't here, that's too bad." To make school more exciting there should be more teacher demonstrations and more people talking, more experiments and a little less reading and writing. Teachers should show you how to do things, because you don't get it only from words. Teachers should lighten up too and let us party.

School should be shorter. Classes start too early and last too long. School would be better if they had better lunches. There should be more free time and more choice time so you could do more things. Use your talents whenever you can.

This is what it's like to be learning disabled.

Being Misunderstood and Unappreciated

Not only did the students labeled learning disabled object to being called retarded, but they were also, as Anna's interview indicates, upset with teachers and students who did not recognize that they could not perform certain tasks as well as their general education peers. It seems that they were frequently being put into niches in which they did not fit. Even their parents sometimes seemed insensitive to their problems. Some would admonish the students to "Do better!" But they were not capable of doing better; they were "trying already to do our best" (see Table 21.3). At other times, parents "love you too much and do your work for you instead of letting you do it for yourself" (see Table 21.3). All of the students told us they felt misunderstood.

TABLE 21.4
Idealized Realization of Anna's Story About Her Relationship with Her Brother

Do you have brothers and sisters?
    I have one brother.

How is he about you being in the LD program?

Stanza 15: Orientation
    58. Well, he was in fourth grade last year.
    59. He told a lot of kids that I wasn't special ed.
    60. And that I did not go, and they noticed that I did not go, to that school either.
    61. (Because I was in special ed, I had to go to a different school.)

Stanza 16: Peer Challenge
    62. And sometimes, I had a half day, like Valentine's Day or some other holiday, and they didn't.
    63. My mom was a room mother for them.
    64. So I had to go with her to watch my little sister.
    65. So my mom took both of us.
    66. And like a few of these kids came up, "Why don't you go to this school?"

Stanza 17: Betrayal
    67. And my brother goes, "Yeah, she doesn't even know times."
    68. Then he goes like, "Yeah, what's this plus this times this?"
    69. And I'm like, "I don't know."
    70. And then his friends like, "Yeah, yeah."

Stanza 18: Coda
    71. And sometimes I just don't get along with them at all.

As a group, the students complained that school was boring. The repetitive drills that teachers said were helpful, the students found boring. They expressed a desire to do more hands-on activities and to have more teacher demonstrations. They complained that teachers used only one avenue of instruction: talking. They wanted more opportunity to use the skills and talents they had, and less reading and writing. We asked about this, because certainly reading and writing are what schooling is about. Although the essay seems somewhat cavalier, the students were really asking for balance. "Use your talents whenever you can," is descriptive of their perception that their gifts go unrecognized and unappreciated, because of the limited ways students are allowed to learn and show their knowledge in classrooms.

Although so many of their comments are negative, these are not hostile, aggressive students. They are instead students who feel the pain of being undervalued and who thrive on whatever attention they can command. The little story Anna tells in Table 21.5 is an example. The

TABLE 21.5
Best School Experience

Best school experience
Uh huh. What's been the best experience that you ever had in school? Can you think of a time that was really a neat experience for you?

Well, last year, for sixth grade, I got this little thing.
(See, we always had lunch time art.
You come in after lunch, which you eat.
She used to have kids eat in there and do work plus,
but it got too messy with food going around.
And so the kids eat and then go in there and did stuff.)
We did this little visual.
We made a little rain forest.
I wasn't there 'cause I thought, "I'm not going to get anything."
(One kid, a boy that was in special ed., went.)
Well, I got something from my art teacher for helping.
A little piece of paper that says, "Thanks for helping."
I thought that was a really great thing.

A school experience that was not fun
Can you think of a time that was not fun?

When I have science, I sometimes need help.
Because the last thing we did for science, because it was going to be summer, you're supposed to make a little placemat.
But we had to read out of the dictionary to see what it was to put the names down.
And I had trouble with that.
I couldn't do it like everybody else.
One thing that's hard for me is when I'm in regular class
And we're supposed to read this piece of paper
(two pages or a story or something),
I'm halfway on the first page and they're done.
And it makes me pretty mad, because I can't do the reading as fast.

---

best experience she had ever had in school was to receive a note of thanks from her art teacher.

Oppression

Oppression by teachers, peers, parents, and siblings and the rigidity of the school structure was another common theme. The students had few choices. They had been found wanting by adults, are tested and staffed by adults, and are instructed by adults. Seldom do they have any input into what happens to them. They want to be like everybody else. They want to spend more time in general education classrooms to get to know their general education peers, instead of being physically set aside.

Furthermore, not once in the interviews or during the discussions did any of the students, including Anna, ever describe *themselves* as learning disabled. In the essay, however, they did use the term, probably because we gave them the essay title. The label itself, like most everything else in their school lives, was imposed by the school because, as the students understood it, they were "having trouble," or "getting bad grades." Most of the students did not have any clear recollection of why they had been labeled in the first place. Wayne commented that "it was just too far off to remember."

In Wayne's cartoon (see Figure 21.1), the teacher is represented as a menacing half-man, half-gorilla with tattoo and cigar, brandishing a spiked bludgeon. On the board is written an impossible assignment demanding that students write an essay with over 31,000 words, "due today." Perhaps the most disturbing part of the picture is the portrayal of the students as three cowering, bewildered dogs. This entire scene of academic "torture" is being recorded on a video camera similar to those used for security systems. The "students" appear to be incarcerated, or, at the very least, "on display." The message is clear: Here there is oppression, and students have no voice.

The Positive Side

The students all agreed that they genuinely enjoyed learning. In their essay they acknowledge that "it's fun to learn new things." In their discussion they talked about how not learning was not fun and how being isolated, punished, or derided for not learning was cruel. They thought that both their parents and their teachers were generally caring and concerned, but that siblings, unless they had been through the same kinds of experiences, were likely to be insensitive. Finally, they were well aware that they were labeled as the result of a process intended to help them. They were grateful for the help they received and were painfully aware that they needed it.

In summary, stories we heard from these students in their interviews and during the group essay writing suggested that they felt isolated, victimized, devalued, and oppressed. They realized that what was done to them was "for their own good," but they would have liked to have had the help without the label and without the isolation.

CONCLUSION

In this chapter we have examined how Anna and her peers use narrative to make sense of their personal experience: When students like

Figure 21.1. Wayne's vision of schooling.

Anna organize their life events into stories with temporal and plausible causal relations, what kind of answers do they get to the question, "Who am I?" Unfortunately, the answer we have gotten from listening to Anna and her peers is something like, "I am a person who is sometimes and in some ways unacceptable as a friend and classmate, as a brother or sister, and as a son or daughter. I am not retarded, but neither am I as able as most of my peers. I am not clear, however, about what my problems are. I am a person who, because of difficulties in school, has little control over my life. I have few choices and little voice in the decisions that affect me. I find life rather hard and people rather intimidating, but I get along with it as best I can."

As we indicated in the opening of this chapter, it is ironic that in a field that was avowedly designed to improve the quality of life for persons with disabilities, we should have come so late to valuing their perspectives. We have constructed a system of intervention in our schools that addresses what we think are their best interests, but we have chosen not to confront the personal damage that that system can inflict on some students. The inclusion movement has begun to redress some of the problems Anna and her peers have raised, especially with respect to social isolation and self-advocacy, but inclusion in its current form does not go far enough.

So long as we continue with our system of "rational nonsense"—with rigid, age-related curriculum demands that are insensitive to natural variations in students' prior experience, including narrative traditions; with measurements that rank order people (and implicitly rank *value* them) along dimensions that are not inherently hierarchical (such as language usage); with a system of education that values only a narrow band of possible talents and intelligences, so that it privileges the children of the middle class while denying the political nature of schooling—we cannot avoid oppression of the students who do not fit the pigeonholes we create for them.

For we do, as a society, *create* many of these categories of disability. We must not lose sight of the fact that handicapping conditions are socially constructed (Foucault, 1965, 1978). Emotional disturbances have been defined by societal norms for behavior—norms that often work against the interests of women, children, and other marginalized populations. Mental retardation has been defined by societal norms for successful schooling: Its primary diagnosis relies on measuring decontextualized cognition against the institutionalized norms for successful schooling as they have been embodied in intelligence tests. Learning disabilities have been defined largely by age-related standards imposed by achievement expectations, when intelligence is not a contributing factor. The difficulty has been that we have reified these conditions, attributing them to students as if they were personal characteristics in the sense of the medical model. Perhaps unintentionally, we have used such labels as a means to justify the exclusion of some students from the system, rather than addressing the question of how to reform our entrenched bureaucratic educational system in ways that will answer their needs. We have paid lip service to the idea that "all children can learn," while simultaneously limiting the potential of many students, including those we have discussed here, by the way we conduct business as usual in our schools.

Language is a pivotal dimension in this regard. Edwards (1989), Gee (1990), Michaels (1991), and others have shown how language is used for the purpose of domination. The quotation we used earlier, about the catch-22 phenomenon, is an example. Students whose home discourse patterns do not match the expectations of school-based language have problems learning to read and write that are not necessarily the direct result of the discourse mismatch, but rather of the way teachers respond to such students as linguistically deficient, deviant, or deprived (Mehan, 1984; Young, 1983). When the student's abilities do not match the often implicit expectations of the teacher, the student's abilities are devalued and, sometimes, in Michaels' (1991) word, dismantled. Anna, for example, is a native speaker of English and a human being with narrative competence, albeit more closely related to the oral tradition. Why has she been isolated, unappreciated, and oppressed in school?

What we can learn from narrative inquiries like the one presented here is that there are powerful inequities in our system that disempower the students we mean to serve. As special educators, we need to invite the voices of our *students*, like Anna and her peers, to negotiate with ours, the voices of the supposed experts, to determine on a one-to-one basis how we can advocate for students like them and help them to advocate for themselves. How can we reform their particular situations so that they can better profit from instruction? How can we develop their talents and show appreciation for their humanity? They know how they experience school, and they can tell us. We need to learn to listen with an open, sensitive, and inquisitive mind and not just our rational judgment. Furthermore, we need to educate ourselves about how our interventions, however well intentioned, produce negative outcomes. We must empower our students, because the answer to the question "Who am I?" leads to decisions about "who I can become."

Authors' Note

This study was funded by a grant from the University of Northern Colorado Research Corporation.

NOTE

It is clear that Anna spends most of her day in a resource room, although she never says so. Her focus throughout the interview is on her painful isolation from the students in the general sixth-grade (actually a fifth/sixth combination) classroom. Even when she is asked specifically about her relationships with students who are also called learning disabled, she glibly mentions that it is "pretty good" to be with them and then shifts immediately to talking about her loneliness. We believe that there are at least two possible reasons for this emphasis on her isolation. First, it is a serious problem for Anna, one that she seems unable to solve. The second reason may be that we tell stories only about those aspects of our lives that are not canonical (Bruner, 1990). We must have a reason to tell stories. They must be about what is out of the ordinary. As storytellers, we do not want to risk having the listener responding with, "So what?"

22. Stories From the Resource Room: Piano Lessons, Imaginary Illness, and Broken-Down Cars

PEGGY ALBINGER

Ongoing controversies in the field of learning disabilities (LD) include (a) the lack of one theoretical definition for learning disabilities (Hammill, 1990), (b) the methodology used to assess children with learning problems (Algozzine & Ysseldyke, 1988; Chalfant, 1989), (c) the impact labeling has on children (Gillung & Rucker, 1977; Hallahan & Kauffman, 1977; Palmer, 1983), (d) the instruction to be provided to children identified with learning disabilities (Bateman, 1992), and (e) the delivery model used for providing services to children with learning disabilities (Bateman, 1992). Inconsistent findings in quantitative research suggest the need for qualitative study of children and their perceptions of learning disabilities (Jenkins & Heinen, 1989; Swanson, 1991). Children are rarely asked or told about the educational decisions that are made on their behalf (Jenkins & Heinen, 1989; Jones, 1974; Vaughn & Bos, 1987).

The process of identifying and labeling children with specific learning disabilities needs to be scrutinized more closely due to the negative connotations that are sometimes inherent in labels (Carlberg & Kavale,

From *Stories From the Resource Room: Piano Lessons, Imaginary Illness, and Broken Down Cars*, by M. A. Albinger, 1993. Copyright 1993 by M. A. Albinger. Adapted with permission.

1980; Gillung & Rucker, 1977; Hrncir & Eisenhart, 1991; Mercer, Algozzine, & Trifiletti, 1988). There is quantitative research suggesting that children identified as learning disabled often have lowered self-esteem and other problems that can lead to school failure or diminished success (Jenkins & Heinen, 1989; McWhirter, McWhirter, & McWhirter, 1985). When children's learning does not meet teachers' or parents' expectations, children are referred for testing to determine what is wrong with them. There are claims that labeling children with learning disabilities places the problem within the child and negates the possibility that the problem may be one of inadequate teaching methods (Armstrong, 1988; Wang, Reynolds, & Walberg, 1986) or the social and cultural changes that are so rapidly taking place today (Hallahan, 1992).

Whether children possess a learning disability or not, little consideration is given to how they feel when labeled with learning disabilities, or what they think about being placed in special education programs (Jenkins & Heinen, 1989).

METHOD

The focus of this ethnomethodology (Bogdan & Biklen, 1992) concerned the microissues formed by children's perceptions and their feelings about being labeled learning disabled. This study used qualitative research methodology and inductive analysis to form a holistic view of children's perspectives regarding their identified learning disabilities and the label assigned to them. Anticipated research questions, referred to as *foreshadowed questions,* were formulated to guide the data collection (McMillan & Schumacher, 1993). The following nine foreshadowed questions were reformulated in the field during data collection:

1. Do children understand their disabilities?

2. Do children understand why they receive resource services?

3. How do children feel about their learning problems?

4. How do children feel about being labeled?

5. How do children with learning disabilities perceive their abilities as compared with their perceptions of their peers' abilities?

6. How do children with learning disabilities feel they are perceived by others?

7. Do children with learning disabilities recognize their strengths?

8. How do children with learning disabilities feel about themselves in their daily world?

9. How do children with learning disabilities feel about coming to the resource room?

Descriptive data were gathered from (a) interviews with the children; (b) their educational portfolios, cumulative school records, and special education confidential files; (c) anecdotal notes; and (d) observational field notes. Predetermined criteria were established for the selection of children in this study. Data collection and analysis were carried out concurrently, thereby facilitating the direction of the interview process and further descriptive data collection. Data analysis was systematic and inductive; patterns of children's perceptions were well grounded in the data collected in this study.

Participants

The children chosen for this study were receiving special education services for specific learning disabilities in a large, suburban school district in southern California. Total student enrollment in the 18 elementary schools, 4 intermediate schools, and 3 high schools was approximately 25,000. The student population consisted of 55.3% White, 36.4% Hispanic, and 8.3% other ethnic groups. At the time of this study, 1,096 children were receiving resource services for specific learning disabilities. Purposeful sampling of children, based on predetermined criteria, was used in this research in order to study the effects of labeling on children who were identified as having specific learning disabilities. The following criteria guided the selection process:

1. Children received special education through the resource specialist program;

2. Children attended one of two schools in my resource specialist program;

3. The sample of children was representative of each grade level (first through sixth);

4. The sample of children was representative of number of years in the resource specialist program (newly identified through 4 years);

5. The sample of children possessed adequate communication skills.

Based on these criteria, 28 children were selected for the study. Letters of consent were sent to the parents explaining the nature of this study. Twenty-five parents responded to the letter; 18 granted permission for their child to be interviewed. Seven parents did not want their child to be interviewed for this study. Two children did not want their interviews to be taped, and five children lacked adequate conversational skills, so taping of their interviews ended. These five children's responses were yes and no answers or a shrug of the shoulders. Eleven children were interviewed and eight children chosen for case study analysis. Three children interviewed were deleted from the case study analyses because their conversations appeared to the observer to be swayed by their desire to please the interviewer.

Procedure

Anecdotal and observational notes were generated over a 6-month period, from September 1992 to February 1993. In February 1993, after the selection process was complete, I started the interviewing process. The interviews were audiotaped for later transcription and analysis so that during the interviews, observations could be made of the children's overt behaviors. All audiotaped interviews took place in the resource room.

Ongoing analysis of the interviews and the emergence of other descriptive data led to further conversations with the children as themes developed. I found that children wanted to clarify thoughts or feelings or add information in the days following their initial audiotaped interviews. Their comments became part of the anecdotal notes.

ANALYSIS OF EMERGING THEMES

Several common themes emerged from the interviews. These themes reflected students' perceptions and coping behaviors regarding being identified as LD. First was the prevalence of invented stories used by the children to justify where they were going when they attended resource. The children resorted to these *fabricated stories* to protect themselves from what they believed others thought of them. The second theme reflected statements indicating that their peers, teachers, or parents had called them "stupid" or some other derogatory name. *Name calling* directed at these children reinforced their low self-esteem. The third theme reflected their expression of memories about their understanding of why they had problems learning. These memories usually were related to events that sent these children the message that *there was something wrong with them*. This mostly happened early in the process of learning to read. The fourth theme emerged out of their statements concerning the implications of *what it meant to go to the resource room* and how much classroom work they missed. Finally, the fifth theme was born of the children's statements regarding what they were *good at*.

Theme 1: Fabricated Stories

Four children attended private schools but came to resource at their neighborhood school, four mornings a week during the first hour of the school day. These children invented stories to justify to their friends why they were late to their respective schools each day. Each one had a story, a kind of secret, only told to inquiring peers.

Kim told her friends that she took piano lessons before school. This invented story continued for 2½ years while she attended resource. She expressed concern that someday someone would want to hear her play the piano—she has never had a piano lesson! I asked her why she told them she was taking piano lessons when she was not; she said, "I wanted to learn to play the piano, but my mom has never let me. I thought someday she would. She says I have to be a good reader first" (she hesitated a moment, then continued), "I guess I won't ever play the piano."

Fred hesitated when I asked him what he told his friends about being late to school four mornings a week. He stated that his friends did not ask him every day, but when they did, he told them his mother's car broke down! He elaborated: "Since my parents got divorced [5 years ago!] my mom don't know how to take care of the car." I pointed out to him that he had a new car. He sank down into his chair and said, "Yes, but you know American cars."

David initially ignored his friends when they asked him why he was late four mornings a week. But when they continued with their questioning, he told a story about having had mononucleosis. He told them that he was so far behind, he had to get tutoring before school. Now, after 2½ years, they have begun asking when he is going to be "caught up"!

Sara did not want her interview taped. However, she told two good friends at school that she was always late because her mom wanted to drop her off on the way to her work. Sara felt this was a good story, as she lived a distance from her school. I asked if her mother knew her story. She said, "No, but my mom wouldn't want me to tell my friends [about resource], because they would say mean things to me." In a conversation with her mother, I asked if Sara's friends knew that Sara went to resource. She stated that Sara had never talked with her about it and that she did not know.

Some children at the public school sites also had stories they clung to when needing to justify where they went when they left the classroom for resource. Carolyn is a sixth grader who has attended resource for a year and was recently placed in a counseling program through the county. She leaves the school three mornings a week, along with two other students from the special day class. She told her friends she goes to resource for help with math. That did not present a problem to her. When I asked her what she tells her friends about going to the counseling groups, she says she does not answer them. The rumor was started that she goes to the bathroom and ditches class for an hour or so. She likes the rumor because she does not have to tell anyone the truth, yet nor does she have to lie. Carolyn thought the story was funny, because her peers believed her teacher was pretty "stupid" not to know that Carolyn was hanging out in the bathroom for so long "three times a week"!

Other responses were given to the question, Where do you tell your friends you are going when you leave the classroom to come to resource? One boy reported going to the reading teacher, even though he knew the difference between the resource room and the reading room. One child stated, "Sometimes I tell them that I have to go see the nurse because I feel like throwing up." Only two of the nine children interviewed told whoever asked that they were going to the resource room; but they said they wished no one knew.

Seven of the eight children interviewed had fabricated stories, to protect themselves from the rejection they feared by their peers. I also discovered other stories while conversing with five parents who did not want their children to be interviewed—stories perpetuated by the parents. One parent called to tell me that she did not believe her son was labeled "learning disabled." Furthermore, she stated that her son did not know he had any problems with his reading. I asked her if she remembered why he was coming to resource. She stated that she knew, but that she did not want *him* to know! This parent believed that it would destroy his self-esteem if he knew. A second parent felt that her daughter should not be in resource with kids who are "dumb," although this parent wanted extra help for her child. She believed that her daughter needed resource because "she had some bad teachers in the other school she went to when she was living with her father."

These stories illustrated how children's self-perception dictated the need for fabricated stories. The question that arises is whether their fabricated stories resulted from being identified as learning disabled, or if stories would have emerged anyway as they recognized their own learning difficulties.

Theme 2: Name-Calling

When I asked the children what they thought their classmates said about them, they brought up such words as *stupid* or *dumb*. One third grader said, "When I read better, no one will laugh at me and call me stupid." When I asked how they felt about being called these names, most children answered, "Sad." One third-grade boy said it made him mad and "someday, something will happen to them and they will know what it feels like."

Fred stated, "I feel stupid because I can't read and write good. My friends are right." Carolyn believed that her friends were wrong when they called her stupid. She stated, "My teacher should do something when I tell her that they call me names, but she never does. Sometimes she just makes me write my name on the board, in the bad list because I'm tattling. I don't understand. Will you tell her to make them stop?" Kim said, "They'd make fun of me and probably call me names." David related that others laughed at him when he received extra help from one of the nuns. Tiffany wanted to avoid the names she believed she would be called in junior high school by getting "fixed" in the special day class.

Carl was frustrated about what other children had said to him; he did not like being called a "retard." Joe believed that everyone thought he was stupid. Fred was convinced that if his friends knew he went to resource they would call him even worse names. I observed Lori's teacher criticize her academic attempts in the presence of the class, telling Lori that she acted like a kindergartner.

Name-calling affected the way these children perceived themselves and reinforced their negative feelings about their learning problems.

Theme 3: There Is Something Wrong with Me

Most children in this study were able to recall when they first were told there was something wrong with their learning. In the interviews, each child told a story about knowing that he or she was having trouble in school. Kim recalled being an "A" book reader and slowly being changed to a lower and lower book, until she finally became a "D" book reader. Daniel recalls sitting alone in kindergarten and knowing that he was not doing as well as other children. Some children were told by a parent or teacher that they just did not try hard enough.

Although these children could recall the beginning of their learning problems, they could not state what their particular learning disabilities were. Fred and Carl were exceptions. Fred made a reference to the fact that he had a hard time remembering words; Carl suggested that he could not write well because his brain did not work right.

Some parents who did not want their children interviewed shared some of their thoughts regarding the label. Three parents expressed the concern that their children's school records would always identify them as learning disabled and that they might not be able to get a good job as a consequence. One parent believed that children should not be told they are in special education when they are placed in the resource program.

Theme 4: What Going to the Resource Room Means

Typically, these children were concerned about having to make up missed work or not knowing how to do the assignments when they returned to the regular classroom. Programmatically, these children should not have to make up missed work; resource is viewed as a punishment when it becomes twice the work. However, these children did not mind leaving the classroom, especially when the class was having to do some really hard work. The two youngest children, one in first and one in second grade, did not seem to be bothered by what they missed.

Theme 5: What I'm Good At

Some of the children came to understand that the LD label told only what they were "bad at" or what they "could not do." One child exclaimed, "I have no disability like someone who is blind, I just can't read good!"

Although each of the children mentioned that they were called derogatory names, they each could find something to say about what they were good at. Carolyn was pleased with her ability to be a cheerleader. Lori knew she could draw well, even though her teacher criticized her other work. Fred was an accomplished baseball player. Joe believed that he could beat me at Nintendo. David was a collector of fossils and also captain of his soccer team. While I was observing Tammy at recess I noticed that she could jump rope well. She said that jumping rope was fun, but she was better at watching television. Kim said, "Acting is everything. I am better than anyone in my class." The activities these children felt they were good at all had to do with something other than traditional academic skills.

Summary

All the children in this study entered the resource room with private stories about why they could not read, or about where they told friends they went, or stories about being called names and feeling bad. The children kept their stories and feelings locked away until asked. It is evident that these children who have been labeled as learning disabled have given up some of their self-respect in order to receive help from the resource program.

ANALYSIS OF FORESHADOWED QUESTIONS

1. *Children's Understanding of Their Identified Learning Disabilities.* In this study, older children were better able to understand their disabilities than were younger children. The children recalled being told at a young age that they were not learning to read, or sometimes to write, like other children (usually at the time they were introduced to reading, in the first grade). However, they did not always recognize the existence of their problems. Only three children could explain their learning disabilities and how these differences interfered with reading or writing. One child stated that he had problems with remembering words (visual memory problem). A second child stated he could not get his thoughts out of his head onto paper because of some problem with the way his brain worked (intermodal transfer problem). A third child stated that she could not concentrate when her teacher was giving directions or giving demonstrations (a type of auditory/visual overloading). The remaining children in this study could state only that they had problems with reading, writing, or math; they could not explain the reason for their difficulties in completing school-related tasks.

2. *Children's Understanding of Why They Go to the Resource Room.* The children stated that they go to the resource room to get help. These children thought they needed help in reading, writing, or math and that what they learned in the resource room helped them in these areas. Typical statements made about the resource program were, "We do more fun things here" and "It gets boring in my class." Although the children in this study all recognized that the resource room was a place to get extra help, not all children knew they were part of a special education program that labeled them learning disabled.

3. *Children's Feelings About Their Learning Problems.* The typical responses to how they felt about their learning problems were "Sad" or "Frustrated." Two days following the interview, one child approached me with the single word "mad." I asked her to tell me why she felt mad. She stated, "It's not fair. I don't try to be a bad reader, what's wrong with me?" These children all expressed the desire to be "good at school" and to "make good grades." However, most expressed the thought that they would never be really good at reading, that school would always be difficult, and that the work in the regular classroom was too hard.

4. *Children's Feelings About Being Labeled.* The children in this study made up stories to justify where they went when they left their classroom to attend resource. Only three out of eight of the children interviewed knew they had learning disabilities and were in the resource program because of those disabilities. Furthermore, the parents who did not wish for their children to be interviewed stated that they did not want their children to discuss their learning problems because it would make them

feel bad. One parent was adamant: If her son knew he was in special education, it would destroy his self-esteem.

Discussions with the children on defining the many uses of labels revealed that seven of eight children believed that the label *learning disabled* told only a little part about who they were. The older children felt that they should not be labeled: "Labeling is bad because it says what we *can't* do."

5. *Children's Perceptions of Their Abilities As Compared to Their Peers'.* In this study, five of the eight children believed that they had more learning problems than the other children in their classes. At the same time, three children felt that there were other children in their classes who could not read or write as well as themselves. Most of the children did not understand why everyone who was failing did not go to resource.

6. *Children's Perceptions of How Others Perceive Them.* All of the children in this study stated that they were called "stupid" (or some other derogatory name) more than once. These children said that whenever derogatory names were used, they felt "bad," "mad," or "frustrated." When asked how they felt about someone calling them names, the responses were, "They're just stupid" (referring to the name-callers); "Well, I must be stupid if they say so"; "I just ignore them"; "It makes me so mad"; and "Someday something bad will happen to them and then they will know how it feels."

7. *Children's Recognition of Their Strengths.* When these children were asked what they thought their strengths were, most thought that the question had to do with something at school. I explained that it meant anything they thought they could do well. Eight children were able to come up with something they did well, all of which had to do with overt acts, for instance, playing baseball, playing soccer, painting, acting, playing Nintendo, and being a cheerleader. One child stated that she "watched TV good." Even though each of these children had difficulty with academic skills, they had found something they could do well.

Self-Esteem

Statements made by the children in this study illustrated issues relating to low self-esteem. Notes I made during an activity that encouraged a discussion about making friends suggested that five of the children who were interviewed liked themselves and had good friends. They made such statements as, "My friends understand that I just need a little extra help"; "I can ride a bike good and I win races"; "My mom says that someday I will be a good reader"; and, "I feel I'm OK." All eight children revealed low self-esteem through statements such as, "No one likes me"; "They think I'm stupid"; "My teacher shouldn't say that in front of my whole class"; "I must be stupid, if they say so"; "I don't feel like I belong anywhere"; "I feel bad that I can't read, everyone makes fun of me"; "You just pretend that you like me"; and "My teacher gives me work that makes me feel dumb." Two children believed that they had no friends, or those they thought were their friends really were not good friends after all.

It is not clear whether low self-esteem comes from what the school does to and for the child, or if the child constructs his or her own view of self, based on self-critical feelings of inadequacy or of perceived judgments from others.

Feelings About Coming to the Resource Room

The children felt that coming to the resource room was something they had to do. They liked the small groups and the individualized help. When given two choices—coming to the resource room or having the resource teacher come to their rooms—the most prevalent reply was having the resource specialist come to their room. They believed that this model would be best because they would not miss so much of their regular classroom work.

IMPLICATIONS AND RECOMMENDATIONS

Children are not always aware of why they see a resource specialist. They know they have problems with not learning "fast enough," or "good enough," but they do not understand that their learning problems are called *specific learning disabilities* by special educators. Children often construct stories to protect themselves from how they perceive others will react to their learning problems. At times, the fabricated stories heard in this study became bigger concerns than the learning problems themselves. Children who are labeled learning disabled often make statements that reflect their low self-esteem. It is not clear if being identified creates the prevalence of low self-esteem, or if low self-esteem results from the way the children perceive themselves in relation to their world.

Children need to be allowed the opportunity to be more involved in the process of identifying learning disabilities. They should be involved in the problem solving and discovering of instructional interventions that may help them with their learning. All too often, meetings are conducted to discuss a child's problems without regard to how the child feels. Identification of learning disabilities is made by people who do not always know the child. When a parent or a child's teacher believes the child has learning disabilities, the child is often tested with inappropriate tests, observed once or twice, labeled, and placed in special education. Rather than a "top-down" approach and testing via some invalid test, we could inform children of the great variety of ways in which their minds work. Then they could be interviewed to help them discover their own learning processes.

Although it is problematic, teachers and parents need to be educated about learning styles and learning differences. At a time when we must be sensitive to ethnic and gender differences, we must also be sensitive to differences in learning styles. Teachers must celebrate the strengths that children possess, and build upon those strengths. Research findings lend support for the theory of multiple intelligences (Armstrong, 1988), but our schools rely on instructional approaches that are mostly linguistic and logical–mathematical.

We need to broaden our view of the many ways that people learn. The human potential is vast, and we do not fully understand it yet. Alternative approaches that involve the child as an active participant in the learning process need to be explored. The process of identifying learning disabilities is derived from the medical model, which values and searches for deficits instead of valuing the uniqueness of the individual. The children in this study knew a great deal about themselves, yet no one had bothered to ask them what they thought, what they wanted, or what they needed. Some of their responses were surprising even to me.

More thought needs to be given to where services are provided. Children should be given the opportunity to decide where they will receive special education services. The eight children interviewed for this study all receive resource support in a pull-out program. The question raised is whether their fabricated stories evolved as a result of their having to leave their classrooms to attend resource.

It was clear in this study that children were not certain about what was "wrong" with them, and they believed they were to blame for not learning. Blaming themselves led to low self-images. The literature indicates that professionals in the field have difficulty defining learning disabilities, and yet children are held responsible for identified deficits that cannot be agreed upon. Perhaps if an alternative approach were employed that respected the children's views, the children would become the informants as to what they need. The question arises as to how we can continue to identify children and label them as learning disabled when there is no consensus as to what a learning disability is. And, without knowing what a learning disability is, how can we continue to use the same testing criteria as tools for identification? Dialogue with children needs to be generated, and we need to listen to their stories.

Epilogue

Longitudinal qualitative studies are needed to determine the long-term effects of labeling from the children's perspectives. The field of special education has not been qualitatively studied in regard to how children feel about being labeled (Stainback & Stainback, 1984). Jones (1974) suggested that children be interviewed about their understanding and perceptions of special services they received at school; and Levine, Clarke, and Ferb (1981) implied that there was value in seeking out the child's view.

This study attempted to look at some of the issues regarding the labeling of children identified as having specific learning disabilities. I learned that the practice of identifying and labeling learning disabilities is not the issue. The issue is the children—their feelings, their strengths, their insecurities, their biases, their perceptions, and their humanness. As I listened to the many stories told by the children, I became embarrassed by my ignorance about their struggles.

The continuing quest to find and label what is defective in children ignores the problems that are inherent in classrooms—classrooms with students who illustrate the concept of normal curves and teaching methods that are often traditionally ineffective and culturally assaultive. The foreshadowed questions of this study emerged from the words of a child who had been in resource for 5 years: "Mrs. Albinger, if you make me keep coming to resource, I'll just be a bum on the street" (he pointed to the window). ". . . All the bums out there went to resource!" I think of this young man often. Several days before the completion of this paper, while standing in line at a store, I saw and spoke to this young man. He had little to say but acknowledged my presence. My heart went out to him in waves of apology for what the system I work within did to him. His affect was blunt, and he looked as if he had lost his spirit. My life has been transformed by what I have learned from the children in this study. The children need to be heard. Qualitative research may provide color to the gray areas about what is known regarding children's learning differences created by a changing world—a world in which schools are often floundering in multibiased, pedagogical ineptness.

23. Bilingual Special Education Teachers' Shifting Paradigms: Complex Responses to Educational Reform

NADEEN T. RUIZ, ROBERT RUEDA, RICHARD A. FIGUEROA,

AND MARGARET BOOTHROYD

In discussing the poor academic outcomes of Latino language-minority students, many educators have called for wide-ranging instructional reforms and institutional restructuring (Cummins, 1989; García, 1991; Mehan, Hubbard, Okamoto, & Villanueva, in press; Moll & Díaz, 1987). In the area of special education for Latino students, reform is critical because of their overrepresentation in the system (Artiles & Trent, 1994; Figueroa, 1990; Ortiz & Yates, 1983). Further, research with Latino students in special education classrooms has shown that the lockstep, teacher-dominated, reductionist teaching practices and materials typical of remedial settings are particularly ineffective instructional contexts for them (Gersten, 1993; chapters 11 and 12 of this book; Ruiz, Figueroa, Rueda, & Beaumont, 1992; Willig & Swedo, 1987). Dramatic changes at the macro level of the special education system, as well as at the micro

Reprinted, with changes, from "Bilingual special education teachers' shifting paradigms: Complex responses to educational reform," by Nadeen T. Ruiz, Robert Rueda, Richard A. Figueroa, and Margaret Boothroyd, *Journal of Learning Disabilities*, Vol. 28, 1995, pp. 622–635. Copyright © 1995 by PRO-ED, Inc.

level of special education classrooms, will require a significant shift in educators' paradigms, that is, their beliefs about teaching and learning.

There is a plethora of ideas for reform and restructuring of schools (Cuban, 1988), including special education programs (Wang, Reynolds, & Walberg, 1987; Will, 1986). Often the prevailing practice is to institute reform by way of top-down policy mandates, with minimal training and without providing long-term follow-up, support, or feedback to teachers. Under these conditions, few significant changes occur, and those that do are frequently temporary (Guskey, 1986).

Adding to the problems is the relative lack of research on how the key reformers—teachers who work daily and directly with students— experience change. The research that is available, however, is particularly informative. It shows that some teachers will see reform as an opportunity to make small, sometimes temporary, modifications in their instruction (Files & Wills, 1992; Peterson, 1990); others will experience conflict when they try to implement an alternative teaching and learning paradigm (Tharp & Gallimore, 1988).

Guskey (1986) proposed a model of teacher change based on large-scale research with general education teachers. He held that three major outcomes are hoped for in staff development programs: (a) change in teachers' classroom practices, (b) change in their beliefs and attitudes, and (c) change in students' learning outcomes. Guskey's model suggests that the process of teacher change begins with a change in classroom practices. If teachers see a positive effect on the students' learning from this change, changes in their belief system follow (see Figure 23.1).

Other researchers looking at teacher change focus on how to encourage teachers to take those initial steps toward changing their classroom practices. Files and Wills (1992) put forth the idea that "what's good for

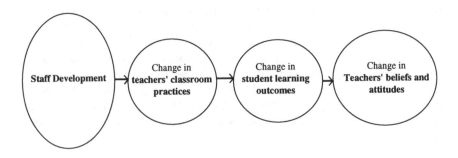

Figure 23.1. A model of the process of teacher change. (*Note.* From "Staff Development and the Process of Teacher Change," by T. R. Guskey, 1986, *Educational Researcher, 15,* p. 7. Copyright 1986 by the American Educational Research Association. Reprinted with permission.)

the children is good for the teachers" (p. 46). Weaver and Henke (1992) suggested that for meaningful and long-lasting change to occur, teachers need ample opportunity to (a) talk and share with colleagues, as well as visit their colleagues' classrooms; (b) interact in an atmosphere that promotes trust and risk-taking over an extended period of time; and (c) exercise choice in the curriculum of their own professional development. Hunsaker and Johnston (1992) added that opportunities for reflective thinking and dialogue support teacher change. Professional development opportunities with these features, then, can facilitate the process of teacher change as Guskey (1986) outlined.

Our own work in teacher change has been in the area of bilingual special education. Specifically, Figueroa and Ruiz (1993) have undertaken a long-term project looking at restructuring instructional and service delivery models for students with learning handicaps in bilingual special education pull-out classrooms in California (The Resource Specialist program). The overall goal of the project has been to develop and implement a specifically designed model of instruction, the Optimal Learning Environment (OLE) Project (Figueroa, Ruiz, & Rueda, 1990). Essentially, the OLE Project rests on an innovative curriculum with a record of success with Latino children in special education (Ruiz, Garcia, & Figueroa, in press; Ortiz, Wilkinson, Robertson-Courtney, & Kushner, 1991). Implementing the innovative curriculum has called for special education teachers to change their classrooms. The present study, then, looks at the process of teacher change within the context of bilingual special education.

THE OLE PROJECT: THEORETICAL FRAMEWORK

We agree with Poplin (1988a) that special education has long been dominated by a single paradigm, a paradigm that she calls reductionism. Reductionism, alternately known as the medical model (Coles, 1987; Mercer, 1973; Rueda, 1989), considers learning disabilities to be a definable phenomenon, essentially unaffected by contextual learning variables and exclusively "owned" by the student. It considers the disability to be treatable, and the treatment entails separating the student into a different educational program, one with its own curriculum, pedagogy, and objectives (captured in the Individualized Education Program [IEP]), and breaking learning into small pieces and rewarding small changes through a wide variety of Skinnerian schedules (Ruiz et al., 1992). In this chapter we will use the terms *reductionism* and *medical model* interchangeably (see Note 1).

The OLE Project operates within a paradigm that directly contrasts with medical model or reductionist assumptions. Once again, we adopt

Poplin's (1988b) term for this alternate paradigm: *holistic/constructivism.* We came to use the term after reviewing the OLE Project's theoretical framework. One of the project's critical organizing principles is the importance of context as a mediator of student performance. Whereas traditional special education views student ability or disability as a stable, within-child trait, a contextualist view of behavior emphasizes the features of the learning situation (e.g., who, what, when, where, and why) as essential factors affecting variability in individual student behavior. Within this paradigm, "learning handicaps" or "pathology" for the most part are viewed as social constructions (Mehan, Hertweck, & Meihls, 1986; Taylor, 1993). It is precisely such a view that has led some investigators to discover hidden competencies in students who are otherwise labeled as incompetent (Gleason, 1989; Hood, McDermott, & Cole, 1981; Taylor, 1991). This finding has been especially true in the case of language-minority students (Diaz, Moll, & Mehan, 1986; Moll & Greenberg, 1990; Moll, Tapia, & Whitmore, 1993; Rueda & Mehan, 1986; chapter 11 of this book).

A second organizing principle of the OLE Project has to do with the effect of the social organization of instruction on children's academic performance. The project draws from research with bilingual students in special education suggesting that certain features of instructional contexts result in more successful student outcomes (Rueda & Mehan, 1986; chapter 12 of this book; Willig & Swedo, 1987). Specifically, when students interact with teachers and peers in holistic/constructivist contexts of instruction (Poplin, 1988b), the upper range of their language and academic competence emerges (Ruiz, 1988). Holistic/constructivist instruction includes offering students choices in meaningful tasks with authentic, real-world functions; providing whole texts; centering curricula on student experiences and knowledge; emphasizing students' meanings over a concern with form in literacy tasks; and providing frequent opportunities for collaboration and mediation in the learning community of teachers and students.

The following two theoretical organizers guide the OLE Project: (a) The academic performance of bilingual children in special education covaries with the contextual features of the learning situation, and (b) certain elements of instruction emanating from both research with bilingual children in special education and a holistic/constructivist paradigm create learning contexts that are linked to greater academic growth. We have chosen to call this theory for explaining learning abilities and disabilities the *contextual performance model.* We consider it to be part of the holistic/constructivist paradigm and will use these terms interchangeably (see Note 2). The theoretical framework outlined here serves as the foundation for the collaborative efforts undertaken by the OLE teachers, paraprofessionals, and researchers to replace the deficit-driven practices of traditional special and remedial education.

The study reported here tracks the changes in the paradigmatic orientations of five special education teachers over a period of 3 years. Two central research questions are addressed:

1. What is the nature and process of change among bilingual special education teachers as they attempt to modify existing belief systems and practices?

2. What factors encourage or inhibit a paradigmatic shift among bilingual special education teachers from a medical model (reductionism) to a contextual performance model (holism/constructivism) for viewing learning abilities and disabilities?

METHOD

The goal of the baseline phase of the OLE Project was to describe the contexts for teaching and learning, as related to the development of literacy, in place before the experimental phase (Ruiz et al., 1992). Later phases of the OLE Project focused on assisting teachers in developing and implementing instructional practices that were more consistent with a holistic/constructivist framework. To this end, teachers and paraprofessionals met periodically with the OLE research and training staff over the 3 years. The present study takes data from both the early, baseline phase and the later, collaboration phase in its longitudinal look at teachers' paradigmatic and instructional changes. Included in this study is a brief but telling look at ourselves (the research and training consultants to the OLE Project) and how we changed the type of assistance we offered to the OLE teachers and paraprofessionals.

Research Sites and Participants

This study focused on five resource specialist (special education pull-out) classrooms in California. Three classrooms were located in a very large, urban school district; the other two classrooms were in rural school districts with a large concentration of migrant, Spanish-speaking students. These five classrooms served approximately 140 children, about 85% of whom were Latino bilinguals. The teachers and paraprofessionals at the sites were a relatively heterogeneous group in terms of ethnicity, language proficiency, and years of experience in special education (see Table 23.1).

One school, "neighborhood school," is the prevalent model in California for special education pull-out programs providing primary lan-

TABLE 23.1
OLE Teachers and Paraprofessionals—School, Languages Spoken, and Years of Experience

School	Resource specialist	Paraprofessional
Neighborhood school (urban)	Ms. Springer, Anglo, non–Spanish-speaking; 0 years in general education, 7 years in special education	Ms. Arellano, Latina, bilingual; 0 years in general education, 10 years in special education
Anderson (urban)	Ms. Rojas, Latina, bilingual; 9 years in general education, 3 years in special education	Ms. Anguiano, Latina, bilingual; 2 years in general education, 8 years in special education
Jefferson (rural)	Ms. Jones, Anglo, bilingual; 10 years in general education, 2 years in special education	Ms. Moreno, Latina, bilingual; 0 years in general education, 6 years in special education
Hillview (urban)	Ms. Avila, Latina, bilingual; 0 years in general education, 12 years in special education	Ms. Saenz, Latina, bilingual; 13 years in general education, 3 years in special education
Oakgrove (rural)	Ms. Hughes, Portuguese American, bilingual; 5 years in general education, 0 years in special education	Ms. Camarena, Latina, bilingual; 10 years in general education, 2 years in special education

guage support: a monolingual (English) teacher teamed with a bilingual paraprofessional. In the other four schools, the teachers spoke Spanish— Ms. Rojas and Ms. Avila as native speakers, and Ms. Jones and Ms. Hughes as second-language speakers who had learned Spanish very well.

Ms. Springer, Ms. Rojas, and Ms. Jones, along with their paraprofessionals, were among the first group of teachers we worked with. When these three teachers withdrew from the project (two because of new job assignments in administrative positions and one because she elected not to continue with the project), Ms. Avila and Ms. Hughes joined.

Intervention/Collaboration Phase

Over the course of their participation in the study, OLE teachers and paraprofessionals attended from 5 to 10 OLE workshops, depending on their individual availability for those sessions. The first session with the first group of OLE teachers occurred near the end of the baseline phase of the project, in the spring of 1989. During that session the OLE teachers and assistants met with project staff and listened to a general description of selected holistic instructional strategies. Those initial strategies, described in detail in the OLE curriculum guide (Ruiz et al., in press), included Writers' Workshop (Graves, 1983), Literature Study (Peterson & Eds, 1990), Reciprocal Teaching (Brown, 1985), and Finding Out/Descubrimiento (De Avila, 1988). Later that summer, the project sent the teachers written descriptions of these strategies and asked for their choice as to the focus of the first training. Unanimously, the teachers asked to begin with Writers' Workshop. Most felt that they needed a specific approach to help their students write better and that Writers' Workshop would fill that need.

For the first workshop, the OLE participants met for a day and listened to general education teachers, all with years of experience using a process approach to writing, describe their programs. Most of the subsequent OLE workshops over the next 2 years followed this general pattern: An OLE literacy consultant or outside trainer presented curriculum strategies to the OLE resource specialists and their paraprofessionals. Although some of these trainers had worked in special education, as researchers, school psychologists, or teachers in special day (self-contained) classes, none had worked specifically as resource specialists. In essence, we as project consultants followed a transmission model of assistance (Cummins, 1989; Weaver, 1992); we set up ourselves and other consultants as experts to dispense new curriculum strategies to the OLE teachers and paraprofessionals, all the while espousing strategies that were antithetical to transmission models of teaching to use in their classrooms.

The one exception to this pattern in the first 2 years of intervention occurred in February 1990. At that workshop, an OLE teacher shared her efforts in launching Writers' Workshop; this exception had a significant and critical impact on teacher change and will be discussed in the Results section. Unfortunately, it was not until a year and a half later that the impact significantly affected the nature of the OLE workshops. At that time, in the fall of 1992, when the second group of OLE teachers came on board, we dramatically changed our workshops. The OLE teachers and professionals became the major providers of information, often taking the whole morning and beyond to share their students' work products, or their successes/problems with the holistic instructional strategies implemented as part of OLE. Outside consultants took up the remainder (and relatively shorter) amount of time, extending participants' knowledge about the instructional strategies through presentations or role-play. Occasionally, the OLE literacy consultants and teachers read professional articles together at these meetings and responded orally or in writing in journals. In short, we had moved from a transmission model of inservice training to more of a holistic/constructivist model—one that allowed teachers to insert their personal experiences and build upon them, to choose the focus of their learning, and to take an active rather than a passive role.

In addition to the periodic workshops, the OLE literacy consultants provided assistance to the teachers in their classrooms when they were invited to do so. Teachers varied in their requests for this on-site demonstration, from no requests to about three or four per year. We also invited the OLE teachers to observe the OLE instructional strategies implemented in one of our literacy consultant's general education bilingual classroom; three of the OLE teachers, with their paraprofessionals, took advantage of that invitation. Finally, all school sites but one invited OLE literacy consultants to make presentations to their entire school faculty on the OLE instructional and assessment strategies.

We need to add here that the thrust of the OLE workshops always involved instructional practices, not paradigmatic stances toward special education. Near the end of the second year of intervention, when we did begin to refer to holism/constructivism in our workshops, we always used the term in the context of an organizing principle for instruction.

Data Sources

Data collection for this study began in 1989 and continued to 1993. Members of the research team visited all classrooms on a regular (monthly) basis and formally interviewed the teachers yearly. The project staff also videotaped the classrooms approximately every 6 weeks and collected classroom work products.

The principal data sources for this study are formal and informal interviews with teachers and paraprofessionals, field notes from classroom observations, videotapes of classrooms and OLE project meetings, and student work products. These data sources form the basis for describing and explaining the process and nature of teacher change over the course of the study.

RESULTS

We consider this study a first look at the intriguing question of teacher paradigmatic change in the area of special education for bilingual children. At this point in our data collection and analysis, we have identified three patterns that characterize the change process: (a) The amount of special education training affects teachers' paradigmatic orientation; (b) change is a transitional and multidimensional process rather than an "all-or-none," unidimensional phenomenon; and (c) change is directly related to the type of assistance and collaboration provided.

Special Education Training and Paradigms

From the beginning of our research, it became evident that although teachers varied in their instructional practices, they incorporated more reductionist practices than the holistic/constructivist practices we advocated as part of an optimal learning context (Beaumont, 1990; Rueda, Betts, & Hami, 1990; Ruiz, 1990). Specifically, we found indicators of a skills-based, remedial, teacher-driven curriculum. Moreover, the teachers viewed the students' low academic success as being due to within-child deficits, often of a perceptual or neurological nature. These deficits were viewed as lifelong disabilities. The following quotes by the OLE teachers while responding to the question "What is a learning disability or learning handicap?" illustrate this orientation. The first two teachers quoted here had extensive special education training.

> Okay. I understand a learning disability to be a deficit in a perceptual area, so the children that I'm working with are having difficulty either taking in information or in expressing themselves, or both. And that could mean verbally, it could mean in their written work, it could mean in their reading skills, it could be reflected in their behavior. So I think that the key word for me is their perception and expression of what is going on around them. (Ms. Springer, June 1989)

> So for my children it's being disabled in one of the processing areas, which is either auditory or visual or memory—which most of mine are. And

severely enough so that they can't process what they need to make good growth. (Ms. Avila, December 1991)

Three other teachers had first been trained as bilingual general education teachers. The first, Ms. Jones, was finishing university courses to receive her learning handicapped credential. When she began to answer the question regarding what a learning disability is, she stopped and replied that she really did not know. After pausing, she continued:

> It's not being able to learn in one area or maybe more than one area in which you're not able to be successful, that inhibits you from learning. . . . It depends on what process it might be. (Ms. Jones, June 1989)

Ms. Rojas had recently finished a credential program in special education. She also defined learning disabilities as a stable, within-child deficit:

> When it has to do with processing, most of us were spiced differently: Some of us were spiced more in the field of auditory discrimination and less in the field of visual discrimination; others were given more in the field of verbal language and not enough in the field of computational skills. It seems like . . . a learning disabled child was given too much spice on one part and not enough spice on another part. Their minds have strengths, but they have weaknesses when they are compared to a regular mind (Ms. Rojas, June 1989).

Although Ms. Rojas's answer above was redolent of the medical model, she added the following, which suggests a less-than-wholehearted acceptance of the term:

> I don't like the label "learning disabled" . . . because in a way they're really not learning disabled, they're just not learning the way a normal or regular or average child learns, because of the deficits. I would like to change that label, though. The children that I teach have weakness but they have a lot of strengths. I have artists in here that go beyond my talent. I've got writers in here that can't spell, but they're writers, and their minds intrigue me.

Ms. Hughes, the bilingual teacher with no specific special education training as yet (she was currently teaching on a waiver program), was the least medically oriented in her response:

> I think a learning disability is something that a child—oh, God, how would I explain it? It's like I feel like I have a learning disability when it comes to spelling. It's something that I haven't been able to work around and maybe it's a mental block in my mind that was set up when I was younger.

Because I was never a good speller then. . . . I think it's just, you know, these students haven't learned to work around a certain area, or find ways to compensate for what—I don't want to use "they're lacking," because it's not lacking—maybe it's something that they never learned. (Ms. Hughes, December 1991)

Ms. Hughes finished answering the question apologetically: "But I haven't taken any special education classes so . . . !"

Later on in the interviews, we asked the teachers if they could tell which of their students may have been misdiagnosed. Ms. Rojas answered that Spanish-speaking children who were transitioned too early from reading Spanish to reading English were often referred for special education placement by English monolingual teachers. She added emphatically that those children were not eligible for services through her program. Ms. Rojas was the only teacher to bring up this ongoing problem of false positives among bilingual children in a medically oriented special education system (Figueroa, 1990). Her answer implied that she kept them out of her program and that the children who were let in were "spiced differently," that is, had learning disabilities.

In essence, four of the five teachers' answers to the learning disability question were highly similar in their medical model orientation. In a related question regarding their opinion as to the cause of learning disabilities, the teachers' answers ranged from heredity to trauma to home environment to "no one really knows," but all of them except for Ms. Hughes indicated that they believed that their students arrived with an internal deficit in learning that they needed to compensate for, as well as internal strengths they needed to capitalize on. Ms. Hughes was somewhat on the fence on this issue, continuing to suggest that the cause of the disability was a "weak area" in the child, and therefore owned by the child, but that the area was "overlooked and overlooked" in the early years of their education, and that caused the disability. No teacher alluded to context as a mediator of their students' performance.

Based on our interviews with the teachers, we devised a 5-point continuum to represent their paradigmatic orientation (see Figure 23.2). A rating of 1 means that teachers consistently projected beliefs associated with a medical model orientation through our interviews with them; a rating of 5 means that they consistently projected a contextual performance orientation. Rueda and García (1994) devised a similar 3-point scale to represent teacher beliefs about reading assessment.

The patterns of teacher responses from our interviews suggest that the more special education training in the teacher's background, the stronger his or her reductionist orientation. These patterns also suggest that teacher preparation in a field outside of special education (here, bilingual education) somewhat tempers this orientation. Supporting these

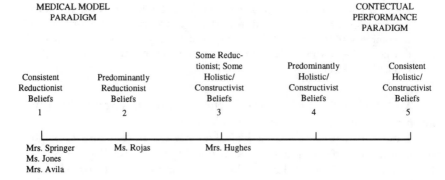

Figure 23.2. Teachers' beliefs on a scale of paradigmatic orientation: Before collaboration.

findings is the work of Rueda and García (1994), who found that of the three groups of educators they studied—bilingual credentialed teachers, bilingual teachers on waiver, and resource specialists—the resource specialists held the most reductionist beliefs and enacted the most reductionist instructional practices.

Change As a Transitional and Multidimensional Process

Following the initial interviews, the OLE project began the intensive collaboration phase with periodic workshops. The OLE teachers gradually began to try out the holistic/constructivist instructional strategies, each teacher with a different schedule and degree of implementation. However, all teachers reported an improvement in their students' literacy skills sometime over the course of the next year and a half, especially in writing. Further, in a study of videotaped lessons in the OLE teachers' classrooms (Ruiz, Figueroa, & Echandía, 1995), before intensive collaboration as well as after collaboration, a random sample of instructional events clearly showed that the lessons became significantly more holistic/constructivist. Table 23.2 presents the mean ratings of eight lessons before intensive collaboration and eight after collaboration. Each lesson was rated by two independent raters using a 5-point scale that defined the features of a holistic/constructivist lesson (e.g., use of student choice, whole–part–whole use of texts, use of students' background knowledge, etc.) and those of a reductionist lesson (teacher-selected content, learning segmented into parts, prepackaged curriculum materials without link to student experiences, etc.). Rating scores ranged from 1, meaning an average of zero observable holistic/constructivist lesson features, to 5, meaning an average of the maximum number of holistic/constructivist

TABLE 23.2
Classroom Practices Rated Along a Holistic/Constructivist Scale:
Before and After Collaboration

Classroom	Mean rating before collaboration	(SD)	Mean rating after collaboration	(SD)	t
Ms. Springer	1.4	.52	4.6	.74	10.14**
Ms. Rojas	2.4	1.18	3.9	1.08	2.65**
Ms. Jones	1.9	.95	3.7	1.39	3.05**
Ms. Avila	3.1	1.78	4.8	.46	2.59**
Ms. Hughes	3.6	1.30	4.6	.52	2.02**

*$p \geq .01$. **$p \geq .05$.

features. The mean interrater reliability coefficient was .95. Table 23.2 presents the means, standard deviations, and t values from this study.

All of the mean values in Table 23.2 are in the expected direction; the lessons became increasingly holistic/constructivist. Four out of the five means show statistically significant increases, particularly in the two classrooms where the OLE Project had no influence on the teachers before baseline data were collected (Springer and Jones). Three of the teachers (Ms. Rojas, Ms. Avila, and Ms. Hughes) began participating at a later period of the study, and their baseline data (before collaboration) were somewhat contaminated by exposure to OLE workshops during the baseline phase. This exposure may have pushed their initial classroom ratings toward holism/constructivism. On the other hand, we feel that the three teachers' limited exposure to holistic/constructivist strategies reflects the real-life situation in schools, whereby many special educators have received at least some inservice training on holistic teaching techniques. Even with this exposure, the ratings in Table 23.2 show that all teachers implemented more holistic/constructivist strategies after long-term collaboration.

In addition to collecting the classroom ratings we interviewed each teacher approximately 1 to 2 years after the interviews previously cited. We were particularly interested in any change in their conception of a learning disability, specifically, away from a medical model orientation (reductionism) and toward a contextual performance model (holism/constructivism). The difference in Ms. Avila's and Ms. Rojas's answers to "What is a learning disability?" were dramatic. Gone are the references to internal processing disorders:

Avila: Well, a learning disability I guess is when you can't learn, huh? And actually it's not that you can't, it's that you're not learning. . . . But it's kind of like we see now that although we do have some kids who even in our rich environment have made little growth, they've made growth. So it's not that you can't, it's maybe that they just are not doing it in the way that you set it up.

Interviewer: Yeah.

Avila: So I don't know what it is. (both laughing) It may not be what I thought it was before.

Ms. Rojas now doubts the very existence of learning disabilities:

> Okay, based upon the experiences that I've had, I believe that there is no such thing as a learning disability. And I firmly believe that learning and intelligence can be molded. Especially if we use the appropriate techniques. I have a feeling that a lot of times it's our instruction that's disabling the child. . . . This is all very new to me still, but I'm really going to focus on, okay, how much have we molded this student? What have we done to make the learning process occur or not occur? I really feel that we want to put quick labels on students and we don't really need to. As a matter of fact we don't even *have* to, given the right molding effect.

Two other teachers in this study did not make such a dramatic shift in their view of learning abilities and disabilities. However, in their second interview there is evidence in their answers that they are beginning to question the medical model, textbook-like definitions they gave before the intervention phase. Here Ms. Jones (recently credentialled in special education) brings up the point that, depending on your approach, almost anyone can seem to have learning disabilities.

> Seems to me Richard asked me that question a few years ago and I think my answer is probably the same almost. (laughs) And I said, "I'm not sure anymore." And the reason I said that and I'd probably still tell you is, because you could probably in some ways, if you want to, depending how you want to define it, you could make anybody be that way. Anybody could be, I guess when you get down to it.

Ms. Jones's answer here implies that she is aware of the social construction of learning disabilities (i.e., our definitions affect who is considered learning disabled). But later on in the interview, her continuing medical model orientation is clearly evident: "Well, definitely there's perceptual things that go on in the brain. Definitely something that is not right. Some message is not being transmitted."

Like Ms. Jones, Ms. Springer (originally credentialled as a special education teacher) also seemed to be in a transitional phase in her view of learning disabilities 2 years later, between a medical model and a contextual performance model. She first gave a textbook-like answer to the learning disability question, nearly mirroring her answer 2 years before. But when asked whether all her students had the neurological problems she had described as characteristic of a learning disability, she responded with uncertainty:

> Well, they're supposed to. (laughs) But I think that sometimes that's difficult to ascertain unless you can do some type of brain scan. (laughs)

Two years before, Ms. Springer had said without hesitation that all her students had learning disabilities. A year later, in her final exit interview with the project, she expounded on her doubts:

> I also think that, especially working with the kids that are bilingual, that it's becoming more difficult for me to make a decision about whether I'm dealing with a learning disability or not. That has changed. I used to think I could tell. I think that how I really feel is that I'm not sure about anything, I don't know if there are learning disabilities.

When we reinterviewed Ms. Hughes (the bilingual special education teacher on waiver to teach in special education), she now had three semesters of special education training toward her learning handicapped credential. She took these courses while participating in the OLE project's collaboration phase. Her contact with the OLE project seemed to temper the medical model orientation that we would have predicted with increased special education training. Here she tells us that she now has acquired a textbook definition, but she does not seem to be buying it:

Hughes: I don't know. I don't know what a learning disability is. I can tell you what my textbook says. I think maybe it's a teaching disability. . . . With some kids I really, seriously think that it's more a teaching disability than a learning disability.
Interviewer: And you mean by a teaching disability . . . ?
Hughes: That the teacher is disabling the child.

Ms. Hughes explains later that taking the wrong instructional approach with a child early on, for example, in reading, can be a source of the problem. Like Ms. Avila and Ms. Rojas, Ms. Hughes does not mention an internal deficit as being responsible for the child's poor performance. All three teachers emphasize the importance of the right or wrong instructional context in a sense "creating" the disability. This conception is much closer to a contextual performance view of learning disabilities.

The data indicated that this type of fundamental change was not a simple, unidimensional process. If teacher change *were* a unidimensional process, we would have expected that once teachers acknowledged in some way the social construction and contextual variation of learning disabilities, they would have concurrently shifted their instructional practices to providing contexts in which they could see the best of their students' abilities. The reverse would also be true: Once teachers had implemented a holistic/constructivist curriculum, we would have expected a shift toward a contextual performance view of disability. This was not the case; rather, we found inconsistencies between beliefs and practices.

One illustration of this inconsistency concerns Ms. Jones. Among the first group of OLE teachers, Ms. Jones was one of the most advanced in terms of adopting Writers' Workshop (Atwell, 1987; Graves, 1983) and Interactive Journals (Flores & Garcia, 1984). These holistic strategies proved crucial to the OLE intervention, because they quickly and clearly helped children who were previously thought to be nonwriters to write well, sometimes even better than their general education peers. Ms. Jones implemented Writers' Workshop so effectively that general education teachers from her school requested her assistance in setting up their writing workshops. She also developed many management techniques for Writers' Workshop, and her classroom became a good demonstration site for modeling a workshop approach in the resource room. Yet, of the five teachers, she alone remained convinced that all of her students had learning disabilities. Ms. Jones continued to view the disability as a neurological problem within the child. So, although she practiced many holistic/constructivist instructional strategies, her belief system and view of her students was typical of reductionist, medical model thinking.

In contrast, Ms. Rojas did not consistently implement holistic/constructivist strategies such as Interactive Journals and Writers' Workshop, as indicated in field notes from classroom observations. (Ms. Rojas did, however, take some of the key holistic/constructivist principles, such as connection to personal experience, and develop her own instructional strategies. One example was a current events circle, where she read the newspaper and children participated actively in the discussion, occasionally writing unedited pieces after discussion.) Yet, a year and a half after the start of the intervention phase, Ms. Rojas announced that only 2 of her 28 students identified as learning disabled in fact had learning disabilities. She came to believe that the other 26 students had experienced ineffective learning environments in school. Because the students' academic functioning in the school setting was judged by school authorities to be evidence of a learning disability, primarily on the basis of biased standardized testing (Figueroa, 1990) or premature transition from Spanish to English reading, she recognized that they were spuriously labeled "disabled." In her exit interview in the fall of 1992, Ms. Rojas clearly transferred the responsibility or cause of the learning handicap from the child to the school system: "It's a system. Some were designed to make some things effective and other things ineffective and I think any system that was designed to make students ineffective is not going to be successful for a very long time."

In short, in this initial study of teacher change in special education we identified *at least* two (we fully expect that there are more) dimensions of teacher change toward holism/constructivism, paradigmatic orientation and instructional practices. These two dimensions did not always go hand in hand, or in a linear fashion. On the basis of this pattern, we constructed a quadrant to represent the two dimensions of practice and paradigmatic orientation toward learning abilities and disabilities (see Figure 23.3). The vertical axis in Figure 23.3 represents the continuum

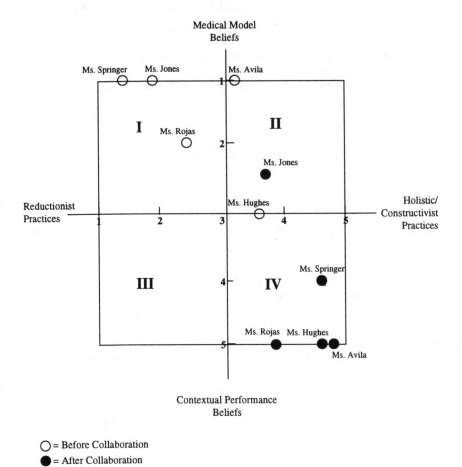

O = Before Collaboration
● = After Collaboration

Figure 23.3. Teacher change in practice and beliefs: Before and after collaboration.

of paradigmatic orientation from Figure 23.2; the horizontal axis represents the classroom ratings of Table 23.2. This two-dimensional figure
allows us to look simultaneously at teacher beliefs and instructional practices and to "place" each teacher within a particular quadrant, observing
change over time as the study progressed.

Using this framework, our data indicate that three of the teachers
began the project somewhere in Quadrant I, that is, with both a reductionist set of beliefs and reductionist practices. The other two teachers,
Ms. Hughes and Ms. Avila, began the study in Quadrant II, with somewhat more holistic/constructivist practices, perhaps because of their exposure to some OLE instructional strategies while they were first being
videotaped. Ms. Hughes, with no special education training and more
experience implementing some holistic/constructivist strategies in her
previous general education setting, actually began close to Quadrant IV.
Again, analyses of videotapes (Ruiz, 1990), student work products (Rueda
et al., 1990), and ongoing interviews cross-validated the teachers' initial
positions in these quadrants.

One and a half to 2 years after beginning to participate in the OLE
workshops, four of the five teachers had moved out of Quadrant I and
into Quadrant IV. Of these teachers, Ms. Avila and Ms. Hughes most
consistently implemented instructional strategies that were holistic/
constructivist in nature, and concurrently rejected a medical model orientation. They acknowledged the powerful effect of context, or an "enriched
environment," as Ms. Avila put it, on their students' performance. Ms.
Avila and the paraprofessional in her class went so far as to make a large,
laminated chart of the OLE conditions and post them in their classroom.
Basically, these conditions are a list of holistic/constructivist principles
combined with other contextual features we had found to promote
optimal academic performance among Latino children (see Table 23.3).
Near the end of the collaboration phase, we co-presented with the teachers at professional conferences, and they had seen us review the OLE
conditions as a theoretical base for optimal academic performance. When
we asked why Ms. Avila and Ms. Saenz had put up this chart, they
responded that it was to help them keep the principles in mind as they
planned their instructional activities. They used it to ask themselves questions such as, "Have we offered the children enough choice in their
literacy projects? Have we made sure to begin and focus our lesson on the
children's background experiences and knowledge?" Ms. Avila and
Ms. Saenz had, in a sense, elected to post their philosophy for all to
see. (Ruiz, Figueroa, and Echandía, 1995, suggested that teachers' meta-
awareness of their philosophical changes is an important element in lasting instructional change.)

In summary, we propose that our findings reflect the teachers'
struggles with changing to a holistic/constructivist paradigm. As others

TABLE 23.3
Conditions for Optimal Language and Literacy Lessons

Student choice	Students exercise choice in their learning: writing topics, books, projects, thematic cycles.
Centered on student interests and background knowledge	Lessons begin and revolve around students' personal experiences, background knowledge, and interests.
Wholeness (whole-part-whole)	Lessons begin with whole texts (e.g., books, poems) to maximize the construction of understanding, then move to the analysis of smaller units of language (e.g., phonics, spelling, punctuation), returning to the text as a whole.
Active participation, peer interaction	Students actively engage in lessons with frequent and long turns of talk.
Primacy of meaning (then form)	Students' good ideas get communicated first, and then move to a focus on correct form or mechanics, such as spelling and grammar.
Authentic purpose	The end products of lessons have a real-life function.
Approximation	Students are encouraged to take risks and successively approximate language and literacy skills (following a developmental course).
Immersion in language and print	The classroom is saturated with different print forms and functions, as well as opportunities to hear and use language for a wide range of purposes.
Demonstration	Teachers demonstrate their own reading and writing and share their ongoing efforts with students.
Immediate response	Students receive a response to their oral and written literacy tasks; they are encouraged to give personal responses to others' efforts.
Community	Students, parents, and teachers form a community of readers, writers, and learners who explore a range of questions relevant to them.
Expectations	Teachers, parents, and the students themselves expect that students will become proficient and independent speakers, readers, and writers.

have done while collaborating with general education teachers, we have identified two dimensions of change: shifts in instructional practices and shifts in beliefs (Guskey, 1986). We also found that both are transitional processes. While in a transitional stage, teachers can change their instructional practices without substantially modifying their belief systems, and vice versa.

We do think, however, that our data suggest that Guskey's (1986) model of teacher change may be an oversimplification. He suggested that there is a chronological order to change: first a change in practices, then observation of their effectiveness, and then a change in beliefs. As we have worked with special education teachers (not only with those mentioned in this study, but in our dissemination efforts in other school districts), we have seen a few teachers that go the route of Ms. Rojas, that is, first a change in beliefs, then a change in practices. Interestingly, all the teachers whom we have observed to go this less frequently traveled route have been Latino. This indicates to us that (a) individual instances of teachers changing are more varied than previously thought, and (b) the impact of other factors on change, such as one's ethnic background, especially in a project focusing on the needs of children from diverse cultural and linguistic backgrounds, needs to be explored.

Change As a Function of Type of Assistance

In the general description of the collaboration phase of OLE, we mentioned that in the early workshops we followed a traditional, transmission sort of teacher-training model. This gave way to a different sort of teacher–researcher collaboration as we continued to work with the OLE teachers and paraprofessionals and note our successes and failures. We considered indices of success to be uptake of holistic/constructivist instructional strategies and continued participation in the project, even when that involved dramatic school-site changes, such as altering the students' class time in the OLE classrooms. We viewed as our failures teachers' continued use of reductionist instructional strategies and withdrawal from the research project.

Causal explanations of these successes and failures are by nature complex, multidimensional, and elusive. They involve individual factors, such as personality, and systemic factors, such as faculty support for restructuring. However, certain features of our changing collaboration with the teachers emerged as highly associated with uptake of holistic/constructivist strategies and with continued participation in the project. We discuss two of those features here: (a) including members of the teachers' occupational community as leaders and (b) a teacher-centered curriculum.

Occupational Community.   In the early OLE workshops, we did not have access to a resource specialist teacher who could lead the teachers into trying the proposed instructional strategies with bilingual students. Many of the OLE teachers were quick to point this out to us. For example, when some general education teachers shared with the OLE teachers their techniques for implementing Writers' Workshop, most of the OLE teachers later commented that their students were different from general education students and therefore they could not take much away from the workshop. We then asked a bilingual special day class teacher to present some of her holistic/constructivist instructional strategies, but, again, we heard from the OLE resource specialists that their children were different from special day class students. Only when one of the OLE resource specialists, influenced more by a bilingual teacher across the hall in her school than by us, decided to try Writers' Workshop did all the OLE teachers begin to try Writers' Workshop (with one exception: Ms. Rojas continued to direct and select the children's topics for writing). From that point on, the OLE workshops have always included practicing resource specialists as leaders. Most of the time these leaders were the OLE teachers themselves, as we invited certain teacher–paraprofessional teams to share their instructional successes with the others. Uptake of instructional strategies dramatically increased when we modified our OLE workshops to include this important feature.

Wagner (1992) wrote of teachers acting as an *occupational community.* We found in the OLE Project that in the initial stages, special education teachers have their own occupational community, separate from general education teachers, at least in the context of professional development. The boundaries of that community are very strong. For the most part, they do not consider general education teachers, educational consultants who have left the classroom, or university professors in the area of special education to be part of that community. Practicing special education teachers who carry the same professional title *are* part of that community.

The critical nature of the latter specification of occupational community—carrying the same title—was made apparent again to us recently as the OLE project began its dissemination phase into a number of large school districts in California. In this phase, special day class teachers participate alongside resource specialists. As the special day class teachers listened to practicing resource specialist teachers share their techniques and impressive student work products, the special day class teachers were quick to point out that their students were different. They continually questioned whether the material presented to them had any relevance to their students.

Around this time in the dissemination phase we were fortunate to discover that one of our participating special day class teachers from another district had begun to implement the OLE instructional strategies. We immediately invited him to present to and speak with this particular group of special day class teachers, believing that we had met the occupational community criterion. But once again, these teachers questioned whether what this teacher had to say applied to them and to their students. It turned out that their designation was *special day class—severely emotionally disturbed,* whereas our other OLE teacher's designation was *special day class—learning handicapped.* It was not enough that *some* of his students carried an emotional disturbance label. One of the teachers responded, "But *all* our students are SED." Luckily for us, the OLE special day class—learning handicapped teacher *had* been a special day class—severely emotionally disturbed teacher in the past and he shared that information with them. This displaying of one's right to be considered a member of an occupational group seems to be a key event in effecting instructional and paradigmatic change among special education teachers. Our data indicate that it cannot be ignored, especially at the beginning stages of collaborating for change.

We further suspect that the notion of occupational community emerges more strongly in special education. Our working hypothesis is that the reductionist paradigm, with its medical stance in explaining students' academic performance, creates an abnormally strong emphasis on labels and categories for children. This emphasis likely begins with university special education training. But special education practice, both microcontexts (e.g., the diagnostic testing session) and macrocontexts (e.g., federal categories of disability for funding purposes) supports the continuing enactment and entrenchment of this paradigm.

It would be easy to become discouraged with the notion of occupational community and its powerful effect on teacher change. However, we have found that it takes just one teacher to take the leap into trying new instructional strategies. Once that teacher does, we have the means to begin to facilitate change among the other members of his or her occupational group. We have also found that as teachers begin to focus on their students' increasing academic success within holistic/instructional lessons, and as they begin to try out new assumptions, both within an atmosphere of trust, special education teachers begin to listen to other educators' voices, not specifically those from special education. For example, OLE teams of teachers and paraprofessionals have now read and listened to whole language leaders such as Ken and Yetta Goodman, Brian Cambourne, Donald Graves, and Lucy Calkins. In the later stages of our collaboration, not once have they dismissed these encounters as being irrelevant to them as special educators. Instead, the OLE teams have listened to these leaders' ideas and integrated them into their beliefs and practices, always adapting them to the specific needs of their students in the resource specialist program.

Teacher-Centered Curriculum. We began with a transmission orientation in our OLE workshops but moved to a constructivist one in the later period of collaboration (Au, 1993). Instead of bringing along our own curriculum topics, we began to invite the OLE teams to bring in their classroom stories and students' work. Our typical procedure was to ask the teachers which area of curriculum or which instructional strategy they wanted assistance with. As a group, the teams would negotiate the general topic for the next workshop. If, for example, they chose Interactive Journals as the topic, we would ask the teachers to bring in at least two student journals, perhaps one in which a student was making significant progress and one in which another student was struggling. As each teacher–paraprofessional team talked about the students and their work, the other OLE teams and researchers would listen, question, react, and sometimes pull out larger themes about literacy development. We would often have a professional article to read and discuss at the workshop. One of the literacy consultants would also bring additional samples to share with the OLE teachers, or lead the participants in actually doing the instructional strategy.

In this atmosphere, the consultants and researchers were *co-learners,* while the OLE teams, who knew the students best, became *co-leaders* of our sessions. OLE teachers who had the benefit of this type of workshop for a longer period of time tended to make the most progress toward Quadrant IV in Figure 3, that is, holistic/constructivist beliefs and practices. Ms. Jones, the teacher in Quadrant II, and Ms. Rojas, the teacher whose practices were not quite as holistic/constructivist as her stated beliefs led us to expect, experienced more of the earlier transmission type of OLE workshop. Consequently, this initial study of bilingual special education teachers' change lends support to others' contentions regarding teacher change in general education (e.g., Weaver & Henke, 1992): The more our collaboration resembles the student-centered and negotiated curriculum of holistic/constructivist classrooms, the more dramatic the change in paradigm and practice.

CONCLUSION

Teachers, paraprofessionals, consultants, and researchers participating in a study of bilingual special education classrooms changed during the course of the project. We all moved from largely a transmission model of instruction to a holistic/constructivist one. Early results from this change indicate that, as researchers and consultants, we became more effective at helping teachers to modify their paradigms and instruction practices. Early results from this change also indicate that students became more proficient readers and writers (Figueroa, Ruiz, & García, 1994). Consequently, we found evidence that the OLE Project effected change in the three target areas of teacher professional development highlighted by Guskey (1986): teachers' beliefs, teachers' practices, and student outcomes.

From our experience in the OLE Project we learned a number of things about the process of teacher change in special education. First, we learned that the more special education training held by practicing resource specialists, the more reductionist their beliefs. We also learned that teacher change in special education, as in general education, has at least two dimensions: instructional practices and beliefs. Change along these two dimensions does not automatically occur simultaneously, nor do all teachers go through the change process in the same sequence. Finally, we discovered that, as in general education, the type of assistance we offered was related to the teachers' change processes. We found a powerful effect from including practicing members of the teachers' occupational community as leaders of change. Further, when we shifted from a transmission model of assistance to one that centered workshops on the teachers' preferences and experiences, we became more effective agents of change.

Based on our experience with teachers in the OLE Project, we have developed a working model for teacher–school district–university collaboration. We are applying that model in three large, urban school districts in California. Our current model consists of a 4- to 5-day summer institute, bimonthly meetings with the teachers and paraprofessionals for the following academic year (on alternate months, the teams meet on their own), another summer institute, and a final year of bimonthly meetings. After these 2 years of collaboration we plan to withdraw from the districts. We expect and hope that reform of instructional practices used with Latino students in learning disabilities programs will continue without our direct assistance. Our findings have led us to believe that the "teacher next door," the comember of the teacher's occupational community, will be a more effective and efficient agent of change than the university researcher or outside training consultant.

In sum, it seems to us that the major lesson to be learned in our initial study of bilingual special education teacher change is that, just as we have to be concerned with setting up optimal learning environments in classrooms for students, we need to be equally concerned with setting up optimal conditions for teacher change. This study has begun to sketch out for us what some of those optimal conditions might be. It has also begun to enlighten this difficult and complex process of special education teacher change.

AUTHORS' NOTES

1. We would like to thank Adriana Echandía, Carolina Oropeza, and Adele Arellano, research personnel for the OLE Research and Dissemination Project, for their assistance in the preparation of this chapter.

2. This work was supported by the California State Department of Education, Specialized Programs Branch (The OLE Research and Dissemination Project), and the CRESS Center, University of California at Davis. Opinions herein are those of the authors and not necessarily those of the aforementioned agencies.

NOTES

1. We consider these two terms part of the same paradigm. However, the term _medical model_ is somewhat clearer in connoting that the paradigm considers the child's learning struggles attributable to an internal processing disorder. On the other hand, this term is less clear in connoting the type of instruction that goes hand in hand with this view. In this case, _reductionism_ projects a clearer sense of the fragmented curriculum traditionally used to correct "processing disorders." For this reason we use both terms throughout the chapter. We also welcome feedback from readers regarding their usage.

2. In a problem parallel to the one described in Note 1, we felt we needed to use two terms for a single paradigm throughout this chapter. The term _contextual performance model_ stresses the social construction of ability and disability. This aspect is not emphasized in Poplin's (1988b) article suggesting _holistic constructivism_ as a term for a contrasting paradigm. Until there is more general acknowledgment of the social construction aspect of disability as part of this paradigm, we feel it necessary to continue to use "contextual performance" as a paradigm descriptor. Once again, however, Poplin's term most clearly connotes the type of instruction and curriculum inherent in this paradigm.

24. Beyond the Herring Sandwich Phenomenon: A Holistic Constructivist Approach to Teacher Education

ELLEN H. BACON AND LISA A. BLOOM

Now logic is a wonderful thing but it has, as the process of evolution discovered, certain drawbacks. Anything that thinks logically can be fooled by something else that thinks at least as logically as it does. The easiest way to fool a completely logical robot is to feed it the same stimulus sequence over and over again so it gets locked in a loop. This was best demonstrated by the famous Herring Sandwich experiments conducted millennia ago at MISPWOSO (the MaxiMegalo Institute of Slowly and Painfully Working Out the Surprisingly Obvious).

A robot was programmed to believe that it liked herring sandwiches. This was actually the most difficult part of the whole experiment. Once the robot had been programmed to believe that it liked herring sandwiches, a herring sandwich was placed in front of it. Whereupon the robot thought to itself, Aha! A herring sandwich! I like herring sandwiches.

Note. From MOSTLY HARMLESS by Douglas Adams. Copyright © 1992 by Douglas Adams. Reprinted by permission of Harmony Books, a division of Crown Publishers, Inc.

Reprinted, with changes, from "Beyond the herring sandwich phenomenon: A holistic constructivist approach to teacher education," by Ellen H. Bacon and Lisa A. Bloom, *Journal of Learning Disabilities*, Vol. 28, 1995, pp. 636–645. Copyright © 1995 by PRO-ED, Inc.

It would then bend over and scoop up the herring sandwich in its herring sandwich scoop, and then straighten up again. Unfortunately for the robot, it was fashioned in such a way that the action of straightening up caused the herring sandwich to slip straight back off its herring sandwich scoop and fall on the floor in front of the robot. Whereupon the robot thought to itself, Ah! A herring sandwich . . . , etc., and repeated the same action over and over and over again. The only thing that prevented the herring sandwich from getting bored with the whole damn business and crawling off in search of other ways of passing the time was that the herring sandwich, being just a bit of dead fish between a couple of slices of bread, was marginally less alert to what was going on than was the robot.

The scientists at the Institute thus discovered the driving force behind all change, development and innovation in life, which was this: herring sandwiches. They published a paper to this effect, which was widely criticized as being extremely stupid. They checked their figures and realized that what they had actually discovered was "boredom," or rather, the practical function of boredom. In a fever of excitement they then went on to discover other emotions like "irritability," "depression," "reluctance," "ickiness" and so on. The next big breakthrough came when they stopped using herring sandwiches, whereupon a whole welter of new emotions became suddenly available to them for study, such as "relief," "joy," "friskiness," "appetite," "satisfaction," and most important of all, the desire for "happiness."

This was the biggest breakthrough of all. (Adams, 1992, pp. 60–62; see Note on p. 397)

Although behavioral theory and practice have given us some systematic tools for examining and changing behavior, many of us who were once students of herring sandwich phenomena find ourselves currently intrigued by the ideas of holistic constructivism. Many constructivist ideas are not new and are clearly presented in the work of Dewey (1968), Montessori (1967), and Ashton-Warner (1963), but there are some fresh perspectives, both theoretical and practical, that have much to contribute to teacher education. One current impetus toward a more holistic approach is coming from a revision in scientific paradigms that has affected many disciplines. As Capra (1988) explained in *The Turning Point,*

> In contrast to the mechanistic Artesian view of the world, the world view emerging from modern physics can be characterized by words like organic, holistic, and ecological. The universe is no longer seen as a machine, made up of a multitude of objects, but has to be pictured as one indivisible, dynamic whole whose parts are essentially interrelated and can be understood only as patterns of a cosmic process. (p. 78)

Modern physics has demonstrated that to understand the universe, we need to understand relations between ever-changing electromagnetic fields. Because forces and fields are ever-changing, what we measure or observe is only a measure of what is happening at the time we are observing, and the phenomenon we measure is affected by our observation. Consequently, we have gained a new understanding through this application of the Heisenberg Principle of the role of observers in shaping and creating what they are observing. Hawking (1988) explained this idea as follows:

> The theory of quantum mechanics is based on an entirely new type of mathematics that no longer describes the real world in terms of particles and waves; it is only the observations of the world that may be described in those terms. (p. 56)

We see in this paradigm a new appreciation of the importance of the observer in science, and how the observer can change what is observed in a study or experiment. Rhodes (1987) applied the idea to special education classes:

> For years I was frustrated by my limited capacity to alter the child's social and physical environment. I knew, for instance, if I could change the teacher's attitude toward the child's behavior, I could make greater inroads into what was viewed as the child's disturbance. But I was relatively helpless to alter, in any significant way, what I saw as the realities of the child's cultural, psychological and physical environment which contributed to the child's "at risk" condition. However, now that I understand quantum logic, I realize I did not give the child as much credit as I should have for her/his inherent power to generate and not simply respond to her/his own environmental reality. (p. 59)

Many of us who have worked in behavioral and prescriptive programs can identify with Rhodes's (1987) frustration over never having enough control to make meaningful changes in a child's environment. With a renewed appreciation of the role of students' understanding of their experiences comes hope that they can generate a different experience in the same environment.

> Therefore, within the expanded framework of quantum logic, I do not have to do so much in the child's environment, I can concentrate upon trying to mediate the child's cognitive capacities for expanding her/his environment, her projection into her environment. (Rhodes, 1987, p. 59)

This idea, that the learner is a generator of her or his own reality, is a basic tenet of the holistic constructivist perspective, in that constructivists view learning as the creation of new meaning by learners within the context of their current knowledge (Heshusius, 1989; Poplin & Stone, 1992).

FOUR PRINCIPLES

As educators explore how to use this paradigm in public school instruction, we believe these ideas must be applied to teacher education programs. We want our students in teacher education to trust their own perceptions of their environment and to rely on their own abilities to make changes. We believe that only by experiencing education as validating and empowering can teachers have an understanding of the types of experiences they can create for their students. With this goal in mind, we redesigned our graduate program in behavior disorders around the following four holistic constructivist principles:

1. *Student work must be individualized and actively involve students in projects they develop to be meaningful to their professional work and development, based on their experiences and background knowledge.*

One of the major premises of holistic constructivism is that learners learn best from experiences connected to their present knowledge and interests and from experiences in which they are passionately involved. Acknowledgment of the learners' experiences, their stories and their voices, is a powerful tool in helping teachers assume ownership of their own learning and in empowering them to initiate changes in their lives. In *We Make The Road By Walking,* Horton and Freire (1990) discuss the importance of engaging students by using the personal and political experiences they bring to their classes. Horton and Freire express this idea eloquently in the following passage.

> When the students come, of course, they bring with them, inside of them, in their bodies, in their lives, they bring their hopes, despair, expectations, knowledge, which they got by living, by fighting, by becoming frustrated. Undoubtedly they don't come here empty. They arrive here full of things. In most of the cases, they bring with them opinions about the world, about life. . . . The question is not to come to the classroom and to make beautiful speeches analyzing, for example, the political authority of the country, but the question is how to take advantage of the reading of reality, which the people are doing, in order to make it possible for students to make a different and much *deeper* reading of reality. (pp. 157–158)

Similarly, O'Loughlin (1992) believed that a fundamental challenge for teacher educators is to construct an environment in which teachers experience the power of constructing their own knowledge and assume ownership of their own learning and thought. He stated,

> In a world in which teachers are often silenced by the institutional structure of schooling, the most powerful antidote is to affirm their personhood and their experiences and provide a space in which they are enabled to voice their thoughts and examine their experiences. (p. 338)

2. *Student work should address problems encountered in the student's classroom, school, and community and should have an audience beyond the teacher and beyond the university.*

Dewey (1968) believed that schools should provide a problem-rich context in which students' minds are put to work, instead of filling their heads with facts. Citing Dewey's work, Skrtic (1991) argued that the role of teachers is to help students learn to solve unanticipated problems and to teach students to think and reason. O'Loughlin (1992), applying constructivist ideas to teacher education, presented the idea of "emancipatory" knowledge construction. He believed that teachers need to learn to understand their own socially constructed nature of reality and to ask themselves critical questions so that they might act on their own vision of a better world. As O'Loughlin noted,

> This is a radical stance because it argues for enabling teachers to make critical curricular and pedagogical decisions for themselves. . . . The advantage of this approach is that it makes it possible to ground the curriculum in teachers' experiences and to include the change process opportunities for modifying teaching practices. (p. 338)

Because teachers are rarely encouraged to question classroom practices or develop methods for addressing problems in their own context, they seldom gain professional recognition for their work, leading to chronic "prestige deprivation," as described by Goodland (1991). Student projects that involve problem solving of real-life issues help students learn to use their own ideas and abilities to address issues of concern. In the process, they gain a new appreciation of their efficacy and the power of their voice. When student work does address real issues from their classrooms, schools, or communities, there is a natural audience for the work in the students' own environment, which gives them new voices and a new sense of power. The importance of an audience for student work is one of the core practices of the Foxfire program. In describing Foxfire pedagogy, Ensminger and Dangel (1992) wrote, "The importance of the audience goes beyond an opportunity for students to share what has been accomplished; it also provides an opportunity for students to have their work recognized as being significant and important" (p. 6). This idea is as true for students in a teacher education program as it is for students enrolled in grade school.

3. *Student work should develop through collaboration and problem solving with faculty and peers.*

Constructivists believe that knowledge and knowing are a result of social interchanges. According to Gergen (1985), knowledge is something people do together, and is not something people possess in their head. Heshusius (1989) described social interchange as a medium for learning. She believes that learners are motivated not by well-designed activities, but by teachers who understand their students and let instruction come from a dialectic with them.

The importance of social interchange was articulated clearly in research by the students, teachers, administrators, staff, and graduate school educators who wrote *Voices from the Inside: A Report on Schooling From Inside the Classroom* (Poplin & Weeres, 1992). Through a year-long process of discussions and analysis, seven issues were defined as being critical to school reform. An issue that dominated the participants' discussions was the importance of relationships. Students' experiences in school were defined by their relationships to their teachers and to other students. Teachers reported that they often felt isolated and unappreciated. Administrators described feeling disconnected from their own staff members and limited in relationships with their teachers and staffs. The authors stated, "This theme was prominently stated by participants and so deeply connected to all other themes in the data that it is believed this may be one of the two most central issues in solving the crisis inside schools" (1992, p. 13). This issue is not just a public school problem. Those of us in higher education programs must respond by providing models of collaborative educational experiences and caring relationships with our students.

4. *Evaluation procedures should be based on authentic assessment of student work, involve self-reflection, and provide an opportunity to learn from mistakes.*

Wiggens (1989) defined authentic assessment as alternative assessment that requires students to go beyond basic recall and demonstrate their knowledge and understanding through a product, performance, or exhibition. Constructivists (Heshusius, 1989; Poplin, 1988) have called for assessment to focus on students' purposeful work in natural settings, with the emphasis on how the learner constructs meaning from a situation. "Errors" become insights into how a child thinks and reasons. Evaluation of students changes from "ranking correct responses to controlled tasks, to documenting and assessing real life processes and accomplishments" (Heshusius, 1989, p. 412).

According to Poplin and Weeres (1992), learning occurs in a spiral in which knowledge is transformed or interpreted differently by each person. Learners select and attend to what needs to be learned based on their own knowledge base, choosing from information and experiences that relate to and are not incongruent with their previous learning. If one adopts this perspective on learning, then evaluation that comprises only right/wrong or pass/fail may become counterproductive in the development of thinking and learning. When learners recognize errors or incongruence and begin to make adjustments and revisions in their work, then they have an opportunity not just to refine their own work, but to become independent learners and thinkers. Evaluation procedures need to encourage students to develop evaluation criteria for their work, to evaluate their work against those criteria, and to make revisions as needed.

IMPLEMENTATION

To implement a constructivist approach in our graduate program in behavior disorders, we developed a portfolio model of evaluation to replace the final master's comprehensive exam. Students now complete a series of projects based on their interests and needs and compile them into a portfolio similar to that of an artist. Like artists' portfolios, students' portfolios include a collection of their best work. The portfolios provide us and our students with a sample of their teaching skills and evidence of their professional development. The portfolio is structured around eight competency areas; students submit projects that demonstrate competency in each area. When completed, each portfolio is unique and reflects the richness and diversity of the students' work in the school and community. Throughout the program, the faculty advisors and the students work together to ensure that there will be projects in the final portfolio that demonstrate competency in each area. Most projects are developed and graded as part of course work, but they may be revised several times after the course before they are submitted as part of a final portfolio.

The process of developing a portfolio, using project proposals, and evaluating competency in each area is presented in Figures 24.1 through 24.4. To describe how the principles and the process are implemented, we asked three of our graduate students to talk about how they experienced the principles of the program, the portfolio, the projects, and the evaluation of the portfolios. We recorded and transcribed their conversation and then invited them back to edit their comments. Other than editing for clarity, the only changes the authors made were to arrange sections of the conversation into topics.

The three students are

* Christine McWhirter, a recent graduate of the program who teaches students with behavior disorders in a self-contained setting at a middle school in a large county system. During part of each day, the class functions as a factory, buying materials, constructing and marketing their product, and spending the profits;

* Diane Milner, a special education teacher in a small city who teaches with an eighth-grade team of four general classroom teachers. This

---

ROLE OF THE FACULTY

*Validate the project as demonstrating competency in required area
*Assist students in identifying projects that are meaningful to them and that are
    professionally relevant
*Assist students with finding information and developing strategies for completing their
    projects
*Assist students in finding an audience for their work

ROLE OF THE STUDENT

*Create a project based on real issues and concerns rising out of current work
*Develop a project proposal defining how the project can be implemented
*Implement the project proposal and make revisions as needed
*Evaluate and revise the project
*Present work to colleagues and professional audiences

Figure 24.1.   Roles of the faculty and the student.

year Diane started a program in which all special education students
in the grade were fully mainstreamed;

• Pat Wishon, a special education teacher in a small, rural elementary
  school, who teaches in a resource room serving students with a wide
  range of disabilities and behavior problems.

Program Principles

Question 1: *Do you think the graduate program is individualized? If so, in
what ways?*

Christine: Oh, I definitely think it's individualized, because my classroom situation was taken into account for everything I did, and I chose
projects that were going to somehow benefit me and that I could use in
my classroom. I didn't feel like I was just regurgitating information, just
learning from books and spitting it back out. I felt like I was really doing
things that I needed to learn or I needed to change in my classroom.

Pat: I have loved being able to be credible in my classes and to be
able to do what I feel I need to be doing. That's the part that I've enjoyed
most, I think, about school. To be able to look at my situation and to have
a lot of input into what's being done. When you're motivated that way,
you just learn so much more and it isn't just regurgitation, it's application, it's synthesis, and it's all those things that make learning, learning.

Diane: And once you've had to do it in the form of a project, you're
more likely to keep doing it.

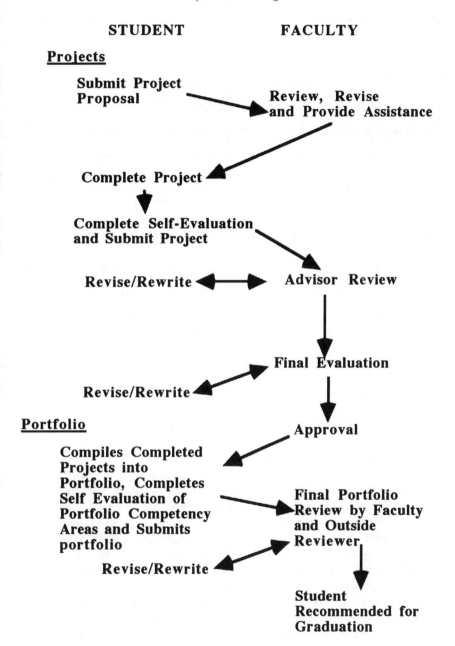

STUDENT   **FACULTY**

Projects

Submit Project
Proposal   Review, Revise
                            and Provide Assistance

Complete Project

Complete Self-Evaluation
and Submit Project

Revise/Rewrite   Advisor Review

                            Final Evaluation

Revise/Rewrite

Portfolio   Approval

Compiles Completed
Projects into
Portfolio, Completes
Self Evaluation of   Final Portfolio
Portfolio Competency   Review by Faculty
Areas and Submits   and Outside
portfolio   Reviewer

Revise/Rewrite

                            Student
                            Recommended for
                            Graduation

Figure 24.2. Process for completing portfolio entries.

COMPETENCY AREAS

Academic interventions. For this area, students are expected to demonstrate "best practices" for improving academic skills of students with behavior disorders in regular classes as well as in resource and self-contained classes.

Behavioral Interventions. For this area, students are expected to demonstrate "best practices" for improving behavioral and social skills of students with behavior disorders in self-contained classrooms as well as resource programs and regular classrooms.

Flexibility and Structure. Students demonstrate the ability to structure a classroom and academic program to meet the needs of students with behavior disorders, but also show flexibility by having a variety of options to use within the structure.

Assessment. For this competency area, students demonstrate use of curriculum-based assessment, anecdotal records and single subject designs to make decisions about student performance.

Collaboration and Coordination of Services. For this competency area, students demonstrate the ability to work collaboratively with parents, teachers, and other professionals to develop comprehensive programs for students with behavior disorders.

Relationships. Students demonstrate the ability to develop appropriate student-teacher relationships with students with behavior disorders for this competency area.

Prevention and Transition. Students demonstrate the ability to develop successful programs for the prevention of behavior disorders and programs for transition services for students with behavior disorders.

Figure 24.3.   Competency areas.

Pat: And to teach that way.

Diane: And to teach that way. And going back to the question, as far as it being individualized, the way it's set up, it's totally individualized. The guidelines are there, the areas are there, but no two of us have identical anything in our portfolios. And I think that's the beauty of it.

Christine: And also, individually, this program has really been helpful in encouraging our professional development through the course work. I've done things that I never would have done on my own, presenting at conferences, teaching classes, and activities that make you feel credible make you feel important, and that your ideas are useful, and make you explore things and help you individually. It also helps you with your peers; professional peers look to you to help out in your school system or any program that you're working in. And I think that it has really helped develop just better classroom situations and school situations by sharing information.

Pat: Well, I think that when you feel competent, that comes across. The more competent you feel, the better you are at what you do.

PROJECT PROPOSALS

Project proposals include the following sections:

a) Importance
This section should present a problem or issue to be addressed. Using previous research findings, the experiences of service providers and a conceptual framework, the applicant should make a convincing argument for the significance of the importance of the proposed project in understanding, remediating or compensating for a problem or issue.

b) Project Goal
In this section, describe the portfolio product you are proposing, describe what your goal is for the project and how your class or school might benefit from the project. Indicate which competency area(s) you plan to cover with this project.

c) Project Objectives
This section should include a description of the expected project and provide a list of procedural objectives which describe the major activities to be implemented during the project.

d) Plan of Operation
This section should describe the tasks to be done including a time line indicating initiation and completion dates for each major task.

e) Evaluation Plan
This section should describe the criteria for how your project should be evaluated. This is not an evaluation of whether a hypothesis proved to be true or not. It is how you think your work on the project should be evaluated. It is how you will evaluate whether or not you have been successful.

f) Key Personnel
If you are working with an instructor in another course or several instructors in different courses or with other teachers or professional, please list them in this section.

g) Resources
This section should list resources which you might need from the university such as a laptop computer, video camera, etc.

Figure 24.4. Project proposal guidelines.

Diane: When I told my students about this project I am working on right now, that my purpose is to become a better teacher, and asked for their help, there was a real closeness there. Also, last year, when they knew they were helping me with my homework, it was kind of neat.

Christine: I think we take the values and the respect that we've been given as students in our course work into our classrooms, and we respect our students and their opinions and are teaching them to learn from within and be part of the learning process, and we're not just throwing information at them. Information wasn't just thrown at us; we had to learn and do and be creative, and I think we are doing that with our students. Especially kids who have problems, they need to feel important and to feel like their ideas are important and that they can succeed at something. I felt a lot more successful professionally, and I think my students are feeling a lot more successful academically because of it.

Question 2: *Has your graduate work had an impact on your school or community?*

Christine: In starting a student-run business, the kids in my behavior disorders class have been recognized as students who are creating something, a product, and selling it. Instead of being separated from the mainstream all the time, they are actually out in the forefront. They're doing something and people are paying attention to them, and they see that they're using this to learn their academics from. And I think that's been real important academically and socially, as well as giving them an opportunity to work with other people, other kids and adults. I think that's had a definite impact. Professionally sharing our projects and ideas with other teachers and other professionals has an impact, you know, and we learn from each other. Schools are open to ideas we want to try, instead of becoming stagnant and doing the same thing over and over. We bring new ideas in.

Diane: My work has had a major impact on our school, because we were at the point that we were switching to a middle school and usually the school scheduled regular ed students first and they work special ed students in wherever they can, and I will truly say this year the school was scheduled around special ed. We looked at the plan, and they saw that pull-out was not going to work. We had nine teams set up, and it was just a nightmare scheduling kids in one place at one time to pull out, so at that point the teachers were ready to listen to some different options. So what we have set up this year, really and truly, we've scheduled for meeting the best interests of special ed kids first, and I think that's wonderful.

Pat: I want to talk about the impact on my school and community. My students have done so much in the last year, year and a half, two years, really since I came back to graduate school, in their school and in their community, and a lot of it has to do with what Christine and Diane have said already—that is, being successful and feeling successful and being involved in a program where they have something important to share. We also had a business last year around Christmas time; they operated the business, they designed the products, they made the product, they marketed the product. Then we took the field trip on the money we made from it. That's one of the things that's really made them to feel credible. Four of my students and I presented our project at a conference at John C. Campbell Folk School and the Association of Experiential Learners at John C. Campbell, last year. I wasn't required to do that. This year I took one student with me to our coordinators meeting and he presented our projects by himself, which was just wonderful. We got so many comments on his presentation. He did a great job. Next week, two of my students are coming to Dr. Bacon's class to teach. And they are so excited about that, because these are students who get shoved back into the resource room and into the special ed program and who get forgotten about, who are now in the forefront, and all the other kids from school are so jealous of these kids that we have kids saying, "How can I get into your program?"

Diane: That's great!!

Pat: I got a note from a parent the other day saying, "My child has permission to be in your class."

Diane: Oh, that's funny. I had one self-referral last year. "I think I need to be in here."

Question 3: *Have you been able to collaborate with other students or faculty on your projects?*

Christine: I feel like a lot of the things we've done in our classes, we've worked together, and we've come up with projects to make changes not just in our own classroom, but in the field in general, and that we've really learned from each other. I don't feel like the faculty are up here and the students are down here, that we all work together and it's been really neat to have a chance to present with a faculty member and write papers together, or work with somebody who's in a totally different county and come up with projects that really are going to have an impact on special education. They're not just something that we're going to sit down and do, and get a grade on it, and when the course is over it stays in a file in the basement. It's something that's ongoing. (Well, some things are still in the basement, but that doesn't mean they're going to stay there.) And it's the same thing we're doing in our classrooms, like you guys were talking about kids' attitudes changing because they were really a part of something, and I think my attitude toward school changed with graduate school, when it wasn't, "My God, I've worked all day and now I have to go home and do something totally different." It was a chance to work on things that were going to help me on my job. It made sense, it was usable, it was practical, and I think our kids are having that same experience. They're being heard, they're doing things that make sense, and their attitudes are changing, and they're more positive so we're more positive. And it really is nice to be working with kids who have behavior problems and not feel negative all the time. Everything is not negative, whereas when the approach was more behavioristic and you were just setting up controls, which worked as far as controls, but there was no real learning or changing in attitudes.

Pat: And it didn't make sense. I enjoy getting together in our classes and, again, having the freedom to exchange ideas and gripes when it's necessary. I think that most of the classes we've been involved in have an atmosphere that's been open to sharing. And I know even in some classes that part of the curriculum is to bring problems to class and let students help each other solve those problems.

Diane: That's so true, and I really didn't realize what we had going here 'til I stepped out of the special education courses and had to go back and take another class, and I realized what support I had there. I just realized that I dread Monday nights and love going on Wednesday nights. There again, I also brought this to my classroom and asked my children's opinions to evaluate something that we're doing right now in our school. They've never been asked their opinion and they felt really good about being asked for input as to whether or not this works.

Christine: Sure.

Diane: I think it's good. We don't do that enough in education, to go to the kids and parents to see if something is working before we make changes. We need their input in the decision making.

Pat: It helped to create an atmosphere of respect.

Diane: Yes, all around.

Pat: We feel respect from the faculty here and from each other, and I think we respect our kids and in turn they respect us.

Christine: Well, it's exciting to feel like there are people who think you can really make a difference and you can really do something good, and I felt really encouraged here to go out and do things I wouldn't have done before, and I like to think that same feeling is happening in the classroom, where the kids feel encouraged and so they are excited and they are proud of themselves and they want to go out and do things that they've always been told that they can't do, you know. Instead of focusing on all the problems they have and all the things they do wrong, we're focusing more on what we can do and encouraging positive things and positive changes.

Pat: I think that says it real well. Looking at the positive instead of the negative. Which is what they've come up with through school, the negative.

Diane: Sometimes in schools, we just feel we're being done *to*. All these changes that happen to us, we have no input, there's nothing we can do about it, the competency-based curriculum, testing, all this stuff that's handed to us. Now, I will honestly say that I just feel that nothing is impossible any more, because I've seen it in our school. We've really been able to make some changes.

Question 4: *How are you involved in evaluation of projects?*
Diane: Well, we set the evaluation criteria, so that's kind of neat. We know what we wanted to put into it and know when we have accomplished what we wanted to accomplish. We can list our criteria, and then an outside party can read those same criteria and decide if our goals have

been met. In a sense, we made our own test.

Christine: One thing that might be helpful to do is more peer evaluation. If it is something that several people are doing, or if others see your presentation, they can give you feedback.

Diane: Yeah, through the courses that we are doing the projects for, we share a whole lot of what we are doing, how we are developing end products, and it would be neat to sit down with peers and say, "What did you want to accom-plish?" and, "How did you do that?" and to learn from each others' projects.

Purpose of Portfolios

Question: *What do you think is the purpose of using a portfolio instead of a comprehensive exam?*

Christine: To have the finished product, to have something tangible that is useful, that people can see the work that you have done and the changes that you have gone through from the beginning to the end and to share that information with other people (see Figures 24.1 and 24.2).

Pat: And learning is progressive. I mean it is not just one shot.

Christine: Right.

Pat: It's progressive, it's a whole process throughout your program, and with comprehensive exams there are going to be questions . . . you might hit on some and miss some. As far as asking the questions, there might not even be some pertinent questions in there, but if you have your own portfolio, your own record of what you have done, then its going to be pertinent to who you are and the job you have done.

Diane: And when you take a test, you finish it and it's over. With portfolios, you have the option to go back and do projects over again if you are not satisfied. You are given the opportunity to improve, until you get it right.

Pat: And in the process, you've learned.

Diane: Right, and I think it's an important carryover to public education.

Christine: Yeah, you are actually using it. You are using it in what you do, and, like you said, it can develop and change over time. It's not over just because the course work is over and it is individual. It is the evaluation of what you have learned and done, not what your neighbor has. You know, the three of us would sit down and take comprehensive exams and they would be real different, but they wouldn't cover everything that we have accomplished on our own.

Diane: We get to share what we have learned. Sometimes when we get back a test, it may only cover a fraction of what you learned. This way you show off all that you have really done.

Pat: Portfolios are much more comprehensive.

Christine: It shows what our values and our philosophies and our abilities are a lot more than a test can. It shows that teachers are capable. I think that has been a problem in education all along, you might produce teachers who have straight As from their course work, but that doesn't necessarily mean that they can work with other people. The portfolios are a much better way of showing the ability to work with others.

Diane: And that was one of the key things that we talked about—being a teacher of students with behavior disorders, it's not a paper-and-pencil kind of thing, you know, it is actual demonstration of skills that you've got, and the portfolio can reflect that, whereas tests really can't.

Demonstration of Competency in Eight Areas

Christine: I think a very important aspect of this program has been that a lot of our learning came from within. We did projects and we came up with different ideas and creative things that we learned by doing and we could actually use in our classrooms, as opposed to reading textbooks and regurgitating information (see Figure 24.3).

Pat: Well, I think it gave us the chance to be practical. With our own situation, I think that we as classroom teachers have a good feel for our students, we have a good feel for our own situation, and I think that having the freedom to use that knowledge that we have has been a big help.

Diane: I really appreciate the freedom of creating projects. I think it was nice to have the framework of the different competency areas that we needed to address, because that kept me aware that I needed to, you know, branch out. One area in particular might be easier for me, but it kept me working on areas that maybe weren't necessarily my strengths. And then, the fact that every project that I think I did helped me a great deal in what I was doing as far as my job in the classroom.

Pat: That's been a bit of a problem for me, addressing the different competency areas, because there is so much overlap. There seems to be a lot of overlap in the projects I do, because I'll come up with a proposal and I start to look at the areas where it might fit and I end up thinking, well, it's going to fit in every one of them somewhere. So that's been personally a problem for me—to fit projects into a niche.

One of my projects, last winter, that I was working on with some other professionals in my school was putting together a care team for the county. Our county is rural and it's so spread out, we felt we needed people with expertise in certain areas whom we could pull together and go to specific locations where there was a problem. That project seemed to address a lot of different competencies.

Diane: We can use one project for several areas, though, right? I thought that part was good.

Pat: Like Diane said, that's good, but when it comes to trying to fit your projects into the competency areas, it can be a problem—just where you're going to put this, where's the best section for it to go in.

Christine: Which is also one of the strengths of the program, that when you are doing a project, it's not just to learn one concept. It does tie in with, you know, everything that makes learning about teaching important. So, even though it was hard and I found the same thing, that projects don't fit neatly into a category, you could show how this one project helped you in many areas.

Diane: Well, my initial feelings were, and it didn't last very long, that, you know, when you get a course syllabus, I was at first looking at the portfolio as being something as extra and outside of class work, and I was overwhelmed at first. I thought, How can I do this, this, and this, AND this?, and now I realize that you do it through the course work. That's been the beauty of it. I've been meeting the portfolio requirements and course requirements, and that's the way it should be, integrated into the program.

Christine: I think we might need to look at some of the competency areas after more people have gone through, and we can look at the course work and what comes out and maybe we could make it fit a little better. Maybe their portfolios could be structured so that students don't feel that they have to have sections under certain competency areas in a file. You know, it somehow needs to be more integrated pieces of work. We need to think of a way to make it a more unified piece of work and still address all of the competency areas.

Project Proposals

Pat: This might be a good place to talk about project proposals. I think project proposals, for me, anyway, helped structure what I wanted to do. It helped me stay structured and it kind of gave me a time line, because there needed to be a time line of sorts in the proposal, to keep things going in the project. So it was a good disciplinary measure for myself (see Figure 24.4).

Diane: It helped me when I'd get into something and I'd start spreading out in a hundred different directions, I always do that when I go to do research; I read journal articles and I think, This one looks good, this one, and then I kind of forget what my purpose was. I'd pull out my proposal and, Oh yeah, this is what I want to do. And that helped. And then, of course, when you're finished, it's a good way to evaluate, did you really do what you said you were going to do. So I think that was a great idea.

Christine: I agree. I really need the structure of a proposal. The only problem I would run into is you needed to have your proposal prepared early on in the course, and a lot of times I didn't know where

I was going to go or have enough information to do a really good job on the proposal. . . .

Pat: That was a problem.

Christine: You know, halfway through the course, a lot of things might change and my project was something different than the original proposal.

Pat: Well, maybe your evaluation procedure might be different after you got into the project. You might want to do something differently and your proposal is already set out. I can identify with that.

Other Suggestions

Christine: Also, I think I've talked to both of you guys about how, a lot of times, with projects, you are doing something new, something different, that you want to do in your classroom. Certain competency areas have already been met because you have been doing them for years, so you don't address these areas in your projects. You know, you don't have to do a brand new project in that area.

Diane: Right, documenting work that you have already done, without doing a whole project just to document something that you have done in the past.

Diane: I think that it is a good idea to have semester reviews, to continually keep track.

Question: *We have a few students in the program who aren't as tuned in to the idea of portfolios, so that when we schedule reviews, they don't show up or don't schedule an appointment to come in and see us. Do you have any suggestions about this problem?*

Christine: Maybe it would be a good idea for some of us to do an orientation with the new students, where they have to come in and talk with old students about their portfolios.

Diane: If new students had a picture of one then they would know in what direction they needed to be heading.

Christine: I would like it, too, because this program is what keeps the spark and, you know, keeps me motivated. It would be nice for all of us to continue to be involved in the program.

Diane: It would keep the network going.

CONCLUSION

As we have revised our teacher education program and implemented constructivist approaches, the energetic and enthusiastic response of our graduate students has continually surprised us. Several years ago, we could have easily written about the difficulty of motivating students who taught all day and had to come to classes at night, or about the difficulty of getting part-time students to read assignments. We ask ourselves, what has really made the difference in these students? Portfolios and projects are good teaching strategies for evaluating student work, but they don't seem powerful enough to transform a whole cohort of students. Our hypothesis is that what Rhodes had to say about the role of the observer is just as true for us and our students as it is for children. By expecting all students to have the creative ability and power to solve their individual problems, all of us see ourselves and each other differently: Students see each other as professionals with important ideas to share, we see our students as serious contributors to solving problems in our region, and they see us as collaborators and assistants in solving these problems. Consequently, we are living all of these roles.

Since we implemented this program, our students have implemented major changes in their classrooms, schools, and communities; presented their programs at state and national conferences; and published their work in professional journals and newsletters. The students' accomplishments, their comments, and their ownership of the program continue to instruct us in the creativity and problem-solving possibilities of teachers in our schools and students in our program. From their work, we are convinced that teacher education programs can be major contributors to school reform via the implementation of constructivist approaches. By collaborating and assisting with students' projects, and by recognizing the importance and creativity of their work, universities and colleges can provide support to teachers who are developing innovative programs in their schools.

Authors' Note

Preparation of this chapter was supported in part by a grant from the U.S. Department of Education, Preparation of Personnel for Careers in Special Education Grant No. HO29B-10063. The opinions herein are those of the authors and not the funding agency's.

25. Addressing the Inevitable Conflicts in Reforming Teacher Education: One Department's Story

JAMES L. PAUL, BETTY EPANCHIN, HILDA ROSSELLI,

BRENDA L. TOWNSEND, ANN CRANSTON-GINGRAS,

AND DAPHNE THOMAS

The Department of Special Education at the University of South Florida is a large program, with approximately 275 undergraduates and 150 master's-level students. In addition, approximately 20 full-time doctoral students are in the department preparing for roles as teacher educators or special education administrators or for leadership positions in the area of child and family policy. The program serves the diverse urban communities of Tampa Bay and the west central Gulf Coast area. In the past 5 years there have been a number of retirements and new additions to the faculty, which precipitated intensive self-study and recommendations for program restructuring.

The faculty adopted a spirit of experimentation and self-study while working to (a) increase recruitment of teacher candidates who reflect the

Reprinted, with changes, from "Addressing the inevitable conflicts in reforming teacher education: One department's story," by James L. Paul, Betty Epanchin, Hilda Rosselli, Brenda L. Townsend, Ann Cranston-Gingras, and Daphne Thomas, *Journal of Learning Disabilities*, Vol. 28, 1995, pp. 646–655. Copyright © 1995 by PRO-ED, Inc.

changing demographics of Florida; (b) redesign curricula to include the use of case studies, cooperative learning, and other constructivist approaches; (c) revise program entrance and exit requirements so that more authentic measurement techniques are used; and (d) develop collaborative school centers serving as research and teacher education sites. These partnerships included a wide array of federally funded, state-funded, and college-funded initiatives supporting the inclusion of students with disabilities, providing cluster sites for practicum and intern placements, and supporting faculty and doctoral assignments at professional development schools.

To engage in any authentic reform of our existing program, it was necessary for us to consider the principles that guided our curriculum as it was described in the catalogue. It was also necessary to examine the values that brought us together as a faculty with our students. This was an iterative process; some things we considered in the beginning, whereas other things we learned and had to accommodate along the way. In the beginning we developed specific statements about our beliefs concerning such basic issues as diversity, power, and learning, and beliefs about ourselves and our students. We also developed grounding positions that provided a foundation for changing our program and our work in it. It became increasingly clear to us that we were working more from a compass to guide our work than from a map of our intentions.

The Department embraced a transformative philosophy for both its undergraduate and its graduate programs that emphasized the constructivist learning paradigm, a collaborative model of work, the value of diversity, the cultivation of reflective practice, an ethic of caring for students, and the importance of a community of learners. These understandings served as markers for planning and as philosophical frameworks to help us think through and articulate our courses of action.

In this chapter we will provide illustrative, rather than extensive, descriptions of fundamental understandings that have guided our work. Specifically, we will briefly describe our perspectives on knowledge, teaching, and the student preparing to teach. We will then discuss some of the conflicts with traditional practice that have emerged from the positions we have taken.

CRITICAL PERSPECTIVES

Ways of Knowing. Historically, teacher education programs have embraced a body of thought and knowledge understood to be empirical. The "common sense," or practical, pedagogy was considered a kind of preknowledge, lore handed down and awaiting verification. The strongest claims for a science of education came in the late 1960s, the 1970s, and part of the 1980s, with applied behavior analysis. The protocols were taught and a culture of training was developed.

During the past decade, some of the changes in philosophy of science and in psychological science have been felt in both special education and teacher education. There has been an increasing sensitivity to paradigm issues and a growing skepticism about the hegemony of empiricism, and in particular, the science of behaviorism. The central issue, from our point of view, is not whether behavioral technologies work and are useful–they do and they are. Rather, our concern is with the context in which behavioral principles are understood and used. We ask our students to examine the nature of empirical knowledge, the ethical issues of power and control, and themselves as interveners in the lives of children whose values and views of life may be very different from their own.

One of the core features of our educational philosophy, therefore, is our belief that it is essential to consider the epistemological foundations of all aspects of our curriculum, from our methods of behavioral management to our relationships with students. While we teach a core content to which we think our students should be exposed, we also seek to make the foundations of that content problematic. We take a critical stance in reviewing the research and philosophical literature, making the moral claims and assumptions of researchers and interpreters of research explicit.

Our teacher education program seeks to focus on the whole child and to help the student teacher appreciate and value the storied nature of each child's behavior. We do not seek the objectification of children. Rather, we ask our students to understand themselves in relation to children in educational settings. Our emphasis is on the constructed nature of our views of children and our approaches to teaching them.

Teaching the Moral and Social Embeddedness of Issues.   Students enter teacher education programs with a wealth of experience as consumers of the views and methods of public education. As students in classrooms, they have logged thousands of hours observing teachers; thus, they approach their own professional preparation program with a socially constructed understanding of what teaching is about. They also have accumulated myriad affects associated with the different teaching practices they have observed. Teacher educators, therefore, do not write the methods they would teach upon a clean slate. Rather, they engage the memories, hopes, and aspirations of students preparing for a teaching career.

Lortie (1975) attributed novice teachers' resistance to practicing new or different ways of teaching to their powerful apprenticeship of observation in classrooms during their childhood prior to entering teacher training. During this time individuals acquire beliefs and understandings about being a teacher that most teacher education programs have not been able to counteract through traditional university-based programs. Lortie also noted that it should not be surprising that novice teachers' ideas are often narrow, limited, and not carefully examined. Persons entering other occupations are more likely to realize how much they still need to know because they feel less familiar with the professional role they are entering. Persons entering teaching, however, think they know the role, and this illusion may limit their learning.

The memories, values, motivations, and goals of student teachers, though not necessarily a conscious part of their imagination about teaching, are nonetheless dynamic aspects of their construction of teaching. So powerful are these constructions that we have long understood that teachers tend to teach as they were taught, rather than as they were taught to teach.

Different teacher education programs have sought to interrupt this continuity. One of the most powerful approaches in teacher preparation programs in this regard has been in the broad genre of behavioral technologies. Behavioral training strategies are designed to teach the objective definition of behavioral events and the careful planning and implementation of interventions to change those events. This data-driven technology involves increasing behavior, decreasing behavior, or teaching new behavior. Noticeably absent from these technologies has been attention to cognitive processes.

We are seeking to interrupt the socialized habits of mind that students bring to our teacher education program. We begin with an acknowledgment of the complexity of education and the understanding that the whole person of the teacher is ultimately involved in the construction of teaching. A primary strategy is the use of teaching cases. We use cases that are layered with the complexity of the real world. For the most part, we use authentic cases—true stories—to illustrate points. Our goals are to teach collaborative analysis and problem solving, empathy for different, legitimate ways of understanding issues, and the existential nature of problems and their solutions. We involve students in the analysis of cases and support them in a collaborative process of examining the following items.

- the importance of context
- the different issues presented
- the nature and significance of nuance
- the moral perspectives embedded in the cases
- the storied nature of the lives revealed in the cases
- the different views of individuals described in the cases

- the technical problems presented to educators

- the constructive nature of teaching

Using this approach we are able to infuse the ethics of teaching, valuing of diversity, and professionalism in all aspects of our curriculum.

Nature of the Student–Teacher Relationship. We view the core of our program, the basic unit of analysis in our teacher education curriculum, to be the relationship between the faculty member and the student. The subject matter and methods of the curriculum are essential, but they are taught in the context of relationships. Fundamental to our view of the faculty–student relationship is the ethic of *care.* We seek to model caring in every aspect of our program, from admission and orientation through academics and field experience. We do this in three ways: First, we emphasize *thoughtfulness.* There are very few rules. We ask students to take responsibility for their actions; whether it be their honest performance on a test, the quality of their portfolio, or the regard they show for children in their internship, we ask them to be conscious of their construction of events and to articulate in a thoughtful way the rationales for their decisions.

Second, we emphasize the *moral content* of our work. This extends into fundamental moral issues, such as racism, sexism, "handicap-ism," classism, and other perspectives and behaviors that devalue members of the human community. We are only beginning to understand the ways in which these issues affect our lives in universities and the lives of children and staff in schools. We have succeeded in gathering a diverse faculty. In our beginning courses, students participate in a field assignment in which the focus of their work is on getting to know a person who has a disability and reflecting on that person's life in relation to their own. We teach a course on families that is heavily focused on diversity, and we are beginning to teach a course on the African American child in the public education system. Whether we are examining ethnic differences in family-participation patterns with regard to school, or intellectual differences in defining issues, we seek to acknowledge and value the different realities represented in problematic events.

Third, realizing that so much that is important in the educational experience of our students occurs in their relationships with faculty, we emphasize *advocacy* for individual students with respect to their particular challenges. Part of this occurs through assigning of undergraduate students to teams. The teams are organized for advisement purposes, but they also serve to help monitor student needs. They provide a context for the support and nurturance of students. Team meetings provide an opportunity for examining issues and demystifying university procedures and policies. Teams can also be useful for examining power issues outside of the classroom environment. This is an important part of the socialization and professionalization process. Teams elect representatives to the student advisory committee, a group composed of both students and faculty members.

Fourth, we recognize the value of *celebration* of our work together. This takes the form of celebratory gatherings, for example, when students present their portfolios. Also, once each year, we have a gathering of the larger community—students, faculty, collaborators in other departments, local school leaders, and others in the community who are interested in our program. We are beginning to learn how important celebration is in a culture of learning that values joy and where both the individual and the community need to be affirmed.

CONFLICTS WITH TRADITIONAL PRACTICE

Diversity Versus Homogeneity. Nonwhite students constitute over 70% of the total student population in 20 of the nation's largest school counties (Center for Education Statistics, 1987). Similarly, the racial and ethnic diversity of Florida's public school population is increasing at a rapid rate. However, despite dramatic demographic shifts in Florida and other states, many teacher education programs continue preparing today's and tomorrow's teachers for yesterday's school populations. Traditional instructional methods, which pay little attention to increasing student diversity, are modeled in university classrooms and emulated in public school classrooms (Franklin, 1992).

Ethnic-minority children and those who come from families who live in poverty have a long history of faring poorly in public school settings. Past criticisms of public schooling for these children (e.g., Dunn, 1968; Johnson, 1969) remain relevant over 25 years later. In addition, 40 years following *Brown v. Board of Education* (1954), it is questionable whether minority children have reaped the educational benefits that school desegregation aimed to provide (Gerard, 1983). Over the years, disproportionate numbers of minority children have received traditional special education services (Byrd, 1994), shown low academic achievement (Banks, 1994), and experienced exclusion from classes for children with gifts and talents (Patton, 1992).

In responding to these circumstances in public schools, our department is pursuing several courses of action. One is monitoring ourselves and the environments in which we place our students. We continually examine biases held by university and school personnel regarding traditionally underrepresented students and families. That involves considerable dialogue among faculty and students about perceptions regarding children who differ on age, ability, ethnicity, class, gender, or other characteristics and their influence on interactions with diverse learners.

As university students and faculty become more involved with schools, we encounter situations involving negative perceptions and/or unequal treatment of diverse students by teaching faculty, administrators, or staff. Dilemmas are created when school philosophies or practices regarding diverse students conflict with the department's philosophy. We provide forums for students and faculty to share their experiences and dilemmas, and create opportunities to problem solve as a group.

Another strategy is to infuse the values of diversity into our curriculum. We infused many of our courses with multicultural perspectives and considerations, so that our students can enhance the academic and social success of individually and culturally different students. Issues involved in understanding and working with diverse families are also taught. As part of their course work, many of our students act as tutors and peer counselors with youth from migrant farmworker families, through a federal project our department has sponsored for the past 7 years.

A third strategy involves employing a diverse faculty and creating a context for learning in which diversity is modeled, valued, and affirmed. Having recognized the importance of mirroring changing demographic trends and affirming diversity, our department faculty includes women and persons from ethnically diverse backgrounds. As schools become increasingly diverse and move toward meeting wider ranges of students' needs in one setting, it becomes critical that teaching faculty also reflect the demographic realities of schools.

Fourth, we are committed to recruiting and retaining students who are members of traditionally underrepresented groups. These include students from ethnic-minority groups and also students from nontraditional age groups, such as women who enter our program with substantial childrearing experience and childcare responsibilities. We are developing strategies in response to factors that challenge our efforts. Nationally, fewer minority students are aspiring to become teachers. Subsequently, a serious decline exists in the number of minority teachers in public schools. It is predicted that by the turn of the century, all ethnic-minority groups will have less than 5% representation in the teaching force, while over 33% of the students will be members of those ethnic groups (King, 1993).

Fifth, we pay attention to the "fit" between our students and their supervising teachers. Having same-ethnicity supervising teachers and mentors in school settings with whom to align student teachers is critical in recruitment. But it must be cautioned that positioning minority teachers and administrators in school settings alone does little to inspire minority children to desire those same positions. We have talked frequently with African American youth regarding their issues with their schooling; many have suggested that their interactions with same-ethnicity teachers and administrators are not always positive. Instead of perceiving those individuals as advocates, many students suggest that faculty and administrators compound the problems they face in school settings. We do not want to overgeneralize; ensuring minority representation is only part of the solution. Representation must not be confused with advocacy. That is, while recruiting minority teachers and administrators, it becomes even more critical to seek individuals who will empower the voices of disenfranchised students to affect policy and practice.

Although the focus of this discussion is on increasing the number of same-ethnicity advocates for minority students, it by no means suggests that dominant-culture individuals cannot, or should not, assume those roles. Thus, we actively recruit students who bring myriad perspectives and experiences to our program from ethnic-minority and -majority cultural backgrounds.

Partnership in Practice Versus Formal Agreement.   When cooperating schools have views and values that are significantly different from those embodied by the teacher education program, conflicts are bound to occur. Although they prefer continuity in field placements, university faculty may uncover unethical practices or philosophies that prevent their student teachers from fully implementing the theory and practices emphasized in the teacher education program. This difficulty is compounded by the semi-permanent structures of *surrounding* long-term placement sites. The situation creates an ethical dilemma in which the university may ask, "What role do we have in influencing the policies and practices of the schools with which we are collaborating?" Also, what are the ethical implications that arise when field placements become a power issue? We may ask, for example, "If the situation continues, will we be able to place our student teachers in this site?"

In our experiences, we have experimented with mostly a priori designations in which a school is identified as a professional development school, teacher education center, or professional practice school affiliated with our program. Duffy (1994) described some of the hazards of this approach, particularly when getting the partnership entity on line becomes more of a priority than developing a spirit of collaboration. In one of our experiences, the designation resulted from over a year of formal planning prior to the school's opening. Although on paper the goals and philosophy of the partnership were congruent with our teacher education program, after a while the site did not embrace the ethic of caring that we encouraged. Over time the differences in philosophy became apparent, causing our department to reconsider affiliation with the school.

There is a perceived "power" used by the university when a field site is designated or "undesignated." Although the first reaction may be to withdraw student teachers from the site, the goals of the partnership must be considered. If progress is being made in other areas of the partnership (e.g., involvement of student teachers from other departments in the college, curriculum-restructuring activities, ongoing collaborative research efforts), this can complicate the decisions to be made. Yet, the scarcity of resources available to support this type of venture emphasizes the need for a good fit between the teacher education program and the school. The very mission of university/school partnerships as defined by Sirotnik and Goodlad (1988), Levine (1992), and the Holmes Group (1986) stresses the need for a collaborative culture, one in which the school and university can explore ideas for change together. This implies compatible core philosophies demonstrated by consistent practices on both sides of the partnership.

Collaboration Versus Isolation.   The current emphasis on inclusion and restructuring in school reform requires changes in the roles of teachers in both general and special education. Co-teaching, team teaching, and collaborative consultation models are replacing resource and self-contained models (where teachers were often isolated with their students). The general education classroom, where many special educators are now working, demands that special education teachers become collaborators with and initiators and advocates for their students (Friend & Cook, 1991; Idol, Paolucci-Whitcomb, & Nevin, 1986). Novice teachers coming into the general education class may feel intimidated and unsure of their roles as consulting teachers. Few teachers have experienced a team- taught class, either in K–12 or postsecondary-level education. The inclusion movement is requiring special education teachers to function in new contexts and, therefore, different needs must be addressed in their professional preparation programs. Teacher education programs in special education must feature practicums and internships where the responsibilities for team teaching or consultative services are part of the student teachers' experiences. This becomes problematic as schools struggle to delineate roles and responsibilities in team-teaching situations. Special education teachers may serve a greater number of students in a team-teaching model yet have less individualized time to work with their students. Teacher education programs that are responsive to these changing delivery models must facilitate experiences that allow student teachers to practice these roles while developing genuine relationships with school, family, and community members that model high regard for student welfare.

Our experiences indicate that when the school administrators and general education faculty at the school site clearly support this type of restructuring, co-teaching and team-teaching models can be effective educational venues. However, the process of changing practices in schools and teacher education programs creates a context within which the policies, philosophies, and institutionalized routines must be addressed. Orchestrating changes in the views and practices of current staff in the school and in teacher education programs requires an environment in which there is mutual respect, trust, and a willingness to change.

Holistic Versus Fragmented Instruction.   Research suggests that the "power of what currently exists tends to dominate the thinking and actions of those who enter" our profession (Pugach, 1992, p. 134). Studies consistently report that within a few years, graduates from very different teacher education programs are indistinguishable, resembling the teachers with whom they work rather than the teachers with whom they graduated (Pugach, 1992). As faculties in teacher education have embraced holistic ways of thinking, some of the traditional ways of doing things have become difficult and objectionable. Traditionally, students sign up for five semesters of courses, each meeting once or twice a week for 15 weeks. Once the course is completed, students may never have contact with that faculty member again. This works well for students seeking diversity of opinions and information and little personal connection with faculty members. However, this instructional design does not lend itself to the development of relationships that influence people to change their behavior.

If teacher education programs want to exert influence on novice teachers' practice, they must do much more than tell students to do things differently. They must create compelling learning environments that are capable of overcoming the 12-year apprenticeship of observation that Lortie (1975) described. For example, faculty need contact with students over the span of the students' education. Isolated 3-hour courses do not lend themselves to reflective learning over time. Course structures need to promote opportunities for students to practice skills and receive feedback about their practice throughout their training. University faculty who are not familiar with applied settings may not be the best persons to teach method courses, even if they do hold the highest degree. Likewise, students need opportunities and support for thoughtful reflection to make sense of their experience and to counteract their intellectual habits and the temptation to do what is most familiar.

A Mentor Versus a Supervisor.   Faculty who promote a collegial atmosphere in their classes at the university may experience a conflict when cooperating teachers assigned to work with the university's interns assume the role of supervisors rather than of coaches or mentors. This role distortion is further reinforced by the carefully defined checklists and summative forms that are often required by the university. The evaluative nature of the internship may be at odds with a constructivist approach to learning, which values experiences as a way to build or link knowledge. One faculty member related her frustrated attempts to model a collegial coaching approach for a teacher who maintained that the intern needed to experience what he had experienced as a first-year teacher: the harsh realities of objective evaluation. Although the faculty member consistently stressed the mentoring nature needed during the student teacher's internship, the presence of both summative and formative evaluation instruments supported another image in the cooperating teacher's mind: that of evaluation rather than collaboration.

One solution that appeared to address this dilemma was the development of action plans following the second formative evaluation. Each area designated as NI (needing assistance) or U (unsatisfactory) was targeted as an area needing growth. The action plan designated specific behaviors that would need to change in order to change the evaluation mark to S (satisfactory). The plan also identified specific strategies to be used by both the cooperating teacher and the university supervisor to assist the intern in reaching a satisfactory level of performance. In addition, needed resources were listed, as well as subsequent checkpoints, prior to the summative evaluation. This action plan then served as a contract among the intern, cooperating teacher, and university faculty member. It also redefined the roles of the cooperating teacher as well as the university supervisor: They were on a team together to structure success for the intern.

Ethic of Caring Versus Controlling.   The ethic of caring that pervades the teacher preparation program at the University of South Florida is not limited to relationships developed between university professors and their graduate and undergraduate students. We expect pre– and inservice teachers to develop and nurture similar relationships with their students and family members. To facilitate teacher–student relationships that reflect sensitivity toward student needs, common university course activities focus on techniques for understanding and appreciating students' experiences in all contexts—school, home, community, and workplace.

As schools restructure for the inclusion of children and youth with disabilities, conflicts arise when teachers expect to develop relationships with their students under conditions resembling traditional service delivery in self-contained settings. When student teachers are placed in inclusive settings, their concern is that the conditions that were conducive to forming bonds with students and that facilitated teacher–student relationships in self-contained and resource room settings are no longer available. Specifically, students with disabilities typically received services in the same classrooms for more than one academic year, often with low teacher–student ratios. Thus, teachers had the benefit of getting to know students and their families over time.

Co-teaching and team teaching are strategies used frequently to facilitate inclusion (Sailor, 1991). As student teachers of students with diverse needs experience the sharing of teaching responsibilities, they initially express frustration regarding working with more students than was traditional and the time constraints associated with doing so. University professors are challenged to facilitate experiences for our students that promote the development of genuine relationships with the children in their classrooms. It is our aim that our students model high regard for student welfare in all contexts.

In preparing teachers for inclusive schools, the changing teacher roles and responsibilities in responding to the needs of children and their families must be understood. In their new roles as collaborators with a variety of individuals, teachers must be skilled at obtaining information from multiple sources to gain insight on student preferences, interests, and experiences. The sources could include students; other school personnel; and family, business, and community members. Ultimately, university professors and teachers in inclusive settings must model the willingness to consider each student's experiences in various contexts.

Advocacy Versus Indifference.   In preparing our teachers for their roles as collaborators, courses addressing consultation and collaboration with other professionals and families are included in their programs of study. The focus is on the roles and responsibilities related to serving as a team member while maintaining a focus on the best interests of children and their families. We expect our pre- and inservice teachers to be advocates for children in various contexts. It is emphasized that large numbers of public school children and their families perceive themselves as powerless and are disenfranchised from the educational enterprise. If we ever hope to accomplish educational parity, teachers' roles must include advocacy when they are interacting with other school personnel, agencies, and businesses.

As a function of advocating for students and their families, teachers must provide them with strategies for self-advocacy. A conflict occurs when faculty or students completing their practica and internship experiences observe situations that warrant child or family advocacy and empowerment. On occasion, that advocacy has not been well received. For example, when a group of minority students were instructed on prosocial and leadership skills to avoid reacting in ways that usually resulted in out-of-school suspensions, they were able to demonstrate ability to negotiate as a means of getting their needs met in school settings. They planned and received approval on several activities they thought would be the most affirming of themselves. After all details were negotiated and agreed upon, school personnel reneged on one of the activities. The students were frustrated and reported the mixed messages they received. They had been told that if they used positive ways to communicate and self-advocate, they would receive certain benefits, but they were misled. We learned that conflicts arise for students and families even when they become empowered to voice their concerns and recommend strategies. In the example used, the faculty member that facilitated the student group should also have prepared school personnel to respond with more sensitivity to the students, who perceived themselves as having more impact on their own educational needs than in reality they did.

We want our students to take more active roles, as teachers, in advocating for the interests of all children, especially those who feel disconnected in school or in society. There are many challenges in meeting the needs of individual students in the classroom, including the constraints of time and school policies that ostensibly reflect students' collective interests, and we believe teachers should be predisposed to advocate for individual interests before situations arise in which individuals are devalued. This is a difficult and complex attitude to promote and a difficult culture to develop and maintain in a setting where norms are defended on the basis of the common good.

Reflection and Self-Disclosure Versus Invasion of Privacy and Unethical Intrusion. Students are encouraged, and sometimes required, to maintain journals for many of their courses and field experiences in our program. The intent of the journal is to encourage reflection on practice and consideration of alternative teaching approaches and ways of understanding. As students think about what they are reading, seeing, and doing, they often relate their current experiences to their own personal histories. This process is an excellent way, perhaps even an essential way, of understanding new information, but it also raises important ethical concerns. Through journal writing students often share intimate information that has not been part of the traditional university faculty–student relationship. One student wrote about her memories of going to school hungry, sleepy, and scared because her alcoholic father spent the family income on his liquor and then behaved abusively toward his wife. She found herself identifying with children from similar backgrounds and struggling with how to support and care for students while also being an authority figure. Another student remembered her own unhappy adolescence and her tendency to act out her anger. Remembering how difficult her own adolescence was made it difficult for her to determine reasonable behavioral expectations. Both of these students wrote copiously in their journals as they sought to clarify their roles and responsibilities and to make meaning of classroom events.

When students engage in such a level of self-disclosure with faculty, the nature of the relationship between professor and student necessarily changes. Faculty may no longer maintain as much distance; they must be capable of dealing with self-disclosure, and willing to do so, so that students do not feel too vulnerable, and they also must protect the confidentiality of information shared by students. Furthermore, because faculty still must grade student products, how does one evaluate personal material? When faculty work with students in personal ways, they can no longer function as judges and dictators of what knowledge must be mastered; rather they become friends, mentors, enablers, and advisers. University traditions dictate otherwise.

Some students are uncomfortable with the level of self-disclosure required of reflective practitioners. They are often uncomfortable with or uncertain of their views; thus they are reluctant to share them. They rarely volunteer information during class discussions and their journals typically contain lists of activities in which they have been involved. Their journals contain comments such as, "Today we discussed assessment tools. I enjoyed learning about them." Little attention is given to their own teaching or to how problems could have been solved differently. One student reported that "all hell broke out in class today so I was tired when I came to class," but she did not describe what happened, what she did, or who the kids were and what their issues were. Because students' understanding of such events is critical in the development of reflective practice, faculty typically ask probing questions and encourage students to tell more. One student wrote, "I don't feel comfortable talking about my fears and worries. I'm being graded." The student's comment underscores the inherent conflict as professors move from judge to facilitator in students' learning.

Another dilemma arises when students' journals disclose personal information that is detrimental to them. One student wrote about overpowering a 4-year-old child in order to force the child to go to sleep during nap time. When describing the event, the student reported that her cooperating teacher commented that the child rarely ever took a nap. Her response was "Oh, boy! I really did a good job!" The faculty member who read the journal was dismayed that the student apparently was not concerned about ethical and legal issues related to physically overpowering a child. Given other observations of the student's marginal performance in class, the faculty member questioned the student's fitness to become a teacher. However, using journal material for evaluation purposes violates the intent and nature of journal writing. The content of another journal raised a faculty member's concerns about whether a child was being psychologically abused by a cooperating teacher; but reporting her concerns would violate the student's right to privacy. When a student wrote in her journal, "I hope I never have to work with any kids who have that breathing thing in their throats, they are disgusting," a faculty member was caught in the conflict between reprimanding the student's insensitivity and encouraging her honesty. If faculty members use journal entries as a means of evaluating students' performance, students will feel reluctant to share their self-reflections, and faculty will be left out of the students' problem solving. However, if faculty ignore the challenging issues that arise from journal entries, they are failing to help students learn how to deal with critical issues.

A Collage Versus a Snapshot Approach to Teacher Evaluation. During the 1970s, the heyday of competency-based teacher education, objectives for a teacher education program were specifically defined, providing candidates with a clear understanding of what was expected. In fact, specificity and explicitness were characteristics that became associated with a sense of fairness (Katz & Raths, 1992). On the other hand, a teacher education program that embraces a philosophy of multiple ways of knowing must search for ways to document not only what teachers know of the subject matter, but also their knowledge of how to help students come to know and understand the content, which combines general pedagogical knowledge and pedagogical content knowledge (Wilson, Shulman, & Richert, 1987). In other words, our student teachers or our graduates must be capable of drawing upon many types of knowledge as they engage in the process of teaching. This more holistic view of teaching requires teacher education programs to depend upon observations of candidates over time. Portfolios honor the need for a collage, rather than a snapshot, approach to evaluation, to capture growth and change in the learner while incorporating reflection as a means of involving teachers in their own professional development and bridging the gap between research and practice (Barton & Collins, 1993; Schon, 1983). The design of portfolios can also explicitly define what is expected of candidates and better integrate the course work with experiences.

At the master's-degree level at USF, we want to insure that all graduates have developed and can demonstrate five domains of practice evident across skill areas in the practice of teaching. Therefore, we have instituted a portfolio assessment that replaces the written comprehensive examination. Specifically, our graduates will be

1. *ethical,* skilled in the negotiation and compromise necessary to preserve the integrity of one's own beliefs and principles;

2. *affirming of diversity,* capable of working productively with a wide range of abilities, cultures, and societal influences reflective of today's society;

3. *reflective practitioners,* able to evaluate their own teaching and continuously learn from it;

4. *professionally competent,* knowledgeable on theory and research and skilled in the best practices of special education; and

5. *users of technology*, comfortable in the use and design of technology-based tools for computer-assisted instruction, assessment, and data management in schools.

Commensurate with the belief that the merging of research and practice is desirable and beneficial, our department of special education has identified five areas in which evidence of these skill domains can be documented:

1. *Assessment*, including norm-referenced, criterion-referenced, dynamic, curriculum-based, and performance-based forms of assessment for the purposes of screening, eligibility/placement, instructional/intervention planning, evaluation of individual/group progress, transition planning, and program evaluation;

2. *Instruction*, including the skills of planning, implementing, and refining successful curricula, methodology, and materials for whole group, small group, team-taught, and/or individual instruction at K–12 levels that are sensitive to students' individual needs and that incorporate exemplary resources;

3. *Classroom management*, incorporating the use of formal and informal systems and theories of learning, reinforcement, and motivation to design and manage learning environments that result in motivated learning, enhanced social skills, competent decision making, and desirable student performance in the classroom;

4. *Collaboration*, encompassing an interpersonal style that may be used in interactions with colleagues, families, and others in order to share responsibilities, resources, and/or accountability and accomplish the goal of educating students; and

5. *Systematic inquiry*, including the skills of planning, design, collection of data, analysis, and interpretation of an investigation using either quantitative and/or qualitative approaches in order to address questions arising from the classroom that may contribute to the knowledge base of our field.

A matrix is used to systematically compile, cluster, and document products, performances, and/or supporting data for students' individualized portfolios that can demonstrate their competence and use of best practices in field-related situations (see Figure 25.1). Each student meets with her or his advisor to assess current strengths, select areas for further growth, and design meaningful projects that will demonstrate competence and skills related to the matrix. Although still undergoing revisions, we believe that this constructivist approach allows students to showcase their teaching skills and evidence of professional development throughout the program. We also see this use of alternative assessment as mirroring and modeling the changing role of assessment in school systems that will employ our teachers.

Skills to Teach Versus Skills to Survive.   Special education is characterized by a high rate of teacher attrition. Estimates of attrition rates among special educators range from 34% to 50% (Morsink, 1988). Research also suggests that the best and the brightest are more likely to leave the field (Darling-Hammond, 1984; Schlechty & Vance, 1983). Clearly, retention of quality teachers is a major challenge in special education; yet year after year, first-year graduates are placed in the most challenging classrooms. Administrators explain that they cannot pull their best teachers from jobs the teachers like because the good teachers would leave; thus, beginning teachers are left to the task. However, when novice teachers flounder in these settings, many schools berate them, attributing their difficulties to personal inadequacies rather than to system failures. This "blame the victim" type of thinking protects the school from

	DOMAINS	**OF**	**PRACTICE**		
	Ethical	Affirming of Diversity	Reflective	Competent (Current)	User of Technology
Assessment					
Instruction					
Classroom Management					
Collaboration					
Systematic Inquiry					

(S K I L L S)

Figure 25.1. Portfolio Development Model developed by the Department of Special Education at the University of South Florida.

examining its problems. As Sarason (1990) pointed out, with "any effort to deal with or prevent a significant problem in a school system that is not based upon reallocation of power, a discernible change in power relationships is doomed" (p. 28). Few initiatives are in place that address the need to support and protect novice teachers as they enter the field, and many of the efforts that are in place (e.g., beginning teacher programs) have quickly become bureaucratic compliance activities rather than real support systems.

Given the realities of the teaching world, university teacher education programs must address the question of what is best for program graduates. Reflective practice is less of an issue than survival. How can programs educate novices in an atmosphere of mutual respect and positive regard while also equipping them with survival skills for the real world of schools? How can novice teachers be inoculated against the pains created by overcrowded classrooms, classrooms that have become dumping grounds, administrators who are overwhelmed by the demands of their responsibilities, and support personnel who have neither the training nor the skill to deal with many of the children schools are serving? Teacher preparation programs need to help restructure, rather than perpetuate, a system that blames the least powerful in order to avoid self-scrutiny and difficult change.

This is a systems problem and, in many ways, is one of the central issues in school reform. The parallel systems of teacher education that exist in universities and in public schools, and the familiar image of the "town–gown" gap that has fostered the separation of theory in "the ivory tower," and practice in "the real world," challenge the efforts of all who would develop research-based and ecologically valid teacher education programs.

Our program has focused on school-sensitive and (to the extent possible) school-based teacher education. We have school-based faculty and doctoral students in a professional development school, faculty and doctoral students who work closely with district and school administrators, and teachers in collaborative school programs. We also involve school district staff in our program. In addition to having a school-sensitive faculty whose education is ongoing, we focus attention in our curriculum on systemic issues as well as clinical and instructional issues.

CONCLUSION

The Department of Special Education at the University of South Florida is deeply involved in a process of change. That change has been guided by the basic principles underpinning school restructuring in general and inclusion in particular. The faculty have been immersed in rethinking the moral, social, and technical foundations of teacher education in special education, and changing the traditional practices that characterized our program. This article presented aspects of the philosophical positions constructed by the faculty, the conflicts these positions posed for practice, and some of the approaches we are taking to address these conflicts.

26. Looking Forward: Using a Sociocultural Perspective to Reframe the Study of Learning Disabilities

VODD GROUP: PATRICIA TEFFT COUSIN, ESTEBAN DIAZ,

BARBARA FLORES, AND JOSÉ HERNANDEZ

Over the past 10 years, discussions about the theoretical perspective that best helps us study and understand learning disabilities (LD) have taken place at conferences and in publications. For many, these discussions are best organized by classifying work according to the two different paradig-matic perspectives currently being used in the field, the reductionist and the constructivist (e.g., Poplin, 1988a, 1988b; Stainback & Stainback, 1992; see the fall 1994 issue of *The Journal of Special Education* and the fall 1993 and winter 1994 issues of *Learning Disability Quarterly*). It is hoped that the chapters in this book, based on constructivist perspectives, have provided additional insights and raised further questions related to the discussion.

The intent of this chapter is to use a sociocultural perspective of teaching and learning to synthesize the chapters of this book and to think about where inquiry in the field of learning disabilities might be headed. First, a short review of constructivist work in the area of learning

Reprinted, with changes, from "Looking foward: Using a sociocultural perspective to reframe the study of learning disabilities," by VODD Group, *Journal of Learning Disabilities*, Vol. 28, 1995, pp. 656–663. Copyright © 1995 by PRO-ED, Inc.

disabilities will be used to develop the background and to provide a foundation for the rest of the chapter. Second, a model based on a sociocultural view of teaching and learning will be presented and discussed. Third, that model will be used to inform our understanding of learning disabilities, with the studies of this book serving to illustrate some of the main points of this application. Finally, this same model will be used to invite discussions and conversations that will hopefully push the field in new directions by reframing how we study and talk about students with learning disabilities. As Poplin stated in her chapter that began this book, "none of us have the answer." Our intent is to create new dialogues about the issues we face as educators today, particularly as we work with students with learning disabilities.

UNDERSTANDING THE CONSTRUCTIVIST PERSPECTIVE

Individuals espousing a constructivist perspective as a means of understanding children with learning disabilities have focused on three different aspects of schooling: teaching and learning, service delivery, and an analysis of the institutional nature of school. The work on learning and teaching has focused on the application of a constructivist perspective to (a) better understand the development of students with learning problems, particularly in respect to literacy, and (b) apply and analyze methods of teaching that are constructivist in nature. Much of this work focused on the literacy development of students with special needs as they participated in authentic literacy events in classrooms (e.g., Cousin, Aragon, & Rojas, 1993; Five, 1990; Katims, 1994; Klenk, 1994; Palincsar & Klenk, 1992; Rueda, 1990; Stires, 1991).

In comparison to the applied work on teaching and learning, the constructivist-oriented work on service delivery and the analysis of the institutional nature of schooling have mainly been critiques of the present system. That collection of work has scrutinized the philosophies and assumptions about learners that have guided our policy decisions and development of programs. Insights regarding how school failure is identified—as the individual failure of a particular student, rather than of the educational program and practices—emerge from this body of work (e.g., Allington, 1994; Coles, 1987; Franklin, 1987, 1994; Hood, McDermott, & Cole, 1980; Lipsky & Gartner, 1987; McDermott, 1993; McDermott & Varenne, 1993; Mehan, Hertweck, & Meihles, 1986; Skrtic, 1991; Sleeter, 1986).

Although an initial understanding of what it means to take a constructivist perspective of learning disabilities has been developed, there is not a fully developed theoretical or conceptual base. This is necessary to both frame and organize current and future work on the study of learning disabilities. The rest of the chapter attempts to begin this process.

SOCIOCULTURAL CONTEXTS MODEL

The model of sociocultural contexts was developed to illustrate the multiple layers of contexts within which individuals develop, particularly focusing on the contexts involved with formal education (see Figure 26.1). The use of this model focuses attention beyond an individual's behavior to consider the embedded nature of his or her behavior in schools.

The basis for this model is cultural historical theory (Cole & Engestrom, 1993; Cole & Griffin, 1987; Forman, Minick, & Stone, 1993; Moll, 1990; Salomon, 1993; Wertsch, 1991, 1994): "The basic goal of the sociocultural (cultural and historical) approach is to create an account of human mental processes that recognizes the essential relationship between these processes and their cultural, historical, and institutional settings" (Wertsch, 1991, p. 6).

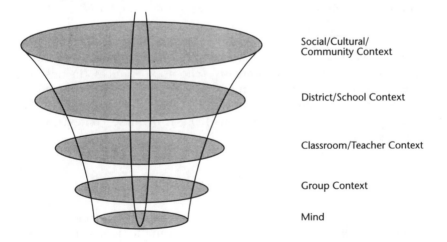

Socio-Cultural Contexts: Framing Learning and Teaching

Social/Cultural/
Community Context

District/School Context

Classroom/Teacher Context

Group Context

Mind

Figure 26.1.   Sociocultural contexts: Framing learning and teaching. Copyright © 1995 by VODD Group. Reprinted by permission.

Activity theory has also informed us in constructing this model (Engestrom, 1991). Using this theoretical view, researchers attempt to explain the relationship between the individual and the system. Thus, "individual actions and situations, as well as failures, disturbances, and innovations are analyzed against the framework of the entire activity system" (Engestrom, Brown, Christopher, & Gregory, 1991, p. 79). Individual development is viewed as dependent on the social interactions that are a part of the daily activities in any given culture. The activities involve and reflect the values of a culture, the tools used to mediate learning, and the institutions of that culture (Rogoff, Mosier, Mistry, & Goncu, 1993). By using this theoretical frame, we are trying to understand how individual development occurs, especially development that occurs within classrooms, across time and space. From a sociocultural, sociohistorical perspective, individuals are ontological constructs of the interactions they participate in within their culture. Thus, we want to look at the complex interactions that take place in school to better understand students' development.

We are particularly interested in understanding the development of students who are underachieving in school contexts. These students encounter a wide range of experiences as they make their way through school. Often those experiences are negative and detrimental to optimal development. This is due to the wide range of misconceptions that organize school experiences for these students and the actual school experiences themselves (Flores, Cousin, & Diaz, 1991). The use of sociocultural and activity theory supports this type of inquiry, because it "highlights the rich interconnections between cultural institutions, social practices, semiotic mediation, interpersonal relationships, and the developing mind" (Forman, 1993, p. 6).

The model presents five interconnected contexts. The intent is to help us illuminate the pathways of ideas, expectations, and activities that either foster or hinder students' school experiences (in this case, those identified as having learning disabilities). These five contexts are (a) social/cultural/community, (b) district/school, (c) classroom/teacher, (d) group, and (e) mind (individual). Each of these contexts will be briefly explained.

Social/Cultural/Community Context

The social/cultural context is the level at which fundamental development takes place. The child's interactions with the significant others in his or her immediate family and community organize the nature of his or her development. Vygotsky's (1978) law of general development explains that any function in children's development appears twice, or on two planes. First it appears on the social plane, and then on the psychological plane. It appears between people, as an interpsychological category, and then within the individual, as an intrapsychological category. In other words, a sociocultural view considers that embedded in the social interactions are the goals for learning. Learning is first shared on a social plane, and then these social interactions become internalized knowledge within the learner's mind—the individual plane.

The everyday experiences organized and sanctioned by the conditions of a child's community create development in very particular ways. In other words, culture, as organized by the everyday interactions in family and community life, "develops" children. As noted by the Laboratory for Comparative Human Cognition (1983), culture organizes for (a) occurrence and nonoccurrence of events, (b) frequency of basic practices, (c) pattern of life experiences, and (d) regulation of task and difficulty. In addition, everyday cultural experiences are also subject to the ecological press of social conditions (such as living in poverty) and the policies that affect neighborhood conditions. The social and political contexts that exist in communities affect the interactions that take place and establish relationships that influence school attitudes, policies, and practices.

District/School Context

Like families and communities, school districts and the individual schools within them exist in social and political contexts that strongly influence their characteristics. Some schools are located in well-to-do areas, others are not. Some schools attract solid, experienced teachers, others see only newly credentialed candidates who leave as quickly as possible. Quantity and quality of resources vary, as do student characteristics. All of these factors, singly and collectively, organize and constrain the development of individuals who go to school at a particular site.

As a result, it is important to see how these institutions influence the development of the individual students who attend them. Schooling is part of the students' cognitive and personal development, and part of who children become is a function of the experiences they have had in school. Those experiences in school, or, rather, the socioeducational contexts in which students participate, continue or disrupt the process of development begun in the home in powerful ways. School experiences are of critical importance for students who are from nonmainstream backgrounds or who have learning disabilities. If the socioeducational contexts support and build on the experiences of these children in their homes and communities, then their individual development may continue in a positive way. However, this is not always the case.

Classroom/Teacher Context

The teacher is the sociocultural mediator of important formal and informal knowledge about the culture and society within which individual children develop (Diaz & Flores, 1991). It is crucial to emphasize the teacher's role in the continuing developmental process of the child. Vygotsky's (1978) zone of proximal development, "the distance between the actual developmental level as determined by individual problem solving and the level of potential development as determined through problem solving under adult guidance or in collaboration with more capable peers" (p. 86), provides a focus for analyzing successful classroom interactions and activities.

The child has been participating in zones of proximal development during the entire course of his or her life until coming to school. Upon entering school, successful negotiations of zones of proximal development in school become critical. The teacher is responsible for helping to create a social system within the classroom that organizes optimal zones for all students. Teaching/learning occurs as a function of the social interactions within the zones that the teacher co-constructs with the student.

The impact of what occurs in the classroom is tremendous, as school success is linked to success or failure in society (Moll, 1990; Vygotsky, 1978). Students enter the classroom at a level of development that has been a function of their everyday familial, cultural, and communal experiences. If the teacher does not properly take these previous experiences into account, the child is put at risk of not being able to participate appropriately in the zones of proximal development organized by the socioeducational contexts. This is where children, particularly those identified as different from the mainstream in some way (e.g., due to learning disabilities, cultural background, language other than English), are likely to begin to fail. The failure, however, is not of their making; it is the direct result of the social interactions set up by the teachers. These interactions reflect personal, school, and cultural norms. If children's experiential, cultural, and linguistic experiences are not included in the socioeducational contexts of the classroom, then they will have great difficulty reaching their highest potential.

And it is not only the teacher's professional knowledge that affects what the teacher organizes, but also his or her beliefs, attitudes, and cultural knowledge about the children he or she teaches (Flores et al., 1991). The materials used in the classroom also have an important impact on the child's development. Those materials reflect the intentions of the author or developer about the learning process, who should use the materials, and what is defined as the goal for instruction. Materials can both create and constrain contexts for learning (Hatano, 1993).

Group Context

The levels of development represented within groups of students vary tremendously across socioeducational contexts. Many levels of potential development exist for all students if social interactions are organized for optimal sharing.

There has been a long history of organizing work for the individual student to complete (Popkewitz, 1987). Teachers were seen as the sole arbiters of knowledge, and its sole dispenser. Hence, there was little need for student group work or conversation. A sociocultural perspective underscores the value of peer and student–teacher interactions in cognitive development. The types of support and mediation that are available in the classroom from both teacher and peers are critical to the learning that occurs there. By studying how children interact in groups, we are able to make these mediations visible. The teacher is also able to create and use mediational structures and processes as tools to facilitate children's social construction of knowledge as they work with each other.

Mind

Mind (individual) is a social construction. It is the internalization of all social interactions, the appropriation of the experiences one has been a part of. In an individual's appropriations we see the trail of his or her social interactions across time. Vygotsky (1978) explained that all of our higher mental functions are the result of internalized social relationships.

There has been a recent movement to rename what is now called "mind" to "consciousness" or "identity." The reason for this is that "mind" tends to be associated primarily with cognitive functioning. A more extensive notion of personhood results when identity is considered to be a function of all the social interactions one has in life. It seems evident that the development of a person is not confined to mere cognitive domains. Rather, a person acts as a whole in whatever she or he does. And who one is and what one does is a culmination of that person's interactions and experiences across time in all contexts (Barone, Eeds, & Mason, 1995; Mead, 1934). Mind must be seen as a sociocultural and sociohistorical construction.

In summary, our intent is for the model to provide a framework for better understanding the relationships that are part of the schooling experience for every child in the Western world. We believe that such a focus will enable us to establish more successful contexts in schools.

REFRAMING THE STUDY OF LEARNING DISABILITIES

So, how does the use of such a model help us reframe both research and practice in the field of learning disabilities? For each context described in the model, we pose a question. Each question reflects the focus that teachers and researchers might take as they try to look at the field of learning disabilities in new ways. All of the questions underscore the embedded and complex nature of learning disabilities, a construct used in Western culture both *to explain why* people might have difficulty learning and *to organize the ways* we deal with this in schools. There has typically been a focus on the individual nature of a learning disability, an orientation developed through the imposition of a medical model on the field of education (Coles, 1987). All of the chapters in this book have rejected such an orientation.

The questions might also provide an opportunity for reflection about the benefits of using a different perspective for understanding how mainstream culture in the Western world interprets and organizes behaviors in response to diversity and differences. There is the potential to develop new understandings regarding how to successfully deal with students encountering difficulty in school. Those in the LD field have typically focused on the individual child, ignoring the embedded nature of an individual's actions within social contexts. The chapters from this book will be used to illustrate what research and practice might look like when we apply these questions to the field of learning disabilities.

Social/Cultural/Community Context

How does mainstream culture interpret differences and diversity among people?
To understand the notion of disability in mainstream culture, we must see the ways that culture "actively organizes ways for people to be disabled" (McDermott & Varenne, 1993, p. 13). Such organization occurs via the institutional structures present in our culture, from the way disability is defined, to who is designated as disabled, to the ways that institutions such as schools are organized to deal with disabilities. "Without the social arrangements for making something of differential rates of learning, there is no such thing as LD" (McDermott, 1993, p. 3). The rate of learning has become the focus of our attention in school, rather than what and how the student is learning (McDermott, 1993; McDermott & Varenne, 1993).

Several of the chapters in this book have focused on providing insight into these social arrangements. Dudley-Marling and Dippo argued that the basic assumptions of schooling, that is, the discourse used to organize thinking about schooling and its role in mainstream culture, also structure interactions involving children encountering difficulty. According to these two authors, this discourse perpetuates the view of differences as *deficiencies*. West challenged us to think of those "deficiencies" from a different perspective. He proposed that the traits, particularly visual–spatial talents, commonly associated with learning difficulties in our present educational system may be viewed as special talents in the educational system and workplace of the 21st century. West's chapter suggested a reexamination of how and what our society defines as disability and talent. In contrast, the chapter by Rhodes and the one by Denti and Katz presented possibilities for a new set of assumptions to inform our work with children. They discussed creating a new discourse, based on liberatory pedagogy, or one of caring, with which to discuss schooling and the teaching/learning process. These chapters also discussed how the use of a new discourse might affect practices for students having difficulty in school.

District/School Context

What policies and practices are organized in our schools for students identified as learning disabled?

Schools as institutions have organized policies, structures, and routines based on the mainstream culture's notion of disabilities as inherent. The model focuses attention on the impact of these organized "ways of doing" currently used in schools. The institutionalized practices that we use to identify, assess, and teach students encountering difficulty in school must be addressed, because these practices structure the interactions that occur among the people participating in them (Forman et al., 1993).

The potential to create new contexts at the district and school level that challenge past ways of acting is there. The chapter by Wiest and Kreil (this book) related how a school psychologist and district director employed a constructivist paradigm in their decision making with teachers, parents, and students. The authors highlighted the tensions and challenges those professionals experienced while confronting patterns of behavior that were based on a view of children and families that they had rejected. In an examination of another aspect of schooling—funding— the chapter by Matsui critiqued the economics of serving students with learning disabilities. The high costs of providing special education services often limits funds for general school operations, setting up competition for funding between special programs and general education services and programs. The chapter by Raskind and Higgins critiqued present views and uses of technology with students with learning disabilities. They provided a thorough examination of one aspect of schooling— technology—and how the context and ethos for its use in schools could limit its effectiveness with the very students who might benefit most through the use of technological tools.

Finally, the chapters by Paul, Epanchin, Rosselli, Townsend, Cranston-Gingras, and Thomas; Bacon and Bloom; and Ruiz, Rueda, Figueroa, and Boothroyd discussed teacher education programs for special educators, relating how programs were reorganized based on constructivist principles. The individuals graduating from these programs have different understandings regarding diversity. Programs like these provide teachers with the potential for establishing different and more effective school environments for students with learning difficulties, thus bringing about changes in school culture.

Classroom/Teacher Context

How do teachers organize their classrooms, instructional activities, and interactions for students identified as learning disabled?

A sociocultural perspective of learning supports the idea that we get what we organize for in schools: Students tend to learn what is available to be learned (McDermott, 1993). Because special educators have a long tradition of organizing instruction to focus on basic skills, it is not surprising that many studies exist showing that children have learned these skills (Chall, 1967; Ekwall, 1989; Haring & Bateman, 1977; Tarver, 1992). Special educators have organized for basic skill learning, but not for sophisticated use and application of these skills. Therefore, students with learning difficulties are typically not able to use the skills for more complex literacy and mathematical tasks (Paris & Oka, 1989; Poplin, 1988a, 1988b; Poplin & Stone, 1992). If the more complex skills are not used in the classroom, then learning does not occur (McDermott, 1993; McDermott & Varenne, 1993).

A number of chapters in this book discussed the need and rationale for organizing curricula in alternative ways—perspectives focused on child-centered, transactional views of learning. The two chapters by Ruiz and those by Hemming and MacInnis, Kugelmass, and Hearne and Stone used sociocognitive perspectives on teaching and learning to discuss why teachers need to restructure learning opportunities for children identified as having learning disabilities. They discussed curricular frameworks that support active engagement in the learning process, and the use of literacy and mathematics for authentic purposes.

Group Context

What opportunities are available for mediation and interaction for students identified as having learning disabilities?

If we argue that it is within social interactions that learning does or does not occur, then we must begin to look at the interactions occurring in the classroom in a more critical light. The ways in which instruction is organized and the instructional materials used by the teacher have a strong impact on the instructional interactions occurring in the classroom. It is not surprising that children have difficulty comprehending books when they spend their language arts instructional time completing skill worksheets by themselves. The students have not had an opportunity to interact with real books or with proficient readers. There must be careful assessment of both the type and the manner of interactions occurring in classrooms involving students identified as LD. These students need effective, socially mediated instruction (Stone & Reid, 1994). In addition, we need to critique the materials used to support these interactions. There is a strong connection between how an individual accomplishes a task in a social situation, for example, in a classroom, and how he or she will accomplish the task alone (Moll & Diaz, 1987).

A number of chapters in this book have investigated classrooms where instruction was organized based on a constructivist view of learning. Authentic uses of literacy were organized and implemented in the classrooms discussed by Goldstein; Jackman; Kau; Lovelace; Palincsar, Parecki, and McPhail; and Thorson. Although the learning difficulties of the students in these classrooms were not "cured," many of the students demonstrated effective reading and writing behaviors for the first time in their educational careers. From a sociocultural perspective, disabilities do not disappear; rather, the interactions in the classroom provide a context for abilities to appear and for children to develop their individual ways of knowing and learning.

Mind

> *How does the student identify him- or herself—as a learner or as a person with disabilities?*

We know that individuals are affected by the personal relationships they are a part of throughout the day. A sociocultural notion of teaching and learning links identity to the social contexts in which an individual has participated. Individuals learn to experience themselves based on the responses they get from others within their social group. Such an orientation provides insight into how an individual labeled as "deficient" begins to enact that identity. When one is identified with a disability, others relate to him or her in particular ways. Thus, it is not enough to examine the classroom activities. There is also a need to critique the student's personal relationships.

> Reexamining what we are asking the learner to do must also include whom we are asking the learner to become. The zone of proximal development describes more than the transmission of cultural knowledge; dyadic roles

and dialogic positions relative to that knowledge have also been internalized. (Libowitz, 1993, p. 191)

Three chapters in this book, by Reid and Button, DuCharme, and Albinger, focused on investigating students' perspectives about their learning problems and the way that schools and teachers have dealt with them and the way they learn. In each chapter, the students' educational histories are reflected in their stories about themselves. Inquiries of this sort underscore the importance of understanding the students' perspectives about their own learning processes and their notions of their learning needs. The authors also pointed out the key role the teacher plays in the teaching/learning process. They highlighted that the interpersonal relationships themselves, in conjunction with the interactions that students participate in while in school, serve a mediating function (Stone, 1993).

LOOKING FORWARD

The chapters of this book have laid out research, organizational-change, and curricular-change agendas that point to where we might direct our thoughts and future work as we continue to better understand and support individuals with learning disabilities. Most of these chapters have focused on *one* of the interrelated contexts that affect instruction and children's learning. The model might help us think about new directions for research, analysis, and interpretation with a focus on ideas, not only *within* contexts, but also *across* contexts.

Looking to the future, there is a need to study and analyze learning and teaching across contexts, because only in this way will the complexity of the social reality of being identified with disabilities in our culture be considered. There is a need to analyze learning taking into account all of the contexts:

> Analysis must consider the broad cultural and institutional content, the local setting as a social meeting place, and the interpersonal relationships that are played out. They are not so much separate levels of reality as they are aspects of social reality linked in the proactive of real persons. (Packer, 1993, p. 264)

What are some possibilities for better studying and understanding these linkages, for better understanding the social reality of students identified with LD? A few examples will be briefly described.

- Reports of successful or unsuccessful practice with children with learning disabilities must be couched in an analysis of other contexts. Change in one context recursively affects another (Cobb, Wood, &

Yackel, 1993). There is a need for studies that document these recursive changes and relationships among contexts.

- Methods need to be developed to study how institutional and social structures used to organize schooling for students with learning disabilities affect such learners across time (Cole & Engestrom, 1993). For example, we might explore the long-term effects of a remedial approach or constructivist approach across time in one student's life.

- The perspectives of students identified with LD on their difficulties and the types of teaching and learning contexts that are most effective for them need to be addressed (Kos, 1991). We know little about using students' self-reflections and beliefs about themselves to plan appropriate curricular interventions.

- There is an increasing interest in considering the role of relationships in the learning process (Chang-Wells & Wells, 1993; Libowitz, 1993; Stone, 1993). We need to better understand the types of teaching relationships that are most supportive and productive for students identified with LD.

- There is a need to develop, implement, and study radically different approaches to meeting the needs of students who require additional support in learning. The data on existing programs are not overly optimistic; it is time to try out some new types of structures (Allington, 1994).

In summary, Mary Poplin, the authors in this book, and the authors of this chapter hope for "remarkably fuller visions" (Allington, 1994, p. 113) of what schooling might be for students with learning disabilities. This book has presented one set of visions. We all agree with McDermott (1993) that

> the question of who is learning what and how much is essentially a question of what conversations they are a part of, and this question is a subset of the more powerful questions of what conversations are around to be had in a given culture. . . . To do this we must give up our preoccupation with individual performance and examine instead the structure of resources and disappointments made available to people in various institutions. (p. 20)

The intent of this book has been to refocus and reframe the conversations engaged in by educators and researchers in the field of learning disabilities and the conversations available for students encountering difficulty in school. We believe that such dialogues are critical for creating more effective learning contexts for students identified with learning disabilities.

References

CHAPTER 1

Five, C. L. (1991). *Special voices.* Portsmouth, NH: Heinemann.

Freire, P. (1970). *Pedagogy of the oppressed.* New York: Continuum.

Freire, P., & Macedo, D. (1987). *Literacy: Reading the word and the world.* South Hadley, MA: Continuum.

Horton, M., & Freire, P. (1990). *We make the road by walking.* New York: Continuum.

Howard, P. (1994). *The death of common sense: How law is suffocating America.* New York: Random House.

Mallory, B. L., & New, R. S. (1994). Social constructivist theory and principles of inclusion: Challenges for early childhood special education. *The Journal of Special Education, 28,* 322–337.

Mehan, H., Hertweck, K., & Meihls, J. (1986). *Handicapping the handicapped.* Palo Alto, CA: Stanford University Press.

Moll, L. C. (Ed.). (1990). *Vygotsky and education: Instructional implications and applications of sociohistorical psychology.* Cambridge, England: Cambridge University Press.

Pine, N. (1992). Three personal theories that suggest models for teacher research. *Teachers College Record, 93,* 657–672.

Poplin, M., & Weeres, J. (1992). *Voices from the inside: A report on schooling from inside the classroom.* Claremont, CA: The Claremont Graduate School, Institute for Education in Transformation.

Poplin, M., Wiest, D., & Thorson, S. (1995). Alternative instructional strategies to reductionism: Constructive, multicultural, feminine and critical pedagogies. In W. Stainback & S. Stainback (Eds.), *Controversial issues confronting special education: Divergent perspectives* (2nd ed.). Boston: Allyn & Bacon.

Rivera, J., & Poplin, M. (1995). Multicultural, critical, feminine and constructive pedagogies seen through the lives of youth: A call for the revisioning of these and beyond—Toward a pedagogy for the next century. In C. Sleeter & P. McLaren (Eds.), *Multicultural education, critical pedagogy, and the politics of difference* (pp. 300–338). Albany, NY: SUNY Press.

Taylor, D. (1990). *Learning denied.* Portsmouth, NH: Heinemann.

Thorson, S. (1995). *Special education and general secondary students' talk about discipline procedures.* Unpublished doctoral dissertation, The Claremont Graduate School.

Valdes, G., & Figueroa, R. A. (1994). *The nature of bilingualism and the nature of testing.* New York: ABLEX.

West, T. (1991). *In the mind's eye.* Buffalo, NY: Prometheus Books.

CHAPTER 2

Bronfenbrenner, U. (1979). The ecology of human development. Cambridge, MA: Harvard University Press.

Capra, F. (1982). The turning point. New York: Bantam Books.

Heshusius, L. (1989). Holistic principles: Not enhancing the old but seeing anew. A rejoinder. Journal of Learning Disabilities, 22, 595–602.

Kuhn, T. S. (1970). The structure of scientific revolution. Chicago: University of Chicago Press.

Poplin, M. (1988a). The reductionistic fallacy in learning disabilities: Replicating the past by reducing the present. Journal of Learning Disabilities, 21, 389–400.

Poplin, M. (1988b). Holistic/constructivist principles of the teaching/learning process: Implications for the field of learning disabilities. Journal of Learning Disabilities, 21, 401–416.

Reid, D. K. (1988). Reflections on the pragmatics of a paradigm shift. Journal of Learning Disabilities, 21, 417–420.

CHAPTER 3

Argyris, C. (1990). Overcoming organizational defenses: Facilitating organizational learning. Boston: Allyn & Bacon.

Barker, J. (1988). Discovering the future: The business of paradigms (2nd ed.). [Videotape]. Burnsville, MN: Charthouse.

Elmore, R. (1980). Backward mapping: Implementation research and policy decisions. Political Science Quarterly, 94, 601–616.

Elmore, R. (1983). Complexity and control: What legislators and administrators can do about implementing public policy. In L. Shullman & F. Sykes (Eds.), Handbook of teaching and policy (pp. 342–369). New York: Longman.

Fullan, M. (1993). Change forces: Probing the depths of educational reform. Briston, PA: The Falmer Press.

Odden, A., & Odden, E. (1984). Education reform, school improvement and state policy. Educational Leadership, 42(2), 13–19.

Rosenholtz, S. J. (1991). Teachers' workplace: The social organization of schools. New York: Teachers College Press.

Sergiovanni, T. (1992). Why we should seek substitutes for leadership. Educational Leadership, 49(5), 41–45.

Slavin, R., Karweit, N., & Wasik, B. (1994). Preventing early school failure. Boston: Allyn & Bacon.

CHAPTER 4

American Association for Children and Adults with Learning Disabilities (ACLD) Board of Directors. (1985). Definitions of the condition of specific learning disabilities. ACLD News Briefs, 158, 1–3.

Apple, M. W. (1982). Curricular form and the logic of technical control: Building the possessive individual. In M. W. Apple (Ed.), Cultural and economic reproduction in education: Essays on class, ideology and the state (pp. 247–274). Boston: Routledge & Kegan Paul.

Bourdieu, P., & Passeron, J. C. (1977). Reproduction in education, society and culture. Beverly Hills, CA: Sage.

Bowles, S., & Gintis, H. (1975). Schooling in capitalist America. New York: Basic Books.

Carrier, J. G. (1986). Learning disability: Social class and the construction of inequality in American education. New York: Greenwood Press.

Coles, G. (1987). The learning mystique: A critical look at "learning disabilities." New York: Random House.

Cremin, L. A. (1988). American education: The metropolitan experience 1876 1980. New York: Harper & Row.

Curtis, B., Livingstone, D. W., & Smaller, H. (1992). Stacking the deck: The streaming of working-class kids in Ontario schools. Toronto: Our Schools/Our Selves Education Foundation.

Edelsky, C. (1991). With literacy and justice for all: Rethinking the social in language and education. Philadelphia: Falmer Press.

Franklin, B. M. (1986). The first crusade for learning disabilities: The movement for the education of backward children. In T. S. Popkewitz (Ed.), The formation of school subjects: The struggle for creating an American institution (pp. 190–209). Philadelphia: Falmer Press.

Fulcher, G. (1989). Disabling policies? A comparative approach to education policy and disability. Philadelphia: Falmer Press.

Gee, J. (1990). Social linguistics and literacies: Ideology in discourses. Philadelphia: Falmer Press.

Greene, M. (1978). Landscapes of learning. New York: Teachers College Press.

Greene, M. (1993). Imagination, community, and the school. The Review of Education, 15, 223–231.

Heshusius, L. (1982). At the heart of the advocacy dilemma: A mechanistic world view. Exceptional Children, 49, 6–13.

Houston, S. E., & Prentice, A. (1988). Schooling and scholars in nineteenth-century Ontario. Toronto: University of Toronto Press.

Iano, R. P. (1986). The study and development of teaching: With implications for the advancement of special education. Remedial and Special Education, 7(5), 50–61.

Jencks, C. (1972). Inequality. New York: Harper Colophon Books.

Kavale, K. A., & Forness, S. R. (1985). The science of learning disabilities. San Diego: College-Hill.

Lerner, J. (1981). Learning disabilities: Theories, diagnosis, and teaching strategies (3rd ed.). Boston: Houghton Mifflin.

Macdonell, D. (1986). Theories of discourse: An introduction. New York: Basil Blackwell.

MacPherson, C. B. (1962). The political theory of possessive individualism. New York: Oxford University Press.

Osborne, K. (1991). Teaching for democratic citizenship. Toronto: Our Schools/Our Selves Education Foundation.

Poplin, M. S. (1984). Toward an holistic view of persons with learning disabilities. Learning Disability Quarterly, 7, 290–294.

Poplin, M. S. (1988). The reductionist fallacy in learning disabilities: Replicating the past by reducing the present. Journal of Learning Disabilities, 21, 389–400.

Rourke, B. P. (1989). Coles's Learning Mystique: The good, the bad, and the irrelevant. Journal of Learning Disabilities, 22, 274–277.

Skrtic, T. M. (1991). Behind special education: A critical analysis of professional culture and school organization. Denver: Love.

Sleeter, C. E. (1987). Why is there learning disabilities? A critical analysis of the birth of the field in its social context. In T. S. Popkewitz (Ed.), The formation of school subjects: The struggle for creating an American institution (pp. 210–237). Philadelphia: Falmer Press.

Ulman, J. D., & Rosenberg, M. S. (1986). Science and superstition in special education. Exceptional Children, 52, 459–460.

CHAPTER 5

Berger, P. L., & Luckman, T. (1966). The social construction of reality: A treatise in the sociology of knowledge. New York: Doubleday.

Coles, G. (1987). The learning mystique: A critical look at learning disabilities. New York: Pantheon.

Collins, M., Brown, A. L., & Newman, R. K. (1990). Cognitive apprenticeship: Teaching the crafts of reading, writing, and mathematics. In L. B. Resnick (Ed.), Knowing, learning, and instruction (pp. 453–494). Hillsdale, NJ: Erlbaum.

Dewey, J. (1916). Democracy and education. New York: Macmillan.

Dunn, L. M. (1968). Special education for the mildly retarded: Is much of it justifiable? Exceptional Children, 35, 5–22.

Ensminger, G. (1991). Defragmenting fragmented learners. Hands-on: A Journal for Teachers, 39, 44–48.

Fuchs, D., & Fuchs, L. S. (1994). Inclusive schools movement and the radicalization of special education reform. Exceptional Children, 60, 294–309.

Gardner, H. (1991). The unschooled mind: How children think and how schools should teach. New York: Basic Books.

Glass, G. V. (1983). Effectiveness of special education. Policy Studies Review, 2, 65–78.

Graham, S., Harris, K. R., & Reid, R. (1993). Developing self-regulated learners. In E. Meyen, G. Vergason, & R. Wheelan (Eds.), Educating students with mild disabilities (pp. 127–149). Denver: Love.

Heshusius, L. (1982). At the heart of the advocacy dilemma: A mechanistic world view. Exceptional Children, 52, 461–465.

Iano, R. P. (1987). Rebuttal: Neither the absolute certainty of prescriptive law nor a surrender to mysticism. Remedial and Special Education, 18(1), 51–56.

James, W. (1962). What makes a life significant. In William James talks to teachers on psychology and to students on some of life's ideals (p. 142). New York: Dover.

Kauffman, J. M. (1991). Restructuring in sociopolitical context: Reservations about the effects of current reform proposals on students with disabilities. In J. W. Lloyd, A. C. Rapp, & N. N. Singh (Eds.), The Regular Education Initiative: Alternative perspectives on concepts, issues, and models (pp. 57–66). Sycamore, IL: Sycamore.

Levin, H. (1988). Accelerated schools for disadvantaged students. Educational Leadership, 44, 19–21.

Madden, N. A., & Slavin, R. R. (1983). Effects of cooperative learning on the social acceptance of mainstreamed academically handicapped students. The Journal of Special Education, 17, 171–182.

Marzanno, R. (1992). A different kind of classroom: Teaching with new dimensions of learning. Alexandria, VA: ASCD.

Mayeroff, M. (1971). On caring. New York: Harper & Row.

Mercer, J. (1973). Labeling the mentally retarded: Clinical and social system perspectives on mental retardation. Berkeley: University of California Press.

Noddings, N. (1984). Caring: A feminine approach to ethics and moral education. Berkeley: University of California Press.

Noddings, N. (1992). The challenge to care in schools: An alternative approach to education. New York: Teachers College Press.

Oakes, J. (1985). Keeping track: How schools structure inequality. New Haven: Yale University Press.

Pirsig, R. M. (1974). Zen and the art of motorcycle maintenance: An inquiry into values. New York: Morrow.

Plato. (1971). The republic. In H. D. P. Lee (Ed. and Trans.), Plato's The republic. Baltimore: Penguin. (Original work published 430–347 B.C.)

Poplin, M. S. (1988a). Holistic/constructivist principles of the teaching/learning process: Implications for the field of learning disabilities. Journal of Learning Disabilities, 21, 401–416.

Poplin, M. S. (1988b). The reductionistic fallacy in learning disabilities: Replicating the past by reducing the present. Journal of Learning Disabilities, 21, 389–400.

Reynolds, M. C., & Lakin, K. C. (1987). Noncategorical special education: Models for research and practice. In M. C. Wang, M. C. Reynolds, & H. J. Walberg (Eds.), Handbook of special education: Research and practice: Learner characteristics and adaptive education (Vol. 1, pp. 331–356). Oxford, England: Pergamon.

Sandel, M. (1982). Liberalism and the limits of justice. New York: Cambridge University Press.

Scruggs, T. E. (1993). Special education and the problems of schooling. Educational Theory, 43, 433–447.

Shinn, M. R., & Hubbard, D. D. (1993). Curriculum-based measurement and problem solving assessment: Basic procedures and outcomes in evaluating students with mild disabilities. In E. Meyen, G. Vergason, & R. Whelan (Eds.), Educating students with mild disabilities (pp. 221–253). Denver: Love.

Skrtic, T. M. (1991). Behind special education: A critical analysis of professional culture and school organization. Denver: Love.

Slavin, R. E. (1990). General education under the Regular Education Initiative: How must it change? Remedial and Special Education, 11(3), 40–50.

Slavin, R. E., Karweit, D., & Madden, N. A. (1989). Effective programs for students at risk. Needham Heights, MD: Allyn & Bacon.

Sleeter, C. E. (1986). Learning disabilities: The social construction of a special education category. Exceptional Children, 53, 46–54.

Stainback, S., & Stainback, W. (1984). A rationale for the merger of special and regular education. Exceptional Children, 51, 102–111.

Thoreau, H. D. (1971). Walden. Princeton, NJ: Princeton University Press.

Tomlinson, S. (1982). A sociology of special education. Boston: Routledge & Kegan Paul.

Will, M. C. (1986). Educating students with learning problems: A shared responsibility. Exceptional Children, 42, 411–415.

Ysseldyke, J. E., & Thurlow, M. L. (1984). Assessment practices in special education: Adequacy and appropriateness. Educational Psychologist, 9, 123–136.

Ysseldyke, J., Thurlow, M., Graden, J., Wesson, C., Deno, S., & Algozzine, B. (1983). Generalizations from five years of research on assessment and decision making. Exceptional Education Quarterly, 4(1), 76–93.

CHAPTER 6

Adelman, H. S., & Taylor, L. (1983). Learning disabilities in perspective. Glenview, IL: Scott, Foresman.

Americans with Disabilities Act of 1990, P.L. 101-336, 42 U.S.C.A. 12, 101-12, 213 (West Supp. 1991).

Barbour, I. (1993). Ethics in an age of technology: The Gifford lectures (Vol. 2). San Francisco: Harper.

Beauchamp, T. L. (1991). Philosophical ethics: An introduction to moral philosophy (2nd ed.). New York: McGraw-Hill.

Beauchamp, T. L., & Walters, L. (1989). Contemporary issues in bioethics (3rd ed.). Belmont, CA: Wadsworth.

Berkow, R. (1992). The Merck manual of diagnosis and therapy (16th ed.). Rathway, NJ: Merck & Co.

Bigler, E. D. (1992). The neurobiology and neuropsychology of adult learning disorders. Journal of Learning Disabilities, 25, 499–506.

Brundin, P., Odin, P., & Widner, H. (1990). Promising new results with transplantation of nerve cells to the brain in Parkinson disease. Lakartidningen, 87, 3761–3763.

Bryan, T. (1974). Peer popularity of learning disabled children. Journal of Learning Disabilities, 7, 261–268.

Bryan, T. (1982). Social skills of learning disabled children and youth: An overview. Learning Disability Quarterly, 5, 322–333.

Charney, D., Reder, L., & Kusbit, G. W. (1990). Goal setting and procedure selection in acquiring computer skills: A comparison of tutorials, problem solving, and learner exploration. Cognition and Instruction, 7, 323–342.

Clouser, K. D. (1989). Bioethics. In T. L. Beauchamp & L. Walters (Eds.), Contemporary issues in bioethics (pp. 54–64). Belmont, CA: Wadsworth.

Collins, T. (1990). The impact of microcomputer word processing on the performance of learning disabled students in a required first year writing course. Computers and Composition, 8, 49–68.

Council for Exceptional Children, Division for Children with Learning Disabilities. (1978). Code of ethics and competencies for teachers of learning disabled children and youth. Kansas City, KS: Author.

Council for Exceptional Children. (1983). Code of ethics and standards for professional practice. Exceptional Children, 50, 8–12.

Dudley-Marling, C., & Edmiaston, R. (1985). Social status of learning disabled children and adolescents: A review. Learning Disability Quarterly, 8, 189–204.

Ellis, E. S., & Sabornie, E. J. (1988). Effective instruction with microcomputers: Promises, practices and preliminary findings. In E. L. Meyer, G. A. Vergason, & R. J. Whelans (Eds.), Effective instructional strategies for exceptional children (pp. 355–379). Denver: Love.

Fifield, M. B. (1989). Psychoeducational testing and the personal computer. Journal of Special Education Technology, 9, 136–143.

Flowers, D. L. (1993). Brain basis for dyslexia: A summary of work in progress. Journal of Learning Disabilities, 26, 575–582.

Galaburda, A. M. (1989). Ordinary and extraordinary brain development: Anatomical variation in developmental dyslexia. Annals of Dyslexia, 39, 67–80.

Geschwind, N. (1982). Why Orton was right. Annals of Dyslexia, 32, 13–30.

Grant, A. H. (1992). Factors influencing hand/eye synchronicity in the computer age. Optometry and Vision Science, 69, 739–744.

Gresham, F. M., & Reschly, D. J. (1986). Social skill deficits and low peer acceptance of mainstreamed learning disabled children. Learning Disability Quarterly, 9, 23–32.

Heavey, C. L., Adelman, H. S., Nelson, P., & Smith, D. C. (1989). Learning problems, anger, perceived control, and misbehavior. Journal of Learning Disabilities, 22, 46–50.

Heshusius, L. (1989). The Newtonian mechanistic paradigm, special education, and contours of alternatives: An overview. Journal of Learning Disabilities, 22, 403–415.

Heshusius, L. (1991). Future perspectives. In D. K. Reid, W. P. Hresko, & L. Swanson (Eds.), A cognitive approach to learning disabilities (pp. 431–467). Austin, TX: PRO-ED.

Hresko, W. P., & Parmar, R. S. (1991a). Educational trends in learning disabilities. In D. K. Reid, W. P. Hresko, & L. Swanson (Eds.), A cognitive approach to learning disabilities (pp. 45–68). Austin, TX: PRO-ED.

Hresko, W. P., & Parmar, R. S. (1991b). The educational perspective. In D. K. Reid, W. P. Hresko, & L. Swanson (Eds.), A cognitive approach to learning disabilities (pp. 3–44). Austin, TX: PRO-ED.

Humphreys, P., Kaufman, W. E., & Galaburda, A. M. (1990). Developmental dyslexia in women: Neuropathological findings in three patients. Annals of Neurology, 28, 727–738.

Hynd, G. W., Marshall, R., & Gonzalez, J. (1991). Learning disabilities and presumed central nervous system dysfunction. Learning Disability Quarterly, 14, 283–296.

Individuals with Disabilities Act of 1990, P.L. 101-476, (1993).

Kroemer, K. H. E. (1993, October). Locating the computer screen: How high, how far? Ergonomics and Design, pp. 7–8.

Larsen, S. (1978). Learning disabilities and the professional educator. Learning Disability Quarterly, 1, 5–12.

Lenz, B. K., & Deshler, D. D. (1994). Ethical issues related to translating research in learning disabilities into practice. In S. Vaughn & C. Bos (Eds.), Research issues in learning disabilities: Theory, methodology, assessment, and ethics (pp. 329–347). New York: Springer–Verlag.

Lewis, R. B. (1993). Special education technology: Classroom applications. Pacific Grove, CA: Brooks/Cole.

Lewis, R. B., Dell, S. J., Lynch, E. W., Harrison, P. J., & Saba, F. (1987). Special education technology in action: Teachers speak out. San Diego, CA: San Diego State University, Department of Special Education.

London, S. J., Thomas, D. C., Bowman, J. D., Sobel, E., Cheng, T. C., & Peters, J. M. (1991). Exposure to electric and magnetic fields and risk of childhood leukemia. American Journal of Epidemiology, 9, 923–940.

Maddux, C. D., Johnson, D. L., & Willis, J. W. (1992). Educational computing. Needham Heights, MA: Allyn & Bacon.

Margalit, M. (1990). Effective technology integration for disabled children: The family perspective. New York: Springer-Verlag.

Margalit, M., & Zak, I. (1984). Anxiety and self-concept of learning disabled children. Journal of Learning Disabilities, 17, 537–539.

National Council on Disability. (1993). Study on the financing of assistive technology devices and services for individuals with disabilities: A report to the President and the Congress of the United States. Washington, DC: Author.

Okolo, C. M., Barh, C. M., & Rieth, H. J. (1993). A retrospective view of computer-based instruction. Journal of Special Education Technology, 12, 1–27.

Olson, R., Wise, B., Conners, F., Rack, J., & Fulker, D. (1989). Specific deficits in component reading and language skills: Genetic and environmental influences. Journal of Learning Disabilities, 22, 339–348.

Omura, Y., & Losco, M. (1993). Electromagnetic fields in the home environment. Acupuncture and Electro-Therapeutics Research, 18, 33–74.

The Panchatantra. (1970). Book V, "Ill-considered action" (A. W. Ryder, Trans.). Bombay: Jaico.

Pennington, B. F., Gilger, J. W., Pauls, D., Smith, S. A., Smith, S. D., & DeFries, J. C. (1991). Evidence for major gene transmission of developmental dyslexia. Journal of the American Medical Association, 266, 1527–1534.

Penso, R. A. (1991). A survey of factors associated with student computer use in resource specialist programs. Unpublished doctoral dissertation, Pepperdine University, Los Angeles.

Poplin, M. (1988a). The reductionist fallacy in learning disabilities: Replicating the past by reducing the present. Journal of Learning Disabilities, 21, 389–400.

Poplin, M. (1988b). Holistic/constructivist principle of the teaching/learning process: Implications for the field of learning disabilities. Journal of Learning Disabilities, 21, 401–416.

Poplin, M. (1995). The dialectic nature of technology and holism: The use of technology for the liberation of the learning disabled. Learning Disability Quarterly, 18, 129–140.

Raskind, M. H. (1993). Assistive technology and adults with learning disabilities: A blueprint for exploration and advancement. Learning Disability Quarterly, 16, 185–198.

Raskind, M. H. (1994). Assistive technology for adults with learning disabilities: A rationale for use. In P. J. Gerber & H. B. Reiff (Eds.), Learning disabilities in adulthood: Persisting problems and evolving issues. Stonem, MA: Andover Medical.

Raskind, M. H., & Higgins, E. (1995). The effects of speech synthesis on the proofreading efficiency of postsecondary students with learning disabilities. Learning Disability Quarterly, 18, 141–158.

Raskind, M. H., & Scott, N. (1993). Technology for postsecondary students with learning disabilities. In S. A. Vogel & P. Adelman (Eds.), Success for postsecondary students with learning disabilities (pp. 240–279). New York: Springer-Verlag.

Rehabilitation Act of 1973, P.L. 92-112, 29 U.S.C. 794 (1980).

Reid, D. K., & Hresko, W. P. (1981). A cognitive approach to learning disabilities. Austin, TX: PRO-ED.

Russell, S. J., Corwin, R., Mokros, J. R., & Kapisovsky, P. M. (1989). Beyond drill and practice: Expanding the computer mainstream. Reston, VA: The Council for Exceptional Children.

Ryder, A. W. (1970). Ill-considered action. In Panchatantra (Book 5). Bombay: Jaico Publishing House. (Translated from the Sanskrit)

Schmaus, D. C. (1990). The risk of carpal tunnel syndrome with computer use. AORN Journal, 52, 383–384.

Sheedy, J. E. (1992). Vision problems at video display terminals: A survey of optometrists. Journal of the American Optometric Association, 63, 687–692.

Smith, D. S. (1987, February). My struggles and triumphs: Dyslexia or "plus-lexia"? Paper presented at the California State University of Northridge Third Annual Conference on the Learning Disabled Adult, Northridge, CA.

Smith, S. D., & Pennington, B. F. (1987). Genetic influences. In K. A. Kavale, S. R. Forness, & M. Bender (Eds.), Handbook of learning disabilities (Vol. 1, pp. 49–75). Boston: Little, Brown.

Stone, W. L., & La Greca, A. M. (1990). The social status of children with learning disabilities: A reexamination. Journal of Learning Disabilities, 23, 32–37.

Sutter, E. (1988). Communication aid utilizing brain responses. In H. J. Murphy (Ed.), Proceedings of the Third Annual Conference on Computer Technology/Special Education/Rehabilitation, 3, 487–498.

Swanson, M. E., & Bray, N. M. (1991). Learning disabilities: The medical view. In D. K. Reid, W. P. Hresko, & L. Swanson (Eds.), A cognitive approach to learning disabilities (pp. 69–102). Austin, TX: PRO-ED.

Technology-Related Assistance for Individuals with Disabilities Act of 1988, P.L. 100-47, 29 U.S.C. 2201, 2202 (1988).

Tindall, L. W., Gugerty, J. J., Heffron, T. J., & Godar, P. G. (1988). Replicating jobs in business and industry for persons with disabilities (Vol. 3). Madison: University of Wisconsin, Vocational Studies Center, School of Education.

Torgesen, J. K., & Barker, T. A. (1995). Computers as aids in the prevention and remediation of reading disabilities. Learning Disability Quarterly, 18, 76–87.

U.S. Congress, Office of Technology Assessment. (1988). Power on! New tools for teaching and learning (OTA-SET-379). Washington, DC: U.S. Government Printing Office.

Vaughn, S., & Lyon, G. R. (1994). Ethical considerations when conducting research with students with learning disabilities. In S. Vaughn & C. Bos (Eds.), Research issues in learning disabilities: Theory, methodology, assessment, and ethics (pp. 315–328). New York: Springer-Verlag.

West, T. C. (1991). In the mind's eye. Buffalo, NY: Prometheus Books.

Woodward, J. P., & Carnine, D. W. (1988). Antecedent knowledge and intelligent computer-assisted instruction. Journal of Learning Disabilities, 21, 131–139.

CHAPTER 7

Andrews, E. (1930). The development of imagination in the pre-school child. University of Iowa Studies in Character, 3(4), 68–74.

Armstrong, T. (1987). In their own way. Los Angeles: Jeremy P. Tarcher.

Atwell, N. (1988). A special writer at work. In T. Newkirk & N. Atwell (Eds.), Understanding writing (pp. 114–129). Portsmouth, NH: Heinemann.

Barken, J. H., & Bernal, E.M. (1991). Gifted education for bilingual and limited English proficient students. Gifted Child Quarterly, 35, 144–148.

Barron, F. (1968). Creativity and personal freedom. Princeton, NJ: Van Nostrand.

Barron, G. (1991). Putting creativity to work. In R. Sternberg (Ed.), The nature of creativity (pp. 76–98). New York: Cambridge University Press.

Baum, S., & Owen, S. (1988). High ability/learning disability students: How are they different? Gifted Child Quarterly, 32, 321–326.

Benesch, R. (1988). Ending remediation: Linking ESL and content in higher education. Alexandria, VA: Teachers of English Speakers.

Bleedom, B. B. (1988). Humor as an indicator of giftedness. Roeper Review, 4(4), 33–34.

Boodoo, G., Bradley, C., Frontera, R., Pitts, J., & Wright, L. B. (1989). A survey of procedures used for identifying gifted learning disabled children. Gifted Child Quarterly, 33, 110–114.

Coles, G. (1987). The learning mystique. New York: Fawcett Columbine.

Dearborn, G. V. (1898). A study of imagination. American Journal of Psychology, 5, 183–190.

DuCharme, C. (1990). The role of drawing in the writing processes of primary grade children. Unpublished doctoral dissertation, Claremont Graduate School, Claremont, CA.

Eisner, E. (1988). The role of discipline-based arts education in America's schools. Los Angeles: Getty Center for Education in the Arts.

Feldman, D. (1986). Nature's gambit. New York: Basic Books.

Finn, C. E. (1990). The biggest reform of all. Phi Delta Kappan, 71, 584–592.

Gardner, H. (1983). Frames of mind. New York: Basic Books.

Gardner, H. (1993). Multiple intelligences: The theory in practice. New York: Basic Books.

Gerber, M. M. (1994). Postmodernism in special education. The Journal of Special Education, 28, 368–378.

Getzels, J. W., & Jackson, P. W. (1962). Creativity and intelligence. New York: Wiley.

Goertzel, V., & Goertzel, M. G. (1962). Cradles of eminence. Boston: Little, Brown.

Guilford, J. P. (1968). Intelligence, creativity, and their educational implications. San Diego, CA: Robert R. Knapp

Harris, K. R., & Graham, S. (1994). Constructivism: Principles, paradigms, and integration. The Journal of Special Education, 28, 233–247.

Hearne, J. D., Poplin, M., Schoneman, C., & O'Shaughnessy, E. (1988). Computer aptitude: An investigation of differences among junior high students with learning disabilities and their non–learning-disabled peers. Journal of Learning Disabilities, 21, 489–492.

Heshusius, L. (1988). The arts, science, and the study of exceptionality. Exceptional Children, 55, 60–65.

Jellen, H. G., & Urban, K. K. (1988). Assessing creative potential worldwide: The first cross-cultural application of the Test for Creative Thinking–Drawing Production. The Creative Child and Adult Quarterly, 14, 151–157.

Kerchner, L. B., & Kistinger, B. (1984). Language processing/word processing: Written expression, computers and learning disabled students. Learning Disability Quarterly, 7, 329–335.

Koestler, A. (1964). The art of creation. New York: Macmillan.

Krantz, B. (1982). Krantz talent identification instrument. Brooklyn, NY: Wiley.

Lazear, D. G. (1992). Teaching for multiple intelligences. Phi Delta Kappa Fastback, No. 342.

Leland, C. H., & Harste, J. C. (1994). Multiple ways of knowing: Curriculum in a new key. Language Arts, 71, 337–345.

McCloy, W., & Meier, N. C. (1931). Recreative imagination. Psychological Monographs, 51(5), 108–116.

Meltzer, L., & Reid, D. K. (1994). New directions in the assessment of students with special needs: The shift toward a constructivist perspective. The Journal of Special Education, 28, 338–355.

Minner, S. (1990). Teacher evaluations of case descriptions of LD gifted children. Gifted Child Quarterly, 34, 37–40.

Moss, P. B. (1989). An autobiography: P. Buckley Moss, the people's artist. Waynesboro, VA: Shenandoah Heritage.

Owen, S. V., & Baum, S. M. (1985). Development of an academic self-efficacy scale for upper elementary school children. Unpublished manuscript, University of Connecticut, Storrs.

Piaget, J. (1926). Judgment and reasoning in the child (M. Warden, Trans.). New York: Harcourt, Brace and World.

Poplin, M. S. (1984). Toward a holistic view of persons with learning disabilities. Learning Disability Quarterly, 7, 290–294.

Poplin, M. S. (1988a). Holistic/constructivist principles of the teaching and learning process: Implications for the field of learning disabilities. Journal of Learning Disabilities, 21, 401–416.

Poplin, M. S. (1988b). The reductionistic fallacy in learning disabilities: Replicating the past by reducing the present. Journal of Learning Disabilities, 21, 389–400.

Poplin, M. S. (1993). Multiple intelligences and the learning disabled. Unpublished manuscript, The Claremont Graduate School, Claremont, CA.

Poplin, M. S., Drew, D. E., & Gable, R. (1984). Computer aptitude, literacy, and interest profile. Austin, TX: PRO-ED.

Poplin, M. S., Gray, R. A., Larsen, S., Banikowski, A., & Mehring, T. (1980). A comparison of written expression abilities in learning disabled and non–learning disabled students at three grade levels. Learning Disability Quarterly, 3, 46–53.

Quinn, D. (1984). Perspective from the other side: A message of hope for learning disability teachers and students. Learning Disability Quarterly, 7, 295–298.

Ramirez, M., & Castaneda, A. (1974). Cultural democracy, bicognitive development and education. New York: Academy Press.

Rimm, S. (1976). GIFT: Group inventory for finding creative talent. Watertown, WI: Educational Assessment Service.

Simpson, R. M. (1922). Creative imagination. American Journal of Psychology, 33, 234–235.

Sleeter, C. E. (1986). Learning disabilities: The social construction of a special education category. Exceptional Children, 53, 46–54.

Sooho, S. (1991). School renewal: Taking responsibility for providing an education of value. In J. I. Goodlad & P. Keating (Eds.), Access to knowledge (pp. 205–221). New York: College Entrance Examination Board.

Sternberg, R. J. (1988). The triarchic mind: A new theory of human intelligence. New York: Viking.

Stolowitz, M. A. (1995). How to achieve academic and creative success in spite of the inflexible, unresponsive higher education system. Journal of Learning Disabilities, 28, 4–6.

Stone, S. (1992). Divergent thinking: Nontraditional or creative talents of monolingual, bilingual, and special education students in an elementary school. Unpublished doctoral dissertation, Claremont Graduate School/San Diego State University, Claremont, CA.

Stone, S., Poplin, M. S., Johnson, J., & Ellis, O. (1993). Non-traditional talents of the learning disabled: Music and art. Unpublished manuscript, Claremont Graduate School, Claremont, CA.

Stone, S., Poplin, M. S., Johnson, J., & Simpson, O. (1992). Non-traditional talents of the learning disabled: Divergent thinking and feeling. Unpublished manuscript, Claremont Graduate School, Claremont, CA.

Tarver, S. G., Ellsworth, P. S., & Rounds, D. J. (1980). Figural and verbal creativity in learning disabled and non-learning-disabled children. Learning Disability Quarterly, 3, 11–18.

Torrance, E. P. (1966). Torrance tests of creative thinking. Lexington, MA: Personnel Press.

Torrance, E. P. (1967). The creative person and the ideal pupil. In L. Nelson & B. Psaltis (Eds.), Fostering creativity (pp. 131–154). New York: Selected Academic Readings.

Torrance, E. P. (1991). The nature of creativity as manifest in its testing. In R. Sternberg (Ed.), The nature of creativity (pp. 43–75). New York: Cambridge University Press.

Weinstein, J. A. (1994). Growing up learning disabled. Journal of Learning Disabilities, 27, 142–143.

Welch, L. (1946). Recombination of ideas in creative thinking. Journal of Applied Psychology, 30, 638–643.

Welsh, G. S. (1975). Creativity and intelligence: A personality approach. Chapel Hill: University of North Carolina.

Williams, F. (1980a). Test of divergent thinking. Buffalo, NY: D.O.K.

Williams, F. (1980b). Test of divergent feeling. Buffalo, NY: D.O.K.

Ziv, A. (1988). Using humor to develop creative thinking. Journal of Children in Contemporary Society, 20, 99–116.

CHAPTER 8

Aaron, P. G., Phillips, S., & Larsen, S., (1988). Specific learning disability in historically famous persons. Journal of Learning Disabilities, 21, 523–545.

Abraham, R. H., & Shaw, C. D. (1984). Dynamics—The geometry of behavior, Part I: Periodic behavior. Santa Cruz, CA: Aerial Press.

Agassi, J. (1971). Faraday as a natural philosopher. Chicago: University of Chicago Press.

Bogen, J. E., & Bogen, G. M. (1969). The other side of the brain III: The corpus callosum and creativity. Bulletin of the Los Angeles Neurological Societies, 34, 191–220.

Brown J. (1991). Images for insight: From the research lab to the classroom. Journal of Computing in Higher Education 3, 104–125.

Campbell, L., & Garnett, W. (1882). The life of James Clerk Maxwell. London: Macmillan.

Cook, T. A.(1979). Curves of life. New York: Dover.

DeFanti, T. A., Brown, M. D., & McCormick, B. H. (1989). Visualization: Expanding scientific and engineering research opportunities. Computer, 22, 12–25.

Einstein, A. (1987). The collected papers of Albert Einstein, Volume 1, The early years: 1879–1902 (J. Stachel, Ed., English translation companion volumes by Anna Beck). Princeton, NJ: Princeton University Press.

Everitt, C. W. F. (1983). Maxwell's scientific creativity. In R. Aris, R. H. Davis, & H. Stuewer (Eds.), Springs of scientific creativity: Essays on founders of modern science. Minneapolis: University of Minnesota Press.

Feynman, R. P., Leighton, R. B., & Sands, M. (1963). The Feynman lectures on physics. Reading, MA: Addison-Wesley.

Forgan, S. (1985). Faraday—From servant to savant. In Faraday rediscovered. New York: Stockton Press.

Frey, W. (1990). Schools miss out on dyslexic engineers. IEEE Spectrum, December, 6.

Gardner, H. (1983). Frames of mind: The theory of multiple intelligences. New York: Basic Books.

Gardner, H. (1987). The theory of multiple intelligences. Annals of Dyslexia, 37, 19–35.

Geschwind, N., & Behan, P. (1982). Left-handedness: Association with immune disease, migraine, and developmental learning disorder. Proceedings of the National Academy of Sciences, 79, 5097–5100.

Geschwind, N., & Galaburda, A. (1985). Cerebral lateralization, biological mechanisms, associations, and pathology: A hypothesis and a program for research, Parts I–III. Archives of Neurology, 42, 428–459, 521–552, 634–654.

Gleick, J. (1987). Chaos: Making a new science. New York: Viking Press.

Götestam, K. O. (1990). Lefthandedness among students of architecture and music. Perceptual and Motor Skills, 70, 1323–1327.

Guyer, B. P. (1988). Dyslexic doctors: A resource in need of discovery. Southern Medical Journal, 81, 1151–1154.

Hadamard, J. (1954). The psychology of invention in the mathematical field. New York: Dover.

Hoffmann, B., & Dukas, H. (1972). Albert Einstein: Creator and rebel. New York: New American Library.

Holton, G. (1972). On trying to understand scientific genius. The American Scholar, 41, 95–110.

Jaffe, C., & Lynch, P. J. (1989). Hypermedia for education in the life sciences. Academic Computing, September, 10–57.

Jolls, K. R. (1989). Understanding thermodynamics through interactive computer graphics. Chemical Engineering Progress, February, 64–69.

Jolls, K. R., & Coy, D. C. (1990). The art of thermodynamics. IRIS Universe: The Magazine of Visual Processing, 12, 31–36.

Jones, B. (1870). The life and letters of Faraday. Philadelphia: Lippincott.

Knaus, W. A., Wagner, D., & Lynn, J. (1991). Short term mortality predictions for critically ill hospitalized adults: Science and ethics. Science, 254, 389–393.

Kolata, G. (1982). Computer graphics comes to statistics. Science, 217, 919–920.

Miller, A. I. (1986). Imagery in scientific thought: Creating 20th-century physics. Cambridge, MA: MIT Press.

Moravec, H. (1989). Human culture: A genetic takeover underway. In Artificial life: Proceedings of an interdisciplinary workshop on the synthesis and simulation of living systems. Redwood City, CA: Addison-Wesley.

Orton, S. T. (1966). "Word blindness" in school children and other papers on strephosymbolia (specific language disability—dyslexia) 1925–1946 (Compiled by June Lynday Orton). Pomfret, CT: Orton Society.

Pearson, E. S. (1966). Some aspects of the geometry of statistics: The use of visual presentation in understanding the theory and application of mathematical statistics. In The selected papers of E. S. Pearson. Los Angeles: University of California Press.

Pestalozzi, J. H. (1973). How Gertrude teaches her children. (L. E. Holland & F. C. Turner, Trans.). New York: Garden. (Reprint of the 1894 English translation from the 1801 German original)

Rheingold, H. (1991). Virtual reality. New York: Summit.

Richards, E. (1989, September 24). The data deluge: Exotic electronic systems may hold key to future success. The Washington Post, p. H1.

Ritchie-Calder, P. (1970). Leonardo and the age of the eye. New York: Simon and Schuster.

Rival, I. (1987). Picture puzzling: Mathematicians are rediscovering the power of pictorial reasoning. The Sciences, January/February, 40–46.

Santillana, G. D. (1966). Man without letters. In M. Philipson (Ed.), Leonardo da Vinci: Aspects of the Renaissance genius. New York: George Braziller.

Satori, G. (1987). Leonardo Da Vinci, Omo Sanza Lettere: A case of surface dysgraphia? Cognitive Neuropsychology, 4, 1–10.

Schultz, B. (1988). Scientific visualization: Transforming numbers into computer pictures. Computer Pictures, 6, 11–16.

Schuster, A. (1910). History of the Cavendish laboratory. London: Macmillan.

Steen, L. A. (1987). Mathematics Education: A predictor of scientific competitiveness. Science, 237, 251–302.

Steen, L. A. (1988). The science of patterns. Science, 240, 611–616.

Thompson, L. (1969). Language disabilities in men of eminence. Bulletin of the Orton Society, 19, 113–120.

Tolstoy, I. (1981). James Clerk Maxwell: A biography. Chicago: University of Chicago Press.

Tyndall, J. (1870). Faraday as a discoverer. London: Longmans, Green.

Weiner, N. (1961). Cybernetics: Control and communication in the animal and in the machine. Cambridge, MA: MIT Press.

West, T. G. (1991). In the mind's eye: Visual thinkers, gifted people with learning difficulties, computer images, and the ironies of creativity. Buffalo, NY: Prometheus Books.

Wolkomir, R. (1989). NASA's data deluge. Air & Space, 4, 78–82.

Zimmermann, W., & Cunningham, S. (Eds.). (1990). Visualization in teaching and learning mathematics. Washington, DC: The Mathematical Association of America.

CHAPTER 9

Education for All Handicapped Children Act of 1975, 20 U.S.C. § 1400 et seq.

Marcuse, H. (1968). One-dimensional man. Boston: Beacon.

Piaget, J. (1954/1986). The construction of reality in the child. New York: Ballantine.

Separate and unequal. (1993, December 13). U.S. News and World Report.

CHAPTER 10

Baca, L. M., & Cervantes, H. T. (1989). The bilingual special education interface. Columbus, OH: Merrill.

Bartolome, L. I. (1994). Beyond the methods fetish: Toward a humanizing pedagogy. Harvard Educational Review, 64, 173–194.

California Administrative Code (1981), Title V, Article 3.1, Section 3030.

California Education Code (1980), Part 30, Special Educational Programs, Article 2.5.

Darder, A. (1991). Culture and power in the classroom: A critical foundation for bicultural education. New York: Bergin & Garvey.

Delpit, L. D. (1990). The silenced dialogue: Power and pedagogy in educating other people's children. In N. M. Hidalgo, C. L. McDowell, & E. V. Siddle (Eds.), Facing racism in education (pp. 84–102). Cambridge, MA: Harvard Educational Review.

Figueroa, R. A. (1989). Psychological testing of linguistic-minority students: Knowledge gaps and regulations. Exceptional Children, 56, 145–152.

Freire, P. (1970). Pedagogy of the oppressed. New York: Seabury.

Freire, P., & Macedo, D. (1987). Literacy: Reading the word and the world. Hadley, MA: Bergin & Garvey.

Giroux, H. (1992). Border crossings: Cultural workers and the politics of education. New York: Routledge.

Lerner, J. W., Cousin, P. T., & Richeck, M. (1992). Critical issues in learning disabilities. Learning Disabilities: Research and Practice, 7, 226–230.

Poplin, M. (1988a). The reductionist fallacy in learning disabilities: Replicating the past by reducing the present. Journal of Learning Disabilities, 21, 389–400.

Poplin, M. (1988b). Holistic/constructivist principles of the teaching/learning process: Implications for the field of learning disabilities. Journal of Learning Disabilities, 21, 401–416.

Ramirez, M., & Castaneda, A. (1974). Cultural democracy, bicognitive development, and education. New York: Academic Press.

Rueda, R. (1989). Defining mild disabilities with language-minority students. Exceptional Children, 56, 121–128.

Ruiz, N. (1989). An optimal learning environment for Rosemary. Exceptional Children, 56, 130–144.

Shor, I. (1980). Critical teaching and everyday life. Chicago, IL: University of Chicago.
Shor, I. (1987). Freire for the classroom. Portsmouth, NH: Heinemann.
U.S. Bureau of the Census. (1992). The Hispanic population in the United States. Washington, DC: U.S. Government Printing Office.

CHAPTER 11

Applebee, A. N. (1978). The child's concept of story: Ages two to seventeen. Chicago: University of Chicago Press.

Applebee, A., & Langer, J. A. (1983). Instructional scaffolding: Reading and writing as natural language activities. Language Arts, 60, 168–175.

Baca, L., & Cervantes, H. (1984). The bilingual special education interface. St. Louis, MO: Times Mirror/Mosby College Publishing.

Brown, R. G., & Yule, J. (1983). Discourse analysis. Cambridge, MA: Cambridge University Press.

Cazden, C. B. (1988). Classroom discourse: The language of teaching and learning. Portsmouth, NH: Heinemann.

Chasty, H. (1985). What is dyslexia? A developmental language perspective. In M. Snowling (Ed.), Children's written language difficulties (pp. 11–27). Philadelphia, PA: NFER-NELSON.

Cook-Gumperz, J., & Gumperz, J. J. (1982). Communicative competence in educational perspective. In L. C. Wilkinson (Ed.), Communicating in the classroom (pp. 13–24). New York: Academic Press.

Cousin, P., Weekley, T., & Gerard, J. (1993). The functional uses of language and literacy by students with severe language and learning problems. Language Arts, 70, 548–556.

Donahue, M. L. (1983). Learning disabled children as conversational partners. Topics in Language Disorders, 4, 15–27.

Donahue, M. (1985). Communicative style in learning disabled children: Some implications for classroom discourse. In D. N. Ripich & F. M. Spinelli (Eds.), School discourse problems (pp. 97–124). San Diego, CA: College-Hill.

Donahue, M. L., Pearl, R., & Bryan, T. (1980). Learning disabled children's conversational competence: Response to inadequate messages. Applied Psycholinguistics, 1, 387–403.

Donahue, M. L., & Prescott, B. (1984, May). Learning disabled children's conversational participating in dispute episodes with peers. Paper presented at the Forum for Language and Culture, Stanford University, Palo Alto, CA.

Echevarría, J., & McDonough, R. (1993). Instructional conversations in special education settings: Issues and accommodations (Education Practice Report 7). Santa Cruz: University of California at Santa Cruz, National Center for Research on Cultural Diversity and Second Language Learning.

Figueroa, R. A. (1986). Diana revisited: Psychological testing policies and practices with Hispanic children in 5 selected school districts in California. Bilingual Education Paper Series 7(7). Los Angeles, CA: Evaluation, Dissemination and Assessment Center, California State University.

Figueroa, R. A. (1990). Assessment of linguistic minority group children. In C. R. Reynolds & R. W. Kamphaus (Eds.), Handbook of psychological and educational assessment of children: Intelligence and achievement. New York: Guilford.

Figueroa, R. A., & Ruiz, N. T. (1993). Bilingual pupils and special education: A reconceptualization. In R. C. Eaves & P. J. McLaughlin (Eds.), Recent advances in special education and rehabilitation (pp. 73–87). Stoneham, MA: Butterworth-Heinemann.

Figueroa, R. A., Ruiz, N. T., & García, E. (1994). The optimal learning environment (OLE) research project in the Los Angeles Unified School District: Report No. 1, reading outcome data. Santa Cruz: California Research Institute on Special Education and Cultural Diversity, University of California.

Figueroa, R. A., Ruiz, N. T., & Rueda, R. (1990). Special education research project for learning handicapped Hispanic pupils: The OLE model (federal proposal). Sacramento: California State Department of Education.

Flores, B., Rueda, R., & Porter, B. (1986). Examining assumptions and instructional practices related to the acquisition of literacy with bilingual special education students. In A. Willig & H. Greenberg (Eds.), Bilingualism and learning disabilities (pp. 149–165). New York: American Library.

Gleason, J. J. (1989). Special education in context: An ethnographic study of persons with developmental disabilities. New York: Cambridge University Press.

Green, J. L. (1983). Research on teaching as a linguistic process: A state of the art. Review of Research in Education, 10, 151–252. Washington, DC: American Educational Research Association.

Green, J., & Wallat, C. (Eds.). (1981). Ethnography and language in educational settings. Norwood, NJ: Ablex.

Heath, S. B. (1983). Ways with words. Cambridge: Cambridge University Press.

Heath, S. B. (1986). Sociocultural contexts of language development. In Beyond language (pp. 143–186). Los Angeles, CA: Evaluation, Dissemination and Assessment Center, California State University.

Hood, L. R., McDermott, R., & Cole, M. (1981). Let's try to make it a good day: Some not so simple ways. Discourse Processes, 3, 155–168.

Hymes, D. (1964). Introduction: Toward ethnographies of communication. American Anthropologist, 66(6), 1–34.

Kirk, S. A. (1972). Educating exceptional children. Boston: Houghton Mifflin.

Legarreta, D. M. (1979). The effects of program models on language acquisition by Spanish-speaking children. TESOL Quarterly, 13, 521–534.

Lutz, F. W. (1981). Ethnography—The wholistic approach to understanding schooling. In J. L. Green & C. Wallat (Eds.), Ethnography and language in educational settings (pp. 51–63). Norwood, NJ: Ablex.

Maldonado-Colón, E. (1984, May). Serving the limited- and non-limited English speakers in programs for the speech/language handicapped: Implications for personnel. Paper presented at the Workshop for Communicative Disorders and Language Proficiency, Los Angeles.

Mehan, H. (1979). Learning lessons: Social organization in the classroom. Cambridge, MA: Harvard University Press.

Mehan, H., Hertweck, H., & Meihls, J. (1986). Handicapping the handicapped. Palo Alto, CA: Stanford University Press.

Mercer, J. (1973). Labeling the mentally retarded. Berkeley: University of California Press.

Neal, S. F. (1993). Students will string five, one-inch beads in one minute or less, or why assessment for special programs must change. Language Arts, 70, 602–610.

Ortiz, A. A., Wilkinson, C. Y., Robertson-Courtney, P., & Kushner, M. I. (1991). AIM for the BESt: Assessment and intervention model for the bilingual exceptional student. Austin: The University of Texas at Austin.

Ortiz, A. A., & Yates, J. R. (1983). Incidence of exceptionality among Hispanics: Implications for manpower planning. NABE Journal, 7, 41–53.

Poplin, M. S. (1988a). The reductionist fallacy in learning disabilities: Replicating the past by reducing the present. Journal of Learning Disabilities, 21, 389–400.

Poplin, M. S. (1988b). Holistic/constructivist principles of the teaching/learning process: Implications for the field of learning disabilities. Journal of Learning Disabilities, 21, 401–416.

Rueda, R. (1989). Defining mild disabilities with language-minority students. Exceptional Children, 56, 121–128.

Rueda, R., & Mehan, H. (1986). Metacognition and passing: Strategic interaction in the lives of students with learning disabilities. Anthropology and Education Quarterly, 17, 145–165.

Ruiz, N. T. (1988). Language for learning in a bilingual special education classroom. Unpublished doctoral dissertation, Stanford University.

Ruiz, N. T. (1989). An optimal learning environment for Rosemary. Exceptional Children, 56, 130–144.

Ruiz, N. T., & Figueroa, R. A. (in press). Latino students in learning handicapped classrooms: The Optimal Learning Environment (OLE) Project. Education and Urban Society.

Ruiz, N. T., Figueroa, R. A., Rueda, R., & Beaumont, C. (1992). History and status of bilingual special education for Hispanic handicapped students. In R. V. Padilla & A. H. Benavides (Eds.), Critical perspectives on bilingual education research (pp. 349–380). Tempe, AZ: Bilingual Press.

Saville-Troike, M. (1982). The ethnography of communication. Baltimore: University Park Press.

Scala, M. A. (1993). What whole language in the mainstream means for children with learning disabilities. Reading Teacher, 47, 222–229.

Silliman, E. (1984). Interactional competencies in the instructional context: The role of teaching discourse in classrooms. In G. P. Wallach & K. G. Butler (Eds.), Language leaning disabilities in school-age children (pp. 288–317). Baltimore: William and Wilkins.

Smilansky, S. (1968). The effects of sociodramatic play on disadvantaged preschool children. New York: Wiley.

Spradley, J. P. (1980). Participant observation. New York: Holt, Rinehart, and Winston.

Taylor, D. (1991). Learning denied. Portsmouth, NH: Heinemann.

Taylor, D. (1993). From the child's point of view. Portsmouth, NH: Heinemann.

Valdés, G., & Figueroa, R. A. (1994). The nature of bilingualism and the nature of testing. Norwood, NJ: Ablex.

Viera, D. R. (1986). Remediating reading problems in a Hispanic learning disabled child from a psycholinguistic perspective: A case study. In A. C. Willig & H. F. Greenberg (Eds.), Bilingualism and learning disabilities (pp. 81–92). New York: American Library.

Wallach, G. P., & Liebergott, J. W. (1984). Who shall be called "learning disabled": Some new direction. In G. P. Wallach & K. G. Butler (Eds.), Language learning disabilities in school-age children (pp. 1–14). Baltimore: Williams & Wilkins.

Wilkinson, L. C. (1982). Introduction: A sociolinguistic approach to communicating in the classroom. In L. C. Wilkinson (Ed.), Communicating in the classroom (pp. 3–11). New York: Academic Press.

Willig, A. C., & Swedo, J. (1987, April). Improving teaching strategies for exceptional Hispanic limited English proficient students: An exploratory study of task engagement and teaching strategies. Paper presented at the annual meeting of the American Educational Research Association, Washington, DC.

CHAPTER 12

Au, K. H. (1993). Literacy instruction in multicultural settings. Fort Worth, TX: Harcourt Brace Jovanovich.

Beaumont, C. (1990). An analysis of IEP's in the OLE classrooms: Baseline phase. Unpublished manuscript, University of California at Davis, Division of Education, The OLE Project.

Cambourne, B., & Turbill, J. (1987). Coping with chaos. Portsmouth, NH: Heinemann.

Cazden, C. (1988). Classroom discourse: The language of teaching and learning. Portsmouth, NH: Heinemann.

Cruttendon, A. (1986). Intonation. New York: Cambridge University Press.

Dickinson, D. (1985). Creating and using formal occasions in the classroom. Anthropology and Education Quarterly, 16, 47–62.

Echevarria, J., & McDonough, R. (1993). Instructional conversations in special education settings: Issues and accommodations (Educational Practice Report No. 7). Santa Cruz: The National Center for Research on Cultural Diversity and Second Language Learning, University of California.

Ervin-Tripp, S. (1972). On sociolinguistic rules: Alternation and co-occurrence. In J. J. Gumperz & D. Hymes (Eds.), Directions in sociolinguistics (pp. 213–250). New York: Holt, Rinehart & Winston.

Figueroa, R. A. (1990). Psychological assessment of linguistic minority group children. In C. R. Reynolds & R. W. Kamphaus (Eds.), Handbook of psychological and educational assessment of children: Vol. 1. Intelligence and achievement. New York: Guilford.

Figueroa, R. A. (1993, April). The Optimal Learning Environment Research Project. Paper presented at the annual conference of the Council for Exceptional Children, San Antonio, TX.

Flores, B., Rueda, R., & Porter, B. (1986). Examining assumptions and instructional practices related to the acquisition of literacy with bilingual special education students. In A. C. Willig & H. F. Greenburg (Eds.), Bilingualism and learning disabilities (pp. 149–165). New York: American Library.

Freeman, Y. S., & Freeman, D. E. (1992). Whole language for second language learners. Portsmouth, NH: Heinemann.

Gallimore, R., & Tharp, R. (1988). Rousing minds to life: Teaching, learning, and schooling in social contexts. New York: Cambridge University Press.

Gleason, J. J. (1989). Special education in context: An ethnographic study of persons with developmental disabilities. New York: Cambridge University Press.

Goldman, S. R., & Rueda, R. (1988). Developing writing skills in bilingual exceptional children. Exceptional Children, 54, 543–551.

Gumperz, J. (1982). Discourse strategies. New York: Cambridge University Press.

Heath, S. B. (1982). Questioning at home and school: A comparative study. In G. Spindler (Ed.), Doing the ethnography of schooling. New York: Holt, Rinehart & Winston.

Heath, S. B. (1983). Ways with words. New York: Cambridge University Press.

Heath, S. B. (1985). Narrative play in second language learning. In L. Galda & A. D. Pelligrini (Eds.), Play, language and stories. Norwood, NJ: Ablex.

Heath, S. B. (1986). Sociocultural contexts of language development. In Beyond language (pp. 143–186). Los Angeles, CA: Evaluation, Dissemination and Assessment Center, California State University.

Hymes, D. (1964). Introduction: Toward ethnographies of communication. American Anthropologist, 66(6), 1–34.

Irvine, J. T. (1979). Formality and informality in communicative events. American Anthropologist, 81, 773–790.

Mehan, H. (1979). Learning lessons: Social organization in the classroom. Cambridge, MA: Harvard University Press.

Mehan, H., Hertweck, H., & Meihls, J. (1986). Handicapping the handicapped. Palo Alto, CA: Stanford University Press.

Pellegrini, A. D. (1985). Relations between preschool children's symbolic play and literate behavior. In L. Galda & A. Pellegrini (Eds.), Play, language and stories (pp. 79–97). Norwood, NJ: Ablex.

Pellegrini, A. D., DeStefano, J. S., & Thompson, D. L. (1983). Saying what you mean: Using play to teach "literate language." Language Arts, 60, 380–384.

Poplin, M. S. (1988a). The reductionist fallacy in learning disabilities: Replicating the past by reducing the present. Journal of Learning Disabilities, 21, 389–400.

Poplin, M. S. (1988b). Holistic/constructivist principles of the teaching/learning process: Implications for the field of learning disabilities. Journal of Learning Disabilities, 21, 401–416.

Rueda, R., Betts, B., & Hami, A. (1990). A descriptive analysis of work products in OLE classroom sites: Baseline phase. Unpublished manuscript, University of California at Davis, Division of Education, The OLE Project.

Rueda, R., Figueroa, R. A., & Ruiz, N. T. (1990, April). An ethnographic analysis of instructional events for Mexican American learning handicapped students. Paper presented at the annual meeting of the American Educational Research Association, Boston.

Rueda, R., & Mehan, H. (1986). Metacognition and passing: Strategic interaction in the lives of students with learning disabilities. Anthropology and Education Quarterly, 17, 145–165.

Ruiz, N. T. (1987). The nature of bilingualism: Implications for special education. Sacramento, CA: Resources in Special Education.

Ruiz, N. T. (1988). Language for learning in a bilingual special education classroom. Unpublished doctoral dissertation, Stanford University.

Ruiz, N. T. (1990). An analysis of instructional events in the OLE classrooms: Baseline phase. Unpublished manuscript, University of California at Davis, Division of Education, The OLE Project.

Ruiz, N. T., Figueroa, R. A., Rueda, R., & Beaumont, C. (1992). History and status of bilingual special education for Hispanic handicapped students. In R. V. Padilla & A. H. Benavides (Eds.), Critical perspectives on bilingual education research (pp. 349–380). Tempe, AZ: Bilingual Press.

Ruiz, N. T., García, E., & Figueroa, R. A. (1995). The OLE curriculum guide. Sacramento, CA: Resources in Special Education.

Sachs, J., Goldman, J., & Chaille, C. (1985). Narratives in preschoolers' sociodramatic play: The role of knowledge and communicative competence. In L. Galda & A. D. Pellegrini (Eds.), Play, language and stories (pp. 45–61). Norwood, NJ: Ablex.

Saravia-Shore, M., & Arvizu, S. F. (Eds.). (1992). Cross-cultural literacy: Ethnographies of communication in multiethnic classrooms (Vol. 3). New York: Garland.

Saville-Troike, M. (1982). The ethnography of communication. Baltimore: University Park Press.

Stern, V. (1984). The symbolic play of lower-class and middle-class children: Mixed messages from the literature. In L. G. Katz (Ed.), Current topics in early childhood education (Vol. 4, pp. 119–141). Norwood, NJ: Ablex.

Taylor, D. (1991). Learning denied. Portsmouth, NH: Heinemann.

Taylor, D. (1993). From the child's point of view. Portsmouth, NH: Heinemann.

Trueba, H. T. (1987, April). Cultural differences or learning handicaps? Towards an understanding of adjustment processes. In Schooling language minority youth: Volume III, Proceedings of the University of California Linguistic Minority Research Project Conference (pp. 45–79). Los Angeles: University of California.

U.S. Department of Education. (1993). Descriptive study of services to limited English proficient students. Washington, DC: Office of Bilingual and Language Minority Affairs.

Viera, D. R. (1986). Remediating reading problems in a Hispanic learning disabled child from a psycholinguistic perspective: A case study. In A. C. Willig & H. F. Greenburg (Eds.), Bilingualism and learning disabilities (pp. 81–92). New York: American Library.

Volk, D. (1992). Communicative competence in a bilingual early childhood classroom. In M. Saravia-Shore & S. F. Arvizu (Eds.), Cross-cultural literacy: Ethnographies of communication in multi-ethnic classrooms (pp. 367–389). New York: Garland.

Willig, A. C., & Swedo, J. (1987). Improving teaching strategies for exceptional Hispanic limited English proficient students: An exploratory study of task engagement and teaching strategies. Paper presented at the annual meeting of the American Educational Research Association, Washington, DC.

CHAPTER 13

Allington, R. L., & McGill-Franzen, A. (1989). School response to reading failure: Instruction for Chapter I and special education students in grades two, four, and eight. Elementary School Journal, 89, 529–542.

Bigelow, B. J., & LaGaipa, J. J. (1980). The development of friendship values and choices. In H. C. Foot, A. J. Chapman, & J. R. Smith (Eds.), Friendship and social relations in children (pp. 15–44). New York: Wiley.

Cosgrove, S. (1982). Morgan and Yew. Los Angeles: Price-Stern-Sloan.

Dimino, J., Gersten, R., Carnine, D., & Blake, G. (1990). Story grammar: An approach for promoting at-risk secondary students' comprehension of literature. Elementary School Journal, 91, 19–32.

El'konin, D. B. (1972). Toward the problem of stages in the mental development of the child. Soviet Psychology, 4, 225–251.

Englert, C. S., & Palincsar, A. S. (1991). Reconsidering instructional research in literacy from a sociocultural perspective. Learning Disabilities Research and Practice, 6, 225–229.

Englert, C. S., Raphael, T. E., & Anderson, L. M. (1988). Students' metacognitive knowledge about informational texts. Learning Disability Quarterly, 11, 18–46.

Furman, W., & Bierman, K. L. (1984). Children's conceptions of friendship: A multimethod study of developmental changes. Developmental Psychology, 20, 925–931.

Golenbock, P. (1992). Teammates. New York: Macmillan.

Graham, S., & Harris, K. (1992). Teaching writing strategies to students with learning disorders: Issues and recommendations. In L. Meltzer (Ed.), Cognitive, linguistic, and developmental perspectives on learning disorders. Boston: College-Hill.

Guerney, D., Gersten, R., Dimino, J., & Carnine, D. (1990). Story grammar: Effective literature instruction for high school students with learning disabilities. Journal of Learning Disabilities, 23, 335–343.

Hartman, D. K. (1991). The intertextual links of readers using multiple passages: A postmodern/semiotic/cognitive view of meaning making. In J. Zutell & S. McCormick (Eds.), Learner factors/teacher factors: Issues in literacy research and instruction (pp. 49–66, 40th Yearbook of the National Reading Conference).

Havill, J. (1990). Jamaica tag-along. Boston: Houghton-Mifflin.

Leont'ev, A. N. (1932). Studies on the cultural development of the child. Journal of Genetic Psychology , 40, 52–83.

Leslie, L., & Caldwell, J. (1990). Qualitative reading inventory. New York: Harper-Collins.

Lipson, M. Y., Valencia, S. W., Wixson, K. K., & Peters, C. W. (1993). Integration and thematic teaching: Integration to improve teaching and learning. Language Arts, 70, 252–263.

Luria, A. R. (1976). Cognitive development: Its cultural and social foundations. Cambridge, MA: Harvard University Press.

Needels, M. C., & Knapp, M. S. (1994). Teaching writing to children who are underserved. Journal of Educational Psychology, 86, 339–349.

Norton, D. E. (1991). Through the eyes of a child. New York: Macmillan.

Perkins, D. N. (1989). Selecting fertile themes for integrated learning. In H. H. Jacobs (Ed.), Interdisciplinary curriculum: Design and implementation (pp. 27–39). Alexandria, VA: Association for Supervision and Curriculum Design.

Poplin, M. S. (1988). The reductionist fallacy in learning disabilities: Replicating the past by reducing the present. Journal of Learning Disabilities, 21, 389–400.

Resch, B. (1991). A place for everyone. Benicia, CA: Atomium Books.

Rueda, R. (1990). Assisted performance in writing instruction with learning disabled students. In L. Moll (Ed.), Vygotsky and education: Instructional implications and applications of sociohistorical psychology (pp. 403–426). Cambridge, England: Cambridge University Press.

Sadler, M. (1992). Elizabeth and Larry. New York: Simon and Schuster.

Smollar, J., & Youniss, J. (1982). Social development through friendship. In K. H. Rubin & H. S. Ross (Eds.), Peer relationships and social skills in childhood (pp. 279–298). New York: Springer-Verlag.

Steig, W. (1990). Amos and Boris. New York: Ferrar-Strauss-Giroux.

Vygotsky, L. S. (1978). Mind in society: The development of higher psychological processes. Cambridge, MA: Harvard University Press.

Williams, J. P., Brown, L. G., Silverstein, A. K., & de Cani, J. S. (in press). An instructional program in comprehension of narrative themes for adolescents with learning disabilities. Learning Disability Quarterly.

Youniss, J., & Volpe, J. (1978). A relational analysis of children's friendship. In W. Damon (Ed.), Social cognition (pp. 1–22). San Francisco: Jossey-Bass.

CHAPTER 14

Adelman, H. S., & Taylor, L. (1982). Learning disabilities in perspective. Glenview, IL: Scott, Foresman.

Altwerger, B., Edelsky, C., & Flores, B. (1987). Whole language: What's new. The Reading Teacher, 41(2), 144–154.

Anderson, V., & Roit, M. (1993). Planning and implementing collaborative strategy instruction for delayed readers in grades 6–10. Elementary School Journal, 94(2), 121–137.

Borkowski, J., Carr, M., & Pressley, M. (1987). "Spontaneous" strategy use: Perspectives from metacognitive theory. Intelligence, 11, 61–75.

Borkowski, J., Johnston, M., & Reid, M. K. (1987). Metacognition, motivation, and controlled performance. In S. J. Ceci (Ed.), Handbook of cognitive, social and neuropsychological aspects of learning disabilities (pp. 147–174). Hillsdale, NJ: Erlbaum.

Brown, A. (1978). Knowing when, where, and how to remember: A problem of metacognition. In R. Glaser (Ed.), Advances in instructional psychology (pp. 55–113). Hillsdale, NJ: Erlbaum.

Brown, A. (1980). Metacognitive development and reading. In R. J. Spiro, B. Bruce, & W. Brewer (Eds.), Theoretical issues in reading and comprehension (pp. 453–481). Hillsdale, NJ: Erlbaum.

Calkins, L. M. (1980). When children want to punctuate: Basic skills belong in context. Language Arts, 57, 567–573.

Ceci, S. (1987). Handbook of cognitive, social and neurological aspects of learning disabilities (Vol. 2). Hillsdale, NJ: Erlbaum.

Chaney, C. (1990). Evaluating the whole language approach to language arts: The pros, the cons. Language, Speech, and Hearing Services in Schools, 21, 244–249.

Cousin, P. T., Prentice, L., Aragon, E., Leonard, C., Rose, L. A., & Weekley, T. (1991). Redefining our role as special educators: Understandings gained from whole language. In S. Stire (Ed.), With promise: Redefining reading and writing for special students (pp. 165–171). Portsmouth, NH: Heinemann.

Deford, D. E., & Harste, J. C. (1982). Child, language, research, and curriculum. Language Arts, 59, 590–600.

Delpit, L. (1988). The silenced dialogue: Power and pedagogy in educating other people's children. Harvard Educational Review, 58(3), 280-298.

Derry, S. (1990). Remediating academic difficulties through strategy training: The acquisition of useful knowledge. Remedial and Special Education, 11(6), 19–31.

Dewey, J. (1938). Experience and education. New York: Collier Macmillan.

Edelsky, C. (1990). Whose agenda is this anyway? A response to McKenna, Robinson, and Miller. Educational Researcher, 19(8), 7–11.

Edelsky, C., Altwerger, B., & Flores, B. (1991). Whole language: What's the difference? Portsmouth, NH: Heinemann.

Freppon, P., & Dahl, K. (1991). Learning about phonics in a whole language classroom. Language Arts, 68, 190–197.

Gaskins, R. W., Gaskins, J. C., & Gaskins, I. W. (1991). A decoding program for poor readers and the rest of the class, too. Language Arts, 68, 213–225.

Gavelek, J., & Palincsar, A. (1988). Contextualism as an alternative worldview of learning disabilities: A response to Swanson's "Toward a metatheory of learning disabilities." Journal of Learning Disabilities, 21, 278–281.

Goodman, K. (1989). Whole language research: Foundations and development. Elementary School Journal, 90, 207–221.

Hallahan, D., Kauffman, J., & Lloyd J. (1985). Introduction to learning disabilities. Englewood Cliffs, NJ: Prentice Hall.

Halliday, M. (1975). Learning how to mean. London: Arnold.

Harste, J. (1989). The future of whole language. Elementary School Journal, 90, 243–249.

Harste, J. (1990). Jerry Harste speaks on reading and writing. The Reading Teacher, 43, 316–318.

Harste, J., Woodward, V., & Burke, C. (1991). Examining instructional assumptions. In B. Power & R. Hubbard (Eds.), Literacy in process (pp. 51–66). Portsmouth, NH: Heinemann.

Heshusius, L. (1989). Holistic principles: Not enhancing the old but seeing a-new. A rejoinder. Journal of Learning Disabilities, 22, 595–602.

Holdaway, D. (1979). The foundations of literacy. Sydney: Ashton Scholastic.

Keogh, B., & Hall, R. (1983). Cognitive training with learning disabled pupils. In A. Myer & W. Craighead (Eds.), Cognitive behavior therapy with children (pp. 163–191). New York: Plenum Press.

Lindquist, D. (1990). Inviting the literacy learner to engage in reading. In D. Stephens (Ed.), What matters? A primer for teaching reading (pp. 15–20). Portsmouth, NH: Heinemann.

Lindsay, C. (1990). An observational study of students with learning disabilities. Unpublished manuscript.

Mastropieri, M., & Scruggs, T. (1987). Effective instruction for special education. Austin, TX: PRO-ED.

Newman, J. (1985). Whole language: Theory in use. Portsmouth, NH: Heinemann.

Newman, J. (1991). Interwoven conversations. Portsmouth, NH: Heinemann.

Newman, J., & Church, S. (1990). Commentary: Myths of whole language. The Reading Teacher, 44, 20–26.

O'Brien, M. (1987). Whole language, the resource teacher and intervention. Reading-Canada-Lecture, 5(3), 165–170.

Palincsar, A., David, Y., Winn, J., & Stevens, D. (1991). Examining the context of strategy instruction. Remedial and Special Education, 12(3), 41–53.

Pearson, P. (1990). Reading and the whole language movement. The Elementary School Journal, 90, 231–241.

Pearson, P. D. (1993). Teaching and learning reading: A research perspective. Language Arts, 70, 502–511.

Poplin, M. (1988a). The reductionist fallacy in learning disabilities: Replicating the past by reducing the present. Journal of Learning Disabilities, 21, 401–416.

Poplin, M. (1988b). Holistic/constructivist principles of the teaching/learning process: Implications for the field of learning disabilities. Journal of Learning Disabilities, 21, 401–416.

Reid, D. K. (1988). Teaching the learning disabled. Boston: Allyn & Bacon.

Reid, D. K., & Stone, C. (1991). Why is cognitive instruction effective? Underlying learning mechanisms. Remedial and Special Education, 12(3), 8–19.

Rhodes, L., & Dudley-Marling, C. (1988). Readers and writers with a difference. Portsmouth, NH: Heinemann.

Shannon, P. (1990). The struggle to continue. Portsmouth, NH: Heinemann.

Smith, C. R. (1983). Learning disabilities: The interaction of learner, task, and setting. Boston: Little, Brown.

Staab, C. (1990). Teacher mediation in one whole language classroom. The Reading Teacher, 43, 548–552.

Stahl, S., & Miller, P. (1989). Whole language and language experience approaches for beginning reading: A quantitative research synthesis. Review of Educational Research, 59, 87–116.

Stone, A. C., & Wertsch, J. (1984). A social interactional analysis of learning disabilities remediation. Journal of Learning Disabilities, 17, 194–199.

Swanson, H. L. (1987). What learning disabled readers fail to retrieve: A problem of encoding, interference or sharing of resources? Journal of Abnormal Child Psychology, 15, 339–351.

Swanson, H. L. (1989). Strategy instruction: Overview of principles and procedures for effective use. Learning Disability Quarterly, 12, 3–14.

Swanson, H. L. (1990). Instruction derived from the strategy deficit model: Overview of principles and procedures. In T. Scruggs & B. Wong (Eds.), Intervention research in learning disabilities (pp. 34–65). New York: Springer-Verlag.

Swanson, H. L. (1991). Learning disabilities and memory. In D. K. Reid, W. P. Hresko, & H. L. Swanson (Eds.), A cognitive approach to learning disabilities. Austin, TX: PRO-ED.

Toomes, J. (1990). Observing learners. In D. Stephens (Ed.), What matters? A primer for teaching reading (pp. 3–14). Portsmouth, NH: Heinemann.

Torgesen, J. (1979). Factors related to poor performance in reading disabled children. Learning Disability Quarterly, 2(3), 17–23.

Vygotsky, L. (1978). Mind in society: The development of higher psychological processes. Cambridge, MA: Harvard University Press.

Watson, D. (1989). Defining and describing whole language. Elementary School Journal, 90, 129–141.

Weaver, C. (1988). Reading process and practice. Portsmouth, NH: Heinemann.

Weins, J. W. (1983). Metacognition and the adolescent passive learner. Journal of Learning Disabilities, 16, 144–149.

Wells, G. (1981). Learning through interaction. New York: Cambridge University Press.

Whitehead, A. N. (1929). The aims of education and other essays. New York: The Free Press.

Winsor, P., & Pearson, P. D. (1992). Children at-risk: Their phonemic awareness development in holistic instruction (Tech. Rep. No. 556). Urbana, IL: Center for the Study of Reading.

Zivian, M. T., & Samuels, S. J. (1986). Performance on a word-likeness task by normal readers and reading-disabled children. Reading Research Quarterly, 21, 150–160.

CHAPTER 15

Anastasiow, N. (1986). Development and disability. Baltimore, MD: Brookes.

Armstrong, T. (1994). Multiple intelligences in the classroom. Alexandria, VA: ASCD.

Bronfenbrenner, U. (1979). The ecology of human development: Experiments by nature and design. Cambridge, MA: Harvard University Press.

Carini, P. (1991). Honoring diversity/striving for inclusion. In K. Jervis & C. Montag (Eds.), Progressive education for the 1990s: Transforming practice (pp. 17–31). New York: Teachers College Press.

Coalition of Essential Schools. (1992). Nine common principles. Providence, RI: Brown University.

Dewey, J. (1964). The child and the curriculum. In R. Archaumbault (Ed.), John Dewey on education (pp. 339–358). Chicago: University of Chicago Press.

Ensminger, E. E., & Dangel, H. L. (1992). The Foxfire approach: A confluence of best practices for special education. Focus on Exceptional Children, 24(7).

Ensminger, G. (1991). Defragmenting fragmented learners. Hands-On: A Journal for Teachers, 39, 44–48.

Ferguson, D. L., & Ginevra, R. (1993). Module 1d—Individually tailored learning: Strategies for designing inclusive curriculum. The Elementary/Secondary System: Supportive Education for Students with Severe Handicaps. Eugene: University of Oregon.

Foxfire Fund. (1991). The Foxfire approach: Perspectives and core practices. Hands-On: A Journal for Teachers, 42, 3–4.

Foxfire Fund. (1994). Annual report, 1992–1993. Mountain City, GA: Author.

Garbarino, J. (1992). Children and families in the social environment. Hawthorne, NY: Aldine De Gruyter.

Gardner, H. (1993). Multiple intelligences: The theory in practice. New York: Basic Books.

Hutchins, P. (1989). Don't forget the bacon. New York: Mulberry Books.

Kauffman, J. M. (1993). How we might achieve the radical reform of special education. Exceptional Children, 60, 6–16.

Kugelmass, J. W. (1991). The ecology of the Foxfire approach. Hands-On: A Journal for Teachers, 42, 14–20.

Poplin, M. S. (1988). The reductionistic fallacy in learning disabilities: Replicating the past by reducing the present. Journal of Learning Disabilities, 21, 401–416.

Sizer, T. R. (1984). Horace's compromise: The dilemma of the American high school. Boston: Houghton Mifflin.

Stainback, W., Stainback, S., & Moravec, J. (1992). Using curriculum to build inclusive classrooms. In S. Stainback & W. Stainback (Eds.), Curriculum considerations in inclusive classrooms: Facilitating learning for all students (pp. 65–84). Baltimore: Brookes.

Vygotsky, L. S. (1962). Thought and language. Cambridge, MA: M.I.T. Press.

CHAPTER 16

Calkins, L. (1986). The art of teaching writing. New York: Teachers College Press.

Suggested Readings

Calkins, L. (1983). Lessons from a child: On the teaching and learning of writing. New York: Teachers College Press.

Hornsby, D., & Parry, J. (1985). Write on: A conference approach to writing. Portsmouth, NH: Heinemann.

CHAPTER 17

Cambourne, B., & Turbill, J. (1987). Coping with chaos. Portsmouth, NH: Heinemann.

CHAPTER 19

Deci, E., & Ryan, R. (1987). Intrinsic motivation and self-determination in human behavior. New York: Plenum Press.

Freire, P. (1990). Pedagogy of the oppressed. New York: Continuum.

Grumet, M. (1988). Bitter milk. Amherst: The University of Massachusetts Press.

Hansberry, L. (1959). A raisin in the sun. New York: Random.

Poplin, M. (1988). Holistic/constructivist principles of the teaching/learning process: Implications for the field of learning disabilities. Journal of Learning Disabilities, 21, 401–416.

CHAPTER 20

Albinger, M. A. (1993). Children labeled learning disabled: Stories from the resource room. Unpublished master's thesis, California State University, Long Beach.

Armstrong, T. (1987). In their own way. Los Angeles: Jeremy P. Tarcher.

Ashton-Warner, S. (1986). Teacher. New York: Simon & Schuster.

Ayers, W. (1993). To teach: The journey of a teacher. New York: Teachers College Press.

Crux, S. C. (1989). Special education legislation: Humanitarianism or legalized deviance and control? Education Canada, 29(1), 24–31.

Five, C. L. (1991). Special voices. Portsmouth, NH: Heinemann.

Gardner, H. (1983). Frames of mind: The theory of multiple intelligences. New York: Basic Books.

Gardner, H. (1991). The unschooled mind: How children think and how schools should teach. New York: Basic Books.

Gould, S. J. (1981). The mismeasure of man. New York: W. W. Norton.

Hrncir, E. J., & Eisenhart, C. E. (1991). Use with caution the "at-risk" label. Young Children, 46, 23–27.

Kohl, H. (1984). Growing minds: On becoming a teacher. New York: Harper & Row.

Martin, A. (1988). Teachers and teaching—Screening, early intervention, and remediation: Obscuring children's potential. Harvard Educational Review, 58, 488–501.

Nieto, S. (1992). Affirming diversity: The sociopolitical context of multicultural education. New York: Longman.

Paley, V. G. (1981). Wally's stories: Conversations in the kindergarten. Cambridge, MA: Harvard University Press.

Paley, V. G. (1991). The boy who would be a helicopter. Cambridge, MA: Harvard University Press.

Perrone, V. (1991). A letter to teachers: Reflections on schooling and the art of teaching. San Francisco: Jossey-Bass.

Poplin, M. S. (1988). The reductionistic fallacy in learning disabilities: Replicating the past by reducing the present. Journal of Learning Disabilities, 21, 389–400.

Shepard, L. (1991). Negative policies for dealing with diversity: When does assessment and diagnosis turn into sorting and segregation? In E. H. Hiebert (Ed.), Literacy for a diverse society: Perspectives, practices, and policies (pp. 279–298). New York: Teachers College Press.

Spodek, B., & Saracho, O. N. (1994). Dealing with individual differences in the early childhood classroom. New York: Longman.

Taylor, D. (1991). Learning denied. Portsmouth, NH: Heinemann.

Taylor, D. (1993). From the child's point of view. Portsmouth, NH: Heinemann.

CHAPTER 21

Ackerman, B. P. (1986). Referential and causal coherence in the story comprehension of children and adults. Journal of Experimental Child Psychology, 41, 336–366.

Bruner, J. (1985). Narrative and paradigmatic modes of thought. In E. Eisner (Ed.), Learning and teaching the ways of knowing (pp. 97–115). Chicago: The National Society for the Study of Education.

Bruner, J. (1990). Acts of meaning. Cambridge, MA: Harvard University Press.

Carter, K. (1993). The place of story in the study of teaching and teacher education. Educational Researcher, 22, 5–11.

Collins, J., & Michaels, S. (1986). Discourse and the acquisition of literacy. In J. Cook-Gumperz (Eds.), The social construction of literacy (pp. 207–222). New York: Cambridge University Press.

Colorado State Board of Education: Department of Education. Colorado Code of Regulations 301-8. Adopted June 11, 1992, and Readopted August 13, 1992. Statutory Authority: Article 20 of Title 22.

Edwards, J. (1989). Language and disadvantage (2nd ed.). London: Whurr.

Ferguson, P. M., Ferguson, D., & Taylor, S. (1992). The future of interpretivism in disabilities studies. In P. M. Ferguson, D. L. Ferguson, & S. J. Taylor (Eds.), Interpreting disability: A qualitative reader (pp. 295–302). New York: Teachers College Press.

Flavell, J. (1992). Cognitive development: Past, present, future. Developmental Psychology, 20, 998–1005.

Foucault, M. (1965). Madness and civilization. New York: Vintage Books.

Foucault, M. (1978). The history of sexuality (Vol. 1). New York: Vintage Books.

Gallagher, J. M., & Reid, D. K. (1983). The learning theory of Piaget and Inhelder. Austin, TX: PRO-ED.

Gee, J. P. (1985). The narrativization of experience in the oral style. Journal of Education, 167(1), 9–35.

Gee, J. P. (1986). Units in the production of narrative discourse. Discourse Processes, 9, 391–422.

Gee, J. P. (1989). Two styles of narrative construction and their linguistic and educational implications. Discourse Processes, 12, 287–307.

Gee, J. P. (1990). Social linguistics and literacies: Ideology in discourse. Bristol, PA: Falmer Press.

Gee, J. P. (1991). A linguistic approach to narrative. Journal of Narrative and Life History, 1, 15–39.

Gee, J. P., Michaels, S., & O'Connor, C. (1992). Discourse analysis. In M. D. LeCompte, W. L. Millroy, & J. Preissle (Eds.), The handbook of qualitative research in education (pp. 227–291). San Diego, CA: Academic Press.

Labov, W. (1972). Language in the inner city: Studies in the black English vernacular. Philadelphia: University of Pennsyl-vania Press.

Liles, B. Z. (1985). Cohesion in the narratives of normal and language disordered children. Journal of Speech and Hearing Research, 28, 123–133.

McAdams, D. P. (1993). Stories we live by. New York: William Morrow.

Mehan, H. (1984). Language and schooling. Sociology of Education, 57, 174–183.

Michaels, D. (1991). The dismantling of narrative. In A. McCate & C. Peterson (Eds.), Developing narrative structure (pp. 303–351). Hillsdale, NJ: Erlbaum.

Michaels, S. (1981). "Sharing Time": Children's narrative styles and differential access to literacy. Language in Society, 10, 423–442.

Michaels, S. (1985). Hearing the connections in children's oral and written discourse. Journal of Education, 167, 36–56.

Michaels, S., & Collins, J. (1984). Oral discourse styles: Classroom interaction and the acquisition of literacy. In D. Tannen (Ed.), Coherence in spoken and written discourse (pp. 219–244). Norwood, NJ: Ablex.

Mishler, E. G. (1986). Research interviewing: Context and narrative. Cambridge, MA: Harvard University Press.

Mishler, E. G. (1990). Validation in inquiry-guided research: The role of exemplars in narrative studies. Harvard Educational Review, 60, 415–442.

Mishler, E. (1992). Work, identity, and narrative: An artist–craftsman's story. In G. Rosenwald & R. Ochberg (Eds.), Storied lives (pp. 21–40). New Haven: Yale University Press.

Mishler, E. G. (1993, June). Missing persons: Recovering developmental stories/histories. Paper presented at the Conference on Ethnographic Approaches to the Study of Human Development, Oakland, CA.

Morris, R., Lyon, G. R., Alexander, D., Gray, D. B., Kavanagh, J., Rourke, B. P., & Swanson, H. L. (1994). Proposed guidelines and criteria for describing samples of persons with learning disabilities. Learning Disability Quarterly, 17, 106–109.

National Institute of Child Health and Human Development, Interagency Committee on Learning Disabilities. (1991). In D. K. Reid, W. P. Hresko, & H. L. Swanson (Eds.), A cognitive approach to learning disabilities (2nd ed., p. 11). Austin, TX: PRO-ED.

Polkinghorne, D. E. (1988). Narrative knowing and the human sciences. Albany: SUNY Press.

Polkinghorne, D. E. (1991). Narrative and self-concept. Journal of Narrative and Life History, 1(2 & 3), 135–153.

Poplin, M. (1984). Research practices in learning disabilities. Learning Disability Quarterly, 7, 2–5.

Prawat, R., & Jones, H. (1977). Constructive memory of normal and learning disabled children. Psycholinguistic Reports, 41, 474–477.

Ricoeur, P. (1981). Hermeneutics and the human sciences. Cambridge, England: Cambridge University Press.

Roth, F. P. (1987). Discourse abilities of learning disabled students: Patterns and intervention strategies. Workshop presented at the Language Disorders and Learning Disabilities Institute, Emerson College, Boston.

Sarbin, T. G. (1986). Narrative psychology: The storied nature of human conduct. New York: Praeger.

Swanson, H. L. (1992). Learning disabilities and memory. In D. K. Reid, W. P. Hresko, & H. L. Swanson (Eds.), A cognitive approach to learning disabilities (pp. 159–182). Austin, TX: PRO-ED.

Thiessen, D. (1987). Curriculum as experienced: Alternative world views from two students with learning disabilities. In B. M. Franklin (Ed.), Learning disability: Dissenting essays (p. 90). Philadelphia, PA: Falmer Press.

Wechsler, D. (1974). Wechsler intelligence scale for children–Revised. San Antonio, TX: Psychological Corp.

Woodcock, R. W. (1977). Woodcock-Johnson psycho-educational battery. Allen, TX: DLM.

Young, R. (1983). A school communication-deficit hypothesis of educational disadvantage. Australian Journal of Education, 27, 3–15.

CHAPTER 22

Algozzine, B., & Ysseldyke, J. E. (1988). Questioning discrepancies: Retaking the first step 20 years later. Learning Disability Quarterly, 11, 307–318.

Armstrong, T. (1988). In their own way. Los Angeles: Jeremy P. Tarcher.

Bateman, B. (1992). Learning disabilities: The changing landscape. Journal of Learning Disabilities, 25, 29–36.

Bogdan, R., & Biklen, S. (1992). Qualitative research for education (2nd ed.). Needham Heights, MA: Allyn and Bacon.

Carlberg, C., & Kavale, K. (1980). The efficacy of special versus regular class placement for exceptional children: A meta-analysis. The Journal of Special Education, 14, 295–309.

Chalfant, J. C. (1989). Learning disabilities: Policy issues and promising approaches. American Psychologist, 44, 392–398.

Gillung, T. B., & Rucker, C. N. (1977). Labels and teacher expectations. Exceptional Children, 43, 464–465.

Hallahan, D. P. (1992). Some thoughts on why the prevalence of learning disabilities has increased. Journal of Learning Disabilities, 25, 523–528.

Hallahan, D. P., & Kauffman, J. M. (1977). Labels, categories, behaviors: ED, LD, EMR reconsidered. The Journal of Special Education, 11, 139–149.

Hammill, D. D. (1990). On defining learning disabilities: An emerging consensus. Journal of Learning Disabilities, 23, 74–84.

Hrncir, E. J., & Eisenhart, C. E. (1991). Use with caution the "at-risk" label. Young Children, 46, 23–27.

Jenkins, J. R., & Heinen, A. (1989). Students' preferences for service delivery: Pull-out, in-class, or integrated models. Exceptional Children, 55, 516–523.

Jones, R. L. (1974). Student views of special placement and their own special classes: A clarification. Exceptional Children, 41, 22–29.

Levine, M. D., Clarke, S., & Ferb, T. (1981). The child as a diagnostic participant: Helping students describe their learning disorders. Journal of Learning Disabilities, 14, 527–530.

McMillan, J. H., & Schumacher, S. (1993). Research in education (3rd ed.). New York: Harper Collins.

McWhirter, J. J., McWhirter, R. J., & McWhirter, M. C. (1985). The learning disabled: A retrospective review. Journal of Learning Disabilities, 18, 315–318.

Mercer, C. D., Algozzine, B., & Trifiletti, J. (1988). Early identification: An analysis of the research. Learning Disability Quarterly, 2, 176–188.

Palmer, D. J. (1983). An attributional perspective on labeling. Exceptional Children, 49, 423–429.

Stainback, W., & Stainback, S. (1984). Broadening the research perspective in special education. Exceptional Children, 50, 400–408.

Swanson, H. L. (1991). Operational definitions and learning disabilities: An overview. Learning Disability Quarterly, 14, 242–254.

Vaughn, S., & Bos, C. S. (1987). Knowledge and perceptions of the resource room: The students' perspective. Journal of Learning Disabilities, 20, 218–223.

Wang, M. C., Reynolds, M., & Walberg, H. J. (1986). Rethinking special education. Educational Leadership, 44, 26–31.

CHAPTER 23

Artiles, A. J., & Trent, S. (1994). Overrepresentation of minority students in special education: A continuing debate. The Journal of Special Education, 27, 410–437.

Atwell, N. (1987). In the middle: Writing, reading and learning with adolescents. Portsmouth, NH: Heinemann.

Au, K. (1993). Literacy instruction in multicultural settings. Orlando, FL: Harcourt Brace Jovanovich.

Beaumont, C. (1990). An analysis of IEP's in the OLE classrooms: Baseline phase. Unpublished manuscript, University of California at Davis, Division of Education, Special Education Demonstration Project.

Brown, A. L. (1985, May). Reciprocal teaching: A cooperative learning environment for fostering comprehension strategies. Paper presented at the annual meeting of the International Reading Association, New Orleans.

Coles, G. (1987). The learning mystique. New York: Pantheon.

Cuban, L. (1988). A fundamental puzzle of school reform. Phi Delta Kappan, 69, 341–344.

Cummins, J. (1989). A theoretical framework for bilingual special education. Exceptional Children, 56, 111–119.

De Avila, E. A. (1988). Finding out/Descubrimiento. Northvale, NJ: Santillana.

Diaz, S., Moll, L., & Mehan, H. (1986). Sociocultural resources in instruction: A context-specific approach. In Bilingual Education Office, California State Department of Education (Eds.), Beyond language: Social and cultural factors in schooling language minority students (pp. 187–230). Los Angeles: California State University, Evaluation, Dissemination, and Assessment Center.

Figueroa, R. A. (1990). Assessment of linguistic minority group children. In C. R. Reynolds & R. W. Kamphaus (Eds.), Handbook of psychological and educational assessment of children: Intelligence and achievement (pp. 671–696). New York: Guilford.

Figueroa, R. A., & Ruiz, N. T. (1993). Bilingual pupils and special education: A reconceptualization. In R. Eaves & P. McLaughlin (Eds.), Recent advances in special education (pp. 73–87).

Figueroa, R. A., Ruiz, N. T., & García, E. (1994). The Optimal Learning Environment (OLE) research project in the Los Angeles Unified School District: Reading outcome data. Santa Cruz: California Research Institute on Special Education and Cultural Diversity, University of California.

Figueroa, R. A., Ruiz, N. T., & Rueda, R. (1990). Special education research project for learning handicapped Hispanic pupils: The OLE model (federal proposal). Sacramento: California State Department of Education.

Files, J., & Wills, P. S. (1992). Learning from teachers how to support their growth. In C. Weaver & L. Henke (Eds.), Supporting whole language: Stories of teacher and institutional change (pp. 43–66). Portsmouth, NH: Heinemann.

Flores, B., & Garcia, E. (1984). A collaborative learning and teaching experience using journal writing. Journal of the National Association of Bilingual Education, 8, 67–83.

García, E. (1991). The education of linguistically and culturally diverse students: Effective instructional practices. Washington, DC: Center for Applied Linguistics.

Gersten, R. (1993, April). The language minority student in transition: Exploring the parameters of effective literacy instruction. Paper presented at the annual meeting of the American Education Research Association, Atlanta, GA.

Gleason, J. J. (1989). Special education in context: An ethnographic study of persons with developmental disabilities. New York: Cambridge University Press.

Graves, D. (1983). Writing: Teachers and children at work. Portsmouth, NH: Heinemann.

Guskey, T. R. (1986). Staff development and the process of teacher change. Educational Researcher, 15, 5–12.

Hood, L. R., McDermott, R., & Cole, M. (1981). Let's try to make it a good day: Some not so simple ways. Discourse Processes, 3, 155–168.

Hunsaker, L., & Johnston, M. (1992). Teacher under construction: A collaborative case study of teacher change. American Educational Research Journal, 29, 350–372.

Mehan, H., Hertweck, H., & Meihls, J. (1986). Handicapping the handicapped. Palo Alto, CA: Stanford University Press.

Mehan, H., Hubbard, L., Okamoto, D., & Villanueva, I. (in press). Untracking high school students in preparation for college: Implications for Latino students. In A. Hurtado & E. E. García (Eds.), The educational achievement of Latinos: Barriers and successes. Santa Cruz: The Latino Eligibility Study.

Mercer, J. (1973). Labeling the mentally retarded. Berkeley: University of California Press.

Moll, L. C., & Díaz, D. (1987). Change as the goal of educational research. Anthropology and Education Quarterly, 18, 300–311.

Moll, L. C., & Greenberg, J. B. (1990). Creating zones of possibilities: Combining social contexts for instruction. In L. C. Moll (Ed.), Vygotsky and education: Instructional implications and applications of sociohistorical psychology (pp. 319–348). New York: Cambridge University Press.

Moll, L. C., Tapia, J., & Whitmore, K. (in press). Living knowledge: The social distribution of cultural resources for thinking. In G. Salomon (Ed.), Distributed cognitions: Psychological and educational considerations (pp. 139–163). Cambridge: Cambridge University Press.

Ortiz, A. A., Wilkinson, C. Y., Robertson-Courtney, P., & Kushner, M. I. (1991). AIM for the BESt: Assessment and intervention model for the bilingual exceptional student. Arlington, VA: Development Associates, Inc.

Ortiz, A. A., & Yates, J. R. (1983). Incidence of exceptionality among Hispanics: Implications for manpower planning. NABE Journal, 7, 41–53.

Peterson, P. P. (1990). Doing more in the same amount of time: Cathy Swift. Educational Evaluation and Policy Analysis, 12, 261–280.

Peterson, R., & Eeds, M. E. (1990). Grand conversations. New York: Scholastic.

Poplin, M. S. (1988a). The reductionistic fallacy in learning disabilities: Replicating the past by reducing the present. Journal of Learning Disabilities, 21, 389–400.

Poplin, M. S. (1988b). Holistic/constructivist principles of the teaching/learning process: Implications for the field of learning disabilities. Journal of Learning Disabilities, 21, 401–416.

Rueda, R. (1989). Defining mild disabilities with language-minority students. Exceptional Children, 56, 121–128.

Rueda, R., Betts, B., & Hami, A. (1990). A descriptive analysis of work products in OLE classroom sites: Baseline phase. Unpublished manuscript, University of California at Davis, Division of Education, Special Education Demonstration Project.

Rueda, R., & Garcia, E. (1994). *Teachers' beliefs about reading assessment with Latino minority students.* Washington, DC: National Center for Research on Cultural Diversity and Second Language Learning.

Rueda, R., & Mehan, H. (1986). Metacognition and passing: Strategic interaction in the lives of students with learning disabilities. *Anthropology and Education Quarterly, 17,* 145–165.

Ruiz, N. T. (1988). *Language for learning in a bilingual special education classroom.* Unpublished doctoral dissertation, Stanford University.

Ruiz, N. T. (1990). *Instructional events in the OLE classrooms: Baseline phase.* Unpublished manuscript, University of California at Davis, Division of Education, Special Education Demonstration Project.

Ruiz, N. T., Figueroa, R. A., & Echandía, A. X. (1995). *Instructional events in bilingual special education classrooms: From reductionism to holistic/constructivism.* Sacramento: The OLE Research and Dissemination Project, California State University.

Ruiz, N. T., Figueroa, R. A., Rueda, R., & Beaumont, C. (1992). History and status of bilingual special education for Hispanic handicapped students. In R. V. Padilla & A. H. Benavides (Eds.), *Critical perspectives on bilingual education research* (pp. 349–380). Tempe, AZ: Bilingual Press.

Ruiz, N. T., Garcia, E., & Figueroa, R. A. (in press). *The OLE curriculum guide: Creating optimal learning environments for students from diverse backgrounds in special and general education.* Sacramento, CA: Resources in Special Education.

Taylor, D. (1991). *Learning denied.* Portsmouth, NH: Heinemann.

Taylor, D. (1993). *From the child's point of view.* Portsmouth, NH: Heinemann.

Tharp, R. G., & Gallimore, R. (1988). *Rousing minds to life: Teaching, learning, and schooling in social contexts.* Cambridge, England: Cambridge University Press.

Wagner, J. (1992, March). *Teacher perspectives on professionalism and school improvement: Studying community among teachers of English.* Paper presented at the Ethnography in Education Forum, University of Pennsylvania, Philadelphia.

Wang, M. C., Reynolds, M. C., & Walberg, H. J. (Eds.). (1987). *Handbook on special education: Research and practice.* New York: Pergamon.

Weaver, C. (1992). A whole language belief system and its implications for teacher and institutional change. In C. Weaver & L. Henke (Eds.), *Supporting whole language: Stories of teacher and institutional change* (pp. 3–23). Portsmouth, NH: Heinemann.

Weaver, C., & Henke, L. (Eds.). (1992). *Supporting whole language: Stories of teacher and institutional change.* Portsmouth, NH: Heinemann.

Will, M. C. (1986). Educating children with learning problems: A shared responsibility. *Exceptional Children, 52,* 411–416.

Willig, A. C., & Swedo, J. (1987, April). *Improving teaching strategies for exceptional Hispanic limited English proficient students: An exploratory study of task engagement and teaching strategies.* Paper presented at the annual meeting of the American Educational Research Association, Washington, DC.

CHAPTER 24

Adams, D. (1992). *Mostly harmless: The fifth book in the increasingly inaccurately named hitchhiker's trilogy.* New York: Harmony Books.

Ashton-Warner, S. (1963). Teacher. New York: Simon & Schuster.

Capra, F. (1988). The turning point. New York: Bantam Books.

Dewey, J. (1968). The child and the curriculum and the school and society. Chicago: University of Chicago.

Ensminger, E. E., & Dangel, H. L. (1992). The Foxfire pedagogy: A confluence of best practices for special education. Focus on Exceptional Children, 24(7), 1–15.

Gergen, K. (1985). The social constructionist movement in modern psychology. American Psychologist, 40, 266–275.

Goodland, J. I. (1991). Why we need a complete redesign of teacher education. Educational Leadership, 49(3), 4–13.

Hawking, S. W. (1988). A brief history of time. New York: Bantam Books.

Heshusius, L. (1989). The Newtonian mechanistic paradigm, special education, and contours of alternatives: An overview. Journal of Learning Disabilities, 22, 403–415.

Horton, M., & Freire, P. (1990). We make the road by walking: Conversations on education and social change. Philadelphia: Temple University Press.

Montessori, M. (1967). The discovery of the child. New York: Ballantine.

O'Loughlin, M. (1992). Engaging teachers in emancipatory knowledge construction. Journal of Teacher Education, 43, 336–347.

Poplin, M. S. (1988). Portfolio assessment and human growth: The case for a changing perspective on teacher assessment. Unpublished manuscript, Claremont Graduate School, Claremont, CA.

Poplin, M. S., & Stone, S. (1992). Paradigm shifts in instructional strategies: From reductionism to holistic/constructivism. In W. Stainback & S. Stainback (Eds.), Controversial issues confronting special education (pp. 153–179). Needham Heights, MA: Allyn and Bacon.

Poplin, M. S., & Weeres, J. (1992). Voices from the inside: A report on schooling from inside the classroom. Claremont, CA: Institute for Education in Transformation at the Claremont Graduate School.

Rhodes, W. C. (1987). Ecology and the new physics. Behavioral Disorders, 13(1), 58–61.

Skrtic, T. M. (1991). Behind special education. Denver: Love.

Wiggens, G. (1989). A true test: Toward more authentic and equitable assessment. Phi Delta Kappan, 70, 703–713.

Chapter 25

Banks, J. A. (1994). Multiethnic education (3rd ed). Boston: Allyn & Bacon.

Barton, J., & Collins, A. (1993). Portfolios in teacher education. Journal of Teacher Education, 44, 200–210.

Brown v. Board of Education of Topeka, Kansas, 347 U.S. 483 (1954).

Byrd, H. B. (1994, April). Inclusive curricula for African-American exceptional students. Paper presented at the annual meeting of the Council for Exceptional Children, Denver.

Center for Education Statistics. (1987). The condition of education. Washington, DC: U.S. Government Printing Office.

Darling-Hammond, L. (1984). Beyond the Commission Reports: The coming crisis in teaching. Santa Monica, CA: Rand Corp.

Duffy, G. (1994). Professional development schools and the disempowerment of teachers and professors. Phi Delta Kappan, 75, 596–600.

Dunn, L. M. (1968). Special education for the mildly retarded: Is much of it justifiable? Exceptional Children, 35, 5–24.

Franklin, M. E. (1992). Culturally sensitive instructional practices for African-American learners with disabilities. Exceptional Children, 59, 115–122.

Friend, M., & Cook, L. (1991). Interactions: Collaboration skills for school professionals. White Plains, NY: Longman.

Gerard, H. B. (1983). School desegregation: The social science role. American Psychologist, 38, 869–877.

Holmes Group. (1986). Tomorrow's teachers: A report of the Holmes Group. East Lansing, MI: Author.

Idol, L., Paolucci-Whitcomb, P., & Nevin, A. (1986). Collaborative consultation. Austin, TX: PRO-ED.

Johnson, J. L. (1969). Special education and the inner city: A challenge for the future or another means for cooling the mark out? The Journal of Special Education, 3, 241–251.

Katz, L., & Raths, J. (1992). Six dilemmas in teacher education. Journal of Teacher Education, 43, 376–385.

King, S. H. (1993). The limited presence of African-American teachers. Review of Educational Research, 63(2), 115–149.

Levine, M. (Ed.). (1992). Professional practice schools: Linking teacher education and school reform. New York: Teachers College Press.

Lortie, D. (1975). Schoolteacher: A sociological study. Chicago: University of Chicago Press.

Morsink, C. V. (1988, February). Changes in the role of special educators: Public perceptions and demands. Exceptional Educators Quarterly, pp. 15–25.

Patton, J. M. (1992). Assessment and identification of African-American learners with gifts and talents. Exceptional Children, 59, 150–159.

Poplin, M. S. (1992). Authentic self assessment and human growth: The case for a changing perspective on teacher assessment. Unpublished manuscript, Claremont Graduate School, Claremont, CA.

Pugach, M. (1992). Unchartered territory: Research on the socialization of special education teachers. Teacher Education and Special Education, 15, 133–147.

Sailor, W. (1991). Special education in the restructured school. Remedial and Special Education, 12(6), 8–22.

Sarason, S. (1990). The predictable failure of education reform. San Francisco: Jossey-Bass.

Schlechty, P., & Vance, V. (1983). Recruitment and retention: The shape of the teaching force. The Elementary School Journal, 83, 469–487.

Schon, D. A. (1983). The reflective practitioner: How professionals think in action. New York: Basic Books.

Sirotnik, K., & Goodlad, J. I. (1988). Introduction. In K. A. Sirotnik & J. I . Goodlad (Eds.), School-university partnerships in action: Concepts, cases, and concerns (pp. vii–xii). New York: Teachers College Press.

Wilson, S., Shulman, L., & Richert, A. (1987). "150 different ways" of knowing: Representations of knowledge in teaching. In J. Calderhead (Ed.), Exploring teachers' thinking. London: Cassell.

CHAPTER 26

Allington, D. (1994). Critical issues: What's special about special programs for children who find learning to read difficult? Journal of Reading Behavior, 26, 95–116.

Barone, T., Eeds, M., & Mason, K. (1995). Literature, the disciplines, and the lives of elementary school children. Language Arts, 72, 30–38.

Chall, J. (1967). Learning to read: The great debate. New York: McGraw-Hill.

Chang-Wells, G. L. M., & Wells, G. (1993). Dynamics of discourse: Literacy and the construction of knowledge. In E. Forman, N. Minick, & C. A. Stone (Eds.), Contexts for learning (pp. 58–90). Oxford, England: Oxford University Press.

Cobb, P., Wood, T., & Yackel, E. (1993). Discourse, mathematical thinking, and classroom practice. In E. Forman, N. Minick, & C. A. Stone (Eds.), Contexts for learning (pp. 91–119). Oxford, England: Oxford University Press.

Cole, M., & Engestrom, Y. (1993). A cultural-historical approach to distributed cognition. In G. Salomon (Ed.), Distributed cognitions: Psychological and educational considerations (pp. 1–46). Cambridge, England: Cambridge University Press.

Cole, M., & Griffin, P. (1987). Contextual factors in education. Madison: Wisconsin Center for Education Research.

Coles, G. (1987). The learning mystique. New York: Pantheon.

Cousin, P. T., Aragon, E., & Rojas, R. (1993). Creating new conversations about literacy: Working with special needs students in a middle-school classroom. Learning Disability Quarterly, 16, 282–298.

Diaz, E., & Flores, B. (1991, May). Teacher as cultural mediator. Paper presented at the Claremont Reading Conference, Claremont, CA.

Ekwall, E. (1989). Locating and correcting reading difficulties. Columbus, OH: Merrill.

Engestrom, Y. (1991). Developmental work research: A paradigm in practice. The Quarterly Newsletter of the Laboratory for Comparative Human Cognition, 13, 79–80.

Engestrom, Y., Brown, K., Christopher, L., & Gregory, J. (1991). Coordination, cooperation, and communication in the courts: Expansive transitions in legal work. The Quarterly Newsletter of the Laboratory for Comparative Human Cognition, 13, 88–97.

Five, C. (1990). Special voices. Portsmouth, NH: Heinemann.

Flores, B., Cousin, P. T., & Diaz, E. (1991). Critiquing deficit myths about language, literacy, and culture. Language Arts, 68, 369–379.

Forman, E., Minick, N., & Stone, C. A. (Eds.). (1993). Contexts for learning. Oxford, England: Oxford University Press.

Franklin, B. (1987). The first crusade for learning disabilities: The movement for the education of backward children. In T. Popkewitz (Ed.), The formation of school subjects (pp. 190–211). Philadelphia: Falmer Press.

Franklin, B. (1994). From "backwardness" to "at risk." Albany, NY: SUNY Press.

Haring, N. G., & Bateman, B. (1977). Teaching the learning disabled child. Englewood Cliffs, NJ: Prentice Hall.

Hatano, G. (1993). Time to move Vygotskian and constructivist conceptions of knowledge acquisition. In E. Forman, N. Minick, & C. A. Stone (Eds.), Contexts for learning (pp. 153–167). Oxford, England: Oxford University Press.

Hood, L., McDermott, R., & Cole, M. (1980). "Let's try to make it a good day"—Some not so simple ways. Discourse Processes, 3, 155–168.

Katims, D. (1994). Emergence of literacy in preschool children with disabilities. Learning Disability Quarterly, 17, 58–69.

Klenk, L. (1994). Case study in reading disability: An emergent literacy perspective. Learning Disability Quarterly, 17, 33–57.

Kos, R. (1991). Persistence of reading disabilities: The voices of four middle school students. American Educational Research Journal, 28, 875–895.

Laboratory for Comparative Human Cognition. (1983). Culture and cognitive development. In P. H. Mussen & W. Kessen (Eds.), Handbook of child psychology: Volume 1 (4th ed., pp. 295–356). New York: Wiley.

Libowitz, B. (1993). Deconstruction in the zone of proximal development. In E. Forman, N. Minick, & C. A. Stone (Eds.), Contexts for learning (pp. 184–196). Oxford, England: Oxford University Press.

Lipsky, D., & Gartner, A. (1987). Beyond separate education. Baltimore: Brookes.

McDermott, R. (1993). The acquisition of a child by a learning disability. In S. Chaiklin & J. Lave (Eds.), Understanding practice: Focus on activity and context. Cambridge, England: Cambridge University Press.

McDermott, R., & Varenne, H. (1993). Culture as disability. Unpublished manuscript, Stanford University.

Mead, G. H. (1934). Mind, self, and society. Chicago: University of Chicago Press.

Mehan, H., Hertweck, A., & Meihles, J. (1986). Handicapping the handicapped. Stanford, CA: Stanford University Press.

Moll, L. (1990). Vygotsky and education: Instructional implications and applications of sociohistorical psychology. Cambridge, England: Cambridge University Press.

Moll, L., & Diaz, E. (1987). Change as the goal of educational research. Anthropology and Education Quarterly, 18, 300–311.

Packer, M. (1993). Away from internalization. In E. Forman, N. Minick, & C. A. Stone (Eds.), Contexts for learning (pp. 254–267). Oxford, England: Oxford University Press.

Palincsar, A., & Klenk, L. (1992). Fostering literacy learning in supportive contexts. Journal of Learning Disabilities, 25, 211–225.

Paris, S., & Oka, E. (1989). Strategies for comprehending text and coping with reading disabilities. Learning Disability Quarterly, 12, 32–42.

Popkewitz, T. (Ed.). (1987). The formation of school subjects. Philadelphia: Falmer Press.

Poplin, M. (1988a). The reductionist fallacy in learning disabilities: Replicating the past by reducing the present. Journal of Learning Disabilities, 21, 389–400.

Poplin, M. (1988b). Holistic/constructivist principles of the teaching/learning process. Implications for the field of learning disabilities. Journal of Learning Disabilities, 21, 389–400.

Poplin, M., & Stone, S. (1992). Paradigm shifts in instructional strategies: From reductionism to holistic/constructivism. In W. Stainback & S. Stainback (Eds.), Controversial issues confronting special education (pp. 153–175). Boston: Allyn & Bacon.

Rogoff, B., Mosier, C., Mistry, J., & Goncu, A. (1993). Toddlers' guided participation with their caregivers in cultural activity. In E. Forman, N. Minick, & C. A. Stone (Eds.), Contexts for learning (pp. 230–253). Oxford, England: Oxford University Press.

Rueda, R. (1990). Assisted performance in writing instruction with LD students. In L. Moll (Ed.), Vygotsky and education (pp. 403–426). Cambridge, England: Cambridge University Press.

Salomon, G. (Ed.). (1993). Distributed cognition. Cambridge, England: Cambridge University Press.

Skrtic, T. (1991). The special education paradox: Equity as the way to excellence. Harvard Educational Review, 61, 148–206.

Sleeter, C. (1986). Learning disabilities: A social construction of a special education category. Exceptional Children, 53, 46–54.

Stainback, W., & Stainback, S. (1992). Controversial issues confronting special education: Divergent perspectives. Boston, MA: Allyn & Bacon.

Stires, S. (Ed.). (1991). With promise: Redefining reading and writing with special students. Portsmouth, NH: Heinemann.

Stone, C. A. (1993). What is missing in the metaphor of scaffolding? In E. Forman, N. Minick, & C. A. Stone (Eds.), Contexts for learning (pp. 169–183). Oxford, England: Oxford University Press.

Stone, C. A., & Reid, D. K. (1994). Social and individual forces in learning: Implications for instruction of children with learning difficulties. Learning Disability Quarterly, 17, 72–86.

Tarver, S. (1992). Direct instruction. In W. Stainback & S. Stainback (Eds.), Controversial issues confronting special education (pp. 141–152). Boston: Allyn & Bacon.

Vygotsky, L. (1978). Mind in society (M. Cole, V. John-Steiner, S. Scribner, & E. Souberman, Trans). Cambridge, MA: Harvard University Press. (Original work published 1930)

Wertsch, J. (1991). Voices of the mind. Cambridge, England: Cambridge University Press.

Wertsch, J. (1994). The primacy of mediated action in sociocultural studies. Mind, Culture, and Activity, 1, 202–208.

Contributors

Peggy Albinger, resource/early childhood specialist, Corona-Norco Unified School District, California

Ellen H. Bacon, associate professor, Western Carolina University

Lisa A. Bloom, associate professor, Western Carolina University

Margaret Boothroyd, educational consultant, San Francisco

Linda J. Button, curriculum coordinator, Weld County District 6 Schools, Colorado

Patricia Tefft Cousin, associate professor, California State University–San Bernardino

Ann Cranston-Gingras, associate professor, University of South Florida

Louis G. Denti, associate professor, San Jose State University

Esteban Diaz, professor, California State University–San Bernardino

Don Dippo, associate professor, York University, Ontario, Canada

Catherine DuCharme, graduate program director, California State University–Long Beach

Curt Dudley-Marling, professor, York University, Ontario, Canada

Betty Epanchin, associate professor, University of South Florida

Richard A. Figueroa, professor, University of California–Davis

Barbara Flores, professor, California State University–San Bernardino

Barbara S. C. Goldstein, resource specialist, Pasadena Unified School District, California

Dixon Hearne, educational consultant, Lake Forest, California

Heather Hemming, lecturer, Acadia University, Nova Scotia, Canada

José Hernandez, associate professor, California State University–San Bernardino

Eleanor L. Higgins, research associate, Frostig Center, Pasadena, California

Jessica A. Jackman, educator, Azusa Unified School District, California

Michael S. Katz, associate professor, San Jose State University

Ina J. Kau, elementary school educator, Claremont, California

Dennis A. Kreil, director of pupil services, Placentia/Yorba Linda Unified School District, California

Judy W. Kugelmass, assistant professor, State University of New York–Binghamton

Laura Lovelace, elementary school educator, Pasadena, California

Carole MacInnis, assistant professor, Acadia University, Nova Scotia, Canada

Bruce I. Matsui, assistant professor, Claremont Graduate School, California

Jean C. McPhail, faculty member, University of Michigan

Annemarie Sullivan Palincsar, professor, University of Michigan

Andrea DeBruin Parecki, doctoral student, University of Michigan

James L. Paul, department chairperson, University of South Florida

Mary S. Poplin, professor, Claremont Graduate School, California

Marshall H. Raskind, director of research, Frostig Center, Pasadena, California

D. Kim Reid, professor, University of Northern Colorado

William C. Rhodes, visiting professor, University of South Florida

Hilda Rosselli, assistant professor, University of South Florida

Robert Rueda, professor, University of Southern California

Nadeen T. Ruiz, associate professor, California State University–Sacramento

Suki Stone, educational consultant, San Diego

Daphne Thomas, assistant professor, University of South Florida

Sue Thorson, assistant professor, University of Maine

Brenda L. Townsend, assistant professor, University of South Florida

Dudley J. Weist, associate professor, California State University–San Bernardino

Thomas G. West, author and founder of the Visualization Research Institute, Inc., Washington, DC

Author Index

Subject Index